2015
南通统计年鉴
NANTONG STATISTICAL YEARBOOK

南 通 市 统 计 局
国家统计局南通调查队 编
NANTONG MUNICIPAL STATISTICS BUREAU
STATE STATISTICS BUREAU NANTONG INVESTIGATION TEAM

中国统计出版社
China Statistics Press

图书在版编目(CIP)数据

南通统计年鉴. 2015 / 南通市统计局, 国家统计局南通调查队编. -- 北京 : 中国统计出版社, 2015.8
ISBN 978-7-5037-7519-2

Ⅰ. ①南… Ⅱ. ①南… ②国… Ⅲ. ①统计资料-南通市-2015-年鉴 Ⅳ. ①C832.533-54

中国版本图书馆 CIP 数据核字(2015)第 181393 号

南通统计年鉴-2015

作　　者/南通市统计局　国家统计局南通调查队
责任编辑/ 陈越月
装帧设计/ 海门日报印务中心
出版发行/ 中国统计出版社
地　　址/ 北京市丰台区西三环南路甲 6 号　邮政编码/100073
电　　话/ 邮购(010)63376909　书店(010)68783171
网　　址/ http://csp.stats.gov.cn
印　　刷/ 南通华民彩印有限公司
经　　销/ 新华书店
开　　本/ 890mm×1240mm　1/16
字　　数/ 130 千字
印　　张/ 45.5
版　　别/ 2015 年 8 月第 1 版
版　　次/ 2015 年 8 月第 1 次印刷
定　　价/280 元

如有印装差错，由本社发行部调换。

编者说明

一、《南通统计年鉴-2015》是一部全面、系统地反映南通市2014年以及历史主要年份国民经济和社会发展情况的资料性年刊和工具书。

二、《年鉴》分为十九部分：综合；国民经济核算；人口、就业；价格指数；人民生活；财政、金融；固定资产投资；对外经济；能源、资源、环境保护；农业；工业；建筑业；交通、邮电；国内贸易；教育、科技；文化、卫生、体育；其它社会事业；城市建设；城市交流。

三、《年鉴》资料大部分来自年度统计报表，一部分来自抽样调查。每部分后附有《主要统计指标解释》。

四、《年鉴》根据统计制度的变化，作了一些调整和改进，并努力与前几年版本在编辑体系、内容结构、指标体系、统计口径等方面保持连续性。读者在使用历史数据时凡与本年鉴有出入的，均以本年鉴为准。

五、《年鉴》中国民经济行业分类按2011年国家标准《国民经济行业分类》(GB/T4754-2011)执行。

六、《年鉴》表中"空格"表示无该项统计数据；"#"表示其中数的主要项；

感谢广大读者多年来对《年鉴》编辑出版工作的支持和帮助，欢迎继续提出宝贵意见，使《年鉴》的形式和内容更趋完善。

《南通统计年鉴-2015》编辑部

2015年7月

Compiler Notes

《Nantong Statistical Yearbook 2015》 is an informative annual publication that comprehensively and systematically reflects the 2014 economy and society development of the Nantong Municipality.

《The Yearbook》 is comprised of 19 parts: General Outlook; National Economy Accounting; Population, Employment; Price Index; People´s Livelihood; Finance, Banking; Fixed Asset Investment; Foreign Economy; Energy, Resource, Environmental Protection; Agriculture; Industry; Construction; Transportation, Post and Telecommunication; Domestic Trade; Education, Technology; Culture, Health, Sports; Other Undertakings; Urban Construction, Intercity Exchange.

The statistics of 《The Yearbook》 mainly comes from the data of annual statistical report,and the rest is from the sampling surveys. And readers can refer to the appendix of each part for the《Explanation of Major Statistical Indicators》.

《The Yearbook》 adjusted and improved in some aspects with the change of the statistical rules,but in the points as compiling system,structure of the contents, indicators and statistical method,it tries to keep coherent.If there are any differences between the historical data of this Yearbook and those of the past Yearbooks, Please refer to this Yearbook as the default correct ones.

In 《The Yearbook》,the group method of National Economy Industry is based on the standard《National Economy Industry》(GB/T4754-2011).

In 《The Yearbook》,(blank)indicates that the figure is not available;# indicates the major component items.

Here we´d like to express our deep thanks to the readers who cared and supported the publication of the Yearbook to enhance the level of our editorial work. We sincerely welcome the continued suggestions so as to improve the form and content of《The Yearbook》.

Editorial Staff

July,2015

地区生产总值（亿元）
GDP(100 million yuan)

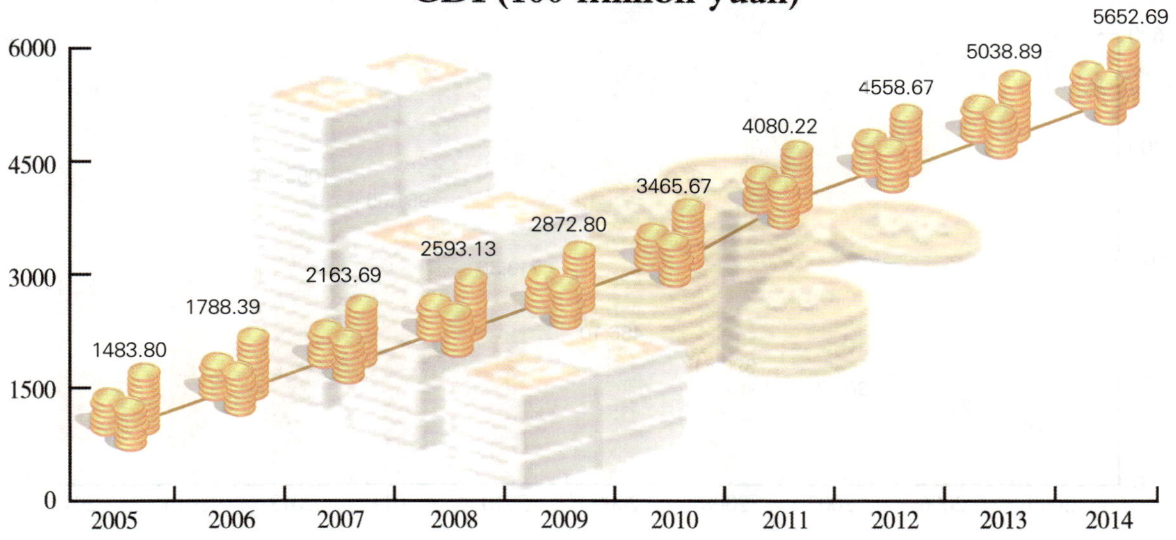

三次产业构成（%）
Composition of Three Industries(%)

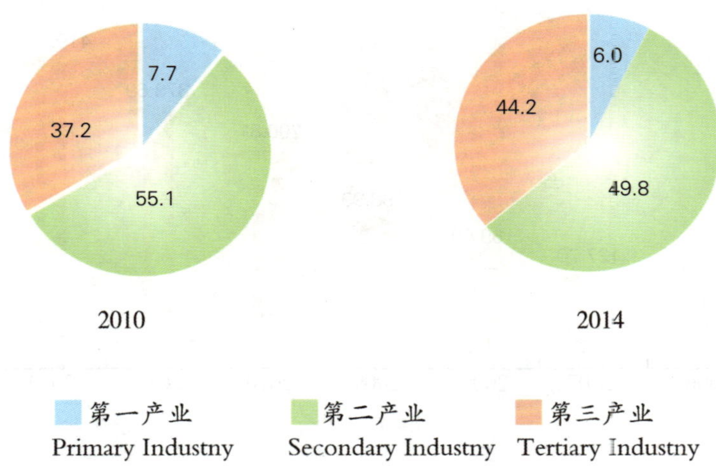

第一产业 Primary Industny　第二产业 Secondary Industny　第三产业 Tertiary Industny

财政总收入（亿元）
Total Financial Revenue(100 million yuan)

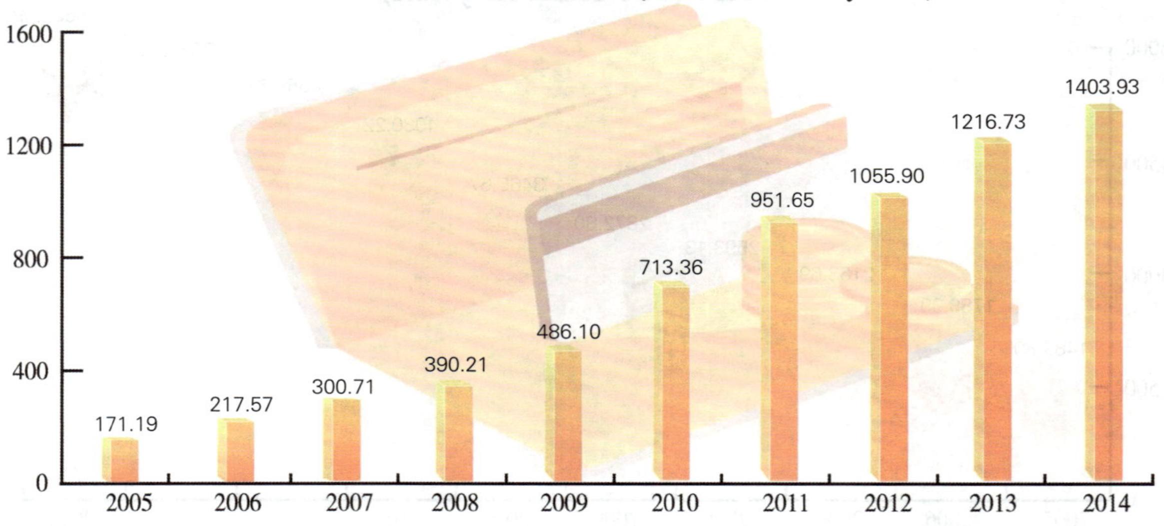

一般公共预算收入（亿元）
General public Budget Revenue(100 million yuan)

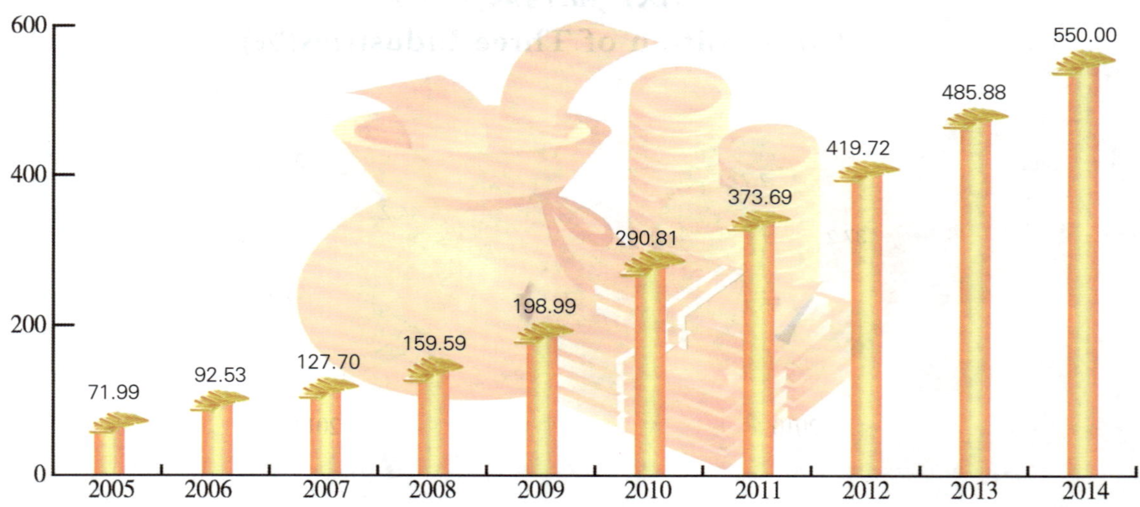

人均地区生产总值（元）
Per Capita GDP(yuan)

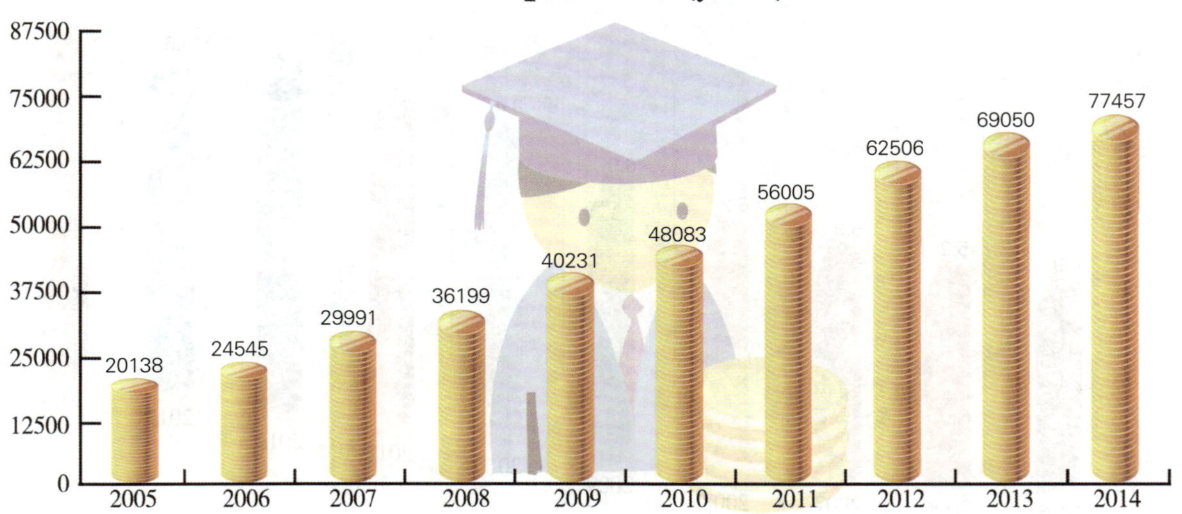

人均一般公共预算收入（元）
Per Capita General public Budget Revenne(yuan)

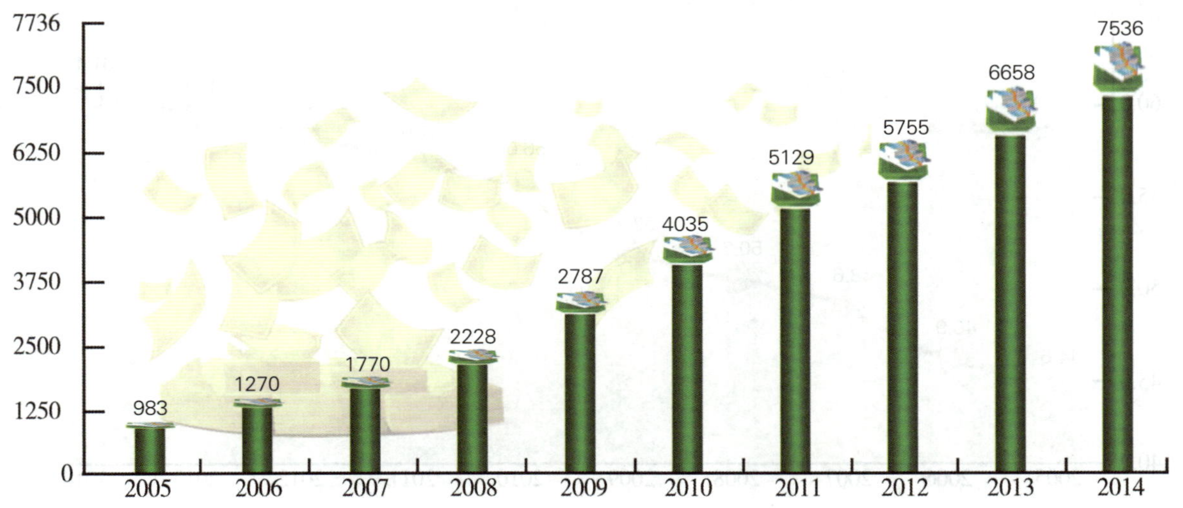

一般公共预算收入占GDP的比重（%）
Ratio of Local Public Budget Revenue to GDP(%)

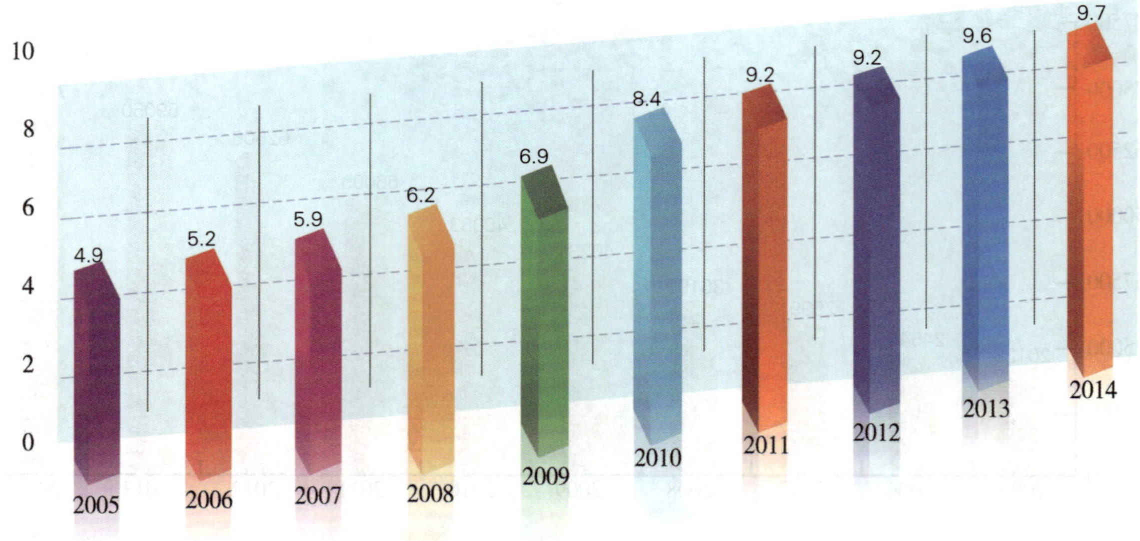

城镇化率（%）
Urbanization Rate(%)

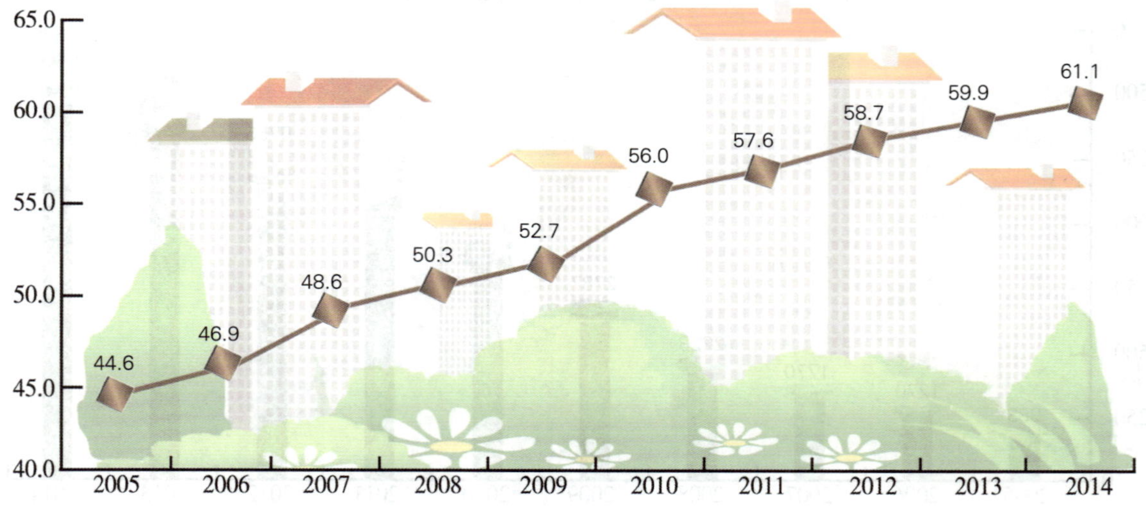

农林牧渔业总产值（亿元）

Total Output Value of Farming, Forestry, Husbandry and Fishery(100 million yuan)

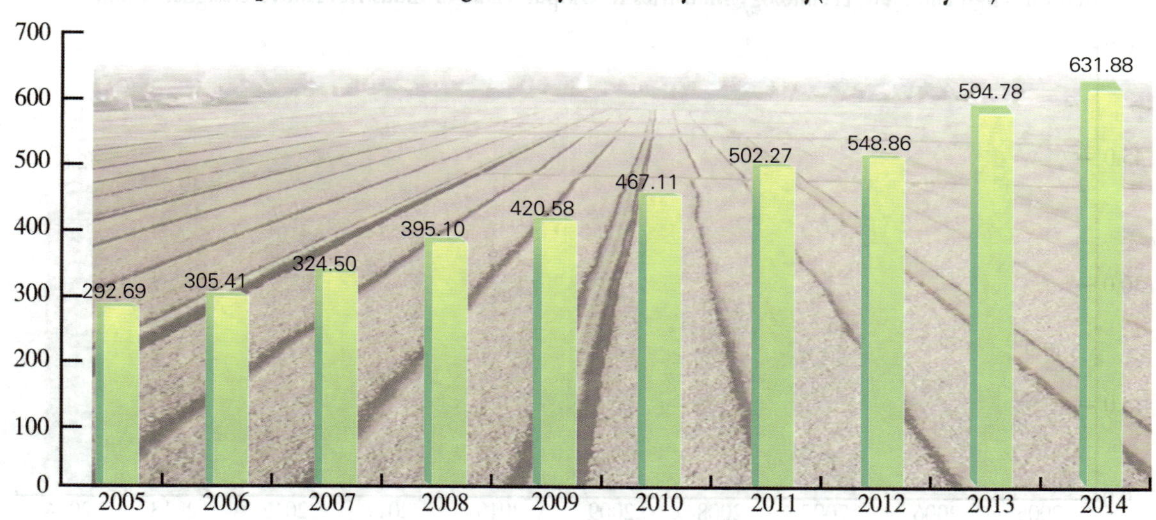

规模以上工业总产值（亿元）

Total Outpnt of Industries Above Designated Size(100 million yuan)

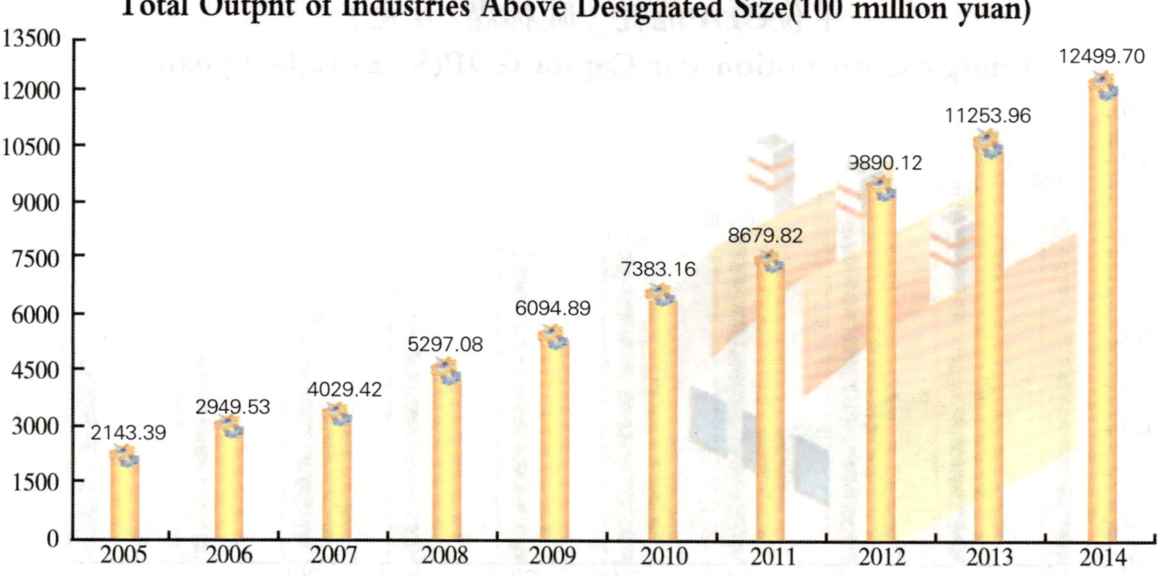

高新技术产业产值占比（%）

Ratio of High and New Technology Industries to Output Value of Industries Above Designated Size(%)

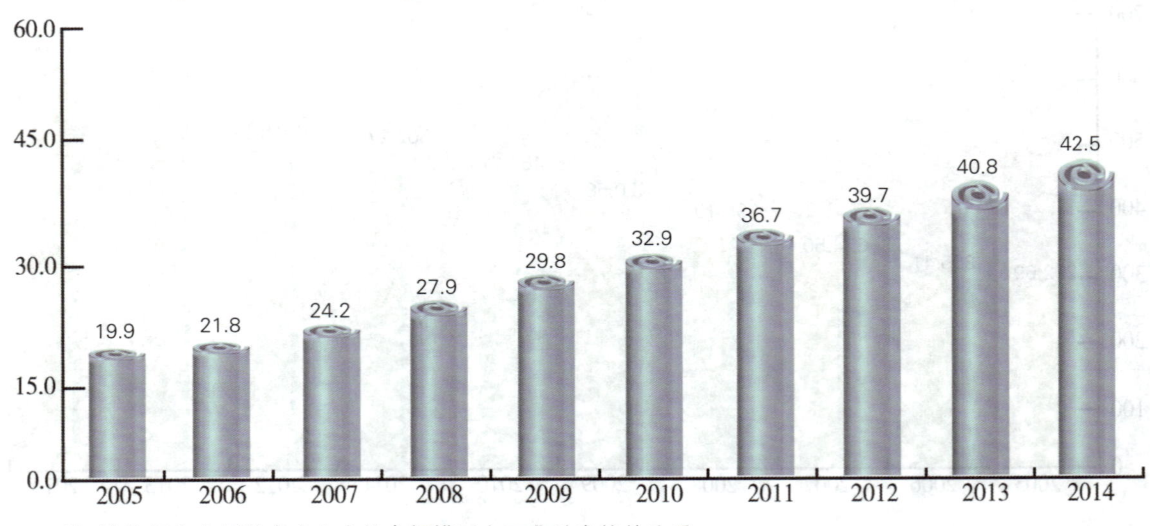

注：该指标为高新技术产业产值占规模以上工业总产值的比重。

单位GDP能耗（吨标煤/万元）

Energy Comsuption Per Capita GDP(SCE/10,000 yuan)

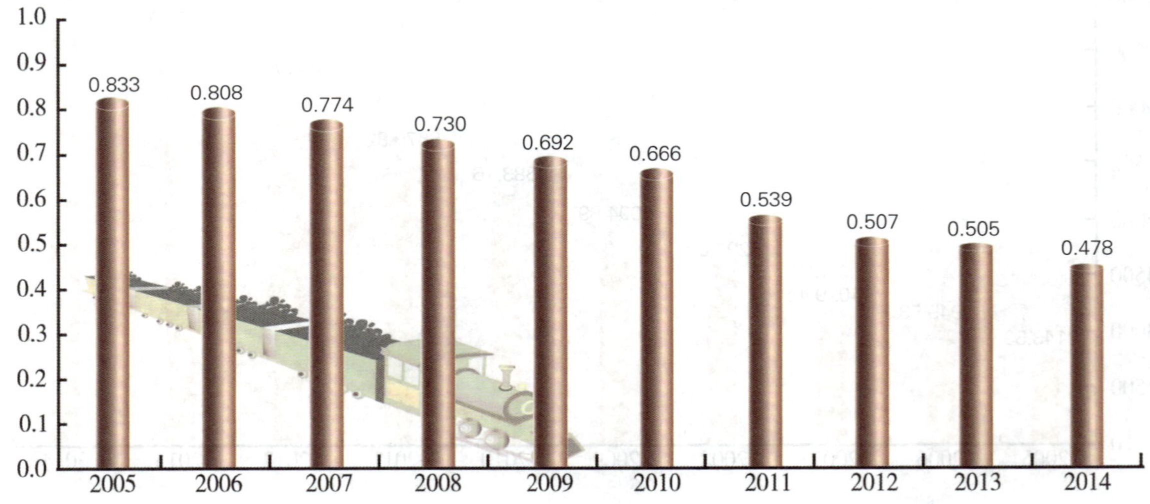

固定资产投资额（亿元）
Fixed-Asset Investment(100 million yuan)

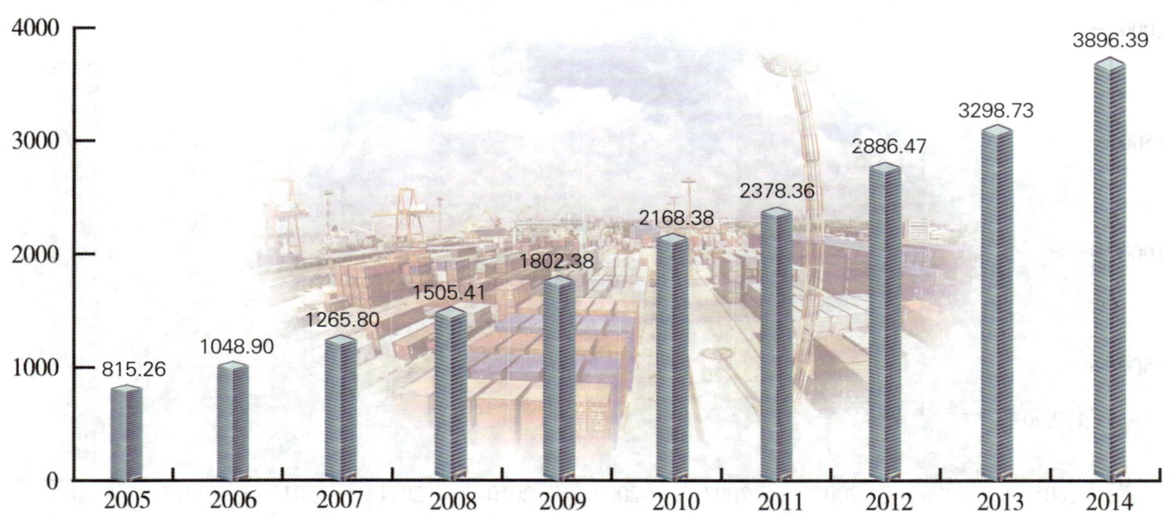

工业固定资产投资额（亿元）
Industrial Fixed-Asset Investment(100 million yuan)

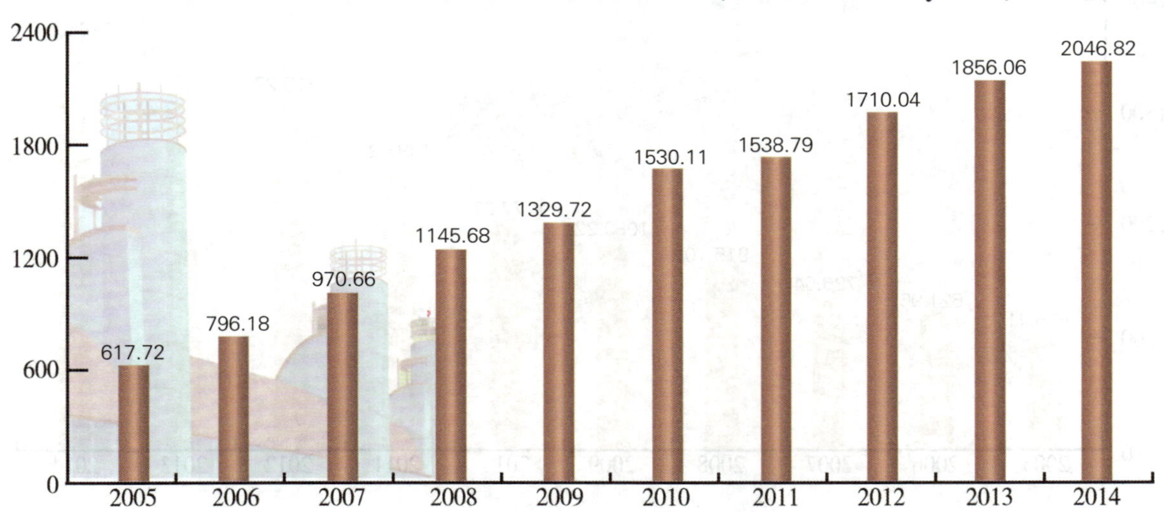

第三产业固定资产投资额（亿元）
Fixed Asset Investment in Tertiary Industries(100 million yuan)

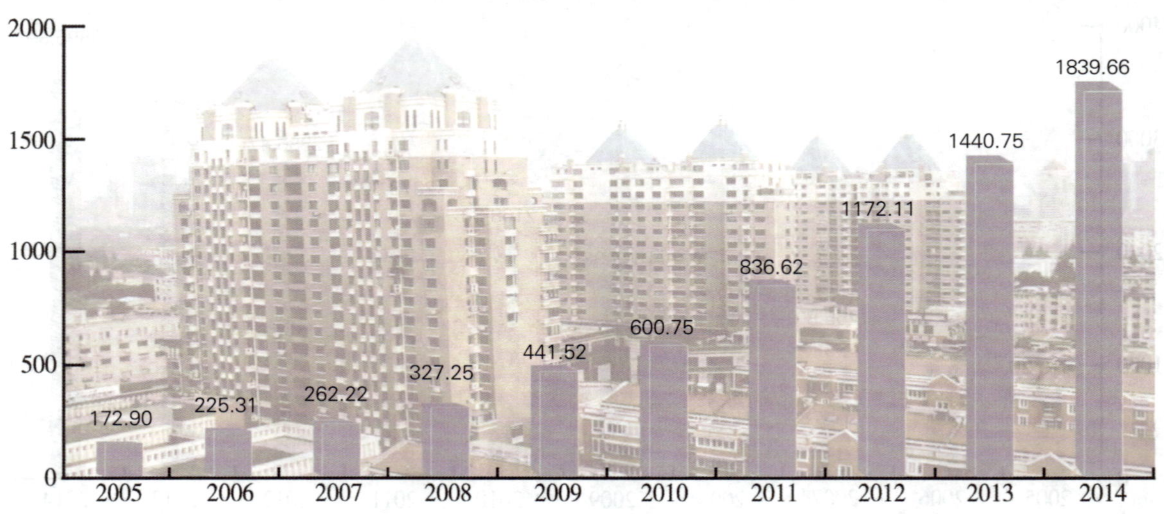

社会消费品零售总额（亿元）
Retail Sales Social Consume Goods(100 million yuan)

进出口总值（亿美元）
Total Output of Imports & Exports(100 million USD)

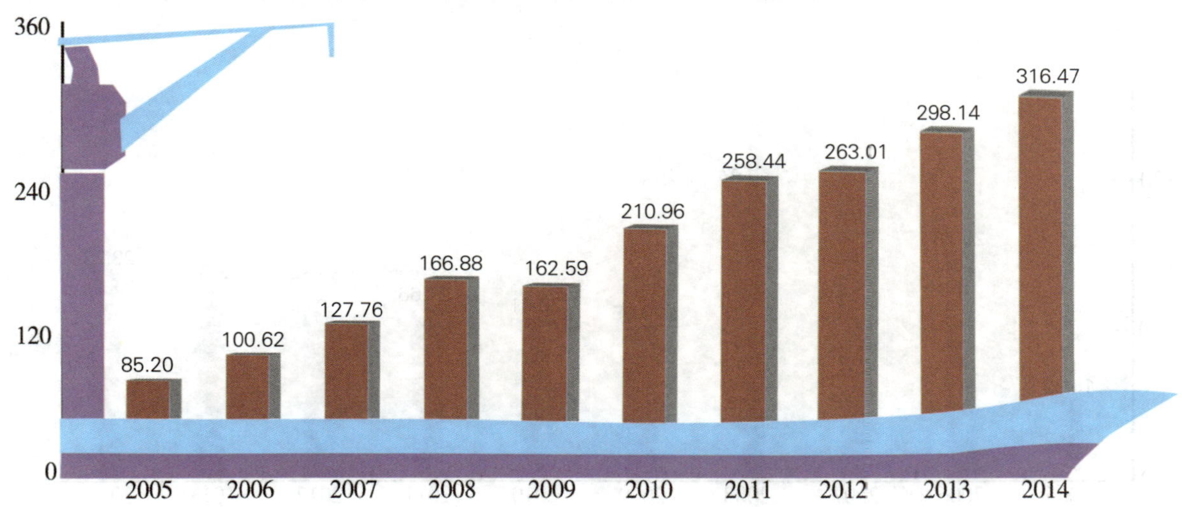

出口总值（亿美元）
Total Output of Exports(100 million USD)

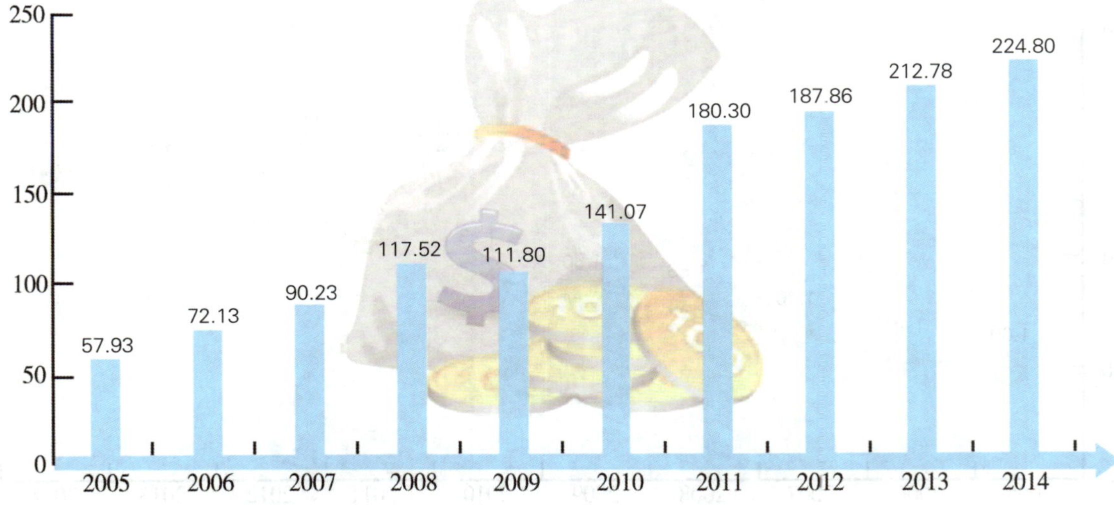

实际利用外资（亿美元）
Actually Utilized Foreign Investment(100 million USD)

全社会研发投入（R&D）占GDP的比重（%）
Ratio of Social R&D Investment to GDP(%)

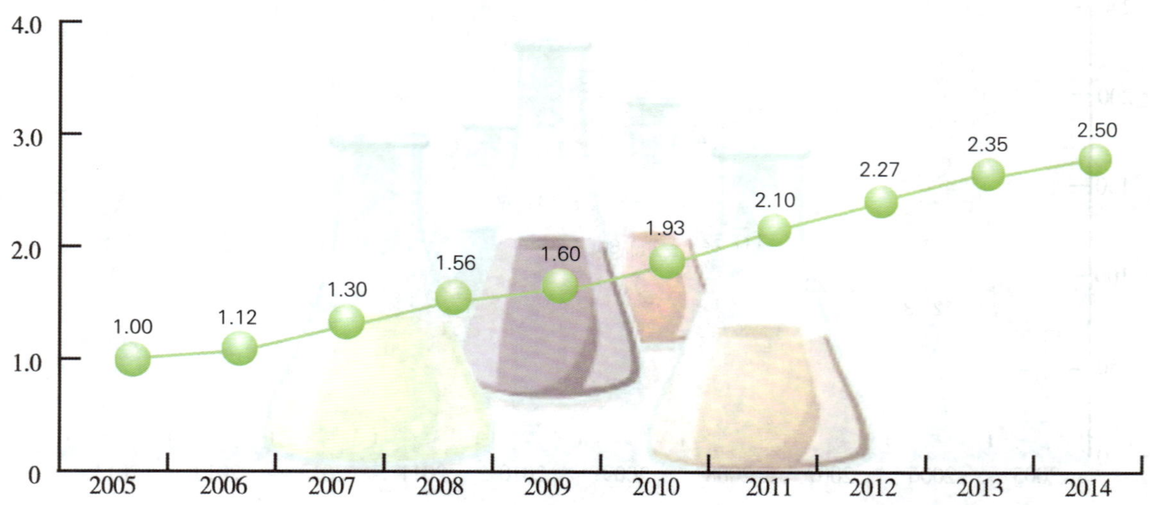

金融机构本外币存款余额（亿元）

Deposit Balance of Domestic and Foreign Currency in Financial Institues(100 million yuan)

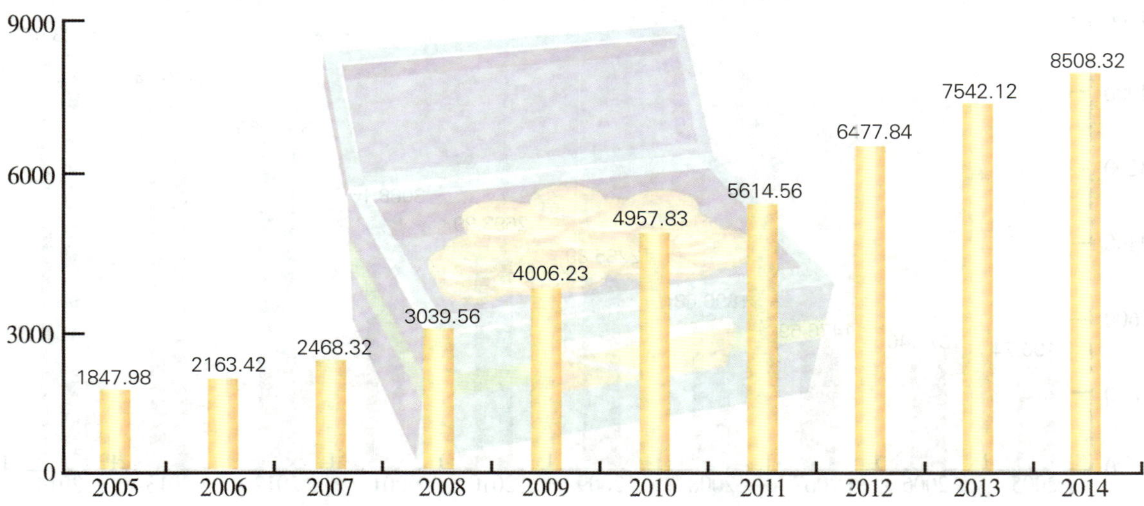

金融机构本外币贷款余额（亿元）

Loan Balance of Domestic and Foreign Currency in Financial Institues(100 million yuan)

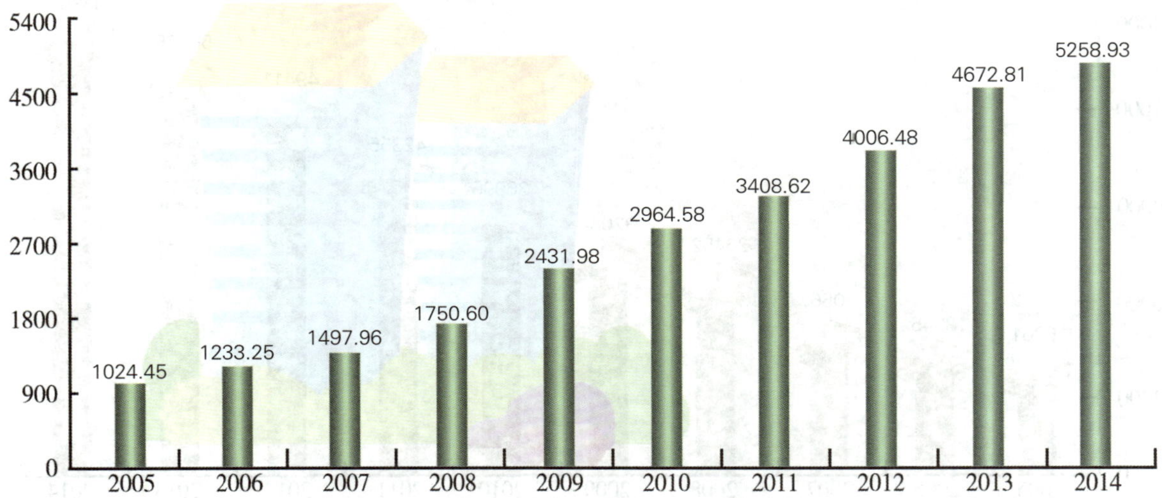

本外币储蓄存款余额（亿元）
Savings Balance of Domestic and Foreign Currency(100 million yuan)

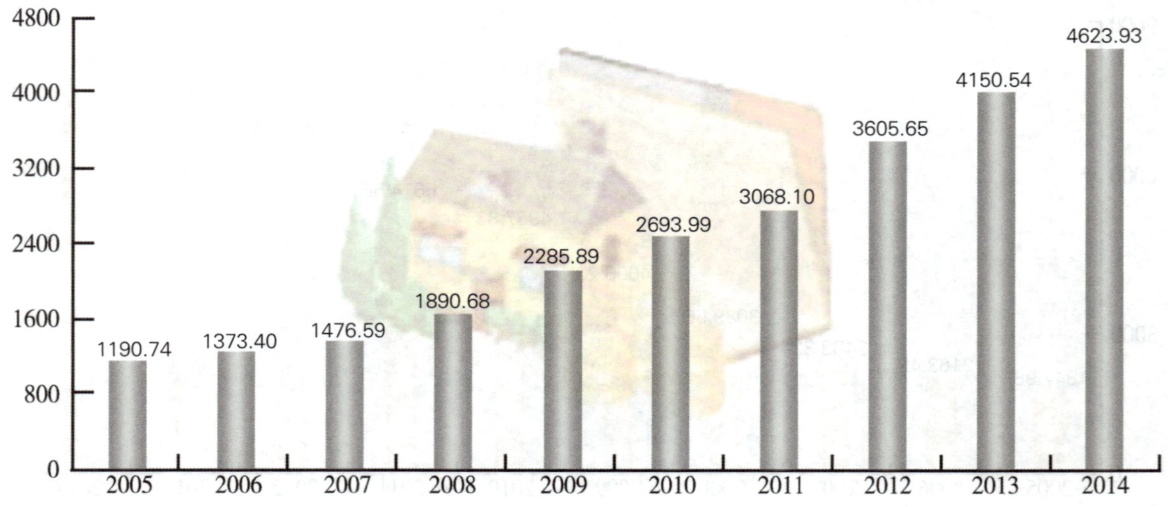

人均储蓄存款（元）
Per Capita Savings(yuan)

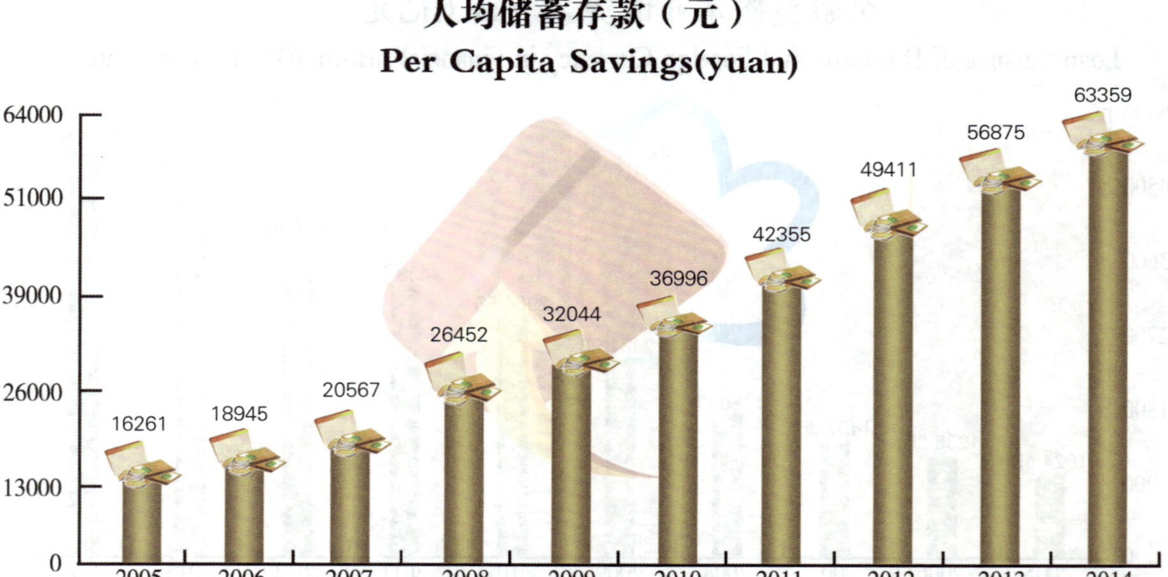

城镇居民人均可支配收入（元）
Urban Per Capita Disposable Income(yuan)

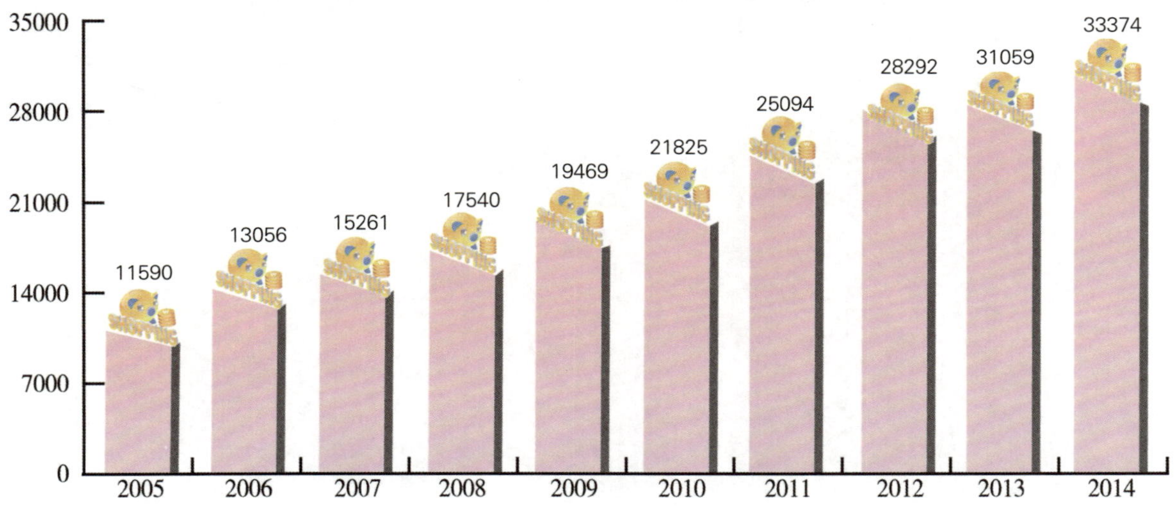

农村居民人均可支配收入（元）
Rural Per Capita Net Income(yuan)

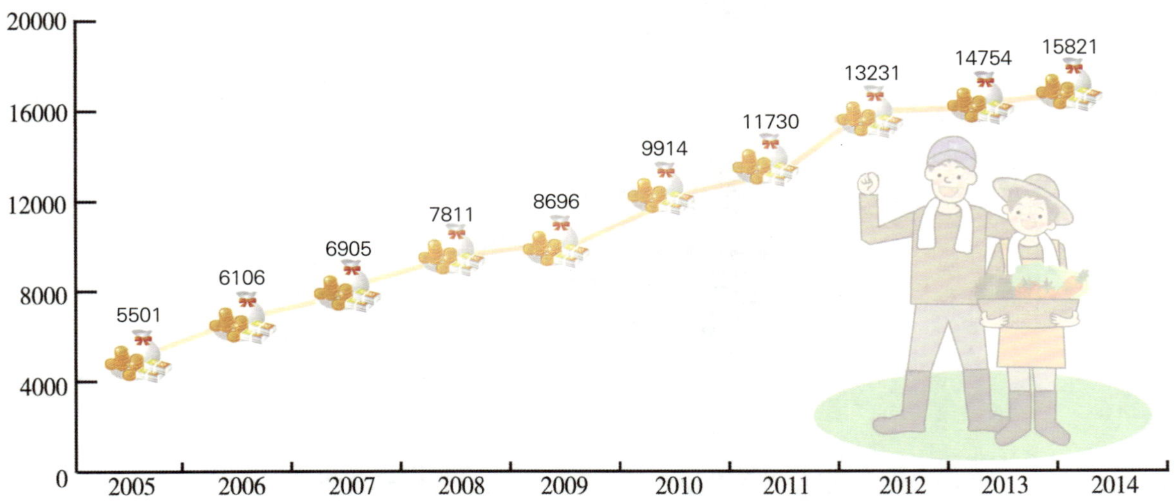

目　录

第一篇　综合

第二篇　国民经济核算

第三篇　人口　就业

第四篇　价格指数

第五篇 人民生活

第六篇 财政　金融

第七篇 固定资产投资

第八篇 对外经济

第九篇 能源 资源 环境保护

第十篇　农业

第十一篇　工业

第十二篇　建筑业

第十三篇 交通 邮电

第十四篇 国内贸易

第十五篇 教育 科技

第十六篇 文化 卫生 体育

第十七篇 其他社会事业

第十八篇 城市建设

第十九篇 城市交流

CONTENTS

CH1 GENERAL SURVEY

CH2 NATIONAL ECONMIC ACCOUTING

CH3 POPULATION AND EMPLOYMENT

CH4 PRICE INDICES

CH5 PEOPLE´S LIVELIHOOD

CH6 GOVERNMENT FINANCE, BANKING

CH7 INVESTMENT IN FIXED ASSETS

CH8 FOREIGN ECONOMY

CH9 ENERGY, RESOURCES AND ENVIRONMENTAL PROTECTION

CH10 AGRICULTURE

CH11 INDUSTRY

CH12 CONSTRUCTION

CH13 TRANSPORTAION AND POST

CH14 DOMESTIC TRADE

CH15 SCIENCE AND TECHNOLOGY

CH16 EDUCATION AND CULTURE

CH17 HEALTH AND SPORT

CH18 OTHER SOCIAL ACTIVITIES

CH19 URBAN CONSTRUCTION AND ENVIRONMENTAL PROTECTION

2014年南通市国民经济和社会发展统计公报

南通市统计局

(2015年3月18日)

2014年，我市全面贯彻中央和省委、省政府决策部署，认真落实习近平总书记系列重要讲话精神和对江苏工作的要求，坚持稳中求进、改革创新，深入实施"八项工程"，全面深化以陆海统筹发展综合配套改革为重点的各项改革，经济运行保持平稳发展态势，总体处于稳健运行的合理区间，转型升级取得新的突破，民生幸福水平取得新的提升，各项社会事业取得新的进展。

一、综合

年末全市常住人口729.8万人，其中，城镇人口达到446.3万人，增长2.1%，城镇化率61.1%，比上年提高1.2个百分点。年末户籍人口767.6万人，比上年增加1.1万人。全市人口出生率7.54‰，人口死亡率8.1‰，人口自然增长率-0.56‰。

就业持续增加。全年新增城镇就业人数9.1万人，新增转移农村劳动力2.78万人。年末从业人员达462.0万人，其中，第一产业101.7万人，第二产业216.0万人，第三产业144.3万人。

2014年年末人口数及构成

指　标	年末数(万人)	比重(%)
年末常住人口	729.80	—
城镇人口	446.27	61.1
乡村人口	283.53	38.9
年末户籍人口	767.63	—
#18岁以下	91.20	11.9
18-35岁	150.99	19.7
35-60岁	325.04	42.3
60岁以上	200.40	26.1
#男性人口	378.28	49.3
女性人口	389.25	50.7

国民经济平稳增长。初步核算，全市实现生产总值②5652.7亿元，按可比价格计算，比上年增长10.5%。其中：第一产业增加值367.1亿元，增长3.5%；第二产业增加值2873.8亿元，增长10.3%；第三产业增加值2411.8亿

元，增长11.9%。人均GDP达到77457元。

2005-2014 年地区生产总值

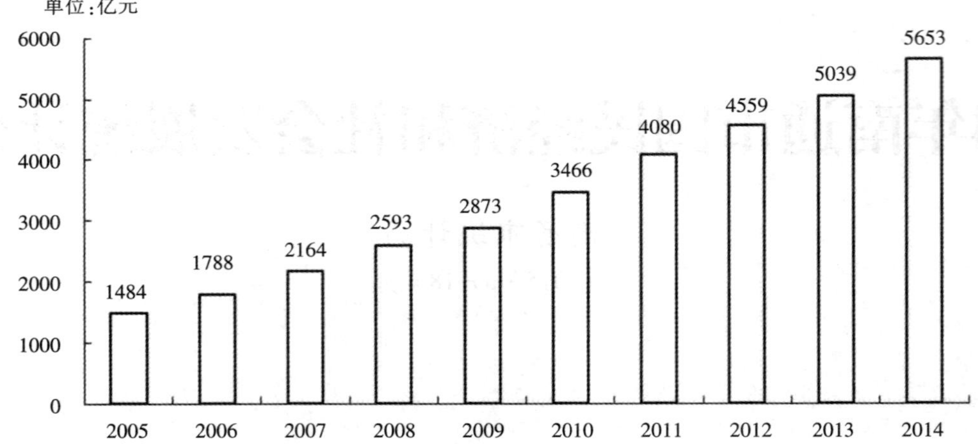

财政收入较快增长。全市实现一般公共预算收入550.0亿元，增长13.2%，其中，税收收入457.3亿元，增长14.4%，税收占比达到83.2%，比上年同期提高0.9个百分点。地方公共财政预算收入占地区生产总值的比重达9.8%，比上年提高0.2个百分点。

劳动生产率稳步提高。全年全员劳动生产率[③]为115481元/人，比上年提高11.3%。

产业结构继续优化。全市三次产业结构由上年的6.8:52.1:41.1调整为6.5:50.8:42.7。全年实现服务业增加值2093.1亿元，增长12.9%，占GDP比重为41.5%，第三产业在国民经济中的比重首次超过工业。"两新"产业较快发展，完成高新技术产业[④]产值5501.2亿元，增长16.7%，占规模以上工业比重达到43.6%，同比提高1.2个百分点。六大新兴产业[⑤]完成产值4179.5亿元，增长20.1%，占规模以上工业的比重达到33.1%，同比提高3.1个百分点。区域经济协调发展，县域经济增速总体快于市区，实现生产总值3558.9亿元，增长10.5%，快于市区增幅0.3个百分点。

全年新登记私营企业1.81万家，年末累计达 22.7万家；新登记私营企业注册资本882.6亿元，年末累计注册资本7425.1亿元。全年新登记个体户5.25万户，年末累计达53.4万户；新登记个体工商户资金数额49.5亿元，年末累计资金数额274.0亿元。年末全市共有规模以上民营工业企业3705家，占全市规模以上工业企业总数的比重达74.0%；全年民营工业增加值1754.2亿元，增长12.4%，占全市规模以上工业的比重达61.2%。

二、人民生活和社会保障

城乡居民收入继续增加。全体居民人均可支配收入[⑥]25340元，比上年增长9.5%，按常住地分，城镇居民人均可支配收入33374元，比上年增长8.9%；农村居民人均可支配收入15821元，比上年增长10.9%。

2014年居民收入构成表

	全体居民			城镇居民			农村居民		
	数值(元)	增长(%)	占比(%)	数值(元)	增长(%)	占比(%)	数值(元)	增长(%)	占比(%)
人均可支配收入	25340	9.5	100.0	33374	8.9	100.0	15821	10.9	100.0
工资性收入	14701	9.4	58.0	19295	8.9	57.8	9259	10.4	58.5
经营净收入	4982	8.7	19.7	6270	7.6	18.8	3453	11.2	21.8
财产性收入	1565	12.0	6.2	2571	12.3	7.7	373	9.7	2.4
转移净收入	4092	9.9	16.1	5238	8.8	15.7	2736	12.3	17.3

全体居民人均消费支出17007元，比上年增长8.1%，按常住地分，城镇居民人均消费支出22035元，增长7.2%；农村居民人均消费支出11051元，增长10.3%。年末，城镇居民家庭每百户拥有电冰箱99.4台，空调181.8台，移动电话232.2部，家用电脑87.8台，家用汽车46辆。农村居民家庭每百户拥有电冰箱99.1台，空调111.8台，移动电话217台，家用电脑55.8台。

年末全市城镇居民人均住房建筑面积46.9平方米，比上年增长4.0%。农村居民人均住房面积56.1平方米，比上年增长0.7%。

市区居民消费价格总指数102.1，物价总水平比上年增长2.1%，其中，服务项目价格上涨2.0%，消费品价格上涨 2.2%。八大类消费价格呈现"六涨二降"的态势。

市区居民消费价格涨跌情况

指　　标	比上年增长(%)
食品类	2.6
其中：粮食类	2.7
肉禽及其制品类	0.1
蛋类	10.9
烟酒及用品类	–1.9
衣着类	6.3
家庭设备用品及维修服务类	3.3
医疗保健和个人用品类	1.1
交通和通讯类	–0.4
娱乐教育文化用品及服务类	2.8
居住类⑦	1.0

2014 年分月居民消费价格指数

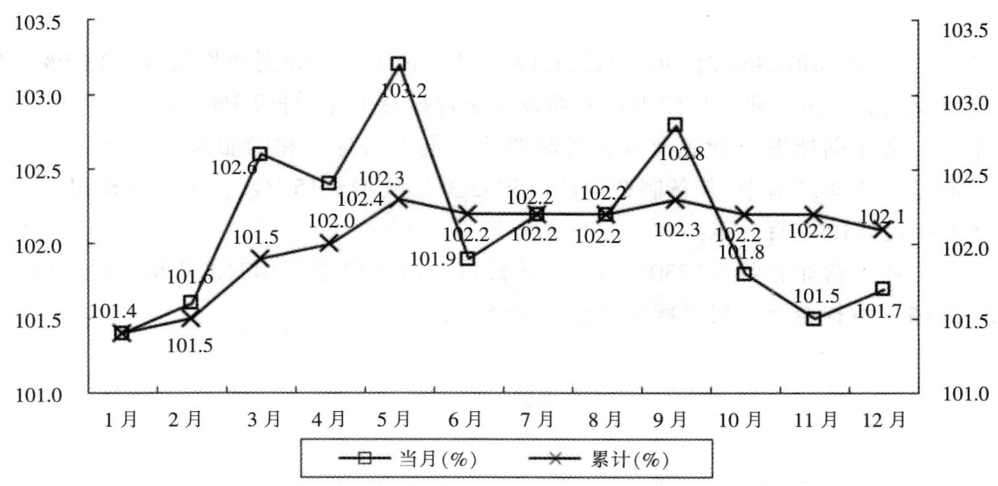

年末全市参加基本养老保险人数314.68万人，比上年末减少5.14万人；参加失业保险人数98.7万人，比上年末增加1.27万人；参加基本医疗保险人数(在职)达128.23万人，比上年末增加4.99万人；参加工伤保险人数为122万人，比上年末增加3万人。

年末全市拥有各类养老机构230家，总床位数56515张(其中养老机构床位数38399张)，农村敬老院96家，床位22760张。年末农村五保对象20924名，集中供养11769人，农村五保集中供养能力达到108.77%。全年结婚登记67616对。

三、农林牧渔业

全市农林牧渔业总产值631.9亿元，按可比价计算，增长3.6%。其中，农业产值278.9亿元，增长2.5%；牧业产值145.1亿元，增长3.6%；渔业产值147.8亿元，增长2.4%。全年粮食亩产432公斤，增长1.0%。粮食播种面积773.3万亩，下降0.8%；棉花种植面积55.8万亩，下降7.3%；油料种植面积190.2万亩，下降3.6%；蔬菜种植面积186.2万亩，增长2.9%。

主要农副产品产量情况

产品名称	计量单位	产量	比上年增长(%)
粮食	万吨	334.02	0.2
棉花	万吨	4.36	–13.8
油料	万吨	39.1	–4.3
蚕茧	万吨	2.00	2.0
生猪存栏	万头	278.52	0.6
生猪出栏	万头	397.37	4.8
羊存栏	万只	227.33	0.8
羊出栏	万只	279.43	Θ2.3
家禽存栏	万羽	4780.86	–3.5
家禽出栏	万羽	10920.05	–0.1
禽蛋	万吨	45.68	持平
水产品	万吨	88.21	1.7

四、工业和建筑业

全市规模以上工业[8]增加值2864.2亿元，增长11.4%，其中，轻重工业分别增长7.5%和13.5%。分经济类型看，集体工业增长5.4%，股份制工业增长12.1%，外商及港澳台投资工业增长9.3%。规模以上工业中，六大主导产业产值全面增长，其中新能源、能源及其装备制造业、电子信息业和船舶海工业等三大产业分别增长18.6%、16.6%和14.6%。工业产值中，装备制造业产值5992.3亿元，增长15.1%，占全市规模以上工业总产值的比重达47.5%，比上年提高1.5个百分点。

全市规模以上工业主营业务收入12308.3亿元，增长11.1%；利税总额1471.8亿元，增长15.0%；利润总额936.4亿元，增长13.9%。亏损企业亏损总额28亿元，下降5.2%。

主要工业产品产量情况

产品名称	计量单位	产量	比上年增长(%)
纱	万吨	62.71	-0.6
布	亿米	32.64	0.5
印染布	亿米	30.51	6.5
服装	亿件	7.63	-0.4
化学纤维	万吨	130.33	27.6
金属集装箱	万立方米	420.70	10.2
电动手提式工具	万台	9181.02	13.4
民用钢质船舶	万载重吨	485.38	4.5
海洋工程及特种船舶	万综合吨	910.25	38.6
通信及电子网络用电缆	万对千米	8.82	5.1
光缆	万芯千米	841.63	15.2
集成电器	亿块	99.32	11.8
半导体分立器件	亿只	80.11	-3.5
发电量	亿千瓦时	403.03	22.4
其中:风力发电量	亿千瓦时	25.26	0.6

初步核算,全市能源消费总量2562.44万吨标准煤,万元地区生产总值能耗[⑨]为0.478吨标准煤,比上年下降5.37%。

十大行业能源消耗情况

指　标	综合能源消费量(万吨标准煤)	单位产值能耗(吨标准煤/万元)	单位产值能耗比上年增长(%)
电力、热力生产和供应业	673.3	4.0884	8.2
化学原料和化学制品制造业	220.2	0.1231	-8.7
纺织业	137.4	0.1041	-1.3
化学纤维制造业	74.6	0.2064	-4.0
金属制品业	51.4	0.0714	-3.0
电气机械和器材制造业	44.3	0.0255	0.3
黑色金属冶炼和压延加工业	37.2	0.1596	-15.6
计算机、通信和其他电子设备制造业	28.2	0.0407	-7.8
非金属矿物制品业	27.3	0.0727	-12.5
文教、工美、体育和娱乐用品制造业	25.7	0.0495	-6.0

2014年,全市建筑业[⑩]增加值507.4亿元,增长 6.6%。建筑企业承建施工面积6.8亿平方米,增长11.4%。全市建筑队伍人数168.57万人,建筑队伍遍及38个国家和地区,年末出国人数0.76万人;年末全市拥有特级资质建筑企业15家,拥有一级建造师7428人。

五、固定资产投资

全年固定资产投资[⑪]额3896.4亿元,比上年增长18.1%,其中,民间投资2895.1亿元,增长20.2%,占固定资产投资的比重达74.3%,提高1.3个百分点;工业投资2046.8亿元,增长10.3%,其中技改投资1220.8亿元,占工业投资的比重达到59.6%,比上年提高6.4个百分点。固定资产投资中,第二产业投资2046.8亿元,增长10.3%;

第三产业投资1839.7亿元，增长27.6%。全年基础设施投资622.8亿元，增长44.0%。

2005-2014 年固定资产投资

单位：亿元

2005	2006	2007	2008	2009	2010	2011	2012	2013	2014
815	1049	1266	1505	1802	2168	2378	2886	3299	3896

全年房地产开发投资678.9亿元，增长13.8%。商品房施工面积5272.2万平方米，增长16.3%，其中，住宅施工面积3951.0万平方米，增长12.2%。全市商品房竣工面积1031.2万平方米，增长11.4%，其中，住宅竣工面积857.6万平方米，增长11.0%。商品房销售面积919.2万平方米，下降11.2%，其中住宅843.4万平方米，下降10.1%。

六、国内贸易和旅游业

全年社会消费品零售总额2153.5亿元，增长11.8%。其中，城市消费品零售额1567.4亿元，增长11.8%；农村消费品零售额586.1亿元，增长11.7%。分行业看，批发和零售业消费品零售额1980.0亿元，增长11.5%；住宿和餐饮业消费品零售额173.5亿元，增长14.3%。

2005-2014 年社会消费品零售额

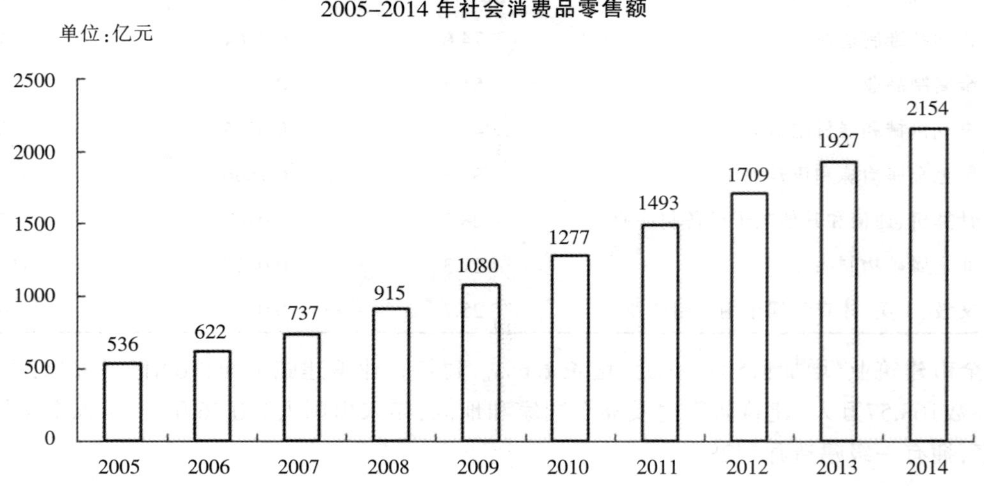

限额以上贸易单位[12]商品零售额中，汽车类零售额比上年增长8.1%，石油及制品类增长19.8%，食品饮料烟酒类下降1.5%，服装鞋帽针织品类增长2.5%，日用品类增长1.7%，化妆品类增长4.6%，金银珠宝类下降2.8%，家用电器和音像器材类增长5.6%。

年末全市拥有旅游星级饭店96家，旅行社140家，A级旅游景区（点）46处，全国农业旅游示范点2个，全国工农业旅游示范点6个。全年实现旅游总收入412.1亿元，增长14.3%，其中，外汇收入1.1亿美元，下降11.0%；国内旅游收入400.6亿元，增长15.0%。全年接待国内旅游者3066.3万人次，增长12.9%；其中旅游住宿设施和居民家中接待过夜海外旅游者18.7万人次，下降13.7%。

七、开放型经济

全年进出口总值316.5亿美元，增长6.2%，其中，出口总值224.8亿美元，增长5.7%；进口总值91.7亿美元，增长7.4%。年末与我市建立进出口贸易关系的国家和地区199个，比上年增加3个。全市有进出口业绩的企业5094家，增加9.8%。

2005-2014 年出口总值

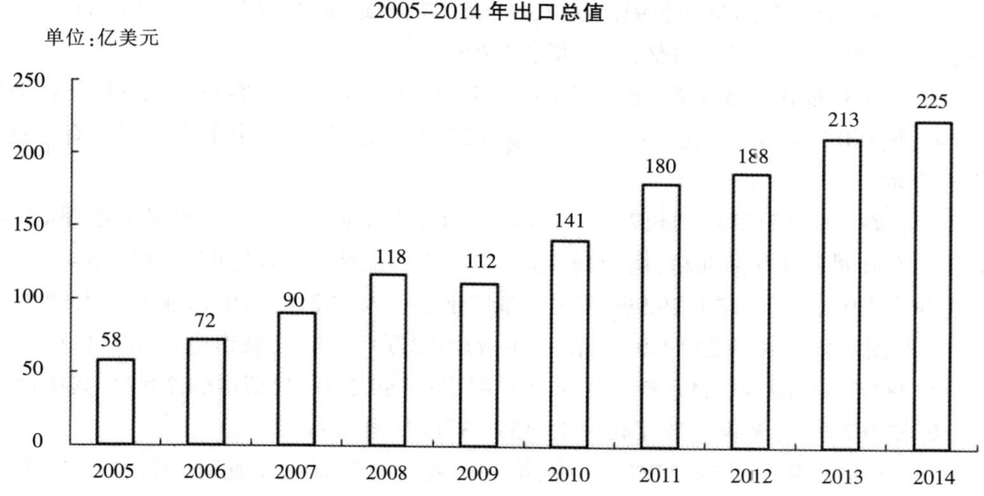

进出口贸易方式及出口地分类情况

指标	总量(亿美元)	比上年增长(%)
进出口总值	316.47	6.2
进口	91.67	7.4
出口	224.80	5.7
# 三资企业	117.78	8.8
私营企业	99.74	11.1
# 一般贸易	147.68	10.3
加工贸易	71.93	-1.5
#纺织品	70.71	5.9
机电产品	92.02	5.7
高新技术产品	24.42	0.2
#船舶及海工	26.31	-7.9
光伏产品	7.37	-0.2
# 亚洲	123.05	4.5
# 东盟	32.80	-3.6
日本	37.58	-2.6
欧洲	40.35	15.5
# 欧盟	34.75	7.2
北美洲	33.49	110.0
# 美国	31.05	11.4

全年新批外商投资项目305个，比上年下降13.3%，其中，千万以上项目140个，比上年下降4.8%；新批协议注册外资55.2亿美元，增长11.5%；实际到账注册外资23.0亿美元，增长0.9%。

全年新批设立境外企业78家，中方协议投资额9.2亿美元。新签对外承包劳务合同额18.6亿美元，增长0.1%；完成对外承包劳务营业额22.7亿美元，增长14.8%；新派劳务人员0.94万人次，下降22.0%；年末在外劳务人员2.3万人，增长3.4%。

八、交通、邮政电信业和电力业

全年交通运输、仓储及邮政业增加值204.4亿元，比上年增长8.2%。年末南通机场民航航线14条，开通周航班量122班，增长25.8%；全年民航货邮吞吐量3.2万吨，增长29.8%；旅客运输量93.2万人次，增长38.0%。年末铁路南通站始发列车13对。全年铁路货运量91.1万吨，增长5.1%；客运量253.4万人次，增长8.0%。全年公路、水路货运量1.8亿吨，增长7.7%；公路客运量1亿人次，增长1.7%。

年末全市机动车保有量194.95万辆，比上年末减少7.52万辆。其中，载客汽车92.54万辆，增加16.27万辆；载货汽车7.02万辆，增加0.28万辆；摩托车94.8万辆，减少23.56万辆。年末全市个人汽车保有量达86.94万辆，比上年末增加15.34万辆。

南通港全年货物吞吐量2.2亿吨，增长7.4%。其中，进港1.3亿吨，增长7.7%；外贸吞吐量4814万吨，比上年增长6.1%。集装箱吞吐量71.1万标准箱，增长18.4%，其中，外贸航线31.6万标准箱，增长3.4%。

全年邮电业务收入93.5亿元，增长19.9%。其中，邮政业务收入28.2亿元，电信业务收入65.2亿元，分别增长27.3%和0.4%。年末固定电话用户232.1万户，比上年减少9.2万户，其中，城市电话用户111.6万户，增加2.2万户；住宅电话用户178.9万户，减少11.4万户。年末互联网用户789.2 万户，新增64.7万户，其中固定宽带互联网用户190.9万户，新增29.7万户，无线宽带互联网用户598.3万户，增加5.0万户。

全年用电量333.23亿千瓦时，增长2.2%。其中，第一产业用电量6.0亿千瓦时，增长11.7%；第二产业用电量248.9亿千瓦时，增长3.7%；工业用电量242.9亿千瓦时，增长3.6%；第三产业用电量34.6亿千瓦时，增长4.2%。城乡居民生活用电量43.7亿千瓦时，下降7.9%。

九、财政、金融

全年一般公共预算收入550亿元，增长13.2%，其中，增值税增长9.7%，营业税增长7.3%。全年一般公共预算支出650亿元，增长12.8%。地方公共财政预算支出中，用于社会保障与就业、科学技术、教育、医疗卫生、环境保护等民生方面的财政投入达371.8亿元，增长15.0%，占一般公共预算支出的比重达到57.2%，比上年提高1.1个百分点。

2005-2014 年地方公共财政预算收入

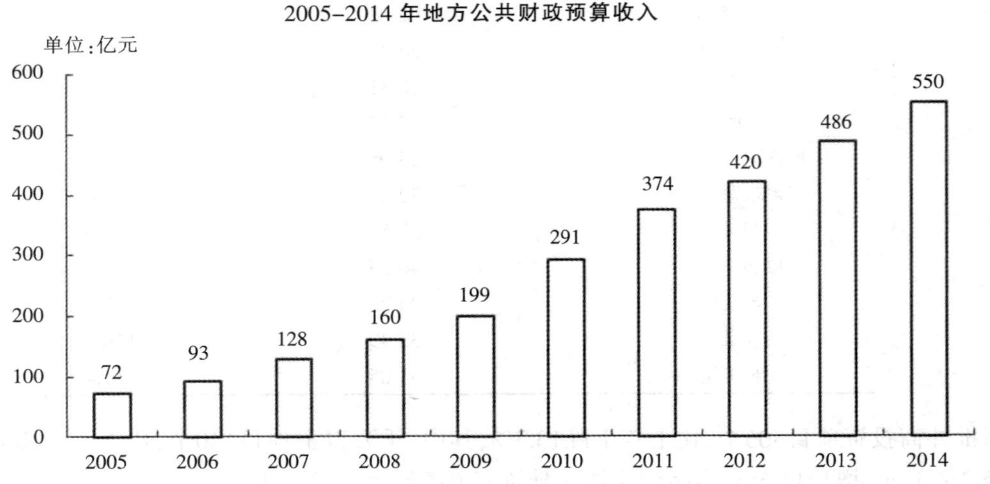

全年金融系统新增存款966.2亿元，年末金融系统存款余额8508.3亿元，比上年末增长12.8%，其中，储蓄存款余额4623.9亿元，增长11.4%；单位存款余额3643.9亿元，增长14.7%。全年金融机构新增贷款586.1亿元，下降12.0%。年末各项贷款余额5258.9亿元，比上年末增长12.5%。全年发放住房公积金贷款 44亿元，比上年下降20.5%；本年提取公积金43.4亿元，增长8.0%。全年新增公积金开户人数10万人，至年末已开户职工人数84.6万人。

全年新增保险机构4家，年末保险机构总数达74家，保险行业从业人员1.6万人。全年保费收入154亿元，比上年增长10.1%，其中，财产险收入49.2亿元，增长24.6%；人寿险收入104.8亿元，增长17.1%。全年已决赔款及给付68.7亿元，增长22.2%。

十、科学技术和教育

年末全市拥有高新技术企业663家；新增省级高新技术产品948项；新建省级企业重点实验室3家，省级工程中心30家，省级企业院士工作站1家；新建市级公共技术服务平台5家，市级工程技术研究中心98家，企业院士工作站3家。全年有18项科技成果获国家及江苏省科技进步奖，其中，国家级二等奖2项；省级二等奖5项，三等奖11项。年末，全市共建成科技孵化器61家，其中国家级9家、省级22家。全年专利申请量27692件，比上年下降32.1%；专利授权量12391件，同比下降43.9%；其中，发明专利申请量8450件，增长5.2%，发明专利授权量932件，增长24.9%，万人发明专利拥有量11.53件，增长80%。全社会研发投入占GDP的比重达到2.42%，比上年提高0.07个百分点。

全市拥有普通高等学校8所，年末在校学生8.74万人；成人高校2所，在校学生2.56万人；中等职业教育学校21所，在校学生6.41万人；普通高中52所，在校学生9.09万人；普通初中163所，在校学生15.65万人；小学321所，在校学生32.04万人；特殊教育学校9所，在校学生0.09万人；各级各类幼儿园396所，在园儿童15.35万人。

十一、文化、卫生和体育

年末全市拥有文化馆9个，文化站99个，公共图书馆11个，“农家书屋”1614个。全市拥有博物馆（纪念馆）21个，年末万人拥有公共文化设施面积1119.5平方米。各级文物保护单位205处，其中全国重点文物保护单位10处，省级文物保护单位22处。市级以上非物质文化遗产106项，其中国家级10项，省级40项。全市拥有广播电视台7座，全年新增有线电视用户9.4万户，年末有线电视用户274.5万户，有线电视入户率达 96.9%。全市文化市场经营单位1204个，印刷发行单位2531个。全市拥有文化产业示范园区（基地）29个，其中国家级2个，省级5个。全年新增4个中国民间文化艺术之乡。

年末全市拥有卫生机构1621个(不含农村社区卫生服务站、村卫生室)。其中，医院、卫生院304个，妇幼保健院(所、站)7个，专科疾病防治院(所、站)3个。全市卫生机构床位数3.51万张，卫生技术人员3.95万人。其中，执业医师和执业助理医师1.64万人，注册护士1.56万人。全市拥有疾病预防控制中心(站)9个，卫生技术人员463人；卫生监督所8个，卫生技术人员265人；乡镇卫生院103个，床位0.73万张，卫生技术人员0.72万人。

市区(不含通州区)共建成城市社区卫生服务中心21个，以街道(镇)为单位建成率100%。累计建成农村社区卫生服务站、村卫生室1641个，行政村覆盖率 100%。全市新型农村合作医疗参合率 99.98%。农村自来水普及率 100%。

全年承办了9项次全国赛事、11项次省级赛事。全市新增晨晚练健身点197个，各级各类全民健身活动参与群众超过21.3万人次。体育彩票销售创历史新高，全年销售额13.4亿元。

十二、环境保护和安全生产

全年市区（含通州区）新增绿地770公顷，城市绿化覆盖率42.3%；日供水能力达到160万立方米，水质综合指标合格率100%；市区燃气普及率、用水普及率、生活垃圾无害化处理率均达到100%。全年市区新增路灯、景观灯55442盏，城市道路亮灯率达到99.7% 。

2014年全市共新建（改造）燃煤火电、热电机组脱硫设备61套、脱硝设施64套、除尘改造64套，锅炉平均脱硫效率达90%以上、综合脱硝效率达70以上，烟尘排放基本达到重点区域特别排放限值。全市各地根据实际划定了禁燃区范围。

2014年全市环境质量保持稳定，环境空气主要污染物年平均值为：二氧化硫26微克/立方米，二氧化氮40微克/立方米，可吸入颗粒物96微克/立方米，PM2.5浓度为62微克/立方米，其中二氧化硫和二氧化氮年均值符合国家空气质量二级标准，可吸入颗粒物和PM2.5年均值超过国家空气质量二级标准；全年空气质量指数达到良好以上的天数达257天，占全年有效监测天数的70.8%。长江南通段主流水质符合国家地面水质环境质量Ⅲ类水质标准，饮用水源地水质达标率100%。区域环境噪声平均值为58.0分贝，交通干线噪声平均平均值为68.1分贝，均符合国家环境噪声质量标准。

全年共发生各类安全生产事故1207起，死亡164人，比上年分别下降4.82%和4.10%。其中，工矿商贸企业（含建筑业）发生生产安全亡人事故19起，死亡27人。全市共发生火灾5985起，死20人，伤20人，直接财产损失1832.2万元。全市共发生一般以上交通事故1285起，死亡437人，伤1172人。

注释：

①公报发布的2014年数据为初步统计数。部分数据因四舍五入的原因，存在着与分项合计不等的情况。

②国内生产总值、各产业增加值绝对数按现价计算，增长速度按不变价格计算；根据第三次全国经济普查结果和国家统计局2012年制定的《三次产业划分规定》对相关数据进行了修订。

③全员劳动生产率为国内生产总值（以2010年不变价格计算）与全部从业人员的比率。

④高新技术产业产值根据江苏省科技厅和江苏省统计局联合下发的《关于发布<江苏省高新技术产业统计分类目录>（2012修订版）的通知》（苏科高[2012]332号）进行统计，包括航空航天制造业、电子计算机及办公设备制造业、电子及通讯设备制造业、医药制造业、仪器仪表制造业、智能装备制造业、新材料制造业和新材料制造业。

⑤新兴产业包括新能源制造业、新材料制造业、生物技术和新医药制造业、智能装备制造业、节能环保制造业和海洋工程装备制造业。

⑥2012年四季度起，国家统计局实施了城乡一体化住户调查改革，统一了城乡居民收入名称、分类和统计标准，在全国统一选取了16万户城乡居民家庭，直接开展调查。在此基础上，计算了城乡可比的新口径全体居民人均可支配收入以及分城乡居民人均可支配收入。耐用消费品拥有量为城乡一体化改革后的调查数据，与以前年份不可比。

⑦居住类价格包括建房及装修材料、住房租金、自有住房和水电燃料等价格。

⑧规模以上工业统计范围为年主营业务收入2000万元及以上的工业企业。

⑨万元国内生产总值能耗按2010年不变价格计算。

⑩建筑业统计范围为有资质的建筑业企业。

⑪固定资产投资统计范围为计划总投资500万元及以上建设项目，房地产投资统计范围为房地产开发经营企业。

⑫社会消费品零售总额统计中限额以上单位是指年主营业务收入2000万元及以上的批发业企业（单位）、500万元及以上的零售业企业（单位）、200万元及以上的住宿和餐饮业企业（单位）。

2014 Nantong Statistical Bulletin of National Economy and Social Development

Statistical Bureau of Nantong Municipal People's Government

March 18, 2015

In 2014, Nantong fully implemented the decisions and deployment of the central and provincial CPC committees and governments, in the spirit of General Secretary Xi Jinping's important speeches and requirement of Jiangsu's development. The city maintained development in stability and realized innovation by reforms, pressed ahead with "Eight Projects", and promoted reforms in all fields with focus on land-and-sea coordinated development overall supporting reforms. As a result, the economy has kept growing stably within a reasonable range. The transformation and upgrading has achieved new breakthrough. The well-being of people's livelihood has been lifted to a higher level. Progress has been made in various social undertakings.

1. General Outlook

At the end of 2014, the city's permanent population reached 7.298 million. The urban population was 4.463 million, with 2.1% increase. The urbanization rete was 61.1%, 1.2 percentage points higher than the previous year. The registered population was 7.676 million, an increase of 11,000 over that of 2013. The birth rate of the city was 7.54‰ and the death rate was 8.1‰, rendering a natural population growth rate of –0.56‰.

The employment kept growing. 91,000 urban working opportunities have been provided throughout the year and 27,800 rural labor forces had been lately transferred. At the end of 2014, the number of employed people reached 4.62 million, 1.017 million of which were for the primary industry, 2.16 million for the secondary industry and 1.443 million for the tertiary industry.

Population and Its Composition at the End of 2014

Item	Year-end Population(Unit: 10,000 persons)	Proportion(%)
Permanent Population at the Year-end	729.80	—
Urban	446.27	61.1
Rural	283.53	38.9
Registered Population at the Year-end	767.63	—
#Aged under 18	91.20	11.9
Aged 18-35	150.99	19.7
Aged 35-60	325.04	42.3
Aged 60 and over	200.40	26.1
#Male	378.28	49.3
Female	389.25	50.7

National economy kept stable grown in 2014. Based on the preliminary accounting, the GDP of the whole city[②] was 565.27 billion yuan, up by 10.5% over the previous year at comparable price. Of the total, the value of the primary industry was 36.71 billion yuan, up by 3.5%, the secondary industry 287.38 billion yuan, up by 10.3%, and the tertiary industry 241.18 billion yuan, up by 11.9%. The per capita GDP reached 77,457 yuan.

2005-2014 Gross Regional Product (GRP)

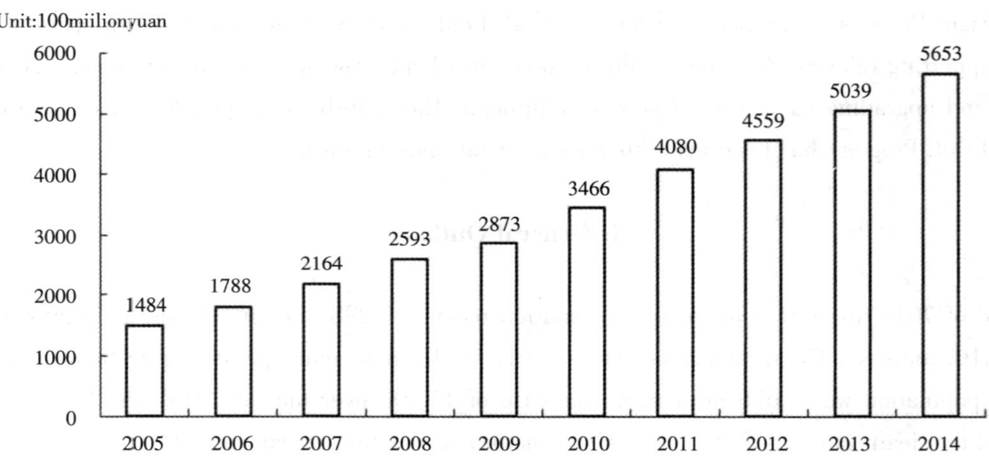

The fiscal revenue grew comparatively fast in 2014. The general public budgetary revenue reached 55 billion yuan, up by 13.2%. The total fiscal revenue accounted for 45.73 billion yuan, up by 14.4%, taking up 83.2% of the total, 0.9 percentage point higher over a year earlier. The local public fiscal budgetary revenue accounted for 9.8% of GRP, 0.2 percentage point higher over the previous year.

The labor productivity increased steadily. The all labor productivity[③] was 115,481 yuan/person, 11.3% higher than that in 2013.

The industrial structure continued to be optimized. The three-industry structure was adjusted from 6.8:52.1: 41.1of 2013 to 6.5:50.8:42.7 in 2014. All year round, the service industry added value registered 209.31 billion yuan, up by 12.9%, accounting for 41.5% of GDP. For the first time, the ratio of the tertiary industry in National economy preceded that of industry. "Two New" industries, namely hi-tech and emerging industries kept developing at a relatively high speed. As for the hi-tech industry[④], the output reached 550.12 billion yuan, up by 16.7%, accounting for 43.6% of all above-scale industries, with a year-on-year growth of 1.2 percentage point. As for the six emerging industries[5], the output reached 417.95 billion yuan, up by 20.1%, accounting for 33.1% of all above-scale industries, with a year-on-year growth of 3.1 percentage point. The coordinated development of regional economy was implemented as the rural area developed faster than the urban area in general. The GDP of rural area was 355.89 billion yuan, up by 10.5%, 0.3 percentage point higher than that of urban area.

There were 18,100 newly-registered private enterprises of the whole year and total number was 227,000 at the end of the year. The whole year's registered capital of the newly-registered private enterprises was 88.26 billion yuan, and the year-end accumulative total was 742.51 billion yuan. There were 52,500 newly-registered individual households of the whole year and the total number reached 534,000 at the end of the year. The registered capital of the newly-registered individual households was 4.95 billion yuan and the year-end accumulative total was 27.4 billion yuan. By the end of the year, there were totally 3,705 above-scale private industrial enterprises, accounting for 74.0% of the whole city's above-scale industrial enterprises. The yearly private industry added value was 175.42 billion yuan, increasing by 12.4%, accounting for 61.2% of total volume of the whole city' industries above designated size.

2. People's Livelihood and Social Security

The income of urban and rural residents kept growing. The per capita disposable income of all residents[6] was 25,340 yuan, up by 9.5% than that of the previous year. According to permanent living areas, the per capita disposable income of urban residents was 33,374 yuan, up by 8.9% than in 2013, while that of rural residents was 15,821 yuan, up by 10.9%.

Composition of Residents' Income in 2014

	All Residents			Urban Residents			Rural Residents		
	Value (yuan)	Increase (%)	Proportion (%)	Value (yuan)	Increase (%)	Proportion (%)	Value (yuan)	Increase (%)	Proportion (%)
Per capita disposable income	25340	9.5	100.0	33374	8.9	100.0	15821	10.9	100.0
Salary income	14701	9.4	58.0	19295	8.9	57.8	9259	10.4	58.5
Net business income	4982	8.7	19.7	6270	7.6	18.8	3453	11.2	21.8
Property income	1565	12.0	6.2	2571	12.3	7.7	373	9.7	2.4
Transfer net income	4092	9.9	16.1	5238	8.8	15.7	2736	12.3	17.3

The per capita consumer spending of all residents reached 17,007 yuan, up by 8.1% than in the previous year. According to permanent living areas, the per capita consumer spending of urban residents was 22,035 yuan, up by 7.2% than in 2013; while that of rural residents was 11,051 yuan, up by 10.3%. By the end of 2014, every 100 urban households possessed 99.4 refrigerators, 181.8 air-conditioners, 232.2 mobile phones, 87.8 PCs, 46 private cars. Every 100 rural households possessed 99.1 refrigerators, 111.8 air-conditioners, 217 mobile phones, 55.8 PCs.

At the end of 2014, the per capita housing construction area was 46.9 ㎡ for urban residents, up by 4.0% than in the previous year. The per capita housing area was 56.1 ㎡ for rural residents, up by 0.7% than in the previous year.

The urban residents' consumer price index was 102.1, which indicated that the general price level increased by 2.1% than in the previous year, among which the price of services rose for 2.0% and the price of consumer goods rose for 2.2%. Eight categories of consumer prices presented the situation of "6 rises and 2 falls".

Rise and Fall of Urban Residents' Consumer Price

Item	Increase than the previous year(%)
Food	2.6
Of which: Grain	2.7
Meat, poultry and other products	0.1
Egg	10.9
Tobacco, liquor and articles	–1.9
Clothing	6.3
Household appliances and maintenance services	3.3
Health care and personal articles	1.1
Transportation and communications	–0.4
Entertainment, education and culture products and services	2.8
Housing⑦	1.0

2014 Monthly Residents' Consumer Price Index

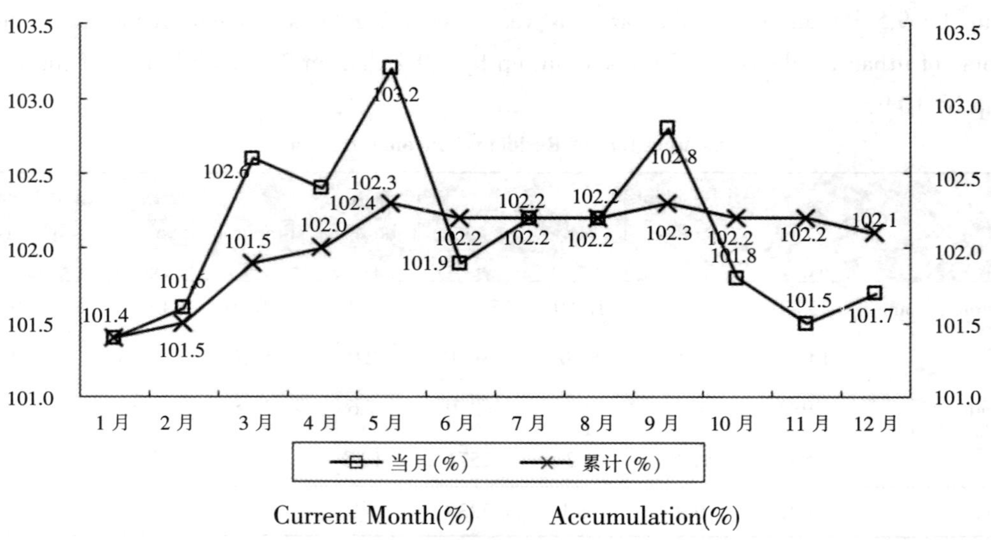

Current Month(%) Accumulation(%)

At the end of 2014, 3.1468 million people attended the basic pension insurance, 51,400 less than that at the end of the previous year. 987,000 people attended the unemployment insurance, 12,700 more than the previous year. 1.2823 million people attended the basic medical insurance (in service), an increase of 49,900. At the end of theyear, 1.22 million people attended the employment injury insurance, an increase of 30,000.

At the end of 2014, there were 230 nursing institutionsfor the aged of various kinds with 56,515 beds in total (among 38,399 beds were within nursing institutions), 96 nursing homes in rural areas with 22,760 beds. The year–end number of rural people who enjoyed the "five guarantees" was 20,924, among which 11,769 were taken care intensively. The nursing capacity of "five guarantees" group reached 108.77%. 67,616 couples registered for marriage of the whole year.

3. Agriculture, Forestry, Husbandry and Fishing Industries

The total output value of the whole city's agriculture, stockbreeding and fishery was 63.19 billion yuan at comparable price, up by 3.6%. Thereinto, the output value of agriculture was 27.89 billion yuan, up by 2.5%;

stockbreeding, 14.51 billion yuan, up by 3.6%; fishery, 14.78 billion yuan, up by 2.4%. The whole year's grain output per mu reached 423 kilograms, up by 1.0%. The sown area of grains was 7.733 million mu, with 0.8% decrease. The sown area of cotton was 558,000 mu, with 7.3% decrease. The sown area of oil plants was 1.902 million mu, with 3.6% decrease. The sown area of vegetable was 1.862 million mu, up by 2.9%.

Output of Main Agricultural and Sideline Products

Product	Unit	Output	Increase than the Previous Year(%)
Grains	10,000 tons	334.02	0.2
Cotton	10,000 tons	4.36	-13.8
Oil Plants	10,000 tons	39.1	-4.3
Silkworm Cocoon	10,000 tons	2.00	2.0
Pigs in Stock	10,000	278.52	0.6
Pigs for Slaughter	10,000	397.37	4.8
Sheep in Stock	10,000	227.33	0.8
Sheep for Slaughter	10,000	279.43	2.3
Poultry in Stock	10,000	4780.86	-3.5
Poultry for Slaughter	10,000	10920.05	-0.1
Poultry Egg	10,000	45.68	持平
Aquatic Products	10,000	88.21	1.7

4. Industry and Construction

The added value of industries above designated size of the whole city⑧ was 286.42 billion yuan, up by 11.4%. Thereinto, the light industry increased by 7.5% and the heavy industry 13.5%. In terms of ownership, the added value of collective industries went up by 5.4%, and that of share-holding industries increased by 12.1%, that of foreign, HK, Macao and Taiwan invested industries increased by 9.3%. Among above-scale industries, the output of six major leading industries all increased. Thereinto, the industry of new energy, energy and equipment manufacturing grew for 18.6%, the industry of electronic information for 16.6% and the industry of shipping and maritime engineering for 14.6% respectively. In terms of industry output, the equipment manufacturing industry took up 599.23 billion yuan, up by 15.1%, accounting for 47.5% among the whole city's total output value of industries above designated value, increasing by 1.5 percentage point than the previous year.

The main business income of the whole city's industries above designated size was 1.23083 trillion yuan, up by 11.1%. The total tax and profit amount was 147.18 billion yuan, up by 15.0%. The total profit amount was 93.64 billion yuan, up by 13.9%. The total loss of loss-suffering enterprises was 2.8 billion yuan, decreasing by 5.2%.

Output of Main Industrial Products

Item	Unit	Output	Increase than the Previous year(%)
Yarn	10,000 tons	62.71	-0.6
Cloth	100 million meters	32.64	0.5
Printed and Dyed Cloth	100 million meters	30.51	6.5
Clothing	100 million	7.63	-0.4
Chemical Fiber	10,000 tons	130.33	27.6
Metal Container	10,000 m^3	420.70	10.2
Electric Portable Tools	10,000 sets	9181.02	13.4
Civil Steel Boats	10,000 deadweight ton	485.38	4.5
Ocean Engineering and Special Boats	10,000 comprehensive ton	910.25	38.6
Communication and Electrcnic Network Cable	10,000 pair km	8.82	5.1
Optical Cable	10,000 core km	841.63	15.2
Integrated Circuit	100 million	99.32	11.8
Semiconductor Discrete Devices	100 million	80.11	-3.5
Power Generation	100 million KWH	403.03	22.4
Of Which: Wind Power Generation	100 million KWH	25.26	0.6

According to preliminary calculation, the whole city's energy consumption equaled 25.6244 million tons of standard coal. The energy consumption for every 10,000 yuan GDP was⑨ 0.478 ton of standard coal, 5.37% decrease than the previous year.

Energy Consumption of 10 Main Industries

Item	Comprehensive Energy Consumption (10,000 tons of standard coal)	Energy Consumption Per Unit Output Value (tons of standard coal/ 10,000 Yuan)	The Growth of Energy Consumption Per Unit Output Value than Last Year (%)
Electric and Heating Power Generation and Supply Industries	673.3	4.0884	8.2
Chemical Raw Material and Chemical Products Manufacturing	220.2	0.1231	-8.7
Textile	137.4	0.1041	-1.3
Chemical Fiber Manufacturing	74.6	0.2064	-4.0
Metal Product Industry	51.4	0.0714	-3.0
Electric Equipment and Machinery Manufacturing	44.3	0.0255	0.3
Ferrous Metal Smelting and Pressing	37.2	0.1596	-15.6
Manufacture of Computers, Communications and Other Electronic Device	28.2	0.0407	-7.8
Non-metallic Mineral Product Manufacturing	27.3	0.0727	-12.5
Manufacture of Culture, Education, Sports and Recreation Products	25.7	0.0495	-6.0

In 2014, the added value of construction industry⑩ was 50.74 billion yuan, up by 6.6%. The construction area undertaken by enterprises was 680 million ㎡, increasing by 11.4%. Of the whole city, there were 1.6857 million people engaged in construction work, with teams extending to 38 countries and regions. At the end of the year, there were 7,600 workers abroad, 15 construction enterprises with premium quality and 7,428 first -grade constructors.

5. Fixed Asset Investment

The whole year's fixed asset investment[11] reached 389.64 billion yuan, 18.1% higher than that of the previous year. Thereinto, the private investment was 289.51 billion yuan with 20.2% increase and accounted for 74.3% of the total fixed-asset investment with 1.3 percentage point increase. The industrial investment was 204.68 billion yuan with 10.3% increase, 59.6% of which was 122.08 billion yuan investment in technological upgrading with 6.4percentage point increase than the previous year. Of all the fixed-asset investment, that of the secondary industry accounted for 204.68 billion yuan, up by 10.3% and that of the tertiary industry 183.97 billion yuan, up by 27.6%. The whole year's infrastructure investment added up to 62.28 billion yuan with 44.0% increase.

2005-2014 Fixed Assets Investment

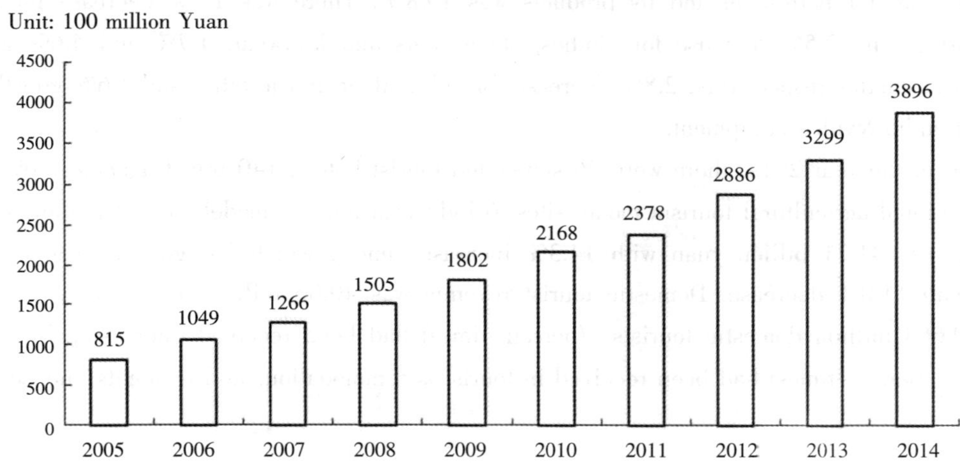

The whole year's investment for real-estate development was 67.89 billion yuan with 13.8% increase. The construction area of commercial housing was 52.722 million m² with 16.3% increase, among which the residential construction area was 39.51 million m² with 12.2% increase. The floor space completed for commercial housing was 10.312 million m² with 11.4% increase, of which the floor space completed for residential building was 8.576 million m² with 11.0% increase. The sales area of commercial housing was 9.192 million m² with 11.2% decrease, of which there were 8.434 million m² for residential building with 10.1% decrease.

6. Domestic Trade and Tourism

The whole year's total social retail sales of consumer goods was 215.35 billion yuan with 11.8% increase, of which it was 156.74 billion yuan with 11.8% increase in urban area and 58.61 billion yuan with 11.7% increase in rural area. As for specific industry, it was 198 billion yuan with 11.5% increase for wholesale and retail sales industry and 17.35 billion yuan with 14.3% increase for accommodation and catering industry.

2005–2014 Social Retail Sales of Consumer Goods

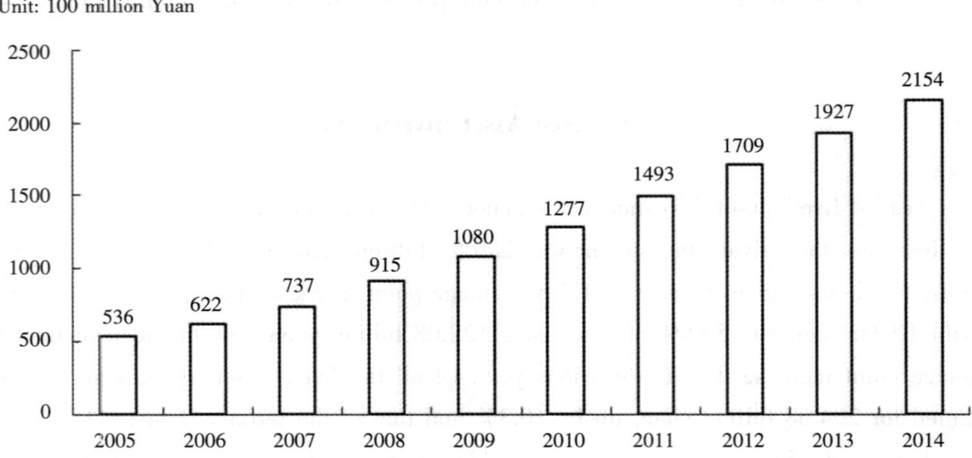

Of total retail sales of enterprises above designated size⑫, the year–on–year growth of sales for motor vehicles was 8.1%, and that for petroleum and its products was 19.8%. There was 1.5% decrease for food, beverage, tobacco and liquor and 2.5% increase for clothes, shoes, hats and knitwear, 1.7% and 4.6% growth for daily necessities and cosmetics respectively, 2.8% decrease for gold, silver and jewelry, and 5.6% growth for household appliances and audio &video equipment.

At the end of the year 2014, there were 96 star–rated tourist hotels, 140 travel agencies, 46 A–Level tourist attractions, 2 national agricultural tourism model sites, 6 industrial tourism model sites. The tourist total income of the whole year was 41.21 billion yuan with 14.3% increase, among which foreign exchange earnings was 110 million USD with 11.0% decrease. Domestic tourist revenue was 40.06 billion yuan, up by 15.0%. As for the whole year, 30.663 million domestic tourists (person–times) had been received, increasing by 12.9%. 187,000 overseas tourists (person–times) had been received in tourist accommodations and residents' houses, decreasing by 13.7%.

7. Open Economy

The total value of goods import and export in 2014 reached 31.65 billion USD, up by 6.2% over the previous year. Of this total, the value of exported goods was 22.48 billion USD, up by 5.7%, and the value of imported goods reached 9.17 billion USD, up by 7.4%. At the end of the year, there were 199 countries and regions which developed import –export trade ties with Nantong. There were 5,094 enterprises with import and export performances, up by 9.8%.

2005-2014 Total Output of Exports

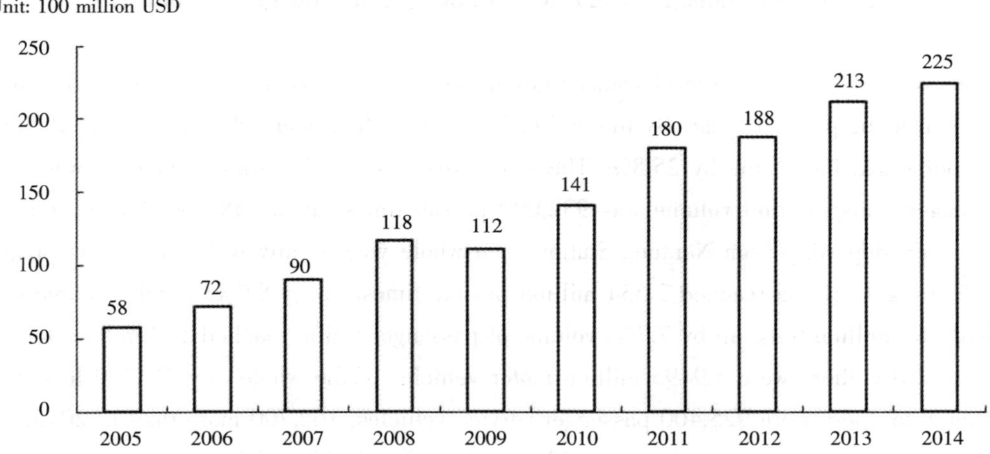

Categorization of Import &Export Modes and Export Market

Item	Volume (100 million USD)	Increase than the Previous Year(%)
Total Value of Imports &Exports	316.47	6.2
Import	91.67	7.4
Export	224.80	5.7
#Joint-venture Enterprises	117.78	8.8
Private Enterprises	99.74	11.1
#General Trade	147.68	10.3
Processing Trade	71.93	-1.5
#Textile Products	70.71	5.9
Mechanical &Electrical Products	92.02	5.7
Hi-tech Products	24.42	0.2
#Shipping &Marine Products	26.31	-7.9
Photovoltaic Products	7.37	-0.2
#Asia	123.05	4.5
#ASEAN	32.80	-3.6
Japan	37.58	-2.6
Europe	40.35	15.5
#EU	34.75	7.2
North America	33.49	110.0
#US	31.05	11.4

There were 305 newly-approved foreign invested projects in 2014, 13.3% lower than the previous year. Thereinto, there were 140 projects over 10 million USD, a 4.8% decrease. The newly-approved registered foreign capital with agreement reached 5.52 billion USD with 11.5% increase. The paid-in registered foreign capital was 2.3 billion USD, up by 0.9%.

There were 78 newly approved and established overseas enterprises and domestic agreement investment reached 920 million USD. As for newly-signed foreign contracted labor agreement, the amount was 1.86 billion USD with 0.1% increase. As for the turnover of foreign contracted labor services, it was 2.27 billion USD with 14.8% increase. As for newly-assigned outsourcing laborers, there were 9,400 person-times, with 22.0% decrease. There were 23,000 laborers aboard at the end of 2014, up by 3.4%.

8. Transportations, Post &Telecommunications and Power Industry

Of the whole year, the added value of transportation, storage and post industries amounted to 20.44 billion yuan, up by 8.2% over the previous year. By the end of 2014, there had been 14 civil airlines at Nantong Airport, with 122 flights per week, increasing by 25.8%. The whole year's civil air cargo throughput was 32,000 tons, up by 29.8%. Passenger transportation volume was 932,000 person times, up by 38.0%. At the end of 2014, there were 13 pairs of train departing from Nantong Station. The whole year's railway freight volume reached 911,000 tons, up by 5.1%; freight volume reached 2.534 million person-times, up by 8.0%; freight volume of highway and waterway reached 180 million tons, up by 7.7%; volume of passenger traffic reached 100 million tons, up by 1.7%.

At the end of 2014, there were 1.9495 million motor vehicles of the whole city, 75,200 less than that at the end of 2013. Thereinto, there were 925,400 passenger service vehicles, 162,700 more than in 2013; 70,200 trucks, 2,800 more than in 2013; 948,000 motor bicycles, 235,600 less than in 2013. The year-end number of private car was 869,400, 153,400 more than in 2013.

For Nantong Port, the whole year's cargo throughput reached 220 million tons, up by 7.4%. Thereinto, inward cargo was 130 million tons, with 7.7% increase; throughput of foreign trade was 48.14 million tons, with 6.1% increase. Container throughput reached 711,000 standard containers, increasing by 18.4%, 316,000 of which were for international lines, increasing by 3.4%.

The turnover of post and telecommunication services totaled 9.35 billion yuan, up by 19.9%. Of the total, there were 2.82 billion yuan for post, 6.52 billion yuan for telecommunication services, up by 27.3% and 0.4% respectively. At the end of 2014, there were 2.321 million fixed-phone users, 92,000 less than the previous year. There were 1.116 million urban fixed phone users, an increase of 22,000, and that of residential phones was 1.789 million, 114,000 less than the previous year. At the end of the year, there were 7.892 million internet users, an increase of 647,000, of which 1.909 million subscribed fixed broadband internet, an increase of 297,000 and 5.983 million subscribed wireless broadband internet, an increase of 50,000.

In 2014, the power consumption was 33.323 billion KWH, up by 2.2%. Thereinto, the power construction for the primary industry accounted for 600 million KWH, up by 11.7%; 24.89 billion KWH for the secondary industry, up by 3.7%; 3.46 billion KWH for the tertiary industry, up by 4.2%. The power consumption for urban and rural residents' living was 4.37 billion KWH, 7.9% lower than the previous year.

9. Finance and Banking

In 2014, the general public budgetary revenue was 55 billion yuan, increasing by 13.2%, among which added value tax grew for 9.7% and turnover tax grew for 7.3%. The whole year's general public budgetary expenditure reached 65 billion yuan, up by 12.8%. 37.17 billion yuan of the local public financial budgetary expenditure was devoted into social security and employment, science &technology, education, medical health, environment protection and other fields of social wellbeing, with 15.0% growth, accounting for 57.2% of the general public budgetary expenditure and increasing by 1.1 percentage points than the previous year.

The whole year's deposit increment of financial institutions was 96.62 billion yuan and the year-end deposit balance was 850.83 billion yuan, increasing by 12.8% than the previous year. Thereinto, saving deposit balance was 462.39 billion yuan, with 11.4% increase; the saving deposit balance of enterprises and public institutions was 364.39 billion yuan, with 14.7% increment. The whole year's new loan of financial system was 58.61 billion yuan, decreasing by 12.0%. At the year end, all loan balance was 525.89 billion yuan, increasing by 12.5% than then end of the previous year. For the whole year, 4.4 billion yuan of housing provident fund loans was released, with 20.5% decrease. 4.34 billion yuan of housing provident fund was withdrawn, with 8.0% increase. There were 100,000 newly-opened accounts for housing fund and the total number had amounted to 846,000 by the end of 2014.

In 2014, there were 4 insurance institutions newly established and the total number reached 74 at the end of the year, with 16,000 employees. The whole year's premium income was 15.4 billion, increasing by 10.1%. Thereinto, the property insurance income was 4.92 billion yuan, up by 24.6%; life insurance income was 10.48 billion yuan, increasing by 17.1%; settled claims and payments were 6.87 billion yuan, up by 22.2%.

10. Science &Technology and Education

By the end of 2014, there were 663 high-tech enterprises. There were 948 newly-added high-tech products, 3 newly-established provincial-level key laboratories, 30 provincial-level engineering centers, 1 provincial-level enterprise academician workshop, 5 newly-built municipal-level public technique service platforms, 98 municipal-level engineering technology research centers, and 3 municipal-level enterprise academician workshops. For the whole year, 18 projects won science &technology advancement prizes, among which 2 won state second prize, 5 won provincial second prize and 11 won provincial third prize. By the end of the year, there had been 61 S&T incubators, including 9 state-level ones and 22 provincial-level ones. There were 27,692 patent applications, with 43.9% decrease than that of the previous year; 12,391 patent authorizations, with 43.9% year-on-year decrease. Thereinto, 8,450 were invention patent applications, up by 5.2%; 932 invention patents had been granted, up by 24.9%. Invention patents per 10,000 people numbered 11.53, increasing by 80%. The social expenditure on research accounted for 2.42% of GDP, 0.07 percentage point higher than the previous year.

Of the whole city, there were 8 general institutes of higher education, with 87,400 students at the end of 2014; 2 adult colleges, with 25,600 students; 21 secondary vocational schools, with 64,100 students; 52 regular high schools, with 90,900 students; 163 regular junior secondary schools, with 156,500 students; 321 primary schools, with 320,400 students; 9 special schools, with 900 students; 396 kindergartens of various kinds, with 153,500 children.

11. Culture, Health and Sports

At the end of the year, there were 9 cultural centers, 99 cultural stations, 11 public libraries, 1,614 "farmer's bookstores" in Nantong. The city boasted 21 museums (memorial halls) and every 10,000 people shared 1,119.5m² area of public cultural facilities. There were 205 historical sites under protection, 10 of which were under state protection and 22 under provincial protection. There were 106 intangible cultural heritages above state level, 10 of which were at state level and 40 were at provincial level. There were 7 broadcast and TV stations, with 94,000 new cable TV subscribers, and the cable TV penetration rate reached 96.9%. There were 1,240 enterprises in cultural market and 2,531 enterprises engaged in printing and distribution. There were 29 cultural industry demonstrative parks (bases), 2 of which were at state level, 5 at provincial level. 4 towns in Nantong were newly honored as China Folk Art Town.

The year-end number of health agencies citywide was 1,621 (exclusive of rural community health stations and town clinics), among which there were 304 hospitals and clinics, 7 maternity and child health care centers (agency or station), 3 specialized subject hospital for disease control and prevention. For the whole city, there were 35,100 health agency beds with 39,500 health workers, including 16,400 practicing and assistant physicians, 15,600 registered nurses. The city owned 9 centers for disease prevention with 463 health workers, 8 health inspection institutes with 265 health workers, 103 township hospitals with 7,300 beds and 7,200 health workers.

There were 21 urban community health service centers in Nantong's downtown are (Tongzhou District excluded), with 100% establishing rate, counting by the unit of sub-districts (township). 1,641 rural community health service stations and village clinics had been established in total with 100% coverage of administrative villages. The whole city's participation rate of new rural cooperative medial health system was 99.98% and the rural tap water coverage rate was 100%.

The city had undertaken 9 national competitions and 11 provincial ones in 2014. There was an increment of 197 sites for morning and evening exercise citywide and a participation of more than 213,000 person-times into various national fitness activities. The yearly sales of sports lottery reached a historical record of 1.34 billion yuan.

12. Environment Protection and Work Safety

There were 770 hectares of new green space in the downtown area (Tongzhou District included), and the urban green coverage reached 42.3%. The daily water supply capacity was 1.6 million m^3, and the pass rate of water quality comprehensive index was 100%. The downtown's penetration rates of gas, tap water and innocuous disposal of domestic garbage all reached 100%. There was an increment of 55,442 road lamps and landscape lights in the downtown area of the whole year, and 99.7% of the urban roads were equipped with lights.

In 2014, there were 61 sets of newly-built (transformed) coal-fired thermal power and thermoelectric desulfurizingequipment, 64 sets of denitration?facilities, 64 sets of dust removing renovation equipment. The average desulfurizing efficiency of boilers reached above 90% and comprehensive denitration efficiency reached above 70%. The dust emission had been basically controlled within the special limit of key areas. There were "no-fly zones" set all around the city.

The whole city's environment quality kept stable. The yearly averages of main ambient air pollutants were 0.026 mg/ m^3 for SO_2, 0.04 mg/ m^3 for NO_2, 0.096 mg/ m^3 for PM10 and 0.062 mg/ m^3 for PM2.5. The annual averages of $SO_2$and NO_2 reached the national secondary level of air quality, while the annual averages of PM10 and PM2.5were above the national secondary level. There were 257 days with good air quality, accounting for 70.8% of the whole year. The mainstream water of Yangtze River in Nantong conformed to national ground water quality Ⅲ standard and the drinking water sources were 100% qualified. The average of regional environment noise in urban area was 58.0 dB, and the average of artery traffic noise was 68.1 dB, both conforming to the national standard.

There were 1,027 work safety accidents and 164 deaths, reducing by 4.82% and 4.10% respectively. Thereinto, there were 19 deadly cases with 27 deaths of industrial and mining business enterprises (including construction industry). In 2014, there were 5,985 fire accidents, causing 20 died, 20 injured, and the direct economic loss reached 18.322 million yuan. For the whole city, there were 1,285 cases of above-average road traffic accidents, causing 437 died and 1,172 injured.

Notes:

① Data of 2014 released in this bulletin are quick statistic data. Due to the rounding-off?reasons, the? subentries may not add up to?theaggregate?totals.

② Gross domestic product and absolute value added of all industries are calculated at current price and growth rates are calculated at constant price. Relevant data were revised according to the 3rd national economic census and the"Regulation on Classification of ThreeSectors "promulgated by NBS in 2012.

③ All labor productivity is the ratio of GDP (calculated at 2010 constant price) to all working labors.

④ Hi-tech industrial output is calculated based on "The Notice on Releasing 'Jiangsu High-tech Industrial Statistics Classified Catalogue'(2012 revised version)"(Jiangsu Hi-tech [2012] No. 332), including aircraft and spacecraft industry, electronic computer and office equipment industry, electronic and telecommunications industry, pharmaceutical industry, instrument and meter industry, intelligent equipment industry, and new material industry.

⑤ Emerging industries comprise new energy industry, new material industry, biological technology and new medicine manufacturing, intelligent equipment industry, energy saving and environment protection industry, as well as oceanic engineering equipment manufacturing.

⑥ Since the fourth quarter of 2012, NBS initiated innovation of urban-rural integration household survey, by making uniform standards for urban and rural residents' income items, classification and statistics. 160,000 urban and rural households were selected for direct survey, based on which two types of data were attained—the comparable new caliber for all residents per capita disposable income and the separateurban and rural residents per capita disposable income. As for the number of durable consumer goodspossessed, it is incomparable to those of previous years as it was first collected after the urban-rural integration reforms.

⑦ Housing prices include those of construction, decoration, residential rents, owner occupied housing, as well as water, electricity and fuels.

⑧ Above-scale industrial statistics refer to industrial enterprises with annual main operation revenue of 20 million yuan and above.

⑨ General energy consumption for every 10,000 yuan GDP was calculated at 2010 fixed price

⑩ Statistics of construction industry refer to qualified construction enterprises

⑪Statistics of fixed asset investment refer to construction projects with 5 million yuan total investment and above. Statistics of real estate refer to real estate development and operation enterprises.

⑫As for statistics of retail sales of social consumer goods, above-designated units refer to whole-sale enterprises (units) with annual main business revenue of 20 million yuan and above, retail enterprises (units) with annual main business revenue of 5 million yuan and above, as well as accommodation and catering enterprises (units) with annual main business revenue of 2 million yuan and above.

第一篇 综合

Chapter 1

General Survey

1-1 行政区划和土地面积(2014年)

ADMINISTRATIVE DIVISION AND LAND AREA(2014)

单位:个 (unit)

地区	Region	街道 Subdistrict	镇 Town	乡 Township	居委会 Neighborhood Committee	村委会 Village Committee	村民小组 Village Group	土地面积(平方公里) Area of Land (sq-km)
全市	**Whole Municipality**	**26**	**73**	**2**	**595**	**1315**	**39625**	**10549**
市区	**Urban Area**	**20**	**19**		**230**	**237**	**10065**	**2140**
崇川区	Chongchuan District	12			113			160
港闸区	Gangzha District	6			37	27	712	152
开发区	Development Zone	2			16	2	49	267
通州区	Tongzhou District		19		64	208	9304	1562
县(市)	**County(City at County Level)**	**6**	**54**	**2**	**365**	**1078**	**29560**	**8409**
海 安	Haian		10		31	207	5097	1184
如 东	Rudong		14		48	213	5627	2791
启 东	Qidong		11	1	36	261	6319	1715
如 皋	Rugao	3	11		181	166	4322	1576
海 门	Haimen	3	8	1	69	231	8195	1144

1-2 分地区乡、镇、街道名单(2014年)

LIST OF COUNTIES,TOWNS AND SUBDISTRICT OFFICES(2014)

地区	Region	乡、镇、街道数(个) Number(unit)	乡、镇、街道名称 Names
市区	**Urban Area**		
崇川区	Chongchuan District	12	钟秀街办、任港街办、文峰街办、城东街办、和平桥街办、新城桥街办、虹桥街办、学田街办、观音山街办、狼山街办、竹行街办、小海街办
富民办	Development Zone	2	新开街办、中兴街办
港闸区	Gangzha District	6	永兴街办、唐闸街办、天生港街办、秦灶街办、陈桥街办、幸福街办
通州区	Tongzhou	19	金沙镇、石港镇、三余镇、平潮镇、十总镇、二甲镇、五接镇、平东镇、刘桥镇、兴仁镇、四安镇、骑岸镇、西亭镇、兴东镇、五甲镇、东社镇、川姜镇、先锋镇、张芝山镇
县(市)	**County(City at County Level)**		
海　安	Haian	10	海安镇、角斜镇、李堡镇、大公镇、城东镇、白甸镇、雅周镇、南莫镇、墩头镇、曲塘镇
如　东	Rudong	14	掘港镇、马塘镇、新店镇、长沙镇、曹埠镇、岔河镇、双甸镇、苴镇、拼茶镇、袁庄镇、大豫镇、河口镇、洋口镇、丰利镇
启　东	Qidong	12	汇龙镇、南阳镇、北新镇、王鲍镇、合作镇、吕四港镇、海复镇、近海镇、惠萍镇、东海镇、寅阳镇、启隆乡
如　皋	Rugao	14	如城街办、城北街办、城南街办、搬经镇、东陈镇、磨头镇、吴窑镇、丁堰镇、九华镇、长江镇、下原镇、白蒲镇、石庄镇、江安镇
海　门	Haimen	12	海门街道、滨江街道、三厂街道、临江镇、三星镇、常乐镇、悦来镇、四甲镇、余东镇、正余镇、包场镇、海永乡

1–3 分月气象情况(2014 年)
MONTHLY CLIMATE CONDITION(2014)

月 份	Month	平均气温（摄氏度）Average Temperature (centigrade)	降水量（毫米）Precipitation (millimeters)	日照时数（小时）Sunshine Hours (hours)	平均相对湿度（%）Average Relative Humidity(%)	平均风力（米/秒）Average Wind Force (m/second)
全年	**Annual Total**	**15.9**	**1326.5**	**1825.0**	**78**	**2.9**
1 月	Jan.	5.1	15.5	171.9	73	2.5
2 月	Feb.	4.8	119.7	84.9	83	3.7
3 月	Mar.	10.3	69.6	164.4	74	3.0
4 月	Apr.	15.0	102.7	163.6	79	3.1
5 月	May	21.4	52.6	227.4	66	3.3
6 月	Jun.	23.1	127.9	107.6	82	2.9
7 月	Jul.	26.6	297.0	153.7	85	3.0
8 月	Aug.	25.4	328.9	104.9	88	2.5
9 月	Sept.	23.1	117.6	97.9	85	3.1
10 月	Oct.	18.6	12.3	209.8	76	2.6
11 月	Nov.	13.1	74.4	140.7	76	2.4
12 月	Dec.	4.2	8.3	198.2	63	2.4

1-4 水文情况(2014年)

HYDROLOGIC CONDITION(2014)

指 标	Item	数 值 Number
汛期(日/月)	Flood Seasons(day/month)	2014年5月1日至2014年10月31日
非汛期(日/月)	Non Flood Seasons(day/month)	2014年1月1日至2014年4月30日 2014年11月1日至2014年12月31日
水位	Water Level	
年最高水位(米)	Annual Highest(meter)	3.50
日期(日/月)	Date(day/month)	8-13
年最低水位(米)	Annual Lowest(meter)	0.20
日期(日/月)	Date(day/month)	4-30
地下水位	Ground Water Level	
年最高地下水位(米)	Annual Highest(meter)	3.08
日期(日/月)	Date(day/month)	8-9
年最低地下水(米)	Annual Lowest(meter)	1.81
日期(日/月)	Date(day/month)	4-8
蒸发量	Evaporation	
年蒸发量(毫米)	Annual Evaporation(mm)	764.4
日最大值(毫米)	Daily Highest(mm)	6.6
日期(日/月)	Date(day/month)	7-23
日最小值(毫米)	Daily Lowest(mm)	0.0
日期(日/月)	Date(day/month)	1-11
降水量	Rainfall	
年降水量(毫米)	Annual Amount(mm)	1509.1
日最大量(毫米)	Daily Largest(mm)	139.4
日期(日/月)	Date(day/month)	8-7
年引水总量(万立方米)	Annual Water Introduction(10,000m^3)	
九圩港闸	Jiuweigang Dam	113700
节制闸	Jiezhizha Dam	67970
年排水总量(万立方米)	Annual Drainage(10,000m^3)	
九圩港闸	Jiuweigang Dam	13240
节制闸	Jiezhizha Dam	8652
最大流量	Largest Flowing	
引水	Water Introduction	
九圩港闸(立方米/秒)	Jiuweigang Dam(m^3/s)	1080
节制闸(立方米/秒)	Jiezhizha Dam(m^3/s)	699
# 日期(日/月)	Date(day/month)	8月11日
排水	Drainage	
九圩港闸(立方米/秒)	Jiuweigang Dam(m^3/s)	867
节制闸(立方米/秒)	Jiezhizha Dam(m^3/s)	589
# 日期(日/月)	Date(day/month)	8月14日

1-5 主要年份国民经济主要指标

指　标	Item	1978	1980	1990
人口	**Population**			
年末户籍人口(万人)	Registered Population at Year-end(10,000 persons)	722.71	729.11	776.01
男	Male	360.80	363.81	390.61
女	Female	361.91	365.30	385.40
年末常住人口(万人)	Permanent Residents at Year-End (10,000 persons)			
城镇	Urban Area			
农村	Rural Area			
劳动力	**Labor Force**			
年末从业人员(万人)	Employees At Year-end(10,000 persons)	400.62	413.95	477.47
#在岗职工	Employed Staff and Workers			
#国有经济	State-Owned Economy	27.16	31.37	42.25
#第一产业	Primary Industry	306.68	302.06	242.88
第二产业	Secondary Industry	56.74	67.77	154.92
第三产业	Tertiary Industry	37.20	44.12	79.67
国民经济核算	**Accounting by National Economy**			
地区生产总值(亿元)	GDP(100 million yuan)	29.39	35.66	134.25
第一产业	Primary Industry	12.28	11.61	42.88
第二产业	Secondary Industry	10.98	16.10	60.46
工业	Industry	9.99	14.58	54.55
建筑业	Construction	0.99	1.52	5.91
第三产业	Tertiary Industry	6.12	7.95	30.90
人均 GDP(元)	Per Capita GDP(yuan)	408	490	1736
财政	**Finance (100 million yuan)**			
财政总收入(亿元)	Financial Revenue	5.49	5.94	12.69
#一般公共预算收入	General public budget revenue			12.69
财政总支出(亿元)	Financial Expenditure (100 million yuan)	1.61	1.74	7.15
财政总收入占 GDP 比重(%)	Percentage of Financial Revenue in GDP	18.7	16.7	9.5
一般公共财政收入占 GDP 比重(%)	Percentage of Local Public Financial Budget Revenue in GDP			9.5
从业人员平均工资	**Average Income of Employees**			
在岗职工平均工资(元)	Average Wage of Employed Workers (Yuan)			
城镇居民人均可支配收入(元)	Per Capita Disposable Income of Urban Residents (Yuan)			
市区城镇居民人均住房建筑面积(M²)	Per Capita Housing Area of Urban Residents (m²)			
农村居民人均可支配收入(元)	Per Capita Net Income of Rural Residents (Yuan)			871
农村居民人均住房面积(M²)	Per Capita Housing Area of Rural Residents (m²)			

注:2010 年起从业人员口径有调整;2013、2014 在岗职工口径调整为城镇非私营。2013 年起城乡居民人均可支配收入按新口径统计。

MAJOR NATIONAL ECONOMIC INDICATORS OVER YEARS

2000	2005	2006	2007	2008	2009	2010	2011	2012	2013	2014
784.53	770.86	769.79	766.13	763.72	762.66	762.92	764.88	765.20	766.51	767.63
391.57	383.20	382.47	380.12	378.56	377.60	377.37	378.01	377.78	378.07	378.28
392.96	387.66	387.32	386.01	385.16	385.06	385.55	386.87	387.42	388.44	389.35
714.77	732.28	724.93	717.95	714.77	713.37	728.18	728.91	729.73	729.77	729.80
359.17	326.60	339.99	348.92	359.17	375.95	407.78	419.85	428.57	437.13	446.27
355.60	405.68	384.94	369.03	355.60	337.42	320.40	309.06	301.16	292.64	283.53
441.46	444.40	449.45	457.23	454.90	460.52	474.00	473.00	468.90	467.20	462.00
62.59	53.29	54.97	57.74	57.55	58.17	58.96	63.04	64.95	146.81	157.88
30.91	19.77	19.41	19.17	18.99	18.81	18.78	20.10	21.01	17.60	18.6
200.04	133.93	108.22	97.36	90.46	84.77	125.50	121.70	114.50	107.30	101.70
138.39	178.30	190.99	203.63	200.97	207.20	211.10	212.80	214.10	216.60	216.00
103.03	132.17	150.24	156.24	163.48	168.55	137.40	138.50	140.30	143.30	144.30
720.59	1483.80	1788.39	2163.69	2593.13	2872.80	3465.67	4080.22	4558.67	5038.89	5652.69
128.64	163.90	176.29	186.80	219.30	236.47	266.22	287.21	319.09	345.41	339.57
361.03	828.79	992.11	1209.96	1451.63	1607.50	1908.56	2221.48	2414.11	2623.50	2812.34
302.69	677.09	821.31	1021.80	1219.60	1319.43	1568.49	1840.41	1992.11	2168.16	2307.64
58.34	151.70	170.80	188.16	232.03	288.07	340.07	381.07	422.00	455.34	507.40
230.92	491.10	620.00	766.93	922.20	1028.84	1290.89	1571.53	1825.47	2069.98	2500.78
9176	20138	24545	29991	36199	40231	48083	56005	62506	69050	77457
53.40	171.19	217.57	300.71	390.21	486.10	713.36	951.65	1055.90	1216.73	1403.93
28.45	71.99	92.53	127.70	159.59	198.99	290.81	373.69	419.72	485.88	550.00
29.31	121.69	152.97	207.07	292.53	387.26	546.18	762.10	937.60	1060.73	1220.52
7.4	11.6	12.4	13.9	15.0	16.9	20.6	23.3	23.2	24.1	24.8
3.9	4.9	5.2	5.9	6.2	6.9	8.4	9.2	9.2	9.6	9.7
9247	18513	21662	25947	30856	35224	39448	44574	49399	57546	61383
	11590	13056	15261	17540	19469	21825	25094	28292	31059	33374
	29.1	29.4	30.0	31.9	32.3	32.8	35.0	35.5	39.8	40.0
3710	5501	6106	6905	7811	8696	9914	11730	13231	14754	15821
	49.6	50.1	51.6	52.5	53.5	53.6	54.5	54.8	55.7	55.9

Note: The calibre of employees has been adjusted since 2010. The calibre of on–post staff was adjusted to non–private workers in 2013、2014.

1–5 续表 1

指 标	Item	1978	1980	1990
物价	**Price of Commodities**			
居民消费价格总指数	General Consumer Price Index	100.2	102.9	102.1
商品零售价格总指数	General Retail Price Index	100.2	103.4	102.7
固定资产投资	**Fixed Assets Investment**			
固定资产投资完成额(亿元)	Completion of Fixed Assets Investment (100 million Yuan)			20.78
#工业	Industry			
服务业	Service Industry			
房屋施工面积(万 M²)	Housing Area under Construction (10,000 m2)			
房屋竣工面积(万 M²)	Housing Area Completed (10,000 m2)			
农业	**Agriculture**			
农林牧渔业总产值(现价)(亿元)	Total Output(current price) (100 million Yuan)			69.77
农业	Agriculture			43.78
林业	Forestry			0.53
牧业	Husbandry			18.96
渔业	Fishery			6.50
农林牧渔服务业	Related Service Industry			
主要农产品产量	Output of Major Agricultural Products			
粮食(万吨)	Grain (10,000 tons)	230.50	219.82	300.73
棉花(万吨)	Cotton (10,000 tons)	20.32	12.99	9.16
油料(万吨)	Oil Products (10,000 tons)	4.34	3.24	18.78
蚕茧(吨)	Silkworm Cocoons (ton)	5807	8795	32594
水产品(万吨)	Aquatic Products (10,000 tons)	10.52	10.68	18.18
生猪出栏数(万头)	Pigs for Slaughter(10,000 heads)	193.16	297.73	231.42
生猪年末存栏数(万头)	Year-end Pigs in Stock(10,000 heads)	310.23	265.40	212.96
工业	**Industry**			
工业总产值(亿元)	Total Industrial Output (100 million Yuan)			
#高新技术产业产值	Output of High &New Tech Industry			
新兴产业产值	Emerging Industry Output			
民营工业产值	Private Industry Output			
主营业务收入(亿元)	Main Business Income (100 million Yuan)			
利税总额(亿元)	Total Pre-tax Profits (100 million Yuan)			
利润总额(亿元)	Total Profits (100 million Yuan)			

CONTINUED 1

2000	2005	2006	2007	2008	2009	2010	2011	2012	2013	2014
98.4	101.2	101.7	105.1	104.8	98.7	103.7	105.0	102.50	102.20	102.10
99.3	99.6	100.3	103.9	105.9	98.6	102.4	104.9	102.30	101.80	101.60
239.50	815.26	1048.90	1265.80	1505.41	1802.38	2168.38	2378.36	2886.47	3298.73	3896.39
82.97	617.72	796.18	970.66	1145.68	1329.72	1530.11	1538.79	1710.04	1856.06	2046.82
			262.22	327.25	441.52	600.75	836.52	1172.11	1440.75	1839.66
	2546	3155	4302	4963	5400	6497	7063	8566	9427	11329
	1289	1231	1585	2007	2164	2517	2930	3168	3002	4125
246.88	292.69	305.41	324.50	371.46	420.58	467.11	502.27	548.86	594.78	631.88
134.14	126.69	129.58	136.04	153.89	175.94	207.46	217.93	243.71	263.63	278.94
1.45	1.92	2.33	2.61	2.80	3.06	3.00	3.07	3.38	3.73	4.07
52.17	77.98	83.19	89.89	107.13	113.21	118.99	133.02	130.48	138.25	145.07
59.12	74.27	77.8	82.26	92.75	105.88	113.10	118.47	131.00	141.11	147.83
	11.83	12.51	13.70	14.89	22.49	24.56	29.78	40.29	48.06	55.97
340.60	294.19	319.48	297.47	319.12	320.62	324.94	329.12	332.97	333.46	334.02
3.25	5.11	5.48	7.84	6.76	5.31	5.95	5.44	5.53	5.07	4.36
39.41	40.67	40.49	34.70	38.07	42.55	42.21	40.00	39.20	40.84	39.06
30253	42625	53360	45924	43371	32632	34383	29100	27229	21175	20008
58.56	69.16	72.28	75.80	76.02	76.00	78.92	82.09	84.80	86.71	88.21
257.93	309.29	303.04	302.22	327.47	348.35	357.28	371.43	391.38	379.28	394.71
254.80	289.83	282.86	283.61	289.19	293.25	284.89	299.98	298.53	276.87	270.76
697.10	2143.39	2949.53	4029.42	5297.08	6094.89	7383.16	8679.82	9890.12	11253.96	12499.70
	426.15	641.75	975.33	1438.02	1815.15	2431.20	3159.24	3936.84	4587.19	5312.93
					1120.73	1615.82	2002.92	2573.69	3404.23	4179.54
			2360.92	3089.93	3581.53	4314.08	4983.45	5782.30	6923.73	7770.49
615.72	2081.14	2919.56	3991.15	5236.83	5957.83	7254.56	8432.59	9690.95	11195.81	12351.36
57.28	162.68	241.32	377.15	673.40	625.74	825.79	1017.50	1160.15	1331.02	1477.71
24.47	99.60	157.05	246.87	303.61	402.10	553.09	694.85	786.59	861.52	937.85

1-5 续表 2

指 标	Item	1978	1980	1990
主要工业产品产量	Output of Major Industrial Products			
纱(万吨)	Yarn (10,000 tons)	5.45	6.83	12.52
布(亿米)	Cloth (100 million meters)	2.71	3.53	6.83
农用化肥(万吨)	Agricultral Fertilizer (10,000 tons)	5.53	7.86	9.24
化学农药(万吨)	Chemical Pesticide (10,000 tons)	0.87	0.90	1.00
烧碱(万吨)	Caustic Soda (10,000 tons)	1.85	2.06	3.24
发电量(亿千瓦时)	Power Generation (TWh)	7.66	14.35	50.35
水泥(万吨)	Cement (10,000 tons)	17.17	24.83	73.07
交通	**Transportation**			
全社会旅客运输量(万人次)	Total Passenger Transportaton (10,000 person-times)	1666	2442	4600
全社会货物运输量(万吨)	Total Cargo Transportation (10,000 tons)	1163	1188	2949
南通港货物吞吐量(万吨)	Nantong Port Cargo Throughput (10,000 tons)	302	293	1043
#外贸吞吐量	Foreign Trade Throughput		5	146
南通港集装箱吞吐量(万标箱)	Nantong Port Container Throughput (10,000 TEU)			1.09
邮电	**Post and Telecommunications**			
邮电业务收入(亿元)	Postal Service Income (100 million Yuan)			
年末固定电话用户(万户)	Year-end Fixed Phone Users (10,000 households)			
年末移动电话用户(万户)	Year-end Mobile Phone Users (10,000 households)			
国际互联网用户(万户)	International Internet Users (10,000 households)			
国内外贸易	**Foreign and Domestic Trade**			
社会消费品零售总额(亿元)	Total Social Consumer Goods Retailing (100 million Yuan)	8.19	13.56	52.45
进出口总值(亿美元)	Total Volume of Imports &Exports (100 million USD)			
进口	Imports			
出口	Exports			
新批协议注册外资(亿美元)	Newly-Approved Contract Registered Foreign Capital (100 million USD)			
实际到账注册外资(亿美元)	Actual Registered Foreign Capital (100 million USD)			0.42
新签对外劳务承包合同额(亿美元)	Newly-Signed Overseas Labor Contract (100 million USD)			
对外劳务承包完成营业额(亿美元)	Completed Revenue of Overseas Labor Contract (100 million USD)			

CONTINUED 2

2000	2005	2006	2007	2008	2009	2010	2011	2012	2013	2014
18.22	38.37	47.20	48.64	54.10	53.61	55.69	49.83	50.28	56.77	62.71
10.80	17.58	22.57	25.29	25.85	27.99	31.10	27.27	27.98	27.54	32.64
8.64	11.02	10.81	7.04	6.32	6.36	5.34	5.57	5.86	2.43	1.74
2.72	7.53	8.85	10.41	9.56	13.82	12.98	15.26	16.09	19.20	18.95
6.23	10.60	16.87	18.65	14.53	13.64	15.56	17.28	17.42	16.76	18.06
97.36	162.11	169.52	160.14	161.81	147.69	279.87	326.84	328.99	328.98	403.03
177.30	519.89	757.25	706.60	815.96	885.81	895.34	860.50	982.80	1049.57	1110.85
7654	9319	10092	11719	13672	14099	16715	19851	21621	22421	10345
6678	9751	10574	12024	12307	15916	20301	24213	26815	30347	18408
2748	8327	10386	12339	13214	13641	15070	17331	18526	20494	22019
491	776	966	1882	2440	2860	2961	3114	3867	4056	4814
18.24	30.12	36.07	42.80	44.33	35.06	46.23	53.98	50.43	60.06	71.10
	35.71	40.41	46.20	51.18	57.64	59.06	65.30	72.18	85.72	76.17
	260	267	300	289	273	243	361	260	253	256
	238.48	281.27	334.20	381.49	510.16	592.89	775.22	809.13	852.03	864.00
	25.30	20.97	30.96	48.60	59.30	82.96	388.66	582.51	729.45	789.22
250.11	536.41	621.96	736.54	915.10	1080.22	1277.07	1493.27	1719.27	1940.39	2166.10
31.56	85.20	100.62	127.76	166.88	162.59	210.96	258.44	263.01	298.14	316.47
11.21	27.27	28.49	37.53	49.36	50.79	69.89	78.14	75.15	85.36	91.67
20.35	57.93	72.13	90.23	117.52	111.80	141.07	180.30	187.86	212.78	224.80
15.30	50.77	69.39	77.40	55.55	55.26	55.15	45.38	45.58	49.52	55.24
1.47	15.32	25.75	31.17	29.37	20.05	20.61	21.66	22.05	22.87	23.23
	5.42	7.11	8.04	9.57	7.72	8.73	9.68	9.00	18.59	18.61
	6.62	7.39	8.49	10.55	11.56	12.53	14.53	16.79	19.76	22.66

1-5 续表 3

指 标	Item	1978	1980	1990
房地产	**Real Estate**			
房地产开发投资额(亿元)	Investment of Real Estate Development (100 million Yuan)			
商品房施工面积(万 M^2)	Space under Construction of Commercial Housing(10,000 m^2)			
商品房竣工面积(万 M^2)	Completed Space of Commercial Housing(10,000 m^2)			
商品房销售面积(万 M^2)	Selling Space of Commercial Housing(10,000 m^2)			
金融	**Banking Institutions**			
金融机构本外币存款余额(亿元)	Foreign and Domestic Deposit Balance of Financial Institutions (100 million Yuan)	6.87	9.46	88.25
# 储蓄存款	Savings Deposit	2.19	3.04	57.48
金融机构本外币贷款余额(亿元)	Foreign and Domestic Loan Balance of Financial Institutions (100 million Yuan)	13.67	17.27	91.22
用电	**Power Consumption**			
全社会用电量(亿千瓦时)	Total Power Consumption (100 milllion KWH)			
# 工业用电量	Industrial Power Consumption			
城乡居民生活用电	Urban and Rural Residents´ Household Power Demand			
万元 GDP 能耗(吨标准煤/万元)	Energy Consumption per 10, 000 Yuan GDP (SCE/10,000 Yuan)			
万元 GDP 能耗下降率(%)	Droprate of Energy Consumption per 10, 000 Yuan GDP (%)			
科技	**S&T**			
全社会研发投入(亿元)	Total R&D Investment (10,000 Yuan)			
专利授权量(件)	Patent Authorization			
# 发明专利	Invention Patent			
全社会研发投入(R&D)占 GDP 比重	Ratio of the Whole Society´s R&D Input to GDP(%)			
社会事业	**Social Undertaking**			
学校数(所)	Number of Schools			
教职工数(万人)	Number of Teaching and Administrative Staff (10,000 Persons)			
专任教师数(万人)	Number of Full-time Teachers (10,000 Persons)			
毕业生数(万人)	Graduates (10,000 Persons)			
在校生数(万人)	Students at School (10,000 Persons)			
卫生机构数(个)	Health Agencies	898	849	1368
# 医院、卫生院	Hospital and Health Centers	898	849	344
卫生技术人员数(万人)	Health Workers(10,000 Persons)	1.47	1.52	2.21
# 医生	Doctors	0.60	0.64	1.05
卫生机构床位数(张)	Beds of Health Institutions	15469	17142	18400

CONTINUED 3

2000	2005	2006	2007	2008	2009	2010	2011	2012	2013	2014
26.11	80.05	107.93	137.43	172.68	200.79	272.78	379.96	481.74	596.52	678.92
334.00	889.43	1168.46	1417.36	1860.76	2008.48	2434.03	2968.64	3795.34	4532.27	5272.22
195.68	327.11	376.64	394.48	518.29	549.68	667.42	773.29	735.30	925.68	1031.15
170.85	326.90	471.75	518.29	419.35	666.64	739.52	677.53	712.49	1035.26	919.17
773.42	1847.98	2163.72	2468.32	3039.56	4006.23	4957.83	5614.56	6477.84	7542.12	8508.32
544.55	1190.74	1373.40	1476.59	1890.68	2285.89	2693.99	3087.27	3605.65	4150.54	4623.93
394.34	1024.45	1233.25	1497.96	1750.60	2431.98	2964.58	3408.62	4006.48	4672.81	5258.93
67.10	138.83	163.60	191.01	203.55	217.45	249.70	280.77	301.79	326.15	333.23
42.00	105.15	126.65	149.39	156.19	165.41	187.84	212.15	222.96	234.38	242.89
15.10	18.11	20.07	22.00	25.47	27.68	32.86	34.87	40.08	47.48	43.73
	0.830	0.808	0.774	0.730	0.692	0.666	0.539	0.507	0.505	0.478
		2.98	4.21	5.69	5.19	3.75	3.65	5.98	4.13	5.37
			28.13	40.45	45.96	66.89	85.68	100.29	118.31	141.32
391.00	792	1709	3756	4102	10722	22644	31335	36247	22086	12391
			63	122	159	294	508	700	746	932
	1.00	1.12	1.30	1.56	1.60	1.93	2.10	2.27	2.35	2.50
2081	894	880	835	762	702	642	627	602	586	578
6.65	6.69	6.71	6.75	6.51	6.46	6.57	6.48	6.46	6.33	6.33
5.32	5.47	5.54	5.59	5.49	5.41	5.38	5.37	5.47	5.39	5.34
22.97	27.92	28.06	27.77	26.59	25.98	24.85	22.82	21.70	21.11	19.67
107.18	104.70	101.67	97.55	93.03	88.35	84.40	81.31	77.72	75.16	73.27
1855	1810	1931	1839	1783	1816	1667	1664	1641	1592	1621
303	319	316	333	331	333	333	328	327	310	304
2.61	2.44	2.57	2.75	2.80	2.96	3.06	3.19	3.40	3.65	3.83
1.30	1.10	1.18	1.29	1.25	1.27	1.32	1.34	1.41	1.56	1.52
18747	21203	22687	22929	24203	24944	26293	29058	31495	33234	35136

1-6 主要年份国民经济主要指标发展速度

指标	Item	2014年为下列各年%	
		1978	1980
人口	**Population**		
年末户籍人口(万人)	Registered Population at Year-end(10,000 persons)	106.2	105.3
男	Male	104.8	104.0
女	Female	107.6	106.6
年末常住人口	Permanent Residents atYear-end(10,000 persons)		
城镇	Urban Area		
农村	Rural Area		
劳动力	**Labor Force**		
年末从业人员	Employees At Year-end	115.3	111.6
国民经济核算	**Accounting of Domestic Economy**		
地区生产总值	GDP	5701	4771
第一产业	Primary Industry	552.9	585.1
第二产业	Secondary Industry	12847	8854
工业	Industry	14102	9732
第三产业	Tertiary Industry	6016	4972
人均 GDP	Per Capita GDP	5266	4448
农业	**Agriculture**		
主要农产品产量	Main Agricultural Products		
粮食	Grain	144.9	152.0
棉花	Cotton Crop	21.5	33.6
油料	Oil-Bearing Crops	900.1	1205.7
蚕茧	Silkworm Cocoons	344.5	227.5
水产品	Aquatic Products	838.5	825.9
生猪出栏数	Pigs for Slaughter	204.3	132.6
生猪年末存栏数	Year-end Pigs in Stock	87.3	102.0
工业	**Industry**		
主要工业产品产量	Main Industrial Products Output		
纱	Yarn	1288	988.5
布	Cloth	123.6	86.9
农用化肥	Agricultural Fertilizers	549.7	531.4
化学农药	Chemical Pesticide	1109	996
烧碱	Caustic Soda	4453	2377
发电量	Power Generation	7012	4849

GROWTH RATE OF MAJOR NATIONAL ECONOMY INDICATORS OF MAIN YEARS

2014 as Perceutage of the Following Years							年均发展速度 Average Annual Growth Rate		
1990	2000	2005	2010	2011	2012	2013	"十五"	"十一五"	2011-2014
98.9	97.8	99.6	100.6	100.4	100.3	100.1	99.6	99.8	100.2
96.8	96.6	98.7	100.2	100.1	100.1	100.1	99.6	99.7	100.1
101.0	99.1	100.4	101.0	100.6	100.5	100.2	99.7	99.9	100.2
		99.7	100.2	100.1	100.0	100.0	100.5	99.9	100.1
		136.6	109.4	106.3	104.1	102.1	98.1	104.5	102.3
		69.9	88.5	91.7	94.1	96.9	102.7	95.4	97.0
96.8	104.7	104.0	97.5	97.7	98.5	98.9	100.1	101.3	99.4
2004	562.1	303.7	154.8	138.1	123.5	110.5	113.1	114.4	111.5
308.4	173.8	140.4	115.7	111.6	106.7	103.5	104.4	103.9	103.7
3051	681.1	324.6	156.1	138.9	123.5	110.3	116.0	115.8	111.8
3368	734.6	341.4	158.2	140.1	124.8	111.1	116.6	116.6	112.1
2512	581.9	322.2	160.6	141.9	126.3	111.9	112.5	114.9	112.6
1988	566.5	300.8	152.9	137.9	123.4	110.5	113.5	114.5	111.2
111.1	98.1	113.5	102.8	101.5	100.3	100.2	97.1	102.0	100.7
47.6	134.3	85.4	73.4	80.2	78.9	86.1	109.5	103.1	92.5
208.0	99.1	28.4	92.5	97.7	99.7	95.7	100.6	100.7	98.1
61.4	66.1	46.9	58.2	68.8	73.5	94.5	107.1	95.8	87.3
485.2	150.6	127.5	111.8	107.5	104.0	101.7	103.4	102.7	102.8
170.6	153.0	127.6	110.5	106.3	100.9	104.1	103.7	102.9	102.5
127.1	106.3	93.4	95.0	90.3	90.7	97.8	102.6	99.7	98.7
510.9	323.1	198.5	112.2	128.0	124.7	110.5	116.1	107.7	102.9
73.9	79.1	62.0	128.0	122.8	116.7	118.5	110.2	112.1	106.4
478.2	175.8	63.5	36.8	31.3	29.7	71.7	105.0	86.5	77.9
633.2	329.3	193.5	131.8	118.7	117.8	98.7	122.6	111.5	107.2
677.5	350.4	210.4	121.9	104.4	103.7	107.7	111.2	108.0	105.1
1648	679.1	231.6	134.5	139.9	122.5	122.5	110.7	111.5	107.7

1-6 续 表

指 标	Item	2014年为下列各年%	
		1978	1980
交通	**Transportation**		
全社会旅客运输量	Total Volume of Passenger Traffic	1374	937.4
全社会货物运输量	Total Volume of Cargo Traffic	2810	2751
南通港货物吞吐量	Cargo Turnover of Nantong Port	7291	7515
国内外贸易	**Domestic & Foreign Trade**		
社会消费品零售总额	Total Consumer Goods Retail Sales	26448	15974
进出口总值	Total Import & Export Volume		
#出口总值	Export Volume		
固定资产投资	**Fixed Asset Investment**		
固定资产投资完成额	Completed Fixed Asset Investment		
#工业	Industry		
服务业	Service Industry		
#房地产开发	Real Estate Development		
房屋施工面积	Floor Space under Construction		
房屋竣工面积	Completed Floor Space		
财政	**Finance**		
财政总收入	General Financial Revenue	25572	23635
#一般公共预算收入	General public budget revenue		
财政总支出	General Financial Expenditure	75809	70145
金融	**Banking Institutions**		
金融机构本外币存款余额	Foreign Deposit Balance of Financial Institutions	123847	89940
#储蓄存款	Savings Deposit	211138	152103
金融机构本外币贷款余额	Foreign Loan Balance of Financial Institutions	38471	30451
人民生活	**People´s Livelihood**		
在岗职工平均工资	Average Wage of Employed Workers		
城镇居民人均可支配收入	Per Capita Disposable Income of Urban Residents		
农村居民人均可支配收入	Farmer´s Per Capita Net Income		
社会事业	**Social Undertaking**		
中学在校学生数	Students at High School	48.6	61.5
小学在校学生数	Students at Primary School	32.7	36.5
卫生机构数	Health Agencies	180.5	190.9
卫生技术人员数	Health Workers	266.0	257.2
卫生机构床位数	Beds of Health Institutions	226.7	205.5

注:2013年起城乡居民人均可支配收入按新口径计算。

CONTINUED

2014 as Perceutage of the Following Years							年均发展速度 Average Annual Growth Rate		
1990	2000	2005	2010	2011	2012	2013	"十五"	"十一五"	2011-2014
497.7	299.1	245.6	137.0	115.3	105.9	102.1	104.0	112.4	108.2
1108	489.4	335.2	161.0	135.0	121.9	107.7	107.9	115.8	112.6
2111	801.3	264.4	146.1	127.0	118.9	107.4	124.8	112.6	109.9
4130	866.1	403.8	169.6	145.1	126.0	111.6	116.5	118.9	114.1
	1002.8	371.4	150.0	122.5	120.3	106.1	122.0	119.9	110.7
	1105	388.1	159.4	124.7	119.7	105.6	123.3	119.5	112.4
18751	1627	477.9	179.7	163.8	135.0	118.1	127.8	121.6	120.5
	2467	331.3	133.8	133.0	119.7	110.3	149.4	119.9	112.4
			306.2	219.9	157.0	127.7			133.7
61164	2600	848.1	248.9	178.7	140.9	113.8	125.1	127.8	125.6
		445.0	174.4	160.4	132.3	120.2		120.6	114.9
		320.0	163.9	140.8	130.2	137.4		114.3	113.1
11063	2629	820.1	196.8	147.5	133.0	115.4	126.2	133.0	118.4
4335	1933	764.0	189.1	147.2	131.0	113.2	120.4	132.2	117.3
17070	4164	1003.0	223.5	160.2	130.2	115.1	132.9	135.0	122.3
9641	1100.1	460.4	171.6	151.5	131.3	112.8	119.0	121.8	114.5
8044	849.1	388.3	171.6	149.8	128.2	111.4	116.9	117.7	114.5
5765	1334	513.3	177.4	154.3	131.3	112.5	121.0	123.7	115.4
	663.8	331.5	155.6	137.7	124.3	106.7	114.9	116.3	115.9
		288.0	152.9	133.0	118.0	107.5		113.5	111.2
1816	426.4	287.6	159.6	134.9	119.6	107.2	108.2	112.5	112.4
87.6	66.6	56.1	73.5	81.1	88.5	95.2	103.5	94.7	92.6
57.4	51.9	73.6	99.1	99.4	100.9	100.7	93.2	94.2	99.8
118.5	87.4	89.6	97.2	97.4	98.8	101.8	99.5	98.4	99.3
176.9	149.8	160.2	127.6	122.6	112.5	104.8	98.7	104.6	106.3
191.0	187.9	165.7	133.6	120.7	111.6	105.7	102.5	104.4	107.5

Note: Since 2013, per capita disposable income of urban and rural residents has been calculated in accordance with new standards.

1-7 主要年份国民经济和社会发展结构指标

单位:%

指 标	Item	2000	2001	2002
人口与就业	**Population and Employment**			
人口	Population			
性别结构	Gender Structure			
男	Male	49.9	49.9	49.8
女	Female	50.1	50.1	50.2
城乡结构	Urban &Rural Structure			
城镇	Urban Area			
农村	Rural Area			
就业	Employment			
产业结构	Industry Structure			
第一产业	Primary Industry	45.3	45.9	42.8
第二产业	Secondary Industry	31.3	32.1	32.5
第三产业	Tertiary Industry	23.4	22.0	24.7
宏观经济	**Macro Economy**			
国民核算	National Account			
地区生产总值产业结构	Regional GDP Structure			
第一产业	Primary Industry	17.9	17.2	16.3
第二产业	Secondary Industry	50.1	50.6	51.6
第三产业	Tertiary Industry	32.0	32.2	32.1
投资	Investment			
产业结构	Industry Structure			
第一产业	Primary Industry			0.2
第二产业	Secondary Industry			43.8
第三产业	Tertiary Industry			56.0
所有制结构	Structure of Ownership			
国有投资	State-owned Investment			
民间投资	Private Investment			
港澳台及外商投资	HK, Macau, Taiwan &Foreign Investment			9.7
财政	Finance			
财政收入结构	Financial Revenue Structure			
中央	Central	45.1	45.0	44.4
地方	Local	54.9	55.0	55.6
财政支出结构	Financial Expenditure Structure			
卫生	Health	7.4	6.6	5.8
教育	Education	23.5	22.7	21.0

STRUCTURAL INDICATORS ON NATIONAL ECONOMY AND SOCIAL DEVELOPMENT OVER THE YEARS

(%)

2003	2004	2005	2006	2007	2008	2009	2010	2011	2012	2013	2014
49.8	49.8	49.7	49.7	49.6	49.6	49.5	49.5	49.4	49.4	49.3	49.3
50.2	50.2	50.3	50.3	50.4	50.4	50.5	50.5	50.6	50.6	50.7	50.7
		44.6	46.9	48.6	50.3	52.7	56.0	57.6	58.7	59.9	61.1
		55.4	53.1	51.4	49.7	47.3	44.0	42.4	41.3	40.1	38.9
39.9	36.6	30.1	24.1	21.3	19.9	18.4	26.5	25.7	24.4	23.0	22.0
37.2	39.6	40.1	42.5	44.5	44.2	45.0	44.5	45.0	45.7	46.4	46.8
22.9	23.8	29.8	33.4	34.2	35.9	36.6	29.0	29.3	29.9	30.7	31.2
15.1	12.9	11.0	9.9	8.6	8.4	8.2	7.7	7.0	7.0	6.3	6.0
53.0	56.0	55.9	55.5	55.9	56.0	56.0	55.1	54.4	53.0	51.6	49.8
32.0	31.1	33.1	34.7	35.4	35.6	35.8	37.2	38.5	40.0	42.1	44.2
0.2	0.1	0.8	0.5	0.1	0.2	0.2	0.2	0.1	0.1	0.1	0.3
55.5	67.3	73.5	71.0	74.2	74.8	72.9	70.0	64.7	59.3	56.2	52.5
44.3	32.6	25.7	28.5	25.7	25.0	26.9	29.8	35.2	40.6	43.7	47.2
29.2	20.2	10.7	9.8	7.9	9.1	12.1	12.6	15.1	17.8	18.9	18.8
51.0	54.4	66.4	69.9	69.4	71.6	67.4	68.5	74.4	74.4	73.1	74.3
19.7	25.4	21.9	17.5	20.1	19.3	11.4	9.0	10.5	7.8	8.0	6.9
40.1	38.8	39.4	38.9	37.1	36.4	32.3	26.9	24.0	21.6	20.9	20.9
59.9	61.2	60.6	61.1	62.9	63.6	67.7	73.1	76.0	78.4	79.1	79.1
6.1	6.1	5.8	6.4	5.7	5.8	6.2	5.5	6.8	6.8	7.2	8.3
13.7	18.3	11.6	14.6	22.8	21.0	21.3	20.5	21.2	21.3	23.0	21.8

1-7 续表 1

单位:%

指　标	Item	2000	2001	2002
进出口	Import &Export			
出口地区结构	Export Region Structure			
亚洲	Asia	66.2	69.2	67.0
欧洲	Europe	12.9	15.8	12.4
北美洲	North America	11.8	14.0	12.3
拉丁美洲	Latin America		5.1	4.7
出口方式结构	Export Way Structure			
一般贸易	General Trade		47.2	55.0
加工贸易	Processing Trade		48.5	44.9
产业经济	**Industrial Economy**			
农业	Agriculture			
农林牧渔业产值结构	Output Value Structure of Farming, Forestry, Husbandry& Fishery Industries			
农业	Farming	54.3	55.9	55.2
林业	Forestry	0.6	1.2	1.3
牧业	Husbandry	21.1	20.2	20.9
渔业	Fishery	23.9	22.7	22.6
农林牧渔服务业	Farming, Forestry, Husbandry& Fishery Service Industry			
工业	Industry			
产值所有制结构	Output Ownership Structure			
内资企业	Domestic Enterprise	66.0	68.6	65.7
港澳台商投资企业	HK, Macau, Taiwan &Foreign Invested Enterprise	10.5	7.6	9.5
外商投资企业	Foreign Invested Enterprise	23.5	23.8	24.8
产值轻重结构	Output Weight Structure			
轻工业	Light Industry	58.0	58.0	56.2
重工业	Heavy Industry	42.0	42.0	43.8
高新技术产业产值占比	Percentage of Hi-tech Industries			
新兴产业产值占比	Percentage of Emerging Industries			
运输业	Transportation			
货运量结构	Cargo Traffic Structure			
铁路	Railway			
公路	Highway	79.6	80.4	81.0
水路	Waterway	20.4	19.6	19.0
客运量结构	Passenger Traffic Structure			
铁路	Railway			
公路	Highway	99.5	99.6	99.9
航空	Aviation	0.1	0.1	0.1

CONTINUED 1

(%)

2003	2004	2005	2006	2007	2008	2009	2010	2011	2012	2013	2014
62.0	56.9	54.2	54.4	51.7	48.7	50.3	44.5	47.4	47.4	55.4	54.7
15.1	19.1	17.9	18.7	21.3	25.9	25.1	26.9	22.7	18.6	16.4	17.9
14.7	15.6	18.3	16.6	16.4	15.7	12.8	14.1	15.3	14.1	14.3	14.9
4.5	3.7	5.5	6.2	4.3	4.7	4.1	9.0	9.1	12.9	5.7	5.7
56.9	58.8	61.4	60.7	62.3	62.5	57.1	60.3	57.7	60.9	62.9	65.7
43.0	41.1	37.8	37.9	36.5	36.4	42.0	38.0	38.3	36.1	34.3	32.0
44.8	44.3	43.3	42.4	41.9	41.2	41.8	44.0	43.4	44.4	44.3	44.1
0.7	0.6	0.7	0.8	0.8	0.7	0.7	0.6	0.6	0.6	0.6	0.6
24.9	26.7	26.6	27.2	27.7	28.4	26.9	25.5	26.5	23.8	23.2	23.0
25.5	24.6	25.4	25.5	25.4	24.7	25.2	24.2	23.6	23.9	23.7	23.4
4.0	3.8	4.0	4.1	4.2	5.0	5.4	5.3	5.9	7.3	8.1	8.9
64.6	64.8	62.4	63.7	62.5	62.3	61.6	60.2	60.9	64.0	65.3	65.9
10.1	10.5	11.1	10.0	11.6	11.7	13.5	15.0	13.6	12.7	12.3	12.5
25.3	24.7	26.5	26.2	25.9	26.0	25.0	24.8	25.5	23.3	22.4	21.6
53.8	49.7	49.8	47.9	45.4	41.1	38.7	38.7	35.8	33.2	33.5	32.0
46.2	50.3	50.2	52.1	54.6	58.9	61.3	61.3	64.2	66.8	66.5	68.0
				24.2	27.9	29.8	32.4	36.7	39.7	40.8	43.6
						18.5	21.6	22.9	25.9	30.0	33.1
	0.3	0.2	0.3	0.6	0.9	1.6	0.5	0.5	0.4	0.3	0.5
80.7	80.1	82.6	82.0	81.7	82.1	76.7	75.8	75.1	75.3	75.1	60.5
19.3	19.6	17.1	17.7	17.7	17.0	21.8	23.7	24.4	24.3	24.6	39.0
	0.4	0.9	1.0	1.8	2.0	1.5	1.6	1.1	1.1	1.0	2.5
99.9	99.5	98.9	98.9	98.1	97.9	98.3	98.3	98.8	98.7	98.7	96.6
0.1	0.1	0.1	0.1	0.1	0.1	0.2	0.2	0.1	0.2	0.3	0.9

1-7 续表 2

单位:%

指　标	Item	2000	2001	2002
旅游业	Tourism			
海外旅游人数结构	Overseas Tourist Structure			
外国人	Foreigners	82.5	78.9	75.0
港、澳、台同胞	HK, Macau &Taiwan Compatriots	17.5	21.1	25.0
金融业	Finance			
存款余额结构	Deposit Balance Structure			
企事业单位存款	Deposit of Enterprises and Institutes	24.4	24.0	24.0
储蓄存款	Savings Deposit	70.4	71.9	69.4
贷款余额结构	Loans Balance Structure			
短期贷款	Short-term Loans	89.0	84.8	81.6
中长期贷款	Medium and Long Term Loans	8.0	12.6	14.2
新增贷款结构	New Loans Structure			
短期贷款	Short-term Loans	88.3	32.7	72.5
中长期贷款	Medium and Long Term Loans	11.7	67.3	32.8
贸易业	Trade			
社会消费品零售额行业结构	Total Consumer Goods Retail Sales Structure			
批发零售业	Wholesale and Retail Sales Industry	69.7	70.4	70.5
住宿餐饮业	Accommodation and Catering Industry	5.1	5.7	6.3
社会事业	**Social Undertaking**			
教育	Education			
在校学生结构	Structure of Students at School			
# 大学生	University Students	1.6	2.5	3.1
中学生	Hign School Students	34.7	38.2	41.5
小学生	Primary School Students	57.6	53.7	49.4
卫生	Health			
卫生机构构成	Health Agency Structure			
医院、卫生院	Hospital and Health Center	16.3	18.8	21.9
门诊部、诊所、卫生所	Out-patient Department and Clinics	80.8	78.4	75.4
卫生技术人员构成	Health Worker Structure			
医生	Doctor	49.9	49.8	45.8
注册护士	Registered Nurses	26.0	26.5	26.8
人民生活	People′s Livelihood			
市区城镇居民恩格尔系数	Engel Coefficient of Downtown Urban Residents	41.4	41.6	39.6
农村居民恩格尔系数	Engel Coefficient of Rural Residents	34.1	35.5	36.1

CONTINUED 2

(%)

2003	2004	2005	2006	2007	2008	2009	2010	2011	2012	2013	2014
75.6	85.3	86.5	87.8	89.2	88.6	89.3	89.0	88.7	88.7	90.6	88.8
24.4	14.7	13.5	12.2	10.8	11.4	10.7	11.0	11.3	11.3	9.4	11.2
24.6	24.7	24.2	24.6	27.9	24.2	27.8	24.3	43.2	41.4	42.1	42.8
66.4	65.0	64.4	63.8	59.8	62.2	57.1	54.3	54.6	55.7	55.0	54.3
77.2	72.7	65.7	64.9	64.7	59.1	50.8	50.9	55.3	57.5	56.9	53.7
16.7	17.9	20.5	25.5	29.1	31.9	38.6	43.3	42.4	40.0	40.2	41.5
71.2	69.0	60.9	44.0	67.1	29.6	29.3	51.8	65.1	72.1	53.5	27.6
28.8	31.0	39.1	56.0	45.1	46.0	55.7	64.9	36.2	24.6	41.1	51.3
91.5	90.6	91.1	91.0	90.4	89.1	92.9	92.0	91.7	91.7	91.5	91.5
6.4	7.1	8.4	8.7	9.4	10.6	7.1	7.1	7.4	7.7	7.8	8.5
4.0	4.7	5.8	7.0	8.3	9.0	10.1	9.8	10.5	11.1	11.4	11.9
43.1	42.8	42.1	41.8	42.3	42.6	41.5	39.9	37.5	35.9	34.6	33.8
45.6	43.4	41.6	39.5	37.7	36.9	37.1	38.3	39.6	40.8	42.3	43.8
23.1	18.7	17.6	16.4	18.1	18.6	18.3	20.0	19.7	19.9	19.5	18.8
73.9	78.9	80.2	81.1	74.6	73.1	72.7	69.8	68.5	68.1	68.1	66.7
45.7	45.3	45.1	48.5	46.9	44.6	42.9	43.1	41.9	42.7	42.7	41.5
28.4	28.4	29.0	28.8	30.1	31.6	32.5	33.8	35.7	28.1	38.0	39.6
40.1	40.4	38.2	36.7	38.5	39.3	36.7	35.7	37.3	36.9	36.0	29.0
39.4	41.3	40.4	38.5	37.9	38.4	37.7	36.2	36.2	36.0	35.4	29.6

1-8 主要年份主要人均指标

MAIN PER CAPITA INDICATORS OF NATIONAL ECONOMY OVER THE YEARS

指 标	Item	2005	2010	2011	2012	2013	2014
地区生产总值(元)	GDP(yuan)	20138	47419	56005	62506	69050	77457
财政收入(元)	Financial Revenue(yuan)	2323	9897	13062	14478	16673	19238
一般公共预算收入(元)	General public budget revenue	983	4035	5129	5755	6658	7536
财政支出(元)	Financial Expenditure(yuan)	1652	7578	10455	12856	14536	16724
固定资产投资完成额(元)	Completed Investment of Fixed Assets(yuan)	11065	30084	32629	39578	45204	53391
社会消费品零售总额(元)	Sales of Social Consumption Goods(yuan)	7280	17718	20486	23574	26590	29681
进出口总额(美元)	Imports and Exports(US$)	1157	2927	3546	3606	4086	4336
主要农产品产量(公斤)	Output of Main Agricultual Products(kg)						
粮食	Grain	399	451	452	457	4570	4577
肉类	Meat	51	64	65	68	656	678
水产品	Aquatic Products	94	109	113	116	1188	1209
禽蛋	Eggs	57	64	63	63	626	626
职工平均工资(元)	Average Wage of Staff and Workers(yuan)	18513	39448	44574	49399	57546	61383
国有经济	State-owned Economy	24912	56939	63230	68893	75759	81383
集体经济	Collective Economy	13177	36666	42303	50892	56963	58454
其它经济	Others	14883	31048	35831	39777	55159	59182
城镇居民人均可支配收入(元)	Per Capita Annual Disposable Income of Urban Households(yuan)		21825	25094	28292	31059	33374
城镇居民人均消费性支出(元)	Living Expenditure of Urban Residents(yuan)		13506	15613	17858	19646	22035
农村居民人均可支配收入(元)	Per Capita Annual Disposable Income of Rural Residents(yuan)	5501	9914	11730	13231	14754	15821
农村居民生活消费支出(元)	Living Expenditure of Rural Residents(yuan)	3858	7240	8510	9839	10931	11051
储蓄存款(元)	Deposits(yuan)	16261	36996	42092	49411	56875	63359
每千人拥有	Possessed Every 1000 Persons:						
固定电话用户(户)	Telephone(unit)	358	334	495	356	346	351
在校学生(人)	Students Enrollment(persons)	143	116	112	107	103	103
# 大学生	#University Students	7.8	11.7	11.7	11.9	11.7	11.7
中专生	Specialized Secondary School Students	8.4	6.9	6.7	6.2	6.4	6.4
中学生	Middle School Students	60.3	46.2	41.9	38.3	35.6	35.6
卫生技术人员(人)	Medical Technical Personnels	3.34	4.21	4.37	4.76	5.00	5.00
# 医生	#Doctors	1.50	1.81	1.84	2.03	2.14	2.13
卫生机构床位数(张)	Beds in Medical Institutions(piece)	2.90	3.61	3.99	4.32	4.55	4.55

1-9 南通的一天(2014年)
ONE DAY IN NANTONG(2014)

指 标	Item	南通的一天 One Day in NanTong
地区生产总值(亿元)	GDP(100 million yuan)	15.49
第一产业	Primary Industry	0.93
第二产业	Secondary Industry	7.71
第三产业	Tertiary Industry	6.85
农林牧渔业总产值(亿元)	Gross Output Value of Agriculture (100 million yuan)	1.73
规模以上工业增加值(亿元)	Value-Added of Industry Above Designed Size(100 million yuan)	7.85
规模以上工业主营业务收入(亿元)	Main Business Income of Industries Above Designed Size(100 million yuan)	33.84
规模以上工业利税总额(亿元)	Total Pre-tax Profits of Industries Above Designed Size(100 million yuan)	4.05
主要工农业产品产量	Output of Main Industrial and Agricultural Products	
粮食(吨)	Grain (ton)	9151.23
棉花(吨)	Cotton (ton)	119.57
油料(吨)	Oil (ton)	1070.24
水产品(吨)	Aquatic Products (ton)	2416.63
肉类(吨)	Meat (ton)	1355.62
发电量(万千瓦时)	Electricity(10,000KWH)	11041.80
纱(吨)	Yarn(ton)	1718.21
布(米)	Cloth (meter)	894.34
水泥(万吨)	Cement(10,000 tons)	3.04
粗钢(吨)	Crude Steel(ton)	1443.88
固定资产投资额(亿元)	Total Investment in Fixed Assets (100 million yuan)	10.68
工业	Industry	5.61
服务业	Service Industry	5.04
建筑业总产值(亿元)	Total Output of Construction Industry (100 million yuan)	17.21
社会消费品零售总额(亿元)	Total Retail Sales of Consumer Goods (100 million yuan)	5.93
进出口总额(万美元)	Total Imports and Exports(10,000 US$)	8670.41
# 出口	#Exports	6158.92
新批协议注册外资(万美元)	Newly-Approved Contracted Foreign Investment(10,000 US$)	1513.35
实际到账注册外资(万美元)	Actual Paid-in Foreign Investment(10,000 US$)	636.46
财政总收入(亿元)	General Financial Revenue(100 million yuan)	3.85
一般公共预算收入	General public budget revenue	1.51
财政总支出(亿元)	General Financial Expenditure(100 million yuan)	3.34
一般公共预算支出	General public budget revenue expenditure	1.78
金融机构人民币存款余额(亿元)	RMB Deposit Balance of Banking Systems (Year End) (100 million yuan)	22.84
# 人民币储蓄存款	#Savings of Urban and Rural Residents	12.61
金融机构人民币贷款余额(亿元)	RMB Loan Balance of Banking Systems(Year End) (100 million yuan)	14.05

1-10 南通国民经济主要指标占全省比重(2014年)

PROPRTION OF NANTONG NATIONAL ECONOMY´S MAJOR INDICATORS IN THE PROVINCE(2014)

指 标	Item	江苏省 Jiangsu Province	南通市 Nantong City	南通占江苏的比重(%) Percentage of Nantong in Jiangsu
土地面积(平方公里)	Land Area(sq,km)	107200	10549	9.8
年末常住人口(万人)	Permanent Residents at Year-end (10,000 persons)	7960.06	729.80	9.2
城镇人口	Urban Residents	5190.76	446.27	8.6
地区生产总值(亿元)	GDP(100 million yuan)	65088.32	5652.69	8.7
第一产业	Primary Industry	3634.33	339.57	9.3
第二产业	Secondary Industry	31057.47	2812.34	9.1
第三产业	Tertiary Industry	30396.52	2500.78	8.2
农林牧渔业总产值(亿元)	Gross Output Value of Agriculture (100 million yuan)	6443.37	631.88	9.8
规模以上工业企业数(个)	Number of Enterprises Above Designed Size	46975	5081	10.8
规模以上工业增加值(亿元)	Value-Added of Industry Above Designed Size(100 million yuan)	31507.87	2864.24	9.1
规模以上工业主营业务收入(亿元)	Sales Income of Industries Above Designed Size(100 million yuan)	142387.86	12351.36	8.7
规模以上工业利税总额(亿元)	Total Pre-tax Profits of Industries Above Designed Size(100 million yuan)	14629.21	1477.71	10.1
主要工农业产品产量	Output of Main Industrial and Agricultural Products			
粮食(万吨)	Grain (10,000 tons)	3490.62	334.02	9.6
棉花(万吨)	Cotton (10,000 tons)	15.95	4.36	27.4
油料(万吨)	Oil (10,000 tons)	146.60	39.06	26.6
水产品(万吨)	Aquatic Products (10,000 tons)	518.84	88.21	17.0
肉类(万吨)	Meat (10,000 tons)	379.46	49.48	13.0
发电量(亿千瓦时)	Electricity(100 million KWH)	4347.07	403.03	9.3
纱(万吨)	Yarn(10,000 tons)	568.33	62.71	11.0
布(亿米)	Cloth (100 million meters)	91.26	32.64	35.8
水泥(万吨)	Cement(10,000 tons)	19360.55	1110.85	5.7
粗钢(万吨)	Crude Steel(10,000 tons)	10195.51	52.70	0.5

1–10 续表
CONTINUED

指　标	Item	江苏省 Jiangsu Province	南通市 Nantong City	南通占江苏的比重(%) Percentage of Nantong in Jiangsu
固定资产投资额(亿元)	Total Investment in Fixed Assets (100 million yuan)	41552.75	3896.39	9.4
工业	Industry	20300.49	2046.82	10.1
服务业	Service Industry	21045.30	1839.66	8.7
# 房地产开发	# Real Estate Development	9857.14	678.92	6.9
建筑业总产值(亿元)	Total Output of Construction Industry (100 million yuan)	24592.93	6281.21	25.5
社会消费品零售总额(亿元)	Total Retail Sales of Consumer Goods (100 million yuan)	23458.07	2166.10	9.2
批发零售业	Wholesale and Retail Sales	21049.02	1982.88	9.4
住宿餐饮业	Accommodation and Catering Services	2159.99	183.21	8.5
进出口总额(亿美元)	Total Imports and Exports(100 million USD)	5637.62	316.47	5.6
# 出口	#Exports	3418 69	224.80	6.6
新批协议注册外资(亿美元)	Newly-Contracted Foreign Investment(100 million USD)	431.87	55.24	12.8
实际到账注册外资(亿美元)	Actually Pald-in Registered Foreign Investment(100 million USD)	281.74	23.23	8.2
财政总收入(亿元)	General Financial Revenue(100 million yuan)	11816.43	1403.93	11.9
一般公共预算收入	General public budget revenue	7233.14	550.00	7.6
一般公共预算支出	General public budget revenue expenditure	8466.48	649.58	7.7
金融机构人民币存款余额(亿元)	RMB Deposits of Banking Systems (Year End) (100 million yuan)	93735.61	8336.79	8.9
# 人民币储蓄存款	#Savings of Urban and Rural Residents	36580.59	4602.87	12.6
金融机构人民币贷款余额(亿元)	RMB Loan Balance of Banking Systems(Year End) (100 million yuan)	69572.67	5127.11	7.4
从业人员平均工资(元)	Average Salary of On-post Staff(yuan)	60867	61383	100.8
全体居民人均可支配收入(元)	All Residents Per-capita Disposable Income(yuan)	27173	25340	93.3
城镇居民人均可支配收入	Urban Residents Per-capita Disposable Income	34346	33374	97.2
农村居民人均可支配收入	Rural Residents Per-capita Disposable Income	14958	15821	105.8

1-11 市区国民经济和社会发展主要指标(2014 年)

指　标	Item	全市 Whole Municipality
乡、镇(街道)数(个)	Number of Township(unit)	101
年末总户数(万户)	Year-end Household (10,000 households)	282.61
年末户籍人口(万人)	Registered Population at Year-end (10,000 persons)	767.63
年平均人口(万人)	Annual Average Population (10,000 persons)	767.07
年出生人口(人)	Annual Birth (person)	57826
人口出生率(‰)	Birth Rate(‰)	7.54
年死亡人口(人)	Annual Death (person)	62098
人口死亡率(‰)	Death Rate(‰)	8.10
人口自然增长率(‰)	Population Natural Growth Rate (‰)	-0.56
年末常住人口(万人)	Permanent Residents at Year-end (10,000 persons)	729.8
#城镇人口	Urban Residents	446.27
年末从业人员(万人)	Employees at Year-end (10,000 persons)	462.0
#在岗职工	#Number of Employed Staff and Workers	157.88
地区生产总值(亿元)	GDP(100 million yuan)	5652.69
第一产业	Primary Industry	339.57
第二产业	Secondary Industry	2812.34
#工业	# Industry	2307.64
第三产业	Tertiary Industry	2500.78
人均 GDP(元)	Average GDP (yuan)	77457
地区生产总值构成(%)	Structure of GDP(%)	100.0
第一产业	Primary Industry	6.0
第二产业	Secondary Industry	49.8
#工业	# Industry	40.8
第三产业	Tertiary Industry	44.2
地区生产总值发展速度(上年为 100)(%)	Developing Rate of GDP(preceding year=100)(%)	110.5
第一产业	Primary Industry	103.5
第二产业	Secondary Industry	110.3
#工业	# Industry	111.1
第三产业	Tertiary Industry	111.9
人均 GDP 发展速度(上年为 100)(%)	Developing Rate of Per CapitaGDP(preceding year=100)(%)	110.5

MAJOR INDICATORS ON NATIONAL ECONOMY AND SOCIAL DEVELOPMENT BY REGION(2014)

市区 Urban Area	崇川区 Chongchuan	港闸区 Gangzha	开发区 Development Zone	通州区 Tongzhou
39	12	6	2	19
82.18	18.86	7.46	6.03	49.84
212.83	52.12	19.22	14.82	126.66
212.57	52.15	19.18	14.78	126.46
18744	4613	1714	1608	10809
8.82	8.85	8.94	10.88	8.55
16849	2912	1679	1025	11233
7.93	5.58	8.75	6.94	8.88
0.89	3.26	0.18	3.95	–0.34
233.55	70.65	28	20.70	114.2
179.36	70.65	24.38	20.70	63.63
136.7	37.2	16.9	12.4	70.2
44.30	11.90	4.88	6.99	20.41
2093.78	574.69	284.14	441.89	860.73
56.54	0.27	2.03	2.00	52.25
1021.67	164.62	168.32	325.86	446.99
852.05	117.20	141.45	308.17	367.49
1015.57	409.81	113.79	114.03	361.49
89766	81545	101660	214340	75363
100.0	100.0	100.0	100.0	100.0
2.7	0.05	0.7	0.5	6.1
48.8	28.6	59.2	73.7	51.9
40.7	20.4	49.8	69.7	42.7
48.5	71.3	40.0	25.8	42.0
110.2	109.5	109.5	110.4	110.8
102.3	59.4	90.1	89.7	103.8
109.8	107.6	108.4	111.0	110.4
110.3	108.6	108.6	110.5	111.5
111.3	110.6	112.5	108.0	112.5
109.9	109.0	109.1	109.3	110.8

1-11 续 表

指　　标	Item	全市 Whole Municipality
农林牧渔业总产值(现价)(亿元)	Gross Output Value of Agriculture (100 million yuan)	631.88
规模以上工业总产值(现价)(亿元)	Gross Industrial Output Above Designated Size(Present Price)(100 million yuan)	12499.70
#高新技术产业产值	High-tech Industy Output Value	5312.93
#新兴产业产值	Emerging Industry Output Value	4179.54
固定资产投资完成额(亿元)	Completed Investment of Fixed Assets(100 million yuan)	3896.39
#工业	Industry	2046.82
服务业	Service Industry	1839.66
房地产开发	Real Estate Development	678.92
#新兴产业投资	High-tech Industy Investment	1196.90
房屋施工面积(万平方米)	Floor Space under Construction (10,000 m^2)	11329.37
房屋竣工面积(万平方米)	Completed Floor Space(10,000 m2)	4124.99
商品房销售面积(万平方米)	Sold Space of Commercial Building (10,000 m^2)	919.17
#住宅	Residence	843.35
商品房销售额(亿元)	Sales ofCommercial Building (100 million Yuan)	479.80
#住宅	Residence	413.73
商品房待售面积(万平方米)	Space of Commercial Building to Sell (10,000 m^2)	689.53
#住宅	Residence	509.38
社会消费品零售总额(亿元)	Total Retail Sales of Consumer Goods (100 million yuan)	2166.10
进出口总额(亿美元)	Total Imports and Exports(100 million US$)	316.37
#出口	Exports	224.80
协议注册外资(亿美元)	Contracted Foreign Investment(100 million US$)	55.24
实际到账注册外资(亿美元)	Actually Paid-in Foreign Investment(100 million US$)	23.23
财政总收入(亿元)	General Financial Revenue(100 million yuan)	1403.93
#一般公共预算收入	General public budget revenue expenditure	550.00
财政总支出(亿元)	General Financial Expenditure(100 million yuan)	1220.52
从业人员平均工资(元)	Auerage Salarg of In-post Employees(yuan)	61383

CONTINUED

市区 Urban Area	崇川区 Chongchuan	港闸区 Gangzha	开发区 Development Zone	通州区 Tongzhou
95.43	0.56	3.64	3.06	88.17
4204.21	381.73	440.19	1526.80	1855.49
1707.24	159.63	153.01	608.95	785.65
1501.55	155.89	132.19	599.47	614.00
1589.61	406.38	239.82	419.09	520.12
594.91	56.26	54.30	172.29	311.14
991.82	350.13	185.33	246.80	206.09
445.70	151.42	152.02	74.46	67.79
413.01	39.94	21.07	107.98	240.72
5101.78	1404.66	1081.19	957.65	1658.27
1631.58	297.67	431.73	224.25	677.94
583.88	145.66	180.02	133.39	124.80
538.42	122.33	175.00	129.38	111.70
265.17	99.04	70.63	50.60	44.90
227.83	76.40	63.97	47.25	40.20
376.05	81.02	153.53	50.71	90.78
290.27	55.18	128.68	39.52	66.89
856.60	334.64	111.91	130.17	279.88
175.54	64.68	29.48	48.19	33.19
127.33	45.99	23.43	28.53	29.38
21.41	2.84	2.62	9.90	6.05
11.08	1.33	0.47	5.96	3.31
643.83	112.44	93.45	94.65	182.01
242.62	68.68	36.45	39.37	70.44
517.70	44.47	61.90	57.83	167.48
61910	67906	53691	72399	60197

1-12 分地区国民经济和社会发展主要指标(2014 年)

指　标	Item	全市 Whole Municipality
土地面积(平方公里)	Land Area(sq.km)	10549
乡、镇(街道)数(个)	Number of Township(unit)	101
# 镇	#Toionship	73
村民委员会(个)	Villagers Committee(unit)	1315
村民小组(个)	Villagers Group(unit)	39625
年末总户数(万户)	Year-end Household (10,000 households)	282.61
年末户籍人口(万人)	Registered Population at Year-end (10,000 persons)	767.63
男性	Male	378.28
女性	Female	389.35
年平均人口(万人)	Annual Average Population(10,000 persons)	767.07
年出生人口(人)	Annual Birth(person)	57826
人口出生率(‰)	Birth Rate(‰)	7.54
年死亡人口(人)	Annual Death(person)	62098
人口死亡率(‰)	Death Rate(‰)	8.10
人口自然增长率(‰)	Population Natural Growth Rate(‰)	0.56
年末常住人口(万人)	Permanent Residents at Year-end (10,000 persons)	729.8
城镇人口	Urban Residents	446.27
年末从业人员(万人)	Employees at Year-end (10,000 persons)	462.00
# 在岗职工人数	#Number of Persons Employed	157.88
第一产业	Primary Industry	101.70
第二产业	Secondary Industry	216.00
# 工业	# Industry	137.40
第三产业	Tertiary Industry	144.30
地区生产总值(亿元)	GDP(100 million yuan)	5652.69
第一产业	Primary Industry	339.57
第二产业	Secondary Industry	2812.34
# 工业	# Industry	2307.64
第三产业	Tertiary Industry	2500.78
人均 GDP(按常住人口计算)(元)	Per Capita GDP(of permanent residents) (yuan)	77457

MAJOR INDICATORS ON NATIONAL ECONOMY AND SOCIAL DEVELOPMENT BY REGION(2014)

市区 Urban Area	通州区 Tongzhou	海安 Haian	如东 Rudong	启东 Qidong	如皋 Rugao	海门 Haimen
2140	1562	1184	2791	1715	1576	1144
39	19	10	14	12	14	12
19	19	10	14	11	11	8
237	208	207	213	261	166	231
10065	9304	5097	5627	6319	4322	8195
82.18	49.84	34.19	37.06	45.37	45.32	38.49
212.83	126.66	94.26	104.37	112.32	143.69	100.16
104.18	61.95	46.70	51.38	55.04	71.68	49.30
108.65	64.71	47.56	52.99	57.28	72.01	50.86
212.57	126.46	94.22	104.37	112.33	143.46	100.11
18744	10809	5966	6341	8101	11465	7209
8.82	8.55	6.33	6.08	7.21	7.99	7.20
16849	11233	7526	9659	8121	11849	8094
7.93	8.88	7.99	9.25	7.23	8.26	8.08
-0.89	0.34	1.66	3.18	0.02	0.27	0.88
233.55	114.2	86.62	98.19	95.60	125.61	90.23
179.36	63.63	46.45	51.67	51.32	67.28	50.19
136.70	70.20	54.50	62.30	67.90	74.70	65.90
44.30	20.41	18.97	17.96	22.56	21.40	32.69
18.40	17.30	11.60	14.10	19.60	20.20	17.80
59.90	33.80	28.80	30.90	29.60	35.10	31.70
40.70	19.90	18.00	19.70	18.20	22.00	18.80
58.40	19.10	14.10	17.30	18.70	19.40	16.40
2093.78	860.73	624.14	615.51	739.13	743.64	836.50
56.54	52.25	51.27	62.17	62.93	57.60	49.07
1021.67	446.99	304.13	297.11	369.03	377.24	443.16
852.05	367.49	245.80	245.42	287.41	311.08	365.88
1015.57	361.49	268.74	256.23	307.17	308.80	344.27
89766	75363	72051	62631	77242	59158	92697

1-12 续表 1

指 标	Item	全市 Whole Municipality
地区生产总值构成(%)	Structure of GDP(%)	100.0
第一产业	Primary Industry	6.0
第二产业	Secondary Industry	49.8
# 工业	# Industry	40.8
第三产业	Tertiary Industry	44.2
地区生产总值发展速度(上年为 100)(%)	Developing Rate of GDP(preceding year=100)(%)	110.5
第一产业	Primary Industry	103.5
第二产业	Secondary Industry	110.3
# 工业	# Industry	111.1
第三产业	Tertiary Industry	111.9
人均 GDP 发展速度(上年为 100)(%)	Developing Rate of Per Capita GDP(preceding year=100)(%)	110.5
农林牧渔业总产值(现价)(亿元)	Gross Output Value of Farming, Forestry, Animal Husbandry and Fishery(presentprice)(100 million yuan)	631.88
农业产值	Farming	278.94
林业产值	Forestry	4.07
牧业产值	Animal Husbandry	145.07
渔业产值	Fishery	147.83
农林牧渔服务业	Farming, Forestry, Animal Husbandry and Fishery Services	55.97
乡村劳动力(万人)	Rural Labor Force(10,000 persons)	302.30
# 农业劳动力	#Agricultural Labor Force	66.66
主要农产品产量	Output of Main Agricultural Products	
粮食(万吨)	Grain(10,000 tons)	334.02
棉花(吨)	Cotton(ton)	43644
油料(万吨)	Oil Crops (10,000 tons)	39.06
蚕茧(吨)	Silkworms(ton)	20008
水产品(万吨)	Aquatic Products(10,000 tons)	88.21
生猪出栏数(万头)	Pigs for Slaughter(10,000 heads)	394.71
生猪年末存栏数(万头)	Year-end Pigs in Stock(10,000 heads)	270.76

CONTINUED 1

市区 Urban Area	通州区 Tongzhou	海安 Haian	如东 Rudong	启东 Qidong	如皋 Rugao	海门 Haimen
100.0	100.0	100.0	100.0	100.0	100.0	100.0
2.7	6.1	8.2	10.1	8.5	7.7	5.9
48.8	51.9	48.7	48.3	49.9	50.7	53.0
40.7	42.7	39.4	39.9	38.9	41.8	43.7
48.5	42.0	43.1	41.6	41.6	41.5	41.2
110.2	110.8	111.0	110.2	110.6	110.5	110.2
102.3	103.8	103.9	103.4	103.2	103.6	103.7
109.8	110.4	111.3	110.2	110.4	110.8	110.6
110.3	111.5	111.5	111.4	110.9	111.4	111.2
111.3	112.5	112.2	112.2	113.0	111.6	110.8
109.9	110.8	111.0	110.4	110.8	110.7	110.2
95.43	88.18	102.71	126.86	121.52	98.98	86.38
50.65	45.76	41.36	48.46	40.58	55.10	42.78
1.16	1.08	0.31	0.97	0.63	0.23	0.72
14.50	13.21	44.45	29.78	12.55	32.14	11.64
15.09	14.49	8.31	40.53	57.40	5.41	21.09
14.03	13.64	8.28	7.12	10.29	6.10	10.15
57.75	52.75	37.45	47.86	50.15	60.10	48.99
12.43	11.45	7.19	8.62	12.81	13.90	11.71
58.52	53.47	64.12	92.74	24.98	74.69	18.96
7429	7366	12	11801	13616	117	10669
10.60	9.86	1.53	4.64	9.38	3.82	9.10
437	437	11228	1625	334	6216	168
5.77	3.50	3.46	30.97	36.02	2.59	9.40
62.93	55.70	76.67	99.09	28.90	113.06	14.06
31.63	27.99	50.10	82.93	15.67	80.52	9.91

1-12 续表 2

指　　标	Item	全市 Whole Municipality
规模以上工业总产值(亿元)	Gross Industrial Output Above Designated Size(Present Price)(100 million yuan)	12499.70
#高新技术产业产值	#High-tech Industy Output Value	5312.93
新兴产业产值	Emerging Industry Output Value	4179.54
主要工业产品产量	Output of Main Industrial Products	
发电量(亿千瓦时)	Electricity(100 million kWh)	403.03
纱(万吨)	Yarn(10,000 tons)	62.71
布(亿米)	Cloth(100 million meters)	32.64
服装(万件)	Garments(10,000 pieces)	76328
化学肥料(吨)	Chemical Fertilizer(tons)	17404
化学农药(万吨)	Chemical Pesticides(10,000 tons)	18.95
水泥(万吨)	Cements(10,000 tons)	1110.85
固定资产投资完成额(亿元)	Investment in Fixed Assets(100 million yuan)	3896.39
#工业	# Industrial	2046.82
服务业	Service Industry	1839.66
房地产开发	#Real Estate Development	678.92
新兴产业投资	High-tech Industy Investment	1196.90
新增固定资产(亿元)	Newly Added Investment in Fixed Assets Above Designated Size(100 million yuan)	5591.65
房屋施工面积(万平方米)	Floor Space of Building Construction (10,000 sq.m)	5272.22
#住宅	# Housing	3951.03
房屋竣工面积(万平方米)	Floor Space of Building Completed (10,000 sq.m)	1031.15
#住宅	# Housing	857.56
商品房销售面积(万平方米)	Floor Space of Commercial Building Sales (10,000 sq.m)	919.17
#住宅	# Housing	843.35
商品房待售面积(万平方米)	Floor Space of Commercial Building to Sell(10,000 sq.m)	689.53
#住宅	# Housing	509.38
商品房销售额(亿元)	Commercial Building Sales(100 million yuan)	479.80
#住宅	# Housing	413.73
社会消费品零售总额(亿元)	Total Retail Sales of Consumer Goods(100 million yuan)	2166.10

CONTINUED 2

市区 Urban Area	通州区 Tongzhou	海安 Haian	如东 Rudong	启东 Qidong	如皋 Rugao	海门 Haimen
4204.21	1855.49	1789.96	1670.98	1508.48	1589.78	1736.29
1707.24	785.65	821.62	678.21	661.52	661.83	782.51
1501.55	614.00	633.58	419.14	558.95	462.80	603.51
224.36	1.07	4.26	24.48	145.77	1.02	3.14
22.55	14.59	12.55	8.37	7.02	7.03	5.20
12.99	6.26	4.21	10.44	0.64	3.68	0.68
36822	28000	4546	16491	2369	13438	2661
				9097	8307	
11.31		0.13	2.48	5.04		
190.46		123.21	180.34	221.40	53.06	342.38
1589.61	520.12	448.95	427.93	483.41	445.08	501.40
594.91	311.14	286.54	280.01	301.94	267.76	315.66
991.82	206.09	158.35	147.42	181.13	176.22	184.73
445.70	67.79	52.48	31.47	47.03	58.53	43.71
413.01	240.72	217.40	127.80	140.79	126.63	171.28
3624.96	479.03	335.12	362.17	435.28	367.16	466.94
3058.38	552.07	590.36	209.41	408.03	550.00	456.04
2231.54	426.29	448.64	155.03	374.23	385.76	355.82
623.63	145.31	84.67	17.77	91.29	94.19	119.60
525.20	128.43	67.85	16.78	89.66	69.00	89.08
583.88	124.80	63.11	29.10	87.84	80.69	74.55
538.42	111.70	57.00	27.73	84.24	65.83	70.12
376.05	90.78	59.94	20.78	53.26	125.04	54.46
290.27	66.89	32.95	14.73	44.94	87.13	39.35
265.17	44.90	37.74	19.00	55.68	46.44	55.78
227.83	40.20	32.08	17.41	52.94	32.71	50.75
856.60	279.88	221.95	257.89	266.41	280.77	282.48

1-12 续表 3

指 标	Item	全市 Whole Municipality
进出口总额(亿美元)	Total Imports and Exports(100 million US$)	316.47
出口	Exports	224.80
新批外商投资项目数(个)	Newly-approved Foreign Inuestment Projects	305
新批协议注册外资(亿美元)	New-Contracted Foreign Investments(100 million)	55.24
实际到账注册外资(亿美元)	Actual Paid-in Foreign Investments(100 million)	23.23
财政总收入(亿元)	Government Revenue (100 million yuan)	1403.93
#一般公共预算收入	#General public budget revenue	550.00
财政总支出(亿元)	Government Expenditure (100 million yuan)	1220.52
#一般公共预算支出	#General public budget revenue expenditure	649.58
金融机构本外币存款余额(亿元)	Deposit Balance of Banking Systems (Year End)(100 million yuan)	8508.32
#本外币储蓄存款	#Savings of Domestic and Foreign Currency	4623.93
金融机构本外币贷款余额(亿元)	Loan Balance of Banking Systems(Year End)(100 million yuan)	5258.93
邮电业务收入(万元)	Postal and Telecommunication Service Revenue(100 million yuan)	10.95
固定电话用户数(万户)	Year-End Telephone Users(10,000 households)	256.13
移动电话用户(万户)	Year-End Mobile Phone Users(10,000 households)	864.00
固定宽带用户(万户)	Broad Band Usage(10,000 households)	182.97
全年用电量(亿千瓦时)	Annual Electricity Use(100 million KWH)	333.23
#工业用电	# Industrial	242.89
城乡居民生活用电	Urban and Rural Residents Power Consumption	43.73
从业人员平均工资(元)	Average Wage of Employed Staff and Workers(yuan)	61383
全体居民可支配收入(元)	Disposable Income of Residents	25340
城镇常住居民可支配收入	Disposable Income of Urban Permanant Residents	33374
农村常住居民可支配收入	Disposable Income of Rural Permanant Residents	15821
在校学生数(万人)	Students At Schools(10,000 persons)	73.18
卫生机构数(个)	Number of Medical Institutions(unit)	3262
卫生技术人员数(人)	Medical Technical Personnels(person)	39481
#执业、助理医师	#Licensed Doctors (Assistants)(person)	16366
卫生机构床位数(张)	Beds in Medical Institutions(unit)	35136

CONTINUED 3

市区 Urban Area	通州区 Tongzhou	海安 Haian	如东 Rudong	启东 Qidong	如皋 Rugao	海门 Haimen
175.54	33.19	24.52	33.11	30.72	32.12	20.36
127.33	29.38	21.44	12.89	23.05	25.55	14.55
119	45	51	47	27	29	32
21.41	6.05	7.20	8.79	5.42	6.26	6.15
11.08	3.31	3.32	3.43	0.55	3.31	1.55
643.83	172.22	127.87	128.35	168.40	173.60	161.88
242.62	68.40	54.10	50.01	67.25	67.45	68.57
517.68	154.81	120.59	134.48	142.21	171.93	133.63
260.88	82.75	70.58	79.20	74.01	91.29	73.62
3959.23	1107.66	984.75	732.13	951.17	860.01	1021.03
1730.37	716.45	567.89	479.89	639.67	577.85	628.24
2495.54	606.81	685.44	344.91	562.52	530.22	640.30
1.68	1.63	1.31	1.43	1.35	2.03	1.52
87.19	35.59	34.09	28.25	36.12	36.56	33.93
315.22	113.35	87.67	86.91	113.72	105.30	82.58
69.42	24.86	21.86	19.71	23.10	30.73	18.16
136.86	47.61	43.01	41.94	26.87	45.76	35.12
99.17	35.66	33.96	31.39	17.35	32.79	24.55
16.26	6.93	4.54	5.02	5.40	7.16	5.35
61910	60197	59299	55105	58341	59089	60725
29960	24836	22842	22454	23908	22391	25262
35568	34565	31597	31557	31708	31026	34280
17051	16835	15155	14494	16762	14210	17419
31.03	8.69	7.57	6.41	7.40	11.99	8.79
1058	505	401	461	426	511	405
18487	5480	4153	3780	3721	5540	3800
7128	2406	1869	1608	1555	2533	1673
15134	5671	4232	3286	3815	5189	3480

1-13　分行业私营企业从业人员(2014年)

单位:户、万人、亿元

指　标	Item
合计	**Total**
农、林、牧、渔业	Farming, Forestry, Husbandry and Fishery
采矿业	Mining
制造业	Manufacturing
电力、热力、燃气及水生产和供应业	Production and Supply of Water, Heat, Gas and Power
建筑业	Construction
批发和零售业	Wholesale and Retail
交通运输、仓储和邮政业	Transportation, Warehousing and Post
住宿和餐饮业	Accomodation and Catering
信息传输、软件和信息技术服务业	Information Transmission, Software and IT Service
金融业	Banking
房地产业	Real Estate
租赁和商务服务业	Leasing and Commercial Service
科学研究、技术服务和地质勘查业	S&T,Technic Services and Geological Suruey
水利、环境和公共设施管理业	Water, Environment and Public Facility Management
居民服务、修理和其他服务业	Service for Residents, Maintenance and Others
教育	Education
卫生和社会工作	Health and Social Work
文化、体育和娱乐业	Culture, Sports and Entertaiment

EMPLOYEES OF PRIVATE ENTERPRISES GROUPED BY SECTOR(2014)

(Units: housholds, 10000 person, 1000 million)

期 末 实 有 Real hold at Final						本期开业 Current Period Opening		
合 计 Total			城 镇 Urban Area					
户数 Housholds	从业人员 Employees	注册资本 Registered Capital	户数 Housholds	从业人员 Employee	注册资本 Registered Capital	户数 Housholds	从业人员 Employee	注册资本 Registered Capital
226878	**250.31**	**7425.11**	**68348**	**67.86**	**2662.71**	**17918**	**9.95**	**870.02**
8133	5.47	183.66	1104	0.71	26.52	312	0.19	11.63
5	0.01	0.94	1	…	0.30			
84065	98.77	2816.54	17834	22.31	652.26	3276	2.49	122.67
158	0.18	11.74	59	0.08	5.23	25	0.01	1.92
8525	58.77	671.28	4361	11.14	265.64	1557	1.26	74.89
98565	58.89	1940.22	28960	17.18	548.85	7646	2.95	152.18
2447	2.09	82.07	1358	1.06	34.83	447	0.20	15.15
795	1.02	11.07	409	0.66	6.66	80	0.05	0.81
2012	1.40	53.63	1457	1.08	42.16	467	0.26	19.81
262	0.27	135.13	159	0.19	89.60	58	0.06	61.25
2073	3.17	380.92	1187	1.90	203.78	289	0.22	22.64
9375	7.95	712.60	6255	4.88	574.06	1942	1.01	311.28
4404	4.82	307.64	2756	2.51	156.03	1201	0.91	63.74
420	0.56	30.94	195	0.29	17.14	73	0.05	3.25
4815	5.98	68.76	1678	3.27	29.63	369	0.19	5.47
179	0.18	0.84	102	0.09	0.48	22	0.02	0.24
54	0.24	2.03	44	0.12	1.26	4	0.01	0.18
589	0.53	15.10	427	0.39	8.27	148	0.07	2.92

1-13 续表

单位:户、万人、亿元

指 标	Item	独资企业 Proprietorship		
		户数 Households	从业人员 Employee	出资额 Capital Contributions
合计	**Total**	**114182**	**64.13**	**1937.02**
农、林、牧、渔业	Farming, Forestry, Husbandry and Fishery	5859	3.14	63.89
农、林、牧、渔服务业	Farming, Forestry, Husbandry and Fishery Service	1596	0.84	13.98
采矿业	Mining	1	…	0.03
制造业	Manufacturing	49918	31.10	919.12
金属制品、机械和设备修理业	Metal Products, Machine and Equipment Maintenance	42	0.03	0.40
电力、热力、燃气及水生产和供应业	Production and Supply of Water, Heat, Gas and Power	29	0.02	0.17
建筑业	Construction	872	0.53	8.60
批发和零售业	Wholesale and Retail	53870	27.49	907.19
交通运输、仓储和邮政业	Transportation, Warehousing and Post	276	0.12	12.21
住宿和餐饮业	Accomodation and Catering	438	0.22	1.20
信息传输、软件和信息技术服务业	Information Transmission, Software and IT Servic	308	0.12	1.10
金融业	Banking	2	…	0.01
房地产业	Real Estate	12	0.01	0.20
租赁和商务服务业	Leasing and Commercial Service	615	0.33	4.91
科学研究和技术服务业	Scientific Research and Technology Service	156	0.08	1.51
水利、环境和公共设施管理业	Water, Environment and Public Facility Management	17	0.01	0.20
居民服务、修理和其他服务业	Service for Residents, Maintenance and Other	1602	0.73	15.01
教育	Education	19	0.02	0.05
卫生和社会工作	Health and Social Work	16	0.02	0.11
文化、体育和娱乐业	Culture, Sports and Entertaiment	172	0.21	1.50

CONTINUED

(Units: housholds, 10000 person, 1000 million)

合伙企业 Partnership			有限责任公司 LLC			股份有限公司 Co. , Ltd.		
户数 Households	从业人员 Employee	实缴出资额 Paid-in Capital Contributions	户数 Households	从业人员 Employee	注册资本 Registered Capital	户数 Households	从业人员 Employee	注册资本 Registered Capital
2035	**2.39**	**83.99**	**103826**	**176.14**	**4376.19**	**474**	**5.06**	**126.66**
42	0.05	0.79	2157	2.27	112.09	3	…	0.75
1	…	0.01	271	0.26	10.39			
			4	0.01	0.91			
1283	1.71	4.94	32937	64.43	1717.85	112	2.49	79.91
			132	0.18	1.68			
15	0.01	0.04	114	0.16	10.21	2	…	0.50
9	0.01	0.03	6686	55.44	530.48	9	1.18	5.55
248	0.16	1.43	41516	29.84	917.85	212	1.02	9.75
8	0.00	0.02	1916	1.94	54.13	1	…	0.52
16	0.02	0.11	376	0.82	11.40	2	…	
28	0.01	0.04	1368	1.09	29.09	22	0.01	1.60
5	0.01	0.54	140	0.13	64.77	65	0.08	7.58
4	…	0.01	1912	3.02	350.25	4	0.02	1.38
274	0.31	74.94	7497	6.66	285.32	25	0.15	9.07
14	0.01	0.03	3204	3.84	210.64	16	0.08	7.68
1	…		362	0.52	22.23	1	0.02	2.38
68	0.06	0.92	3172	5.33	46.03			
5	…	0.01	151	0.16	0.52			
2	…	0.01	36	0.23	1.84			
13	0.01	0.12	278	0.26	10.58			

1-14 分行业个体从业人员(2014年)

单位:人

指　标	Item
合 计	**Total**
农、林、牧、渔业	Farming, Forestry, Husbandry and Fishery
采矿业	Mining
制造业	Manufacturing
电力、热力、燃气及水生产和供应业	Production and Supply of Water, Heat, Gas and Power
建筑业	Construction
批发和零售业	Wholesale and Retail
交通运输、仓储和邮政业	Transportation, Warehousing and Post
住宿和餐饮业	Accomodation and Catering
信息传输、软件和信息技术服务业	Information Transmission, Software and IT Servic
金融业	Banking
房地产业	Real Estate
租赁和商务服务业	Leasing and Commercial Service
科学研究和技术服务业	Scientific Research and Technology Service
水利、环境和公共设施管理业	Water, Environment and Public Facility Management
居民服务、修理和其他服务业	Service for Residents, Maintenance and Others
教育	Education
卫生和社会工作	Health and Social Work
文化、体育和娱乐业	Culture, Sports and Entertainment
其他	Others

INDIVIDUAL JOBHOLDERS GROUPED BY SECTOR(2014)

(Unit: person)

期末实有 Term-end Actual Sum				本期开业 Current Period Opening	
合计 Total		城镇 Urban Area			
户数(户) Households(household)	从业人员 Employees	户数(户) Households(household)	从业人员 Employees	户数(户) Households(household)	从业人员 Employees
534077	**736327**	**165448**	**250553**	**52656**	**91894**
17038	20955	3423	4265	1057	2304
31	51	6	10		
79013	147297	14698	28487	7813	19946
43	59	15	19	1	5
1741	2788	373	679	85	154
362650	443827	112052	148203	31901	45201
5791	6792	1550	1934	632	920
19060	42467	10839	28709	4972	12261
867	1162	445	608	260	435
6	8	3	5	2	2
1427	1891	1254	1672	90	152
5945	8618	3132	4803	1214	1944
1266	2008	645	1214	180	336
41	77	23	53	2	3
37473	54479	15954	27040	4199	7568
165	353	127	295	34	76
131	184	48	89	24	45
1384	3303	861	2468	189	539
5	8			1	3

1-15 全市各类法人单位分布情况(2014 年)

单位:个

指 标	Item	合计 Total
总　　计	**Total**	**114404**
按地区分组	**Grouped by Regions**	
南通市	Municipality	114404
市区	Urban Area	43230
崇川区	Chongchuan	15199
港闸区	Gangzha	6336
开发区	Development Zone	5216
通州区	Tongzhou	16479
海安县	Haian	14587
如东县	Rudong	14655
启东市	Qidong	12236
如皋市	Rugao	17239
海门市	Haimen	12457
按国民经济行业门类分组	Grouped by National Economic Sectors	
农、林、牧、渔业	Farming, Forestry, Husbandry and Fishery	4058
采矿业	Mining	6
制造业	Manufacturing	38895
电力、燃气及水的生产和供应业	Production and Supply of Power, Heat, Gas and Water	342
建筑业	Construction	5088
交通运输、仓储和邮政业	Transportation, Storage and Postal Industry	2152
信息传输、计算机服务和软件业	Information Transmission, Software and IT Service	1573
批发和零售业	Wholesale and Retail	33123
住宿和餐饮业	Accomodation and Catering Services	897
金融业	Banking	313
房地产业	Real Estate	2425
租赁和商务服务业	Leasing and Commercial Service	7208
科学研究、技术服务和地质勘查业	S&T, Technic Services and Geological Survey	3907
水利、环境和公共设施管理业	Water, Environment and Public Facility Management	578
居民服务和其他服务业	Service for Residents, Maintenance and Others	1737
教育	Education	1942
卫生、社会保障和社会福利业	Health, Social Security and Social Welfare	2574
文化、体育和娱乐业	Culture, Sports and Entertainment	1165
公共管理和社会组织	Public Administration and Social Organiztions	6421

DISTRIBUTION OF VARIOUS TYPES OF LEGAL ENTITIES(2014)

(Unit)

企业 Enterprise	事业 Public Institution	机关 Organ	社会团体 Social Group	民办非企业 Private Nonenterprise	其他组织机构 Others
99070	**3727**	**889**	**2167**	**2629**	**5922**
99070	3727	889	2167	2629	5922
38372	1130	331	988	947	1462
13425	405	153	486	489	241
5657	159	54	61	288	117
4850	46	12	209	20	79
14440	520	112	232	150	1025
12368	605	108	256	548	702
12898	590	106	210	283	568
9912	399	122	308	410	1085
14801	541	118	193	235	1351
10719	462	104	212	206	754
1827	42			29	2160
6					
38895					
342					
5088					
2108	32			2	10
1534	29			5	5
33123	0				
892	0				5
305	1			2	5
2372	36				17
6671	164			78	295
3023	358			95	431
376	178			8	16
1366	40			262	69
318	1020			528	76
88	501		37	1464	484
736	194		7	154	74
	1132	889	2123	2	2275

1-15 续表

指 标	Item	合计 Total
按登记注册类型分组	**Grouped by Types of Registration**	
内资	Domestic Enterprise	111183
国有	State-owned Enterprise	4929
集体	Collective Enterprise	1804
股份合作	Joint Equity Cooperative Enterprise	281
联营	Joint Venture	97
国有联营	State-owned Joint Venture	7
集体联营	Collective Joint Venture	43
国有与集体联营	State-owned and Collective Joint Venture	8
其他联营	Others	39
有限责任公司	Limited Liability Company	10864
国有独资公司	State-owned Sole Proprietorship	86
其他有限责任公司	Others	10778
股份有限公司	Joint Stock Company	710
私营	Private Company	80793
私营独资	Private Sole Proprietorship	19490
私营合伙	Private Partnership	1711
私营有限责任公司	Private Limited Liablity Company	58404
私营股份有限公司	Private Joint Stock Company	1188
其他内资	Other Domestic Capital	11705
港澳台商投资	HK, Macau or Taiwan Invested Company	1297
与港澳台商合资经营	Joint Venture(HK, Macau or Taiwan)	421
与港澳台商合作经营	Cooperative Enterprise (HK, Macau or Taiwan)	16
港澳台商独资	Sole Proprietorship (HK, Macau or Taiwan)	833
港澳台商投资股份有限公司	Shareholding Limited Company (HK, Macau or Taiwan)	17
其他港、澳、台商投资	Others	10
外商投资	Foreign InvestedCompany	1924
中外合资经营	Sino-foreign Joint Venture	789
中外合作经营	Sino-foreign Cooperative Enterprise	31
外资企业	Foreign Funded Enterprise	1048
外商投资股份有限公司	Foreign Funded Joint Stock Company	40
其他外商投资	Others	16

CONTINUED

企业 Enterprise	事业 Public Institution	机关 Organ	社会团体 Social Group	民办非企业 Private Nonenterprise	其他组织机构 Others
95859	3727	889	2161	2628	5919
326	3087	889	555	14	58
740	542		160	292	70
257			2	8	14
80	1			13	3
6				1	
33				7	3
5	1			2	
36				3	
10851			1	1	11
86					
10765			1	1	11
705			2	1	2
80508			19	129	137
19374			6	78	32
1664			2	18	27
58288			9	31	76
1182			2	2	2
2392	97		1422	2170	5624
1296				1	
421					
16					
832				1	
17					
10					
1915			6		3
789					
31					
1040			6		2
40					
15					1

1-16 全市多产法人单位所属各类产业活动单位分布情况(2014 年)

单位:个

指 标	Item	合计 Total
总 计	**Total**	**15192**
按地区分组	**Grouped by Regions**	
南通市	Municipality	15192
市区	Downtown Area	6582
崇川区	Chongchuan	2535
港闸区	Gangzha	531
开发区	Development Zone	284
通州区	Tongzhou	3232
海安县	Haian	1784
如东县	Rudong	1324
启东市	Qidong	1859
如皋市	Rugao	1093
海门市	Haimen	2550
按国民经济行业门类分组	Grouped by National Economic Sectors	
农、林、牧、渔业	Farming, Forestry, Husbandry and Fishery	75
采矿业	Mining	
制造业	Manufacturing	1011
电力、燃气及水的生产和供应业	Production and Supply of Power, Heat, Gas and Water	73
建筑业	Construction	613
交通运输、仓储和邮政业	Transportation, Storage and Postal Industry	796
信息传输、计算机服务和软件业	Information Transmission, Software and IT Service	830
批发和零售业	Wholesale and Retail	5400
住宿和餐饮业	Accomodation and Catering Services	572
金融业	Banking	1830
房地产业	Real Estate	427
租赁和商务服务业	Leasing and Commercial Service	601
科学研究、技术服务和地质勘查业	S&T, Technic Services and Geological Survey	242
水利、环境和公共设施管理业	Water, Environment and Public Facility Management	46
居民服务和其他服务业	Service for Residents, Maintenance and Others	120
教育	Education	245
卫生、社会保障和社会福利业	Health, Social Security and Social Welfare	1178
文化、体育和娱乐业	Culture, Sports and Entertainment	61
公共管理和社会组织	Public Administration and Social Organiztions	1072

DISTRIBUTION OF VARIOUS TYPES OF LEGAL ENTITIES AND THEIR PROLIFIC INDUSTIRIAL, ACTIVITIES(2014)

企业 Enterprise	事业 Public Institution	机关 Organ	社会团体 Social Group	其他组织机构 Others
12405	**913**	**501**	**119**	**1254**
12405	913	501	119	1254
5422	197	130	89	744
2349	53	23	67	43
482	22	19	3	5
274	1	1	2	6
2317	121	87	17	690
1384	106	80	4	210
1219	24	41	5	35
1280	378	73	9	119
999	6	68	6	14
2101	202	109	6	132
67	2			6
1011				
72				1
613				
750	24			22
795	9			26
5400				0
483	12			77
1796	4	3		27
399	7			21
569	13			19
228	11			3
18	15			13
102	6			12
60	158			27
7	503			668
35	23			3
	126	498	119	329

1-16 续表

指 标	Item	合计 Total
按登记注册类型分组	**Grouped by Types of Registration**	
内资	Domestic Enterprise	14543
国有	State-owned Enterprise	2457
集体	Collective Enterprise	1198
股份合作	Joint Equity Cooperative Enterprise	110
联营	Joint Venture	36
国有联营	State-owned Joint Venture	6
集体联营	Collective Joint Venture	9
国有与集体联营	State-owned and Collective Joint Venture	4
其他联营	Others	17
有限责任公司	Limited Liability Company	1434
国有独资公司	State-owned Sole Proprietorship	19
其他有限责任公司	Others	1415
股份有限公司	Joint Stock Company	1774
私营	Private Company	5845
私营独资	Private Sole Proprietorship	1307
私营合伙	Private Partnership	124
私营有限责任公司	Private Limited Liablity Company	4202
私营股份有限公司	Private Joint Stock Company	212
其他内资	Other Domestic Capital	1689
港澳台商投资	HK, Macau or Taiwan Invested Company	342
与港澳台商合资经营	Joint Venture(HK, Macau or Taiwan)	78
与港澳台商合作经营	Cooperative Enterprise (HK, Macau or Taiwan)	2
港澳台商独资	Sole Proprietorship (HK, Macau or Taiwan)	250
港澳台商投资股份有限公司	Shareholding Limited Company (HK, Macau or Taiwan)	12
外商投资	Foreign InvestedCompany	307
中外合资经营	Sino-foreign Joint Venture	132
中外合作经营	Sino-foreign Cooperative Enterprise	1
外资企业	Foreign Funded Enterprise	152
外商投资股份有限公司	Foreign Funded Joint Stock Company	21
其他外商投资	Others	1

CONTINUED

企业 Enterprise	事业 Public Institution	机关 Organ	社会团体 Social Group	其他组织机构 Others
11759	913	501	119	1251
1231	568	501	98	59
689	333		4	172
105	4			1
34				2
6				
8				1
3				1
17				
1420				14
19				
1401				14
1748				26
5798				47
1285				22
120				4
4182				20
211				1
734	8		17	930
341				1
78				
2				
249				1
12				
305				2
132				
1				
150				2
21				
1				

1-17 按地区、行业大类、注册类型分组法人单位及产业活动单位数(2014年)

(单位：个)

指 标	Item
总　计	**Total**
按地区分组	**Grouped by Regions**
南通市	Municipality
市区	Downtown Area
崇川区	Chongchuan
港闸区	Gangzha
开发区	Development Zone
通州区	Tongzhou
海安县	Haian
如东县	Rudong
启东市	Qidong
如皋市	Rugao
海门市	Haimen
按国民经济行业门类分组	Grouped by National Economic Sectors
农、林、牧、渔业	Farming, Forestry, Husbandry and Fishery
采矿业	Mining
制造业	Manufacturing
电力、燃气及水的生产和供应业	Production and Supply of Power, Heat, Gas and Water
建筑业	Construction
交通运输、仓储和邮政业	Transportation, Storage and Postal Industry
信息传输、计算机服务和软件业	Information Transmission, Software and IT Service
批发和零售业	Wholesale and Retail
住宿和餐饮业	Accomodation and Catering Services
金融业	Banking
房地产业	Real Estate
租赁和商务服务业	Leasing and Commercial Service
科学研究、技术服务和地质勘查业	S&T, Technic Services and Geological Survey
水利、环境和公共设施管理业	Water, Environment and Public Facility Management
居民服务和其他服务业	Service for Residents, Maintenance and Others
教育	Education
卫生、社会保障和社会福利业	Health, Social Security and Social Welfare
文化、体育和娱乐业	Culture, Sports and Entertainment
公共管理和社会组织	Public Administration and Social Organiztions

NUMBER OF LEGAL ENTITIES AND INDUSTRIAL ESTABLISHMENTS GROUPED BY REGION, INDUSTRY AND REGISTRATION TYPES (2014)

(Unit)

法人单位数 Number of Legal Entities			产业活动单位数 Number of Industrial Establishments			
合计 Total	单产法人单位 Single Industry Legal Entities	多产法人单位 Multi-industry Legal Entites	合计 In total	多产法人所属的产业活动单位 Establishments of Multi-industry Legal Entities	产业本地 Local	产业外地 Non-local
114404	111476	2928	126668	15192	13568	1624
114404	111476	2928	126668	15192	13568	1624
43230	41492	1738	48074	6582	7805	870
15199	14560	639	17095	2535	4539	615
6336	6128	208	6659	531	423	62
5216	5097	119	5381	284	304	45
16479	15707	772	18939	3232	2539	148
14587	14365	222	16149	1784	1205	178
14655	14509	146	15833	1324	976	61
12236	11990	246	13849	1859	1312	178
17239	17076	163	18169	1093	463	122
12457	12044	413	14594	2550	1807	215
4058	4042	16	4117	75	69	6
6	6		6			
38895	38239	656	39250	1011	895	116
342	333	9	406	73	55	18
5088	4807	281	5420	613	439	174
2152	2067	85	2863	796	631	165
1573	1555	18	2385	830	787	43
33123	32492	631	37892	5400	5019	381
897	859	38	1431	572	471	101
313	230	83	2060	1830	1631	199
2425	2288	137	2715	427	318	109
7208	7020	188	7621	601	430	171
3907	3829	78	4071	242	151	91
578	572	6	618	46	38	8
1737	1709	28	1829	120	100	20
1942	1789	153	2034	245	240	5
2574	2470	104	3648	1178	1178	
1165	1150	15	1211	61	44	17
6421	6019	402	7091	1072	1072	

1-17 续表

指 标	Item
按登记注册类型分组	**Grouped by Types of Registration**
内资	Domestic Enterprise
国有	State-owned Enterprise
集体	Collective Enterprise
股份合作	Joint Equity Cooperative Enterprise
联营	Joint Venture
国有联营	State-owned Joint Venture
集体联营	Collective Joint Venture
国有与集体联营	State-owned and Collective Joint Venture
其他联营	Others
有限责任公司	Limited Liability Company
国有独资公司	State-owned Sole Proprietorship
其他有限责任公司	Others
股份有限公司	Joint Stock Company
私营	Private Company
私营独资	Private Sole Proprietorship
私营合伙	Private Partnership
私营有限责任公司	Private Limited Liablity Company
私营股份有限公司	Private Joint Stock Company
其他内资	Other Domestic Capital
港澳台商投资	HK, Macau or Taiwan Invested Company
与港澳台商合资经营	Joint Venture(HK, Macau or Taiwan)
与港澳台商合作经营	Cooperative Enterprise (HK, Macau or Taiwan)
港澳台商独资	Sole Proprietorship (HK, Macau or Taiwan)
港澳台商投资股份有限公司	Shareholding Limited Company (HK, Macau or Taiwan)
其他港、澳、台商投资	Others
外商投资	Foreign InvestedCompany
中外合资经营	Sino-foreign Joint Venture
中外合作经营	Sino-foreign Cooperative Enterprise
外资企业	Foreign Funded Enterprise
外商投资股份有限公司	Foreign Funded Joint Stock Company
其他外商投资	Others

CONTINUED

法人单位数 Number of Legal Entities			产业活动单位数 Number of Industrial Establishments			
合计 Total	单产法人单位 Single Industry Legal Entities	多产法人单位 Multi-industry Legal Entites	合计 In total	多产法人所属的产业活动单位 Establishments of Multi-industry Legal Entities	产业本地 Local	产业外地 Non-local
111183	108426	2757	122969	14543	13143	1400
4929	4592	337	7049	2457	2391	66
1804	1659	145	2857	1198	1186	12
281	263	18	373	110	101	9
97	90	7	126	36	34	2
7	6	1	12	6	4	2
43	38	5	47	9	9	
8	7	1	11	4	4	
39	39		56	17	17	
10864	10418	446	11852	1434	1163	271
86	76	10	95	19	14	5
10778	10342	436	11757	1415	1149	266
710	607	103	2381	1774	1638	136
80793	79403	1390	85248	5845	5021	824
19490	19377	113	20684	1307	1216	91
1711	1688	23	1812	124	115	9
58404	57197	1207	61399	4202	3521	681
1188	1141	47	1353	212	169	43
11705	11394	311	13083	1689	1609	80
1297	1228	69	1570	342	270	72
421	388	33	466	78	50	28
16	15	1	17	2	1	1
833	798	35	1048	250	213	37
17	17		29	12	6	6
10	10		10			
1924	1822	102	2129	307	155	152
789	739	50	871	132	73	59
31	31		32	1	1	
1048	999	49	1151	152	72	80
40	37	3	58	21	9	12
16	16		17	1		1

1-18　分地区法人单位基本情况(2014 年)

单位:个

指　标	Item	全市 Total	市区 Urban Area
按国民经济行业门类分组	**Total**	114404	43230
农、林、牧、渔业	Farming, Forestry, Husbandry and Fishery	4058	841
采矿业	Mining	6	0
制造业	Manufacturing	38895	13203
电力、燃气及水的生产和供应业	Production and Supply of Power, Heat, Gas and Water	342	86
建筑业	Construction	5088	1744
交通运输、仓储和邮政业	Transportation, Storage and Postal Industry	2152	1101
信息传输、计算机服务和软件业	Information Transmission, Software and IT Service	1573	842
批发和零售业	Wholesale and Retail	33123	14082
住宿和餐饮业	Accomodation and Catering Services	897	337
金融业	Banking	313	214
房地产业	Real Estate	2425	932
租赁和商务服务业	Leasing and Commercial Service	7208	3394
科学研究、技术服务和地质勘查业	S&T, Technic Services and Geological Survey	3907	1419
水利、环境和公共设施管理业	Water, Environment and Public Facility Management	578	156
居民服务和其他服务业	Service for Residents, Maintenance and Others	1737	819
教育	Education	1942	676
卫生、社会保障和社会福利业	Health, Social Security and Social Welfare	2574	747
文化、体育和娱乐业	Culture, Sports and Entertainment	1165	419
公共管理和社会组织	Public Administration and Social Organiztions	6421	2218

BASIC STATISTICS OF LEGAL ENTITIES BY REGIONS(2014)

(Unit)

崇川区 Chongchuan	港闸区 Gangzha	开发区 Development Zone	通州区 Tongzhou	海安 Haian	如东 Rudong	启东 Qidong	如皋 Rugao	海门 Haimen
15199	6336	5216	16479	14587	14655	12236	17239	12457
21	39	103	678	656	444	782	774	561
0	0	0	0	0	1	3	2	0
1683	2278	2225	7017	6191	4385	4554	6526	4036
13	7	14	52	46	69	43	54	44
654	253	181	656	693	394	832	870	555
433	290	139	239	262	134	164	368	123
491	138	65	148	217	70	107	245	92
6552	1901	1366	4263	2701	6305	1914	3820	4301
218	28	24	67	76	55	166	197	66
175	11	10	18	29	28	14	20	8
435	117	91	289	293	176	316	495	213
1720	377	394	903	896	452	806	1031	629
589	146	140	544	515	408	462	754	349
59	15	27	55	108	78	83	72	81
430	163	76	150	235	153	199	237	94
305	74	38	259	280	217	260	287	222
324	180	39	204	424	292	409	509	193
197	94	24	104	135	173	195	132	111
900	225	260	833	830	821	927	846	779

第二篇

国民经济核算 Chapter 2

National Economic Accounting

2-1 历年地区生产总值

GROSS DOMESTIC PRODUCT OVER THE YEARS

单位:万元 (10,000 yuan)

年份 Year	地区生产总值 Gross Domestic Product	第一产业 Primary Industry	第二产业 Secondary Industry	工业 Industry	建筑业 Construction	第三产业 Tertiary Industry	人均地区生产总值(元) Per Capita GDP(yuan)
1978	293861	122813	109818	99949	9869	61230	408
1979	324508	125937	129643	116545	13098	68928	448
1980	356579	116090	160983	145803	15180	79506	490
1985	672429	232625	297730	275031	22699	142074	904
1990	1342454	428817	604618	545542	59076	309019	1736
1991	1489165	434820	689181	610178	79003	365164	1916
1992	1865012	482288	926342	812105	114237	456382	2393
1993	2408383	570959	1277766	1126839	150927	559658	3086
1994	3430404	844346	1756522	1541088	215434	829536	4388
1995	4630977	1080469	2378654	1969112	409542	1171854	5912
1996	5248682	1220064	2515908	2050675	465233	1512710	6688
1997	5689912	1211513	2761956	2259753	502203	1716443	7241
1998	6148681	1233687	2996515	2436578	559937	1918479	7814
1999	6576020	1268003	3212679	2644786	567893	2095338	8359
2000	7205859	1286388	3610291	3026898	583393	2309180	9176
2001	7896123	1358106	3992877	3365434	627443	2545140	10078
2002	8651791	1407972	4464239	3718124	746115	2779580	11073
2003	9801814	1476696	5192842	4285973	906869	3132276	12584
2004	11957426	1545226	6698400	5420100	1278300	3713800	15415
2005	14837976	1639040	8287902	6770924	1516978	4911035	20138
2006	17883938	1762866	9921068	8213105	1707963	6200003	24545
2007	21636878	1867992	12099580	10217962	1881618	7669305	29991
2008	25931300	2193000	14516300	12196000	2320300	9222000	36199
2009	28728038	2364711	16074976	13194276	2880700	10288351	40231
2010	34656712	2662212	19085636	15684936	3400700	12908864	48083
2011	40802182	2872082	22214804	18404104	3810700	15715297	56005
2012	45586742	3190881	24141149	19921149	4220000	18254712	62506
2013	51500108	3223125	26583759	21926359	4682400	21693224	70572
2014	56526943	3395747	28123382	23076364	5074000	25007772	77457

注:1.本表2013-2014年数据在全国第三次经济普查后进行了调整。

2.自2013年开始,第一产业是指农、林、牧、渔业(不含农、林、牧、渔服务业);第二产业是指采矿业(不含开采辅助活动),制造业(不含金属制品、机械和设备修理业),电力、热力、燃气及水生产和供应业,建筑业;第三产业即服务业,是指除第一产业、第二产业以外的其他行业。

3.人均地区生产总值自2005年起调整为按常住人口计算。

Note:1.2013-2014 data have been adjusted after the third national economic census.

2.Since 2013, primary industry refers to agriculture, forestry, husbandry and fishing Sccondary industry refers to mining industry cexclusine of support activities), manufacturing cexdusine of metal product, machionery or equipment repair, electric power, thermal power, gas, water production and supply, and construction; tertiary industry refers to service industry other than the previous two industries.

3. The calculation of percapita GDP has heen. adjusted in accordance to the permanent residence population.

2-2 历年地区生产总值构成

COMPOSITION OF GROSS DOMESTIC PRODUCT OVER THE YEARS

单位:% (%)

年份 Year	地区生产总值 Gross Domestic Product	第一产业 Primary Industry	第二产业 Secondary Industry	工业 Industry	第三产业 Tertiary Industry
1978	100.0	41.8	37.4	34.0	20.8
1979	100.0	38.8	40.0	35.9	21.2
1980	100.0	32.6	45.1	40.9	22.3
1985	100.0	34.6	44.3	40.9	21.1
1990	100.0	31.9	45.1	40.6	23.0
1991	100.0	29.2	46.3	41.0	24.5
1992	100.0	25.8	49.7	43.5	24.5
1993	100.0	23.7	53.1	46.8	23.2
1994	100.0	24.6	51.2	44.9	24.2
1995	100.0	23.3	51.4	42.5	25.3
1996	100.0	23.2	48.0	39.2	28.8
1997	100.0	21.3	48.5	39.7	30.2
1998	100.0	20.1	48.7	39.6	31.2
1999	100.0	19.2	48.9	40.2	31.9
2000	100.0	17.9	50.1	42.0	32.0
2001	100.0	17.2	50.6	42.6	32.2
2002	100.0	16.3	51.6	43.0	32.1
2003	100.0	15.0	53.0	43.7	32.0
2004	100.0	12.9	56.0	45.3	31.1
2005	100.0	11.0	55.9	45.6	33.1
2006	100.0	9.8	55.5	45.9	34.7
2007	100.0	8.6	55.9	47.2	35.5
2008	100.0	8.4	56.0	47.0	35.6
2009	100.0	8.2	56.0	45.9	35.8
2010	100.0	7.7	55.1	45.3	37.2
2011	100.0	7.0	54.5	45.1	38.5
2012	100.0	7.0	53.0	43.7	40.0
2013	100.0	6.3	51.6	42.6	42.1
2014	100.0	6.0	49.8	40.8	44.2

注:1.本表 2013-2014 年数据在全国第三次经济普查后进行了调整。

2.自 2013 年开始,第一产业是指农、林、牧、渔业(不含农、林、牧、渔服务业);第二产业是指采矿业(不含开采辅助活动),制造业(不含金属制品、机械和设备修理业),电力、热力、燃气及水生产和供应业,建筑业;第三产业即服务业,是指除第一产业、第二产业以外的其他行业。

Note:1.2013-2014 data have been adjusted after the third national economic census.

2.Since 2013, primary industry refers to agriculture, forestry, husbandry and fishing Sccondary industry refers to mining industry cexclusine of support activities), manufacturing cexdusine of metal product, machionery or equipment repair, electric power, thermal power, gas, water production and supply, and construction; tertiary industry refers to service industry other than the previous two industries.

2-3 历年地区生产总值指数

INDICES OF GROSS DOMESTIC PRODUCT OVER THE YEARS

按可比价计算,1978=100 (At comparable price,1978=100)

年份 Year	地区生产总值 Gross Domestic Product	第一产业 Primary Industry	第二产业 Secondary Industry	工业 Industry	建筑业 Construction	第三产业 Tertiary Industry	人均地区生产总值 Per Capita GDP
1978	100.0	100.0	100.0	100.0	100.0	100.0	100.0
1979	109.9	102.5	117.0	116.2	124.6	111.1	109.4
1980	119.5	94.5	145.1	144.9	147.5	121.0	118.4
1985	206.2	160.5	264.5	269.6	213.9	188.3	200.2
1990	284.5	179.3	421.1	418.7	444.4	239.5	264.9
1991	305.6	178.0	462.8	452.6	565.3	272.8	283.5
1992	365.2	193.1	582.7	568.5	727.7	329.0	338.5
1993	414.5	193.3	708.0	712.3	661.5	368.5	383.4
1994	492.8	206.3	866.6	871.9	807.0	455.1	454.6
1995	603.7	242.8	1068.5	1038.4	1367.1	568.9	555.9
1996	681.0	274.1	1191.4	1164.0	1461.4	655.4	625.9
1997	751.8	284.0	1330.8	1310.7	1525.7	744.5	690.4
1998	830.7	291.1	1503.8	1489.0	1646.2	831.6	762.8
1999	914.6	302.7	1672.2	1678.1	1628.1	932.2	839.1
2000	1014.3	318.1	1886.2	1919.7	1585.8	1033.8	929.7
2001	1116.7	333.1	2106.9	2169.3	1635.0	1143.4	1026.4
2002	1240.7	349.4	2382.9	2455.6	1842.6	1270.3	1143.4
2003	1407.0	363.7	2780.8	2892.7	2012.1	1430.4	1301.2
2004	1626.5	383.0	3323.1	3453.9	2422.6	1632.0	1510.7
2005	1877.0	393.7	3957.8	4130.9	2822.3	1867.0	1751.0
2006	2171.7	409.8	4662.3	4924.0	3149.7	2160.1	2031.2
2007	2522.5	423.3	5516.9	5955.5	3334.3	2509.6	2366.4
2008	2858.5	440.8	6273.7	6853.9	3532.9	2884.9	2693.0
2009	3258.7	459.3	7239.9	7799.7	4419.6	3297.5	3078.1
2010	3682.4	477.7	8231.7	8915.1	4883.7	3745.9	3444.3
2011	4127.9	495.4	9252.5	10065.1	5372.1	4240.4	3819.8
2012	4615.0	518.2	10399.8	11303.1	6075.8	4762.0	4266.7
2013	5158.3	529.9	11650.1	12698.7	6713.1	5377.8	4766.1
2014	5700.8	543.6	12854.3	14111.9	7153.0	6020.6	5267.2

注:自 2013 年开始,第一产业是指农、林、牧、渔业(不含农、林、牧、渔服务业);第二产业是指采矿业(不含开采辅助活动),制造业(不含金属制品、机械和设备修理业),电力、热力、燃气及水生产和供应业,建筑业;第三产业即服务业,是指除第一产业、第二产业以外的其他行业。

Note: Since 2013, primary industry refers to agriculture, forestry, husbandry and fishing Sccondary industry refers to mining industry cexclusine of support activities), manufacturing cexdusine of metal product, machionery or equipment repair, electric power, thermal power, gas, water production and supply, and construction; tertiary industry refers to service industry other than the previous two industries.

2-4　市区历年生产总值

GROSS DOMESTIC PRODUCT OVER THE YEARS IN URBAN DISTRICT

单位:万元　　　　(10,000 yuan)

年份 Year	地区生产总值 Gross Domestic Product	第一产业 Primary Industry	第二产业 Secondary Industry	工业 Industry	建筑业 Construction	第三产业 Tertiary Industry	人均地区生产总值(元) Per Capita GDP(yuan)
1978	118707	29908	66595	62259	4336	22204	655
1979	129933	28161	76113	69807	6306	25659	710
1980	146130	23331	92587	85217	7370	30212	793
1985	276128	58725	157082	148209	8873	60321	1444
1990	527159	88872	310488	287957	22531	127799	2619
1991	595681	89107	348516	316270	32246	158058	2938
1992	759164	96885	453813	403557	50256	208466	3727
1993	930109	96334	583183	520251	62932	250592	4544
1994	1293163	144027	793824	700627	93197	355312	6286
1995	1694285	211968	999453	832912	166541	482864	8208
1996	1970127	238750	1078369	887430	190939	653008	9505
1997	2177176	212603	1235683	994296	241387	728890	10452
1998	2330956	213064	1244389	987287	257102	873503	11152
1999	2527668	222017	1339530	1106291	233239	966121	12077
2000	2900826	229928	1620829	1375183	245646	1050069	13881
2001	3174795	246279	1794361	1511611	282750	1134155	15149
2002	3481456	223432	2036059	1716391	319668	1221965	16571
2003	3982268	246244	2367390	1996418	370972	1368634	18892
2004	4894600	263590	3036300	2537000	499300	1594710	23161
2005	6174129	284317	3750713	3131776	618937	2139098	27769
2006	7408524	307249	4361942	3700187	661755	2739332	33517
2007	9009822	332522	5220806	4506904	713902	3456494	40943
2008	10333385	387700	5900600	5023700	876900	4045085	47003
2009	11449035	413198	6526990	5428272	1098718	4508847	51924
2010	13928054	459427	7502731	6208509	1294221	5965896	62132
2011	15940744	494293	8561956	7247534	1314422	6884495	69705
2012	17581293	540817	9226092	7645360	1580733	7814383	76060
2013	19217731	538969	10103142	8519591	1508551	8575620	82612
2014	20937816	565404	10216678	8520493	1723167	10155744	89766

注:1.本表2013-2014年数据在全国第三次经济普查后进行了调整。

2.自2013年开始,第一产业是指农、林、牧、渔业(不含农、林、牧、渔服务业);第二产业是指采矿业(不含开采辅助活动),制造业(不含金属制品、机械和设备修理业),电力、热力、燃气及水生产和供应业,建筑业;第三产业即服务业,是指除第一产业、第二产业以外的其他行业。

3.人均地区生产总值自2005年起调整为按常住人口计算。

Note:1.2013-2014 data have been adjusted after the third national economic census.

2.Since 2013, primary industry refers to agriculture, forestry, husbandry and fishing Sccondary industry refers to mining industry cexclusine of support activities), manufacturing cexdusine of metal product, machionery or equipment repair, electric power, thermal power, gas, water production and supply, and construction; tertiary industry refers to service industry other than the previous two industries.

3. The calculation of percapita GDP has heen. adjusted in accordance to the permanent residence population.

2-5 市区历年生产总值构成

COMPOSITION OF GROSS DOMESTIC PRODUCT OVER THE YEARS IN URBAN AREA

单位:% (%)

年份 Year	地区 生产总值 Gross Domestic Product	第一产业 Primary Industry	第二产业 Secondary Industry	工业 Industry	第三产业 Tertiary Industry
1978	100.0	25.2	56.1	52.4	18.7
1979	100.0	21.7	58.6	53.7	19.7
1980	100.0	16.0	63.4	58.3	20.7
1985	100.0	21.3	56.9	53.7	21.8
1990	100.0	16.9	58.9	54.6	24.2
1991	100.0	15.0	58.5	53.1	26.5
1992	100.0	12.8	59.8	53.2	27.5
1993	100.0	10.4	62.7	55.9	26.9
1994	100.0	11.1	61.4	54.2	27.5
1995	100.0	12.5	59.0	49.2	28.5
1996	100.0	12.1	54.7	45.0	33.1
1997	100.0	9.8	56.8	45.7	33.5
1998	100.0	9.1	53.4	42.4	37.5
1999	100.0	8.8	53.0	43.8	38.2
2000	100.0	7.9	55.9	47.4	36.2
2001	100.0	7.8	56.5	47.6	35.7
2002	100.0	6.4	58.5	49.3	35.1
2003	100.0	6.2	59.4	50.1	34.4
2004	100.0	5.4	62.0	51.8	32.6
2005	100.0	4.6	60.7	50.7	34.6
2006	100.0	4.1	58.9	49.9	37.0
2007	100.0	3.7	57.9	50.0	38.4
2008	100.0	3.8	57.1	48.6	39.1
2009	100.0	3.6	57.0	47.4	39.4
2010	100.0	3.3	53.9	44.6	42.8
2011	100.0	3.1	53.7	45.5	43.2
2012	100.0	3.1	52.5	43.5	44.4
2013	100.0	2.8	52.6	44.3	44.6
2014	100.0	2.7	48.8	40.7	48.5

注:1.本表2013-2014年数据在全国第三次经济普查后进行了调整。

2.自2013年开始,第一产业是指农、林、牧、渔业(不含农、林、牧、渔服务业);第二产业是指采矿业(不含开采辅助活动),制造业(不含金属制品、机械和设备修理业),电力、热力、燃气及水生产和供应业,建筑业;第三产业即服务业,是指除第一产业、第二产业以外的其他行业。

Note:1.2013-2014 data have been adjusted after the third national economic census.

2.Since 2013, primary industry refers to agriculture, forestry, husbandry and fishing Sccondary industry refers to mining industry cexclusine of support activities), manufacturing cexdusine of metal product, machionery or equipment repair, electric power, thermal power, gas, water production and supply, and construction; tertiary industry refers to service industry other than the previous two industries.

2-6 市区历年生产总值指数

INDICES OF GROSS DOMESTIC PRODUCT OVER THE YEARS IN URBAN AREA

按可比价计算,1978=100 (At comparable price,1978=100)

年份 Year	地区生产总值 Gross Domestic Product	第一产业 Primary Industry	第二产业 Secondary Industry			第三产业 Tertiary Industry	人均地区生产总值 Per Capita GDP
				工业 Industry	建筑业 Construction		
1978	100.0	100.0	100.0	100.0	100.0	100.0	100.0
1979	108.9	94.2	113.5	111.9	143.2	114.1	311.5
1980	121.6	78.0	138.7	136.8	166.2	126.9	346.9
1985	213.5	166.9	238.8	245.8	206.6	220.8	501.5
1990	291.9	152.6	369.5	368.2	394.4	273.9	648.6
1991	321.2	157.9	401.4	394.8	548.6	325.3	708.3
1992	389.9	167.4	521.1	510.8	757.6	402.0	835.3
1993	424.3	163.0	616.6	630.6	634.2	448.5	869.9
1994	507.3	180.3	767.9	785.2	802.9	535.9	1013.9
1995	599.3	230.2	869.7	844.7	1277.6	645.7	1181.9
1996	670.1	258.2	920.0	904.2	1422.4	772.1	1317.5
1997	751.4	244.7	1115.4	1071.0	1732.7	859.7	1440.0
1998	818.8	254.1	1249.3	1242.0	1817.4	1008.8	1536.5
1999	912.3	267.4	1416.7	1423.0	1578.0	1131.6	1694.7
2000	1041.6	271.9	1500.0	1497.1	1617.0	1256.8	1833.1
2001	1142.1	283.6	1705.2	1726.5	1806.6	1358.6	1997.5
2002	1268.3	304.1	1957.9	2021.4	1933.9	1458.5	2177.6
2003	1428.8	316.9	2269.3	2393.4	2097.6	1625.6	2409.6
2004	1662.7	336.1	2711.9	2893.7	2480.8	1843.6	2766.2
2005	1920.2	348.7	3151.6	3388.0	2997.1	2141.2	3164.0
2006	2219.9	364.7	3751.1	4093.3	3262.5	2482.1	3623.1
2007	2568.4	379.5	4380.1	4836.8	3433.8	2884.0	4167.1
2008	2929.1	397.4	5145.5	5782.1	3681.9	3305.7	4744.5
2009	3339.1	415.4	5918.2	6592.3	4487.7	3778.7	5408.8
2010	3783.2	427.4	6717.2	7495.5	5044.2	4311.6	6030.9
2011	4244.8	438.5	7523.3	8432.4	5518.4	4880.7	6633.9
2012	4741.4	452.1	8373.4	9368.4	6213.7	5524.9	7330.5
2013	5288.6	461.3	9327.4	10410.9	7022.3	6222.5	8124.8
2014	5827.2	471.9	10243.1	11487.8	7499.1	6925.5	8928.3

注:自2013年开始,第一产业是指农、林、牧、渔业(不含农、林、牧、渔服务业);第二产业是指采矿业(不含开采辅助活动),制造业(不含金属制品、机械和设备修理业),电力、热力、燃气及水生产和供应业,建筑业;第三产业即服务业,是指除第一产业、第二产业以外的其他行业。

Note:Since 2013, primary industry refers to agriculture, forestry, husbandry and fishing Sccondary industry refers to mining industry cexclusine of support activities), manufacturing cexdusine of metal product, machionery or equipment repair, electric power, thermal power, gas, water production and supply, and construction; tertiary industry refers to service industry other than the previous two industries.

2-7 通州区历年生产总值

GROSS DOMESTIC PRODUCT OF TONGZHOU DISTRICT OVER THE YEARS

单位:万元 (10,000 yuan)

年份 Year	地区生产总值 Gross Domestic Product	第一产业 Primary Industry	第二产业 Secondary Industry	工业 Industry	建筑业 Construction	第三产业 Tertiary Industry	人均地区生产总值(元) Per Capita GDP(yuan)
1978	48423	25538	15089	13001	2088	7796	355
1979	51683	24218	18317	15909	2408	9148	378
1980	54844	19835	24150	20863	3287	10859	401
1985	119596	51296	48208	45112	3096	20092	859
1990	212050	76002	94274	82709	11565	41774	1470
1991	234548	77021	106557	93658	12899	50970	1617
1992	310667	84591	154986	134639	20347	71090	2135
1993	406879	83941	233159	206552	26607	89779	2794
1994	585305	128015	330533	289875	40658	126757	4015
1995	774388	189580	404380	325576	78804	180428	5309
1996	868454	213849	406338	328200	78138	248267	5960
1997	968719	190480	500846	383209	117637	277393	6654
1998	1055531	192453	546147	428752	117395	316931	7259
1999	1140817	199927	595920	474034	121886	344970	7871
2000	1091951	184346	561805	442911	118894	345800	8323
2001	1201002	193149	636415	505702	130713	371438	9174
2002	1315451	180717	733804	590343	143461	400930	10142
2003	1496234	201004	857456	700810	156646	437774	11628
2004	1805700	216990	1097700	898200	199500	491010	14147
2005	2214922	236396	1318639	1094929	223710	659887	19173
2006	2692259	256977	1599285	1344735	254550	835998	23726
2007	3211782	281604	1900087	1611962	288125	1030091	28792
2008	3902498	335000	2271000	1907300	363700	1296498	35286
2009	4323207	362161	2522800	2073600	449200	1438246	39393
2010	5079983	404021	2958912	2421444	537468	1717050	45538
2011	6047109	439735	3431320	2804666	626654	2176054	53084
2012	6801193	487452	3743024	3104819	638205	2570716	59607
2013	7796430	490828	4130830	3387444	743385	3174772	68264
2014	8607259	522451	4469923	3674923	795000	3614885	75363

注:1.本表2013-2014年数据在全国第三次经济普查后进行了调整。

2.自2013年开始,第一产业是指农、林、牧、渔业(不含农、林、牧、渔服务业);第二产业是指采矿业(不含开采辅助活动),制造业(不含金属制品、机械和设备修理业),电力、热力、燃气及水生产和供应业,建筑业;第三产业即服务业,是指除第一产业、第二产业以外的其他行业。

3.人均地区生产总值自2005年起调整为按常住人口计算。

Note:1.2013-2014 data have been adjusted after the third national economic census.

2.Since 2013, primary industry refers to agriculture, forestry, husbandry and fishing Sccondary industry refers to mining industry cexclusine of support activities), manufacturing cexdusine of metal product, machionery or equipment repair, electric power, thermal power, gas, water production and supply, and construction; tertiary industry refers to service industry other than the previous two industries.

3. The calculation of percapita GDP has heen. adjusted in accordance to the permanent residence population.

2-8 通州区历年生产总值构成

COMPOSITION OF GROSS DOMESTIC PRODUCT OF TONGZHOU DISTRICT OVER THE YEARS

单位:% (%)

年份 Year	地 区 生产总值 Gross Domestic Product	第一产业 Primary Industry	第二产业 Secondary Industry	工业 Industry	第三产业 Tertiary Industry
1978	100.0	52.7	31.2	26.8	16.1
1979	100.0	46.9	35.4	30.8	17.7
1980	100.0	36.2	44.0	38.0	19.8
1985	100.0	42.9	40.3	37.7	16.8
1990	100.0	35.8	44.5	39.0	19.7
1991	100.0	32.8	45.4	39.9	21.7
1992	100.0	27.2	49.9	43.3	22.9
1993	100.0	20.6	57.3	50.8	22.1
1994	100.0	21.9	56.5	49.5	21.7
1995	100.0	24.5	52.2	42.0	23.3
1996	100.0	24.6	46.8	37.8	28.6
1997	100.0	19.7	51.7	39.6	28.6
1998	100.0	18.2	51.7	40.6	30.0
1999	100.0	17.5	52.2	41.6	30.2
2000	100.0	16.9	51.4	40.6	31.7
2001	100.0	16.1	53.0	42.1	30.9
2002	100.0	13.7	55.8	44.9	30.5
2003	100.0	13.4	57.3	46.8	29.3
2004	100.0	12.0	60.8	49.7	27.2
2005	101.0	10.7	59.5	49.4	29.8
2006	100.0	9.5	59.4	49.9	31.1
2007	100.0	8.8	59.2	50.2	32.1
2008	100.0	8.6	58.2	48.9	33.2
2009	100.0	8.4	58.4	48.0	33.3
2010	100.0	8.0	58.2	47.7	33.8
2011	100.0	7.3	56.7	46.4	36.0
2012	100.0	7.2	55.0	45.7	37.8
2013	100.0	6.3	53.0	43.4	40.7
2014	100.0	6.1	51.9	42.7	42.0

注:1.本表 2013−2014 年数据在全国第三次经济普查后进行了调整。

2.自 2013 年开始,第一产业是指农、林、牧、渔业(不含农、林、牧、渔服务业);第二产业是指采矿业(不含开采辅助活动),制造业(不含金属制品、机械和设备修理业),电力、热力、燃气及水生产和供应业,建筑业;第三产业即服务业,是指除第一产业、第二产业以外的其他行业。

Note:1.2013−2014 data have been adjusted after the third national economic census.

2.Since 2013, primary industry refers to agriculture, forestry, husbandry and fishing Sccondary industry refers to mining industry cexclusine of support activities), manufacturing cexdusine of metal product, machionery or equipment repair, electric power, thermal power, gas, water production and supply, and construction; tertiary industry refers to service industry other than the previous two industries.

2-9 通州区历年生产总值指数

INDICES OF GROSS DOMESTIC PRODUCT OF TONGZHOU DISTRICT OVER THE YEARS

按可比价计算，1978=100 (At comparable price,1978=100)

年份 Year	地区生产总值 Gross Domestic Product	第一产业 Primary Industry	第二产业 Secondary Industry			第三产业 Tertiary Industry	人均地区生产总值 Per Capita GDP
				工业 Industry	建筑业 Construction		
1978	100.0	100.0	100.0	100.0	100.0	100.0	100.0
1979	106.4	94.8	120.1	121.9	109.2	115.8	106.2
1980	112.2	77.7	158.4	159.2	153.1	129.8	111.9
1985	222.1	170.2	311.9	339.5	139.9	209.2	217.5
1990	274.0	152.8	478.6	488.2	418.7	254.3	259.2
1991	301.1	160.3	525.0	537.5	445.1	304.4	283.3
1992	380.3	170.7	732.9	749.3	628.5	394.2	356.1
1993	436.2	167.3	905.9	963.6	538.6	456.9	407.3
1994	530.9	184.7	1144.2	1214.1	699.1	560.2	494.3
1995	632.3	237.7	1283.8	1295.4	1207.3	711.5	587.1
1996	713.2	267.2	1383.9	1430.1	1110.7	873.0	661.6
1997	809.5	252.5	1698.0	1713.3	1602.7	1001.3	751.6
1998	915.5	263.4	1947.7	2019.9	1537.0	1165.5	850.8
1999	1021.7	277.6	2212.5	2331.0	1541.6	1306.6	952.9
2000	1134.1	293.4	2484.7	2664.3	1466.1	1463.4	1061.5
2001	1253.2	308.4	2859.9	3122.6	1529.1	1571.7	1173.0
2002	1391.1	328.4	3257.4	3631.6	1518.4	1716.3	1313.8
2003	1583.1	340.9	3837.2	4365.2	1529.0	1925.7	1506.9
2004	1833.2	361.3	4600.8	5294.9	1646.7	2181.8	1758.6
2005	2117.3	373.9	5475.0	6327.4	1915.1	2485.1	2046.1
2006	2456.0	391.1	6482.4	7611.8	2089.4	2865.3	2387.8
2007	2855.3	406.7	7664.8	9145.6	2249.0	3326.0	2791.1
2008	3272.6	424.6	8855.0	10712.2	2374.7	3843.3	3215.3
2009	3730.8	443.3	10209.8	12211.9	2920.9	4385.2	3675.1
2010	4234.4	461.5	11700.4	13970.4	3385.3	4994.7	4105.1
2011	4755.2	479.0	13139.5	15786.6	3703.5	5704.0	4515.6
2012	5330.6	500.5	14716.3	17775.7	4033.1	6491.1	5053.0
2013	5978.9	517.1	16549.2	19991.6	4533.3	7361.7	5662.0
2014	6622.8	536.7	18278.4	22300.2	4767.2	8285.3	6271.8

注：自2013年开始，第一产业是指农、林、牧、渔业（不含农、林、牧、渔服务业）；第二产业是指采矿业（不含开采辅助活动），制造业（不含金属制品、机械和设备修理业），电力、热力、燃气及水生产和供应业，建筑业；第三产业即服务业，是指除第一产业、第二产业以外的其他行业。

Note:Since 2013, primary industry refers to agriculture, forestry, husbandry and fishing Sccondary industry refers to mining industry cexclusine of support activities), manufacturing cexdusine of metal product, machionery or equipment repair, electric power, thermal power, gas, water production and supply, and construction; tertiary industry refers to service industry other than the previous two industries.

2-10 海安县历年生产总值

GROSS DOMESTIC PRODUCT OF HAIAN COUNTY OVER THE YEARS

单位:万元 (10,000 yuan)

年份 Year	地区生产总值 Gross Domestic Product	第一产业 Primary Industry	第二产业 Secondary Industry	工业 Industry	建筑业 Construction	第三产业 Tertiary Industry	人均地区生产总值(元) Per Capita GDP(yuan)
1978	31533	18045	7749	6922	827	5739	346
1979	35165	19007	8738	7349	1389	7420	383
1980	33280	14137	10557	8995	1562	8586	361
1985	69632	31319	22855	20430	2425	15458	739
1990	136322	56462	45507	37335	8172	34353	1393
1991	145000	53439	53663	45364	8299	37898	1476
1992	174968	63722	66913	56868	10045	44333	1777
1993	224300	65392	103856	88448	15408	55052	2275
1994	337388	97141	156679	134698	21981	83568	3416
1995	460342	158824	184915	151328	33587	116603	4653
1996	506083	174403	170485	136828	33657	161195	5112
1997	558238	183939	189022	149846	39176	185277	5634
1998	607425	186421	220967	170938	50029	200037	6134
1999	650681	190363	248339	189379	58960	211979	6593
2000	705285	193603	282964	217268	65696	228718	7173
2001	783558	205922	322304	249505	72799	255332	7998
2002	870067	216219	369501	285435	84066	284347	8922
2003	998097	222687	456618	355140	101478	318792	10300
2004	1236500	233700	618200	475000	143200	384600	12845
2005	1498633	245772	761411	598225	163186	491449	16848
2006	1785824	264467	923801	732611	191190	597555	20380
2007	2165405	276730	1152484	937683	214800	736191	24766
2008	2709960	321200	1462000	1190000	272000	926760	30900
2009	3007545	347027	1629986	1294105	335882	1030531	35234
2010	3555718	382537	1932590	1575279	357311	1240591	41374
2011	4295193	429429	2280074	1861630	418444	1585689	49598
2012	4801406	476897	2463012	2043259	419753	1861497	55443
2013	5648316	482188	2800174	2300789	499385	2365954	65212
2014	6241389	512686	3041312	2457979	583333	2687391	72051

注:1.本表 2013-2014 年数据在全国第三次经济普查后进行了调整。

2.自 2013 年开始,第一产业是指农、林、牧、渔业(不含农、林、牧、渔服务业);第二产业是指采矿业(不含开采辅助活动),制造业(不含金属制品、机械和设备修理业),电力、热力、燃气及水生产和供应业,建筑业;第三产业即服务业,是指除第一产业、第二产业以外的其他行业。

3.人均地区生产总值自 2005 年起调整为按常住人口计算。

Note:1.2013-2014 data have been adjusted after the third national economic census.

2.Since 2013, primary industry refers to agriculture, forestry, husbandry and fishing Secondary industry refers to mining industry cexclusine of support activities), manufacturing cexdusine of metal product, machionery or equipment repair, electric power, thermal power, gas, water production and supply, and construction; tertiary industry refers to service industry other than the previous two industries.

3. The calculation of percapita GDP has heen. adjusted in accordance to the permanent residence population.

2-11 海安县历年生产总值构成

COMPOSITION OF GROSS DOMESTIC PRODUCT OF HAIAN COUNTY OVER THE YEARS

单位:% (%)

年份 Year	地 区 生产总值 Gross Domestic Product	第一产业 Primary Industry	第二产业 Secondary Industry	工业 Industry	第三产业 Tertiary Industry
1978	100.0	57.2	24.6	22.0	18.2
1979	100.0	54.1	24.8	20.9	21.1
1980	100.0	42.5	31.7	27.0	25.8
1985	100.0	45.0	32.8	29.3	22.2
1990	100.0	41.4	33.4	27.4	25.2
1991	100.0	36.9	37.0	31.3	26.1
1992	100.0	36.4	38.2	32.5	25.3
1993	100.0	29.2	46.3	39.4	24.5
1994	100.0	28.8	46.4	39.9	24.8
1995	100.0	34.5	40.2	32.9	25.3
1996	100.0	34.5	33.7	27.0	31.9
1997	100.0	32.9	33.9	26.8	33.2
1998	100.0	30.7	36.4	28.1	32.9
1999	100.0	29.3	38.2	29.1	32.6
2000	100.0	27.5	40.1	30.8	32.4
2001	100.0	26.3	41.1	31.8	32.6
2002	100.0	24.9	42.5	32.8	32.7
2003	100.0	22.3	45.7	35.6	31.9
2004	100.0	18.9	50.0	38.4	31.1
2005	100.0	16.4	50.8	39.9	32.8
2006	100.0	14.8	51.7	41.0	33.5
2007	100.0	12.8	53.2	43.3	34.0
2008	100.0	11.9	53.9	43.9	34.2
2009	100.0	11.5	54.2	43.0	34.3
2010	100.0	10.8	54.4	44.3	34.9
2011	100.0	10.0	53.1	43.3	36.9
2012	100.0	9.9	51.3	42.6	38.8
2013	100.0	8.5	49.6	40.7	41.9
2014	100.0	8.2	48.7	39.4	43.1

注:1.本表2013-2014年数据在全国第三次经济普查后进行了调整。

2.自2013年开始,第一产业是指农、林、牧、渔业(不含农、林、牧、渔服务业);第二产业是指采矿业(不含开采辅助活动),制造业(不含金属制品、机械和设备修理业),电力、热力、燃气及水生产和供应业,建筑业;第三产业即服务业,是指除第一产业、第二产业以外的其他行业。

Note:1.2013-2014 data have been adjusted after the third national economic census.

2.Since 2013, primary industry refers to agriculture, forestry, husbandry and fishing Sccondary industry refers to mining industry cexclusine of support activities), manufacturing cexdusine of metal product, machionery or equipment repair, electric power, thermal power, gas, water production and supply, and construction; tertiary industry refers to service industry other than the previous two industries.

2-12 海安县历年生产总值指数

INDICES OF GROSS DOMESTIC PRODUCT OF HAIAN COUNTY OVER THE YEARS

按可比价计算,1978=100 (At comparable price,1978=100)

年份 Year	地区生产总值 Gross Domestic Product	第一产业 Primary Industry	第二产业 Secondary Industry	工业 Industry	建筑业 Construction	第三产业 Tertiary Industry	人均地区生产总值 Per Capita GDP
1978	100.0	100.0	100.0	100.0	100.0	100.0	100.0
1979	110.0	105.3	111.4	105.7	159.0	127.6	109.3
1980	104.0	78.3	134.7	128.9	183.7	139.4	103.0
1985	191.8	139.4	287.5	288.8	276.6	218.6	186.0
1990	251.5	152.3	449.4	413.9	746.9	280.1	234.4
1991	270.4	154.9	515.0	485.9	758.9	300.3	251.3
1992	308.0	173.2	606.7	585.0	782.4	334.8	286.0
1993	358.5	178.7	806.3	801.5	829.3	372.3	331.6
1994	447.0	205.5	1066.7	1070.0	1012.6	463.5	412.4
1995	506.0	235.3	1159.5	1131.0	1386.2	558.5	465.5
1996	526.2	256.4	1067.9	1033.7	1341.8	650.1	483.2
1997	577.8	268.2	1199.3	1158.8	1522.9	729.4	530.1
1998	640.2	271.4	1433.1	1385.9	1815.3	799.4	587.8
1999	698.4	283.6	1630.9	1575.8	2073.1	858.6	643.7
2000	761.3	296.1	1823.3	1779.0	2185.1	939.3	705.5
2001	835.9	309.4	2074.9	2058.3	2322.8	1029.5	774.6
2002	927.8	325.8	2394.4	2404.1	2543.5	1137.6	863.7
2003	1054.9	338.8	2894.8	2961.9	2813.1	1275.2	982.0
2004	1226.8	359.5	3592.4	3693.5	3395.4	1446.1	1149.9
2005	1420.6	370.6	4375.5	4517.2	4064.3	1654.3	1339.6
2006	1649.3	389.1	5254.9	5506.4	4608.9	1910.7	1563.3
2007	1918.1	403.9	6280.6	6764.4	4884.5	2229.2	1828.5
2008	2204.8	420.9	7352.8	8061.6	5232.3	2578.8	2115.6
2009	2517.9	438.5	8551.3	9287.0	6372.9	2945.0	2422.3
2010	2872.9	456.5	9928.1	10791.5	7367.1	3360.3	2744.5
2011	3229.2	476.2	11208.8	12291.5	8000.6	3837.4	3062.9
2012	3623.1	498.5	12576.3	13926.3	8552.7	4382.3	3436.5
2013	4074.9	515.5	14186.7	15738.8	9559.9	5009.2	3864.4
2014	4523.1	535.8	15786.9	17548.9	10533.1	5621.9	4289.0

注:自 2013 年开始,第一产业是指农、林、牧、渔业(不含农、林、牧、渔服务业);第二产业是指采矿业(不含开采辅助活动),制造业(不含金属制品、机械和设备修理业),电力、热力、燃气及水生产和供应业,建筑业;第三产业即服务业,是指除第一产业、第二产业以外的其他行业。

Note:Since 2013, primary industry refers to agriculture, forestry, husbandry and fishing Sccondary industry refers to mining industry cexclusine of support activities), manufacturing cexdusine of metal product, machionery or equipment repair, electric power, thermal power, gas, water production and supply, and construction; tertiary industry refers to service industry other than the previous two industries.

2-13 如东县历年生产总值

GROSS DOMESTIC PRODUCT OF RUDONG COUNTY OVER THE YEARS

单位：万元 (10,000 yuan)

年份 Year	地区生产总值 Gross Domestic Product	第一产业 Primary Industry	第二产业 Secondary Industry	工业 Industry	建筑业 Construction	第三产业 Tertiary Industry	人均地区生产总值(元) Per Capita GDP(yuan)
1978	36564	22699	6413	5648	765	7452	341
1979	40348	23863	8144	7147	997	8341	375
1980	42819	22648	10234	9160	1074	9937	398
1985	77269	44303	19212	16907	2305	13754	709
1990	180495	93907	52980	47765	5215	33608	1604
1991	198980	101071	58548	52464	6084	39361	1762
1992	244169	108493	88138	76884	11254	47538	2158
1993	296795	124181	118723	106412	12311	53891	2620
1994	450299	202953	158627	137032	21595	88719	3973
1995	589148	251195	213344	176509	36835	124609	5196
1996	628019	268662	202666	154548	48118	156691	5542
1997	640517	252765	216152	174804	41348	171600	5666
1998	685443	256034	238785	181810	56975	190624	6081
1999	714688	258921	257036	202875	54161	198731	6364
2000	773261	257282	285513	222556	62957	230466	6917
2001	844356	270398	320297	248270	72027	253661	7593
2002	919738	284108	358842	279448	79394	276788	8323
2003	1029746	293221	421829	324305	97524	314696	9384
2004	1243376	302176	567200	433100	134100	374000	11417
2005	1471784	303340	702816	554519	148297	465629	14388
2006	1768460	316833	867487	691131	176355	584140	17450
2007	2160229	326615	1109294	914144	195150	724320	21354
2008	2692000	377800	1415000	1165000	250000	899200	26668
2009	2975011	407667	1570700	1261400	309300	996644	30199
2010	3523571	450977	1882513	1520114	362400	1190081	35593
2011	4254475	504966	2231274	1806578	424697	1518235	42843
2012	4780018	565628	2430255	1978707	451548	1784136	48364
2013	5586461	593426	2724282	2189696	534586	2268754	56727
2014	6155108	621700	2971100	2454200	516900	2562300	62631

注：1.本表 2013－2014 年数据在全国第三次经济普查后进行了调整。

2.自 2013 年开始，第一产业是指农、林、牧、渔业(不含农、林、牧、渔服务业)；第二产业是指采矿业(不含开采辅助活动)，制造业(不含金属制品、机械和设备修理业)，电力、热力、燃气及水生产和供应业，建筑业；第三产业即服务业，是指除第一产业、第二产业以外的其他行业。

3.人均地区生产总值自 2005 年起调整为按常住人口计算。

Note:1.2013−2014 data have been adjusted after the third national economic census.

2.Since 2013, primary industry refers to agriculture, forestry, husbandry and fishing Sccondary industry refers to mining industry cexclusine of support activities), manufacturing cexdusine of metal product, machionery or equipment repair, electric power, thermal power, gas, water production and supply, and construction; tertiary industry refers to service industry other than the previous two industries.

3. The calculation of percapita GDP has heen. adjusted in accordance to the permanent residence population.

2-14 如东县历年生产总值构成

COMPOSITION OF GROSS DOMESTIC PRODUCT OF RUDONG COUNTY OVER THE YEARS

单位:% (%)

年份 Year	地区生产总值 Gross Domestic Product	第一产业 Primary Industry	第二产业 Secondary Industry	工业 Industry	第三产业 Tertiary Industry
1978	100.0	62.1	17.5	15.4	20.4
1979	100.0	59.1	20.2	17.7	20.7
1980	100.0	52.9	23.9	21.4	23.2
1985	100.0	57.3	24.9	21.9	17.8
1990	100.0	52.0	29.4	26.5	18.6
1991	100.0	50.8	29.4	26.4	19.8
1992	100.0	44.4	36.1	31.5	19.5
1993	100.0	41.8	40.0	35.9	18.2
1994	100.0	45.1	35.2	30.4	19.7
1995	100.0	42.6	36.2	30.0	21.2
1996	100.0	42.8	32.3	24.6	25.0
1997	100.0	39.5	33.7	27.3	26.8
1998	100.0	37.4	34.8	26.5	27.8
1999	100.0	36.2	36.0	28.4	27.8
2000	100.0	33.3	36.9	28.8	29.8
2001	100.0	32.0	37.9	29.4	30.0
2002	100.0	30.9	39.0	30.4	30.1
2003	100.0	28.5	41.0	31.5	30.6
2004	100.0	24.3	45.6	34.8	30.1
2005	100.0	20.6	47.8	37.7	31.6
2006	100.0	17.9	49.1	39.1	33.0
2007	100.0	15.1	51.4	42.3	33.5
2008	100.0	14.0	52.6	43.3	33.4
2009	100.0	13.7	52.8	42.4	33.5
2010	100.0	12.8	53.4	43.1	33.8
2011	100.0	11.9	52.4	42.5	35.7
2012	100.0	11.8	50.9	41.4	37.3
2013	100.0	10.6	48.8	39.2	40.6
2014	100.0	10.1	48.3	39.9	41.6

注:1.本表2013-2014年数据在全国第三次经济普查后进行了调整。

2.自2013年开始,第一产业是指农、林、牧、渔业(不含农、林、牧、渔服务业);第二产业是指采矿业(不含开采辅助活动),制造业(不含金属制品、机械和设备修理业),电力、热力、燃气及水生产和供应业,建筑业;第三产业即服务业,是指除第一产业、第二产业以外的其他行业。

Note:1.2013-2014 data have been adjusted after the third national economic census.

2.Since 2013, primary industry refers to agriculture, forestry, husbandry and fishing Sccondary industry refers to mining industry cexclusine of support activities), manufacturing cexdusine of metal product, machionery or equipment repair, electric power, thermal power, gas, water production and supply, and construction; tertiary industry refers to service industry other than the previous two industries.

2-15 如东县历年生产总值指数

INDICES OF GROSS DOMESTIC PRODUCT OF RUDONG COUNTY OVER THE YEARS

按可比价计算,1978=100 (At comparable price,1978=100)

年份 Year	地区生产总值 Gross Domestic Product	第一产业 Primary Industry	第二产业 Secondary Industry	工业 Industry	建筑业 Construction	第三产业 Tertiary Industry	人均地区生产总值 Per Capita GDP
1978	100.0	100.0	100.0	100.0	100.0	100.0	100.0
1979	110.0	105.1	125.7	126.0	123.4	110.5	109.9
1980	115.5	99.8	158.0	160.9	136.6	124.3	115.2
1985	185.0	165.4	291.9	292.9	284.3	149.8	182.4
1990	289.0	212.4	633.1	649.0	515.3	214.0	275.5
1991	309.2	216.9	714.1	733.4	570.4	239.5	293.9
1992	366.4	221.7	1041.9	1055.4	934.9	282.1	348.0
1993	384.0	214.2	1222.1	1295.0	698.4	279.3	363.3
1994	476.9	269.7	1437.2	1486.7	1077.6	378.2	450.3
1995	568.9	304.8	1764.9	1790.0	1577.6	473.9	536.2
1996	616.1	333.8	1840.8	1818.6	1924.7	532.2	580.7
1997	641.4	329.1	1982.5	2044.1	1584.0	578.0	606.3
1998	699.1	342.6	2216.5	2226.0	2102.0	651.4	662.6
1999	753.6	355.6	2475.8	2557.7	1933.8	702.8	717.0
2000	818.4	366.3	2693.7	2782.8	2111.8	814.6	782.2
2001	892.1	383.2	3016.9	3136.2	2299.7	898.5	852.6
2002	978.6	402.0	3427.2	3625.4	2384.8	991.9	941.3
2003	1105.8	417.3	4133.2	4365.0	2895.1	1122.8	1071.2
2004	1271.7	435.7	5129.3	5473.7	3378.6	1273.3	1240.4
2005	1457.4	441.8	6283.4	6721.7	4084.7	1454.1	1432.5
2006	1680.4	458.6	7540.0	8153.4	4721.9	1682.4	1661.7
2007	1945.7	464.1	9058.5	10003.4	5264.9	1961.7	1936.2
2008	2207.2	480.1	10420.6	11734.1	5611.5	2264.2	2211.1
2009	2509.6	501.2	12056.6	13353.4	7076.1	2588.0	2525.1
2010	2861.0	521.3	14046.0	15516.6	8328.5	2947.7	2863.5
2011	3207.1	543.2	15843.9	17673.4	9003.2	3360.4	3198.5
2012	3588.8	568.2	17856.0	20024.0	9930.5	3793.9	3595.1
2013	4025.1	587.5	20190.5	22611.1	11298.2	4307.3	4046.7
2014	4435.6	607.5	22248.3	25188.8	11834.8	4832.8	4468.8

注:自2013年开始,第一产业是指农、林、牧、渔业(不含农、林、牧、渔服务业);第二产业是指采矿业(不含开采辅助活动),制造业(不含金属制品、机械和设备修理业),电力、热力、燃气及水生产和供应业,建筑业;第三产业即服务业,是指除第一产业、第二产业以外的其他行业。

Note:Since 2013, primary industry refers to agriculture, forestry, husbandry and fishing Sccondary industry refers to mining industry cexclusine of support activities), manufacturing cexdusine of metal product, machionery or equipment repair, electric power, thermal power, gas, water production and supply, and construction; tertiary industry refers to service industry other than the previous two industries.

2-16 启东市历年生产总值

GROSS DOMESTIC PRODUCT OF QIDONG CITY OVER THE YEARS

单位：万元 (10,000 yuan)

年份 Year	地区生产总值 Gross Domestic Product	第一产业 Primary Industry	第二产业 Secondary Industry	工业 Industry	建筑业 Construction	第三产业 Tertiary Industry	人均地区生产总值(元) Per Capita GDP(yuan)
1978	43738	20679	11512	9864	1648	11547	402
1979	48731	21458	15090	13240	1850	12183	446
1980	53916	21272	19165	17146	2019	13479	492
1985	88325	34193	34789	31714	3075	19343	788
1990	186945	71332	71307	63889	7418	44306	1619
1991	218124	80641	87275	76594	10681	50208	1879
1992	276603	101158	114049	96032	18017	61396	2378
1993	399585	128955	194111	168415	25696	76519	3433
1994	552074	168984	257559	226315	31244	125531	4742
1995	771790	212190	368552	319278	49274	191048	6630
1996	811438	233233	365491	313494	51997	212714	6963
1997	880148	240693	389662	324685	64977	249793	7540
1998	950864	247669	416800	348619	68181	286395	8150
1999	1010928	257714	442944	372931	70013	310270	8690
2000	1092955	265608	490189	410943	79246	337158	9409
2001	1190355	276761	546111	459846	86265	367483	10268
2002	1225485	282026	561484	469211	92273	381975	10619
2003	1359237	295033	652430	519439	132991	411774	11845
2004	1604100	313100	820600	630400	190200	470400	14085
2005	1993113	339935	1020945	796577	224368	632233	20129
2006	2377087	367184	1226432	967322	259110	783471	24326
2007	2814906	391228	1479538	1197069	282469	944139	29229
2008	3250000	456400	1695100	1382300	312800	1098500	34112
2009	3595015	492882	1884800	1498500	386300	1217333	37747
2010	4300395	544910	2299798	1833709	466089	1455686	44744
2011	5201749	559581	2771063	2191898	579165	1871105	53629
2012	5891385	614819	3060885	2406246	654639	2215681	61127
2013	6695000	606249	3384517	2631700	752817	2704234	69820
2014	7391280	629318	3690256	2874056	816200	3071706	77242

注：1.本表2013-2014年数据在全国第三次经济普查后进行了调整。

2.自2013年开始，第一产业是指农、林、牧、渔业（不含农、林、牧、渔服务业）；第二产业是指采矿业（不含开采辅助活动），制造业（不含金属制品、机械和设备修理业），电力、热力、燃气及水生产和供应业，建筑业；第三产业即服务业，是指除第一产业、第二产业以外的其他行业。

3.人均地区生产总值自2005年起调整为按常住人口计算。

Note:1.2013-2014 data have been adjusted after the third national economic census.

2.Since 2013, primary industry refers to agriculture, forestry, husbandry and fishing Sccondary industry refers to mining industry cexclusine of support activities), manufacturing cexdusine of metal product, machionery or equipment repair, electric power, thermal power, gas, water production and supply, and construction; tertiary industry refers to service industry other than the previous two industries.

3. The calculation of percapita GDP has heen. adjusted in accordance to the permanent residence population.

2-17 启东市历年生产总值构成

COMPOSITION OF GROSS DOMESTIC PRODUCT OF QIDONG CITY OVER THE YEARS

单位:% (%)

年份 Year	地区 生产总值 Gross Domestic Product	第一产业 Primary Industry	第二产业 Secondary Industry	工业 Industry	第三产业 Tertiary Industry
1978	100.0	47.3	26.3	22.6	26.4
1979	100.0	44.0	31.0	27.2	25.0
1980	100.0	39.5	35.5	31.8	25.0
1985	100.0	38.7	39.4	35.9	21.9
1990	100.0	38.2	38.1	34.2	23.7
1991	100.0	37.0	40.0	35.1	23.0
1992	100.0	36.6	41.2	34.7	22.2
1993	100.0	32.3	48.6	42.1	19.1
1994	100.0	30.6	46.7	41.0	22.7
1995	100.0	27.5	47.8	41.4	24.8
1996	100.0	28.7	45.0	38.6	26.2
1997	100.0	27.3	44.3	36.9	28.4
1998	100.0	26.0	43.8	36.7	30.1
1999	100.0	25.5	43.8	36.9	30.7
2000	100.0	24.3	44.8	37.6	30.8
2001	100.0	23.3	45.9	38.6	30.9
2002	100.0	23.0	45.8	38.3	31.2
2003	100.0	21.7	48.0	38.2	30.3
2004	100.0	19.5	51.2	39.3	29.3
2005	101.0	17.1	51.2	40.0	31.7
2006	100.0	15.4	51.6	40.7	33.0
2007	100.0	13.9	52.6	42.5	33.5
2008	100.0	14.0	52.2	42.5	33.8
2009	100.0	13.7	52.4	41.7	33.9
2010	100.0	12.7	53.5	42.6	33.9
2011	100.0	10.8	53.2	42.1	36.0
2012	100.0	10.4	52.0	40.8	37.6
2013	100.0	9.0	50.6	39.3	40.4
2014	100.0	8.5	49.9	38.9	41.6

注:1.本表 2013-2014 年数据在全国第三次经济普查后进行了调整。

2.自 2013 年开始,第一产业是指农、林、牧、渔业(不含农、林、牧、渔服务业);第二产业是指采矿业(不含开采辅助活动),制造业(不含金属制品、机械和设备修理业),电力、热力、燃气及水生产和供应业,建筑业;第三产业即服务业,是指除第一产业、第二产业以外的其他行业。

Note:1.2013-2014 data have been adjusted after the third national economic census.

2.Since 2013, primary industry refers to agriculture, forestry, husbandry and fishing Sccondary industry refers to mining industry cexclusine of support activities), manufacturing cexdusine of metal product, machionery or equipment repair, electric power, thermal power, gas, water production and supply, and construction; tertiary industry refers to service industry other than the previous two industries.

2-18 启东市历年生产总值指数

INDICES OF GROSS DOMESTIC PRODUCT OF QIDONG CITY OVER THE YEARS

按可比价计算,1978=100

(At comparable price,1978=100)

年份 Year	地区生产总值 Gross Domestic Product	第一产业 Primary Industry	第二产业 Secondary Industry	工业 Industry	建筑业 Construction	第三产业 Tertiary Industry	人均地区生产总值 Per Capita GDP
1978	100.0	100.0	100.0	100.0	100.0	100.0	100.0
1979	110.9	103.8	129.8	133.7	106.3	104.2	110.6
1980	121.2	102.9	164.8	172.4	119.2	108.8	120.4
1985	180.7	140.1	294.8	314.6	176.0	136.0	175.6
1990	258.7	177.1	474.6	497.1	340.2	182.1	243.4
1991	316.4	211.6	629.3	657.7	462.3	199.8	296.5
1992	352.2	242.9	663.9	660.3	691.6	239.8	330.1
1993	447.3	270.6	986.6	1038.0	679.8	275.3	417.6
1994	518.4	264.6	1193.8	1265.3	762.1	368.1	482.7
1995	670.8	300.6	1630.7	1733.5	1013.6	489.6	622.8
1996	707.7	341.8	1643.7	1747.4	1012.6	524.4	655.3
1997	777.1	358.9	1763.7	1852.2	1221.2	626.1	717.6
1998	864.9	372.9	1975.3	2094.9	1245.6	732.6	799.4
1999	954.8	394.9	2163.0	2312.8	1251.8	845.4	884.9
2000	1055.1	410.3	2396.6	2569.5	1342.0	971.4	979.6
2001	1162.7	429.6	2708.2	2934.4	1405.1	1072.4	1079.5
2002	1225.5	440.3	2846.3	3095.8	1429.0	1153.9	1143.2
2003	1375.0	459.2	3301.7	3535.4	1856.3	1293.5	1289.5
2004	1586.7	483.0	4018.2	4299.0	2277.7	1466.8	1499.5
2005	1831.0	497.0	4874.1	5141.6	2929.1	1670.7	1741.5
2006	2124.0	518.4	5849.3	6185.3	3476.8	1929.6	2027.1
2007	2462.8	538.8	6971.2	7468.7	3937.1	2243.3	2361.2
2008	2806.5	560.4	8051.5	8829.7	4113.9	2589.9	2703.6
2009	3193.8	582.8	9339.8	10110.1	5064.2	2960.3	3079.4
2010	3644.1	606.1	10918.2	11828.8	5874.5	3365.8	3479.7
2011	4092.3	609.1	12424.9	13461.1	6673.4	3853.9	3872.9
2012	4575.2	636.5	14002.9	15211.1	7447.6	4331.8	4357.0
2013	5118.4	649.2	15856.0	17149.4	8579.1	4883.8	4899.2
2014	5661.0	670.0	17501.3	19018.7	9293.7	5518.7	5429.9

注:自2013年开始,第一产业是指农、林、牧、渔业(不含农、林、牧、渔服务业);第二产业是指采矿业(不含开采辅助活动),制造业(不含金属制品、机械和设备修理业),电力、热力、燃气及水生产和供应业,建筑业;第三产业即服务业,是指除第一产业、第二产业以外的其他行业。

Note:Since 2013, primary industry refers to agriculture, forestry, husbandry and fishing Sccondary industry refers to mining industry cexclusine of support activities), manufacturing cexdusine of metal product, machionery or equipment repair, electric power, thermal power, gas, water production and supply, and construction; tertiary industry refers to service industry other than the previous two industries.

2-19 如皋市历年生产总值

GROSS DOMESTIC PRODUCT OF RUGAO CITY OVER THE YEARS

单位:万元 (10,000 yuan)

年份 Year	地区生产总值 Gross Domestic Product	第一产业 Primary Industry	第二产业 Secondary Industry	工业 Industry	建筑业 Construction	第三产业 Tertiary Industry	人均地区生产总值(元) Per Capita GDP(yuan)
1978	35947	17298	10054	8556	1498	8595	266
1979	40551	19113	12099	10485	1614	9339	298
1980	45577	18985	16620	14632	1988	9972	334
1985	83290	35495	30387	26795	3592	17408	603
1990	159200	65371	57882	49280	8602	35947	1105
1991	173267	65950	66240	55011	11229	41077	1196
1992	210130	74884	86328	72158	14170	48918	1450
1993	282117	84539	136609	120104	16505	60969	1951
1994	376423	130040	167981	149564	18417	78402	2604
1995	502135	161990	218488	173445	45043	121657	3465
1996	598413	178187	257588	209064	48524	162638	4122
1997	627272	172129	265678	212777	52901	189465	4318
1998	663497	172013	279101	221807	57294	212383	4546
1999	693646	178979	285580	224315	61265	229087	4739
2000	733704	180551	305557	239603	65954	247596	5027
2001	804437	189087	336998	268059	68939	278352	5530
2002	879540	198496	375645	297609	78036	305399	6069
2003	1028140	208852	469966	374535	95431	349322	7129
2004	1259800	219600	627200	498900	128300	413000	8795
2005	1549659	238726	802838	651619	151220	508095	11456
2006	1914203	259091	1007451	835563	171888	647661	13922
2007	2385155	283104	1290257	1097201	193056	811794	17001
2008	3199952	342300	1807700	1549700	258000	1049952	22206
2009	3551519	369685	1982800	1671200	311600	1199034	28394
2010	4309975	413466	2448488	2075908	372580	1448021	34296
2011	5206735	469898	2888200	2450347	437853	1848637	41178
2012	5901668	527722	3184929	2690135	494794	2189018	46801
2013	6748100	539203	3478444	2896483	581961	2730453	53599
2014	7436400	575976	3772400	3110800	661600	3087980	59158

注:1.本表 2013-2014 年数据在全国第三次经济普查后进行了调整。

2.自 2013 年开始,第一产业是指农、林、牧、渔业(不含农、林、牧、渔服务业);第二产业是指采矿业(不含开采辅助活动),制造业(不含金属制品、机械和设备修理业),电力、热力、燃气及水生产和供应业,建筑业;第三产业即服务业,是指除第一产业、第二产业以外的其他行业。

3.人均地区生产总值自 2005 年起调整为按常住人口计算。

Note:1.2013-2014 data have been adjusted after the third national economic census.

2.Since 2013, primary industry refers to agriculture, forestry, husbandry and fishing Sccondary industry refers to mining industry cexclusine of support activities), manufacturing cexdusine of metal product, machionery or equipment repair, electric power, thermal power, gas, water production and supply, and construction; tertiary industry refers to service industry other than the previous two industries.

3. The calculation of percapita GDP has heen. adjusted in accordance to the permanent residence population.

2-20 如皋市历年生产总值构成

COMPOSITION OF GROSS DOMESTIC PRODUCT OF RUGAO CITY OVER THE YEARS

单位:% (%)

年份 Year	地区 生产总值 Gross Domestic Product	第一产业 Primary Industry	第二产业 Secondary Industry	工业 Industry	第三产业 Tertiary Industry
1978	100.0	48.1	28.0	23.8	23.9
1979	100.0	47.1	29.8	25.9	23.0
1980	100.0	41.7	36.5	32.1	21.9
1985	100.0	42.6	36.5	32.2	20.9
1990	100.0	41.1	36.4	31.0	22.6
1991	100.0	38.1	38.2	31.7	23.7
1992	100.0	35.6	41.1	34.3	23.3
1993	100.0	30.0	48.4	42.6	21.6
1994	100.0	34.5	44.6	39.7	20.8
1995	100.0	32.3	43.5	34.5	24.2
1996	100.0	29.8	43.0	34.9	27.2
1997	100.0	27.4	42.4	33.9	30.2
1998	100.0	25.9	42.1	33.4	32.0
1999	100.0	25.8	41.2	32.3	33.0
2000	100.0	24.6	41.6	32.7	33.7
2001	100.0	23.5	41.9	33.3	34.6
2002	100.0	22.6	42.7	33.8	34.7
2003	100.0	20.3	45.7	36.4	34.0
2004	100.0	17.4	49.8	39.6	32.8
2005	100.0	15.4	51.8	42.0	32.8
2006	100.0	13.5	52.6	43.7	33.8
2007	100.0	11.9	54.1	46.0	34.0
2008	100.0	10.7	56.5	48.4	32.8
2009	100.0	10.4	55.8	47.1	33.8
2010	100.0	9.6	56.8	48.2	33.6
2011	100.0	9.0	55.5	47.1	35.5
2012	100.0	8.9	54.0	45.6	37.1
2013	100.0	8.0	51.5	42.9	40.5
2014	100.0	7.8	50.7	41.8	41.5

注:1.本表2013-2014年数据在全国第三次经济普查后进行了调整。

2.自2013年开始,第一产业是指农、林、牧、渔业(不含农、林、牧、渔服务业);第二产业是指采矿业(不含开采辅助活动),制造业(不含金属制品、机械和设备修理业),电力、热力、燃气及水生产和供应业,建筑业;第三产业即服务业,是指除第一产业、第二产业以外的其他行业。

Note:1.2013-2014 data have been adjusted after the third national economic census.

2.Since 2013, primary industry refers to agriculture, forestry, husbandry and fishing Sccondary industry refers to mining industry cexclusine of support activities), manufacturing cexdusine of metal product, machionery or ecuipment repair, electric power, thermal power, gas, water production and supply, and construction; tertiary industry refers to service industry other than the previous two industries.

2-21 如皋市历年生产总值指数

INDICES OF GROSS DOMESTIC PRODUCT OF RUGAO CITY OVER THE YEARS

按可比价计算,1978=100 (At comparable price,1978=100)

年份 Year	地区生产总值 Gross Domestic Product	第一产业 Primary Industry	第二产业 Secondary Industry	工业 Industry	建筑业 Construction	第三产业 Tertiary Industry	人均地区生产总值 Per Capita GDP
1978	100.0	100.0	100.0	100.0	100.0	100.0	100.0
1979	112.2	110.5	119.1	122.1	102.0	107.3	111.8
1980	124.8	109.8	163.7	169.7	129.1	108.1	123.9
1985	206.2	173.9	294.5	306.4	226.2	164.4	202.4
1990	265.9	194.0	440.8	442.0	434.0	198.5	249.4
1991	293.6	200.0	526.8	524.7	538.2	218.0	274.6
1992	339.7	214.4	652.2	661.6	602.8	239.1	318.4
1993	386.2	216.5	828.3	887.9	511.2	262.3	360.9
1994	420.2	210.4	984.0	1075.2	497.9	274.6	391.2
1995	500.9	237.1	1147.3	1164.4	1059.0	367.7	463.8
1996	542.5	259.6	1196.6	1183.0	1292.0	412.9	501.4
1997	590.8	279.8	1226.5	1190.1	1417.3	489.3	545.5
1998	644.0	287.7	1355.3	1324.6	1496.7	548.0	591.9
1999	691.0	299.8	1454.2	1426.6	1567.0	601.2	633.3
2000	746.9	312.1	1573.5	1547.8	1664.2	666.7	686.5
2001	814.1	327.4	1735.6	1741.3	1682.5	735.4	748.3
2002	895.5	343.1	1954.3	1976.4	1822.1	811.9	826.1
2003	1024.5	357.5	2370.6	2436.9	2033.5	913.4	950.0
2004	1191.5	377.5	2925.3	3043.7	2342.6	1036.7	1112.4
2005	1378.6	388.4	3545.5	3707.2	2780.7	1187.0	1295.3
2006	1603.3	407.8	4265.2	4541.3	3092.1	1369.8	1510.3
2007	1867.7	424.1	5115.7	5560.4	3359.3	1592.3	1765.8
2008	2144.5	441.5	5976.5	6626.4	3522.8	1839.8	2034.2
2009	2449.0	460.0	6944.7	7633.6	4329.5	2099.3	2325.1
2010	2799.2	478.9	8062.8	8870.2	4996.3	2395.3	2643.6
2011	3135.1	499.5	9038.3	10005.6	5401.0	2733.0	2942.4
2012	3505.1	522.5	10186.2	11316.4	5941.1	3066.4	3298.4
2013	3917.4	538.7	11438.3	12641.6	6877.9	3464.8	3692.3
2014	4328.7	558.0	12669.1	14082.8	7366.2	3866.3	4086.3

注:自 2013 年开始,第一产业是指农、林、牧、渔业(不含农、林、牧、渔服务业);第二产业是指采矿业(不含开采辅助活动),制造业(不含金属制品、机械和设备修理业),电力、热力、燃气及水生产和供应业,建筑业;第三产业即服务业,是指除第一产业、第二产业以外的其他行业。

Note:Since 2013, primary industry refers to agriculture, forestry, husbandry and fishing Sccondary industry refers to mining industry cexclusine of support activities), manufacturing cexdusine of metal product, machionery or equipment repair, electric power, thermal power, gas, water production and supply, and construction; tertiary industry refers to service industry other than the previous two industries.

2-22 海门市历年生产总值

GROSS DOMESTIC PRODUCT OF HAIMEN CITY OVER THE YEARS

单位:万元 (10,000 yuan)

年份 Year	地区生产总值 Gross Domestic Product	第一产业 Primary Industry	第二产业 Secondary Industry	工业 Industry	建筑业 Construction	第三产业 Tertiary Industry	人均地区生产总值(元) Per Capita GDP(yuan)
1978	27372	14184	7495	6700	795	5693	283
1979	29780	14335	9459	8517	942	5986	307
1980	34857	15717	11820	10653	1167	7320	358
1985	77785	28590	33405	30976	2429	15790	783
1990	152333	52873	66454	59316	7138	33006	1493
1991	158113	44612	74939	64475	10464	38562	1541
1992	199978	47753	106494	95999	10495	45731	1944
1993	286509	70723	154054	136104	17950	61732	2783
1994	420778	103522	226774	197839	28935	90482	4084
1995	654534	118005	375771	305411	70360	160758	6338
1996	758815	135683	383246	314552	68694	239886	7335
1997	831323	146971	416327	354813	61514	268025	8043
1998	907798	156658	458543	386930	71613	292597	8770
1999	976756	160190	506363	423503	82860	310203	9416
2000	1075073	164834	574244	476458	97786	335995	10374
2001	1172650	178985	629162	542025	87137	364503	11346
2002	1276995	190504	695463	593560	101903	391028	12405
2003	1429704	199406	815866	675121	140745	414432	13943
2004	1719000	212409	1028900	845700	183200	477691	16841
2005	2115157	227110	1243053	1029230	213823	644994	22761
2006	2600795	248406	1521102	1271281	249821	831287	28159
2007	3092712	258431	1827895	1544881	283014	1006385	34024
2008	3746000	307600	2235900	1885300	350600	1202500	41705
2009	4150029	334286	2479700	2040800	438900	1336043	46431
2010	5001041	372939	3019515	2471417	548098	1608587	55635
2011	5903286	413915	3482236	2846117	636119	2007136	65226
2012	6630972	464998	3775976	3157442	618534	2389997	73473
2013	7604500	463090	4093200	3388100	705100	3048210	84270
2014	8364950	490663	4431636	3658836	772800	3442651	92697

注:1.本表2013-2014年数据在全国第三次经济普查后进行了调整。

2.自2013年开始,第一产业是指农、林、牧、渔业(不含农、林、牧、渔服务业);第二产业是指采矿业(不含开采辅助活动),制造业(不含金属制品、机械和设备修理业),电力、热力、燃气及水生产和供应业,建筑业;第三产业即服务业,是指除第一产业、第二产业以外的其他行业。

3.人均地区生产总值自2005年起调整为按常住人口计算。

Note:1.2013-2014 data have been adjusted after the third national economic census.

2.Since 2013, primary industry refers to agriculture, forestry, husbandry and fishing Sccondary industry refers to mining industry cexclusine of support activities), manufacturing cexdusine of metal product, machionery or equipment repair, electric power, thermal power, gas, water production and supply, and construction; tertiary industry refers to service industry other than the previous two industries.

3. The calculation of percapita GDP has heen. adjusted in accordance to the permanent residence population.

2-23 海门市历年生产总值构成

COMPOSITION OF GROSS DOMESTIC PRODUCT OF HAIMEN CITY OVER THE YEARS

单位:% (%)

年份 Year	地区 生产总值 Gross Domestic Product	第一产业 Primary Industry	第二产业 Secondary Industry	工业 Industry	第三产业 Tertiary Industry
1978	100.0	51.8	27.4	24.5	20.8
1979	100.0	48.1	31.8	28.6	20.1
1980	100.0	45.1	33.9	30.6	21.0
1985	100.0	36.8	42.9	39.8	20.3
1990	100.0	34.7	43.6	38.9	21.7
1991	100.0	28.2	47.4	40.8	24.4
1992	100.0	23.9	53.3	48.0	22.9
1993	100.0	24.7	53.8	47.5	21.5
1994	100.0	24.6	53.9	47.0	21.5
1995	100.0	18.0	57.4	46.7	24.6
1996	100.0	17.9	50.5	41.5	31.6
1997	100.0	17.7	50.1	42.7	32.2
1998	100.0	17.3	50.5	42.6	32.2
1999	100.0	16.4	51.8	43.4	31.8
2000	100.0	15.3	53.4	44.3	31.3
2001	100.0	15.3	53.7	46.2	31.1
2002	100.0	14.9	54.5	46.5	30.6
2003	100.0	13.9	57.1	47.2	29.0
2004	100.0	12.4	59.9	49.2	27.8
2005	100.0	10.7	58.8	48.7	30.5
2006	100.0	9.6	58.5	48.9	32.0
2007	100.0	8.4	59.1	50.0	32.5
2008	100.0	8.2	59.7	50.3	32.1
2009	100.0	8.1	59.8	49.2	32.2
2010	100.0	7.5	60.4	49.4	32.2
2011	100.0	7.0	59.0	48.2	34.0
2012	100.0	7.0	57.0	47.6	36.0
2013	100.0	6.1	53.8	44.6	40.1
2014	100.0	5.9	53.0	43.7	41.2

注:1.本表 2013-2014 年数据在全国第三次经济普查后进行了调整。

2.自 2013 年开始,第一产业是指农、林、牧、渔业(不含农、林、牧、渔服务业);第二产业是指采矿业(不含开采辅助活动),制造业(不含金属制品、机械和设备修理业),电力、热力、燃气及水生产和供应业,建筑业;第三产业即服务业,是指除第一产业、第二产业以外的其他行业。

Note:1.2013-2014 data have been adjusted after the third national economic census.

2.Since 2013, primary industry refers to agriculture, forestry, husbandry and fishing Sccondary industry refers to mining industry cexclusine of support activities), manufacturing cexdusine of metal product, machionery or equipment repair, electric power, thermal power, gas, water production and supply, and construction; tertiary industry refers to service industry other than the previous two industries.

2-24 海门市历年生产总值指数

INDICES OF GROSS DOMESTIC PRODUCT OF HAIMEN CITY OVER THE YEARS

按可比价计算,1978=100 (At comparable price,1978=100)

年份 Year	地区生产总值 Gross Domestic Product	第一产业 Primary Industry	第二产业 Secondary Industry	工业 Industry	建筑业 Construction	第三产业 Tertiary Industry	人均地区生产总值 Per Capita GDP
1978	100.0	100.0	100.0	100.0	100.0	100.0	100.0
1979	108.4	101.1	125.1	126.6	112.2	103.8	108.1
1980	125.5	110.8	156.1	157.7	142.8	119.8	124.8
1985	256.8	170.8	435.0	452.4	288.2	225.1	250.5
1990	346.6	191.4	679.3	679.4	678.7	275.2	328.2
1991	346.9	163.6	741.1	717.4	946.8	287.6	327.3
1992	435.4	185.2	988.6	1004.4	850.2	357.8	410.0
1993	530.8	194.3	1299.0	1334.8	986.2	430.1	498.9
1994	658.7	213.3	1695.2	1736.6	1334.3	526.0	617.3
1995	947.9	257.2	2502.1	2427.8	3139.6	817.9	886.7
1996	1062.6	301.4	2537.1	2495.8	2860.2	1103.3	992.2
1997	1217.7	339.1	2877.1	2915.1	2459.8	1303.0	1136.1
1998	1340.7	320.8	3282.7	3308.6	2983.7	1473.7	1248.5
1999	1494.9	333.0	3762.0	3831.4	3049.3	1627.0	1389.6
2000	1660.9	347.3	4254.8	4344.8	3360.4	1809.2	1545.3
2001	1833.6	362.9	4790.9	5061.7	2836.2	1984.7	1706.0
2002	2044.5	384.3	5428.1	5750.1	3105.6	2205.0	1909.0
2003	2328.7	401.2	6475.7	6836.9	3810.6	2423.3	2182.0
2004	2698.9	425.6	7770.8	8272.6	4187.8	2745.6	2541.0
2005	3117.2	440.9	9231.7	9869.2	4853.7	3127.2	2949.0
2006	3619.1	459.0	10958.0	11882.5	5353.6	3605.6	3435.6
2007	4200.3	468.2	12953.4	14275.6	5769.6	4185.0	4001.4
2008	4786.3	488.3	14809.1	16550.9	6035.4	4839.2	4581.6
2009	5456.4	508.4	17045.3	18901.1	7290.8	5526.3	5241.4
2010	6236.7	528.7	19721.4	21792.9	8595.9	6316.6	5959.4
2011	6985.1	550.4	22107.7	24560.6	9403.9	7182.0	6626.9
2012	7823.3	575.7	24650.1	27802.6	9733.0	8216.2	7442.0
2013	8768.0	594.7	27781.6	31240.9	11136.2	9255.5	8341.6
2014	9665.8	616.7	30723.7	34725.7	12001.5	10252.1	9195.7

注:自2013年开始,第一产业是指农、林、牧、渔业(不含农、林、牧、渔服务业);第二产业是指采矿业(不含开采辅助活动),制造业(不含金属制品、机械和设备修理业),电力、热力、燃气及水生产和供应业,建筑业;第三产业即服务业,是指除第一产业、第二产业以外的其他行业。

Note:Since 2013, primary industry refers to agriculture, forestry, husbandry and fishing Sccondary industry refers to mining industry cexclusine of support activities), manufacturing cexdusine of metal product, machionery or equipment repair, electric power, thermal power, gas, water production and supply, and construction; tertiary industry refers to service industry other than the previous two industries.

2-25 南通市生产总值要素构成(2014年)

单位:亿元

指 标	Item
地区生产总值	**Gross Domestic Product**
农、林、牧、渔业	Agiculture, Forestry, Animal Husbandry and Fishery
农业	Farming
林业	Forestry
畜牧业	Husbandry
渔业	Fishery
农、林、牧、渔服务业	Services in Sapport of Agricultare
工业	Industry
制造业	Manufacturing
#金属制品、机械和设备修理业	Metal Product, Machinery and Equipment Repair
电力、燃气及水的生产和供应	Production and Supply of Electricily, Gas and Water
建筑业	Construction
批发和零售业	Wholesale and Retail Trades
批发业	Wholesale Trades
零售业	Retail Trades
交通运输、仓储和邮政业	Transportation, Storage and Postal Industry
住宿和餐饮业	Hotels and Catering Services
住宿业	Hotel Industry
餐饮业	Catering Services
信息传输、计算机服务和软件业	Information Transmission, Computer Services and Software
金融业	Financial Intermediation
房地产业	Real Estate
租赁和商务服务业	Leasing and Business Services
科学研究、技术服务和地质勘查业	Scientific Research,Technical Services and Geologic Prospecting
水利、环境和公共设施管理业	Managementof Water Conservancy, Environment and Public Facilities
居民服务和其他服务业	Services to Households and Other Services
教育	Education
卫生和社会工作	Health and Social work
文化、体育和娱乐业	Culture, Sports and Entertainment
公共管理、社会保障和社会组织	Public Administration, Social Security and Social Organizateions
第一产业	Primary Industry
第二产业	Secondary Industry
第三产业	Tertiary Industry

注:第一产业是指农、林、牧、渔业(不含农、林、牧、渔服务业);第二产业是指采矿业(不含开采辅助活动),制造业(不含金属制品、机械和设备修理业),电力、热力、燃气及水生产和供应业,建筑业;第三产业即服务业,是指除第一产业、第二产业以外的其他行业。

COMPONONTS OF GROSS DOMESTIC PRODUCT OF NANTONG CITY(2014)

(100 million yuan)

地区生产总值 Gross Product	劳动者报酬 Compensation of Employees	生产税净额 Net Taxes on Production	固定资产折旧 Depreciation of Fixed Assets	营业盈余 Operating Surplus
5652.69	**2050.78**	**1112.79**	**690.00**	**1799.12**
367.11	325.66	-6.88	16.09	32.24
197.12	177.64	-6.88	8.78	17.58
2.41	2.10		0.10	0.21
56.60	49.29		2.44	4.88
83.44	72.65		3.59	7.19
27.53	23.97		1.18	2.37
2307.64	554.62	517.94	285.60	949.47
2227.73	547.15	505.46	263.64	911.47
2.70	2.40	0.60	0.43	-0.73
79.91	7.47	12.48	21.96	38.01
507.40	361.88	60.25	6.00	79.27
619.33	123.08	241.46	36.84	217.95
407.13	49.47	171.14	15.04	171.48
212.20	73.61	70.32	21.80	46.47
210.85	111.51	17.62	26.92	54.81
118.28	67.24	20.31	26.35	4.38
15.40	9.63	3.85	5.78	-3.85
102.88	57.61	16.46	20.58	8.23
69.01	18.48	9.09	16.54	24.89
318.31	48.71	24.82	33.88	210.90
367.98	54.50	148.96	133.73	30.79
193.78	44.96	27.53	38.54	82.76
70.66	28.69	11.02	4.86	26.09
18.60	5.07	4.40	2.03	7.10
96.03	60.02	12.00	4.00	20.01
120.80	57.78	15.76	15.76	31.51
78.75	38.46	3.66	16.48	20.15
33.65	14.42	4.12	9.62	5.49
154.50	135.71	0.72	16.76	1.31
339.57	301.68	-6.88	14.90	29.86
2812.34	914.10	577.59	291.18	1029.47
2500.78	835.00	542.07	383.92	739.79

Note:primary industry refers to agriculture, forestry, husbandry and fishing Sccondary industry refers to mining industry cexclusine of support activities), manufacturing cexdusine of metal product, machionery or equipment repair, electric power, thermal power, gas, water production and supply, and construction; tertiary industry refers to service industry other than the previous two industries.

2-26 分地区生产总值(2014年)

单位:亿元

指 标	Item	全市 Whole City
地区生产总值	**Gross Domestic Product**	**5652.69**
农、林、牧、渔业	Agiculture, Forestry, Animal Husbandry and Fishery	367.11
工业	Industry	2307.64
建筑业	Construction	507.40
批发和零售业	Wholesale and Retail Trades	619.33
批发业	Wholesale Trades	407.13
零售业	Retail Trades	212.20
交通运输、仓储和邮政业	Transportat, Storage and Post	210.85
住宿和餐饮业	Hotel and Catering Services	118.28
住宿业	Hotel Industry	15.40
餐饮业	Catering Services	102.88
金融业	Financial Intermediation	318.31
房地产业	Real Estate	367.98
其他服务业	Others	835.78
营利性服务业	Profit-Oriented Service	392.47
非营利性服务业	Nonprofit-Oriented Service	443.31
第一产业	Primary Industry	339.57
第二产业	Secondary Industry	2812.34
第三产业	Tertiary Industry	2500.78

注:第一产业是指农、林、牧、渔业(不含农、林、牧、渔服务业);第二产业是指采矿业(不含开采辅助活动),制造业(不含金属制品、机械和设备修理业),电力、热力、燃气及水生产和供应业,建筑业;第三产业即服务业,是指除第一产业、第二产业以外的其他行业。

GROSS DOMESTIC PRODUCT BY REGION(2014)

(100 million yuan)

市区 Urban Area	市区 通州区 Tongzhou	海安 Haian	如东 Rudong	启东 Qidong	如皋 Rugao	海门 Haimen
2093.78	**860.73**	**624.14**	**615.51**	**739.13**	**743.64**	**836.50**
61.57	57.05	56.00	65.30	68.55	61.14	54.55
852.05	367.49	245.80	245.42	287.41	311.08	365.88
172.32	79.50	58.33	51.69	81.62	66.16	77.28
255.54	98.37	51.78	60.32	89.72	59.58	102.39
167.17	82.87	35.19	35.79	61.49	40.12	67.37
88.37	15.50	16.59	24.53	28.23	19.47	35.02
76.58	43.16	35.64	20.75	18.39	38.80	20.70
32.53	12.41	11.80	11.35	19.74	20.16	22.70
3.58	0.61	2.52	1.74	1.17	1.16	5.23
28.96	11.81	9.27	9.61	18.57	19.00	17.47
143.24	35.83	42.21	23.22	33.27	39.47	36.90
184.81	50.42	30.29	29.83	32.84	49.08	41.12
315.12	116.49	92.30	107.63	107.59	98.17	114.97
183.54	55.49	29.38	50.81	48.13	33.79	46.82
131.58	61.00	62.91	56.82	59.46	64.38	68.16
56.54	52.25	51.27	62.17	62.93	57.60	49.07
1021.67	446.99	304.13	297.11	369.03	377.24	443.16
1015.57	361.49	268.74	256.23	307.17	308.80	344.27

Note:primary industry refers to agriculture, forestry, husbandry and fishing Sccondary industry refers to mining industry cexclusine of support activities), manufacturing cexdusine of metal product, machionery or equipment repair, electric power, thermal power, gas, water production and supply, and construction; tertiary industry refers to service industry other than the previous two industries.

2-27 分地区生产总值发展速度(2014年)

按可比价计算,2013年=100

指 标	Item	全市 Whole City
地区生产总值	**GDP**	**110.5**
农、林、牧、渔业	Agiculture, Forestry, Animal Husbandry and Fishery	103.5
工业	Industry	111.1
建筑业	Construction	106.6
批发和零售业	Wholesale and Retail Trades	110.7
批发业	Wholesale Trades	111.1
零售业	Retail Trades	109.8
交通运输、仓储和邮政业	Transportation, Storage and Post	108.2
住宿和餐饮业	Hotel and Catering Services	112.2
住宿业	Hotel Industry	111.3
餐饮业	Catering Services	112.4
金融业	Financial Intermediation	117.8
房地产业	Real Estate	103.5
其他服务业	Others	115.9
营利性服务业	Profit-Oriented Service	121.4
非营利性服务业	Nonprofit-Oriented Service	111.7
第一产业	Primary Industry	102.6
第二产业	Secondary Industry	110.3
第三产业	Tertiary Industry	112.0

注:第一产业是指农、林、牧、渔业(不含农、林、牧、渔服务业);第二产业是指采矿业(不含开采辅助活动),制造业(不含金属制品、机械和设备修理业),电力、热力、燃气及水生产和供应业,建筑业;第三产业即服务业,是指除第一产业、第二产业以外的其他行业。

GROSS DOMESTIC PRODUCT GROWTH RATE BY REGION(2014)

(At Comparable Price,2013=100)

市区 Urban Area	通州区 Tongzhou	海安 Haian	如东 Rudong	启东 Qidong	如皋 Rugao	海门 Haimen
110.2	**110.8**	**111.0**	**110.2**	**110.6**	**110.5**	**110.2**
102.3	103.8	103.9	103.4	103.2	103.6	103.7
110.3	111.6	111.5	111.4	110.9	111.4	111.2
106.8	105.2	110.2	104.8	108.3	107.1	107.8
109.3	110.1	109.8	112.9	107.2	111.5	111.4
109.3	110.0	111.4	113.9	107.8	112.1	111.9
109.2	110.7	106.6	111.5	106.0	110.4	110.3
110.9	110.8	111.0	113.9	108.3	110.9	106.2
107.2	107.1	107.5	111.3	108.9	109.1	112.1
108.2	107.7	110.1	111.1	112.1	107.8	113.2
106.9	107.0	106.9	111.4	108.5	109.2	111.8
109.7	113.8	118.1	112.1	117.0	115.5	108.9
108.6	110.1	103.4	97.8	106.6	108.1	106.3
115.4	117.4	116.5	116.1	121.4	112.7	113.2
115.4	120.3	115.3	118.2	130.9	118.0	118.3
115.4	114.9	117.1	114.2	114.7	112.0	110.1
102.3	103.8	103.9	103.4	103.2	103.6	103.7
109.8	110.4	111.3	110.2	110.4	110.8	110.6
111.3	112.5	112.2	112.2	113.0	111.6	110.8

Note:primary industry refers to agriculture, forestry, husbandry and fishing Sccondary industry refers to mining industry cexclusine of support activities), manufacturing cexdusine of metal product, machionery or equipment repair, electric power, thermal power, gas, water production and supply, and construction; tertiary industry refers to service industry other than the previous two industries.

2-28 规模以上服务业企业主要经济指标(2014年)

单位:万元

指 标	Item	单位数 Number of Units	年初存货 Inventory at the Beginning of the Year	流动资产 Current Assets
总计	**Total**	**2033**	**1005558**	**10038613**
按登记注册类型分组	**Grouped by Types of Registration**			
内资企业	Domestic Funded Enterprises	1993	763570	9451483
国有企业	State-owned Enterprises	41	198302	1008485
集体企业	Collective-owned Enterprises	49	1326	407162
股份合作企业	Cooperative Enterprises	2		
联营企业	Joint Ownership Enterprises	1	28	1726
有限责任公司	Limited Liability Corporations	720	291801	4580994
股份有限公司	Share-holding Corporations Ltd	25	7497	239299
私营企业	Private Enterprises	850	244935	3129228
其他企业	Other Enterprises	305	19681	84589
港、澳、台商投资企业	Enterprises With Funds From Hongkong, Macou and Taiwan	14	239265	497678
外商投资企业	Foreign Funded Enterprises	26	2723	89452
按企业控股情况分组	**Grouped by Types of Share Holding**			
国有控股	State-holding	129	275669	3006163
集体控股	Collective-holding	77	9956	639230
私人控股	Private-holding	1546	440115	4588352
港澳台商控股	HK, Macau or Taiwan Holding	12	236462	397962
外商控股	Foreign Holding	19	294	76364
其他	Others	233	42518	1324934
按地区分组	**Grouped by Regions**			
市区	Urban Area	617	37647	538851
崇川区	Chongchuan	176	97021	1322151
港闸区	Gangzha	113	14315	819496
开发区	Development Zone	77	96354	2022659
通州区	Tongzhou	251	168777	1224201
海安县	Haian	302	132830	1450856
如东县	Rudong	278	27820	395908
启东市	Qidong	265	343683	1385517
如皋市	Rugao	296	96712	665263
海门市	Haimen	275	28048	752563

MAJOR ECONMIC INDICATORS OF KEY SERVICE INDUSTRY ENTERPRISES(2014)

(Unit: 10,000 Yuan)

其中:应收账款 of which:Receivable Accounts	存货 Deposits	固定资产原价 Fixed Assets At cost	本年折旧 Depreciation of the year	资产总计 Total Assets	负债合计 Total Liabilities	所有者权益合计 Total Ownership Interests	营业收入 Operating Revenue	其中:主营业务收入 Of which:Main Business Income	营业成本 Operating Cost	其中:主营业务成本 Of which:Main Business Cost
1298729	**921030**	**7921750**	**580863**	**31597199**	**19154081**	**12443118**	**8260657**	**8102340**	**5878246**	**5759684**
1050051	749358	7141086	538843	30255722	18302602	11953120	7920730	7772514	5641067	5532966
59682	65070	376119	50551	1597552	1015558	581994	482147	465781	417251	399345
7217	755	86119	5712	519158	345894	173264	207208	207102	136052	134892
		3545	240	4294	2936	1358	2857	2643	2364	2364
710	31	1086	162	2814	1137	1677	1650	1650	1123	1123
529750	225516	3784951	292630	20096406	12724385	7372020	3427459	3331518	2274076	2225784
21434	6308	1090657	50601	1651636	1029689	621947	417957	413024	279596	273555
392099	440742	1636828	122712	6063031	3072019	2991011	2886680	2859647	2134891	2104294
39161	10937	161782	16236	320831	110983	209848	494773	491150	395714	391609
235127	171388	657429	34950	1140969	787461	353508	278388	268375	193892	184307
13550	284	123235	7070	200509	64018	136491	61539	61451	43287	42412
84880	127062	2992151	228672	10154263	5943196	4211067	2041961	1951915	1289424	1232119
25373	4132	149969	9897	1192628	603946	588683	349372	346227	253053	250090
799488	609201	3025631	223966	14638004	9325519	5312485	5027856	4975025	3749470	3704918
209929	169282	271040	16289	543161	469990	73171	109322	102066	73660	64852
12399	231	84243	4996	167781	55381	112400	45454	45431	29410	29328
163382	10742	1369604	96209	4852928	2729791	2123137	666490	661560	432647	428778
58951	53528	510846	32078	1244164	680712	563452	374921	363227	259704	251432
108734	50846	2740096	203477	5386409	3014679	2371730	1664356	1605065	1044652	1008369
35416	27839	443798	33138	1353011	976478	376532	544813	496205	441117	427983
239849	90240	1293064	30325	2447203	1488220	958983	601879	601112	333345	326546
205510	366351	631501	53844	3255019	1327740	1927279	938164	929888	777922	751423
48558	6372	638236	45298	2595814	1491613	1104201	1144337	1141758	908021	901789
23028	8797	193874	16598	1484152	649843	834309	544968	539265	410519	402151
268321	280135	707261	51428	3592820	2220225	1372595	788122	768022	569676	558947
138771	35631	851899	114211	9833452	7214852	2618600	897985	887880	678333	672141
230543	54820	422023	32544	1649320	770431	878888	1136033	1133146	714663	710334

2-28 续表 1

单位：万元

指 标	Item	单位数 Number of Units	年初存货 Inventory at the Beginning of the Year	流动资产 Current Assets
按行业分组	**Grouped by Industries**			
道路运输业	Road Transportation	252	11549.3	449911
水上运输业	Waterway Transportation	39	7456.3	979420
航空运输业	Airway Transportation	2	28.5	14075
管道运输业	Pipeline Transportation	1	0	1642
装卸搬运和运输代理业	Handling and Transportation Agent	77	1639.8	295325
仓储业	Storage	46	202793.7	282217
邮政业	Post	17	408.9	28464
电信、广播电视和卫星传输服务	Telecommunication, TV Broadcasting and Satellite Transmission Services	10	10936.7	107091
互联网和相关服务	Internet and Related Services	9	211	-11515
软件和信息技术服务业	Software and IT Services	61	4319.7	46479
房地产业(物业管理、房地产中介服务)	Real Estate(Property Management,Real Estate Agency)	109	1670.4	229884
租赁业	Leasing Industry	31	423.6	43408
商务服务业	Commercial Services	538	429274.6	6224698
研究和试验发展	R&D	35	8111.2	38419
专业技术服务业	Special Technique Service	225	33016.1	274193
科技推广和应用服务业	S&T Promotion & Application	316	32473.5	189548
水利管理业	Water Conservancy	2		34126
生态保护和环境治理业	Ecological Protection and Environment Management	15	806.2	127071
公共设施管理业	Public Facility Management	31	5487.9	52545
居民服务业	Resident Services	10	39.8	2795
机动车、电子产品和日用产品修理业	Repair of Automobile, Electronic Product and Daily Use Items	39	2660.8	11643
其他服务业	Others	14	145.5	2176
教育	Education	44	1615.2	8643
卫生	Health	36	5320.9	82396
社会工作	Social Work	1		
新闻和出版业	Media and Publication Industry	2	185.1	46654
广播、电视、电影和影视录音制作业	Broadcasting, TV, Movie and Recording	12	734.5	53190
文化艺术业	Culture and Arts	8	7759.9	17690
体育	Sports	4	203.3	2993
娱乐业	Entertainment	47	236286	403435

CONTINUED 1

(Unit: 10,000 Yuan)

其中:应收账款 of which:Receivable Accounts	存货 Deposits	固定资产原价 Fixed Assets At cost	本年折旧 Depreciation of the year	资产总计 Total Assets	负债合计 Total Liabilities	所有者权益合计 Total Ownership Interests	营业收入 Operating Revenue	其中:主营业务收入 Of which:Main Business Income	营业成本 Operating Cost	其中:主营业务成本 Of which:Main Business Cost
79777	12002	816816	71474	1895603	1159132	736471	1182423	1166480	942259	930447
129319	5511	1473971	35947	666350	409505	256845	233752	231447	168679	167752
1205	30	48328	2111	91888	23503	68385	11898	10725	12779	11964
649		2543	16	5044	1044	4000	1025	1025	885	885
15323	1375	371661	21958	308765	178359	130406	653580	639670	506217	505383
31869	61338	310886	27612	637028	392302	244726	461257	454163	413851	389320
14042	2395	73707	30724	85775	22535	63240	163159	160322	132602	127877
80273	10029	1671375	105121	1019029	780039	238990	681679	672429	327013	314587
12201	778	46049	2946	38267	7585	30682	72401	72401	16182	16182
8285	1748	23809	3002	83982	22062	61920	123127	123127	98115	97729
19867	8470	64325	3400	297590	145931	151658	146663	141111	95042	94009
23466	640	65826	5047	129211	76459	52752	108509	107455	64682	64414
437638	545972	2119789	208334	23386966	14264169	9122797	2602763	2536166	1722068	1691242
10414	4677	51155	3489	173602	84394	89208	88416	88269	65901	65779
77850	26191	173307	12579	668160	321650	346510	547812	540561	407975	401764
42430	34699	178796	14070	494868	201300	293567	602530	592347	446974	437257
14437	11250	8263	523	109114	33873	75241	23498	23498	14773	14773
46203	706	68888	3717	278387	138297	140090	50453	50453	37715	33133
12823	6534	36721	1873	173890	86780	87110	139499	139357	112181	112178
528	91	1769	181	16178	10131	6046	11083	9265	8957	7138
3698	2572	8090	612	19715	10700	9016	40685	39536	29894	28949
689	225	4761	532	8793	3704	5089	15842	15797	11842	11714
1493	118	39264	2699	68480	39215	29265	59163	59061	75475	75027
26044	5561	68918	8788	143033	80280	62753	111322	110210	81618	80168
		551	11	552	520	32	1480	1480	1287	1287
1683	141	6977	510	57057	33649	23408	15194	6102	11571	7835
665	52	27973	1798	111082	68925	42158	27449	26517	16240	15931
523	10532	2952	743	50644	38056	12588	15412	15162	10478	10476
122	9	2132	210	5358	3250	2108	3135	3135	1650	1650
205214	167387	152150	10838	572791	516732	56060	65449	65072	43341	42836

2-28 续表 2

单位：万元

指 标	Item	营业税金及附加 Business Tax and Surcharges	#主营业务税金及附加 Of which: Main Business Tax and Surcharges	销售费用 Selling Expenses
总计	**Total**	**249982**	**242885**	**286087**
按登记注册类型分组	**Grouped by Types of Registration**			
内资企业	Domestic Funded Enterprises	244792	237879	270895
国有企业	State-owned Enterprises	4516	3739	7208
集体企业	Collective-owned Enterprises	7162	7158	3010
股份合作企业	Cooperative Enterprises	36	36	0
联营企业	Joint Ownership Enterprises	102	102	0
有限责任公司	Limited Liability Corporations	107626	102021	130500
股份有限公司	Share-holding Corporations Ltd	8890	8760	48241
私营企业	Private Enterprises	105268	105009	71592
其他企业	Other Enterprises	11193	11056	10345
港、澳、台商投资企业	Enterprises With Funds From Hongkong, Macou and Taiwan	4771	4589	13279
外商投资企业	Foreign Funded Enterprises	418	417	1913
按企业控股情况分组	**Grouped by Types of Share Holding**			
国有控股	State-holding	41974	39294	154524
集体控股	Collective-holding	9171	9036	3400
私人控股	Private-holding	179787	176413	106815
港澳台商控股	HK, Macau or Taiwan Holding	4225	4064	12677
外商控股	Foreign Holding	387	387	1801
其他	Others	14154	13409	6593
按地区分组	**Grouped by Regions**			
市区	Urban Area	6499	5977	22109
崇川区	Chongchuan	23259	20851	171717
港闸区	Gangzha	11027	8867	11128
开发区	Development Zone	15356	15256	26214
通州区	Tongzhou	15346	14793	12026
海安县	Haian	73390	73287	13076
如东县	Rudong	8988	8644	10822
启东市	Qidong	28552	27850	15695
如皋市	Rugao	18935	18268	10516
海门市	Haimen	55130	55071	14892

CONTINUED 2

(Unit: 10,000 Yuan)

管理费用 Management Expenses	其中:税金 Of which: Taxes	财务费用 Financial Expenses	其中:利息收入 Of which:Interest Income	其中:利息支出 Interest Cost	投资收益 Investment Revenue	营业利润 Operating Profit	营业外收入 Non-operating Income	补贴收入 Subsidy Income	营业外支出 Non-operating Expense	利润总额 Total Profits	应交所得税 Income Tax Payable	应付职工薪酬 Payroll Payable	应交增值税 Value Added Tax Payable
664562	**39004**	**245529**	**20342**	**148681**	**95860**	**1002424**	**124982**	**51564**	**52809**	**1044915**	**174255**	**978161**	**153429**
628710	36738	231537	19551	134458	95488	968931	122748	51482	51260	1010352	162800	913700	147469
46844	1516	14063	2417	11852	810	−3508	26991	24698	1355	29678	2653	89891	2948
26969	946	6016	74	671	106	29023	4590	4580	105	27400	4086	41024	4919
194	19	−1				42				55	16	812	199
133	0	−2				295	6		20	280	70	2127	1
238339	19108	123579	14845	73352	17105	522657	68255	10844	42161	537099	85400	337808	63178
21523	1173	9710	1337	1751	−218	51640	5687	2354	4468	51827	12986	49860	554
266084	11409	73749	869	44042	77675	287892	16944	8738	2866	287399	44524	328008	56011
28625	2568	4423	8	2791	12	80892	275	268	287	76615	13067	64172	19660
24852	1658	13415	414	12889	368	28675	1950		1340	29058	2363	47143	5395
11000	608	577	377	1334	3	4818	284	81	208	5505	9092	17318	565
167175	8516	111533	9515	59740	8258	261760	95461	36549	48320	315068	71672	280013	24534
38817	1403	6637	235	1248	106	41725	5047	4665	137	38198	6706	58233	6206
392951	19650	102652	9244	68413	84288	528477	21843	9816	3952	525909	79266	538563	79936
4892	462	2238	1	1421	−101	11668	256		143	11705	394	6535	1908
9213	451	707	211	1227		3478	205	80	56	4154	701	15252	409
50550	8503	21731	1136	16625	3309	154540	2170	453	131	149086	15471	75095	40428
36191	1345	15606	1647	9942	9385	41198	10979	4490	5015	46337	9679	54391	7029
176422	6726	54268	8087	28133	30057	220988	39621	26172	8254	254635	53854	290892	28615
24822	1659	19093	2675	11158	21	−3539	47862	897	39861	2410	2935	43575	18343
95483	1934	38202	2106	36015	496	101920	5697	3587	1298	105852	26728	102155	8928
65186	3134	44496	3600	24119	63272	92607	16607	14242	734	100468	13276	107287	14404
64301	3315	10875	830	7040	241	58827	3388	2866	954	63975	3358	77093	4228
28199	2351	7276	284	1971	613	70716	3191	166	190	71316	21556	60998	22783
48731	3927	29753	1942	10020	427	80453	3394	2237	158	81015	12809	90111	13861
63663	9016	32657	603	26525	273	137185	4073	549	790	131668	11362	99095	27379
97756	6941	8909	215	3701	460	243266	1147	849	569	233576	28378	106956	14889

2-28 续表 3

单位：万元

指 标	Item	营业税金及附加 Business Tax and Surcharges	#主营业务税金及附加 Of which: Main Business Tax and Surcharges	销售费用 Selling Expenses
按行业分组	**Grouped by Industries**			
道路运输业	Road Transportation	27784	25660	20390
水上运输业	Waterway Transportation	1255	1189	4812
航空运输业	Airway Transportation	22		
管道运输业	Pipeline Transportation	14	14	16
装卸搬运和运输代理业	Handling and Transportation Agent	38195	38120	3133
仓储业	Storage	2939	2361	5034
邮政业	Post	1239	1239	1462
电信、广播电视和卫星传输服务	Telecommunication, TV Broadcasting and Satellite Transmission Services	11743	9993	147557
互联网和相关服务	Internet and Related Services	3089	3089	2278
软件和信息技术服务业	Software and IT Services	3962	3962	4366
房地产业(物业管理、房地产中介服务)	Real Estate(Property Management and Intermediate Services)	6479	6260	2034
租赁业	Leasing Industry	8915	8896	857
商务服务业	Business Services	93123	91415	45684
研究和试验发展	R&D	1109	1102	2211
专业技术服务业	Special Technique Service	18613	18592	8006
科技推广和应用服务业	S&T Promotion & Application	12832	12693	11928
水利管理业	Water Conservancy	1227	1227	0
生态保护和环境治理业	Ecological Protection and Environment Management	2195	2195	163
公共设施管理业	Public Facility Management	5921	5822	2545
居民服务业	Resident Services	441	441	557
机动车、电子产品和日用产品修理业	Repair of Automobile, Electronic Product and Daily Use Items	1367	1365	459
其他服务业	Others	408	318	653
教育	Education	1805	1805	2220
卫生	Health	819	759	6129
社会工作	Social Work	13	13	14
新闻和出版业	Press and Publication Industry	276	169	841
广播、电视、电影和影视录音制作业	Broadcasting, TV, Movie and Recording	922	914	2680
文化艺术业	Culture and Arts	530	530	4153
体育	Sports	76	76	165
娱乐业	Entertainment	2669	2668	5740

CONTINUED 3

(Unit: 10,000 Yuan)

管理费用 Management Expenses	其中:税金 Of which: Taxes	财务费用 Financial Expenses	其中:利息收入 Of which:Interest Income	其中:利息支出 Interest Cost	投资收益 Investment Revenue	营业利润 Operating Profit	营业外收入 Non-operating Income	补贴收入 Subsidy Income	营业外支出 Non-operating Expense	利润总额 Total Profits	应交所得税 Income Tax Payable	应付职工薪酬 Payroll Payable	应交增值税 Value Added Tax Payable
76744	3481	43728	1912	42130	246	82163	34254	25753	1942	109055	25649	159438	28366
26367	1155	17898	932	7365	560	16114	1618	1037	1265	15735	3474	50509	6403
2645	35	−15	48			−3533	4274	4267	135	606	224	3833	119
5		5				101				101	12	140	
38530	2477	1882	153	513	214	52831	1526	238	191	53343	4261	17075	3835
14950	1980	15733	1565	14125	2866	14146	5745	4933	398	22822	3471	16692	2638
13702	809	169	133	221		14039	521	453	10	14512	577	62438	2232
29570	1603	1228	425	1267		161588	3899		5538	160424	38513	60436	13596
51960	56	222	7	0		−1450	1784	970	2	350	592	41537	92
10941	528	381	122	351	6	5840	1401	491	8	6529	1985	21875	1360
22183	773	801	167	368	13	16094	3219	161	1080	18552	3542	37388	1271
9723	644	1905	17	644		22027	75		5	22022	2149	9403	1916
219948	16044	145370	12737	72503	91354	410417	59039	7840	40142	408102	45579	236309	52808
8637	288	297	10	440	−338	10885	161	46	83	10699	1567	14726	2221
55763	2798	4234	654	1905	240	53097	1053	452	416	53709	18554	99816	8047
29505	2709	3107	46	1426	14	96943	815	498	695	96853	14749	62895	19636
1308	162	41				6078				6078	177	1366	259
4831	349	1463	6	58		5453	864	864	2	5232	1293	3986	162
6537	722	1770	17	414	219	9105	2565	2178	158	11089	2121	10038	1748
1112	59	33		7		82	102	62	41	129	175	2546	163
3449	364	85	7	23		3969	1		4	4053	577	6201	929
1656	149	36		27		1282	73	27	19	1336	330	5862	149
5046	226	119	53	66	247	6460	425	2	452	6574	1219	11126	2117
14512	349	3513	11	3157		10471	234	191	150	6437	1259	21364	667
21	2	17				128				128	32	96	44
2733	34	−198	914	709	76	−28	12		21	39	3	1463	562
3199	108	40	3	6		3807	186	16	20	4006	507	3772	510
2368	119	105	20	123	−33	−2493	1090	1078	23	−1178	194	2251	63
668	34	134		130		442	9	9		527	127	809	70
5951	947	1429	383	705	175	6366	40		10	7054	1345	12775	1447

2-29 联网直报企业信息化情况(2014)

指 标	Item	企业数（个）Number of Enterprises	使用计算机的企业 Enterprises usingcomputes
合计	**Total**	**10934**	**10922**
按行业分	**Grouped by Industries**		
制造业	Manufacturing	5025	5021
电力、热力、燃气及水生产和供应业	Production and Supply of Power, Fuel and Water	49	49
建筑业	Construction	1010	1007
批发和零售业	Wholesale and Retail Trades	2053	2052
交通运输、仓储和邮政业	Transport, Storage and Post	434	434
住宿和餐饮业	Hotel and Catering Services	241	241
信息传输、软件和信息技术服务业	Information Transmission,Computer Servivce and Software	80	80
房地产业	Real Estate	649	646
租赁和商务服务业	Leasing and Commercial Service	568	568
科学研究和技术服务业	Scientific Research and Technology Service	569	569
水利、环境和公共设施管理业	Management of Water Conservancy,Environment and Public Facility	47	47
居民服务、修理和其他服务业	Service for Residents, Maintenance and Other	63	62
教育	Education	42	42
卫生和社会工作	Healith and Social Work	31	31
文化、体育和娱乐业	Culture, Sports and Entertainment	73	73
按地区分			
崇川区	Chongchuan	807	805
港闸区	Gangzha	602	600
通州区	Tongzhou	1505	1503
海安县	Haian	1673	1673
如东县	Rudong	1349	1347
开发区	Development Zone	738	737
启东市	Rudong	1207	1207
如皋市	Rugao	1615	1613
海门市	Haimen	1438	1437

INFORMATIATION OF NETWORKING REPORT ENTERPRISES(2014)

有信息技术人员的企业 Enterprises with IT Professionals	有局域网的企业 Enterprises with LAN	使用信息化管理的企业 Enterprises of Informatization	有信息化投入的企业 Enterprises whit Informatization	使用互联网的企业 Enterprises with access to Internet	连接宽带的企业 Enterprises with Broadhand Internet	有网站的企业 Enterprises whit websites	通过互联网对本企业进行宣传和推广的企业 Enterprises with on-line Promotion
7984	**6458**	**10665**	**8914**	**10835**	**10702**	**5199**	**9013**
4085	3060	4955	4239	5000	4962	3046	4443
45	42	49	43	49	49	34	39
721	638	998	799	999	994	449	797
1218	1074	1947	1520	2011	1964	611	1449
297	256	425	352	429	425	156	342
147	146	224	178	240	214	108	189
80	60	79	76	80	80	39	77
417	416	627	540	644	644	271	525
368	319	557	454	564	561	182	464
409	316	554	490	564	558	204	467
36	22	47	38	47	47	10	38
40	25	59	54	62	60	18	51
32	20	42	38	42	41	16	35
29	25	31	30	31	30	19	28
60	39	71	63	73	73	36	69
615	592	785	624	797	793	505	665
469	409	583	440	593	593	332	489
877	669	1460	1220	1496	1493	445	1185
1329	984	1652	1585	1657	1628	871	1450
1060	824	1315	1061	1337	1330	702	1116
606	505	730	437	733	733	459	617
838	678	1164	848	1187	1134	507	988
1186	945	1573	1470	1610	1604	769	1368
1004	852	1403	1229	1425	1394	609	1135

2–29 续表 1

指标	Item	期末使用计算机(台) Term–end Number of Computers
合计	**Total**	**429846**
按行业分	**Grouped by Industries**	
制造业	Manufacturing	200169
电力、热力、燃气及水生产和供应业	Production and Supply of Power, Fuel and Water	7074
建筑业	Construction	95888
批发和零售业	Wholesale and Retail Trades	32913
交通运输、仓储和邮政业	Transport, Storage and Post	12263
住宿和餐饮业	Hotel and Catering Services	12774
信息传输、软件和信息技术服务业	Information Transmission,Computer Servivce and Software	20535
房地产业	Real Estate	9880
租赁和商务服务业	Leasing and Commercial Service	14216
科学研究和技术服务业	Scientific Research and Technology Service	8535
水利、环境和公共设施管理业	Management of Water Conservancy,Environment and Public Facility	766
居民服务、修理和其他服务业	Service for Residents, Maintenance and Other	1243
教育	Education	380
卫生和社会工作	Health and Social Work	1661
文化、体育和娱乐业	Culture, Sports and Entertainment	1669
按地区分		
崇川区	Chongchuan	47511
港闸区	Gangzha	16622
通州区	Tongzhou	37722
海安县	Haian	31312
如东县	Rudong	25006
开发区	Development Zone	31057
启东市	Rudong	47416
如皋市	Rugao	44748
海门市	Haimen	38300

CONTINUED 1

台式机 Desktop	笔记本电脑 Laptop	平板电脑 Tablet Computer	信息化投入（万元）Informatization Input (10,000 yuan)	一次性投入 One-off Input			运营维护投入 Operation and maintenance Input
				合计 Total	硬件投入 Hardwore Input	软件投入 Softurare Input	
338868	**81048**	**9930**	**406119**	**277079**	**210970**	**66109**	**129039**
168843	26911	4415	219354	130554	92885	37668	88800
5810	1176	88	3572	2510	1775	735	1063
56956	35493	3439	42247	27908	18505	9402	14340
28508	3830	575	29829	21687	16153	5534	8142
10706	1271	286	8746	6170	4503	1667	2577
10666	1832	276	26947	25222	24136	1086	1725
17879	2602	54	22599	21075	20384	691	1524
8056	1654	170	19140	15189	12145	3044	3951
11462	2534	220	4608	3780	2901	879	828
6854	1516	165	5766	4221	2508	1712	1546
644	103	19	1122	1081	1057	24	41
1147	82	14	1810	1507	1240	267	303
295	83	2	64	40	31	10	24
1568	78	15	679	520	237	283	159
1418	229	22	494	428	363	65	66
39523	7522	466	57102	45175	38414	6761	11927
13484	2880	258	9745	7251	4259	2992	2494
30533	6253	936	32501	22183	14326	7857	10318
24426	5842	1044	27746	20939	15365	5574	6807
18384	5431	1191	18287	15812	12410	3402	2475
26274	4429	354	14981	10185	7079	3106	4796
34202	12035	1179	25564	18195	12087	6108	7369
36341	6800	1607	45353	25109	17429	7679	20244
23502	14012	786	40750	22168	17487	4681	18582

2-30 联网直报企业电子商务主要指标(2014)

指 标	Item	企业数 Number of Eneerprises	有电子商务交易的企业数 with E-Business Transactions
合计	**Total**	**10934**	**930**
按行业分	**Grouped by Industries**		
制造业	Manufacturing	5025	641
电力、热力、燃气及水生产和供应业	Production and Supply of Power, Fuel and Water	49	4
建筑业	Construction	1010	53
批发和零售业	Wholesale and Retail Trades	2053	75
交通运输、仓储和邮政业	Transport, Storage and Post	434	19
住宿和餐饮业	Hotel and Catering Services	241	54
信息传输、软件和信息技术服务业	Information Transmission,Computer Servivce and Software	80	12
房地产业	Real Estate	649	14
租赁和商务服务业	Leasing and Commercial Service	568	21
科学研究和技术服务业	Scientific Research and Technology Service	569	17
水利、环境和公共设施管理业	Management of Water Conservancy,Environment and Public Facility	47	1
居民服务、修理和其他服务业	Service for Residents, Maintenance and Other	63	2
教育	Education	42	
卫生和社会工作	Helith and Social Work	31	2
文化、体育和娱乐业	Culture, Sports and Entertainment	73	15
按地区分			
崇川区	Chongchuan	807	78
港闸区	Gangzha	602	43
通州区	Tongzhou	1505	93
海安县	Haian	1673	186
如东县	Rudong	1349	128
开发区	Development Zone	738	29
启东市	Rudong	1207	56
如皋市	Rugao	1615	162
海门市	Haimen	1438	155

MAIN E-BUSINESS INDICATORS NETWORKING REPORT ENTERPRISES(2014)

有电子商务销售的企业数 with E-business Sales	按销售方式分 Grouped by sales Method		按销售对象分 Grouped by sales target			有电子商务采购的企业数 with E-business purchase	按采购方式分 Grouped by purchase way		按采购内容分 Grouped by Purchase object	
	通过自营平台 Self-managed platform	通过第三方电子商务平台 Third-party E-business Platfrom	B2B	B2G	B2C		通过自营平台 Self-managed platform	通过第三方电子商务平台 Third-party E-business Platfrom	商品采购 Commodity purchase	服务采购 Service Purchase
754	**108**	**587**	**581**	**50**	**274**	**598**	**66**	**450**	**583**	**103**
559	76	423	474	31	147	418	47	309	418	58
1			1		1	4	1	1	4	1
14	4	10	13	2	2	51	5	37	48	11
59	7	50	37	1	36	48	5	38	47	9
16	3	14	12	2	7	11		11	7	5
54	2	52	17	10	47	8	1	7	8	1
10	6	5	8	1	5	8	2	7	7	3
6	2	4	3		3	9	0	7	8	2
13	3	11	8	1	9	19	2	14	15	8
6	4	4	6	1	2	15	3	13	15	2
1		1			1					
						2		2	2	
2					2					
13	1	13	2	1	12	5		4	4	3
54	17	36	30	7	36	48	12	33	43	10
31	5	26	26	2	9	29	6	21	28	5
73	9	45	55	6	28	60	8	34	59	11
174		163	139	8	52	115	3	100	115	19
109	25	83	97	6	27	87	11	66	85	16
21	8	15	16	1	8	18	3	13	18	4
45	7	28	37	5	24	39	4	27	37	10
106	23	66	90	13	32	118	13	83	116	15
141	14	125	91	2	58	84	6	73	82	13

2-30 续表1

指 标	Item	电子商务销售额 E-business Sales Value	按销售方式分 Grouped by sales Method	
			通过自营平台 Self-managed platform	通过第三方电子商务平台 Third-party E-business Platfrom
合计	**Total**	**2996633**	**1288621.5**	**1384825.5**
按行业分	**Grouped by Industries**			
制造业	Manufacturing	2021088	551816.2	1164038.1
电力、热力、燃气及水生产和供应业	Production and Supply of Power, Fuel and Water	214.5		
建筑业	Construction	7876.9	1157	6434
批发和零售业	Wholesale and Retail Trades	861790.6	708226	144107.3
交通运输、仓储和邮政业	Transport, Storage and Post	32222.3	10172.8	16255.4
住宿和餐饮业	Hotel and Catering Services	8618.1	161.2	8198.9
信息传输、软件和信息技术服务业	Information Transmission,Computer Servivce and Software	22445.6	10199.3	12246.3
房地产业	Real Estate	22250.1	0.4	22249.7
租赁和商务服务业	Leasing and Commercial Service	15729.5	6572.6	8701.8
科学研究和技术服务业	Scientific Research and Technology Service	964.1	315	649.1
水利、环境和公共设施管理业	Management of Water Conservancy,Environment and Public Facility	24.9		24.9
居民服务、修理和其他服务业	Service for Residents, Maintenance and Other			
教育	Education			
卫生和社会工作	Heilith and Social Work	1487.4		
文化、体育和娱乐业	Culture, Sports and Entertainment	1921	1	1920
按地区分				
崇川区	Chongchuan	817512.9	720010.9	78454.1
港闸区	Gangzha	101444.4	16672.3	81037.6
通州区	Tongzhou	308984.7	118525.8	121746.2
海安县	Haian	350218.9		326259.9
如东县	Rudong	346192.2	90098.9	187128.6
开发区	Development Zone	82178.9	28508.7	50385.2
启东市	Rudong	285444.3	2864.9	255599.6
如皋市	Rugao	416506.4	305633.5	72638.6
海门市	Haimen	288150.3	6306.5	211575.7

CONTINUED 1

按销售对象分 Grouped by sales target			电子商务采购额 E-business Purchase Value	按采购方式分 Grouped by purchase way		按采购内容分 Grouped by Purchase object	
B2B	B2G	B2C		通过自营平台 Self-managed platform	通过第三方电子商务平台 Third-party E-business Platfrom	商品采购 Commodity Purchase	服务采购 Service Purchase
2484738.9	**78354**	**433540.1**	**2671889.8**	**1449566.1**	**1023689.6**	**2582831.7**	**89058.1**
1614165	73111.8	333811.2	1837504.3	887019.4	770191.3	1754734.9	82769.4
146.2		68.3	17679.2	6786.3	10000	17656.8	22.4
7341.9	170	365	70602.5	707.4	65674.4	70236.4	366.1
818435.2	4295.3	39060.1	691174.4	522622.3	157832.3	690404.6	769.8
22685.5	50.1	9486.7	8727.1		8726.2	5231.5	3495.6
2884.8	296.5	5436.8	1304.1	21	1201.1	1303.1	1
9519.2	426	12500.4	35638	30755.1	4882.9	35407.4	230.6
955.5	0	21294.6	581.9		531.4	118.7	463.2
7458.4	3.2	8267.9	5394.1	1602.6	3432.8	4516.2	877.9
917.1	1	46	3048.7	52	996.7	3007.7	41
		24.9					
			187		187	187	
		1487.4					
230.1	0.1	1690.8	48.5		33.5	27.4	21.1
784901.9	4555.9	28055.1	832669.2	797450.9	27682.6	828716.4	3952.8
93525.9	3155	4763.5	140967.1	15864.4	124285.2	140745	222.1
252743.5	2470.6	53770.6	201793.8	93091.8	65660.6	168632.7	33161.1
300812.4	3012.7	46393.8	274631.6	3590.7	263149.7	273450.1	1181.5
324258.8	1138.5	20794.9	175390.4	29622.8	126694.1	168657.5	6732.9
76326.4	3	5849.5	37651.4	16558.5	15205.7	37360.8	290.6
141764.8	61019.9	82659.6	485901.1	213606.2	203900.4	447379.4	38521.7
318933.7	2543.8	95028.9	335949.7	274772.2	41408.9	333035.6	2914.1
191471.5	454.6	96224.2	186935.5	5008.6	150702.4	184854.2	2081.3

2-31　规模以上服务业企业资产30强(2014年)

TOP 30 KEY SERVICE ENTERPRISES IN TERMS OF ASSETS(2014)

序号 No.	单位名称 Name of the Enterprises	地　址 Address
1	如皋市华玉新农村基础设施开发有限公司	如皋市长江镇长江东路8号
2	如皋沿江开发投资有限公司	如皋市长江镇海坝居委会
3	南通综艺投资有限公司	通州区兴东镇黄金村
4	如皋市交通投资发展有限公司	如皋市行政中心B座4楼
5	南通产业控股集团有限公司	崇川区工农路486号
6	江苏苏通大桥有限责任公司	开发区星湖大道1088号
7	南通沿海开发集团有限公司	崇川区工农南路150号政务中心综合楼十五层
8	江苏炜赋集团公司	开发区中央路29号星湖大厦
9	海安投资建设有限公司	海安县海安镇中坝南路12号建设大厦11楼育才社区
10	如皋市城建投资有限公司	如皋市如城镇宁海路2号
11	海安县城建开发投资有限责任公司	海安县海安镇中坝南路9号开发大厦5楼
12	江苏洋口港股份有限公司	如东县长沙镇洋口港开发区
13	江苏省吕四海洋经济开发区开发建设有限公司	启东市吕四港镇海洋经济开发区
14	南通国有置业集团有限公司	崇川区人民中路10号
15	启东滨海工业园开发有限公司	启东市滨海工业园
16	启东国有资产投资控股有限公司	启东市汇龙镇人民中路526号银洲大厦7楼
17	启东经济开发区总公司	启东市汇龙镇人民西路898号
18	启东江洲生态科技发展有限公司	启东市启隆生态产业园
19	中国电信股份有限公司南通分公司	崇川区环城南路88号
20	江苏文峰集团有限公司	崇川区青年东路1号
21	如皋港务集团有限公司	如皋市长江镇(如皋港区)疏港路6号
22	南通汽运实业集团有限公司	崇川区长江中路99号
23	中国移动通信集团江苏有限公司南通分公司	崇川区洪江路69号
24	江苏洋口港建设发展有限公司	如东县经济开发区
25	海安县交通建设投资有限公司	海安县海安镇江海西路1号
26	南通云地实业股份有限公司	港闸区永兴街道永兴村社区
27	南通港口集团有限公司	崇川区青年西路38号
28	南通汇仁劳务派遣有限公司	海安县城东镇南阳村15组103号
29	如皋港现代物流开发投资有限公司	如皋市长江镇长新街50号331-332室
30	南通创和实业股份有限公司	港闸区越江路口城港路28号城镇房地产10楼

2-32 规模以上服务业企业营业收入30强(2014年)

TOP 30 KEY SERVICE ENTERPRISES IN TERMS OF BUSINESS INCOME (2014)

序号 No.	单位名称 Name of the Enterprises	地址 Address
1	海安国龙物流有限公司	海安县城东镇长江东路2号701室
2	中国移动通信集团江苏有限公司南通分公司	南通市崇川区洪江路69号
3	中国电信股份有限公司南通分公司	崇川区环城南路88号
4	南通综艺投资有限公司	通州区兴东镇黄金村
5	林森物流集团有限公司	港闸区幸福街道秦西村16组
6	江苏苏通大桥有限责任公司	开发区星湖大道1088号
7	如皋沿江开发投资有限公司	如皋市长江镇海坝居委会
8	南通邮政局	崇川区人民中路83号
9	南通汽运实业集团有限公司	崇川区长江中路99号
10	南通港口集团有限公司	崇川区青年西路38号
11	南通潮盛投资有限公司	通州区平潮镇民主居
12	如皋市交通投资发展有限公司	如皋市行政中心B座4楼
13	中国联合网络通信有限公司南通市分公司	崇川区人民东路55号
14	南通丰源食品城有限公司	海安县城东镇迎宾路266号
15	海安亚太亿发物流有限公司	海安县城东镇三丰村9组
16	海门沿海投资发展有限公司	海门市滨海新区港西大道999号
17	南通东方石油化工储运有限公司	如皋市长江镇石化园区
18	中央储备粮如东直属库	如东县马塘镇潮桥街国库路1号
19	携程信息技术(南通)有限公司	开发区长川路1号
20	江苏远恒物流有限公司	海安县城东镇刘觖村5组
21	中国供销集团南通国际棉花有限公司	通州经济开发区南区锦绣路北希望大道西
22	南通好一家投资管理有限公司	开发区新开工业集中区
23	启东经济开发区科技创业中心有限公司	启东市经济开发区凯旋路1号
24	南通棉花现货交易有限公司	崇川开发区崇川路46号
25	南通五水投资发展有限公司	港闸区城港路118号
26	江苏叠石桥物流有限公司	海门市三星镇工贸园区
27	南通化学危险品运输有限公司	港闸区唐闸南市街103号
28	海门市港口发展有限责任公司	海门市海门镇静海路192号
29	江苏大唐航运股份有限公司	崇川区崇川路1号
30	启东市新城建设发展有限公司	启东市汇龙镇公园中路842号

2-33 规模以上服务业企业利税 30 强(2014 年)

TOP 30 KEY SERVICE ENTERPRISES IN TERMS OF PROFITS &TAXES(2014)

序号 No.	单 位 名 称 Name of the Enterprises	地 址 Address
1	中国移动通信集团江苏有限公司南通分公司	崇川区洪江路 69 号
2	海安国龙物流有限公司	海安县城东镇长江东路 2 号 701 室
3	如皋市交通投资发展有限公司	如皋市行政中心 B 座 4 楼
4	江苏苏通大桥有限责任公司	开发区星湖大道 1088 号
5	中国电信股份有限公司南通分公司	崇川区环城南路 88 号
6	如皋沿江开发投资有限公司	如皋市长江镇海坝居委会
7	南通综艺投资有限公司	通州区兴东镇黄金村
8	江苏文峰集团有限公司	崇川区青年东路 1 号
9	林森物流集团有限公司	港闸区幸福街道秦西村 16 组
10	海门沿海投资发展有限公司	海门市滨海新区港西大道 999 号
11	南通好一家投资管理有限公司	开发区新开工业集中区
12	南通港口集团有限公司	崇川区青年西路 38 号
13	海门市港口发展有限责任公司	海门市海门镇静海路 192 号
14	江苏叠石桥绣品城有限公司	海门市三星镇叠石桥大岛路 188 号
15	南通邮政局	崇川区人民中路 88 号
16	南通汽运实业集团有限公司	崇川区长江中路 99 号
17	达海投资有限公司	通州区世纪大道 999 号
18	启东国有资产投资控股有限公司	启东市汇龙镇人民中路 526 号银洲大厦 7 楼
19	如皋市城建投资有限公司	如皋市如城镇宁海路 2 号
20	中国联合网络通信有限公司南通市分公司	崇川区人民东路 55 号
21	启东市长江船舶工业投资发展有限公司	启东市汇龙镇人民中路 526 号
22	海门市鹏天交通建设有限责任公司	海门市海门镇静海路 192 号
23	中南控股集团有限公司	海门市常乐镇
24	海安亚太亿发物流有限公司	海安县城东镇三丰村 9 组
25	江苏骅东投资有限公司	启东市汇龙镇人民中路 888 号
26	江苏景瑞农业科技发展有限公司	南通市通州区东社镇新街村
27	海门市海天交通建设投资有限责任公司	海门市海门镇静海路 192 号
28	南通一德物流有限公司	开发区东方红农场内
29	海门市滨江建设发展有限公司	海门市海门镇解放中路文化弄 9 号
30	海门市三星叠石桥集贸市场服务所	海门市三星镇叠石村

主要统计指标解释

国内生产总值(GDP)　指按市场价格计算的一个国家(或地区)所有常住单位在一定时期内生产活动的最终成果。国内生产总值有三种表现形态,即价值形态、收入形态和产品形态。从价值形态看,它是所有常住单位在一定时期内生产的全部货物和服务价值与同期投入的全部非固定资产货物和服务价值的差额,即所有常住单位的增加值之和;从收入形态看,它是所有常住单位在一定时期内创造并分配给常住单位和非常住单位的初次收入之和;从产品形态看,它是所有常住单位在一定时期内最终使用的货物和服务价值与货物和服务净出口价值之和。在实际核算中,国内生产总值有三种计算方法,即生产法、收入法和支出法。三种方法分别从不同的方面反映国内生产总值及其构成。对于一个地区来说,称为地区生产总值或地区 GDP。

三次产业　三产业的划分是世界上较为常用的产业结构分类,但各国的划分不尽一致。我国的三次产业划分是:

第一产业　指农、林、牧、渔业(不含农、林、牧、渔服务业)。

第二产业　指采矿业(不含开采辅助活动),制造业(不含金属制品、机械和设备修理业),电力、热力、燃气及水生产和供应业,建筑业。

第三产业　指服务业,是指除第一产业、第二产业以外的其他行业。第三产业包括:批发和零售业,交通运输、仓储和邮政业,住宿和餐饮业,信息传输、软件和信息技术服务业,金融业,房地产业,租赁和商务服务业,科学研究和技术服务业,水利、环境和公共设施管理业,居民服务、修理和其他服务业,教育,卫生和社会工作,文化、体育和娱乐业,公共管理、社会保障和社会组织,国际组织,以及农、林、牧、渔业中的农、林、牧、渔服务业,采矿业中的开采辅助活动,制造业中的金属制品、机械和设备修理业。

劳动者报酬　指劳动者因从事生产活动所获得的全部报酬。包括劳动者获得的各种形式的工资、奖金和津贴,既包括货币形式的,也包括实物形式的,还包括劳动者所享受的公费医疗和医药卫生费、上下班交通补贴、单位支付的社会保险费、住房公积金等。

生产税净额　指生产税减生产补贴后的余额。生产税指政府对生产单位从事生产、销售和经营活动以及因从事生产活动使用某些生产要素(如固定资产、土地、劳动力)所征收的各种税、附加费和规费。生产补贴与生产税相反,指政府对生产单位的单方面转移支出,因此视为负生产税,包括政策亏损补贴、价格补贴等。

固定资产折旧　指一定时期内为弥补固定资产损耗按照规定的固定资产折旧率提取的固定资产折旧,或按国民经济核算统一规定的折旧率虚拟计算的固定资产折旧。它反映了固定资产在当期生产中的转移价值。各类企业和企业化管理的事业单位的固定资产折旧是指实际计提的折旧费;不计提折旧的政府机关、非企业化管理的事业单位和居民住房的固定资产折旧是按照统一规定的折旧率和固定资产原值计算的虚拟折旧。原则上,固定资产折旧应按固定资产的重置价值计算,但是目前我国尚不具备对全社会固定资产进行重估价的基础,所以暂时只能采用上述办法。

营业盈余　指常住单位创造的增加值扣除劳动者报酬、生产税净额和固定资产折旧后的余额。它相当于企业的营业利润加上生产补贴,但要扣除从利润中开支的工资和福利等。

规模以上服务业　辖区内年营业收入 1000 万元及以上,或年末从业人员 50 人及以上服务业法人单位。包括:交通运输、仓储和邮政业,信息传输、软件和信息技术服务业,租赁和商务服务业,科学研究和技术服务业,水利、环境和公共设施管理业,教育,卫生和社会工作;以及物业管理、房地产中介服务等行业。

辖区内年营业收入 500 万元及以上,或年末从业人员 50 人及以上服务业法人单位。包括:居民服务、修理和其他服务业,文化、体育和娱乐业。

联网直报企业　指规模以上工业、有资质的建筑业、限额以上批发和零售业、限额以上住宿和餐饮业、全部房地产开发经营业以及规模以上服务业法人单位。

计算机数　指报告期末企业(单位)使用的计算机数量,包括台式机、笔记本电脑和平板电脑。

信息技术人员　指专职从事信息技术系统的制定、设计、开发、安装、操作、维护、管理和评估的人员。

局域网(LAN)　指在局部区域,如单一建筑物、独立部门,连接计算机的网络,可以是无线网络。

信息化投入 包括企业(单位)一次性投入和运营维护投入。

一次性投入 包括企业(单位)购置各类硬件和软件的实际支出。

硬件投入 包括企业(单位)购置计算机、服务器、交换机等信息通信硬件设备的实际支出。

软件投入 包括企业(单位)购置计算机各种软件产品的实际支出。

运营维护投入 包括企业(单位)更新维护各类信息通信硬件和软件的实际支出。

互联网 指在世界范围内的公共计算机网络。它提供一系列通信服务(包括万维网)的接入,并传送电子邮件、新闻、娱乐和数据文件等。

固定宽带 指一个或两个方向速度至少为256kbit/s的技术,如DSL(数字用户线路)、电缆调制解调器、高速租用线路、光纤入户、输电线、微型、固定无线、无线局域网和WiMAX。

移动宽带 指一个或两个方向速度至少为256kbit/s的技术,如宽带CDMA(W-CDMA),可通过任何装置(如平板电脑、笔记本电脑或者移动电话等)接入。

网站数 指报告期末企业拥有和维护的,在互联网上可浏览的网站数,不包括企业内网。网站是指在公共互联网上,面向公众使用的,基于TCP/IP协议的计算机系统,以域名本身或者"WWW.+域名"为网址的web站点,由地址、软件、硬件和内容组成。

电子商务平台 是为企业(单位)或个人提供网上交易洽谈的平台,可提供网上交易和管理等全过程的服务,一般具有广告宣传、咨询洽谈、网上订购、网上支付、电子账户、服务传递、意见征询、交易管理等各项功能。

全年电子商务销售金额 指报告期内企业(单位)借助网络订单而销售的商品和服务总额。借助网络订单指通过网络接受订单,付款和配送可以不借助于网络。

全年电子商务采购金额 指报告期内企业(单位)借助网络订单而采购的商品和服务总额。借助网络订单指通过网络发送订单,付款和配送可以不借助于网络。

自营电子商务交易平台 指为企业自己开展电子商务交易活动提供服务的平台。

第三方电子商务交易平台 指为其他单位或个人开展电子商务交易活动提供服务的平台。

B2B交易 是指企业与企业之间实现的交易。

B2G交易 是指企业与政府或其他公共机构之间实现的交易。

B2C交易 是指企业与消费者个人之间实现的交易。

C2C交易 是指消费者与消费者之间实现的交易

第三方电子商务交易平台交易金额 报告期内买卖双方借助第三方电子商务交易平台生成网络订单实现的交易总金额。

第三篇

人口　就业

Chapter 3

Population and Employment

3-1 主要年份年末户籍总人口

单位：万人

年份 Year	全市 Municipaility	按地区分 Grouped by Districts						
		市区 Urban Area	通州区 Tongzhou	海安 Haian	如东 Rudong	启东 Qidong	如皋 Rugao	海门 Haimen
1949	464.52	113.71	94.28	60.93	69.97	60.79	94.30	64.82
1952	495.80	124.92	102.55	64.33	74.92	65.24	99.00	67.39
1957	550.45	139.27	114.08	72.34	82.54	77.04	105.63	73.63
1962	567.51	142.57	115.02	72.59	84.84	83.94	107.51	76.06
1965	610.44	153.48	125.29	76.69	91.67	91.41	114.62	82.57
1970	682.26	170.03	140.69	86.80	102.80	101.79	128.86	91.98
1975	710.22	178.07	146.09	90.07	106.06	106.67	133.82	95.53
1980	729.11	185.09	148.15	92.35	107.83	109.69	136.59	97.56
1986	749.07	193.04	151.08	94.89	109.82	112.55	139.07	99.70
1990	776.01	202.19	156.51	98.09	112.78	115.86	144.68	102.41
1991	778.84	203.27	145.38	98.36	113.04	116.26	145.10	102.81
1992	779.86	204.11	145.66	98.51	113.21	116.33	144.73	102.97
1993	781.20	205.34	145.64	98.69	113.36	116.44	144.42	102.95
1994	782.43	206.09	145.89	98.85	113.31	116.41	144.67	103.10
1995	784.24	206.76	145.86	99.00	113.46	116.41	145.18	103.43
1996	785.24	207.78	145.57	99.00	113.20	116.66	145.14	103.46
1997	786.30	208.83	145.60	99.16	112.90	116.79	145.37	103.25
1998	787.49	209.20	145.23	98.90	112.52	116.54	146.55	103.78
1999	785.99	209.39	144.66	98.48	112.09	116.13	146.21	103.69
2000	784.53	209.42	144.28	98.18	111.50	116.19	145.67	103.57
2001	782.46	209.73	130.19	97.76	110.89	115.67	145.28	103.13
2002	780.26	210.44	129.21	97.27	110.11	115.13	144.56	102.75
2003	777.62	211.14	128.13	96.54	109.36	114.38	143.87	102.33
2004	773.79	211.52	127.14	95.98	108.46	113.40	142.61	101.82
2005	770.86	211.61	126.25	95.33	107.68	112.87	142.01	101.36
2006	769.79	212.28	125.64	95.03	107.14	112.44	141.85	101.05
2007	766.13	212.14	124.89	94.19	106.30	111.84	141.01	100.65
2008	763.72	211.79	124.27	93.81	105.67	111.41	140.92	100.12
2009	762.66	211.54	124.16	93.68	105.30	111.58	140.72	99.84
2010	762.92	211.54	124.64	93.42	104.84	112.05	141.21	99.86
2011	764.88	211.70	125.26	93.72	104.80	112.41	142.26	99.99
2012	765.20	211.88	125.74	93.87	104.60	112.38	142.50	99.97
2013	766.51	212.31	126.27	94.18	104.38	112.36	143.23	100.06
2014	767.63	212.83	126.66	94.26	104.37	112.32	143.69	100.16

REGISTERED POPULATION AT YEAR-END OF MAIN YEARS

(Unit:10,000 persons)

按性别分 Grouped by Gender		按农业、非农业分 Grouped by Agriculture and Non-agriculture		年平均人口 Annual Average Population	户平均人口(人) Average Household Population	人口密度 (人/km²) Population Density
男性 Male	女性 Female	农业人口 Agricultural Population	非农业人口 Non-agricultural Population			
228.47	236.05	430.18	34.45		3.89	581
244.79	251.01	463.23	32.57	491.18	3.91	620
272.57	277.88	505.89	44.56	545.78	3.95	688
280.34	287.17	526.02	41.49	559.77	3.70	709
303.28	307.16	567.44	43.00	602.91	3.91	763
338.63	343.63	642.54	39.72	675.45	4.03	853
354.18	356.04	663.70	46.52	707.59	3.90	888
363.81	365.30	669.09	60.02	727.72	3.69	911
376.75	372.32	599.70	149.73	746.90	3.38	936
390.61	385.40	622.62	153.39	773.28	3.06	969
392.08	386.76	623.17	155.67	777.43	3.03	972
392.64	387.22	618.21	161.65	779.35	3.00	974
393.16	388.04	590.07	191.13	780.53	2.99	975
393.34	389.09	578.96	203.47	781.82	2.99	977
394.02	390.22	572.63	211.61	783.34	2.97	979
393.91	391.33	545.00	240.24	784.74	2.97	980
393.56	392.75	541.94	244.36	785.77	2.97	982
393.84	393.65	540.28	247.21	786.90	2.96	983
392.74	393.25	537.53	248.46	786.74	2.93	981
391.57	392.96	531.94	252.59	785.26	2.89	979
390.11	392.35	524.70	257.76	783.50	2.88	977
388.80	391.46	517.45	262.81	781.36	2.84	975
387.21	390.41	542.70	234.92	778.94	2.81	971
384.97	388.82	533.17	240.62	775.70	2.79	967
383.20	387.66	523.70	247.16	772.33	2.77	963
382.47	387.32	505.49	264.30	770.33	2.76	962
380.12	386.01	474.20	291.93	767.96	2.74	958
378.56	385.16	442.12	321.60	764.93	2.72	955
377.60	385.06	405.01	357.65	763.19	2.73	953
377.37	385.55	403.76	359.16	762.79	2.69	954
378.01	386.87	398.17	366.71	763.90	2.71	956
377.78	387.42	390.37	374.83	765.04	2.72	956
378.07	388.44	385.03	381.48	765.86	2.71	958
378.28	389.35	373.83	393.80	767.07	2.71	959

3-2 主要年份年末总户数

TOTAL NUMBER OF HOUSEHOLDS OF MAIN YEARS

单位：万户 (Unit: 10,000 households)

年份 Year	全市 Municipaility	市区 Urban Area	通州区 Tongzhou	海安 Haian	如东 Rudong	启东 Qidong	如皋 Rugao	海门 Haimen
1949	119.61	28.55	24.30	15.41	18.93	15.49	22.72	18.51
1952	126.85	32.29	27.42	15.56	20.02	16.70	23.32	18.96
1957	139.41	36.80	31.43	17.01	22.04	18.33	25.25	19.98
1962	153.45	38.80	33.01	19.42	24.43	22.23	27.78	20.79
1965	156.23	39.30	33.35	19.54	24.61	23.00	27.93	21.85
1970	169.15	42.51	36.26	20.78	27.12	25.70	29.39	23.65
1975	182.06	46.72	39.10	22.25	28.54	28.29	31.04	25.22
1978	193.28	49.50	41.35	23.63	30.85	30.41	32.34	26.55
1980	197.39	50.57	41.87	24.15	30.60	31.51	32.69	27.87
1985	220.33	56.46	45.12	29.92	31.82	37.12	34.17	30.84
1990	253.96	67.29	53.50	30.67	37.42	42.70	40.73	35.15
1991	257.10	68.34	49.90	30.64	37.63	43.57	41.39	35.53
1992	259.91	69.28	50.07	31.00	38.14	44.19	41.48	35.82
1993	261.40	69.83	50.32	30.81	38.07	44.56	41.70	36.43
1994	261.92	70.43	50.78	30.75	38.05	44.71	42.02	35.96
1995	264.29	70.81	51.00	31.94	38.21	44.78	42.32	36.23
1996	264.73	70.19	50.06	32.20	37.78	45.28	42.50	36.78
1997	264.53	71.02	50.50	32.20	37.51	45.20	42.75	35.85
1998	266.03	72.06	51.31	31.95	37.72	44.58	43.47	36.25
1999	268.45	72.85	51.71	32.39	37.94	45.16	43.69	36.42
2000	271.25	73.70	52.27	33.04	38.23	45.98	43.62	36.68
2001	271.64	74.26	47.38	31.59	38.30	46.25	44.50	36.74
2002	274.77	75.60	47.64	32.93	38.12	46.33	44.58	37.21
2003	276.33	76.73	47.90	33.03	38.19	46.53	44.63	37.22
2004	277.47	77.53	48.09	33.08	38.13	46.71	44.56	37.46
2005	278.72	78.21	48.20	33.23	38.07	46.90	44.64	37.67
2006	278.77	77.18	46.67	33.52	38.02	47.38	44.82	37.85
2007	279.47	77.40	46.58	33.73	37.77	47.66	44.91	38.00
2008	280.74	79.60	48.48	33.99	37.82	45.86	45.23	38.24
2009	279.03	80.03	48.62	34.36	37.80	46.02	45.46	35.36
2010	283.17	80.23	48.47	34.75	37.72	46.30	45.77	38.40
2011	282.76	80.12	48.12	34.72	37.60	46.18	45.79	38.35
2012	281.22	79.69	47.64	34.47	37.46	45.82	45.48	38.30
2013	283.35	79.79	47.34	37.04	37.31	45.55	45.31	38.37
2014	283.35	82.19	49.84	34.19	37.06	45.37	45.32	38.49

3-3 主要年份人口自然变动情况

NATURAL CHANGE OF POPULATION OF MAIN YEARS

年份 Year	出 生 Birth		死 亡 Death		自然增长 Natural Growth	
	人数(人) Number of People(person)	出生率(‰) Birth Rate(‰)	人数(人) Number of People(person)	死亡率(‰) Death Rate(‰)	人数(人) Number of People(person)	自然增长率(‰) Natural Growth Rate(‰)
1957	179009	32.80	55237	10.12	123772	22.68
1962	166863	29.81	62514	11.17	104349	18.64
1965	223477	37.07	62057	10.29	161420	26.78
1970	181998	26.94	48560	7.19	133438	19.75
1975	94524	13.36	47295	6.68	47229	6.68
1978	88559	12.29	44127	6.12	44432	6.17
1980	72334	9.94	46684	6.42	25650	3.52
1985	71852	9.66	49415	6.64	22437	3.02
1986	95827	12.83	50364	6.74	45463	6.09
1987	115612	15.37	50755	6.75	64857	8.62
1988	113077	14.90	50055	6.59	63022	8.31
1989	125607	16.40	49661	6.50	75946	9.90
1990	114386	14.80	53979	7.00	60407	7.80
1991	87344	11.24	52128	6.71	35216	4.53
1992	78299	10.05	55432	7.11	22867	2.94
1993	79556	10.19	54597	6.99	24959	3.20
1994	79493	10.17	54751	7.00	24742	3.17
1995	81255	10.37	56201	7.17	25054	3.20
1996	70655	9.00	55610	7.09	15045	1.91
1997	68241	8.68	54783	6.97	13458	1.71
1998	72031	9.15	59291	7.53	12740	1.62
1999	59235	7.53	56459	7.18	2776	0.35
2000	69090	8.80	55954	7.12	13136	1.68
2001	51825	6.61	51340	6.55	485	0.06
2002	52483	6.72	54143	6.93	−1660	−0.21
2003	44876	5.76	56353	7.23	−11477	−1.47
2004	50863	6.56	58808	7.58	−7945	−1.02
2005	49274	6.38	57628	7.46	−8354	−1.08
2006	48886	6.35	55143	7.16	−6257	−0.81
2007	46715	6.08	59656	7.77	−12941	−1.69
2008	45825	5.99	58063	7.59	−12238	−1.60
2009	47646	6.24	59162	7.75	−11516	−1.51
2010	53385	7.00	60138	7.88	−6753	−0.88
2011	51665	6.8	58864	7.71	−7199	−0.9
2012	56647	7.4	67708	8.85	−11061	−1.45
2013	54137	7.07	61249	8.00	−7112	−0.93
2014	57826	7.54	62098	8.10	−4272	−0.56

3-4 分乡、镇、街道人口基本情况

单位：人

地　区	Region	年末总户数(户) Total Number of Households at Year-end (household)	年末总人口 Total Population at Year-end	男性 Male	女性 Female	非农业人口 Non-agricultural population
南通市区	**Urban Area of Nantong**	**821818**	**2128278**	**1041786**	**1086492**	**1357410**
崇川区	**Chongchuan**	**248892**	**669458**	**328842**	**340616**	**669424**
学田街办	Xuetian Subdistrict	12879	37127	18311	18816	37127
虹桥街办	Hongqiao Subdistrict	23587	69577	34518	35059	69577
新城桥街办	Xincheng Subdistrict	15208	41469	20282	21187	41469
城东街办	Chengdong Subdistrict	24135	67713	33336	34377	67713
任港街办	Rengang Subdistrict	20841	58235	29516	28719	58235
和平桥街办	Hepingqiao Subdistrict	21979	62801	30725	32076	62801
文峰街办	Wenfeng Subdistrict	20362	52204	25387	26817	52204
钟秀街办	Zhongxiu Subdistrict	10820	26684	12804	13880	26684
中兴街办	Zhongxing Subdistrict	8948	24450	11986	12464	24442
南通农场	Nantong Farm	6531	17527	8589	8938	17522
新开镇	Xinkai	15597	39292	19704	19588	39280
狼山镇	Langshan	15567	40808	19817	20991	40808
小海镇	Xiaohai	15455	35807	17369	18438	35800
竹行镇	Zhuhang	13737	31166	15172	15994	31164
观音山镇	Guanyinshan	23244	64349	31187	33162	64349
其他	Others	2	249	139	110	249
港闸区	**Gangzha**	**74555**	**192236**	**93408**	**98828**	**192236**
永兴街办	Yongxing Subdistrict	13337	30881	15114	15767	30881
陈桥街办	Chenqiao Subdistrict	11132	29036	14083	14953	29036
幸福街办	Xingfu Subdistrict	9124	25211	12162	13049	25211
天生港镇街办	Tianshenggang Subdistrict	15355	38766	18704	20062	38766
唐闸镇街办	Tangzha Subdistrict	16956	43879	21603	22276	43879
秦灶镇街办	Qinzao Subdistrict	8651	24463	11742	12721	24463

BASIC STATISTICS OF POPULATION BY TOWNSHIP, TOWN AND SUBDISTRICT

(Unit:person)

出生人数 Birth	男性 Male	女性 Female	死亡人数 Death Toll	男性 Male	女性 Female	年初总人口 Total Population at Year-beginning
18744	**9512**	**9232**	**16849**	**9154**	**7695**	**2123120**
6221	**3247**	**2974**	**3937**	**2236**	**1701**	**669071**
280	146	134	145	91	54	38114
481	232	249	351	202	149	71494
300	170	130	234	145	89	41477
524	285	239	358	212	146	67616
477	251	226	336	188	148	58629
480	241	239	350	200	150	63819
660	336	324	259	153	106	50671
242	129	113	162	78	84	26095
278	142	136	148	79	69	24142
146	74	72	140	88	52	17475
490	250	240	232	133	99	38820
338	187	151	284	146	138	41615
424	214	210	259	138	121	35561
270	144	126	246	128	118	31272
831	446	385	432	254	178	61941
0	0	0	1	1	0	330
1714	**844**	**870**	**1679**	**917**	**762**	**191380**
336	149	187	210	120	90	30646
243	111	132	297	153	134	29075
232	117	115	237	124	113	25129
265	139	126	407	212	195	38867
372	188	184	345	200	145	43536
266	140	126	183	98	85	24127

3-4 续表 1

单位:人

地 区	Region	年末总户数(户) Total Number of Households at Year-end (household)	年末总人口 Total Population at Year-end	男性 Male	女性 Female	非农业人口 Non-agricultural population
通州区	**Tongzhou**	**498371**	**1266584**	**619536**	**647048**	**495750**
金沙镇	Jinsha	107416	271680	132973	138707	144116
西亭镇	Xiting	16688	44531	21810	22721	16622
二甲镇	Erjia	30534	71956	35453	36503	21967
东社镇	Dongshe	21320	60993	30425	30568	16489
三余镇	Sanyu	48284	126897	62310	64587	34953
十总镇	Shizong	14041	36203	17773	18430	15509
骑岸镇	Qi´an	19733	47987	23499	24488	10452
五甲镇	Wujia	11300	32667	16249	16418	10262
石港镇	Shigang	27994	67879	33067	34812	21240
四安镇	Si´an	14665	39867	19385	20482	12218
刘桥镇	Liuqiao	27803	76351	37165	39186	30142
平潮镇	Pingchao	28237	78766	38188	40578	36794
平东镇	Pingdong	15729	44263	21578	22685	13837
五接镇	Wujie	14788	38797	19087	19710	17483
兴仁镇	Xingren	18514	44274	21294	22980	15537
兴东镇	Xingdong	11787	32683	15768	16915	10996
张芝山镇	Zhangzhishan	25868	55137	26874	28263	28573
先锋镇	Xianfeng	16495	37007	18158	18849	11590
川姜镇	Chuanjiang	27175	58646	28480	30166	26970

CONTINUED 1

(Unit:person)

出生人数 Birth	男性 Male	女性 Female	死亡人数 Death Toll	男性 Male	女性 Female	年初总人口 Total Population at Year-beginning
10809	**5421**	**5388**	**11233**	**6001**	**5232**	**1262669**
2641	1296	1345	1940	1091	849	269960
343	173	170	493	274	219	44475
572	288	284	662	329	333	71819
494	245	249	552	290	262	60932
909	442	467	1088	538	550	126880
236	126	110	365	194	171	36247
295	164	131	495	264	231	47986
270	143	127	302	164	138	32642
453	232	221	736	402	334	67957
282	151	131	423	225	197	39803
591	288	303	758	389	369	76211
705	339	366	700	370	330	78680
355	169	186	416	220	196	43987
399	204	195	306	171	135	38571
388	193	195	427	220	207	43911
310	173	137	303	175	128	32493
445	216	229	501	255	246	55153
443	229	214	267	160	107	36670
678	350	328	499	269	230	58292

3-4 续表 2

单位：人

地　区	Region	年末总户数(户) Total Number of Households at Year-end (household)	年末总人口 Total Population at Year-end	男性 Male	女性 Female	非农业人口 Non-agricultural population
海安县	**Hai´an**	**341914**	**942630**	**467035**	**475595**	**588817**
海安镇	Hai´an	102917	274022	135592	138430	274022
雅周镇	Yazhou	22193	58730	29349	29381	12087
角斜镇	Jiaoxie	22213	66777	32851	33926	16650
李堡镇	Libao	29206	81595	40219	41376	48390
白甸镇	Baidian	11696	31917	15937	15980	6657
墩头镇	Duntou	24429	65419	32697	32722	13060
南莫镇	Nanmo	20238	53063	26579	26484	17588
曲塘镇	Qutang	36497	96460	47985	48475	58275
大公镇	Dagong	23187	64797	32180	32617	17232
城东镇	Chengdong	49338	149850	73646	76204	124856

CONTINUED 2

(Unit:person)

出生人数 Birth	男性 Male	女性 Female	死亡人数 Death Toll	男性 Male	女性 Female	年初总人口 Total Population at Year-beginning
5966	**3120**	**2846**	**7526**	**4036**	**3490**	**941794**
2051	1085	966	1637	889	748	271774
269	142	127	595	323	272	58960
535	289	246	636	342	294	66820
465	234	231	747	398	349	81905
120	64	56	269	154	115	32007
339	162	177	604	336	268	65810
208	111	97	513	262	251	53364
573	303	270	876	473	403	96918
328	172	156	552	290	262	65059
1078	558	520	1097	569	528	149177

3-4 续表3

单位:人

地 区	Region	年末总户数(户) Total Number of Households at Year-end (household)	年末总人口 Total Population at Year-end	男性 Male	女性 Female	非农业人口 Non-agricultural population
如东县	**Rudong**	**370623**	**1043668**	**513757**	**529911**	**190434**
掘港镇	Juegang	79045	213599	105068	108531	65640
长沙镇	Changsha	13335	38272	18794	19478	1565
大豫镇	Dayu	38979	102183	50173	52010	5919
袁庄镇	Yuanzhuang	18277	58363	28805	29558	3343
河口镇	Hekou	21368	63738	31100	32638	15316
岔河镇	Chahe	27881	82155	40290	41865	30166
新店镇	Xindian	13687	37456	18365	19091	7371
双甸镇	Shuangdian	23338	72667	35697	36970	6946
马塘镇	Matang	29420	80147	39846	40301	16312
曹埠镇	Caofu	16961	46915	23198	23717	1775
丰利镇	Fengli	29226	80899	39810	41089	9517
苴 镇	Juzhen	13084	36935	18389	18546	2544
栟茶镇	Bengcha	20490	57375	28141	29234	21392
洋口镇	Yangkou	25532	72964	36081	36883	2628
启东市	**Qidong**	**453653**	**1123163**	**550406**	**572757**	**322667**
汇龙镇	Huilong	96499	251930	123685	128245	251930
南阳镇	Nanyang	43146	104888	51585	53303	9257
北新镇	Beixin	30931	74203	36307	37896	4781
王鲍镇	Wangbao	36271	91029	44566	46463	5353
合作镇	Hezuo	26070	63850	31373	32477	6943
吕四镇	Lvsi	69871	178422	87203	91219	17857
海复镇	Haifu	22217	55686	27279	28407	5194
近海镇	Jinhai	26065	62951	30786	32165	3092
寅阳镇	Yingyang	31206	75860	37052	38808	8817
惠萍镇	Huiping	39315	91271	44423	46848	4773
东海镇	Donghai	30083	69198	34063	35135	4670
启隆乡	Qilong	1979	3875	2084	1791	0

CONTINUED 3

(Unit:person)

出生人数 Birth	男性 Male	女性 Female	死亡人数 Death Toll	男性 Male	女性 Female	年初总人口 Total Population at Year-beginning
6341	**3217**	**3124**	**9659**	**5262**	**4397**	**1043811**
1541	763	778	1674	907	767	211797
247	129	118	340	191	149	38376
461	228	233	909	475	433	102584
341	171	170	532	302	230	58415
413	220	193	607	318	289	63763
521	281	240	818	439	379	82204
224	120	104	371	214	157	37622
570	297	273	706	369	337	72649
401	199	202	825	481	344	80610
260	118	142	445	249	196	47033
472	228	244	766	428	338	81112
205	105	100	358	196	162	37107
272	146	126	506	264	242	57302
413	212	201	802	428	374	73237
8101	**4137**	**3964**	**8121**	**4251**	**3870**	**1123545**
2399	1224	1175	1344	758	586	248630
718	388	330	1042	529	513	105568
557	290	267	539	278	261	74398
532	264	268	671	335	336	91835
445	213	232	469	238	231	64412
1216	631	585	1328	694	634	178224
304	152	152	398	201	197	56008
389	197	192	467	245	222	63247
495	244	251	580	300	280	76248
665	336	329	751	409	342	91362
362	191	171	511	251	260	69764
19	7	12	21	13	8	3849

3-4 续表 4

单位:人

地 区	Region	年末总户数(户) Total Number of Households at Year-end (household)	年末总人口 Total Population at Year-end	男性 Male	女性 Female	非农业人口 Non-agricultural population
如皋市	**Rugao**	**453234**	**1436920**	**716818**	**720102**	**901000**
如城镇街道办事处	Rucheng	59749	183348	89910	93438	183348
东陈镇	Dongchen	26506	81147	39963	41184	40018
丁堰镇	Dingyan	16521	52744	25778	26966	31980
白蒲镇	Baipu	37492	123326	60591	62735	63954
下原镇	Xiayuan	16921	59848	29807	30041	34762
九华镇	Jiuhua	22287	70659	34906	35753	28741
石庄镇	Shizhuang	25503	85744	43446	42298	45936
长江镇	Changjiang	51306	139366	68972	70394	119671
吴窑镇	Wuyao	19260	65383	33270	32113	32563
江安镇	Jiang´an	37008	120458	62000	58458	60067
搬经镇	Banjing	43756	139395	70518	68877	79670
磨头镇	Motou	24620	82877	42098	40779	31683
城北街道办事处	Chengbei Subdistrict	54073	168067	83428	84639	108744
城南街道办事处	Chengnan Subdistrict	18232	64558	32131	32427	39863

注:学岸镇和东陈镇合并;林梓镇和白蒲镇合并;长江镇和郭园镇合并;江安和高明镇一部分;搬经镇和高明镇一部分合并;城北街道办事处是袁桥镇和柴湾镇合并;城南街道办事处是桃园和部分村镇合并;石庄镇和常青镇一部分合并。

Note: Xuean is now part of Dongchen; Lizi part of Baipu; Guoyuan part of Changjiang part of Gaoming belongs to Jiangan, the other part belongs to Banjing; Yuangiao and Chaiwan merger to Chengbei Subdistrict, Tiaoyuan and some other towns merger to Chennan Subdistrict, part of Changqing belongs to Shizhang now.

CONTINUED 4

(pUnit:person)

出生人数 Birth	男性 Male	女性 Female	死亡人数 Death Toll	男性 Male	女性 Female	年初总人口 Total Population at Year-beginning
11465	**5870**	**5595**	**11849**	**6616**	**5233**	**1432253**
1613	838	775	1188	688	500	181539
519	245	274	785	429	356	81326
363	190	173	442	251	191	52840
941	477	464	1111	596	515	123357
418	217	201	547	294	253	59714
509	243	266	616	329	287	70525
598	330	268	645	365	279	85577
1150	590	560	1002	596	406	138892
464	239	225	505	282	223	65124
1120	569	551	1186	701	485	119541
1105	582	523	1148	608	540	139225
856	431	425	847	452	395	82771
1282	650	632	1243	714	529	167325
527	269	258	584	310	274	64497

3-4 续表 5

单位:人

地　区	Region	年末总户数(户) Total Number of Households at Year-end (household)	年末总人口 Total Population at Year-end	男性 Male	女性 Female	非农业人口 Non-agricultural population
海门市	**Haimen**	**384900**	**1001634**	**492951**	**508683**	**577651**
海门镇	Haimen	82643	223698	108967	114731	223698
三星镇	Sanxing	36723	93116	45727	47389	93116
三场街道办事处	Sanchang	19674	53242	26066	27176	53242
常乐镇	Changle	30869	76902	38012	38890	4030
悦来镇	Yuelai	43106	107534	53347	54187	6670
四甲镇	Sijia	32037	86168	42982	43186	10090
包场镇	Baochang	55456	145589	72028	73561	94235
余东镇	Yudong	23963	63280	31177	32103	4898
正余镇	Zhengyu	22834	61413	30208	31205	2519
临江镇	Linjiang	21606	53258	26070	27188	53258
海永乡	Haiyong	2439	5539	2663	2876	0
江心沙农场	Jiangxinsha Farm	2419	5979	2901	3078	5979
滨江街道办事处	Binjiang Subdistrict	11131	25916	12803	13113	25916

注:德胜镇并入工业园区;麒麟镇并入常乐镇;万年镇和三阳镇并入悦来镇;货隆镇并入四平镇;王浩镇并入正余镇,树勋镇并入余东镇;刘浩镇、包场镇并入海门滨江街道办事处。

Note:Desheng is now part of the Industrial Park; Qilin part of Changle; Wannian and Sanyang part of Yuelai; Huolong part of Siping; Wanghao part of Zhengyu; Shuxun part of Yudong; Liuhao and Baochang part of Bingjian Shbdistric.

CONTINUED 5

(Unit:person)

出生人数 Birth	男性 Male	女性 Female	死亡人数 Death Toll	男性 Male	女性 Female	年初总人口 Total Population at Year-beginning
7209	**3663**	**3546**	**8094**	**4330**	**3764**	**1000580**
1924	967	957	1067	547	520	221605
690	344	346	770	377	393	93116
351	180	171	473	255	218	53497
388	190	198	795	411	384	77368
655	336	319	1041	571	470	107928
597	301	296	819	430	389	86395
1171	626	545	1133	653	480	145227
413	214	199	607	313	294	63330
447	228	219	533	288	245	61354
317	148	169	541	321	220	53481
58	29	29	49	24	25	5470
40	19	21	43	24	19	5959
158	81	77	223	116	107	25850

3-5 历年全社会从业人员

STATISTCS ON EMPLOYMENT BY SECTOR OVER THE YEARS

单位：万人 (10,000 persons)

年份 Year	从业人员 Employment	第一产业 Primary Industry	第二产业 Secondary Industry	工业 Industry	第三产业 Tertiary Industry
1978	400.62	306.68	56.74		37.20
1979	406.64	309.28	58.58		38.78
1980	413.95	302.06	67.77		44.12
1985	457.54	242.72	139.71	106.96	75.11
1990	477.47	242.88	154.92	113.58	79.67
1991	485.38	251.49	154.36	113.10	79.53
1992	487.44	248.46	151.83	108.45	87.15
1993	491.60	243.00	157.00	110.10	91.60
1994	492.70	239.30	159.20	109.90	94.20
1995	489.40	226.40	164.60	111.20	98.40
1996	476.80	209.90	164.30	109.50	102.60
1997	481.20	208.30	164.50	106.90	108.40
1998	459.84	205.66	148.62	92.17	105.56
1999	446.26	203.88	138.69	81.96	103.69
2000	441.46	200.04	138.39	80.20	103.03
2001	426.33	195.55	136.88	76.74	93.90
2002	432.04	185.02	140.24	78.67	106.78
2003	430.87	172.07	160.14	92.46	98.66
2004	432.69	158.45	171.19	100.45	103.05
2005	444.40	133.93	178.30	108.31	132.17
2006	449.45	108.22	190.99	119.15	150.24
2007	457.23	97.36	203.63	126.98	156.24
2008	454.90	90.45	200.96	128.87	163.49
2009	460.52	84.77	207.20	131.32	168.55
2010	474.00	125.50	211.10	133.74	137.40
2011	473.00	121.70	212.80	135.23	138.50
2012	468.90	114.50	214.10	138.00	140.30
2013	467.20	107.30	216.60	138.00	143.30
2014	462.00	101.70	216.00		144.30

注：2010年起从业人员口径有调整。

Note:The Caliber of employee adjusted since 2010.

3-6 主要年份职工年末人数

NUMBER OF STAFF AND WORKERS AT YEAR-END OF MAIN YEARS

单位：万人 (Units:10000 persons)

年份 Year	全市 Municipaility	市区 Urban Areas	通州区 Tongzhou	海安 Haian	如东 Rudong	启东 Qidong	如皋 Rugao	海门 Haimen
1978	51.13	23.52	8.72	5.07	5.65	5.55	7.00	4.34
1979	53.84	25.12	8.99	4.81	6.02	5.89	7.19	4.81
1980	57.89	26.45	9.08	5.15	6.91	6.11	7.66	5.61
1985	72.26	33.26	10.61	6.83	8.57	7.52	9.13	6.95
1990	84.93	39.07	12.42	8.65	10.02	8.83	10.12	8.23
1991	86.97	39.40	12.12	8.84	10.45	9.19	10.56	8.53
1992	87.26	39.04	12.20	8.91	10.25	9.37	10.73	8.96
1993	87.34	40.21	12.30	9.15	9.73	9.29	10.56	8.40
1994	87.16	40.16	12.24	9.33	9.74	9.01	10.53	8.39
1995	87.17	39.82	11.59	9.35	9.51	9.26	10.64	8.59
1996	83.47	37.43	10.93	9.62	9.33	8.93	10.15	8.01
1997	81.02	35.55	10.25	9.66	9.19	8.83	10.11	7.68
1998	69.08	30.65	8.99	7.82	7.95	7.96	8.00	6.70
1999	65.73	29.45	8.74	7.27	7.49	7.74	7.38	6.41
2000	62.59	28.07	8.40	6.93	6.91	7.72	7.07	5.90
2001	56.74	26.13	5.99	5.52	6.11	6.85	6.43	5.70
2002	51.12	24.61	5.42	5.27	5.01	5.26	5.61	5.35
2003	50.71	24.45	5.24	5.44	5.17	5.32	5.11	5.23
2004	50.94	24.43	5.44	5.46	5.22	5.47	5.06	5.29
2005	53.29	25.28	5.57	5.78	5.25	5.81	5.50	5.68
2006	54.97	25.66	6.74	6.03	5.54	5.85	5.96	5.94
2007	57.74	26.51	6.92	7.06	5.91	5.87	6.21	6.18
2008	57.55	26.25	6.91	6.76	6.23	5.85	6.23	6.23
2009	58.17	26.97	6.95	6.55	6.21	5.75	6.10	6.60
2010	58.96	27.67	7.41	6.41	6.53	5.79	6.08	6.48
2011	63.04	30.01	7.63	7.01	6.87	6.53	6.16	6.46
2012	64.95	30.79	7.56	7.40	6.81	7.06	6.36	6.53
2013	146.81	39.53	19.38	13.90	17.77	21.48	25.01	29.12
2014	157.88	44.30	20.41	18.97	17.96	22.56	21.40	32.69

注：自 1998 年起为在岗职工年末人数。

Notes:Number of Employed Staff and Workers at Year-end since 1998.

3-7 主要年份职工平均工资

单位:元 (Units:Yuan)

年份 Year	全 市 Municipaility	市区 Urban Areas	通州区 Tongzhou
1978	496	520	462
1979	543	572	508
1980	634	669	581
1985	1042	1133	1019
1986	1260	1364	1158
1987	1429	1551	1341
1988	1683	1809	1493
1989	1771	1911	1661
1990	1984	2172	1809
1991	2125	2326	1905
1992	2593	2857	2307
1993	3346	3838	3170
1994	4781	5358	4559
1995	5779	6406	5311
1996	6232	6954	6111
1997	6664	7529	6506
1998	7438	8474	7009
1999	8310	9614	7913
2000	9247	10810	8811
2001	10588	12243	10057
2002	12110	14073	11677
2003	13547	15747	13195
2004	15901	18534	15217
2005	18513	21394	17589
2006	21662	24649	20735
2007	25947	28766	24884
2008	30856	34136	29013
2009	35224	38763	32451
2010	39448	43500	36664
2011	44574	47771	43479
2012	49399	52572	47781
2013	57546	57560	53413
2014	61383	61910	60197

注:自 1998 年起为在岗职工平均工资。

Notes:Average Wage of Employed Staff and Workers since 1998.

AVERAGE WAGE OF STAFF AND WORKERS IN MAIN YEARS

单位：元 (Units:Yuan)

海安 Haian	如东 Rudong	启东 Qidong	如皋 Rugao	海门 Haimen
491	453	510	455	469
493	493	532	486	612
590	574	606	587	689
960	956	1051	965	1021
1155	1145	1223	1143	1209
1316	1283	1396	1280	1390
1610	1493	1668	1520	1609
1730	1518	1776	1590	1677
1907	1746	1927	1741	1833
2032	1894	2006	1871	2012
2323	2372	2437	2267	2509
2864	2894	3036	2766	3106
4224	4390	4550	3965	4366
5009	5271	5485	5039	5473
5249	5889	5902	5142	6130
5785	6297	6092	5448	6421
6014	6779	6917	6345	7071
6735	7292	7531	7031	7687
7300	7868	8176	7872	8690
8706	8978	9146	9086	10039
10532	10240	9977	10171	11016
11550	11622	6692	11288	12370
13746	13189	12354	13036	15204
16462	15548	14680	15252	17576
19825	18436	18011	17937	20833
24422	22598	22346	22594	25491
28564	27402	26680	26895	30797
33406	31907	30164	31753	33272
37065	35894	34103	35957	36173
41974	40655	42113	41562	42354
46226	46063	45604	46686	48578
51828	51670	52072	52248	53494
59299	55105	58341	59089	60725

3-8 城镇集体以上分地区从业人员数(2014年)

单位:人

指 标	Item
总 计	**Total**
#女性	#Female
按企业、事业、机关分	**Grouped by Administrative Relationship**
企业	Enterprises
事业	Public Units
机关	Government Units
民间非营利组织	Non-profit and Non-governmental Organization
其他	Others
按行业分	**Grouped by Sector**
农、林、牧、渔业	Farming,Forestry,Animal Husbandry and Fishery
制 造 业	Manufacturing Industry
电力、热力、燃气及水生产和供应业	Electric Power,Gas,Water Production and Supply
建筑业	Construction
批发和零售业	Transportation, Storage and Postal Service
交通运输、仓储和邮政业	Information Transmision, Computer Services and Software
住宿和餐饮业	Wholesale and Retail Trade
信息传输、软件和信息技术服务业	Hotel and Catering Trade
金融业	Banking
房地产业	Real Estate
租赁和商务服务业	Leasing and Commercial Services
科学研究、技术服务业	Scientific Research,Technical Services and Geological Prospecting
水利、环境和公共设施管理业	Water Conservancy, Environment and Public Facility Management
居民服务、修理和其他服务业	Resident Services and others
教育	Education
卫生和社会工作	Health, Social Security and Social Welfare
文化、体育和娱乐业	Culture,Sports and Entertainment Industry
公共管理、社会保障和社会组织	Public Administration and Social Organization

NUMBER OF EMPLOYEES IN DIFFERENT REGIONS ABOVE URBAN COLLECTIVE(YEAR 2014)

(Units:Person)

全市 Municipaility	市区 Urban Areas		海安 Haian	如东 Rudong	启东 Qidong	如皋 Rugao	海门 Haimen
		通州区 Tongzhou					
2212696	**769594**	**413474**	**279620**	**192784**	**347420**	**286004**	**337274**
439475	182071	68917	51019	41409	57614	57507	49855
2023116	686599	383870	258974	173614	326636	259494	317799
136276	59411	19282	15758	12328	14912	20065	13802
51622	22763	10175	4888	6772	5667	6339	5193
588	76	44			36		476
1094	745	103		70	169	106	4
6369	1475	710	105	2958	170	432	1229
465413	199640	87429	60665	39333	44001	67304	54470
11340	6531	661	754	1261	1117	779	898
1349822	379841	277268	181870	113923	263931	165685	244572
39235	23463	2288	4480	2347	1718	3895	3332
29517	19386	2404	1849	1758	2093	2739	1692
5173	2294	12	517	842	653	228	639
11058	6500	607	829	527	663	2056	483
35475	23531	2555	1974	2805	2989	1985	2191
13112	5997	1447	906	369	1799	3093	948
32567	12594	7258	1473	4882	4583	4821	4214
21425	6840	1837	3586	2383	1751	4506	2359
10469	3863	1051	1392	809	1341	1025	2039
2425	1350	151	183	91	609	123	69
77911	30634	12356	8944	8217	8755	13165	8196
39465	17974	4380	4029	3070	4730	5699	3963
5049	1974	505	275	691	273	1194	642
56871	25707	10555	5789	6518	6244	7275	5338

3-9 分所有制从业人员人数、劳动报酬(2014年)

指　　标	Item
总　计	Total
按企业、事业、机关分	Grouped by Administrative Relationship
企业	Enterprises
事业	Public Units
机关	Government Units
民间非营利组织	Non-profit and Non-governmental Organization
其他	Others
按行业分	Grouped by Sector
农、林、牧、渔业	Farming,Forestry,Animal Husbandry and Fishery
制 造 业	Manufacturing Industry
电力、热力、燃气及水生产和供应业	Electric Power,Gas,Water Production and Supply
建筑业	Construction
批发和零售业	Transportation, Storage and Postal Service
交通运输、仓储和邮政业	Information Transmision, Computer Services and Software
住宿和餐饮业	Wholesale and Retail Trade
信息传输、软件和信息技术服务业	Hotel and Catering Trade
金融业	Banking
房地产业	Real Estate
租赁和商务服务业	Leasing and Commercial Services
科学研究、技术服务业	Scientific Research,Polytechnical Services and Geological Prospecting
水利、环境和公共设施管理业	Water Conservancy, Environment and Public Facility Management
居民服务、修理和其他服务业	Resident Services and others
教育	Education
卫生和社会工作	Health, Social Security, and Social Welfare
文化、体育和娱乐业	Culture,Sports and Entertainment Industry
公共管理、社会保障和社会组织	Public Administration and Social Organization

LABOR REMUNERATIONS AND NUMBER OF EMPLYEES BY TYPE OF OWNERSHIP(YEAR 2014)

从业人员(人) Employees (Persons)	国有 State-owned	集体 Collective	其他 Others	劳动报酬(万元) Labor Remunerations (10000 Yuan)	国有 State-owned	集体 Collective	其他 Others
2212696	**213129**	**37741**	**1961826**	**12909212**	**1710874**	**201409**	**10996930**
2023116	37046	29779	1956291	11418701	282015	165816	10970870
136276	124290	7507	4479	1049495	992475	33696	23324
51622	51622			435179	435179		
588		7	581	1287		21	1266
1094	171	448	475	4551	1205	1876	1470
6369	6167	10	192	19204	18671	37	496
465413	608	2044	462761	2754582	4161	7812	2742609
11340	4757	304	6279	132419	74757	1473	56189
1349822	1177	14123	1334522	7444384	6126	84780	7353477
39235	1891	479	36865	170584	11763	1668	157153
29517	8168	1148	20201	169299	54740	5447	109112
5173	222	31	4920	20789	885	78	19826
11058	2230		8828	74756	15403		59353
35475	8089	2032	25354	293977	81887	31552	180538
13112	869	90	12153	78211	5436	164	72611
32567	4326	9110	19131	147425	21571	32725	93129
21425	3141	477	17807	123242	24383	2930	95929
10469	2679	4787	3003	44425	16064	17514	10847
2425	395	582	1448	8793	2816	892	5086
77911	75445	724	1742	627820	614273	3706	9842
39465	32372	1633	5460	294932	259490	9641	25801
5049	3815	167	1067	31670	26123	990	4556
56871	56778		93	472701	472326		375

3-10 在岗职工年末人数(2014年)

单位:人

指 标	Item
总 计	**Total**
按企业、事业、机关分	**Grouped by Administrative Relationship**
企业	Enterprises
事业	Public Units
机关	Government Units
民间非营利组织	Non-profit and Non-governmental Organization
其他	Others
按行业分	**Grouped by Sector**
农、林、牧、渔业	Farming,Forestry,Animal Husbandry and Fishery
制 造 业	Manufacturing Industry
电力、热力、燃气及水生产和供应业	Electric Power,Gas,Water Production and Supply
建筑业	Construction
批发和零售业	Transportation, Storage and Postal Service
交通运输、仓储和邮政业	Information Transmision, Computer Services and Software
住宿和餐饮业	Wholesale and Retail Trade
信息传输、软件和信息技术服务业	Hotel and Catering Trade
金融业	Banking
房地产业	Real Estate
租赁和商务服务业	Leasing and Commercial Services
科学研究、技术服务业	Scientific Research,Technical Services and Geological Prospecting
水利、环境和公共设施管理业	Water Conservancy, Environment and Public Facility Management
居民服务、修理和其他服务业	Resident Services and others
教育	Education
卫生和社会工作	Health, Social Security and Social Welfare
文化、体育和娱乐业	Culture,Sports and Entertainment Industry
公共管理、社会保障和社会组织	Public Administration and Social Organization

NUMBER OF EMPLOYED STAFF AND WORKERS AT YEAR-END(YEAR 2014)

(person)

全市 Municipality	市区 Urban Areas	通州区 Tongzhou	海安 Haian	如东 Rudong	启东 Qidong	如皋 Rugao	海门 Haimen
1578795	**443036**	**204134**	**189659**	**179603**	**225605**	**214001**	**326891**
1412210	373607	177876	172227	161380	206686	189522	308788
118720	48217	17082	13372	11924	13749	18758	12700
46630	20838	9044	4060	6229	4965	5615	4923
588		44			36		476
647		88		70	169	106	4
6270	1475	710	105	2956	128	381	1225
424863	169591	72835	60570	39150	41100	61172	53280
10737	6241	623	700	1236	952	759	849
818833	120549	88550	96318	106979	150214	106847	237926
37732	22409	2017	4381	2256	1661	3843	3182
20867	13216	1546	1361	1072	1369	2258	1591
4986	2188	12	517	842	588	218	633
8598	4780	541	675	351	653	1780	359
22156	13234	2373	1780	1480	2142	1874	1646
11065	5310	1157	839	360	1382	2244	930
24299	9366	6323	1469	2301	3837	3144	4182
18858	6126	1740	3521	2274	1710	3005	2222
8184	2689	460	769	751	1297	1025	1653
1698	926	140	183	89	320	120	60
72068	26803	11625	7879	7902	8678	12852	7954
32815	13507	3797	3420	2946	3899	5478	3565
3838	1539	340	257	491	228	695	628
50928	23087	9345	4915	6167	5447	6306	5006

3-11　分所有制在岗职工年末人数(2014年)

单位:人

指　标	Item
总　计	**Total**
按企业、事业、机关分	**Grouped by Administrative Relationship**
企业	Enterprises
事业	Public Units
机关	Government Units
民间非营利组织	Non-profit and Non-governmental Organization
其他	Others
按行业分	**Grouped by Sector**
农、林、牧、渔业	Farming,Forestry,Animal Husbandry and Fishery
制 造 业	Manufacturing Industry
电力、热力、燃气及水生产和供应业	Electric Power,Gas,Water Production and Supply
建筑业	Construction
批发和零售业	Transportation, Storage and Postal Service
交通运输、仓储和邮政业	Information Transmision, Computer Services and Software
住宿和餐饮业	Wholesale and Retail Trade
信息传输、软件和信息技术服务业	Hotel and Catering Trade
金融业	Banking
房地产业	Real Estate
租赁和商务服务业	Leasing and Commercial Services
科学研究、技术服务业	Scientific Research,Technical Services and Geological Prospecting
水利、环境和公共设施管理业	Water Conservancy, Environment and Public Facility Management
居民服务、修理和其他服务业	Resident Services and others
教育	Education
卫生和社会工作	Health, Social Security and Social Welfare
文化、体育和娱乐业	Culture,Sports and Entertainment Industry
公共管理、社会保障和社会组织	Public Administration and Social Organization

NUMBER OF EMPLOYED STAFF AND WORKERS AT YEAR-END BY TYPE OF OWNERSHIP(YEAR 2014)

(Units:Person)

国有 State-Owned		集体 Collective		其他 Others	
全市 Municipality	市区 Urban Areas	全市 Municipality	市区 Urban Areas	全市 Municipality	市区 Urban Areas
186793	**78061**	**24782**	**13351**	**1367220**	**351624**
3759	11246	1938	11747	1362143	35614
19311	45935	5373	1556	436	726
4663	2838				
		7		581	76
93	42	94	48	46	28
674	145	1		186	7
427	37	229	937	42247	168347
4574	2189	288	71	5875	3981
892	869	7368	5748	81573	113932
1637	569	477	96	35618	21744
535	3836	637	171	1488	929
216		31	9	4739	2179
1828	316			677	4464
786	1764	1941		13129	1147
712	529	9	5	1263	4776
393	1351	5952	4541	15254	3474
2661	157	476	21	15721	449
2284	929	2963	597	2937	1163
33	126	293	29	175	771
69821	2626	616	342	1631	435
26279	12337	1461	558	575	612
2694	946	15	37	994	556
5835	2355			93	32

主要统计指标解释

人口数 指一定时间、一定地区范围的有生命的个人的总和。年度统计的年末人口数是指每年12月31日24时的人口数。

出生率(又称粗出生率) 指在一定时期内(通常为一年)出生的人数与同期平均人数(或期中人数)的比率，一般用千分率表示。

计算公式：$出生率=\frac{年出生人数}{年平均人数}\times1000‰$

出生人数是指活产婴儿，即胎儿脱离母体时(不管怀孕月数)，有过呼吸或其他生命现象。

目前出生率的计算，在市级有公安的户籍口径、计生委的常住人口统计口径；国家、省级还有年度人口抽样调查公布口径等。本年鉴用的为公安口径出生数，包括了补报往年出生数在内。

死亡率(又称粗死亡率) 指在一定时期内(通常为一年)一定地区的死亡人数与同期平均人数(或期中人数)之比，一般用千分率表示。

计算公式：$死亡率=\frac{年死亡数}{年平均人数}\times1000‰$

人口自然增长率 指在一定时期内(通常为一年)人口自然增加数(出生人数减死亡人数)与该时期内平均人数(或期中人数)之比，一般用千分率表示。

计算公式：$人口自然增长率=\frac{本年出生人数-本年死亡人数}{年平均人数}\times1000‰$

人口预期寿命 指在一定年龄组死亡率水平下，对某一确定的年龄日后平均还能继续生存的年数(或该年龄组未来的平均预期寿命)。

单位从业人员 各单位的从业人员指在各级国家机关、政党机关、社会团体及企业、事业单位中工作，取得工资或其他形式的劳动报酬的全部人员。包括：在岗职工、再就业的离退休人员、民办教师以及在各单位中工作的外方人员和港澳台方人员、兼职人员、借用的外单位人员和第二职业者。不包括离开单位仍保留劳动关系的职工。

在岗职工 指在本单位工作并由单位支付工资的人员，以及有工作岗位，但由于学习、病伤产假等原因暂未工作，仍由单位支付工资的人员。

其他从业人员 指劳动统计制度规定不作职工统计，但实际参加各单位生产或工作并取得劳动报酬的人员。包括：再就业的离退休人员、民办教师以及在各单位中工作的外方人员和港、澳、台方人员、兼职人员、借用的外单位人员和第二职业者。但不包括在单位中打工领取劳动报酬的在校学生。

离开本单位仍保留劳动关系的职工 指由于各种原因，已经离开本人的生产或工作岗位，并已不在本单位从事其他工作，但仍与用人单位保留劳动关系的职工。

内部退养职工 指接近正常退休年龄但因各种原因退出工作岗位，并办理了内退手续，在办理正式退休手续前由单位按月发给一定生活费的职工。

平均人数 指报告期内每天平均拥有的人数。计算方法：报告期每天实有人数之和/报告期日历天数或(报告期初人数+报告期末人数)/2。

离、退休、退职离、退休 指根据有关规定，离开生产或工作岗位，正式办理离职手续，并享受离、退休待遇的人员。退职指职工本人自愿、或因丧失工作能力，又不具备退休条件而办理离职手续享受相应待遇的人员。

从业人员劳动报酬 指各单位在一定时期内直接支付给本单位全部从业人员的劳动报酬总额。包括在岗职工工资总额和本单位其他从业人员劳动报酬两部分。

工资总额 指各单位在一定时期内直接支付给本单位全部在岗职工的劳动报酬总额。目前工资总额只对在岗职工进行统计。不在岗职工生活费另作统计。职工工资总额反映了一定时期职工从单位得到的全部工资，是计算地区生产总值的基础性指标，也是研究劳动者收入状况和居民购买力的主要依据。工资总额包括计时工资、计件工资、奖金、计件超额工资、各种津贴和补贴、加班加点工资、特殊情况下支付的工资(其他工资)等。

工资总额的计算应以直接支付给职工的全部劳动报酬为依据。各单位支付给本单位全部职工的劳动报酬，不论是计入成本还是不计入成本，不论是以货币形式支付还是以实物形式支付，不论是单位自筹的资金还是上级(或政府财政部门)下拨的资金，不论是厂级单位筹集的资金还是下属车间(科室)及附属经营单位筹集的资金，均应列入工资总额计算的范围。

平均工资 指一定时期内平均每人所得的工资额，表明一定时期内职工工资收入的高低程度，是反映职工工资水平的主要指标。

计算公式：职工平均工资=报告期实际支付的全部职工工资总额/报告期全部职工平均人数。

第四篇

价格指数 Chapter 4

Price Indices

4-1 历年主要价格指数

MAIN PRICE INDICATORS OVER THE YEARS

(以上年价格为100) (Preceding Year=100)

年份 Year	居民消费价格指数 General Consumer Price Index		商品零售价格指数 General Retail Price Index		农业生产资料价格指数(启东市) Price Index of Means of Agricultural Products
	市区 Urban Area	启东 Qidong	市区 City Proper	启东 Qidong	
1978	100.2		100.2		
1979	100.9		101.0		
1980	103.4		102.9		
1985	110.6		111.5		
1990	102.7		102.1		
1991	107.5		107.5		
1992	108.6		107.4		
1993	123.4		120.7		
1994	124.9		120.9		
1995	115.3		113.0		
1996	110.5	108.5	106.5	107.3	
1997	100.7	101.2	98.8	99.2	
1998	99.9	98.4	97.5	97.6	
1999	97.6	97.3	95.9	96.3	
2000	99.3	100.3	98.4	98.6	
2001	100.8	100.7	98.3	99.0	
2002	100.0	100.8	97.6	98.2	
2003	101.6	101.1	98.5	100.5	
2004	104.5	104.7	103.4	104.7	
2005	101.2	101.4	99.6	101.0	103.8
2006	101.7	101.4	100.3	101.9	102.9
2007	105.1	104.4	103.9	103.8	105.5
2008	104.8	105.7	105.9	103.5	114.3
2009	98.7	99.2	98.6	98.8	102.0
2010	103.7	103.6	102.4	103.6	99.1
2011	105.0	106.7	104.9	107.1	102.9
2012	102.5	102.5	102.3	102.6	103.4
2013	102.2	102.9	101.8	101.7	101.8
2014	102.1	102.6	101.6	101.3	98.7

4-2 历年市区居民消费价格总指数及分类指数

GENERAL INDICES AND INDICATORS BY CATEGORY OF CONSUMPTION PRICE OVER THE YEARS OF URBAN RESIDENT

(以上年价格为 100) (preceding year=100)

年份 Year	居民消费价格总指数 General Residents Consumption Price Index	其中 of which				
		食品类 Food	衣着类 Clothing	家庭设备用品及维修服务 Household Facilities	居住 Inhabitation	服务项目 Services
1978	100.2	100.1	99.9	110.1		100.0
1979	100.9	101.5	99.9	101.2		100.5
1980	103.4	105.7	100.0	100.6		100.4
1985	110.6	116.0	100.2	100.8		102.8
1990	102.7	99.8	111.8	106.1		110.6
1991	107.5	109.2	111.8	103.0		106.9
1992	108.6	109.8	104.6	102.1		121.8
1993	123.4	120.8	123.1	120.4		152.2
1994	124.9	131.5	132.3	110.3	115.2	127.3
1995	115.3	118.7	120.6	103.8	113.0	125.0
1996	110.5	111.8	111.0	102.1	118.0	109.4
1997	100.7	97.0	104.8	98.2	107.2	112.5
1998	99.9	97.9	96.5	98.2	111.9	105.0
1999	97.6	94.2	98.2	97.7	105.2	106.6
2000	99.3	96.7	98.9	98.1	108.1	106.0
2001	100.8	98.4	99.1	96.8	103.5	112.5
2002	100.0	100.9	94.0	98.5	99.2	104.8
2003	101.6	103.9	98.4	98.7	102.6	103.5
2004	104.5	111.4	102.5	99.4	102.7	101.9
2005	101.2	102.2	93.8	99.8	109.9	103.3
2006	101.7	101.7	100.5	100.5	106.9	104.2
2007	105.1	113.5	98.9	102.1	103.9	100.8
2008	104.8	112.6	99.9	104.3	101.6	100.2
2009	98.7	100.0	99.8	99.9	95.0	98.2
2010	103.7	104.9	103.7	99.9	109.2	106.0
2011	105.0	111.3	107.1	102.4	102.1	102.1
2012	102.5	105.2	104.4	104.1	100.4	101.3
2013	102.2	103.8	102.8	102.0	102.4	101.9
2014	102.1	102.6	106.3	102.3	101.0	102.0

4-3 主要年份市区商品零售价格指数

(以上年价格为 100)

指 标	Item	2000	2001	2002	2003
商品零售价格总指数	**General Retail Price Index**	**98.4**	**98.3**	**97.6**	**98.5**
食品	Food	97.2	98.2	100.1	103.2
# 粮食	Grain	87.8	105.3	97.7	100.8
肉禽及其制品	Meat and Poultry	95.1	99.5	99.0	105.6
水产品	Aquatic Products	96.9	99.9	93.7	98.4
鲜菜	Fresh Vegetables	116.7	94.1	109.1	118.2
饮料、烟酒	Beverages, Tobacco and Liquor	92.7	100.8	96.1	100.4
服装、鞋帽	Garments,shoes and Hats	99.3	97.2	92.5	97.7
纺织品	Textiles	100.1	104.5	101.9	99.4
家用电器及音像器材	Household Facilities and Moviolas	94.0	90.0	91.6	91.0
文化办公用品	Cultural and Office Appliances				84.3
日用品类	Articles for Daily Use	99.6	98.9	99.6	98.7
体育娱乐用品	Sports and Recreation Articles				97.9
交通、通信用品	Transportation and Telecommunications				77.0
家具	Furniture	99.8	98.7	100.0	99.8
化妆品	Cosmetics	96.8	99.6	94.7	101.0
金银珠宝	Gold, Silver and Jewelry	99.8	89.9	97.6	110.7
中、西药品类及医疗保健品	Chinese and Western Medicine	98.2	107.4	102.1	96.3
书报杂志及电子出版物	Books,Newspapers,Magazines and Electronic Publications	105.0	115.2	96.8	100.3
燃料	Fuels	121.8	96.8	99.5	109.1
建筑材料及五金电料	Building Materials and Hardware	96.4	99.2	102.1	100.5

RETAIL PRICE INDICATORS OF COMMODITIES IN CITY PROPER OVER TNE YEARS

(preceding year=100)

2004	2005	2006	2007	2008	2009	2010	2011	2012	2013	2014
103.4	**99.6**	**100.3**	**103.9**	**105.9**	**98.6**	**102.4**	**104.9**	**102.3**	**101.8**	**101.6**
110.2	102.5	101.7	113.5	112.9	100.6	105.3	111.1	105.4	103.8	102.9
143.3	97.7	106.6	108.3	104.4	104.7	112.6	112.9	100.6	101.6	102.7
118.6	98.3	95.9	128.9	122.5	87.9	100.6	123.6	101.2	101.7	100.1
105.3	101.9	103.4	113.7	107.4	95.1	105.1	109.1	111.3	104.9	102.7
104.4	124.8	106.2	114.6	98.0	111.3	108.4	99.3	110.1	111.9	102.6
102.8	100.5	100.2	101.0	105.6	101.6	101.7	102.6	101.9	101.2	99.3
103.7	93.3	100.2	98.2	99.7	99.0	103.3	106.7	104.5	102.9	106.1
100.1	100.4	98.9	99.9	105.6	102.6	103.2	107.0	103.3	100.3	101.0
94.7	95.8	94.2	91.4	101.8	95.2	96.7	100.5	101.2	101.6	101.7
91.5	94.1	92.7	95.3	95.3	94.8	91.0	96.9	95.3	100.1	102.9
101.5	102.7	100.3	100.5	103.1	100.1	99.7	102.3	105.8	101.3	100.6
98.0	101.0	103.8	99.6	97.7	88.5	96.1	101.4	101.2	100.0	103.8
87.0	88.2	89.5	93.3	94.6	91.9	96.1	96.7	97.3	99.2	100.3
98.7	102.4	100.9	104.8	103.3	99.6	98.6	107.4	107.0	99.4	101.6
99.7	99.0	102.9	99.9	99.1	103.3	100.3	98.0	104.3	103.3	101.6
118.7	103.5	120.6	109.2	123.7	91.0	116.2	116.6	102.5	92.8	88.6
93.0	97.1	100.5	100.0	98.1	102.6	99.9	103.5	100.7	101.0	102.7
101.6	100.5	102.7	101.0	107.4	117.5	104.4	100.1	101.8	105.4	103.7
108.7	116.1	111.1	103.1	110.0	90.8	109.6	107.3	101.4	101.3	99.3
103.3	103.8	108.9	108.1	107.0	93.6	105.1	104.7	97.1	100.7	100.5

4-4 分地区居民消费价格指数(2014年)

CONSUMER PRICE INDICATORS BY REGION(2014)

(以上年价格为100) (preceding year=100)

指 标	Item	市区 Urban Areas	启东 Qidong
居民消费价格总指数	**General Consumption Price Index of Residents**	**102.1**	**102.6**
非食品价格指数	Non-food Price Index	101.9	102.1
服务项目价格指数	Services Price Index	102.0	103.9
工业品价格指数	Industrial Products Price Index	101.8	100.8
扣除食品和能源价格指数	Price Index of Food and Energy Excluded	102.1	102.4
扣除鲜菜鲜果总指数	Allow for Fresh Vegetables and Fruits Price Index	101.8	102.3
消费品价格指数	Overall Retail Price Index	102.2	102.0
食品	Food	102.6	103.5
粮食	Grain	102.7	102.9
油脂	Oil and Fat	98.1	95.6
肉禽及其制品	Meat,Poultry and Their Products	100.1	99.8
蛋	Eggs	110.9	106.0
水产品	Aquatic Products	102.7	102.4
菜	Vegetables	102.6	101.5
#鲜菜	Fresh Vegetables	102.6	100.9
烟酒	Tobacco,Liquor and Utensil	98.1	98.9
衣着	Clothing	106.3	102.5
服装	Garments	106.8	100.9
衣着材料	Clothing Material	101.2	102.2
鞋袜帽	Shoes,socks and Hats	104.7	107.1
家庭设备用品及维修服务	Household Facilities and Repair Services	103.3	101.8
医疗保健和个人用品	Health Protection and Articles for Personal Use	101.1	103.6
医疗保健	Medicine and Medical Care	101.9	104.2
#中药材及中成药	Chinese Medicine	102.7	109.8
西药	Western Medicine	100.2	100.2
医疗保健服务	Medicine and Medical Services	100.0	103.6
个人用品及服务	Services and Articles for Personal use	100.4	102.7
交通和通讯	Transportation and Telecommunications	99.6	100.0
交通	Transportation	99.5	100.0
通信	Telecommunication Tools	99.7	100.0
娱乐教育文化用品及服务	Recreation,Education and Culture Articles and other Services	102.8	103.6
文娱用耐用消费品及服务	Cultural and Recreational Durables and Services	102.5	98.5
教育	Education	101.1	102.6
#教材及参考书	Teaching Materials and Referenes Books	97.9	96.3
#教育服务	Education and Child-Care Fee	101.1	103.0
居住	Residence	101.0	102.3
建房及装修材料	Building Materials	101.5	101.4
住房租金	Rent room	101.5	101.5
水、电、燃料	Water,Electricity and Fuels	100.1	100.2

4-5 分地区商品零售价格指数(2014 年)

RETAIL PRICE INDICES BY REGIONS(2014)

(以上年价格为 100) (preceding year=100)

指 标	Item	市区 Urban Areas	启东 Qidong
商品零售价格总指数	**General Retail Price Index**	**101.6**	**101.3**
食品	Food	102.9	103.2
#粮食	Grain	102.7	102.9
油脂	Oil and Fat	98.1	95.6
肉禽及其制品	Meat,Poultry and Their Products	100.1	99.7
蛋	Eggs	110.9	105.6
水产品	Aquatic Products	102.7	102.4
菜	Vegetables	102.6	101.5
饮料、烟酒	Beverage,Tobacco and Liquor	99.3	100.6
服装、鞋帽	Garments,shoes and Hats	106.1	102.1
#服装	Garments	106.8	100.9
鞋袜帽	Shoes,socks and Hats	104.7	107.1
纺织品	Textiles	101.0	105.1
家用电器及音像器材	Household Facilities and Moviolas	101.7	99.7
#家庭设备	Household Facilities	102.4	101.5
文娱用耐用消费品	Cultural and Recreational Durables	102.0	94.1
专业音像器材类	Moviolas	97.0	100.0
文化办公用品	Cultural and Office Articles	102.9	100.3
日用品	Articles for Daily Use	100.6	99.9
体育娱乐用品	Sports and Recreation Articles	103.8	104.2
交通、通信用品	Transportation and Telecommunications	100.3	100.0
#交通运输机械	Transport Tools	99.9	100.0
通讯器材	Communications Tools	101.1	100.1
家具	Furniture	101.6	103.7
化妆品	Cosmetics	101.6	100.4
金银珠宝	Treasures	88.6	88.6
中西药品及医疗保健用品	Chinese and Western Medicine and Health Appliances	102.7	102.6
#中药材及中成药	Chinese Medicine	102.7	109.8
西药	Western Medicine	100.4	100.2
保健器具及用品	Health Appliances	104.8	106.0
书报杂志及电子出版物	Books,Newspapers,Magazines and Electronic Publications	103.7	107.1
燃料	Fuels	99.3	99.4
#煤炭及制品	Coal and Its Products	100.0	100.0
石油及制品	Petroleum and Its Products	99.3	99.4
建筑材料及五金电料	Building and Hardware Materials	100.5	100.2
#建筑装璜材料	Building Decoration Materials	100.2	100.3
五金电料	Hardware Materials	101.0	99.8

4-6 市区年度及分月居民消费价格同期比指数(2014 年)

(以上年同期价格为 100)

指 标	Item	全年 Annual Total	1 月 Jan
居民消费价格总指数	**General Consumption Price Index of Resident**	**102.1**	**101.4**
非食品价格指数	Non-food Price Index	101.9	101.0
服务项目价格指数	Services Price Index	102.0	101.0
工业品价格指数	Industrial Products Price Index	101.8	100.9
扣除食品和能源价格指数	Price Index of Food and Energy Excluded	102.1	101.1
扣除鲜菜鲜果总指数	Allow for Fresh Vegetables and Fruits Price Index	101.8	101.3
消费品价格指数	Overall Retail Price Index	102.2	101.5
一、食品	**Food**	**102.6**	**102.2**
1.粮食	Grain	102.7	101.7
2.淀粉	Starches	107.0	97.6
3.干豆类及豆制品	Bean and Its Products	104.5	103.2
4.油脂	Oil and Fat	98.1	95.0
5.肉禽及其制品	Meat,Poultry and Their Products	100.1	100.6
6.蛋	Eggs	110.9	101.1
7.水产品	Aquatic Products	102.7	107.1
8.菜	Vegetables	102.6	92.4
#鲜菜	Fresh Vegetables	102.6	91.2
9.调味品	Flavoring	99.7	99.2
10.糖	Carbonhydrate	99.3	96.8
11.茶及饮料	Tea and Beverage	102.0	105.7
12.干鲜瓜果	Dried Fruit	115.5	120.4
#鲜瓜果	Fresh Fruit	118.4	124.7
13.糕点饼干面包	Cake,biscuit and Bread	103.4	104.2
14.液体乳及乳制品	Milk and Dairy Products	108.6	111.4
15.在外用膳食品	Dine Out	100.1	100.9
16.其它食品	Others	97.2	94.1
二、烟酒	**Tobacco,Liquor and Utensil**	**98.1**	**98.5**
1.烟草	Tobacco	100.0	100.0
2.酒	Liquor	95.1	96.3
三、衣着	**Clothing**	**106.3**	**107.0**
1.服装	Garments	106.8	105.9
2.衣着材料	Clothing Material	101.2	99.2
3.鞋袜帽	Shoes,socks and Hats	104.7	111.2
4.衣着加工服务费	Clothing Processing	110.7	104.6
四、家庭设备用品及维修服务	**Household Facilities and Repair Services**	**103.3**	**101.8**
1.耐用消费品	Durable Consuming Goods	102.2	101.7
家具	Furniture	101.6	101.2
家庭设备	Household Facilities	102.4	101.8
2.室内装饰品	Interior Decorations	101.9	99.9

CONSUMER PRICE INDICATORS IN CITY PROPER BY YEAR AND MONTH COMPARED WITH THE YEAR BEFORE(2014)

(preceding year=100)

2月 Feb	3月 Mar	4月 Apr	5月 May	6月 Jun	7月 Jul	8月 Aug	9月 Sept	10月 Oct	11月 Nov	12月 Dec
101.5	**101.9**	**102.0**	**102.3**	**102.2**	**102.2**	**102.2**	**102.3**	**102.2**	**102.2**	**102.1**
101.2	101.5	101.7	101.9	101.9	102.0	102.0	102.0	102.0	101.9	101.9
101.3	101.4	101.6	101.7	101.7	101.7	101.8	102.0	101.9	102.0	102.0
101.2	101.6	101.8	102.0	102.2	102.2	102.2	102.1	102.0	101.9	101.8
101.4	101.7	101.9	102.1	102.1	102.1	102.2	102.2	102.2	102.1	102.1
101.3	101.5	101.6	101.8	101.8	101.8	101.9	101.9	101.9	101.8	101.8
101.6	102.1	102.2	102.6	102.5	102.4	102.4	102.4	102.4	102.3	102.2
102.1	**102.7**	**102.7**	**103.2**	**102.9**	**102.7**	**102.7**	**102.8**	**102.7**	**102.7**	**102.6**
101.1	101.2	101.7	102.3	102.5	102.6	102.6	102.7	102.7	102.7	102.7
97.1	98.8	100.6	101.2	101.6	102.5	103.9	104.9	105.7	106.5	107.0
102.7	102.7	103.0	103.5	103.9	104.2	104.4	104.5	104.6	104.5	104.5
95.9	96.1	96.2	96.1	96.3	96.7	97.1	97.0	97.4	98.1	98.1
99.2	98.7	98.5	99.2	99.5	99.7	100.0	100.1	100.2	100.1	100.1
101.1	101.4	102.9	105.7	107.1	108.7	109.8	110.0	110.5	110.7	110.9
105.7	106.3	106.2	105.8	105.1	104.2	103.8	103.4	103.1	102.9	102.7
94.8	101.0	101.5	103.8	101.9	101.8	101.2	102.7	102.4	102.2	102.6
94.3	101.4	102.0	104.7	102.3	102.1	101.3	103.0	102.5	102.3	102.6
98.8	98.6	98.3	98.2	98.5	98.6	98.7	98.9	99.4	99.7	99.7
97.6	98.4	98.2	98.2	98.2	98.4	98.5	98.6	98.8	99.0	99.3
106.0	105.9	107.0	108.1	106.6	105.2	103.7	102.7	102.0	102.0	102.0
119.8	118.5	118.0	117.9	118.2	117.6	117.7	117.6	117.3	116.6	115.5
123.8	122.1	121.5	121.4	121.6	121.0	121.2	121.1	120.6	119.8	118.4
104.6	103.5	103.1	102.9	102.8	102.8	102.6	102.7	102.9	103.2	103.4
110.9	110.6	110.1	110.0	109.5	109.5	109.3	109.2	109.4	109.3	108.6
100.8	100.6	100.6	100.5	100.4	100.3	100.2	100.1	100.1	100.1	100.1
95.3	96.3	96.2	96.1	95.5	95.0	94.9	95.4	96.0	96.5	97.2
98.0	**97.9**	**98.0**	**97.9**	**97.9**	**97.9**	**97.9**	**97.9**	**97.9**	**98.0**	**98.1**
100.0	100.0	100.0	100.0	100.0	100.0	100.0	100.0	100.0	100.0	100.0
94.9	94.8	94.8	94.5	94.5	94.6	94.6	94.6	94.7	94.9	95.1
108.0	**109.4**	**109.8**	**110.1**	**109.8**	**109.4**	**108.9**	**108.4**	**107.8**	**107.0**	**106.3**
106.8	108.0	108.6	109.3	109.3	109.1	108.8	108.7	108.4	107.7	106.8
99.2	99.2	99.2	99.6	100.0	100.3	100.5	100.7	100.9	101.1	101.2
112.8	114.8	114.3	113.4	112.0	110.8	109.8	108.0	106.4	105.0	104.7
104.6	105.7	106.6	107.8	108.8	109.6	110.1	110.5	110.7	110.9	110.7
101.6	**101.9**	**102.1**	**102.2**	**102.5**	**102.5**	**102.7**	**102.8**	**103.0**	**103.1**	**103.3**
101.7	101.9	101.8	101.8	101.9	101.9	102.1	102.1	102.2	102.2	102.2
101.1	101.0	101.0	101.0	101.1	101.3	101.3	101.4	101.4	101.5	101.6
101.9	102.1	101.9	101.9	102.0	102.1	102.2	102.3	102.4	102.4	102.4
99.2	99.5	99.9	100.4	100.9	101.2	101.4	101.5	101.7	101.8	101.9

4-6 续表

(以上年同期价格为 100)

指　标	Item	全年 Annual Total	1月 Jan
3.床上用品	Beding Articles	100.8	101.0
4.家庭日用杂品	Daily Use Household Articles	100.3	101.3
5.家庭服务及加工维修服务	Farmily Services and Upkeep	120.2	105.0
五、医疗保健和个人用品	**Health Protection and Articles for Personal Use**	**101.1**	**100.3**
1.医疗保健	Medicine and Medical Care	101.9	102.3
医疗器具及用品	Medical Facilities	105.8	100.0
中药材及中成药	Chinese Medicine	102.7	105.7
西药	Western Medicine	100.2	100.1
保健器具及用品	Health Appliances	104.8	104.2
医疗保健服务	Medicine and Medical Care	100.0	100.0
2.个人用品及服务	Services and Articles for Personal use	100.4	98.3
化妆美容用品	Beauty Utensil	102.5	103.7
清洁类化妆品	Sanitation Articles	102.7	99.9
个人饰品	Aticles for Personal Adornment	91.0	88.0
个人服务	Personal Services	105.2	102.6
六、交通和通讯	**Transportation and Telecommunications**	**99.6**	**98.9**
1.交通	Transportation	99.5	99.6
交通工具	Transportation Tools	99.6	99.5
车用燃料及零配件	Fuels and Spares for Vehicle	97.8	99.5
车辆使用及维修费	Services and Repair for Vehicle	100.9	100.0
市区公共交通费	Urban Public Traffic	100.0	100.0
城市间交通费	Traffic Within cities	100.5	99.7
2.通信	Telecommunications	99.7	97.6
通信工具	Telecommunications Tools	98.6	87.5
通信服务	Telecommunications Services	100.0	100.0
七、娱乐教育文化用品及服务	**Recreation,Education and Culture Articles and other Services**	**102.8**	**100.5**
1.文娱用耐用消费品及服务	Cultural and Recreational Durables and Services	102.5	92.2
2.教育	Education	101.1	100.1
教材及参考书	Teaching Materials and Referenes Books	97.9	97.9
教育服务	Education and Child-Care Fee	101.1	100.2
3.文化娱乐类	Cultural and Recreational Articles	101.2	101.0
文化娱乐用品	Culture and Recreation	101.0	101.3
书报杂志	Books,Newspapers and Magazines	105.1	105.1
文娱费	Cultural expenses	100.5	100.0
4.旅游	Travel and outing	107.8	106.4
八、居住	**Residence**	**101.0**	**100.2**
1.建房及装修材料	Building Materials	101.5	98.6
2.住房租金	Rent room	101.5	101.1
#公房房租	Rent for State-owned House	100.0	100.0
#私房房租	Rent for Private House	101.5	101.3
3.自有住房	Private Residence	100.9	100.2
4.水、电、燃料	Water,Electricity and Fuels	100.1	100.2

CONTINUED

(preceding year=100)

2月 Feb	3月 Mar	4月 Apr	5月 May	6月 Jun	7月 Jul	8月 Aug	9月 Sept	10月 Oct	11月 Nov	12月 Dec
101.0	101.0	101.0	101.0	101.0	101.0	101.0	100.9	100.8	100.8	100.8
101.4	101.1	100.9	100.5	100.3	100.0	99.9	99.9	100.0	100.1	100.3
102.4	105.5	109.0	111.5	113.5	115.0	116.2	117.3	118.5	119.4	120.2
100.5	**100.8**	**100.7**	**100.7**	**100.8**	**100.9**	**101.0**	**101.0**	**101.1**	**101.1**	**101.1**
102.2	102.2	102.1	102.0	101.9	101.8	101.8	101.8	101.8	101.8	101.9
100.0	100.8	101.8	102.4	103.3	103.7	104.3	104.8	105.2	105.5	105.8
105.6	105.9	105.1	104.6	103.9	103.3	102.9	102.7	102.4	102.6	102.7
100.1	100.1	100.1	100.1	100.1	100.1	100.1	100.2	100.2	100.2	100.2
103.9	103.8	103.8	103.7	104.0	104.2	104.4	104.5	104.6	104.7	104.8
100.0	100.0	100.0	100.0	100.0	100.0	100.0	100.0	100.0	100.0	100.0
98.8	99.3	99.4	99.4	99.7	100.0	100.2	100.3	100.3	100.3	100.4
102.8	102.5	101.9	101.7	101.6	101.9	102.0	102.1	102.2	102.3	102.5
100.3	100.9	101.2	101.5	102.0	102.2	102.3	102.5	102.6	102.6	102.7
88.9	89.8	90.0	89.8	90.2	91.1	91.3	91.3	91.3	91.1	91.0
103.6	104.2	104.6	104.7	104.9	105.0	105.0	105.1	105.1	105.2	105.2
98.8	**98.9**	**99.1**	**99.4**	**99.7**	**99.8**	**99.9**	**99.8**	**99.8**	**99.7**	**99.6**
99.5	99.4	99.5	99.8	100.0	100.2	100.2	100.1	99.9	99.8	99.5
99.8	99.8	99.7	99.6	99.6	99.6	99.6	99.6	99.6	99.6	99.6
98.8	98.5	98.8	99.8	100.5	101.0	100.8	100.2	99.6	98.7	97.8
100.0	100.0	100.0	100.0	100.0	100.3	100.4	100.6	100.7	100.8	100.9
100.0	100.0	100.0	100.0	100.0	100.0	100.0	100.0	100.0	100.0	100.0
98.9	98.7	99.2	99.9	100.0	100.2	100.3	100.5	100.6	100.6	100.5
97.6	98.1	98.4	98.8	99.1	99.2	99.3	99.4	99.4	99.6	99.7
87.6	89.9	91.7	93.7	95.4	95.9	96.1	96.7	97.0	97.9	98.6
100.0	100.0	100.0	100.0	100.0	100.0	100.0	100.0	100.0	100.0	100.0
100.8	**101.2**	**101.7**	**102.1**	**102.2**	**102.3**	**102.4**	**102.7**	**102.6**	**102.7**	**102.8**
92.9	94.0	95.9	97.6	98.3	98.8	99.2	100.0	100.7	101.7	102.5
100.2	100.2	100.2	100.2	100.2	100.2	100.2	100.5	100.7	100.9	101.1
98.9	99.2	99.4	99.5	99.6	99.6	99.6	99.1	98.6	98.3	97.9
100.2	100.2	100.2	100.2	100.2	100.2	100.2	100.5	100.8	101.0	101.1
100.9	101.0	100.9	100.9	100.9	101.4	101.3	101.3	101.3	101.2	101.2
101.1	101.1	100.9	100.9	100.8	100.8	100.8	100.8	100.9	100.9	101.0
105.1	105.1	105.1	105.1	105.1	105.1	105.1	105.1	105.1	105.1	105.1
100.0	100.0	100.0	100.0	100.0	100.9	100.8	100.7	100.6	100.6	100.5
107.1	108.3	109.6	110.2	110.2	110.1	110.1	110.4	109.0	108.2	107.8
100.6	**100.4**	**100.4**	**100.4**	**100.4**	**100.4**	**100.6**	**100.7**	**100.8**	**100.8**	**101.0**
98.6	98.6	98.6	98.6	99.3	99.9	100.4	100.7	101.0	101.3	101.5
101.4	101.3	101.2	101.2	101.1	101.1	101.2	101.3	101.4	101.4	101.5
100.0	100.0	100.0	100.0	100.0	100.0	100.0	100.0	100.0	100.0	100.0
101.5	101.4	101.3	101.3	101.1	101.1	101.2	101.3	101.4	101.4	101.5
100.9	100.7	100.6	100.6	100.4	100.4	100.6	100.6	100.7	100.7	100.9
100.1	100.0	100.0	100.0	100.0	100.0	100.0	100.1	100.1	100.1	100.1

4-7 市区分月居民消费价格定基比指数(2014年)

(以2000年价格为100)

指　标	Item	1月 Jan	2月 Feb
居民消费价格总指数	**General Consumption Price Index of Resident**	**136.7**	**138.1**
非食品价格指数	Non-food Price Index	112.2	113.2
服务项目价格指数	Services Price Index	135.9	137.9
扣除鲜菜鲜果总指数	Fresh Vegetables and Fruits Excluded Price Index	132.0	132.8
消费品价格指数	Overall Retail Price Index	139.0	140.0
一、食品	**Food**	**206.0**	**208.8**
1.粮食	Grain	232.9	232.2
2.淀粉	Starches	175.4	175.5
3.干豆类及豆制品	Bean and Its Products	250.6	247.8
4.油脂	Oil and Fat	150.5	152.0
5.肉禽及其制品	Meat,Poultry and Their Products	227.8	226.4
6.蛋	Eggs	219.2	218.6
7.水产品	Aquatic Products	192.7	195.9
8.菜	Vegetables	285.7	297.3
#鲜菜	Fresh Vegetables	302.2	315.9
9.调味品	Flavoring	142.0	140.9
10.糖	Carbonhydrate	172.3	173.4
11.茶及饮料	Tea and Beverage	118.3	118.7
12.干鲜瓜果	Dried Fruit	264.4	293.3
#鲜瓜果	Fresh Fruit	275.5	308.6
13.糕点饼干面包	Cake,biscuit and Bread	151.3	152.0
14.液体乳及乳制品	Mike and Its Products	211.7	212.9
15.在外用膳食品	Dine Out	166.9	166.7
16.其它食品	Others	0.0	0.0
二、烟酒	**Tobacco,Liquor and Utensil**	**113.1**	**111.2**
1.烟草	Tobacco	100.1	100.1
2.酒	Liquor	142.3	136.0
三、衣着	**Clothing**	**116.1**	**117.1**
1.服装	Garments	116.9	117.0
2.衣着材料	Clothing Material	136.1	136.1
3.鞋袜帽	Shoes,socks and Hats	109.1	113.0
4.衣着加工服务费	Clothing Processing	150.3	150.3
四、家庭设备用品及维修服务	**Household Facilities and Repair Services**	**112.6**	**113.0**
1.耐用消费品	Durable Consuming Goods	97.4	97.5
家具	Furniture	117.2	117.1
家庭设备	Household Facilities	90.5	90.7
2.室内装饰品	Interior Decorations	95.6	94.9

INDICATORS OF CONSUMER PRICE RELATINE OF A FIXED BASE(2014)

(price in 2000=100)

3月 Mar	4月 Apr	5月 May	6月 Jun	7月 Jul	8月 Aug	9月 Sept	10月 Oct	11月 Nov	12月 Dec
138.5	**138.6**	**139.0**	**138.4**	**138.8**	**139.2**	**139.5**	**138.4**	**137.8**	**138.2**
114.4	114.8	114.7	114.5	114.6	114.3	114.1	113.9	113.9	114.1
139.6	140.0	139.3	138.9	139.2	139.1	139.3	139.7	139.9	140.1
133.6	133.7	133.9	133.7	133.9	134.1	133.9	133.6	133.4	133.7
139.8	139.7	140.6	140.0	140.5	141.2	141.5	139.6	138.5	139.0
206.0	**204.9**	**206.7**	**204.9**	**206.6**	**210.0**	**212.1**	**207.2**	**204.5**	**205.2**
234.6	237.9	239.6	240.0	238.9	240.0	241.8	240.6	241.0	241.4
178.5	182.2	182.8	187.3	196.9	203.4	200.8	195.0	196.4	195.7
249.2	252.9	255.6	257.2	257.0	256.1	256.3	256.6	256.2	256.4
151.7	151.2	149.5	150.0	151.0	151.0	149.6	151.2	153.4	148.1
219.6	212.3	218.3	222.5	224.5	229.3	229.9	228.1	225.8	225.3
215.4	217.5	231.2	226.9	235.5	247.6	250.5	245.4	240.9	239.6
194.6	193.7	191.1	185.8	186.8	192.6	189.3	186.9	186.5	188.7
284.0	285.8	308.3	283.3	307.2	333.4	357.8	301.6	273.2	281.4
296.4	297.0	326.2	296.4	325.8	357.7	387.9	319.2	284.8	294.6
139.6	138.4	138.2	141.2	140.7	139.8	141.1	145.2	145.1	141.7
171.7	170.7	170.4	174.2	177.4	176.5	176.7	177.1	176.0	179.7
118.5	122.7	123.4	119.4	115.8	110.6	110.2	111.1	117.5	120.0
290.1	289.3	267.1	266.9	250.6	241.6	245.9	249.3	253.7	249.5
305.0	304.2	279.3	278.9	260.1	249.3	254.3	257.8	263.0	255.7
148.1	150.1	152.0	153.1	153.0	150.5	149.5	148.5	149.0	152.5
212.9	212.0	210.7	211.3	212.0	212.5	212.9	211.8	206.9	205.5
166.7	167.0	167.2	167.2	167.2	167.2	167.2	167.5	167.7	167.7
0.0	0.0	0.0	0.0	0.0	0.0	0.0	0.0	0.0	0.0
111.8	**111.7**	**111.2**	**111.2**	**111.3**	**111.3**	**111.0**	**112.0**	**112.2**	**112.3**
100.1	100.1	100.1	100.1	100.1	100.1	100.1	100.1	100.1	100.1
138.0	137.8	136.0	135.9	136.2	136.4	135.2	138.5	139.1	139.6
119.3	119.5	120.4	118.5	117.4	115.4	114.2	112.6	112.0	113.7
118.2	**118.4**	**119.9**	**118.6**	**117.6**	**116.0**	**115.1**	**114.0**	**113.2**	**113.6**
136.1	136.1	138.6	140.0	140.0	140.0	140.0	140.0	140.0	140.0
118.1	118.2	117.2	113.3	111.6	108.3	106.4	103.2	102.8	108.8
155.4	157.0	161.4	164.0	164.0	164.0	164.0	164.0	164.0	164.0
114.6	**115.7**	**115.5**	**116.4**	**115.9**	**116.4**	**116.6**	**117.0**	**117.3**	**117.8**
97.9	98.0	98.5	99.3	99.3	99.6	99.6	99.5	99.4	99.6
117.1	117.1	117.1	117.4	117.7	117.5	117.5	117.5	118.0	118.4
91.2	91.3	91.9	92.7	92.7	93.0	93.1	92.9	92.7	92.9
96.0	96.5	97.5	98.6	98.7	98.7	97.7	98.3	98.4	98.8

4-7 续 表

(以 2000 年价格为 100)

指　标	Item	1 月 Jan	2 月 Feb
3.床上用品	Bedding Articles	111.5	111.5
4.家庭日用杂品	Daily Use Household Articles	121.2	122.1
5.家庭服务及加工维修服务	Farmily Services and Upkeep	177.7	177.7
五、医疗保健和个人用品	**Health Protection and Aticles for Personal Use**	**117.6**	**117.9**
1.医疗保健	Medicine and Medical Care	110.8	110.9
医疗器具及用品	Medical Facilities	106.2	106.2
中药材及中成药	Chinese Medicine	172.5	174.1
西药	Western Medicine	70.9	70.9
保健器具及用品	Health Appliances	107.6	107.0
医疗保健服务	Medicine and Medical Care	137.7	137.7
2.个人用品及服务	Services and Articles for Personal use	132.7	133.3
化妆美容用品	Beauty Utensil	97.5	96.6
清洁类化妆品	Health Utensil	113.4	113.5
个人饰品	Articales for Personal Adornment	166.1	166.5
个人服务	Personal Services	152.4	155.3
六、交通和通讯	**Transportation and Telecommunications**	**81.5**	**81.5**
1.交通	Transportation	103.1	103.0
交通工具	Transportation Tools	69.6	70.0
车用燃料及零配件	Fuels and Spares for Vehicle	190.5	188.9
车辆使用及维修费	Services and Repair for Vehicle	108.5	108.5
市区公共交通费	Urban Public Tratlic	125.4	125.4
城市间交通费	Traffic Within Cities	121.7	120.4
2.通信	Telecommunications	60.3	60.3
通信工具	Telecommunications Tools	8.6	8.6
通信服务	Telecommunications Services	95.4	95.4
七、娱乐教育文化用品及服务	**Recreation,Education and Culture Articles and other Services**	**118.9**	**120.3**
1.文娱用耐用消费品及服务	Cultural and Recreational Durables and Services	25.8	26.2
2.教育	Education	159.1	159.1
教材及参考书	Teaching Materials and Referenes Books	135.0	135.0
教育服务	Education and Child-Care Fee	160.6	160.6
3.文化娱乐类	Cultural and Recreational Articles	121.1	125.5
文化娱乐用品	Culture and Recreation	93.8	93.5
书报杂志	Books,Newspapers and Magazines	147.9	147.9
文娱费	Cultural expenses	145.6	155.1
4.旅游	Travel and outing	123.6	124.7
八、居住	**Residence**	**125.7**	**127.7**
1.建房及装修材料	Building Materials	133.2	133.2
2.住房租金	Rent room	151.6	154.1
3.自有住房	Private Residence	91.9	94.3
4.水、电、燃料	Water,Electricity and Fuels	136.9	136.9

CONTINUED

(price in 2000=100)

3月 Mar	4月 Apr	5月 May	6月 Jun	7月 Jul	8月 Aug	9月 Sept	10月 Oct	11月 Nov	12月 Dec
111.5	111.6	111.4	111.4	111.4	111.4	111.4	111.5	111.8	112.1
122.2	122.5	120.4	121.2	119.6	120.3	120.2	120.9	121.8	122.8
198.3	212.2	215.4	219.8	219.8	221.7	224.2	228.6	228.6	228.6
118.7	**118.1**	**118.0**	**118.5**	**119.1**	**118.6**	**118.4**	**118.1**	**118.3**	**118.2**
111.1	110.8	110.9	111.1	111.2	111.3	111.4	111.2	112.3	112.1
108.9	111.4	111.4	114.4	112.6	115.5	115.5	115.5	115.5	115.5
175.9	173.2	174.1	172.4	172.0	172.3	173.0	171.8	179.4	177.9
70.9	70.9	70.9	71.0	71.0	71.0	71.0	71.0	71.0	71.0
107.0	107.0	107.0	108.5	109.1	109.1	109.1	109.1	108.8	108.8
137.7	137.7	137.7	137.7	137.7	137.7	137.7	137.7	137.7	137.7
134.7	133.7	133.5	134.3	135.7	134.5	133.9	133.3	132.5	132.6
95.6	94.9	95.6	97.2	98.9	98.7	99.2	99.3	99.3	99.5
116.7	116.3	115.5	115.7	114.9	114.9	116.0	115.6	115.4	117.1
169.3	165.9	164.8	166.0	171.5	165.5	160.1	157.3	153.5	151.7
156.7	156.7	156.7	156.7	156.7	156.7	156.7	156.7	156.7	156.7
81.8	**82.0**	**82.3**	**82.5**	**83.0**	**82.7**	**82.3**	**81.8**	**81.1**	**80.4**
103.3	103.2	103.5	103.6	104.6	103.9	103.1	102.5	101.0	100.0
69.8	69.4	69.5	69.6	69.6	69.6	69.6	69.6	69.6	69.4
191.7	189.9	192.5	193.5	194.4	190.6	185.8	180.6	171.8	166.9
108.5	108.5	108.5	108.5	110.4	110.4	110.4	110.4	110.4	110.4
125.4	125.4	125.4	125.4	125.4	125.4	125.4	125.4	125.4	125.4
119.9	124.8	124.0	122.8	127.7	125.9	124.1	125.9	122.6	120.2
60.7	61.3	61.7	61.7	61.9	62.0	61.9	61.5	61.6	61.4
8.9	9.5	9.7	9.8	10.0	10.1	10.0	9.7	9.7	9.6
95.4	95.4	95.4	95.4	95.4	95.4	95.4	95.4	95.4	95.4
121.4	**123.0**	**123.3**	**122.7**	**122.7**	**122.0**	**123.5**	**124.5**	**124.5**	**124.6**
26.9	28.7	29.7	28.9	29.0	29.2	29.3	29.3	29.5	29.5
159.1	159.1	159.1	159.1	159.1	159.1	163.5	163.5	163.5	163.5
135.0	135.0	135.0	135.0	135.0	135.0	127.8	127.8	127.8	127.8
160.6	160.6	160.6	160.6	160.6	160.6	165.5	165.5	165.5	165.5
125.6	125.4	125.5	125.5	125.6	121.1	121.2	125.8	125.8	125.9
93.7	93.2	93.4	93.5	93.7	93.9	94.2	94.3	94.3	94.5
147.9	147.9	147.9	147.9	147.9	147.9	147.9	147.9	147.9	147.9
155.1	155.1	155.1	155.1	155.1	145.6	145.6	155.1	155.1	155.1
127.8	129.8	128.6	127.8	127.8	127.8	127.9	127.9	127.9	127.9
129.3	**129.3**	**128.2**	**128.3**	**128.5**	**129.1**	**128.3**	**128.0**	**128.4**	**128.8**
133.2	133.0	133.1	137.6	137.8	138.7	138.7	138.7	138.7	138.7
156.8	156.8	155.3	154.5	154.8	155.5	154.4	153.9	154.5	155.1
95.9	95.9	94.7	94.2	94.4	94.9	94.0	93.7	94.2	94.6
136.9	136.9	136.9	136.9	136.9	136.9	136.9	136.9	136.9	136.9

4-8 市区全年及分月商品零售价格指数(2014 年)

(以上年同期价格为 100)

指 标	Item	全年 Annual Total	1 月 Jan
商品零售价格总指数	**General Retail Price Index**	**101.6**	**101.0**
一、食品	Food	102.9	102.6
1.粮食	Grain	102.7	101.7
2.淀粉	Starches	107.0	97.6
3.干豆类及豆制品	Bean and Its Products	104.5	103.2
4.油脂	Oil and Fat	98.1	95.0
5.肉禽及其制品	Meat,Poultry and Their Products	100.1	100.5
食用畜肉及副产品	Edible Poultry and Their By-Products	99.5	101.5
禽	Poultry	101.6	98.9
肉禽加工制品	Meat and Poultry Products	100.8	99.1
6.蛋	Eggs	110.9	101.1
7.水产品	Aquatic Products	102.7	107.1
鱼	Fish	100.5	105.4
其它水产品	Others	104.8	108.7
8.菜	Vegetables	102.6	92.4
9.调味品	Flavoring	99.7	99.2
10.糖	Carbonhydrate	99.3	96.8
11.干鲜瓜果	Dried Fruit	115.5	120.4
12.糕点饼干面包	Cake,biscuit and Bread	103.4	104.2
13.液体乳及乳制品	Milk and Its Products	108.6	111.4
14.在外用膳食品	Dine Out	100.1	100.9
15.其它食品	Others	97.2	94.1
二、饮料、烟酒	Beverage,Tobacco and Liquor	99.3	100.8
1.茶及饮料	Tea and Beverage	102.0	105.7
茶叶	Tea	100.0	99.1
饮料	Beverage	102.5	107.7
2.烟草	Tobacco	100.0	100.0
3.酒	Liquor	95.1	96.3
三、服装、鞋帽	Garments,Shoes and Hats	106.1	106.9
1.服装	Garments	106.8	105.9
男式服装	Men's Wear	108.0	104.7
女式服装	Women's Wear	105.7	106.8
儿童服装	Children's Wear	108.3	107.7
2.鞋袜帽	Shoes,socks and Hats	104.7	111.2
鞋	Shoes	105.1	112.7
袜子	Socks	100.2	100.3
帽子	Hats	106.2	104.1
3.其它	Others	97.8	94.1

RETAIL PRICE INDICATORS OF COMMODITIES IN CITY PROPER BY MONTH(2014)

(preceding year=100)

2月 Feb	3月 Mar	4月 Apr	5月 May	6月 Jun	7月 Jul	8月 Aug	9月 Sept	10月 Oct	11月 Nov	12月 Dec
101.0	**101.4**	**101.5**	**101.8**	**101.8**	**101.7**	**101.7**	**101.7**	**101.7**	**101.7**	**101.6**
102.4	103.0	103.1	103.4	103.2	103.0	102.9	103.1	103.0	103.0	102.9
101.1	101.2	101.7	102.3	102.5	102.6	102.6	102.7	102.7	102.7	102.7
97.1	98.8	100.6	101.2	101.6	102.5	103.9	104.9	105.7	106.5	107.0
102.7	102.7	103.0	103.5	103.9	104.2	104.4	104.5	104.6	104.5	104.5
95.9	96.1	96.2	96.1	96.3	96.7	97.1	97.0	97.4	98.1	98.1
99.2	98.7	98.5	99.2	99.5	99.7	100.0	100.1	100.2	100.1	100.1
100.0	99.4	99.2	99.8	100.0	100.1	100.3	100.2	100.0	99.7	99.5
96.8	95.6	95.6	97.1	97.8	98.5	99.2	99.9	100.6	101.1	101.6
98.6	98.8	98.6	98.8	99.2	99.4	99.8	100.1	100.5	100.7	100.8
101.1	101.4	102.9	105.7	107.1	108.7	109.8	110.0	110.5	110.7	110.9
105.7	106.3	106.2	105.8	105.1	104.2	103.8	103.4	103.1	102.9	102.7
102.9	102.7	102.2	102.2	101.6	100.9	100.1	100.0	100.2	100.3	100.5
108.5	109.8	110.0	109.4	108.5	107.5	107.4	106.7	106.1	105.4	104.8
94.8	101.0	101.5	103.8	101.9	101.8	101.2	102.7	102.4	102.2	102.6
98.8	98.6	98.3	98.2	98.5	98.6	98.7	98.9	99.4	99.7	99.7
97.6	98.4	98.2	98.2	98.2	98.4	98.5	98.6	98.8	99.0	99.3
119.8	118.5	118.0	117.9	118.2	117.6	117.7	117.6	117.3	116.6	115.5
104.6	103.5	103.1	102.9	102.8	102.8	102.6	102.7	102.9	103.2	103.4
110.9	110.6	110.1	110.0	109.5	109.5	109.3	109.2	109.4	109.3	108.6
100.8	100.6	100.6	100.5	100.4	100.3	100.2	100.1	100.1	100.1	100.1
95.3	96.3	96.2	96.1	95.5	95.0	94.9	95.4	96.0	96.5	97.2
100.5	100.4	100.8	101.0	100.6	100.2	99.7	99.4	99.3	99.3	99.3
106.0	105.9	107.0	108.1	106.6	105.2	103.7	102.7	102.0	102.0	102.0
99.1	99.1	99.1	99.1	99.1	99.1	99.3	99.5	99.7	99.9	100.0
108.0	107.8	109.3	110.7	108.7	107.0	105.0	103.6	102.7	102.5	102.5
100.0	100.0	100.0	100.0	100.0	100.0	100.0	100.0	100.0	100.0	100.0
94.9	94.8	94.8	94.5	94.5	94.6	94.6	94.6	94.7	94.9	95.1
107.9	109.2	109.6	109.9	109.6	109.2	108.8	108.3	107.7	106.8	106.1
106.8	108.0	108.6	109.3	109.3	109.1	108.8	108.7	108.4	107.7	106.8
106.1	107.8	108.7	109.5	109.7	109.6	109.5	109.4	109.1	108.6	108.0
107.2	108.0	108.5	109.1	108.9	108.6	108.2	108.0	107.7	106.7	105.7
108.1	109.0	108.6	108.9	108.6	108.5	108.7	109.1	109.6	109.2	108.3
112.8	114.8	114.3	113.4	112.0	110.8	109.8	108.0	106.4	105.0	104.7
114.4	116.7	116.0	115.0	113.3	112.0	110.8	108.8	107.0	105.4	105.1
100.7	100.4	100.8	101.0	100.9	100.8	100.7	100.6	100.4	100.3	100.2
104.8	106.5	108.0	108.0	107.9	107.8	107.4	107.2	106.9	106.6	106.2
94.1	94.0	94.0	95.0	95.8	96.3	96.8	97.1	97.4	97.6	97.8

4-8 续 表

(以上年同期价格为 100)

指 标	Item	全年 Annual Total	1月 Jan
四、纺织品	Textiles	101.0	100.8
1.衣着材料	Clothing Material	101.2	99.2
2.床上用品	Bedding Articles	101.0	101.5
五、家用电器及音像器材	Household Facilities and Moviolas	101.7	98.4
1.家庭设备	Household Facilities	102.4	101.8
2.文娱用耐用消费品	Cultural and Recreational Durables	102.0	89.2
3.专业音像器材	Moviolas	97.0	97.0
六、文化办公用品	Cultural and Office Articles	102.9	98.6
七、日用品	Articles for Daily Use	100.6	99.9
1.日用百货	Articles of Daily Use	101.2	100.0
2.日用杂品	Sundries for Daily Use	103.4	104.0
3.洗涤用品	Detergent	98.7	99.5
4.其它日用品	Others	101.4	98.8
八、体育娱乐用品	Sports and Recreation Articles	103.8	104.6
1.体育用品	Sports Goods	106.0	105.6
2.娱乐用品	Recreation Articles	101.9	103.7
九、交通、通信用品	Transportation and Telecommunications	100.3	96.8
1.交通运输机械	Transport Tools	99.9	99.9
2.通信器材	Communications tools	101.1	89.7
十、家具	Furniture	101.6	101.2
十一、化妆品	Cosmetics	101.6	100.2
十二、金银珠宝	Treasures	88.6	82.7
十三、中西药品及医疗保健用品	Chinese and Western Medicine and Health Appliances	102.7	103.1
1.医疗器具及用品	Medical Facilities	105.8	100.0
2.中药材及中成药	Chinese Medicine	102.7	105.7
3.西药	Western Medicine	100.4	100.1
4.保健品及器具	Health Appliances	104.8	104.1
十四、书报杂志及电子出版物	Books,Newspapers,Magazines and Electronic Publications	103.7	104.4
1.教材及参考书	Teaching Materials and Referenes Books	97.9	97.9
2.书报杂志	Books,Newspapers and Magazines	105.1	105.1
3.电子音像制品	Electronic Moviolas Products	101.9	110.2
十五、燃料类	Fuels	99.3	100.3
1.煤炭及制品	Coal and Its Products	100.0	100.0
2.石油及制品	Petroleum and Its Products	99.3	100.3
十六、建筑材料及五金电料	Building and Hardware Materials	100.5	98.9
1.建筑装璜材料	Building Decoration Movterials	100.2	97.9
2.五金电料	Hardware Materials	101.0	100.4

CONTINUED

(preceding year=100)

2月 Feb	3月 Mar	4月 Apr	5月 May	6月 Jun	7月 Jul	8月 Aug.	9月 Sept	10月 Oct	11月 Nov	12月 Dec
100.8	100.8	100.8	100.9	101.0	101.1	101.1	101.1	101.1	101.1	101.0
99.2	99.2	99.2	99.6	100.0	100.3	100.5	100.7	100.9	101.1	101.2
101.5	101.5	101.5	101.4	101.4	101.4	101.4	101.3	101.2	101.0	101.0
98.6	98.8	99.3	99.8	100.2	100.4	100.7	101.0	101.3	101.5	101.7
101.9	102.1	101.9	101.9	102.0	102.1	102.2	102.3	102.4	102.4	102.4
89.8	90.6	93.0	95.5	96.7	97.6	98.3	99.2	100.1	101.1	102.0
96.5	96.4	96.3	96.2	96.2	96.2	96.2	96.4	96.6	96.8	97.0
98.8	99.5	100.1	100.5	100.6	100.8	101.1	101.5	101.9	102.4	102.9
100.4	100.6	100.8	100.8	100.7	100.6	100.5	100.4	100.4	100.5	100.6
100.9	101.0	100.9	100.8	100.9	101.0	101.1	101.1	101.2	101.2	101.2
103.0	102.9	103.2	103.1	103.2	103.1	103.2	103.3	103.3	103.3	103.4
100.5	100.8	101.1	100.8	100.3	99.5	99.1	98.7	98.5	98.5	98.7
98.6	99.0	99.4	99.7	100.1	100.6	100.8	101.0	101.2	101.3	101.4
104.3	104.2	104.1	104.0	104.0	104.0	104.0	104.0	103.9	103.9	103.8
105.7	105.9	106.0	106.0	106.0	106.0	106.0	106.0	105.9	105.9	106.0
102.9	102.6	102.3	102.1	102.1	102.1	102.1	102.1	102.1	102.1	101.9
96.9	97.6	98.1	98.6	99.1	99.3	99.4	99.6	99.8	100.1	100.3
100.0	100.0	100.0	100.0	100.0	100.0	100.0	100.0	100.0	100.0	99.9
89.9	92.0	93.7	95.4	97.1	97.8	98.1	98.8	99.3	100.3	101.1
101.1	101.0	101.0	101.0	101.1	101.3	101.3	101.4	101.4	101.5	101.6
100.2	100.5	100.3	100.4	100.6	100.8	100.9	101.1	101.2	101.4	101.6
83.8	85.4	85.9	86.0	86.6	87.9	88.4	88.5	88.6	88.5	88.6
103.1	103.2	103.0	102.8	102.7	102.6	102.6	102.6	102.6	102.6	102.7
100.0	100.8	101.8	102.4	103.3	103.7	104.3	104.8	105.2	105.5	105.8
105.6	105.9	105.1	104.6	103.9	103.3	102.9	102.7	102.4	102.6	102.7
100.1	100.2	100.2	100.2	100.3	100.3	100.4	100.4	100.4	100.4	100.4
104.0	103.9	103.9	103.9	104.1	104.3	104.5	104.6	104.7	104.7	104.8
104.5	104.5	104.4	104.4	104.3	104.2	104.1	104.0	103.9	103.8	103.7
98.9	99.2	99.4	99.5	99.6	99.6	99.6	99.1	98.6	98.3	97.9
105.1	105.1	105.1	105.1	105.1	105.1	105.1	105.1	105.1	105.1	105.1
109.6	109.2	108.0	106.7	105.6	104.7	103.8	103.2	102.7	102.3	101.9
99.7	99.4	99.5	99.9	100.2	100.5	100.5	100.3	100.1	99.7	99.3
100.0	100.0	100.0	100.0	100.0	100.0	100.0	100.0	100.0	100.0	100.0
99.7	99.3	99.4	99.9	100.2	100.5	100.5	100.3	100.1	99.7	99.3
98.7	98.6	98.6	98.6	99.1	99.5	99.8	100.0	100.2	100.4	100.5
97.7	97.5	97.5	97.6	98.1	98.7	99.2	99.5	99.8	100.0	100.2
100.4	100.4	100.4	100.3	100.6	100.7	100.8	100.9	100.9	101.0	101.0

主要统计指标解释

居民消费价格指数是反映一定时期内城乡居民所购买的生活消费品和服务项目价格变动趋势和程度的相对数，是对城市居民消费价格指数和农村居民消费价格指数进行综合汇总计算的结果。通过该指数可以观察和分析消费品的零售价格和服务项目价格变动对城乡居民实际生活费支出的影响程度。

城市居民消费价格指数是反映一定时期内城市居民家庭所购买的生活消费品价格和服务项目价格变动趋势和程度的相对数。通过该指数可以观察和分析消费品的零售价格和服务项目价格变动对城镇居民收入和消费支出的影响。

农村居民消费价格指数是反映一定时期内农村居民家庭所购买的生活消费品价格和服务项目价格变动趋势和程度的相对数。该指数可以观察农村消费品的零售价格和服务项目价格变动对农村居民收入和生活消费支出的影响。

商品零售价格指数是反映一定时期内城乡商品零售价格变动趋势和程度的相对数。商品零售价格的变动与国家的财政收入、市场供需的平衡、消费与积累的比例关系有关。因此,该指数可以从一个侧面对上述经济活动进行观察和分析。

农业生产资料价格指数指反映一定时期内农业生产资料价格变动趋势和程度的相对数。其编制目的是了解农业生产中投入物质资料价格的变动状况,服务于国民经济核算。1994 年以前,农业生产资料价格指数仅仅是商品零售价格指数的一个类别,此后,从商品零售价格指数中分离出来,单独编制。

农产品生产价格指数是反映一定时期内,农产品生产者出售农产品价格水平变动趋势及幅度的相对数。该指数可以客观反映全国农产品生产价格水平和结构变动情况,满足农业与国民经济核算需要。其中某代表品生产价格指数是通过对全部有出售该产品行为的调查单位的个体指数进行几何平均求得的,类价格指数是通过对其所属的类(或代表品)的价格指数进行加权平均求得的。季度累计价格指数的计算方法与分季指数的计算方法相同。

工业生产者出厂价格指数是反映一定时期内全部工业产品出厂价格总水平的变动趋势和程度的相对数，包括工业企业售给本企业以外所有单位的各种产品和直接售给居民用于生活消费的产品。该指数可以观察出厂价格变动对工业总产值及增加值的影响。

工业生产者购进价格指数是反映工业企业作为生产投入,而从物资交易市场和能源、原材料生产企业购买原材料、燃料和动力产品时,所支付的价格水平变动趋势和程度的统计指标,是扣除工业企业物质消耗成本中的价格变动影响的重要依据。

目前,我国编制的工业生产者购进价格指数所调查的产品包括燃料动力、黑色金属、有色金属、化工、建材等九大类。

固定资产投资价格指数是反映一定时期内固定资产投资品及取费项目的价格变动趋势和程度的相对数。固定资产投资额是由建筑安装工程投资完成额、设备工器具购置投资完成额和其他费用投资完成额三部分组成的。编制固定资产投资价格指数应首先分别编制上述三部分投资的价格指数,然后采用加权算术平均法求出固定资产投资价格总指数。

该指数可以准确地反映固定资产投资中涉及的各类投资品和取费项目价格变动趋势和变动幅度，消除按现价计算的固定资产投资指标中的价格变动因素,真实地反映固定资产投资的规模、速度、结构和效益,为国家科学地制定、检查固定资产投资计划并提高宏观调控水平,为完善国民经济核算体系提供科学的、可靠的依据。

第五篇

人民生活 Chapter 5

People's livelihood

5-1 历年城乡居民收支

单位:元

年份 Year	全市城镇居民人均可支配收入 Per Capita Disposable Income of Urban Residents	全市城镇居民人均消费性支出 Per Capita Expense of Urban Residents	食品烟酒 Food
1985			
1990			
1991			
1992			
1993			
1994			
1995			
1996			
1997			
1998			
1999			
2000			
2001			
2002			
2003			
2004			
2005	11590	7805	2950
2006	13056	8366	3120
2007	15261	9413	3560
2008	17540	10864	4151
2009	19469	11908	4336
2010	21825	13506	4803
2011	25094	15613	5651
2012	28292	17858	6211
2013	31059	19646	6776
2014	33374	22035	6399

注:2014年以前市区城镇居民人均可支配收入及消费性支出数据不包括通州区。2014年以前农村居民人均可支配收入指标名称为农民人均纯收入。

INCOME AND EXPENSES OF URBAN AND RURAL RESIDENTS OVER THE YEARS

(yuan)

市区城镇居民人均可支配收入 Per Capita Disposable Income in Urban Area	市区城镇居民人均消费性支出 Per Capita Expense in Urban Area	食品烟酒 Food	人均可支配收入 Per Capita Net Income of Rural Residents	农村居民人均生活消费性支出 Per Capita Nonproductive Expense of Rural Residents	食品烟酒 Food
	733	405	452	437	226
	1551	875	871	828	423
	1817	992	886	884	478
2592	2001	1100	1008	999	499
3291	2769	1314	1167	1064	482
4889	3693	1832	1820	1752	820
5531	4319	2443	2547	2213	1040
5915	4640	2484	3168	2834	1274
6506	4909	2507	3388	2717	1165
6899	5701	2614	3504	2660	1108
7416	5835	2575	3585	2547	1011
7911	5898	2439	3710	2897	989
8485	5959	2478	3926	2776	986
8640	5852	2318	4133	2907	1050
9598	6808	2730	4393	2976	1173
10937	7768	3140	4929	3342	1381
12384	8573	3274	5501	3858	1559
14058	9332	3425	6106	4313	1659
16451	10188	3921	6905	4911	1863
18903	11613	4560	7811	5653	2172
21001	13103	4804	8696	6448	2433
23541	14492	5173	9914	7240	2623
26778	16666	6220	11730	8510	3077
30206	18981	7000	13231	9839	3546
33136	20978	7562	14754	10931	3864
35568	21099	6127	15821	11051	3271

Note:Per capita disposable income and Expenses of urban residents before 2014 did not include Tongzhou District Before 2014, the indicator of per capita disposable income of rural residents was referred as per capitea net income of farmers.

5-2 分地区全体居民家庭收入消费情况

单位:元

指 标	Item	南通市 Nantong
人均可支配收入	**Per Capita Disposable Income**	**25340**
工资性收入	Salary	14701
经营净收入	Net Income From Operations	4982
财产净收入	Income from Property	1565
转移净收入	Transfer Income	4092
生活消费支出	**Expenses**	**17007**
食品	Food	4967
衣着	Clothing	1181
居住	Housing	3828
生活用品及服务	Family Equipments and Services	992
交通通信	Transprotation&Communication	2740
教育文化娱乐	Education,Culture and Entertainment	1707
医疗保健	Medical Care	1053
其他用品和服务	Grocery &Services	539

注:本表为全体居民新口径数据,市区包括通州区。

REVENUE AND EXPENDITURE OF URBAN FAMILIES BY REGION

(Unit: Yuan)

市区 Urban Area	通州区 Tongzhou	海安 Haian	如东 Rudong	启东 Qidong	如皋 Rugao	海门 Haimen
29960	**24836**	**22842**	**22454**	**23908**	**22391**	**25262**
17358	14801	13051	13441	15764	13717	16114
5786	4969	4530	5558	3586	3803	5226
2032	1265	1450	713	1688	1728	524
4784	3801	3811	2742	2870	3143	3398
18352	**15903**	**16036**	**14609**	**18776**	**14550**	**17081**
5350	4933	4767	4429	5887	4583	5090
1323	1097	1157	1134	1522	1091	1838
4235	2653	2603	1260	2903	2430	1688
1070	843	959	977	1138	844	1051
2879	2067	2120	2587	2423	1818	3215
1775	2854	2946	2731	3376	2241	2523
1154	982	1063	919	1058	1208	1108
566	474	421	572	469	335	568

Note:Data of this table are in accordance with urban old standards. Tongzhou District is not included in downtown area.

5-3 分地区城镇常住居民家庭收入消费情况

单位:元

指 标	Item	南通市 Nantong
人均可支配收入	**Per Capita Disposable Income**	**33374**
工资性收入	Salary	19295
经营净收入	Net Income From Operations	6270
财产净收入	Income from Property	2571
转移净收入	Transfer Income	5238
生活消费支出	**Expenses**	**22035**
食品烟酒	Food	6399
衣着	Clothing	1707
居住	Housing	5037
生活用品及服务	Family Equipments and Services	1283
交通通信	Transprotation&Communication	3268
教育文化娱乐	Education,Culture and Entertainment	2270
医疗保健	Medical Care	1430
其他用品和服务	Grocery &Services	641

注:本表为城镇新口径数据,市区包括通州区。

INCOME AND EXPENDITURE OF URBAN PERMANENT FAMILIES BY REGION

(Unit: Yuan)

市区 Urban Area	通州区 Tongzhou	海安 Haian	如东 Rudong	启东 Qidong	如皋 Rugao	海门 Haimen
35568	**34565**	**31597**	**31557**	**31708**	**31026**	**34280**
20563	20807	18320	19887	19976	19194	23311
6683	5238	5630	5745	4756	3490	4614
2740	2218	2539	1062	3171	2646	762
5582	6302	5108	4863	3805	5696	5592
21099	**20501**	**20125**	**18819**	**26248**	**19116**	**22830**
6127	6217	5745	6512	8076	5830	6803
1634	1532	1660	1601	2421	1587	2960
4920	3513	3296	1291	4283	3326	1620
1228	1116	1150	1128	1517	1090	1291
3129	2339	2677	3127	3211	2370	4201
2078	3697	3753	3483	4851	2925	4155
1369	1476	1264	1026	1431	1510	999
614	611	580	651	409	478	801

Note: Data of this table are in accordance with urban new standards. Tongzhou District is included in downtown area.

5-4 分地区农村常住居民家庭收入消费情况

单位：元

指 标	Item	南通市 Nantong
人均可支配收入	**Per Capita Net Income**	**15821**
工资性收入	Salary	9259
家庭净收入	Net Income From Operations	3453
财产净收入	Income from Property	373
转移净收入	Transfer Income	2736
家庭经营性费用支出	Operating cost	2130
购置生产性固定资产支出	Purchase of productive fixed assets	3225
生活消费支出	**Living Expenditure**	**11051**
食品烟酒	Food	3271
衣着	Clothing	558
居住	Housing	2394
生活用品及服务	Family Equipments and Services	648
交通通信	Medical Care	2115
教育文化娱乐	Transprotation&Communication	1040
医疗保健	Education,Culture and Entertainment	607
其他用品和服务	Others	418
财产性支出	Property Expenditure	5
转移性支出	Transfer Expenditures	543
现金支出	Cash Outlay	21511
生产费用	Operating cost	2054

注：本表为农村新口径数据，市区包括通州。

INCOME AND EXPENDITURE OF RURAL PERMANENT FAMILIES BY REGION

(Unit: Yuan)

市区 Urban Area	通州区 Tongzhou	海安 Haian	如东 Rudong	启东 Qidong	如皋 Rugao	海门 Haimen
17051	**16835**	**15155**	**14494**	**16762**	**14210**	**17419**
9979	9861	8426	7804	11566	7853	9633
3721	4748	3564	5394	2514	3902	6037
402	482	493	409	670	536	603
2949	1744	2672	887	2012	1919	1146
1054	1477	2601	9202	575	1525	1729
1596	3730	806	115	1993	146	2156
12030	**12122**	**12447**	**10928**	**11931**	**10225**	**12081**
3561	3877	3908	2608	3814	3272	3600
608	740	716	725	933	664	888
2660	1945	1991	1233	1686	1636	1921
705	619	788	845	752	654	853
2302	1843	1624	826	1667	1299	1262
1078	2161	2251	2115	2146	1585	2091
661	576	887	2073	710	859	1201
455	361	282	504	223	256	265
6	5	99	4			1
516	615	888	1006	1046	467	166
18998	24426	23140	24937	14970	23610	17679
1814	1465	2494	1838	572	1502	1729

Note: Data of this table are in accordance with urban new standards. Tongzhou District is included in downtown area.

5-5 市区居民家庭基本情况(2014 年)

STATISTICS OF URBAN FAMILIES (2014)

单位:元/人 (Unit: Yuan/person)

指 标	Item	2014 年	2013 年	2014 年为 2013 年% Percentage to2013
调查户数(户)	Residents Surveyed (household)	340	312	109.0
户均家庭人口数(人)	Average Residents Per Household (person)	3.02	3.00	100.7
户均就业人口数(人)	Average Emplyees Per Household (person)	1.86	1.94	95.9
人均住房建筑面积(平方米)	Floor Space Per Capita (m2)	51.4	52.4	98.1
可支配收入	Disposable Income	29960	27456	109.1
工资性收入	Salary Income	17358	15917	109.0
经营净收入	Operation Net Income	5786	5348	108.2
财产净收入	Property Income	2032	1815	112.0
转移净收入	Transfer Income	4784	4376	109.3
# 离退休金	Pensions	3719	3154	117.9
出售财物收入	Income from Selling Property	70	451	15.4
借贷收入	Income from Debt and Credit	1779	1908	93.2
# 提取储蓄存款	Dissaving	1714	1671	102.6
生活消费支出	Nonproductive Expenses	18352	17053	107.6
借贷支出	Borrowing Costs	4514	4121	109.6
# 存入储蓄款	Savings Deposits	3825	3397	112.6

注:本表为全体居民新口径数据,市区包括通州。

Note: Data of this table are in accordance with urban new standards. Tongzhou District is included in downtown area.

5-6 市区城镇常住居民家庭基本情况(2014年)

STATISTICS OF URBAN PERMANENT FAMILIES (2014)

单位:元/人

(Unit: Yuan/person)

指 标	Item	2014年	2013年	2014年为2013年% Percentage to2013
调查户数(户)	Residents Surveyed (household)	240	212	113.2
户均家庭人口数(人)	Average Residents Per Household (person)	2.94	2.95	99.7
户均就业人口数(人)	Average Emplyees Per Household (person)	1.68	1.76	95.5
人均住房建筑面积(平方米)	Floor Space Per Capita (m2)	45.5	45.4	100.2
可支配收入	Disposable Income	35568	32696	108.8
工资性收入	Salary Income	20563	18902	108.8
经营净收入	Operation Net Income	6683	6216	107.5
财产净收入	Property Income	2740	2443	112.2
转移净收入	Transfer Income	5582	5135	108.7
#离退休金	Pensions	4609	4005	115.1
出售财物收入	Income from Selling Property	88	656	13.4
借贷收入	Income from Debt and Credit	1612	2531	63.7
#提取储蓄存款	Dissaving	1522	2243	67.9
生活消费支出	Nonproductive Expenses	21099	19719	107.0
借贷支出	Borrowing Costs	4411	5895	74.8
#存入储蓄款	Savings Deposits	3364	4806	70.0

注:本表为城镇居民新口径数据,市区包括通州。

Note: Data of this table are in accordance with urban new standards. Tongzhou District is included in downtown area.

5-7 市区农村常住居民家庭基本情况(2014 年)

STATISTICS OF RURAL PERMANENT FAMILIES (2014)

单位:元/人 (Unit: Yuan/person)

指　标	Item	2014 年	2013 年	2014 年为 2013 年% Percentage to2013
调查户数(户)	Residents Surveyed (household)	100	100	100.0
户均家庭人口数(人)	Average Residents Per Household (person)	3.21	3.10	103.5
户均就业人口数(人)	Average Emplyees Per Household (person)	2.30	2.32	99.1
人均住房建筑面积(平方米)	Floor Space Per Capita (m2)	64.5	66.3	97.3
可支配收入	Disposable Income	17051	15395	110.8
工资性收入	Salary Income	9979	9048	110.3
经营净收入	Operation Net Income	3721	3350	111.1
财产净收入	Property Income	402	367	109.5
转移净收入	Transfer Income	2949	2630	112.1
# 离退休金	Pensions	1258	1026	122.6
出售财物收入	Income from Selling Property	27	10	280.3
借贷收入	Income from Debt and Credit	1890	522	361.9
# 提取储蓄存款	Dissaving	1878	403	466.1
生活消费支出	Nonproductive Expenses	12030	10917	110.2
借贷支出	Borrowing Costs	4897	1269	385.9
# 存入储蓄款	Savings Deposits	4788	1136	421.4

注:本表为农村新口径数据,市区包括通州。

Note: Data of this table are in accordance with urban new standards. Tongzhou District is included in downtown area.

主要统计指标解释

可支配收入 指调查户在调查期内获得的、可用于最终消费支出和储蓄的总和,即调查户可以用来自由支配的收入。可支配收入既包括现金,也包括实物收入。按照收入的来源,可支配收入包含四项,分别为:工资性收入、经营净收入、财产净收入、转移净收入。计算公式为:

可支配收入 = 工资性收入 + 经营净收入 + 财产净收入 + 转移净收入

其中:经营净收入 = 经营收入 - 经营费用 - 生产性固定资产折旧 - 生产税

财产净收入 = 财产性收入 - 财产性支出

转移净收入 = 转移性收入 - 转移性支出

工资性收入 指就业人员通过各种途径得到的全部劳动报酬和各种福利,包括受雇于单位或个人、从事各种自由职业、兼职和零星劳动得到的全部劳动报酬和福利。

消费支出 指住户用于满足家庭日常生活消费需要的全部支出,包括用于消费品的支出和用于服务性消费的支出。根据用途不同,消费支出可划分为食品烟酒、衣着、居住、生活用品及服务、交通通信、教育文化娱乐、医疗保健、其他用品及服务八大类。根据来源不同,消费支出可划分为现金消费支出、实物消费支出(含自产自用、来自单位、来自政府和其他社会组织)。

第六篇

财政 金融

Chapter 6

Government Finance, Banking

6-1 历年财政收入

GOVERNMENT REVENUE OVER THE YEARS

单位：万元 (10,000 Yuan)

年份 Year	全市 Total	市区 Urban Area	通州区 Tongzhou	海安 Haian	如东 Rudong	启东 Qidong	如皋 Rugao	海门 Haimen
1978	54878	35401	6051	2963	3674	4460	3747	4633
1979	55382	34179	6318	3109	3981	5018	3907	5188
1980	59421	37859	6757	3331	3950	5695	3731	4855
1985	88750	49252	12229	6661	6651	9914	7317	8955
1990	126870	68064	19487	10046	10209	14609	10690	13252
1991	124296	67178	18187	8937	10235	14102	10663	13181
1992	139849	73253	20501	10909	12109	16496	12041	15041
1993	193560	101212	25866	18127	15641	22759	16709	19112
1994	227811	118469	30466	20004	19344	26622	20619	22753
1995	272751	136622	36351	24538	23452	33390	25847	28902
1996	307839	151069	43393	26289	29162	38467	28011	34841
1997	364398	182043	49270	29471	34352	44716	31131	42685
1998	402701	207952	55286	31131	35986	48788	32178	46666
1999	416248	231212	56672	32351	35590	44295	29817	42983
2000	534025	319048	70797	36831	39370	51370	35376	52030
2001	667483	390062	81621	49151	51924	60111	51593	64642
2002	874086	517144	100031	62552	71291	69669	65518	87912
2003	1169933	690169	131376	85088	88711	100188	90358	115419
2004	1387200	801250	147730	102710	96105	133062	106788	147285
2005	1711871	1010657	200331	125140	110462	160111	130166	175335
2006	2175697	1261107	241318	159519	155503	200239	175010	224319
2007	3007122	1706798	339390	228675	220159	262010	270693	318787
2008	3902076	2146310	416082	305039	300915	348392	391141	410279
2009	4861042	2556053	553823	402131	401442	453669	517513	530234
2010	7133642	3890193	778652	505436	503824	750592	780841	702756
2011	9516538	4955494	1001531	724080	657922	1035559	1107470	1036013
2012	10558988	5008596	1219538	1001445	803630	1233468	1290984	1220865
2013	12167339	5729732	1457074	1151937	1024246	1395121	1464161	1402142
2014	14039281	6438340	1722185	1278748	1283453	1683986	1735962	1618792

6-2 历年一般公共预算收入

GENERAL PUBLIC BUDGET REVENUE OVER THE YEARS

单位：万元　　(10,000 yuan)

年份 Year	全市 Total	市区 Urban Area	通州区 Tongzhou	海安 Haian	如东 Rudong	启东 Qidong	如皋 Rugao	海门 Haimen
1985	88750	49252	12229	6661	6651	9914	7317	8955
1986	91226	49972	13182	7033	7197	10096	7375	9553
1987	99303	53843	14570	7743	7846	11183	8227	10461
1988	111043	59826	16465	8713	8749	12773	9416	11566
1989	121430	65056	18368	9541	9781	13874	10372	12806
1990	126870	68064	19487	10046	10209	14609	10690	13252
1991	124296	67178	18187	8937	10235	14102	10663	13181
1992	139849	73253	20501	10909	12109	16496	12041	15041
1993	193560	101212	25866	18127	15641	22759	16709	19112
1994	110640	57205	14420	9692	10297	13493	9494	10459
1995	139256	69485	17324	12564	12618	17726	12582	14281
1996	160108	75319	21142	13925	16650	21043	14995	18176
1997	177909	87593	21760	14322	18130	21951	15613	20300
1998	207951	106277	24912	16351	19471	25518	17053	23281
1999	223666	109566	17551	20489	25459	17468	26553	24131
2000	284549	164099	35263	19395	22210	29426	20074	29345
2001	352853	201478	41293	25011	29363	33376	27891	35734
2002	387298	220232	39661	27061	32468	33887	31378	42272
2003	488063	273932	52804	36566	37077	46954	38398	55136
2004	525893	293150	57301	37528	35593	55987	39428	64207
2005	719903	423987	86395	47330	44472	73289	54520	76305
2006	925330	538635	105655	61501	61568	92387	75086	96153
2007	1276956	725064	140101	93588	90188	122006	115089	131021
2008	1595895	857542	165822	125656	121156	162166	164288	165087
2009	1989873	1023914	241912	155797	153346	213132	216529	227155
2010	2908061	1550372	338858	205188	190398	312558	336880	312665
2011	3736858	1877357	424002	285060	253906	440716	456307	423512
2012	4197225	1926012	525194	375279	321681	522149	536012	516092
2013	4858818	2187487	611832	466342	406572	585350	601318	611749
2014	5500019	2426245	684012	541022	500127	672463	674450	685712

6-3 历年财政支出

GOVERNMENT EXPENDITURE OVER THE YEARS

单位：万元 (10,000 Yuan)

年份 Year	全市 Total	市区 Urban Area	通州区 Tongzhou	海安 Haian	如东 Rudong	启东 Qidong	如皋 Rugao	海门 Haimen
1978	16109	7188	2011	1779	1906	1652	2174	1410
1979	16074	7352	2009	1589	1589	1737	2159	1648
1980	17447	6894	2276	1879	2047	2275	2512	1840
1985	32531	13395	4652	3626	3621	3871	4348	3670
1990	71461	29949	11105	7691	8242	8577	9305	7697
1991	76948	32580	11515	8367	8946	9380	9495	8180
1992	80858	33374	11848	8698	9821	10037	10054	8874
1993	108606	44354	14858	13486	12876	13492	13648	10750
1994	145949	62035	20014	16429	17004	17997	17129	15355
1995	173140	77234	22098	17893	19523	21376	18690	18424
1996	201871	86904	25585	20934	23214	25872	22262	22685
1997	238890	105483	28849	24248	26877	29398	24639	28245
1998	270733	125019	34242	26881	29187	32176	26369	31101
1999	304364	143419	38167	29565	33274	35293	28625	34188
2000	347893	175177	46170	31533	37353	36669	31108	36053
2001	437273	213745	53728	39970	48175	45422	42103	47858
2002	595402	302849	73507	51615	64617	56895	56802	62624
2003	826768	442225	93527	64228	80091	78427	80742	81055
2004	1014614	538539	112436	83061	94361	101395	95222	102036
2005	1216879	637308	134013	102522	110682	122849	124387	119131
2006	1529734	794723	166222	130693	140687	158753	157749	147129
2007	2070672	1011622	239255	197083	204644	209806	224741	222776
2008	2925337	1468818	321025	254978	307961	244326	352213	297041
2009	3872631	1918539	419108	359475	400417	326505	474775	392920
2010	5461761	2630285	609286	484127	529382	567140	696741	554086
2011	7621044	3655843	833199	677506	638797	815717	993749	839432
2012	9375855	4265526	1075977	960008	814093	1108301	1215639	1012288
2013	10607312	4613028	1305357	1107652	1035276	1230291	1448932	1172133
2014	12205232	5176795	1548080	1205872	1344771	1422140	1719338	1336316

6-4 历年一般公共预算支出

GENERAL PUBLIC BUDGET EXPENDITURE OVER THE YEARS

单位：万元 (10,000 yuan)

年份 Year	全市 Total	市区 Urban Area	通州区 Tongzhou	海安 Haian	如东 Rudong	启东 Qidong	如皋 Rugao	海门 Haimen
1983	23878	9123	3100	2871	3087	2844	3391	2562
1984	29445	11613	4572	3309	3366	3815	4029	3313
1985	32531	13395	4652	3626	3621	3871	4348	3670
1986	44790	19256	6280	5017	4849	5132	5727	4809
1987	44461	18901	6196	4715	5310	5270	5655	4610
1988	54047	23405	7585	5772	6181	6109	6354	6226
1989	65939	26984	9431	7633	7608	7584	8959	7171
1990	71461	29949	11105	7691	8242	8577	9305	7697
1991	76948	32580	11515	8367	8946	9380	9495	8180
1992	80858	33374	11848	8698	9821	10037	10054	8874
1993	108606	44354	14858	13486	12876	13492	13648	10750
1994	145949	62035	20014	16429	17004	17997	17129	15355
1995	173140	77234	22098	17893	19523	21376	18690	18424
1996	201871	86904	25585	20934	23214	25872	22262	22685
1997	226693	99584	28042	23083	25859	28466	23535	26166
1998	265013	122102	32908	26573	28801	31521	26124	29892
1999	298584	140350	36950	29353	32995	34801	28106	32979
2000	340298	170715	44525	31295	37249	36104	30615	34320
2001	426640	210312	50900	39901	46667	43317	40824	45619
2002	506480	248555	59802	45341	56551	51123	51606	53304
2003	620379	308842	70336	52016	65421	65122	64874	64104
2004	756486	378951	88844	62411	74658	81452	76613	82401
2005	895895	439144	108025	74432	89889	97921	102378	92131
2006	1126224	547212	131385	96418	114035	124377	130929	113253
2007	1470696	701630	180920	131504	155445	161705	172388	148024
2008	1962186	885822	221065	185640	224928	198628	271202	195966
2009	2374668	1023903	298661	231221	274427	258473	338918	247726
2010	3167489	1328663	415348	333728	348117	341138	474512	341331
2011	4194492	1724869	533768	430909	424067	532719	605433	476495
2012	5352831	2280585	694892	573747	584769	608469	727628	577633
2013	5764110	2260019	772412	645808	671073	688660	834858	663692
2014	6495797	2608831	827497	705844	791961	740076	912914	736171

6-5 分地区财政收入(2014年)

单位：万元

指标	Item	全市 Total	市区 Urban Area
财政收入	**Financial Revenue**	**14039281**	**6438340**
中央财政收入	Central Financial Revenue	2929133	1479406
增值税(75%)	Value Added Tax	1579675	745411
消费税	Consumption Tax	49855	43683
企业所得税(60%)	Corporate Income Tax	671693	346213
个人所得税(60%)	Individual Income Tax	627910	344099
地方财政收入	Local Financial Revenue	11110148	4958934
一般公共预算收入	General public budget revenue	5500019	2426245
增值税(25%)	Value Added Tax	644823	328413
营业税	Business Tax	1603434	687228
企业所得税(40%)	Corporate Income Tax	447794	230808
个人所得税(40%)	Individual Income Tax	418606	229399
资源税	Resource Tax	1874	53
城市维护建设税	City Maintenance and Construction Tax	254270	130432
房产税	House Property Tax	139293	71101
印花税	Stamp Tax	62065	25886
城镇土地使用税	Urban Land Use Tax	178795	56469
土地增值税	Land Appreciation Tax	395287	99976
车船使用和牌照税	Vehicle and Vessels Lisence Tax	30783	15288
耕地占用税	Farm Land Occupation Tax	40968	14798
契税	Deed Tax	355426	117244
专项收入	Special Program Receipts	138691	64426
行政事业性收费收入	Charge of Administrative and Institutional Units	318878	163842
罚没收入	Penalty Receipts	77454	38237
国有资产经营收益	Operation Income of State-owned Assets	228798	61601
国有资源有偿使用收入	Income from Use of State-owned Resources	133525	61789
其他收入	Others	29255	29255
政府性基金收入	Revenue from Government-controlled Funds	4384738	1887900
工交部门	Department of Industry and Traffic	15254	9838
文教部门	Department of Culture and Education	84903	40336
农业部门	Department of Agriculture	33648	26200
地方财政税费附加收入	Local Finance Taxes and Fees Additional Income	22039	7787
土地有偿使用收入	Revenue of Land Compensable Use	4186411	1773395
其他部门基金收入	Fund Revenue of Other Departments	42483	30344
缴库社会保险基金收入	**Fund Revenue of Social Insurance**	**1225391**	**644789**

FINANCIAL REVENUE BY REGION(2014)

(10,000 Yuan)

崇川区 Chongchuan	港闸区 Gangzha	通州区 Tongzhou	海安 Haian	如东 Rudong	启东 Qidong	如皋 Rugao	海门 Haimen
1266230	**1066917**	**1722185**	**1278748**	**1283453**	**1683986**	**1735962**	**1618792**
464865	290565	332074	250577	256041	337671	272178	333260
202030	139752	190484	163623	152236	182187	182738	153480
4335	4	4599	1344	420	440	1367	2601
129333	54698	70202	59817	49907	36241	57197	72318
129167	96111	66789	25793	53478	68803	30876	104861
801365	776352	1390111	1028171	1027412	1346315	1463784	1285532
686813	364513	684012	541022	500127	672463	674450	685712
96320	74082	70677	64356	57159	56514	71105	57276
205859	84834	259682	108654	99061	251381	235032	212078
86222	36464	46801	39878	33271	57494	38131	48212
86111	64074	44526	17195	35652	45869	20584	69907
		46	1455	69	167	55	75
36203	21985	32451	17805	15503	31000	30829	28701
22595	9948	16666	11355	10079	15387	14696	16675
7186	4320	7247	7776	7149	6520	8124	6610
12983	9900	13853	16685	51989	15128	21103	17421
41194	11927	36544	82652	52549	11884	72816	75410
517	10	2717	2649	2470	2982	4062	3332
2266	2749	4963	11601	3646	3296	3735	3892
39486	24049	32723	80211	46707	41391	40275	29598
15611	9490	18096	12008	11597	18004	17000	15656
22664	5564	55836	14362	15726	34413	19435	71100
2771	245	8076	8528	7667	5962	10573	6487
2700	5245		43650	46870	53477		23200
5341	745	33108	202	2963	1594	66895	82
1157							
114552	411839	603697	366090	396149	581106	669757	483736
		770	1482	1066	367	2301	200
11622	6191	11032	7319	6321	11033	10475	9419
		2	1800			4108	1540
		1968	2150	1844	7435	2768	55
100589	404492	588502	351721	385437	560389	644769	470700
2341	1156	1423	1618	1481	1882	5336	1822
		102402	**121059**	**131136**	**92746**	**119577**	**116084**

6-6 分地区财政支出(2014年)

单位:万元

指 标	Item	全市 Total	市区 Urban Area
财政支出	**Financial Expenditure**	**12205232**	**5176795**
一般公共预算支出	General public budget revenue expenditure	6495797	2608831
一般公共服务	General Public Services	736057	274627
国防	National Defense	9616	4447
公共安全	Public Security	352330	169545
教育	Education	1418762	498796
科学技术	Science & Technology	217879	92335
文化体育与传媒	Culture, Sports and Media	105921	43864
社会保障和就业	Social Security and Employment	572048	235717
医疗卫生	Medical Treatment and Health Care	538285	201455
环境保护	Environment Protection	125509	57807
城乡社区事务	Urban and Rural Community Affairs	732226	386325
农林水事务	Agriculture, Forestry andWater Affairs	749721	162573
交通运输	Transportation	98303	31694
工业商业金融等事务	Industrial, Commercial and Financial Affairs	383055	218943
其他支出	Others	456085	230703
基金支出	Fund Expenditure	5709435	2567964
政府性基金支出	Expenditure of Governmental Fund	4484044	1923175
社会保险基金支出	Expenditure of Social Security Fund	1225391	644789

FINANCIAL EXPENDITURE BY REGION(2014)

(10,000 Yuan)

崇川区 Chongchuan	港闸区 Gangzha	通州区 Tongzhou	海安 Haian	如东 Rudong	启东 Qidong	如皋 Rugao	海门 Haimen
444722	**619012**	**1548080**	**1205872**	**1344771**	**1422140**	**1719338**	**1336316**
337874	205423	827497	705844	791961	740076	912914	736171
34677	27966	94732	74408	102351	138089	75101	71481
	21	3033	927	946	1488	1808	
15213	6384	44034	32836	33241	35381	42814	38513
77728	42179	230205	179067	172533	185284	174495	208587
10692	4515	29953	28873	21684	35010	25181	14796
6058	1973	16687	12469	8375	9958	14156	17099
18666	68255	73393	47119	57645	30422	85006	66139
12409	7982	76582	51791	60333	73187	77024	74495
312	1526	17432	11928	18422	10129	19163	8060
76531	21290	89331	42324	49079	18477	197872	38149
15168	10013	97045	134289	144239	86082	86784	135754
		7139	10467	15151	27759	5383	7849
66939	3927	23645	10708	86196	8145	30485	28578
3481	9392	24286	68638	21766	30665	77642	26671
106848	413589	720583	500028	552810	682064	806424	600145
106848	413589	618181	378969	421674	589318	686847	484061
		102402	121059	131136	92746	119577	116084

6-7 历年财政收入占地区生产总值的比重

FINANCIAL REVENUE AS PERCENTAGE TO GROSS DOMESTIC PRODUCT OVER THE TEARS

单位:万元 (10,000 Yuan)

年份 Year	财政收入 Financial Revenue	地区生产总值 Regional GDP	财政收入占地区生产总值的比重(%) Percentage of Financial Revenue to GDP(%)
1978	54878	293861	18.7
1979	55382	324508	17.1
1980	59421	356579	16.7
1985	88750	672429	13.2
1990	126870	1342454	9.5
1991	124296	1489165	8.3
1992	139849	1865012	7.5
1993	193560	2408383	8.0
1994	227811	3430404	6.6
1995	272751	4630977	5.9
1996	307839	5248682	5.9
1997	364398	5689912	6.4
1998	402701	6148681	6.5
1999	416248	6576020	6.3
2000	534025	7205859	7.4
2001	667483	7896123	8.5
2002	874086	8651791	10.1
2003	1169933	9801814	11.9
2004	1387200	11957426	11.6
2005	1711871	14720776	11.6
2006	2175697	17583392	12.4
2007	3007122	21118792	14.2
2008	3902076	25101257	15.5
2009	4861042	28728038	16.9
2010	7133642	34656712	20.6
2011	9516538	40802182	23.3
2012	10558988	45586742	23.2
2013	12167339	50388916	24.1
2014	14039281	56526943	24.8

6-8 历年金融机构存贷款与现金收支

DEPOSITS LOANS AND CASH BALANCES OF FINANCIAL INSTITUTIONS OVER THE YEARS

单位：亿元 (100 million yuan)

年份 Year	存款余额 Deposits Balance	城乡居民储蓄 Urban and Rural Savings Deposits	人均储蓄存款（元） Per Capita Savings Deposits	贷款余额 Loans Balance	现金收入 Cash Income	现金支出 Cash Expenditure	货币投放(+)回笼(−) Monetary Issuance(+) or Currency Withdrawal (−)
1978	6.87	2.19	30	13.67	8.68	9.55	0.87
1979	10.01	2.30	32	15.73	11.53	11.90	0.34
1980	9.46	3.04	42	17.27	16.80	17.85	1.05
1985	23.07	12.00	161	36.98	41.03	41.81	0.78
1990	88.25	57.48	741	91.22	120.89	123.07	2.19
1991	112.94	77.93	1001	108.69	142.43	147.88	5.45
1992	141.16	98.55	1264	130.45	201.91	215.17	13.26
1993	179.39	121.33	1553	152.56	314.84	326.58	11.74
1994	259.04	172.77	2210	204.93	458.89	478.25	19.36
1995	365.28	246.40	3142	264.23	599.73	616.70	16.98
1996	456.27	321.81	4098	301.71	681.41	708.07	26.66
1997	534.56	381.23	4848	344.05	676.69	668.24	−8.45
1998	620.28	450.15	5716	368.89	1257.04	1260.04	3.00
1999	698.12	500.92	6368	377.21	1470.75	1481.90	11.15
2000	773.42	544.55	6935	394.34	1712.67	1722.24	9.57
2001	916.96	649.18	8297	433.42	2083.00	2081.67	−1.33
2002	1087.42	754.71	9672	526.90	2353.91	2358.71	4.80
2003	1332.96	882.12	11344	726.87	3174.26	3170.30	−3.96
2004	1574.40	1017.26	13146	880.70	4168.48	4148.47	−20.01
2005	1847.98	1190.74	16261	1024.45	5001.68	4980.99	−20.69
2006	2163.42	1373.40	18945	1233.25	5759.15	5746.18	−12.97
2007	2468.32	1476.59	20567	1497.96	6936.06	6921.60	−14.46
2008	3039.56	1890.68	26452	1750.60	6620.20	6587.91	−32.29
2009	4006.23	2285.89	32044	2431.98	7073.23	7039.30	−33.93
2010	4957.83	2693.99	36996	2964.58	7844.19	7825.99	−18.20
2011	5614.56	3068.10	42355	3408.62	−	−	−
2012	6477.84	3605.65	49411	4006.48	−	−	−
2013	7542.12	4150.54	56876	4672.81	−	−	−
2014	8508.32	4623.93	63359	5258.93	−	−	−

注：自2005年起，人均储蓄存款为按常住人口计算。

Note: Since 2005, the per capita savings deposits are calculated according to permanent residents.

6-9 分地区金融机构本外币存贷款(2014 年末)

单位:万元(折合人民币)

指 标	Item	全市 Total	市区 Urban Area
各项存款	**Deposits**	**8508.32**	**3959.23**
1.单位存款	Deposits	3643.87	2045.12
活期存款	Demand Deposits	1153.76	542.26
定期存款	Time Deposits	1242.27	724.83
2.个人存款	Personal Deposits	4692.96	1772.29
储蓄存款	Savings Deposits	4623.93	1730.37
结构性存款	Structural Deposits	61.57	37.49
委托存款	Designated Deposits	12.42	7.94
其他存款	Others	108.86	99.45
各项贷款	**Loans**	**5258.93**	**2495.54**
短期贷款	Short-Term Loans	2822.12	1267.10
中长期贷款	Medium & Long-Term Loans	2179.94	1116.74
票据融资	Bill Financing	253.58	109.37
各项垫款	Advances	2.91	2.04

LOCAL&FOREIGN CURRENCY DEPOSITS AND LOANS OF BANKING INSTITUTIONS BY REGION(AT 2014 END)

(10,000 Yuan)(To RMB)

通州区 Tongzhou	海安 Haian	如东 Rudong	启东 Qidong	如皋 Rugao	海门 Haimen
1107.66	**984.75**	**732.13**	**951.17**	**860.01**	**1021.03**
376.70	406.28	243.19	293.19	274.46	381.64
137.89	115.46	107.24	131.65	78.30	178.84
132.44	145.58	67.60	85.42	108.30	110.54
722.35	572.31	484.82	646.38	583.50	633.66
716.45	567.89	479.89	639.67	577.85	628.24
4.78	3.74	4.91	5.25	4.98	5.19
1.88	2.19	0.74	1.10		0.44
1.78	0.38	0.70	6.00	0.60	1.73
606.81	**685.44**	**344.91**	**562.52**	**530.22**	**640.30**
344.46	442.58	181.71	322.84	261.14	346.75
217.70	224.18	146.18	210.32	219.25	263.26
44.61	18.20	17.00	29.12	49.81	30.08
0.01	0.48		0.19		0.20

6-10 分地区金融机构人民币存贷款(2014年末)

单位：万元

指 标	Item	全市 Total	市区 Urban Area
各项存款	**Deposits**	**8336.79**	**3828.42**
1.单位存款	Corporate Deposits	3498.85	1931.80
2.个人存款	Individual Deposits	4671.48	1759.78
#储蓄存款	Savings Deposits	4602.87	1718.21
3.财政性存款	Fiscal Deposits	30.44	18.09
4.临时性存款	Temporary Deposits	19.64	16.25
5.委托存款	Entrusted Deposits	12.42	7.94
6.其他存款	Others	103.97	94.56
各项贷款	**Loans**	**5127.11**	**2401.39**
短期贷款	Short-term Loans	2713.73	1191.46
个人贷款及透支	Individual Loans and Overdrafts	415.79	145.18
#个人消费贷款	Loans for Individual Consumption	42.54	24.76
单位普通贷款及透支	Ordinary Loans and Overdraft	2211.29	995.73
#经营性贷款	Operating Loans	2113.80	967.92
固定资产贷款	Fixed-asset Loans	95.55	27.11
银团贷款	Syndicated Loans	6.09	3.80
贸易融资	Trade Financing	80.56	46.75
中长期贷款	Medium&Long-term Loans	2157.45	1099.16
个人贷款	Individual Loans	628.09	339.50
#个人消费贷款	Individual Consumption Loans	518.00	276.52
单位贷款	Corporate Loans	1355.22	664.51
#经营贷款	Operating Loans	74.68	27.25
固定资产贷款	Fixed-asset Loans	1280.54	637.26
普通并购贷款	Ordinary M&A Loans	0.20	0.20
银团贷款	Syndicated Loans	173.94	94.95
票据融资	Bill Financing	253.39	109.19
各项垫款	Advances	2.16	1.29

DEPOSITS AND LOANS OF BANKING INSTITUTIONS BY REGION(AT 2014 END)

(10,000 Yuan)

通州区 Tongzhou	海安 Haian	如东 Rudong	启东 Qidong	如皋 Rugao	海门 Haimen
1099.19	**975.91**	**723.57**	**944.22**	**849.56**	**1015.12**
369.67	399.99	235.79	287.98	265.61	377.66
720.90	569.75	483.66	644.64	581.91	631.74
715.02	565.35	478.73	637.96	576.27	626.34
4.23	3.23	2.52	3.79	1.03	1.79
0.71	0.37	0.16	0.71	0.40	1.75
1.88	2.19	0.74	1.10		0.44
1.78	0.38	0.70	6.00	0.60	1.73
604.67	**682.49**	**342.90**	**550.04**	**519.70**	**630.58**
342.47	439.63	179.71	313.62	252.29	337.03
60.03	63.07	22.05	75.46	48.99	61.04
2.57	5.46	2.22	3.11	3.28	3.71
270.53	362.89	154.38	233.75	197.88	266.66
263.05	338.75	139.13	220.19	193.18	254.63
7.23	24.14	14.85	13.56	4.70	11.18
0.40	1.12	0.09	0.38	0.70	
11.51	12.55	3.19	4.03	4.72	9.33
217.55	224.18	146.18	207.07	217.59	263.26
46.97	62.63	27.80	61.89	60.27	76.01
34.37	55.26	23.19	55.57	46.71	60.75
160.65	137.84	108.72	142.77	141.55	159.84
6.48	13.90	2.51	6.27	17.99	6.75
154.17	123.93	106.21	136.49	123.56	153.09
9.93	23.71	9.67	2.41	15.77	27.42
44.61	18.20	17.00	29.12	49.81	30.08
0.01	0.48		0.19		0.20

6-11 历年分地区城乡居民储蓄存款余

URBAN AND RURAL RESIDENTS´ DEPOSITS OVER THE YEARS BY REGION

单位:亿元 (100 million Yuan)

年份 Year	全市 Total	市区 Urban Area	通州区 Tongzhou	海安 Haian	如东 Rudong	启东 Qidong	如皋 Rugao	海门 Haimen
1978	2.19	0.69	0.35	0.19	0.32	0.49	0.16	0.33
1979	2.30	0.86	0.37	0.23	0.34	0.35	0.19	0.34
1980	3.04	1.09	0.48	0.33	0.40	0.52	0.29	0.41
1985	12.00	3.86	2.14	1.45	1.51	2.17	1.25	1.76
1990	57.48	18.92	10.12	6.94	7.70	10.36	5.38	8.18
1991	77.93	25.76	13.84	9.46	10.21	14.11	7.44	10.94
1992	98.55	33.38	16.82	11.99	12.92	17.21	9.42	13.63
1993	121.33	40.10	21.30	14.75	15.67	20.55	12.92	17.34
1994	172.77	59.74	29.09	19.87	22.05	29.42	17.81	23.88
1995	246.40	86.86	39.65	28.73	30.90	41.04	24.86	34.01
1996	321.81	116.87	52.16	37.70	35.84	53.95	32.23	45.22
1997	381.23	139.97	60.66	45.07	39.98	62.41	38.97	54.83
1998	450.15	166.77	72.07	54.14	45.63	72.43	46.43	64.76
1999	500.92	187.68	80.69	61.11	48.19	79.11	52.00	72.83
2000	544.55	197.78	87.35	68.81	54.46	86.47	57.66	79.37
2001	649.18	241.45	91.25	80.12	64.74	99.13	69.61	94.14
2002	754.71	287.87	105.89	91.30	73.63	112.06	80.76	109.08
2003	882.12	340.56	123.24	105.16	85.26	128.29	95.31	127.53
2004	1017.26	396.35	143.60	122.01	98.93	144.43	111.20	144.34
2005	1190.74	465.06	170.17	142.48	116.00	168.03	131.77	167.40
2006	1373.40	542.85	198.35	162.01	131.02	189.63	155.40	192.48
2007	1476.59	574.55	219.61	176.72	145.33	202.27	175.12	202.60
2008	1890.68	755.22	281.10	217.97	187.06	254.32	221.04	255.07
2009	2285.89	937.02	336.31	260.04	215.78	300.34	263.80	308.90
2010	2693.99	1099.30	396.71	308.11	251.45	354.47	316.80	363.86
2011	3068.10	770.68	1223.05	358.03	297.46	407.39	371.25	410.92
2012	3605.65	1423.73	533.14	428.33	349.46	483.41	437.24	483.48
2013	4150.54	1606.03	630.04	499.84	411.99	565.97	507.48	559.23
2014	4623.93	1730.37	716.45	567.89	479.89	639.67	577.85	628.24

主要统计指标解释

财政收入 是国家(各级政府)通过财政各个环节筹集的财政资金的总称,它是保证国家和各级政府行使其职能不可缺少的财力。

财政支出 是国家政权为行使其职能,对筹集的财政资金进行有计划的分配使用的总体。国家财政支出,体现政府的活动范围和方向反映财政资金的分配关系。

中央财政和地方财政 财政是国家为了实现其职能,凭借政治权力,对一部分社会产品进行分配和再分配的经济活动。中央财政和地方财政,是指财政体制上划分中央政府和地方政府以及地方各级政府之间财政管理权限的一项分配制度。它是经济管理体制的重要组成部分。它在财政管理中居于主导地位。它具体规定了各级政府筹集資金、支配使用资金的权力、范围和责任,使各级政府在财政管理上有责有权。这对于正确处理中央和地方,以及地方各级之间的分配关系,充分发挥各级政府的积极性,更好地完成国家财政收支任务,促进社会主义建设有着极其重要的意义。中央财政收入和地方财政收入,是指中央和地方各级负责组织征收的收入,不是按财政体制计算的收入分成数。其收入中还包括了国外借款。

在现行分税制财政管理体制下,财政总收入又分为中央级收入和地方级收入。中央级收入主要包括消费税和增值税的75%部分,以及其他属中央预算固定收入科目的收入,如关税。地方级财政收入主要是指财政收入中扣除中央级收入后的部分。

存款 企业、机关、团体或居民根据可以收回的原则,把货币资金存入银行或其他信用机构保管并取得一定利息的一种信用活动形式。根据存款对象的不同可划分为企业存款、财政存款、机关团体存款、基本建设存款、城镇储蓄存款、农村存款等项目。它是银行信贷资金的主要来源。

贷款 银行或其他信用机构根据必须归还的原则,按一定利率,为企业、个人等提供资金的一种信用活动形式。我国银行贷款,分流动资金贷款、固定资金贷款、城乡个体工商户贷款以及农户贷款等科目。

保费 又叫保险费。是保险人根据保险合同的有关规定,为被保险人取得因约定危险事故发生所造成的经济损失补偿(或给付)权利,付给保险人的代价。包括财产险和人身险储金收入。

赔款 保险事故发生后,经查证确属保险责任范围以内的保险标的损失,保险人根据保险合同的规定赔偿义务,给予被保险人的款项叫做赔款,赔款可分为已决赔款和未决赔款两种。

第七篇

固定资产投资

Chapter 7

Investment in Fixed Assets

7-1 主要年份固定资产投资完成额

COMPLETION OF FIXED-ASSET INVESTMENT OF MAIN YEARS

单位:万元　　(Unit: 10,000 Yuan)

年 份 Year	固定资产投资额 Investment of Fixed Assets	工业投资 Industrial Investment	房地产开发投资 Investment for Real-estate Development
1986	141110		
1987	238789		
1988	298060		
1989	217214		
1990	207830		1113
1991	334127		13431
1992	504782		18179
1993	890069		46789
1994	1262149		86607
1995	1933063		229837
1996	1988584		201248
1997	2220498	914662	178391
1998	2566701	1027315	172521
1999	2122386	630252	216046
2000	2395047	829676	261062
2001	2580869	803675	331316
2002	3098867	1237981	359613
2003	4484170	2403729	483169
2004	6051657	4003732	593879
2005	8152635	6177247	800498
2006	10488974	7961793	1079295
2007	12657961	9706640	1374262
2008	15054081	11456835	1726846
2009	18023780	13297225	2007915
2010	21683751	15301124	2727825
2011	23783559	15387851	3799617
2012	28864699	17100432	4817428
2013	32987297	18560630	5965201
2014	38963893	20468162	6789218

注:2011 年之前固定资产投资、工业投资口径为全社会。

Note:The Calibre for fixed-asset investment and industrial investment before 2011 is the whole Society.

7-2 1978-2014 年分地区固定资产投资完成额

COMPLETION OF FIXED-ASSET INVESTMENT BY DISTRICTS 1978-2014

单位：万元 (Unit: 10,000 Yuan)

年份 Year	全市 Municipality	市区 Urban Areas	崇川区 Chongchuan	港闸区 Gangzha	开发区 Development Zone	通州区 Tongzhou	海安 Haian	如东 Rudong	启东 Qidong	如皋 Rugao	海门 Haimen
1978	13406	8638				795	639	594	1472	1714	349
1979	18212	13103				764	1144	1078	1086	1305	496
1980	27439	20004				1853	1368	1301	1859	1718	1189
1985	59793	38350			535	7247	3477	4516	4232	6241	2977
1986	141110	74625			3015	25778	13577	14003	16219	11383	11303
1987	238789	142069			7711	37758	16701	19834	22144	20906	17135
1988	298060	166231			5149	43337	28124	23877	32709	27311	19808
1989	217214	105644			2048	33930	21293	13458	31222	17750	27847
1990	207830	110140			3698	49286	18327	21109	18901	19447	19906
1991	334127	158005			3899	58264	26970	33087	42850	41396	31819
1992	504782	247363	7879		18925	79817	39039	35266	72050	52452	58612
1993	890069	428320	14204		19210	165115	81957	67039	126674	83226	102853
1994	1262149	524343	25081		37034	204664	114960	105167	211011	132706	173962
1995	1933063	838615	32574		40333	345002	143313	171288	268856	191763	319228
1996	1988584	899067	40469		40562	343754	139282	193076	270902	211073	275184
1997	2286261	1205499	53760	41091	156065	430488	160890	127385	268486	246390	277611
1998	2566701	1332341	45664	32363	140432	433058	163235	218839	291983	236892	323410
1999	2122386	900612	46102	35182	42144	408491	177092	206143	301687	236071	300781
2000	2395047	1044142	52479	51927	56453	414984	205806	218319	342306	247435	337039
2001	2580869	1180054	74957	48428	79156	399227	223659	237762	356844	261250	321300
2002	3098867	1371170	102654	100363	121755	467930	299586	302582	379171	309790	436568
2003	4484170	1977142	154794	216666	210479	676453	423038	418349	566975	433419	665247
2004	6051657	2570052	227854	305868	326972	848415	630479	602768	795955	644835	807568
2005	8152635	3179249	758463	451291	501371	1215991	881021	866472	1100051	937104	1188738
2006	10488974	3981935	924992	593081	706051	1520946	1173668	1164808	1448079	1245407	1475077
2007	12657961	4847373	1205118	745842	927190	1802103	1436498	1431525	1711635	1520335	1710595
2008	15054081	5806319	1468843	950618	1222014	2095364	1718671	1700455	2012746	1808468	2007422
2009	18023780	7192342	1814763	1166199	1575084	2518116	2006105	1974326	2364679	2131130	2355198
2010	21683751	8757300	2172125	1434889	2084241	2990104	2419631	2351377	2807454	2533727	2814262
2011	23783559	9918182	2511445	1653158	2463421	3130452	2601235	2507515	3029895	2720169	3006563
2012	28864699	11927621	3012080	1711544	3038905	3779884	3226554	3107935	3595336	3298620	3708633
2013	32987297	13596890	3472321	2009728	3518088	4363553	3742826	3592362	4071717	3748616	4234886
2014	38963893	15896124	4063848	2398229	4190912	5201158	4489468	4279317	4834148	4450849	5013987

注：2011 年之前固定资产投资口径为全社会。

Note: The calibre for fixed-asset investment before 2011 is the whole society.

7-3 分地区固定资产投资完成情况(2014年)

单位:万元

指 标	Item	全市 Municipality	市区 Urban Areas
一、计划投资	**Planned Investment**		
计划总投资	Total Planned Investment	91418022	41841494
本年新开工	New Projects of the Year	28797489	9276089
二、本年完成投资	**Completed Investment of the Year**	**38963893**	**15896124**
本年新开工	New Projects of the Year	23545143	8458942
(一)按隶属关系分	Grouped by Relationship of Administrative Surbodination		
中央	Central	374646	251346
省	Province	321842	209691
省辖市	Provincially Administered Municipality	798673	761887
县(市)、区	County(city) and District	2563986	1733819
其他	Others	34904746	12939381
(二)按产业分	Grouped by Industries		
第一产业	Primary Industry	99154	28919
第二产业	Secondary Industry	20468162	5949050
#工业	Industry	20468162	5949050
第三产业	Tertiary Industry	18396577	9918155
(三)按建设性质分	Grouped by Types of Construction		
新建	New Construction	14570138	4336479
扩建	Extension	8931325	3731232
改建	Reconstruction	7024029	1938313
单纯建造生活设施	Construction of Livelihood Facilities	89480	89480
其他	Others	8348921	5800620
(四)按工程构成分	Grouped by Project Structures		
建筑工程	Construction Project	19281734	9081049
安装工程	Installation Project	1162956	320617
设备工器具购置	Purchase of Equipment and Instruments	16102054	5102619
其他费用	Others	2417149	1391839
建设用地费	Construction Land Fee	1938743	1063065
(五)按登记注册类型分	Grouped by Types of Registration		
内资	Domestic Capital	36287439	14217069
#国有经济	State-owned Economy	7336185	4947085
#民营经济	Private Economy	28951254	9269984
#私营个体	Private Individual Economy	20117983	5545719
港澳台商投资	HK,Macau &Taiwan Funded	1079173	495100
外商投资	Foreign Investment	1597281	1183955
(六)按国民经济行业分	Grouped by National Economic Sectors		
农、林、牧、渔业	Agriculture, Forestry, Husbandry and Fishery	107954	28919
农业	Agriculture	48637	26669
林业	Forestry	6894	
畜牧业	Husbandry	32853	
渔业	Fishery	10770	2250
农、林、牧、渔服务业	Related Service Industry	8800	
制造业	Manufacturing	19502534	5548736
农副食品加工业	Agrifood Processing	333997	63800
食品制造业	Food Production	130948	13157
酒、饮料和精制茶制造业	Alcohol, Beverage and Refined Tea Production	31099	1950
烟草制品业	Tobacco Industries	11830	11830
纺织业	Textile	2316007	1065785
纺织服装、服饰业	Textile and Garment, Dress and Personal Adornment	587417	233128
皮革、毛皮、羽毛及其制品和制鞋业	Leather, Fur, Feather(Fuzz) and Related Products	107872	19261
木材加工和木、竹、藤、棕、草制品业	Wood Processing and Industries of Wood, Bamboo, Rattan, Palm and Grass Products	67245	15728
家具制造业	Furniture Manufacturing	232575	37189

COMPLETION OF FIXED-ASSET INVESTMENT BY DISTRICTS (2014)

(10,000 yuan)

崇川区 Chongchuan	港闸区 Gangzha	开发区 Developing Zone	通州区 Tongzhou	海安 Haian	如东 Rudong	启东 Qidong	如皋 Rugao	海门 Haimen
12565895	6914808	10530251	11742540	13910763	6634520	8269748	9848710	10912787
1625258	561504	2273505	4815822	2449758	3756098	4496605	4128179	4690760
4063848	**2398229**	**4190912**	**5201158**	**4489468**	**4279317**	**4834148**	**4450849**	**5013987**
1680409	970880	2321495	3486158	1031089	3153277	4086970	2892866	3921999
231346	20000				117000			6300
209691				73431		30416	6426	1878
679881	4488	35541			29200		7586	
523342	505970	495068	209439	185978	89556	360699	109930	84004
2419588	1867771	3660303	4991719	4230059	4043561	4443033	4326907	4921805
			28919	40627	5000	3500	11038	10070
562598	542958	1722874	3111364	2865378	2800107	3019381	2677612	3156634
562598	542958	1722874	3111364	2865378	2800107	3019381	2677612	3156634
3501250	1855271	2468038	2060875	1583463	1474210	1811267	1762199	1847283
1139171	356010	1002880	1796441	1824287	1891225	2106226	2038617	2373304
323932	42596	1887399	1477305	1198931	808509	1618745	204331	1369577
333564	199568	230217	1174964	875235	1188963	638830	1548728	833960
29887		2693	56900					
2237294	1800055	1067723	695548	591015	390620	470347	659173	437146
2314850	1482543	2846664	2404271	2433848	1495056	2274403	2200855	1796523
140448	20224	33580	125309	45674	178029	143656	74042	400938
1296766	458461	1185133	2158259	1786602	2502255	2052781	1985496	2672301
311784	437001	125535	513319	223344	103977	363308	190456	144225
261988	398934	85375	316768	174278	94804	318170	156141	132285
3792659	2172890	3172370	5037173	4465844	4111497	4450846	4348226	4693957
1817106	724548	1917867	445587	112219	532808	711510	386548	646015
1975553	1448342	1254503	4591586	4353625	3578689	3739336	3961678	4047942
1297201	813818	982661	2452039	1671863	2868715	2926285	3451131	3654270
189619	196369	81631	27481	19951	94353	158950	54634	256185
81570	28970	936911	136504	3673	73467	224352	47989	63845
			28919	40627	5000	7100	11038	15270
			26669	8398		3500		10070
				1894	5000			
				24585			8268	
			2250	5750			2770	
						3600		5200
544388	408760	1596055	2999533	2829366	2425990	2933651	2631835	3132956
5360		11070	47370	67384	63836	54380	57217	27380
10210		2947		5555	50416	27970	7730	26120
1950							22969	6180
11830								
203055	37899	248112	576719	142933	388548	84010	151261	483470
31463	16850	73780	111035	38525	98890	43840	108964	64070
2340	2770	5460	8691		31206	31200	14205	12000
	2968	2500	10260	12625		5950	10362	22580
	5000	11060	21129	151702	12280	5910	19614	5880

7-3 续表1

单位：万元

指 标	Item	全市 Municipality	市区 Urban Areas
造纸和纸制品业	Paper Making and Industries of Paper Products	371019	274352
印刷和记录媒介复制业	Printing and Record Medium Reproduction	68699	33139
文教、工美、体育和娱乐用品制造业	Industries of Culture, Education, Arts, Sports and Recreational Products	311164	55153
石油加工、炼焦和核燃料加工业	Petroleum Processing, Coking and Nuclear Fuel Processing Industries	61868	8290
化学原料和化学制品制造业	Production of Chemical Raw Materials and Chemical Products	1357986	284190
医药制造业	Pharmaceutical Industry	356121	138679
化学纤维制造业	Chemical Fiber Manufacturing	590835	173110
橡胶和塑料制品业	Industry of Rubber and Plastic Products	404377	111387
非金属矿物制品业	Industry of Nonmetallic Mineral Products	1247257	187129
黑色金属冶炼和压延加工业	Ferrous Metal Smelting and Pressing	238023	8050
有色金属冶炼和压延加工业	Non-Ferrous Metal Smelting and Pressing	269483	66643
金属制品业	Manufacture of Metal Products	1128172	575907
通用设备制造业	Manufacture of General Purpose Machinery	2785046	765546
专用设备制造业	Manufacture of Equipment for Special Purpose	2004079	230076
汽车制造业	Automobile Industry	451837	134102
铁路、船舶、航空航天和其他运输设备制造业	Manufacture of Railroad, Shipping, Aerospace and Other Transportation Equipments	412611	132728
电气机械和器材制造业	Manufacture of Electrical Machinery and Equipments	1753927	350699
计算机、通信和其他电子设备制造业	Manufacture of Computer, Communications and Other Electronic Products	1210727	419909
仪器仪表制造业	Instrument Manufacturing	538940	102294
其他制造业	Others	55763	33055
废弃资源综合利用业	Comprehensive Utilization of Waste Resources	43110	2470
金属制品、机械和设备修理业	Metal Product, Machinery and Equipment Repair Industry	22500	
电力、热力、燃气及水生产和供应业	Generation and Supply of Electric and Heating Power, Gas and Water	988128	400314
电力、热力生产和供应业	Generation and Supply of Electric Power and Heating Power	606716	221370
燃气生产和供应业	Generation and Supply of Gas	129900	25100
水的生产和供应业	Generation and Supply of Water	251512	153844
批发和零售业	Wholesale and Retail Sales	1343192	562270
批发业	Wholesale	723727	340273
零售业	Retail Sales	619465	221997
交通运输、仓储和邮政业	Transportaion, Storage and Postal Industries	2245681	821176
铁路运输业	Railway Transport	19336	19336
道路运输业	Road Transport	696963	330842
水上运输业	Waterway Transport	863870	309820
航空运输业	Aviation Transportation	28932	25982
管道运输业	Pipeline Transport	11656	
装卸搬运和运输代理业	Handling and Shipping Agency Industries	41376	17857
仓储业	Storage Industry	566298	117339
邮政业	Postal Industry	17250	
住宿和餐饮业	Accommodation and Catering Services	390573	150792
住宿业	Accommodation Industry	282733	92772
餐饮业	Catering Industry	107840	58020
信息传输、软件和信息技术服务业	Information Transmission, Software and IT Services	445852	347134
电信、广播电视和卫星传输服务	Telecom, Broadcasting and Satellite Transmission Services	9409	6429
互联网和相关服务	Internet and Related Services	206789	195099
软件和信息技术服务业	Software and IT Services	229654	145606
金融业	Banking Industry	166157	128170
货币金融服务	Monetary and Financial Services	53327	24240
资本市场服务	Capital Market Services	2500	
其他金融业	Others	110330	103930
房地产业	Real Estate Industry	1127118	411413
房地产业	Real Estate	1127118	411413
租赁和商务服务业	Renting and Commercial Services	542547	335279
租赁业	Renting	31135	28155
商务服务业	Commercial Services	511412	307124

CONTINUED 1

(10,000 yuan)

崇川区 Chongchuan	港闸区 Gangzha	开发区 Developing Zone	通州区 Tongzhou	海安 Haian	如东 Rudong	启东 Qidong	如皋 Rugao	海门 Haimen
520	2840	257602	13390	9093	19775	18010	27599	22190
24784	1250	3700	3405		10920	2960		21680
6930	14480	11240	22503	1573	107400	47710	37698	61630
	2980	5310		709	38100		2769	12000
5529	5500	237335	35826	102972	402601	192051	205252	170920
4480		89480	44719	27614	20627	58176	31785	79240
7261	4037	10660	151152	327871	56864	5970	21260	5760
8883	8480	24020	70004	44384	36304	55900	45502	110900
3780	27698	43905	111746	155100	171577	71352	397226	264873
		8050		163069	10320	2850	17134	36600
		1010	65633	73988	10000	2860	28502	87490
8605	70480	167768	329054	55490	89995	102900	119030	184850
57728	101053	117735	489030	476173	156749	799410	269968	317200
44119	14896	37870	133191	123008	230545	685295	172439	562716
2487		42424	89191	158010	200	2800	128765	27960
23541	29850	27712	51625	55800		110550	90483	23050
5867	42679	77845	224308	300735	300273	265432	268409	268379
70496	17050	50100	282263	200248	58424	104110	232228	195808
3170		27360	71764	124249		149125	139162	24110
			33055	10556		2930	4302	4920
			2470		37640			3000
					22500			
18210	134198	126819	111831	36012	396617	85730	45777	23678
5400	134198	42230	39542	32555	300570	27950	9413	14858
10100			15000		59000	45800		
2710		84589	57289	3457	37047	11980	36364	8820
181880	39978	234650	105762	135889	125578	142629	163036	213790
151644	23910	120400	44319	82087	15653	101179	33245	151290
30236	16068	114250	61443	53802	109925	41450	129791	62500
352125	62570	90040	316441	205128	326359	457663	211124	224231
			19336					
114611	41770	22050	152411	45558	216456	8130	32799	63178
187990		11080	110750	53354	16400	433633		50663
			25982					2950
					9556			2100
9887		7970		4941	7078	2900		8600
39637	20800	48940	7962	101275	73369	13000	177175	84140
					3500		1150	12600
82582	22830	9000	36380	117542	20700	25445	32409	43685
70872	5820		16080	117542	20700	22545	20509	8665
11710	17010	9000	20300			2900	11900	35020
238871	68560	31668	8035	10066	11200	20500	30172	26780
4429			2000					2980
186739		8360					9690	2000
47703	68560	23308	6035	10066	11200	20500	20482	21800
34070		91500	2600		7495		21292	9200
21640			2600		7495		21292	300
								2500
12430		91500						6400
54590	17700	10330	328793	290065	62167	24220	339253	
54590	17700	10330	328793	290065	62167	24220	339253	
145259	81740	19780	88500	30461	26750	23880	16797	109380
23255	2020	2880				2980		
122004	79720	16900	88500	30461	26750	20900	16797	109380

7-3 续表 2

单位:万元

指　标	Item	全市 Municipality	市区 Urban Areas
科学研究和技术服务业	Scientific Research and Technology Services	430362	193607
研究和试验发展	Research and Experimental Development	181249	80486
专业技术服务业	Special Technical Services	149958	77428
科技推广和应用服务业	S&T Promotion and Application Services	99155	35693
水利、环境和公共设施管理业	Water Conservancy, Environment & Public Facilities Management	3343825	1826294
水利管理业	Water Conservancy Management	248449	154734
生态保护和环境治理业	Ecological Protection and Environmental Management	133019	89155
公共设施管理业	Public Facilities Management	2962357	1582405
居民服务、修理和其他服务业	Resident Service, Repair and Other Services	91254	48238
居民服务业	Resident Service	39128	17362
机动车、电子产品和日用产品修理业	Mobile, Electronic Product and Daily-use Product Repair Services	49326	28076
其他服务业	Other Services	2800	2800
教育	Education	511616	222519
教育	Education	511616	222519
卫生和社会工作	Health and Social Work	306697	106723
卫生	Health	244923	76819
社会工作	Social Work	61774	29904
文化、体育和娱乐业	Culture, Sports and Entertainment	342795	128387
新闻和出版业	News and Publishing Industry	3000	3000
广播、电视、电影和影视录音制作业	Broadcasting, TV, Film, Video&Audio Recording Industry	25263	
文化艺术业	Culture & Arts Industry	128473	55503
体育	Sports	55090	37284
娱乐业	Entertainment	130969	32600
公共管理、社会保障和社会组织	Public Administration, Social Security and Social Organizations	288390	179124
中国共产党机关	Party Institutions of CPC	3750	3750
国家机构	State Institutions	207961	114857
群众团体、社会团体和其他成员组织	Mass Organization, Social Organization & Other Membership Organizations	24821	11509
基层群众自治组织	Self-governing Mass Organizations at the Grass-roots Level	51858	49008
三、本年新增固定资产	**Newly Increased Fixed Assets of the Year**	**55916479**	**36249647**
四、项目个数(个)	**Number of Projects**		
施工项目个数	Projects under Construction	5746	2102
#新开工项目个数	Newly-started Projects	4648	1793
本年投产项目个数	New Production Projects of the Year	4628	1755
五、房屋建筑面积(万平方米)	**Contruction Area of the Building (10,000 m²)**		
本年施工房屋面积	Construction Area of the Year	11329.37	5101.78
其中:住宅	Of which: Residence	4401.09	2518.12
本年竣工房屋面积	Floor Space Completed of the Year	4124.99	1631.58
其中:住宅	Of which: Residence	1007.18	608.24
六、资金来源	**Capital Sources**		
本年资金来源合计	Total Capital Sources of Last Year	44851611	17707971
1.上年末结余资金	Cash Balance at the end of Last Year	2296510	1560266
2.本年资金来源小计	Subtotal of Capital Sources of the Year	42555101	16147705
(1)国家预算内资金	State Budgetary Appropriation	1799600	1475998
(2)国内贷款	Domestic Loans	3312326	1848955
(3)债券	Bond		
(4)利用外资	Utilization of Foreign Capital	494725	53851
其中:外商直接投资	Of which: Foreign Direct Investment	200265	45950
(5)自筹资金	Self-raised Funds	33360890	10919302
其中:企、事业单位自有资金	Of which: Self-owned Capital by Enterprises and Institutes	15136953	3196764
(6)其他资金来源	Others	3587560	1849599
各项应付款合计	Total Payables	3834696	2770756
其中:工程款	Of which: Project Funds	1911522	1383598

CONTINUED 2

(10,000 yuan)

崇川区 Chongchuan	港闸区 Gangzha	开发区 Developing Zone	通州区 Tongzhou	海安 Hai´an	如东 Rudong	启东 Qidong	如皋 Rugao	海门 Haimen
85469	13680	24750	69708	13766	108835	38946	9300	65908
13396	8560	14000	44530		77635	2000	4550	16578
59208	5120	10750	2350	12700	4000	10880	4750	40200
12865			22828	1066	27200	26066		9130
457931		1080348	255294	189976	357860	479753	255140	234802
33365		79407	41962	20985	25669		500	46561
15222		8600	65333		23664			20200
409344		992341	147999	168991	308527	479753	254640	168041
25651	5470	8300	8817	3266	5200		4100	30450
8545			8817	336	5200		2580	13650
17106	5470	5500		2930			1520	16800
		2800						
58513	7500	82499	74007	4965	26700	54045	52825	150562
58513	7500	82499	74007	4965	26700	54045	52825	150562
73345		17000	16378	21697	48200	28707	9560	91810
55341		8500	12978	21697	47500	23307	5360	70240
18004		8500	3400		700	5400	4200	21570
79414	2640		46333	25905	10000	13968	21936	142599
3000								
				10463		6000		8800
55503				15442		2568	7850	47110
20911			16373				436	17370
	2640		29960		10000	5400	13650	69319
117327	12368	23550	25879	9962		27564	10000	61740
3750								
66269	4468	23550	20570	7450		22564	10000	53090
	7900		3609	2512		5000		5800
47308			1700					2850
26650957	**2383085**	**2425277**	**4790328**	**3351242**	**3621701**	**4352840**	**3671613**	**4669436**
500	88	756	755	651	302	615	1063	1013
461	68	678	586	294	242	578	881	860
447	69	691	548	340	260	567	857	849
1404.66	1081.19	957.65	1658.27	2279.47	540.25	890.61	1509.7	1007.58
614.92	666.99	523.34	712.87	448.64	155.03	374.23	549.25	355.82
297.67	431.73	224.25	677.94	647.05	267.91	491.83	658.99	427.61
78.05	276.96	41.76	211.48	67.85	16.78	89.66	135.57	89.08
5711106	2380792	4749794	4855534	5320677	4693179	5372149	5749112	6008523
645040	192051	599428	123747	355016	31938	109030	162321	77939
5066066	2188741	4150366	4731787	4965661	4661241	5263119	5586791	5930584
563984	46368	854901		23250	6500	213338	7514	73000
716423	204812	214066	713654	331389	91772	254739	508441	277030
	2920	2801	48130	5700	84196	21885	63833	265260
			45950	1000	83195	21885	41735	6500
3017922	1595430	2709219	3596731	4216821	4286085	4301603	4629736	5007343
1397008	84050	465	1715241	1093694	938997	4209396	2619640	3078462
767737	339211	369379	373272	388501	192688	471554	377267	307951
667457	932273	158448	980471	243236	239381	196867	198413	186043
363684	203028	67360	736970	130020	43956	110468	118380	125100

7-4 分地区项目投资完成情况(2014年)

单位:万元

指 标	Item	全市 Municipality	市区 Urban Areas
一、计划投资	**Planned Investment**		
计划总投资	Total Planned Investment	58066871	21724107
本年新开工	New Projects of the Year	28797489	9276089
二、本年完成投资	**Completed Investment of the Year**	**32174675**	**11439095**
本年新开工	New Projects of the Year	21563967	7119427
(一)按隶属关系分	Grouped by Relationship of Administrative Surbodination		
中央	Central	374646	251346
省	Province	243009	130858
省辖市	Provincially Administered Municipality	580452	580452
县(市)、区	County(city) and District	1049946	307899
其他	Others	29926622	10168540
(二)按产业分	Grouped by Industries		
第一产业	Primary Industry	99154	28919
第二产业	Secondary Industry	20468162	5949050
#工业	Industry	20468162	5949050
第三产业	Tertiary Industry	11607359	5461126
(三)按建设性质分	Grouped by Types of Construction		
新建	New Construction	14570138	4336479
扩建	Extension	8931325	3731232
改建	Reconstruction	7024029	1938313
单纯建造生活设施	Construction of Livelihood Facilities	89480	89480
其他	Others	1559703	1343591
(四)按工程构成分	Grouped by Project Structures		
建筑工程	Construction Project	13992475	5699980
安装工程	Installation Project	1026531	211901
设备工器具购置	Purchase of Equipment and Instruments	16005800	5033791
其他费用	Others	1149869	493423
建设用地费	Construction Land Fee	792469	263810
(五)按登记注册类型分	Grouped by Types of Registration		
内资	Domestic Capital	30124552	10128913
#国有经济	State-owned Economy	5649145	3336358
#民营经济	Private Economy	24475407	6792555
#私营个体	Private Individual Economy	17554143	4202058
港澳台商投资	HK,Macau &Taiwan Funded	552363	155346
外商投资	Foreign Investment	1497760	1154836
(六)按国民经济行业分	Grouped by National Economic Sectors		
农、林、牧、渔业	Agriculture, Forestry, Husbandry and Fishery	107954	28919
农业	Agriculture	48637	26669
林业	Forestry	6894	
畜牧业	Husbandry	32853	
渔业	Fishery	10770	2250
农、林、牧、渔服务业	Related Services	8800	
制造业	Manufacturing	19502534	5548736
农副食品加工业	Agrifood Processing	333997	63800
食品制造业	Food Production	130948	13157
酒、饮料和精制茶制造业	Alcohol, Beverage and Refined Tea Production	31099	1950
烟草制品业	Tobacco Industries	11830	11830
纺织业	Textile	2316007	1065785
纺织服装、服饰业	Textile and Garment, Dress and Personal Adornment	587417	233128
皮革、毛皮、羽毛及其制品和制鞋业	Leather, Fur, Feather(Fuzz) and Related Products	107872	19261
木材加工和木、竹、藤、棕、草制品业	Wood Processing and Industries of Wood, Bamboo, Rattan, Palm and Grass Products	67245	15728
家具制造业	Furniture Manufacturing	232575	37189

COMPLETION OF PROJECT INVESTMENT BY REGIONS(2014)

(10,000 yuan)

崇川区 Chongchuan	港闸区 Gangzha	开发区 Developing Zone	通州区 Tongzhou	海安 Haian	如东 Rudong	启东 Qidong	如皋 Rugao	海门 Haimen
4508499	2222201	6216363	8689044	10581859	5492753	5722252	7020085	7525815
1625258	561504	2273505	4815822	2449758	3756098	4496605	4128179	4690760
2549625	**877994**	**3446289**	**4523210**	**3964693**	**3964651**	**4363801**	**3865594**	**4576841**
1402776	405297	2098499	3212855	929192	2993915	3961051	2826528	3733854
231346	20000				117000			6300
130858				73431		30416	6426	1878
528957	4488	5030						
128530			179369	152814	82456	352532	82456	71789
1529934	853506	3441259	4343841	3738448	3765195	3980853	3776712	4496874
			28919	40627	5000	3500	11038	10070
562598	542958	1722874	3111364	2865378	2800107	3019381	2677612	3156634
562598	542958	1722874	3111364	2865378	2800107	3019381	2677612	3156634
1987027	335036	1723415	1382927	1058688	1159544	1340920	1176944	1410137
1139171	356010	1002880	1796441	1824287	1891225	2106226	2038617	2373304
323932	42596	1887399	1477305	1198931	808509	1618745	204331	1369577
333564	199568	230217	1174964	875235	1188963	638830	1548728	833960
29887		2693	56900					
723071	279820	323100	17600	66240	75954		73918	
1124715	374380	2220119	1948045	2018627	1247006	1870958	1757650	1398254
88105	7000	25624	90116	45028	157806	140866	70172	400758
1252717	457157	1176318	2143599	1783367	2496310	2043667	1976518	2672147
84088	39457	24228	341450	117671	63529	308310	61254	105682
59846	31829	11463	160672	71742	59064	268552	33937	95364
2449122	797166	2448138	4392510	3942321	3798668	4159512	3816617	4278521
1217656	210178	1446530	420017	112219	509755	704180	386548	600085
1231466	586988	1001608	3972493	3830102	3288913	3455332	3430069	3678436
805519	459092	797128	2140319	1414353	2648641	2793035	3025666	3470390
19343	51858	77795	6350	18901	94316	37150	2850	243800
81160	28970	920356	124350	3471	71667	167139	46127	54520
			28919	40627	5000	7100	11038	15270
			26669	8398		3500		10070
				1894	5000			
				24585			8268	
			2250	5750			2770	
						3600		5200
544388	408760	1596055	2999533	2829366	2425990	2933651	2631835	3132956
5360		11070	47370	67384	63836	54380	57217	27380
10210		2947		5555	50416	27970	7730	26120
1950							22969	6180
11830								
203055	37899	248112	576719	142933	388548	84010	151261	483470
31463	16850	73780	111035	38525	98890	43840	108964	64070
2340	2770	5460	8691		31206	31200	14205	12000
	2968	2500	10260	12625		5950	10362	22580
	5000	11060	21129	151702	12280	5910	19614	5880

7-4 续表 1

单位：万元

指 标	Item	全市 Municipality	市区 Urban Areas
造纸和纸制品业	Paper Making and Industries of Paper Products	371019	274352
印刷和记录媒介复制业	Printing and Record Medium Reproduction	68699	33139
文教、工美、体育和娱乐用品制造业	Industries of Culture, Education, Arts, Sports and Recreational Products	311164	55153
石油加工、炼焦和核燃料加工业	Petroleum Processing, Coking and Nuclear Fuel Processing Industries	61868	8290
化学原料和化学制品制造业	Production of Chemical Raw Materials and Chemical Products	1357986	284190
医药制造业	Pharmaceutical Industry	356121	138679
化学纤维制造业	Chemical Fiber Manufacturing	590835	173110
橡胶和塑料制品业	Industry of Rubber and Plastic Products	404377	111387
非金属矿物制品业	Industry of Nonmetallic Mineral Products	1247257	187129
黑色金属冶炼和压延加工业	Ferrous Metal Smelting and Pressing	238023	8050
有色金属冶炼和压延加工业	Non-Ferrous Metal Smelting and Pressing	269483	66643
金属制品业	Manufacture of Metal Products	1128172	575907
通用设备制造业	Manufacture of General Purpose Machinery	2785046	765546
专用设备制造业	Manufacture of Equipment for Special Purpose	2004079	230076
汽车制造业	Automobile Industry	451837	134102
铁路、船舶、航空航天和其他运输设备制造业	Manufacture of Railroad, Shipping, Aerospace and Other Transportation Equipments	412611	132728
电气机械和器材制造业	Manufacture of Electrical Machinery and Equipments	1753927	350699
计算机、通信和其他电子设备制造业	Manufacture of Computer, Communications and Other Electronic Products	1210727	419909
仪器仪表制造业	Instrument Manufacturing	538940	102294
其他制造业	Others	55763	33055
废弃资源综合利用业	Comprehensive Utilization of Waste Resources	43110	2470
金属制品、机械和设备修理业	Metal Product, Machinery and Equipment Repair Industry	22500	
电力、热力、燃气及水生产和供应业	Generation and Supply of Electric and Heating Power, Gas and Water	988128	400314
电力、热力生产和供应业	Generation and Supply of Electric Power and Heating Power	606716	221370
燃气生产和供应业	Generation and Supply of Gas	129900	25100
水的生产和供应业	Generation and Supply of Water	251512	153844
批发和零售业	Wholesale and Retail Sales	1343192	562270
批发业	Wholesale	723727	340273
零售业	Retail Sales	619465	221997
交通运输、仓储和邮政业	Transportaion, Storage and Postal Industries	2245681	821176
铁路运输业	Railway Transport	19336	19336
道路运输业	Road Transport	696963	330842
水上运输业	Waterway Transport	863870	309820
航空运输业	Aviation Transportation	28932	25982
管道运输业	Pipeline Transport	11656	
装卸搬运和运输代理业	Handling and Shipping Agency Industries	41376	17857
仓储业	Storage Industry	566298	117339
邮政业	Postal Industry	17250	
住宿和餐饮业	Accomodation and Catering Services	390573	150792
住宿业	Accomodation Industry	282733	92772
餐饮业	Catering Industry	107840	58020
信息传输、软件和信息技术服务业	Information Transmission, Software and IT Services	445852	347134
电信、广播电视和卫星传输服务	Telecom, Broadcasting and Satellite Transmission Services	9409	6429
互联网和相关服务	Internet and Related Services	206789	195099
软件和信息技术服务业	Software and IT Services	229654	145606
金融业	Banking Industry	166157	128170
货币金融服务	Monetary and Financial Services	53327	24240
资本市场服务	Capital Market Services	2500	
其他金融业	Others	110330	103930
房地产业	Real Estate Industry	1127118	411413
房地产业	Real Estate	1127118	411413
租赁和商务服务业	Renting and Commercial Services	542547	335279
租赁业	Renting	31135	28155
商务服务业	Commercial Services	511412	307124

CONTINUED 1

(10,000 yuan)

崇川区 Chongchuan	港闸区 Gangzha	开发区 Developing Zone	通州区 Tongzhou	海安 Haian	如东 Rudong	启东 Qidong	如皋 Rugao	海门 Haimen
520	2840	257602	13390	9093	19775	18010	27599	22190
24784	1250	3700	3405		10920	2960		21680
6930	14480	11240	22503	1573	107400	47710	37698	61630
	2980	5310		709	38100		2769	12000
5529	5500	237335	35826	102972	402601	192051	205252	170920
4480		89480	44719	27614	20627	58176	31785	79240
7261	4037	10660	151152	327871	56864	5970	21260	5760
8883	8480	24020	70004	44384	36304	55900	45502	110900
3780	27698	43905	111746	155100	171577	71352	397226	264873
		8050		163069	10320	2850	17134	36600
		1010	65633	73988	10000	2860	28502	87490
8605	70480	167768	329054	55490	89995	102900	119030	184850
57728	101053	117735	489030	476173	156749	799410	269968	317200
44119	14896	37870	133191	123008	230545	685295	172439	562716
2487		42424	89191	158010	200	2800	128765	27960
23541	29850	27712	51625	55800		110550	90483	23050
5867	42679	77845	224308	300735	300273	265432	268409	268379
70496	17050	50100	282263	200248	58424	104110	232228	195808
3170		27360	71764	124249		149125	139162	24110
			33055	10556		2930	4302	4920
			2470		37640			3000
					22500			
18210	134198	126819	111831	36012	396617	85730	45777	23678
5400	134198	42230	39542	32555	300570	27950	9413	14858
10100			15000		59000	45800		
2710		84589	57289	3457	37047	11980	36364	8820
181880	39978	234650	105762	135889	125578	142629	163036	213790
151644	23910	120400	44319	82087	15653	101179	33245	151290
30236	16068	114250	61443	53802	109925	41450	129791	62500
352125	62570	90040	316441	205128	326359	457663	211124	224231
			19336					
114611	41770	22050	152411	45558	216456	8130	32799	63178
187990		11080	110750	53354	16400	433633		50663
			25982					2950
					9556			2100
9887		7970		4941	7078	2900		8600
39637	20800	48940	7962	101275	73369	13000	177175	84140
					3500		1150	12600
82582	22830	9000	36380	117542	20700	25445	32409	43685
70872	5820		16080	117542	20700	22545	20509	8665
11710	17010	9000	20300			2900	11900	35020
238871	68560	31668	8035	10066	11200	20500	30172	26780
4429			2000					2980
186739		8360					9690	2000
47703	68560	23308	6035	10066	11200	20500	20482	21800
34070		91500	2600		7495		21292	9200
21640			2600		7495		21292	300
								2500
12430		91500						6400
54590	17700	10330	328793	290065	62167	24220	339253	
54590	17700	10330	328793	290065	62167	24220	339253	
145259	81740	19780	88500	30461	26750	23880	16797	109380
23255	2020	2880				2980		
122004	79720	16900	88500	30461	26750	20900	16797	109380

7-4 续表 2

单位：万元

指 标	Item	全市 Municipality	市区 Urban Areas
科学研究和技术服务业	Scientific Research and Technology Services	430362	193607
研究和试验发展	Research and Experimental Development	181249	80486
专业技术服务业	Special Technical Services	149958	77428
科技推广和应用服务业	S&T Promotion and Application Services	99155	35693
水利、环境和公共设施管理业	Water Conservancy, Environment & Public Facilities Management	3343825	1826294
水利管理业	Water Conservancy Management	248449	154734
生态保护和环境治理业	Ecological Protection and Environmental Management	133019	89155
公共设施管理业	Public Facilities Management	2962357	1582405
居民服务、修理和其他服务业	Resident Service, Repair and Other Services	91254	48238
居民服务业	Resident Service	39128	17362
机动车、电子产品和日用产品修理业	Mobile, Electronic Product and Daily-use Product Repair Services	49326	28076
其他服务业	Other Services	2800	2800
教育	Education	511616	222519
教育	Education	511616	222519
卫生和社会工作	Health and Social Work	306697	106723
卫生	Health	244923	76819
社会工作	Social Work	61774	29904
文化、体育和娱乐业	Culture, Sports and Entertainment	342795	128387
新闻和出版业	News and Publishing Industry	3000	3000
广播、电视、电影和影视录音制作业	Broadcasting, TV, Film, Video&Audio Recording Industry	25263	
文化艺术业	Culture & Arts Industry	128473	55503
体育	Sports	55090	37284
娱乐业	Entertainment	130969	32600
公共管理、社会保障和社会组织	Public Administration, Social Security and Social Organizations	288390	179124
中国共产党机关	Party Institutions of CPC	3750	3750
国家机构	State Institutions	207961	114857
群众团体、社会团体和其他成员组织	Mass Organization, Social Organization & Other Membership Organizations	24821	11509
基层群众自治组织	Self-governing Mass Organizations at the Grass-roots Level	51858	49008
三、本年新增固定资产	**Newly Increased Fixed Assets of the Year**	**52281362**	**34116891**
四、项目个数(个)	**Number of Projects**		
施工项目个数	Projects under Construction	5746	2102
#新开工项目个数	Newly-started Projects	4648	1793
本年投产项目个数	New Production Projects of the Year	4628	1755
五、房屋建筑面积(万平方米)	**Contruction Area of the Building (10,000 m²)**		
本年施工房屋面积	Construction Area of the Year	6057.15	2043.4
其中：住宅	Of which: Residence	450.06	286.58
本年竣工房屋面积	Floor Space Completed of the Year	3093.84	1007.95
其中：住宅	Of which: Residence	149.62	83.04
六、资金来源	**Capital Sources**		
本年资金来源合计	Total Capital Sources of Last Year	33221169	10873227
1.上年末结余资金	Cash Balance at the end of Last Year	179027	172507
2.本年资金来源小计	Subtotal of Capital Sources of the Year	33042142	10700720
(1)国家预算内资金	State Budgetary Appropriation	1799600	1475998
(2)国内贷款	Domestic Loans	1161178	406554
(3)债券	Bond		
(4)利用外资	Utilization of Foreign Capital	494725	53851
其中：外商直接投资	Of which: Foreign Direct Investment	200265	45950
(5)自筹资金	Self-raised Funds	29432346	8659824
其中：企、事业单位自有资金	Of which: Self-owned Capital by Enterprises and Institutes	13624899	2528580
(6)其他资金来源	Others	154293	104493
各项应付款合计	Total Payables	1105660	1034083
其中：工程款	Of which: Project Funds	748415	748365

CONTINUED 2

(10,000 yuan)

崇川区 Chongchuan	港闸区 Gangzha	开发区 Developing Zone	通州区 Tongzhou	海安 Hai'an	如东 Rudong	启东 Qidong	如皋 Rugao	海门 Haimen
85469	13680	24750	69708	13766	108835	38946	9300	65908
13396	8560	14000	44530		77635	2000	4550	16578
59208	5120	10750	2350	12700	4000	10880	4750	40200
12865			22828	1066	27200	26066		9130
457931		1080348	255294	189976	357860	479753	255140	234802
33365		79407	41962	20985	25669		500	46561
15222		8600	65333		23664			20200
409344		992341	147999	168991	308527	479753	254640	168041
25651	5470	8300	8817	3266	5200		4100	30450
8545			8817	336	5200		2580	13650
17106	5470	5500		2930			1520	16800
		2800						
58513	7500	82499	74007	4965	26700	54045	52825	150562
58513	7500	82499	74007	4965	26700	54045	52825	150562
73345		17000	16378	21697	48200	28707	9560	91810
55341		8500	12978	21697	47500	23307	5360	70240
18004		8500	3400		700	5400	4200	21570
79414	2640		46333	25905	10000	13968	21936	142599
3000								
				10463		6000		8800
55503				15442		2568	7850	47110
20911			16373				436	17370
	2640		29960		10000	5400	13650	69319
117327	12368	23550	25879	9962		27564	10000	61740
3750								
66269	4468	23550	20570	7450		22564	10000	53090
	7900		3609	2512		5000		5800
47308			1700					2850
26275241	**1417897**	**2179966**	**4243787**	**3031700**	**3531495**	**3935138**	**3373599**	**4292539**
500	88	756	755	651	302	615	1063	1013
461	68	678	586	294	242	578	881	860
447	69	691	548	340	260	567	857	849
352.03	285.67	299.51	1106.2	1689.1	330.84	482.57	959.7	551.54
			286.58				163.48	
189.5	119.56	166.27	532.63	562.38	250.15	400.54	564.81	308.01
			83.04				66.58	
2608761	850538	3497422	3905761	4375923	4252000	4388650	4649276	4682093
6400		166107				6520		
2602361	850538	3331315	3905761	4375923	4252000	4382130	4649276	4682093
563984	46368	854901		23250	6500	213338	7514	73000
49843			356711	202322	30662	31700	342240	147700
	2920	2801	48130	5700	84196	21885	63833	265260
			45950	1000	83195	21885	41735	6500
1978640	801250	2473613	3406321	4144651	4080842	4115207	4235689	4196133
879076			1649504	1092599	916969	4115207	2526527	2445017
9894			94599		49800			
195197	44900		761879	1250	66527		900	2900
114714	42400		578695				50	

7-5 按计划总投资分组项目投资分地区情况(2014年)

单位:万元

指标	Item	全市 Municipality	市区 Urban Area
固定资产投资项目	Fixed-asset Investment Project		
计划总投资	Planned Investment in Total	58066871	21724107
#本年新开工	Newly-started Projects of the Year	28797489	9276089
本年完成投资	Investment Completed of the Year	32174675	11439095
#本年新开工	Newly-started Projects of the Year	21563967	7119427
#设备工器具购置	Purchase of Equipment and Instruments	16005800	5033791
施工项目个数	Number of Construction Projects	5746	2102
#本年新开工	Newly-started Projects of the Year	4648	1793
本年投产项目个数	Production Projects of the Year	4628	1755
3000万元以上项目	Projects above 30 million Yuan		
计划总投资	Planned Investment in Total	48210699	17106544
#本年新开工	Newly-started Projects of the Year	20595823	5836511
本年完成投资	Investment Completed of the Year	22973800	6977183
#本年新开工	Newly-started Projects of the Year	13652682	3748977
施工项目个数	Number of Construction Projects	2180	586
#本年新开工	Newly-started Projects of the Year	1328	334
本年投产项目个数	Production Projects of the Year	1355	311
亿元以上项目	Projects above 100 million Yuan		
计划总投资	Planned Investment in Total	42123772	15453986
#本年新开工	Newly-started Projects of the Year	16148979	4645686
本年完成投资	Investment Completed of the Year	18599424	5831442
#本年新开工	Newly-started Projects of the Year	10062619	2792670
施工项目个数	Number of Construction Projects	1197	322
#本年新开工	Newly-started Projects of the Year	615	148
本年投产项目个数	Production Projects of the Year	653	138
5亿元以上项目	Projects above 500 million Yuan		
计划总投资	Planned Investment in Total	21217066	8874881
#本年新开工	Newly-started Projects of the Year	4773180	1295665
本年完成投资	Investment Completed of the Year	6483063	2161186
#本年新开工	Newly-started Projects of the Year	2057054	449251
施工项目个数	Number of Construction Projects	190	68
#本年新开工	Newly-started Projects of the Year	46	14
本年投产项目个数	Production Projects of the Year	65	22
10亿元以上项目	Projects above 1 billion Yuan		
计划总投资	Planned Investment in Total	13920642	5990453
#本年新开工	Newly-started Projects of the Year	2723681	400000
本年完成投资	Investment Completed of the Year	3730146	1229736
#本年新开工	Newly-started Projects of the Year	1066633	79080
施工项目个数	Number of Construction Projects	79	25
#本年新开工	Newly-started Projects of the Year	17	2
本年投产项目个数	Production Projects of the Year	25	7
20亿元以上项目	Projects above 2 billion Yuan		
计划总投资	Planned Investment in Total	6299008	4357048
#本年新开工	Newly-started Projects of the Year	923102	400000
本年完成投资	Investment Completed of the Year	1337553	717585
#本年新开工	Newly-started Projects of the Year	217880	79080
施工项目个数	Number of Construction Projects	19	13
#本年新开工	Newly-started Projects of the Year	4	2
本年投产项目个数	Production Projects of the Year	7	4

GROUPED PROJECTS BY DISTRICT GROUPED BY TOTAL PLANNED INVESTMENT (2014)

(10,000 yuan)

崇川区 Chongchuan	港闸区 Gangzha	开发区 Developing Zone	通州区 Tongzhou	海安 Haian	如东 Rudong	启东 Qidong	如皋 Rugao	海门 Haimen
4508499	2222201	6216363	8689044	10581859	5492753	5722252	7020085	7525815
1625258	561504	2273505	4815822	2449758	3756098	4496605	4128179	4690760
2549625	877994	3446289	4523210	3964693	3964651	4363801	3865594	4576841
1402776	405297	2098499	3212855	929192	2993915	3961051	2826528	3733854
1252717	457157	1176318	2143599	1783367	2496310	2043667	1976518	2672147
500	88	756	755	651	302	615	1063	1013
461	68	678	586	294	242	578	881	860
447	69	691	548	340	260	567	857	849
3220704	1832286	4185434	7780120	10328132	5492753	4759717	4982457	5541096
870074	433722	518106	4014609	2253039	3756098	3575220	2312974	2861981
1269299	491082	1419360	3755465	3786412	3964651	3429716	2067896	2747942
653191	277255	343100	2475431	775885	2993915	3041616	1124094	1968195
88	36	98	361	523	302	266	219	284
51	20	23	240	191	242	244	127	190
41	17	33	220	253	260	219	126	186
2979945	1776813	4101977	6507251	8920679	4916922	3633506	4603395	4595284
663036	405737	486231	3090682	1611266	3251687	2475446	2041737	2123157
1093366	462976	1373335	2859788	3123632	3463194	2349685	1794834	2036637
491669	255967	323500	1721534	533051	2525852	1974822	900806	1335418
56	28	85	150	286	205	97	156	131
23	16	18	91	80	158	80	79	70
20	10	26	82	128	173	66	73	75
1569401	1309848	2496273	3499359	4768014	1541733	1744958	1951455	2336025
81000	122000	69000	1023665	333248	743537	842369	628307	930054
346751	228669	690408	895358	1371803	754763	925744	576218	693349
70219	68560	69000	241472	92473	258671	627755	192164	436740
11	6	23	28	51	12	15	22	22
1	2	1	10	4	5	9	6	8
4	1	9	8	6	6	10	11	10
1235224	1059148	1330845	2365236	2955290	1093153	1088115	984177	1809454
			400000	140940	634457	419213	350617	778454
219674	102059	343499	564504	753311	458856	498923	294940	494380
			79080	43472	186000	249421	134650	374010
6	2	5	12	23	5	5	7	14
			2	1	3	3	2	6
2	1	1	3	2	1	3	5	7
752635	1059148	1006845	1538420	400000	556391	556902	228667	200000
			400000		294435		228667	
167701	102059	221974	225851	30800	253456	204102	80800	50810
			79080		58000		80800	
3	2	2	6	1	2	1	1	1
			2		1		1	
1	1		2		1	1	0	1

7-6 按计划总投资分组工业项目分地区情况(2014年)

单位:万元

指标	Item	全市 Municipality	市区 Urban Area
固定资产投资项目	Fixed-asset Investment Project		
计划总投资	Planned Investment in Total	35078459	11684357
#本年新开工	Newly-started Projects of the Year	18873471	4807684
本年完成投资	Investment Completed of the Year	20468162	5949050
#本年新开工	Newly-started Projects of the Year	14471556	3839461
#设备工器具购置	Purchase of Equipment and Instruments	13811757	4080043
施工项目个数	Number of Construction Projects	3624	1044
#本年新开工	Newly-started Projects of the Year	2947	866
本年投产项目个数	Production Projects of the Year	2990	869
3000万元以上项目	Projects above 30 million Yuan		
计划总投资	Planned Investment in Total	28877184	9433208
#本年新开工	Newly-started Projects of the Year	13623522	3273198
本年完成投资	Investment Completed of the Year	14650727	3818819
#本年新开工	Newly-started Projects of the Year	9387584	2349789
施工项目个数	Number of Construction Projects	1447	338
#本年新开工	Newly-started Projects of the Year	903	205
本年投产项目个数	Production Projects of the Year	963	205
亿元以上项目	Projects above 100 million Yuan		
计划总投资	Planned Investment in Total	24590300	8381447
#本年新开工	Newly-started Projects of the Year	10557417	2517146
本年完成投资	Investment Completed of the Year	11529671	3074552
#本年新开工	Newly-started Projects of the Year	6867873	1709810
施工项目个数	Number of Construction Projects	764	168
#本年新开工	Newly-started Projects of the Year	420	85
本年投产项目个数	Production Projects of the Year	462	86
5亿元以上项目	Projects above 500 million Yuan		
计划总投资	Planned Investment in Total	11742136	5107491
#本年新开工	Newly-started Projects of the Year	2777588	449165
本年完成投资	Investment Completed of the Year	3571241	1042609
#本年新开工	Newly-started Projects of the Year	1159447	133189
施工项目个数	Number of Construction Projects	101	36
#本年新开工	Newly-started Projects of the Year	22	4
本年投产项目个数	Production Projects of the Year	39	15
10亿元以上项目	Projects above 1 billion Yuan		
计划总投资	Planned Investment in Total	8085013	3501121
#本年新开工	Newly-started Projects of the Year	1999339	200000
本年完成投资	Investment Completed of the Year	2213658	683830
#本年新开工	Newly-started Projects of the Year	763242	61000
施工项目个数	Number of Construction Projects	47	12
#本年新开工	Newly-started Projects of the Year	12	1
本年投产项目个数	Production Projects of the Year	18	6
20亿元以上项目	Projects above 2 billion Yuan		
计划总投资	Planned Investment in Total	3330634	2807532
#本年新开工	Newly-started Projects of the Year	723102	200000
本年完成投资	Investment Completed of the Year	636132	497332
#本年新开工	Newly-started Projects of the Year	199800	61000
施工项目个数	Number of Construction Projects	9	7
#本年新开工	Newly-started Projects of the Year	3	1
本年投产项目个数	Production Projects of the Year	3	3

INDUSTRIAL PROJECTS BY DISTRICTS GROUPED BY TOTAL PLANNED INVESTMENT (2014)

(10,000 yuan)

崇川区 Chongchuan	港闸区 Gangzha	开发区 Developing Zone	通州区 Tongzhou	海安 Haian	如东 Rudong	启东 Qidong	如皋 Rugao	海门 Haimen
1203233	1375239	3656170	5416715	6800052	3907090	3480911	4570531	4635518
398820	244496	858062	3306306	1743431	2859597	3262575	3020232	3179952
562598	542958	1722874	3111364	2865378	2800107	3019381	2677612	3156634
359120	154549	745397	2580395	685597	2215903	2923851	2084628	2722116
396778	440373	1169739	2069153	1741222	2177933	1820041	1775283	2217235
203	30	261	549	447	212	482	732	707
192	22	212	440	186	174	460	634	627
196	19	221	433	264	176	456	593	632
790466	1090380	2838193	4681169	6637382	3907090	2667048	3041107	3191349
73700	218752	310165	2670581	1614096	2859597	2489862	1581466	1805303
150831	259594	906597	2492541	2743584	2800107	2232018	1285134	1771065
35000	128805	197500	1988484	578259	2215903	2151138	726928	1365567
13	19	59	246	373	212	191	150	183
2	12	11	180	127	174	184	85	128
7	8	19	171	207	176	165	81	129
782466	1054595	2817892	3693494	5542756	3584868	1737248	2819147	2524834
73700	195767	307105	1940574	1182760	2586795	1579742	1436786	1254188
147331	240876	901303	1775786	2201605	2525679	1338398	1142730	1246707
35000	112517	195000	1367293	415747	1968849	1269498	614560	889409
12	14	55	86	193	162	56	112	73
2	9	10	64	55	132	53	59	36
6	4	17	59	100	134	45	50	47
585766	786000	1791140	1944585	2829714	984855	652288	864363	1303425
			449165	230482	526515	540288	425684	605454
75831	102059	458026	406693	1013686	389407	428150	258209	439180
			133189	68187	105171	382750	134980	335170
6	1	17	12	31	8	6	8	12
			4	2	3	5	3	5
3	1	6	5	5	4	4	5	6
332589	786000	894112	1488420	1738393	671175	394893	680977	1098454
			200000	140940	474435	282893	350617	550454
18973	102059	276027	286771	596688	157400	190400	236310	349030
			61000	43472	80000	145000	134650	299120
2	1	3	6	15	3	3	5	9
			1	1	2	2	2	4
1	1	1	3	2		2	3	5
	786000	683112	1338420		294435		228667	
			200000		294435		228667	
	102059	187502	207771		58000		80800	
			61000		58000		80800	
	1	1	5		1		1	
			1		1		1	
	1		2					

7-7 按计划总投资分组三产项目分地区资情况(2014年)

单位:万元

指 标	Item	全市 Municipality	市区 Urban Area
固定资产投资项目	Fixed-asset Investment Project		
计划总投资	Planned Investment in Total	22861110	10001304
#本年新开工	Newly-started Projects of the Year	9801046	4434289
本年完成投资	Investment Completed of the Year	11607359	5461126
#本年新开工	Newly-started Projects of the Year	6993787	3251577
#设备工器具购置	Purchase of Equipment and Instruments	2171759	945331
施工项目个数	Number of Construction Projects	2058	1043
#本年新开工	Newly-started Projects of the Year	1638	913
本年投产项目个数	Production Projects of the Year	1600	874
3000万元以上项目	Projects above 30 million Yuan		
计划总投资	Planned Investment in Total	19285295	7661186
#本年新开工	Newly-started Projects of the Year	6928411	2555493
本年完成投资	Investment Completed of the Year	8289858	3154677
#本年新开工	Newly-started Projects of the Year	4232413	1396031
施工项目个数	Number of Construction Projects	723	246
#本年新开工	Newly-started Projects of the Year	416	128
本年投产项目个数	Production Projects of the Year	386	105
亿元以上项目	Projects above 100 million Yuan		
计划总投资	Planned Investment in Total	17523472	7072539
#本年新开工	Newly-started Projects of the Year	5581562	2128540
本年完成投资	Investment Completed of the Year	7064753	2756890
#本年新开工	Newly-started Projects of the Year	3189746	1082860
施工项目个数	Number of Construction Projects	432	154
#本年新开工	Newly-started Projects of the Year	194	63
本年投产项目个数	Production Projects of the Year	191	52
5亿元以上项目	Projects above 500 million Yuan		
计划总投资	Planned Investment in Total	9474930	3767390
#本年新开工	Newly-started Projects of the Year	1995592	846500
本年完成投资	Investment Completed of the Year	2911822	1118577
#本年新开工	Newly-started Projects of the Year	897607	316062
施工项目个数	Number of Construction Projects	89	32
#本年新开工	Newly-started Projects of the Year	24	10
本年投产项目个数	Production Projects of the Year	26	7
10亿元以上项目	Projects above 1 billion Yuan		
计划总投资	Planned Investment in Total	5835629	2489332
#本年新开工	Newly-started Projects of the Year	724342	200000
本年完成投资	Investment Completed of the Year	1516488	545906
#本年新开工	Newly-started Projects of the Year	303391	18080
施工项目个数	Number of Construction Projects	32	13
#本年新开工	Newly-started Projects of the Year	5	1
本年投产项目个数	Production Projects of the Year	7	1
20亿元以上项目	Projects above 2 billion Yuan		
计划总投资	Planned Investment in Total	2968374	1549516
#本年新开工	Newly-started Projects of the Year	200000	200000
本年完成投资	Investment Completed of the Year	701421	220253
#本年新开工	Newly-started Projects of the Year	18080	18080
施工项目个数	Number of Construction Projects	10	6
#本年新开工	Newly-started Projects of the Year	1	1
本年投产项目个数	Production Projects of the Year	4	1

TERTIARY INDUSTRY PROJECTS BY DISTRICT GROUPED BY TOTAL PLANNED INVESTMENT (2014)

(10,000 yuan)

崇川区 Chongchuan	港闸区 Gangzha	开发区 Developing Zone	通州区 Tongzhou	海安 Haian	如东 Rudong	启东 Qidong	如皋 Rugao	海门 Haimen
3305266	846962	2560193	3233883	3737547	1575663	2237841	2432048	2876707
1226438	317008	1415443	1475400	662067	886501	1230530	1090441	1497218
1987027	335036	1723415	1382927	1058688	1159544	1340920	1176944	1410137
1043656	250748	1353102	604071	202968	773012	1033700	730862	1001668
855939	16784	6579	66029	36458	314377	222176	200805	452612
297	58	495	191	176	89	132	318	300
269	46	466	132	80	67	117	234	227
251	50	470	103	59	84	110	260	213
2430238	741906	1347241	3086801	3668180	1575663	2089169	1941350	2349747
796374	214970	207941	1336208	616373	886501	1081858	731508	1056678
1118468	231488	512763	1259237	1021800	1159544	1194198	782762	976877
618191	148450	145600	483790	176598	773012	886978	397166	602628
75	17	39	113	144	89	74	69	101
49	8	12	59	58	67	59	42	62
34	9	14	48	42	84	53	45	57
2197479	722218	1284085	2813757	3377923	1322054	1896258	1784248	2070450
589336	209970	179126	1150108	428506	654892	895704	604951	868969
946035	222100	472032	1084002	922027	932515	1011287	652104	789930
456669	143450	128500	354241	117304	552003	705324	286246	446009
44	14	30	64	93	42	41	44	58
21	7	8	27	25	25	27	20	34
14	6	9	23	28	39	21	23	28
983635	523848	705133	1554774	1938300	556878	1092670	1087092	1032600
81000	122000	69000	574500	102766	217022	302081	202623	324600
270920	126610	232382	488665	358117	365356	497594	318009	254169
70219	68560	69000	108283	24286	153500	245005	57184	101570
5	5	6	16	20	4	9	14	10
1	2	1	6	2	2	4	3	3
1		3	3	1	2	6	6	4
902635	273148	436733	876816	1216897	421978	693222	303200	711000
0	0	0	200000		160022	136320		228000
200701	0	67472	277733	156623	301456	308523	58630	145350
			18080		106000	104421		74890
4	1	2	6	8	2	2	2	5
			1		1	1		2
1					1	1	2	2
752635	273148	323733	200000	400000	261956	556902		200000
			200000					
167701		34472	18080	30800	195456	204102		50810
			18080					
3	1	1	1	1	1	1		1
			1					
1					1	1		1

7-8 固定资产投资主要比例(2014年)

指 标	Item	全市 Municipality	市区 Urban Areas
固定资产投资额(万元)	Investment of Fixed Assets (10,000 Yuan)	38963893	15896124
按产业分	Grouped by Industries		
第一产业	Primary Industry	99154	28919
第二产业	Secondary Industry	20468162	5949050
#工业	Industry	20468162	5949050
第三产业	Tertiary Industry	18396577	9918155
#房地产业	Real Estate	6789218	4457029
按建设性质分	Grouped by Types of Construction		
新建	New Construction	14570138	4336479
扩建	Extension	8931325	3731232
改建	Reconstruction	7024029	1938313
其他	Others	8438401	5890100
投资比例(%)	Investment Proportion (%)		
三次产业投资比例(%)	Three Industrial Investment Proportion (%)		
第一产业	Primary Industry	0.3	0.2
第二产业	Secondary Industry	52.5	37.4
#工业	Industry	52.5	37.4
第三产业	Tertiary Industry	47.2	62.4
#房地产业	Real Estate	17.4	28.0
建设性质投资比例	Investment Proportion by Types of Construction		
新建	New Construction	37.4	27.3
扩建	Extension	22.9	23.5
改建	Reconstruction	18.0	12.2
其他	Others	21.7	37.1

MAJOR PROPORTIONS OF FIXED-ASSET INVESTMENT(2014)

崇川区 Chongchuan	港闸区 Gangzha	开发区 Developing Zone	通州区 Tongzhou	海安 Haian	如东 Rudong	启东 Qidong	如皋 Rugao	海门 Haimen
4063848	2398229	4190912	5201158	4489468	4279317	4834148	4450849	5013987
			28919	40627	5000	3500	11038	10070
562598	542958	1722874	3111364	2865378	2800107	3019381	2677612	3156634
562598	542958	1722874	3111364	2865378	2800107	3019381	2677612	3156634
3501250	1855271	2468038	2060875	1583463	1474210	1811267	1762199	1847283
1514223	1520235	744623	677948	524775	314666	470347	585255	437146
1139171	356010	1002880	1796441	1824287	1891225	2106226	2038617	2373304
323932	42596	1887399	1477305	1198931	808509	1618745	204331	1369577
333564	199568	230217	1174964	875235	1188963	638830	1548728	833960
2267181	1800055	1070416	752448	591015	390620	470347	659173	437146
			0.6	0.9	0.1	0.1	0.2	0.2
13.8	22.6	41.1	59.8	63.8	65.4	62.5	60.2	63.0
13.8	22.6	41.1	59.8	63.8	65.4	62.5	60.2	63.0
86.2	77.4	58.9	39.6	35.3	34.4	37.5	39.6	36.8
37.3	63.4	17.8	13.0	11.7	7.4	9.7	13.1	8.7
28.0	14.8	23.9	34.5	40.6	44.2	43.6	45.8	47.3
8.0	1.8	45.0	28.4	26.7	18.9	33.5	4.6	27.3
8.2	8.3	5.5	22.6	19.5	27.8	13.2	34.8	16.6
55.8	75.1	25.5	14.5	13.2	9.1	9.7	14.8	8.7

7-9 房地产开发投资完成额(2014 年)

单位:万元

指 标	Item	全市 Municipality	市区 Urban Areas
计划投资	Planned Investment		
计划总投资	Total Planned Investment	33351151	20117387
本年完成投资	**Completed Investment of the Year**	**6789218**	**4457029**
按隶属关系分	Grouped by Relationship of Administrative Surbodination		
中央	Central	7586	
省	Province	36061	36061
省辖市	Provincially Administered Municipality	210635	181435
县(市)、区	County(city) and District	1454358	1375238
其他	Others	5080578	2864295
按登记注册类型分	Grouped by Types of Registration		
内资	Domestic Capital	6170510	4088156
#国有经济	State-owned Economy	1701238	1617339
#民营经济	Private Economy	4469272	2470817
#私营个体	Private Individual Economy	2569469	1358730
港澳台商投资	HK,Macau &Taiwan Funded	519187	339754
外商投资	Foreign Investment	99521	29119
按资质等级分	Grouped by Grades of Qualifications		
一级	1st Grade	978100	877330
二级	2nd Grade	2123167	1653139
三级	3rd Grade	103872	35843
四级	4th Grade	920	
暂定	Tentative	3385375	1766325
其他	Others	197784	124392
按构成分	Grouped by Use of Funds		
建筑工程	Construction Project	5289259	3381069
安装工程	Installation Project	136425	108716
设备工器具购置	Purchase of Equipment and Instruments	96254	68828
其他费用	Others	1267280	898416
旧建筑物购置费	Purchase Expense of Old Buildings	1392	892
土地购置费	Land Purchase Fee	1146274	799255
按工程用途分	Grouped by Use of Projects		
住宅	Residence	4926656	3094109
90 平方米以下	Below 90 m^2	542017	352259
144 平方米以上	Above 144 m^2	641409	332479
别墅、高档公寓	Villa and High-end Apartment	153325	68834
办公楼	Office Building	437738	396381
商业营业用房	Commercial Building	1003423	695296
其他	Others	421401	271243
本年新增固定资产	Newly-increased Fixed Asset of the Year	3635117	2132756
土地开发	Land Development		
待开发土地面积(万平方米)	Land to be Developed (10,000 m^2)	284.67	111.72
本年土地购置面积(万平方米)	Land Purchased of the Year (10,000 m^2)	329.83	198.15
本年土地成交价款(万元)	Price of Transaction this Year (10,000 Yuan)	955858	499430
资金来源	Capital Sources		
本年实际到位资金合计	Total Actual Investment of the Year	11630442	6834744
上年末结余资金	Balance of Cash by the End of the Year	2117483	1387759
本年实际到位资金小计	Subtotal Actual Investment of the Year	9512959	5446985
国内贷款	Domestic Loans	2151148	1442401
利用外资	Utilization of Foreign Investment		
外商直接投资	Direct Foreign Investment		
自筹资金	Self-raised Funds	3928544	2259478
自有资金	Equity Fund	1512054	668184
其他资金来源	Others	3433267	1745106
定金及预收款	Advance Deposit and Receipts	2336424	1268334
个人按揭贷款	Personal Mortgage Loan	676118	335685
本年各项应付款合计	Total Payables of the Year	2729036	1736673
工程款	Project Funds	1163107	635233

COMPLETED INVESTMENT OF REAL ESTATE DEVELOPMENT(2014)

(10,000 yuan)

崇川区 Chongchuan	港闸区 Gangzha	开发区 Developing Zone	通州区 Tongzhou	海安 Haian	如东 Rudong	启东 Qidong	如皋 Rugao	海门 Haimen
8057396	4692607	4313888	3053496	3328904	1141767	2547496	2828625	3386972
1514223	**1520235**	**744623**	**677948**	**524775**	**314666**	**470347**	**585255**	**437146**
							7586	
36061								
150924		30511			29200			
394812	505970	444386	30070	33164	7100	8167	27474	3215
932426	1014265	269726	647878	491611	278366	462180	550195	433931
1343537	1375724	724232	644663	523523	312866	291334	539195	415436
599450	514370	477949	25570		23053	7330	7586	45930
744087	861354	246283	619093	523523	289813	284004	531609	369506
491682	354726	200602	311720	257510	220111	133250	415988	183880
170276	144511	3836	21131	1050		121800	44198	12385
410		16555	12154	202	1800	57213	1862	9325
433044		332381	111905			51825		48945
561887	719919	128501	242832	32036	87799	67042	142134	141017
21750		970	13123	202	5334	30510	18458	13525
				920				
497542	800316	226975	241492	488806	221533	298727	415343	194641
		55796	68596	2811		22243	9320	39018
1190135	1108163	626545	456226	415221	248050	403445	443205	398269
52343	13224	7956	35193	646	20223	2790	3870	180
44049	1304	8815	14660	3235	5945	9114	8978	154
227696	397544	101307	171869	105673	40448	54998	129202	38543
892					500			
202142	367105	73912	156096	102536	35740	49618	122204	36921
812281	1114322	615037	552469	415309	240541	429590	400764	346343
112526	109121	67334	63278	19304	41984	42275	27548	58647
126354	87406	44817	73902	49206	27837	96315	67623	67949
14288		6400	48146	16360	8242	27651	7199	25039
280391	79947	33219	2824	6528	3266	18249	2391	10923
327405	224751	67287	75853	48107	46218	14031	133055	66716
94146	101215	29080	46802	54831	24641	8477	49045	13164
375716	965188	245311	546541	319542	90206	417702	298014	376897
13.99	69.8	24.8	3.13	41.41	32.94	21.4	74.42	2.78
23.35	48.19	62.18	64.43	16.52	39.51	21.63	28.15	25.87
69456	151148	100416	178410	29381	99005	88249	92290	147503
3102345	1530254	1252372	949773	944754	441179	983499	1099836	1326430
638640	192051	433321	123747	355016	31938	102510	162321	77939
2463705	1338203	819051	826026	589738	409241	880989	937515	1248491
666580	204812	214066	356943	129067	61110	223039	166201	129330
1039282	794180	235606	190410	72170	205243	186396	394047	811210
517932	84050	465	65737	1095	22028	94189	93113	633445
757843	339211	369379	278673	388501	142888	471554	377267	307951
608880	253512	232019	173923	246458	40772	354210	179624	247026
138266	77709	66255	53455	111065	45265	63355	78728	42020
472260	887373	158448	218592	241986	172854	196867	197513	183143
248970	160628	67360	158275	130020	43956	110468	118330	125100

7-10 房地产开发房屋施工、竣工面积及竣工价值(2014年)

单位:万平方米、万元

指 标	Item	全市 Municipality	市区 Urban Areas
施工面积	Floor Space under Construction	5272.22	3058.38
住宅	Residence	3951.03	2231.54
90平方米以下	Below 90 m^2	408.26	247.01
144平方米以上	Above 144 m^2	555.38	230.52
别墅、高档公寓	Villa and High-end Apartment	124.66	55.61
办公楼	Office Building	255.74	213.07
商业营业用房	Commercial & Business Occupancy	578.95	354.45
其他	Others	486.5	259.31
新开工面积	Floor Space of New Construction	1523.55	846.86
住宅	Residence	1103.38	615.13
90平方米以下	Below 90 m^2	113.34	45.35
144平方米以上	Above 144 m^2	112.25	39.59
别墅、高档公寓	Villa and High-end Apartment	25.98	17.29
办公楼	Office Building	60.58	46.69
商业营业用房	Commercial & Business Occupancy	172.43	99.64
其他	Others	187.16	85.4
竣工面积	Floor Space Completed	1031.15	623.63
住宅	Residence	857.56	525.2
90平方米以下	Below 90 m^2	76	55.71
144平方米以上	Above 144 m^2	91.55	16.35
别墅、高档公寓	Villa and High-end Apartment	13.99	3.37
办公楼	Office Building	32.06	28.05
商业营业用房	Commercial & Business Occupancy	82.38	38.02
其他	Others	59.15	32.35
竣工住宅套数	Completion of Residential Properties	70024	45106
90平方米以下	Below 90 m^2	8875	6330
144平方米以上	Above 144 m^2	4875	856
别墅、高档公寓	Villa and High-end Apartment	576	113
竣工房屋价值	Value of Buildings Completed	2986800	1625799
住宅	Residence	2452119	1323620
90平方米以下	Below 90 m^2	164599	107084
144平方米以上	Above 144 m^2	387260	101680
别墅、高档公寓	Villa and Hign-end Apartment	100193	50354
办公楼	Office Building	128861	118467
商业营业用房	Commercial & Business Occupancy	272278	121637
其他	Others	133542	62075

FLOOR SPACE UNDER CONSTRUCTION &COMPLETED AND VALUE OF BUILDING COMPLETED FOR REAL ESTATE DEVELOPMENT (2014)

(10000m²,10000 yuan)

崇川区 Chongchuan	港闸区 Gangzha	开发区 Developing Zone	通州区 Tongzhou	海安 Haian	如东 Rudong	启东 Qidong	如皋 Rugao	海门 Haimen
1052.63	795.52	658.15	552.07	590.36	209.41	408.03	550	456.04
614.92	666.99	523.34	426.29	448.64	155.03	374.23	385.76	355.82
86.45	45.35	55.74	59.47	18.24	11.01	50.4	32.64	48.96
78.2	31.78	69.65	50.89	84.73	9.01	87.11	81.45	62.56
11.37		9.62	34.63	8.42	8.91	32.75	10.24	8.73
136.1	34.71	37.53	4.73	11.38	7.08	7.72	2.09	14.39
179.61	58.53	50.87	65.45	38.72	17.27	12.26	95.16	61.09
122.01	35.3	46.4	55.6	91.61	30.03	13.82	66.99	24.74
154.7	250.88	225.31	215.97	143.99	57.7	125.8	175.4	173.8
72.85	187.99	177.1	177.19	102.84	30.63	105.96	104.42	144.4
1.65	22.24	11.12	10.34	9.8	5.37	24.63	6.38	21.8
4.36	5.62	8.6	21.01	17.27	3.5	1.67	20.07	30.15
3.5		1.2	12.59		0.51	0.06	6.29	1.83
18.57	20.48	6.94	0.7	0.06		5.89	1.46	6.48
33.87	25.27	23.29	17.21	9.03	6.58	4.74	39.24	13.21
29.42	17.14	17.97	20.87	32.06	20.48	9.21	30.29	9.71
108.17	312.17	57.98	145.31	84.67	17.77	91.29	94.19	119.6
78.05	276.96	41.76	128.43	67.85	16.78	89.66	69	89.08
2.59	8.23	2.4	42.49	1.55		8.89	5.56	4.28
0.16	11.76	2.8	1.64	27.01	0.9	22.84	15.42	9.04
		2.57	0.8	0.61	1.83	1.7	3.14	3.34
7.52	10.68	9.85			0.08		0.63	3.29
12.85	18.16	3.88	3.14	6.75	0.55	0.88	17.84	18.33
9.75	6.37	2.5	13.74	10.08	0.35	0.75	6.72	8.9
7385	22399	3816	11506	4839	1504	6691	5268	6616
327	989	268	4746	191		1103	704	547
10	658	92	96	1286	50	1247	862	574
		78	35	18	98	42	123	182
332321	836213	230242	227023	238212	65909	415717	276855	364308
244643	714568	167568	196841	193005	63798	407817	199826	264053
11615	31180	14160	50129	4653		26405	17676	8781
480	46808	48926	5466	79962	2303	118166	55375	29774
		47569	2785	1699	14652	14306	6945	12237
36220	45347	36900			189		2825	7380
30594	62588	16312	12143	15436	1423	3709	57842	72231
20864	13710	9462	18039	29771	499	4191	16362	20644

7-11 房地产开发销售情况(2014 年)

单位:万平方米、万元

指 标	Item	全市 Municipality	市区 Urban Areas
商品房销售面积	Sales Area of Commercial Buildings	919.17	583.88
住宅	Residence	843.35	538.42
90 平方米以下	Below 90 m^2	64.92	40.98
144 平方米以上	Above 144 m^2	77.28	39.69
别墅、高档公寓	Villa and High-end Apartment	11.98	5.41
办公楼	Office Building	19.05	15.44
商业营业用房	Commercial & Business Occupancy	38.94	15.88
其他	Others	17.84	14.14
现房销售面积	Sales Area of Completed Housing	287.77	224.19
住宅	Residence	264.03	208.71
90 平方米以下	Below 90 m^2	29.85	25.6
144 平方米以上	Above 144 m^2	25.2	14.21
别墅、高档公寓	Villa and High-end Apartment	2.39	0.22
办公楼	Office Building	1.31	1.22
商业营业用房	Commercial & Business Occupancy	8.11	1.97
其他	Others	14.32	12.29
期房销售面积	Sales Area of Future Housing	631.4	359.69
住宅	Residence	579.32	329.71
90 平方米以下	Below 90 m^2	35.07	15.38
144 平方米以上	Above 144 m^2	52.07	25.48
别墅、高档公寓	Villa and High-end Apartment	9.59	5.19
办公楼	Office Building	17.74	14.22
商业营业用房	Commercial & Business Occupancy	30.83	13.91
其他	Others	3.52	1.85
出租面积	Renting Area	12.36	11.59
住宅	Residence	0.16	0.16
90 平方米以下	Below 90 m^2	0.16	0.16
144 平方米以上	Above 144 m^2		
别墅、高档公寓	Villa and High-end Apartment		
办公楼	Office Building		
商业营业用房	Commercial & Business Occupancy	12.21	11.44
其他	Others		
待售面积	For-sale Area	689.53	376.05
住宅	Residence	509.38	290.27
90 平方米以下	Below 90 m^2	43.32	32.89
144 平方米以上	Above 144 m^2	119.52	35.18
别墅、高档公寓	Villa and High-end Apartment	21.24	4.35
办公楼	Office Building	19.95	14.93
商业营业用房	Commercial & Business Occupancy	113.33	41
其他	Others	46.87	29.85

SALES OF REAL ESTATE DEVELOPMENT (2014)

(10000m², 10000 yuan)

崇川区 Chongchuan	港闸区 Gangzha	开发区 Developing Zone	通州区 Tongzhou	海安 Haian	如东 Rudong	启东 Qidong	如皋 Rugao	海门 Haimen
145.66	180.02	133.39	124.8	63.11	29.1	87.84	80.69	74.55
122.33	175	129.38	111.7	57	27.73	84.24	65.83	70.12
6.35	6.01	2.23	26.38	2.14	0.8	11.48	2.44	7.09
20.72	5.04	2.61	11.32	4.51	1.38	8.65	11.37	11.68
2.22		0.06	3.12	0.39		1.67	1.06	3.46
13.9	1.42	0.12		1.35	0.07	2.06		0.13
5.29	3.6	2.48	4.5	4.04	1.27	1.52	12.23	4.01
4.14		1.41	8.59	0.73	0.03	0.02	2.63	0.29
81.6	45.8	26	70.79	5.45	3.37	18.69	23.19	12.88
76.74	44.89	24.2	62.87	3.96	3.2	17.78	18.89	11.49
1.51	0.52	0.09	23.48	0.05	0.05	2.01	0.41	1.73
10.42	1.48	0.67	1.64	0.74	0.05	3.71	4.82	1.67
0.1		0.06	0.05	0.08		0.54	0.34	1.22
0.39	0.78	0.05				0.09		
1.12	0.12	0.34	0.38	1.37	0.14	0.82	2.72	1.1
3.35		1.41	7.53	0.12	0.03		1.59	0.29
64.06	134.22	107.39	54.01	57.66	25.73	69.15	57.51	61.67
45.59	130.11	105.18	48.83	53.04	24.54	66.46	46.94	58.63
4.84	5.49	2.14	2.91	2.09	0.75	9.47	2.03	5.36
10.29	3.56	1.93	9.69	3.77	1.33	4.94	6.55	10.01
2.12			3.07	0.31		1.13	0.72	2.24
13.51	0.64	0.07		1.35	0.07	1.97		0.13
4.18	3.47	2.14	4.12	2.67	1.12	0.7	9.52	2.91
0.78			1.06	0.61		0.02	1.05	
11.2	0.39			0.77				
0.16								
0.16								
11.04	0.39			0.77				
81.02	153.53	50.71	90.78	59.94	20.78	53.26	125.04	54.46
55.18	128.68	39.52	66.89	32.95	14.73	44.94	87.13	39.35
9.74	3.05	2.09	18.01	0.84		4.16	4.26	1.16
18.32	4.26	4.13	8.47	15.23	1.61	19.25	35.44	12.82
1.04		1.48	1.83	0.36		6.63	3.92	5.98
6.02	8.04	0.82	0.05	0.09		1.97	0.63	2.33
11.91	13.03	6.85	9.21	22.51	5.73	6.33	29.11	8.66
7.91	3.79	3.51	14.64	4.38	0.33	0.02	8.17	4.12

7-11 续表

单位:万平方米、万元

指 标	Item	全市 Municipality	市区 Urban Areas
待售一至三年(含一年)	For Sale 1-3 Years (Including 1 Year)	303.23	148.42
住宅	Residence	226.09	116.2
90 平方米以下	Below 90 m^2	34.68	27.56
144 平方米以上	Above 144 m^2	57.78	23.14
别墅、高档公寓	Villa and High-end Apartment	9.41	2.55
办公楼	Office Building	6.54	2.98
商业营业用房	Commercial & Business Occupancy	50.29	15.6
其他	Others	20.32	13.65
待售三年以上(含三年)	For Sale above 3 Years (Including 3 Years)	7.1	2.89
住宅	Residence	3.27	1.64
90 平方米以下	Below 90 m^2	0.49	0.48
144 平方米以上	Above 144 m^2	2.06	0.91
别墅、高档公寓	Villa and High-end Apartment	0.6	0.4
办公楼	Office Building	0.3	0.3
商业营业用房	Commercial & Business Occupancy	2.56	0.66
其他	Others	0.97	0.28
商品房销售额	Sales of Commercial Buildings	4798036	2651689
住宅	Residence	4137302	2278304
90 平方米以下	Below 90 m^2	266538	131845
144 平方米以上	Above 144 m^2	720582	430789
别墅、高档公寓	Villa and High-end Apartment	117302	56336
办公楼	Office Building	155303	129434
商业营业用房	Commercial & Business Occupancy	468842	217574
其他	Others	36589	26377
现房销售额	Sales of Completed Housing	964669	667497
住宅	Residence	873757	623589
90 平方米以下	Below 90 m^2	53111	40572
144 平方米以上	Above 144 m^2	214273	152539
别墅、高档公寓	Villa and High-end Apartment	22273	3133
办公楼	Office Building	10800	9920
商业营业用房	Commercial & Business Occupancy	59491	18708
其他	Others	20621	15280
期房销售额	Sales of Future Housing	3833367	1984192
住宅	Residence	3263545	1654715
90 平方米以下	Below 90 m^2	213427	91273
144 平方米以上	Above 144 m^2	506309	278250
别墅、高档公寓	Villa and High-end Apartment	95029	53203
办公楼	Office Building	144503	119514
商业营业用房	Commercial & Business Occupancy	409351	198866
其他	Others	15968	11097

CONTINUED

(10000m², 10000 yuan)

崇川区 Chongchuan	港闸区 Gangzha	开发区 Developing Zone	通州区 Tongzhou	海安 Haian	如东 Rudong	启东 Qidong	如皋 Rugao	海门 Haimen
42.67	13.75	19.86	72.14	16.49	15.83	45.07	48.47	28.95
27.98	13.75	12.83	61.65	7.6	12.43	37.43	32.72	19.72
6.46	1.01	2.09	17.99	0.04		4.15	2.83	0.1
10.65	3.15	2.42	6.92	1	1.61	12.97	10.57	8.48
0.88			1.67	0.36		0.85	1.41	4.24
2.11		0.82	0.05	0.09		1.63	0.61	1.23
7.66		4.94	2.99	7.32	3.4	5.99	10.28	7.7
4.93		1.27	7.45	1.49		0.02	4.86	0.3
2.31	0.33	0.24		0.27			3.94	
1.07	0.33	0.24					1.63	
0.14	0.33						0.01	
0.91							1.15	
0.16		0.24					0.2	
0.3								
0.66				0.27			1.63	
0.28							0.68	
990442	706301	505974	448972	377425	189950	556831	464374	557767
764001	639749	472522	402032	320833	174125	529445	327077	507518
41164	37262	8591	44828	12001	4592	63741	12214	42145
272949	36650	31009	90181	33568	5960	64798	57982	127485
23562		718	32056	3198		18934	6813	32021
119357	9304	773		11196	1229	12920		524
92594	57248	31724	36008	42950	14450	14426	130162	49280
14490		955	10932	2446	146	40	7135	445
334338	147586	80876	104697	31745	13030	83872	109490	59035
312921	141660	76751	92257	20424	11864	77905	88986	50989
10155	2714	463	27240	289	181	6566	2002	3501
123492	10401	9296	9350	5457	152	22636	19527	13962
1820		718	595	559		4837	1280	12464
4582	4872	466				880		
9445	1054	2704	5505	10806	1020	5087	16269	7601
7390		955	6935	515	146		4235	445
656104	558715	425098	344275	345680	176920	472959	354884	498732
451080	498089	395771	309775	300409	162261	451540	238091	456529
31009	34548	8128	17588	11712	4411	57175	10212	38644
149457	26249	21713	80831	28111	5808	42162	38455	113523
21742			31461	2639		14097	5533	19557
114775	4432	307		11196	1229	12040		524
83149	56194	29020	30503	32144	13430	9339	113893	41679
7100			3997	1931		40	2900	

7-12 房地产开发经营情况(2014 年)

单位:万元

指 标	Item	全市 Municipality	市区 Urban Areas
企业个数	Number of Enterprises	577	231
一、年初存货	BOY Inventory	13346758	7621013
二、期末资产负债	Balance Sheet at the End of the Period		
流动资产合计	Total Current Assets	26060312	15806976
存货	Inventory	16889972	9899837
应收账款	Receivable Accounts	776523	435760
固定资产合计	Total Fixed Assets	699387	529156
固定资产原价	Fixed Assets at Cost	841080	612412
累计折旧	Accmulated Depreciation	196269	132660
其中:本年折旧	Of which: Depreciation of the Year	43450	28909
在建工程	Construction in Progress	621836	400782
资产总计	Total Assets	30472759	18472393
流动负债合计	Total Current Liabilities	19032039	10968496
其中:应付账款	Of which: Payable Accounts	2770094	1664865
非流动负债合计	Total Non-current Liabilities	4844346	3340969
负债合计	Total Liabilities	23876384	14309465
所有者权益合计	Total Ownership Interests	6596374	4162928
其中:实收资本	Of which: Paid-in Capital	5447463	3609849
三、损益及分配	Profit&Loss and Distribution		
营业收入	Operating Revenue	5316089	2988127
主营业务收入	Main Business Income	5292974	2978992
土地转让收入	Land Transfer Income	31521	27186
商品房屋销售收入	Sales Revenue of Commercial Building	5012765	2724735
房屋出租收入	Rental Income	25877	21239
其他收入	Others	222811	205832
营业成本	Operating Cost	4455980	2664397
主营业务成本	Main Business Cost	4423825	2661535
营业税金及附加	Business Tax and Surcharges	366896	191533
主营业务税金及附加	Main Business Tax and Surcharges	362841	190924
其他业务利润	Others	7241	2593
销售费用	Selling Expenses	150573	84830
管理费用	Management Expenses	207105	119658
其中:税金	Of which: Tax	12135	6267
财务费用	Financial Expenses	107772	68798
其中:利息收入	Of which: Interest Income	13041	10356
其中:利息支出	Of which: Interest Expense	76490	49996
资产减值损失	Asset Impairment Loss	3631	1415
公允价值变动收益	Changes in Fair Value	2030	2050
投资收益	Income from Investment	19453	15383
营业利润	Operating Profit	50431	-120831
营业外收入	Non-operating Income	175244	150397
其中:补贴收入	Of which: Subsidy Income	22246	15876
营业外支出	Non-operating Expense	54644	40672
利润总额	Total Profit	172151	-10159
应交所得税	Income Tax Payable	45368	20483
四、人工成本	Labor Cost		
本年应付工资总额(贷方累计发生额)	Total Payable Salary of the Year (Total Credit Ammount)	110875	56348

OPERATION OF REAL ESTATE DEVELOPMENT(2014)

(10,000 yuan)

崇川区 Chongchuan	港闸区 Gangzha	开发区 Developing Zone	通州区 Tongzhou	海安 Haian	如东 Rudong	启东 Qidong	如皋 Rugao	海门 Haimen
124	31	29	47	66	28	55	104	93
3802413	1338136	1399937	1080527	1282265	473833	1008694	1331095	1629858
6913433	3947642	2946520	1999381	1864603	929128	2242869	2545218	2671517
4434754	2452977	1571241	1440865	1299580	670911	1357077	1719673	1942894
169878	121945	54534	89403	67262	79739	38484	115723	39556
340557	44789	61435	82376	48596	7051	38334	46506	29743
427267	60501	72569	52076	60547	8941	51994	62265	44920
92699	15915	11188	12857	14520	2123	14960	15967	16040
18306	3941	3384	3279	4085	546	2747	3529	3634
64204	38418	235537	62623	2700	7870	49039	52035	109409
8509626	4137297	3583261	2242209	2120551	965339	2462118	3150836	3301522
4644714	3005245	2062254	1256283	1385865	587229	1624065	2246205	2220179
808891	421455	264158	170360	171822	84671	310394	287019	251325
1595869	431417	763739	549944	327534	160937	372342	254510	388054
6240583	3436662	2825994	1806227	1713399	743166	1996407	2500714	2608233
2269044	700635	757268	435982	407152	217173	465711	650122	693288
1915272	589328	755211	350038	292710	119302	330539	570836	524227
1143468	653040	693157	498463	463280	201894	466971	554130	641687
1138755	652226	692852	495159	458730	201567	461954	553797	637934
		27186				2290	2038	8
1111426	642658	477455	493197	445442	200573	458553	550640	632823
10213	9134	1614	277	1014	660	453	905	1607
17116	435	186597	1684	12275	334	658	215	3497
987215	679825	559330	438026	351982	170087	369616	393699	506200
985178	679211	559328	437818	348147	169787	366238	390801	487319
95234	39854	26843	29602	34283	18861	37995	36398	47825
95122	39768	26840	29194	32700	17676	37993	36322	47227
3635	102	-1562	418	1187	325	904	202	2031
37860	18660	15445	12865	13984	6160	16350	13553	15697
65905	21291	15707	16755	18057	4884	18223	17037	29247
3884	816	1596	-28	1126	515	1326	1241	1660
28994	10305	13777	15722	13186	-120	15054	3307	7547
3726	1347	5071	212	133	147	1288	429	688
22120	9746	11368	6761	10989	-275	10402	3297	2081
1609	-122	-72				15	206	1995
2050								
							-20	
14745	388	207	44	22		135	202	3711
-57403	-116385	60494	-7537	31811	2072	9854	90110	37415
35244	87724	24616	2813	524	506	8343	76	15398
801	2103	10951	2022	82	152	5954	13	169
3312	2378	32597	2385	1881	488	9576	671	1356
-24524	-31039	52513	-7109	30455	2215	8620	89522	51498
17944	-560	1570	1528	5314	782	3634	3252	11902
23078	11592	10524	11154	9719	6161	11063	13947	13637

7-13　计划总投资10亿元以上在建项目(2014年)

单位名称	项目名称
江苏省吕四海洋经济开发区开发建设有限公司	挖入式港池匡围工程
江苏天赋力现代物流有限公司	海安现代综合物流园
南通苏通科技产业园控股发展有限公司	东方大道快速化改造
江苏恒科新材料有限公司	差别化纤维项目
江苏恒科新材料有限公司	差别化纤维项目(二期)
南通综艺新材料有限公司	综艺一期薄膜太阳
中广核风电有限公司	中广核如东海上风电场项目
南通农副产品物流有限公司	农副产品物流中心
上海市北高新集团(南通)有限公司	市北科技城市政配套工程
如东洋口港经济开发区	临海高等级公路如东段
江苏省交通工程建设局	南通至洋口港区高速公路一期工程
南通滨江投资有限公司	南通滨江洲际酒店
东升南通石材产业园有限公司	新建年加工1000万平方米高档石材项目
宝钢物流(江苏)有限公司	海宝码头工程物流
南通高新区科技城投资发展有限公司	科技之窗项目建设
江苏甬金金属科技有限公司	机械零部件加工
南通新江海动力电子有限公司	电子元器件制造
江苏三一重工塔机有限公司	特种装备车辆生产项目
南通醋酸纤维有限公司	五期扩建工程
广汇能源综合物流发展有限责任公司	广汇能源LNG分销转运站项目
招商局重工(江苏)有限公司	海门海工基地填平补齐项目
中石油江苏液化天然气公司	LNG二期
南通市通州区交通运输局	345国道南通东绕城段工程
江苏旭明投资集团有限公司	物流中心项目
江苏洋通开发投资有限公司	江苏小洋口温泉生态休闲旅游配套设施建设项目
江苏海临实业发展有限公司	临江新区国际中小企业科技园
海安宏腾特种精密铸造有限公司	合金铸件技改项目
海门市蛎蚜山投资开发有限公司	东灶国家中心渔港
江苏海安县工业园区发展有限公司	苏中汽车城内部道路景观绿化及水电气管线设施建设项目
江苏弘盛新材料股份有限公司	人造纤维短纤维生产项目
南通新东区投资发展有限公司	总部经济产业园一期
南通同洲电子有限责任公司	新建生产厂房
南通里下河投资开发有限公司	水韵里下河项目
南通市通州区新志浩实业有限公司	家用纺织品生产
南通市通州港区新世界开发建设有限公司	通用码头建设
江苏东材新材料有限责任公司	功能膜材料生产项目
南通市通州区张芝山镇人民政府	农民集中安置居住区建设
江苏通光海洋光电科技有限公司	海底光电元件
江苏省吕四海洋经济开发区开发建设有限公司	环抱式港池进港航道一期工程

PROJECTS WITH PLANNED INVESTMENT OF MORE THAN 1 BILLION YUAN UNDER CONSTRUCTION(2014)

单位名称	项目名称
江苏融达再生资源加工配送有限公司	新建再生资源加工，配送，码头项目
江苏陆地方舟新能源电动汽车有限公司	年产5万台场地电动车及关键零部件
中交二航江苏投资有限公司	围填海工程
南通叠石桥大智城信息服务产业园有限公司	伊顿数据中心产业基地
海安远东新材料有限公司	高档精密不锈钢冷轧生产项目
江苏永通新材料科技有限公司	规模化锦纶6联合纺丝生产线项目
江苏天楹环保科技有限公司	水质污染监测设备制造项目
康迪电动汽车江苏有限公司	新建电动汽车车身总成制造项目
南通市通州区交通运输局	225省道改线工程
南通好一家投资管理有限公司	工业博览城一期
江苏神通阀门股份有限公司	环保设备及核电配套设备生产
丝路咖精机（南通）有限公司	精密零部件项目
江苏德晋塑料包装有限公司	年产各类塑料包装制品3亿件
复旦科技园江苏有限公司	海门复旦科技园
江苏信拓建设（集团）股份有限公司	总部经济大厦工程建设项目
江苏老坝港沿海开发有限公司	河道整治建设项目
江苏鹰球集团有限公司	软磁铁氧体磁元件生产项目
江苏海新船务重工有限公司	年产1.5万吨海工装备部件
江苏鹏飞集团股份有限公司	30万吨高效节能粉磨技术装备制造项目
南通英普环保科技有限公司	绿色安防产业一体化建设项目
人民电器集团江苏斯诺成套设备工程有限公司	智能电网控制系统及终端节能配电装备产业化项目
南通富通城市建设有限公司	南山湖公园基础设施
上柴动力海安有限公司	新一代环保型车用柴油机机体、缸盖铸件制造项目
江苏新天下能源有限公司	电脑及其配件
上海现代制药海门有限公司	新型原料药于中间体
江苏佳铝实业股份有限公司	年产15万吨建筑节能型材及铝合金材料项目
江苏省海门中等专业学校	海门张謇职业技术学校工程
江苏瑞马汽车有限公司	年产12.5万套新能源汽车车身系统零部件建设项目一期工程
欧贝黎新能源科技股份有限公司	年产1000MW太阳能电池组件项目
南通大青节能科技有限公司	节能变频电机生产项目
上海神舟汽车节能环保海安有限公司	电动车及电动汽车节能系统生产一期建设工程项目
江苏美勒家具有限公司	高档家具制造项目
海安县交通运输局	221省道扩建工程项目
江苏省邦瑞实业有限公司	王府邦瑞国际大酒店项目
东部全球家具采购中心（海安）有限公司	全球家具采购中心项目一期工程项目
如皋市经济贸易开发总公司	标准厂房、污水厂
江苏聚源电气有限公司	智能组合电器（GIS）产业化项目
江苏尼欧凯汽车研发有限公司	动力电池项目

7-14 房地产企业主营业务收入排名50强(2014年)

TOP 50 REAL ESTATE ENTERPRISES OF MAIN BUSINESS INCOME(2014)

序号	企业名称	序号	企业名称
1	江苏炜赋集团建设开发有限公司	26	南通榕达置业有限公司
2	南通市城镇房地产开发公司	27	南通中瑾置业有限公司
3	海门中南世纪城开发有限公司	28	南通星浩房地产发展有限公司
4	南通五洲国际投资有限公司	29	江苏大唐房地产有限公司
5	江苏致豪房地产开发有限公司	30	华润置地(南通)有限公司
6	南通市碧桂园房地产开发有限公司	31	南通环中置业有限公司通州分公司
7	上海西部企业集团海门威斯特置业有限公司	32	南通华鹏置业有限公司
8	南通天一置业有限公司	33	启东市御和湾置业有限公司
9	南通中南世纪花城投资有限公司	34	南通东宝房地产开发有限公司
10	江苏运杰置业有限公司	35	海安苏中动漫城有限公司
11	南通中港置业有限公司	36	南通锋富置业有限公司
12	恒盛炜达(南通)房地产开发有限公司	37	江苏星源房地产综合开发有限公司
13	深圳华强(南通)投资有限公司	38	江苏炜赋集团天鹏置业有限公司
14	南通中南新世界中心开发有限公司	39	如东和园房地产开发有限公司
15	启东通誉置业有限公司	40	南通德诚房地产有限公司
16	南通神辉置业有限公司	41	南通金凤置业有限公司
17	南通银洲房地产开发有限公司	42	南通盛华置业有限公司
18	海安保障性住房投资建设有限公司	43	南通市润南置业有限公司
19	南通万科投资有限公司	44	启东中邦房地产开发有限公司
20	南通翡翠苑置业有限公司	45	南通恒丰房地产开发有限公司
21	华润置地(南通)发展有限公司	46	海安亚伦房地产开发有限公司
22	南通意邦投资有限公司	47	江苏帝奥地产发展有限公司南通分公司
23	南通盈丰房地产投资发展有限公司	48	如皋市万都置业有限公司
24	骏和地产(江苏)有限公司	49	南通京扬天下置业有限公司
25	江苏华恒置业发展有限公司	50	江苏星湖置业有限公司

主要统计指标解释

固定资产投资　固定资产投资是社会固定资产再生产的主要手段。固定资产投资额是以货币表现的建造和购置固定资产活动的工作量，它是反映固定资产投资规模、速度、比例关系和使用方向的综合性指标。

房地产开发投资　包括各种经济类型的房地产开发公司、商品房建设公司及其他房地产开发单位统一开发的包括统代建、拆迁还建的住宅、厂房、仓库、饭店、宾馆、度假村、写字楼、办公楼等房屋建筑物和配套的服务设施、土地开发工程，如道路、给水、排水、供电、供热、通讯、平整场地等基础设施工程的投资。还包括非房地产企业实际从事房地产开发或经营活动，不包括单纯的土地交易活动。

固定资产投资的资金来源　根据固定资产投资的资金来源不同，分为上年末结余资金、本年资金来源。其中本年资金来源又分为国家预算内资金、国内贷款、债券、利用外资、自筹资金和其他资金来源6种。

固定资产投资按国民经济行业分　建设项目归哪个行业，按其建成投产后的主要产品或主要用途及社会经济活动性质来确定。一般情况下，一个建设项目或一个企业、事业单位只能属于一种国民经济行业。为了更准确地反映国民经济各行业之间的比例关系，联合企业(总厂)所属分厂属于不同行业的，原则上按分厂划分行业。

固定资产投资按构成分　固定资产投资活动按其工作内容和实现方式分为建筑工程、安装工程、设备、工具、器具购置，其他费用4个部分。

施工项目　指报告期内曾进行建筑或安装工程施工活动的建设项目。包括报告期内新开工项目、报告期以前开工跨人报告期继续施工的项目以及报告期施过工并在报告期内全部构建成投产或停缓建的项目。

全部建成投产项目　工业项目是指设计文件规定形成生产能力的主体工程及其相应配套的辅助设施全部构成，经负荷试运转，证明具备生产设计规定合格产品的条件，并经过验收鉴定合格或达到竣工验收标准，与生产性工程配套的生产福利设施可以满足近期正常生产的需要，正式移交生产的建设项目。非工业项目是指设计文件规定的主体工程和相应的配套工程全部建成，能够发挥设计规定的全部效益，经验收鉴定合格或达到竣工验收标准，正式移交使用的建设项目。

新增生产能力　指通过固定资产投资活动而增加的设计能力或工程效益，它是用实物形态表示的固定资产投资的成果。新增生产能力的计算，是以能独立发挥生产能力或效益的单项工程(或项目)为对象。当单项工程(或项目)建成，经有关部门鉴定合格，正式移交投入生产，即可计算新增生产能力。

新增生产能力或工程效益有以下几种表现形式：

(1)以建设项目或单项工程建成后的年产能力表示。如煤炭开采，石油开采等。

(2)以建设项目或单项工程建成后处理原料的能力表示。如选矿工程的年处理矿石能力，洗煤厂年洗原煤能力等。

(3)以新增的主要设备数量或容量表示。如棉纺定枚数，发电机组容量等。

(4)以建筑物容积、容量、面积或长度表示。如水库容量，铁路公路里程等。

新增生产能力的数量一般按设计能力计算。设计能力是指设计文件中规定的正常情况下能够达到的生产能力，而不论投产后的实际产量如何。以设备数量、建筑物容积、面积、长度等表示的新增生产能力(或效益)则按建成的实际数量计算。

施工房屋建筑面积　房屋建筑面积是从房屋外墙线算起的各层平面面积的总和，包括房屋结构(如柱、墙)占用的面积和地下室面积。多层建筑按各自然层面积总和计算，包括房屋内的楼隔层、突出墙面的眺望间、门斗、有柱雨罩的面积。不包括突出墙面结构的构件、艺术装饰等所占的面积，如台阶等。凹阳台，挑阳台按其水平投影面积一半计算建筑面积。

竣工房屋建筑面积　指在报告期内房屋建筑按照设计要求，已全部完工，达到住人和使用条件，经验收鉴定合格，正式移交使用单位的建筑面积。

房屋建筑面积竣工率　指一定时期内房屋竣工面积占同期房屋施工面积的比率。它是从房屋建筑施工速度的角度反映投资效果和建筑业经济效益的指标。

新增固定资产　指通过投资活动所形成的新的固定资产价值。包括已经建成投入生产或交付使用的工程价值和达到固定资产标准的设备、工具、器具的价值及有关应摊人的费用。它是以价值形式表示的固定资产投资成果的综合性指标，可以综合反映不同时期、不同部门、不同地区的固定资产投资成果。

建设项目投产率 指一时期内全部建成投人生产项目个数占同期正式施工项目个数的比率。它是从项目建设速度的角度反映投资效果的指标。

固定资产交付使用率 指一定时期新增固定资产与同期完成投资额的比率。它是反映各个时期固定资产动用速度,衡量建设过程中投资效果的一个综合性指标。

规模以上固定资产投资 具体包括:1.计划总投资或实际需要总投资500万元及以上的项目投资;2.房地产开发投资。

第八篇 对外经济

Chapter 8

Foreign Economy

8-1 主要年份出口总额

TOTAL EXPORTS OVER THE YEARS 1986-2014

单位：万美元 (Unit: 10,000 USD)

年份 Year	全市 Total	市区 Urban Area	崇川区 Chongchuan	港闸区 Gangzha	开发区 Develop Area	通州区 Tongzhou	海安 Haian	如东 Rudong	启东 Qidong	如皋 Rugao	海门 Haimen
1986	553										
1990	15576										
1991	21604										
1992	35217										
1993	55194	45871				4091	497	3849	2267	1193	1517
1994	94786	70857				9019	2198	8020	7552	2635	3524
1995	136604	95499				14109	4401	12620	11303	5549	7232
1996	168928	113452				18845	7064	17676	14947	7204	8585
1997	174044	121904				21274	9657	11561	11618	10007	9297
1998	133128	103354				15691	2570	7957	6841	5930	6476
1999	159550	125881				21348	2654	9017	7385	8213	6400
2000	203523	157714				30449	3511	12916	9932	11269	8181
2001	208352	157335				29068	3963	15296	10441	11631	9686
2002	253138	191976				33685	6498	16835	12554	12637	12638
2003	328471	254908				41764	7468	19056	13341	16023	17675
2004	434940	325433				59251	14333	26805	17356	23882	27130
2005	579315	427528	146571	79093	102770	80024	24049	36847	25941	32145	32805
2006	721275	516850	183723	94391	118061	95937	31881	41703	38028	44906	47907
2007	902258	615036	223597	114215	133602	120194	47336	53692	67108	57437	61649
2008	1175216	756509	282154	151865	176496	145994	72865	74206	117943	82246	71447
2009	1118045	708839	318294	107419	140425	142701	58793	61307	122065	99542	67498
2010	1410748	854082	327502	140944	191255	194381	90305	80779	191823	100470	93282
2011	1803038	1114127	472627	195777	231288	214435	102705	100701	182833	187659	113812
2012	1878633	1146347	456168	206312	251623	232244	127888	99854	144300	237164	123813
2013	2127783	1163827	422112	211738	270058	259919	200649	106632	265069	237197	154409
2014	2248006	1273295	459886	234293	285313	293803	214359	128918	230497	255539	145459

注：1998 年开始出口总量为海关统计资料。

Note: The data since 1998 are provided by Nantong Customs.

8-2 主要年份实际利用外资

ACTUALLY UTILIZED FOREIGN INVESTMENT OVER THE YEARS 1986-2014

单位:万美元 (Unit: 10,000 USD)

年份 Year	全市 Total	市区 Urban Area	崇川区 Chongchuan	港闸区 Gangzha	开发区 Develop Area	通州区 Tongzhou	海安 Haian	如东 Rudong	启东 Qidong	如皋 Rugao	海门 Haimen
1986	3866										
1990	4216										
1991	5009										
1992	6039										
1993	15090	9435				1981	526	1904	1357	873	995
1994	29022	20957				1673	367	2566	2758	802	1572
1995	41304	24005				1811	2771	5870	3890	1415	3353
1996	50324	33132				4035	3069	6267	4246	1344	2266
1997	61410	52438				4019	1812	1992	1444	550	3174
1998	61077	56445				2506	505	932	2022	211	962
1999	30705	27594				1244	521	653	1150	360	427
2000	14669	9510				1171	763	1557	534	1006	1299
2001	17523	11106				1245	1009	1186	1311	401	2510
2002	23848	15541				2651	1219	1632	1421	1385	2650
2003	73092	40085				10529	5265	5518	5009	6219	10996
2004	101986	54104				12432	9058	10344	11626	10483	14819
2005	153162	75658	7021	11362	35104	22171	15018	19746	17070	21886	25390
2006	257497	90065	11887	9745	23446	44987	28469	32079	42441	32604	48707
2007	311745	87000	6374	11046	36073	33507	33442	38184	43743	69808	39566
2008	293710	99572	9614	4865	59286	25807	37599	23752	38286	64731	29770
2009	200481	60607	5348	5265	43929	6065	13478	23496	12318	58418	32163
2010	206056	70015	9092	5375	47572	7976	14184	27913	24968	34048	34925
2011	216644	74052	12005	2789	51384	7874	15851	29538	38287	47609	11305
2012	220542	105875	12108	13234	59677	23109	25176	32016	23874	21396	12205
2013	228743	100306	5899	12014	56128	26265	26146	27356	25357	24812	24770
2014	232309	110765	13344	4676	59641	33104	33151	34338	5466	33071	15518

注:从2002年开始,利用外资实际金额采用新口径。

2006年"实际利用外资"总数来源于商务部、分县(市)区数来源于市商务局。

Note: From 2002, the accounting of actually utilized foreign investment was operated in a new way;

The totality of Actually Otilized Foreign Investment in 2006 is provideel by Ministry of Commerce and county-leuel figures are provided by Nantong Bureau of Commerce.

8-3 主要年份新批外商投资项目数

NUMBER OF FOREIGN INVESTMENT UTILIZATION CONTRACTS OVER THE YEARS 1986-2014

单位:个 (unit)

年份 Year	全市 Total	市区 Urban Area	崇川区 Chongchuan	港闸区 Gangzha	开发区 Develop Area	通州区 Tongzhou	海安 Haian	如东 Rudong	启东 Qidong	如皋 Rugao	海门 Haimen
1986	35										
1990	45										
1991	98										
1992	591										
1993	1181	498				205	76	134	197	134	142
1994	429	201				44	19	41	71	28	69
1995	498	206				97	41	54	78	33	86
1996	232	115				37	17	15	33	20	32
1997	148	63				14	13	11	34	14	13
1998	122	53				16	12	10	19	16	12
1999	136	64				16	8	13	22	12	17
2000	234	126				34	18	22	29	11	28
2001	233	122				39	14	15	35	16	31
2002	369	159				71	32	25	54	38	61
2003	906	305				181	79	95	112	87	228
2004	1033	352				200	106	119	144	88	224
2005	998	298	32	64	57	145	131	138	135	106	190
2006	964	289	39	46	84	120	124	140	111	120	180
2007	744	211	32	56	29	94	111	104	77	110	131
2008	416	128	30	26	30	42	68	74	32	43	71
2009	401	121	20	30	21	50	47	52	32	58	91
2010	364	121	25	22	29	45	35	52	37	59	60
2011	327	134	32	22	35	45	40	52	31	44	26
2012	349	128	36	8	38	46	58	50	27	48	38
2013	354	125	26	4	45	50	54	61	46	43	25
2014	305	119	22	9	43	45	51	47	27	29	32

注:2005 年前数据来源于市商务局,2005 年后来源于南通工商局。

Note:The data before 2005 were provided by Nantong Bureau of Commerce. The data after 2005 are provided by Nantong Administration for Industry and Commerce.

8-4 主要年份新批协议注册外资额

CONTRACTED FOREIGN INVESTMENT OVER THE YEARS 1986-2014

单位:万美元

(Unit:10,000 USD)

年份 Year	全市 Total	市区 Urban Area	崇川区 Chongchuan	港闸区 Gangzha	开发区 Develop Area	通州区 Tongzhou	海安 Haian	如东 Rudong	启东 Qidong	如皋 Rugao	海门 Haimen
1986	2748										
1990	5098										
1991	6636										
1992	30664										
1993	52458	29942				6271	1610	4409	9582	3001	3914
1994	50992	38134				2411	1171	4147	4086	1343	2111
1995	153006	109656				8756	4912	11314	11089	5540	10495
1996	83447	64313				5100	1680	6170	5196	2338	3750
1997	56037	38510				6352	4746	4016	2241	1280	5244
1998	53182	36323				1184	1218	3294	3050	1175	8122
1999	34868	25021				2147	1584	1099	1847	1881	3434
2000	33315	20241				2418	1614	2149	1407	2112	5792
2001	42201	31008				3420	1334	1623	2462	1184	4590
2002	49441	27860				8373	3891	3708	4535	3268	6179
2003	231084	118493				35062	10715	21620	23455	22019	34782
2004	378226	150134				58140	32879	32078	56077	50908	56150
2005	507694	209294	27309	37937	73215	70833	35363	46408	63424	82072	71133
2006	693862	235657	27625	30942	116179	60911	47010	89812	112643	114195	94545
2007	773985	250757	36611	44171	86483	83492	77528	98114	102335	160622	84629
2008	555472	148851	29208	40788	49480	29375	74106	99227	64911	98789	69588
2009	552648	140736	26765	26238	43937	43796	38082	68180	88792	157589	59269
2010	551453	187706	34911	29496	72756	50543	44298	63456	57738	139559	58696
2011	453808	174627	28215	28681	74057	43674	44228	57028	66769	92484	18672
2012	455768	164655	28866	25568	78855	31366	57922	57318	50059	95143	30671
2013	495242	201208	31290	25203	93058	51657	61964	65310	47348	65317	54095
2014	552371	214087	28378	26206	98975	60528	72027	87943	54173	62639	61502

注:上表数据来源于市商务局。

Note:The figures above are provided by Nantong Bureau of Commerce.

8-5 外向型经济主要指标(2014 年)

指 标	Item	全市 Total
对外贸易(海关口径)	Foreign Trade (Calculated by Customs)	
进出口总额(万美元)	Total Value Imports and Exports(10,000 USD)	1755402
进口总额	Total Imports	482106
出口总额	Total Exports	1273296
利用外资	Foreign Capital Utilized	
新批外商投资项目数(个)	Newly Approved Foreign Investment Projects	119
新批协议注册外资额(万美元)	Newly Approved Contracted Registered Foreign Investment (10,000 USD)	214087
实际利用外资额(万美元)	Actually Utilized Foreign Capital (10,000 USD)	110765
境外投资	Overseas Investment	
境外投资项目数(个)	Project	40
境外投资中方协议投资额(万美元)	Investment Amount(10,000 USD)	34484
对外承包劳务	Overseas Contracted Labor Services	
合同额(万美元)	Contract Amount (10,000 USD)	81999
营业额(万美元)	Turnover (10,000 USD)	75983
期末在外人数(人)	Term-end Number of Labors Overseas (person)	5004

MAIN INDICATORS OF EXPORT-ORIENTED ECONOMY(2014)

崇川区 Chongzhuan	港闸区 Gangzha	开发区 Developing Area	通州区 Tongzhou	海安 Haian	如东 Rudong	启东 Qidong	如皋 Rugao	海门 Haimen
646809	294801	481904	331888	245194	331116	307209	321231	203581
186923	60508	196591	38084	30835	202198	76712	65692	58122
459886	234293	285313	293804	214359	128918	230497	255539	145459
22	9	43	45	51	47	27	29	32
28378	26206	98975	60528	72027	87943	54173	62639	61502
13344	4676	59641	33104	33151	34338	5466	33071	15518
7	6	10	17	10	5	5	10	8
7097	1489	7836	18062	10684	350	8786	24919	12781
41348	1221	27950	11480	11940	2715	18338	25934	45174
55621	2001	9587	8774	6978	7260	45835	23993	66534
2743	617		1644	2396	2076	1584	6799	5539

8-6 按贸易方式分进口总额(2014)

单位：万美元

指　　标	Item	合计 Total	国有 State-owned	外商投资企业 Foreign-invested Enterprises
总　　计	**Total**	**915665**	**216533**	**548263**
一般贸易	General Trade	511307	194159	239777
加工贸易	Processing Trade	325239	20890	268998
来料加工装配贸易	Contract Processing & Assembling Trade	20922	566	11037
进料加工贸易	Processing Trade with Imported Materials	304317	20324	257961
外商投资进口设备	Foreign Invested Imported Equipments	14283		14283
保税仓库进出境货物	Bonded Houseware Exit & Entry Cargos	59473	1440	23101
其它	Others	5363	44	2104

8-7 按贸易方式分出口总额(2014 年)

单位：万美元

指　　标	Item	合计 Total	国有 State-owned	外商投资企业 Foreign-invested Enterprises
总　　计	**Total**	**2248068**	**49442**	**1177762**
一般贸易	General Trade	1476837	45810	487568
加工贸易	Processing Trade	719299	3602	648368
来料加工装配贸易	Contract Processing & Assembling Trade	47128	746	28801
进料加工贸易	Processing Trade with Imported Materials	672171	2856	619567
对外承包工程出口	Foreign Invested Imported Equipments	1402		
保税仓库进出境货物	Bonded Houseware Exit & Entry Cargos	48564	30	41411
其它	Others	1966		415

TOTAL IMPORTS GROUPED BY THE WAY OF TRADE(2014)

(Unit: 10,000 USD)

合作 Cooperative	合资 Joint-Venture	独资 Sole Proprietorship	集体 Collective	私营及其他 Private and Others
59	**241731**	**306473**	**8930**	**141939**
28	81769	157980	1971	75400
29	138614	130355	332	35019
27	6200	4810		9319
2	132414	125545	332	25700
	1743	12540		
	18903	4198	6591	28341
2	702	1400	36	3179

TOTAL EXPORTS GROUPED BY THE WAY OF TRADE(2014)

(Unit: 10,000 USD)

合作 Cooperative	合资 Joint-Venture	独资 Sole Proprietorship	集体 Collective	私营及其他 Private and Others
4911	**578920**	**593931**	**22661**	**998203**
4856	209897	272815	18212	925247
55	327622	320691	865	66464
55	11521	17225		17581
	316101	303466	865	48883
			18	1384
	41337	74	3565	3558
	64	351	1	1550

8-8 对主要国家或地区进出口情况(2014年)

IMPORT AND EXPORT TO MAJOR COUNTRIES OR REGIONS(2014)

单位:万美元 (Unit: 10,000 Yuan)

地区	Region	进出口总额 Total Value of Import and Export	出口 Exports	进口 Imports
总 计	**Total**	**3163733**	**2248068**	**915665**
亚洲	**Asia**	**1817466**	**1230499**	**586967**
#香港	Hong Kong	209270	206643	2627
印度	India	60566	50871	9696
印度尼西亚	Indonisia	83328	50395	32933
日本	Japan	477981	375820	102162
马来西亚	Malaysia	83506	42980	40526
沙特阿拉伯	Saudi Arabia	32096	20066	12029
卡塔尔	Katar	173170	1602	171568
新加坡	Singapore	145144	98292	46852
韩国	Korea	153841	97644	56197
泰国	Thailand	101033	59452	41581
越南	Vietnam	48556	45224	3332
台湾	Taiwan	73455	36117	37338
#东盟	ASEAN	499228	327962	171266
非洲	**Africa**	**107954**	**95160**	**12794**
#纳米比亚	Namibia	10645	10645	
尼日利亚	Nigeria	13650	8194	5457
南非(阿扎尼亚)	South Africa (Azania)	16686	16673	13
欧洲	**Europe**	**567924**	**403456**	**164468**
#比利时	Belgium	46631	34098	12533
丹麦	Denmark	23978	21750	2228
英国	UK	71543	64261	7282
德国	Germany	75541	42135	33406
法国	France	37126	23286	13840
意大利	Italy	31863	18584	13279
荷兰	Netherlands	71164	46662	24502
西班牙	Spain	24955	21044	3910
俄罗斯	Russia	39845	39348	497
#欧盟	EU	484799	347520	137279
拉丁美洲	**Latin America**	**146112**	**127824**	**18288**
#巴西	Brazil	55060	40258	14802
墨西哥	Mexico	19621	19383	238
巴拿马	Panama	25423	25423	
北美洲	**North America**	**458797**	**334897**	**123900**
#加拿大	Canada	30487	24374	6113
美国	America	428299	310511	117788
大洋洲	**Oceania**	**65432**	**56232**	**9200**
#澳大利亚	Australia	48676	39980	8696

8-9 主要商品进出口总额(2014年)

Total Exports of Main Commodities(2014)

单位:万美元 (Unit: 10,000 USD)

指 标	Item	进出口总额 Total Exports and Imports	出口 Exports	进口 Imports
总 计	**Total**	**3163733**	**2248068**	**915665**
活动物、动物产品	Live Animals and Animal Products	19707	16742	2965
植物产品	Vegetable Products	51709	7060	44649
动植物油脂蜡及其分解产品	Animal or Vegetable Fats and Oils and Their Cleavage Products	40340	121	40220
食品饮料酒及醋、烟草及制品	Food, Beverage, Alcohol, Vinegar Tobacco and Their Products	31744	29784	1960
矿产品	Mineral Products	254384	5795	248589
化学工业及相关工业产品	Chemical Industry and Related Products	306584	196536	110049
塑料、橡胶及其制品	Plastics,Rubber and Their Products	147373	98165	49209
生皮皮革毛皮及制品	Leather, Furs, and Related Products	25320	21048	4271
木、木制品及其它编织材料制品	Wood, Wood Products and other Woven Products	11987	5564	6424
纸、纸浆、纸板及制品	Paper Pulp, Paper Board and Other Products	35455	7388	28067
纺织原料及纺织制品	Textile and Textile Articals	743590	691797	51793
鞋帽伞杖鞭羽毛制品人造花	Shoes,Hats,Umbrella Crane,Whip,Feather and Artificial Flowens	43663	43340	323
石料、陶瓷玻璃及制品	Stone,Cements,Ceramics and Glass Products	25094	22026	3068
珍珠宝石贵金属仿首饰及硬币	Pearl,Natural Jewellery, Noble Metal, Artificial Jewellery and Coins	4658	2118	2540
贱金属及制品	Base Metals and Articles of Base Metal	172075	112675	59399
机器电子产品电子设备及零件	Machinery,Electric Equipmems and Spare Parts	594647	355076	239571
车辆航空器船舶及运输设备	Vehicles,Aircraft,Ship and Transportation Equipment	407740	406174	1566
光学照相电影计量检验医疗设备	Camera,Film, Measuring and Examing Medical Instrument	34925	20032	14893
武器弹药及其零附件	Arms, Ammunition and Spare Parts	158	158	
杂项制品	Miscellaneous Manufactured Articles	212166	206056	6109
艺术品收藏品及古物	Works of Art, Collectables Pieces and Antiques	412	412	
特殊交易品及分类商品	Special and Classified Commodities			

8-10 分国别地区外商直接投资(2014年)

FOREIGN DIRECT INVESTMENT BY COUNTRIES AND REGION(2014)

单位:万美元 (Unit: 10,000 USD)

地区	Region	项目数(个) Project Number (unit)	合同外资 Contract Foreign Capital	实际投资 Actual Investment
总计	**Total**	**307**	**509926**	**230479**
亚洲	**Asia**	**249**	**427464**	**186302**
#香港	Hongkong	135	298285	135676
台湾	Taiwan	46	46597	14199
日本	Japan	20	28453	14653
澳门	Macao	4	1905	390
马来西亚	Malaysia	4	3788	59
菲律宾	Philippines	2	4812	4350
新加坡	Singapore´	18	17853	11477
韩国	Korea	11	8560	2773
非洲	**Africa**	**3**	**6813**	**805**
#毛里求斯	Mauritius	1	3030	150
纳米比亚	Namibia	2	3695	
欧洲	**Europe**	**12**	**15230**	**10733**
#英国	# Britain	3	7312	2768
德国	Germany	1	84	1633
法国	France		369	378
爱尔兰	Ireland	1	2737	1372
荷兰	Netherands	2	1299	245
希腊	Greece	1	261	
西班牙	Romalia	1	1059	378
奥地利	Austria	2	1811	938
俄罗斯	Russia	1	600	
南美洲		**7**	**28134**	**13256**
#巴西	#Brazil	1	5500	2100
开曼群岛	Cayman Islands	1	1200	980
智利	Chile	3	1915	
英属维尔京群岛	British Virgin Islands	2	19519	10051
北美洲	**North America**	**24**	**17817**	**4022**
#加拿大	#Canada	9	10854	1298
美国	America	15	6963	2724
大洋洲	**Oceanic**	**13**	**6909**	**2802**
#澳大利亚	#Australia	9	5048	1244
萨摩亚	Samoa	4	2162	1500

8-11 分行业外商直接投资(2014 年)

FOREIGN DIRECT INVESTMENT BY SECTOR(2014)

单位:万美元 (Unit: 10,000 USD)

地区	Region	项目数(个) Project Number (unit)	合同外资 Contract Foreign Capital	实际投资 Actual Investment
总计	**Total**	**307**	**509926**	**230479**
农、林、牧、渔业	Agiculture, Forestry, Animal Husbandry and Fishery	30	21532	4674
#农业	Agiculture	28	20911	4674
采矿业	Mining	2	13998	2000
#石油和天然气开采业	Petroleum and Natural Gas Mining	1	8000	
非金属矿采选业	Nonmetal Minerals Mining and Dressing	1	2998	1000
制造业	Manufacturing	96	191507	116798
#农副食品加工业	Agricultural Process and By-products Processing	3	11908	4233
食品制造业	Food	2	1470	2050
饮料制造业	Beuerage	1	3045	1372
纺织业	Textile	6	4839	6981
纺织服装、鞋、帽制造业	Garment, Shoe sand Hats	9	6397	3763
家具制造业	Furniture	2	3375	23
印刷业和记录媒介的复制	Printing and Copy of Record Medium	1	200	
文教体育用品制造业	Culture, Education, sports product manufacturing	1	568	123
化学原料及化学制品制造业	Chemicals and Chemical Product Manufacturing	3	8482	19115
医药制造业	Medicine Manufacturing	4	6434	7648
化学纤维制造业	Chemical Fiber Manufacturing	1	1500	991
塑料制品业	Plastic Products	3	8835	1730
非金属矿物制品业	Nonmetal Mineral Products	3	10096	4755
金属制品业	Manufacture of Metal Products	6	12278	4460
通用设备制造业	General Equipment Manufacturing	18	29190	13023
专用设备制造业	Special Equipment Manufacturing	12	12711	5276
交通运输设备制造业	Manufacture of Transport Facilities	5	15485	21659
电气机械及器材制造业	Electric Apparatus and Equipment Manufacturing	5	22148	10671
通讯设备、计算机及其他电子设备制造业	Manufacture of Telecommunication Equipment,Computer and Other Electronic Equipments	10	20572	4478
废弃资源和废旧材料回收加工业	Waste Resoure and Material Recouery Processing	1	2988	1347
电力、燃料及水的生产和供应业	Production and Supply of Power, Fuel and Water	2	981	936
建筑业	Construction	8	38113	7012
交通运输、仓储和邮政业	Transport, Storage and Post	11	52706	31258
信息传输、计算机服务和软件业	Information Transmission,Computer Service and Software	3	2395	550
批发和零售业	Wholesale and Retail Trades	110	95203	21555
住宿和餐饮业	Hotel and Catering Services	2	-875	
金融业	Financial Industry	2	4000	850
房地产业	Real Estate	5	14859	28300
租赁和商务服务业	Leasing and Business Services	18	21164	8095
科学研究、技术服务和地质勘察业	Scientific Research,Technology Service and Geological Prospection	7	4574	2583
水利、环境和公共设施管理业	Management of Water Conservancy,Environment and Public Facility	10	48669	4568
居民服务和其他服务业	Services to Housebolds and Other Services	1	1100	1300
文化、体育和娱乐业	Culture, Sports and Entertainment			

8-12 出口总额前50家内资企业名录(2014年)

TOP 50 DOMESTIC ENTERPRISES OF EXPORT VOLUME(2014)

序号 No.	企业名称 Names of the Enterprises	序号 No.	企业名称 Names of the Enterprises
1	南通江山农药化工股份有限公司	26	南通市常海食品添加剂有限公司
2	南通卓钦贸易有限公司	27	海安永再进出口有限公司
3	南通鹏江贸易有限公司	28	南通联发印染有限公司
4	中天世贸有限公司	29	如东县铁链厂有限公司
5	南通恒康海绵制品有限公司	30	海安溪新进出口有限公司
6	南通赛轩国际贸易有限公司	31	海安日隆贸易有限公司
7	南通开发区炜赋对外贸易有限公司	32	江苏东成机电工具有限公司
8	海安骏明威贸易有限公司	33	海安溪峰进出口有限公司
9	南通三润贸易有限公司	34	如皋市神速超导器材有限公司
10	南通四方罐式储运设备制造有限公司	35	南通市沃思特工贸有限公司
11	南通醋酸化工股份有限公司	36	南通三荣贸易有限公司
12	百川化工(如皋)有限公司	37	南通千色时装有限公司
13	海安瑞振贸易有限公司	38	鑫缘茧丝绸集团股份有限公司
14	海安涛澜日用百货有限公司	39	江苏铁锚电动工具有限公司
15	海安日辉进出口有限公司	40	海安县联发制衣有限公司
16	江苏九鼎新材料股份有限公司	41	南通铁人经贸有限公司
17	江苏鹏飞集团股份有限公司	42	南通中燃船舶燃料有限公司
18	海安标盛贸易有限公司	43	如皋市逸人服装有限公司
19	海安纺格思进出口贸易有限公司	44	海安广辉进出口有限公司
20	南通润邦重机有限公司	45	江苏中瑾投资发展有限公司
21	南通阳印进出口有限公司	46	南通开源国际贸易有限公司
22	海门市悦翔百货贸易有限公司	47	江苏力星通用钢球股份有限公司
23	南通市通润汽车零部件有限公司	48	南通仁寿食品有限公司
24	南通昶岳商贸有限公司	49	保真超导科技如皋有限公司
25	海安标信进出口有限公司	50	南通星辰合成材料有限公司

8-13 出口总额前50家三资企业名录(2014年)

TOP 50 JOINT-VENTURE ENTERPRISES OF EXPORT VOLUME(2014)

序号 No.	企业名称 Names of the Enterprises	序号 No.	企业名称 Names of the Enterprises
1	南通中远川崎船舶工程有限公司	26	创斯达(南通)机电有限公司
2	韩华新能源(启东)有限公司	27	精技电子(南道)有限公司
3	南通中远船务工程有限公司	28	江苏宝众宝达药业有限公司
4	江苏熔盛重工有限公司	29	南通刚正薄板有限公司
5	南通中集罐式储运设备制造有限公司	30	富加宜电子(南通)有限公司
6	南通富士通微电子股份有限公司	31	路特利举升机(海门)有限公司
7	启东胜狮能源装备有限公司	32	卡姆丹克太阳能(江苏)有限公司
8	江苏联发纺织股份有限公司	33	东丽酒伊织染(南通)有限公司
9	启东太平物流装备有限公司	34	江苏飞亚化学工业有限责任公司
10	江苏韩通船舶重工有限公司	35	江苏皇室食品工业有限公司
11	江苏好收成韦恩农药化工有限公司	36	南通华盛新材料有限公司
12	南通太平洋海洋工程有限公司	37	惠生(南通)重工有限公司
13	南通荣威塑胶工业有限公司	38	江苏永兴多媒体有限公司
14	南通中集顺达集装箱有限公司	39	南通艺源家用纺织品有限公司
15	南通中集特种运输设备制造有限公司	40	南通泰禾化工有限公司
16	南通诚晖石油化工有限公司	41	万高(南通)电机制造有限公司
17	三大雅精细化学品(南通)有限公司	42	南通伟越电器有限公司
18	嘉吉粮油(南通)有限公司	43	南通江海电容器有限公司
19	南通好瑞吉家用纺织品有限公司	44	东丽合成纤维(南通)有限公司
20	先正达南通作物保护有限公司	45	南通三荣实业有限公司
21	台橡(南通)实业有限公司	46	南通东润实业有限公司
22	江苏三友集团股份有限公司	47	南通泰慕士服装有限公司
23	南通强生安全防护科技有限公司	48	汇鸿(南通)安全用品有限公司
24	东丽高新聚化(南通)有限公司	49	南通延锋江森座椅面套有限公司
25	迈图高新材料(南通)有限公司	50	南通金飞祥服装有限公司

主要统计指标解释

利用外资 指我国各级政府、部门、企业和其他经济组织通过对外借款、吸收外商直接投资以及用其他方式筹措境外现汇、设备、技术等。

新签协议个数 是指报告期内新批准的外国政府贷款和国际金融组织贷款等对外借款协议项目个数、新批准设立的外商直接投资企业个数、海洋石油勘探开发以签订的独立勘探开发的合同份数、新签订的外商其他投资合同份数。

协议外资金额 指报告期内新签协议(合同)中规定的外资金额。具体包括:①经批准对外正式签订的借款协议中规定的借款金额;②新批外商直接投资企业的合同规定的外商投资额(即合同外资金额);③新签订的加工装配和补偿贸易协议中规定的商提供设备价款,以及国际租赁协议中我方应付的设备租金。

合同外资金额 指新批外商投资企业的合同规定的可使用的外方投资额。

实际利用外资 是指协议(合同)正式签订并经批准后,在协议(合同)执行过程中实际发生的资本拨交价值。它是衡量一个国家或地区实际利用外资规模的总量指标。具体包括:①实际提取的对外借款数或拨交使用金额;②外商投资企业中外方实际投入的资本(即外商实际投资),包括现金、实物、工业产权、专有技术等,外商投资收益的再投资也包括在内;③"三来一补"(加工装配和补偿贸易)业务中外商作价提供的设备实际进口到货金额(即我方应付的设备款),以及国际租赁业务中租赁的设备实际进口到货后,我方应付的租金总额等。

进出口总额 指实际进出我国国境的货物总金额。包括对外贸易实际进出口货物、来料加工装配进出口货物,国家间、联合国及国际组织无偿援助物资和赠送品,华侨、港澳台同胞和外籍华人捐赠品,租赁期满归承租人所有的租赁货物,进料加工进出口货物,边境地方贸易及边境地区小额贸易进出口货物(边民互市贸易除外),外商投资企业进出口货物和公用物品,到、离岸价格在规定限额以上的进出口货样和广告品(无商业价值、无使用价值和免费提供出口的除外),从保税仓库提取在中国境内销售的进口货物以及其他进出口货物。进出口总额用以观察一个国家或地区在对外贸易方面的总规模,海关统计制度规定:出口货物按离岸价格统计,进口货物按到岸价格统计。

对外劳务合作 指以收取工资的形式向业主或承包商提供技术和劳动服务的活动。我国对外承包公司在境外开办的合营企业,中国公司同时有提供劳务的,其劳务部分也纳入劳务合作统计。劳务合作营业额按报告期内向雇主提交的结算数(包括工资、加班费和奖金等)统计。

对外承包劳务合同额 指对外承包劳务企业在报告期内签订的对外承包工程、劳务合作和设计咨询项目的合同金额。

对外承包劳务营业额 指对外承包劳务企业在报告期内完成的以货币表现的承包工程工作量、劳务合作收入、设计咨询收入(包括以前年度签订合同和本年新签订的合同在报告期完成的工作量)。

国际旅游接待人数 指来我国参观、访问、旅行、探亲、访友、休养、考察、参加会议和从事经济、科技、文化、教育、体育、宗教等活动的外国人、港澳台同胞的人数。不包括外国在我国的常驻机构,如使领馆、通讯社、企业办事处的工作人员和来我国常驻的外国专家、留学生以及在口岸逗留不过夜人员。

外 国 人 是指外国国籍的人。外籍华人应包括在外国人中,它是指加入外国国籍的中国血统华人。

华　　侨 是指居住在国外但未加入居住国和其他国家国籍的中国同胞。

港澳同胞 是指居住在我国港澳地区的中国同胞。

台湾同胞 是指居住在我国台湾省的同胞。凡以加入外国国籍,或定居在其他国家、地区的台湾同胞应分别统计在"外国人"或"华侨"项内。

国际旅游外汇收入 指入境旅游的外国人、港澳台同胞在中国大陆旅游过程中发生的一切旅游支出,对于国家或地区来说就是国际旅游外汇收入。

国内旅游人数 指报告期内在中国(大陆)观光游览、度假、探亲访友、就医疗养、购物、参加会议或从事经济、文化、体育、学教活动的中国(大陆)居民,其出游的目的不是通过所从事的活动得取报酬。统计时,国内游客按每出游一次统计1人次。

第九篇

能源 资源 环境保护

Chapter 9

Energy, Resources and Environmental Protection

9-1 2007-2014 年分地区单位 GDP 能耗

ENERGY CONSUMPTION PER UNIT GDP BY REGIONS 2007-2014

指 标 Item	全市 Municipality	市区 (不含通州) Urban Areas (Tongzhou Excluded)	崇川区 Chongchuan	港闸区 Gangzha	开发区 Development Area	通州区 Tongzhou	海安 Haian	如东 Rudong	启东 Qidong	如皋 Rugao	海门 Haimen
单位 GDP 能耗(吨标煤/万元)	Energy Consumption per unit GDP			Unit: ton of SCE(standard coal equivalent)/ 10,000 Yuan							
2014 年	0.478		0.491	0.671	0.836	0.425	0.485	0.471	0.326	0.486	0.412
2013 年	0.505		0.533	0.790	0.880	0.437	0.511	0.493	0.349	0.533	0.444
2012 年	0.507		0.549	0.846	0.901	0.446	0.524	0.502	0.356	0.551	0.462
2011 年	0.539		0.643	0.997	0.924	0.471	0.504	0.521	0.356	0.529	0.480
2010 年	0.666	0.996				0.545	0.586	0.606	0.419	0.628	0.565
2009 年	0.692	1.037				0.566	0.610	0.628	0.434	0.654	0.587
2008 年	0.730	1.089				0.598	0.640	0.662	0.456	0.688	0.618
2007 年	0.774	1.163				0.634	0.675	0.703	0.480	0.725	0.655
单位 GDP 能耗增幅(%)	Increase of Energy Consumption per unit GDP (%)										
2014 年	−5.37		−7.82	−15.08	−5.06	−2.75	−5.20	−4.32	−6.64	−8.85	−7.15
2013 年	−4.13		−4.03	−5.80	−4.75	−3.01	−3.32	−3.12	−2.93	−4.90	−3.89
2012 年	−5.98		−4.12	−9.28	−4.87	−5.18	−3.65	−3.61	−6.47	−5.05	−3.73
2011 年	−3.65		−3.91	−3.78	−3.43	−3.65	−3.58	−3.56	−3.62	−3.60	−3.67
2010 年	−3.75	−3.95				−3.73	−3.91	−3.56	−3.51	−3.98	−3.75
2009 年	−5.19	−5.51				−5.27	−4.70	−5.21	−4.75	−4.97	−5.08
2008 年	−5.69	−6.36				−5.63	−5.09	−5.78	−5.01	−5.06	−5.65

9-2 2007-2014 年分地区单位 GDP 电耗

POWER CONSUMPTION PER UNIT GDP BY REGIONS 2007-2014

指 标 Item	全市 Municipality	市区 (不含通州) Urban Areas (Tongzhou Excluded)	崇川区 Chongchuan	港闸区 Gangzha	开发区 Development Area	通州区 Tongzhou	海安 Haian	如东 Rudong	启东 Qidong	如皋 Rugao	海门 Haimen
单位 GDP 电耗 (千瓦时/万元)	Power Consumption per unit GDP (kilowatt/10,000 Yuan)										
2014年	621.1		598.9	583.3	1039.0	599.7	768.5	768.1	402.5	686.5	453.2
2013 年	671.8		686.6	726.6	1090.7	610.2	838.5	802.4	443.4	752.1	492.0
2012 年	694.8		722.1	817.6	1153.1	613.0	856.1	832.8	448.3	792.2	500.5
2011 年	723.0		739.3	941.6	1243.0	627.9	882.8	800.1	462.9	815.9	515.1
2010 年	857.7	1026.2				698.2	984.2	882.7	525.2	932.5	590.0
2009 年	844.4	1007.4				668.1	940.7	853.2	519.5	891.9	594.1
2008 年	896.5	1161.0				737.9	966.3	986.2	481.1	1108.2	618.7
2007 年	956.8	1297.3				786.4	974.1	1079.0	495.6	1124.3	668.5
单位 GDP 电耗增幅 (%)	Increase of Power Consumption per unit GDP (%)										
2014年	−7.6		−12.8	−20.4	−4.4	−1.7	−8.3	−4.3	−9.2	−8.7	−7.9
2013 年	−3.3		−4.9	−10.8	−5.2	−0.5	−2.1	−3.7	−1.1	−5.1	−1.7
2012 年	−3.9		−2.3	−13.2	−7.2	−2.4	−3.0	4.1	−3.2	−2.8	−2.8
2011 年	0.4		−9.1	−2.5	2.2	0.3	0.6	1.7	0.0	0.2	−1.0
2010 年	1.6	1.9				4.5	4.6	3.5	1.1	4.6	−0.7
2009 年	−6.3	−11.8				−8.4	2.2	−8.3	1.5	−1.5	−4.0
2008 年	−6.3	−10.5				−6.2	−0.8	−8.6	−2.9	−1.4	−7.5

注:1.2007−2010 年单位 GDP 能耗、单位 GDP 电耗的指标值计算,GDP 使用的 2005 价格。

2.2011 年以后单位 GDP 能耗、单位 GDP 电耗的指标值计算,GDP 使用的 2010 价格。

3.2011 年起,崇川区、港闸区、开发区能耗分开核算。

Note:1. 1. As for the calculation of 2007−2010 energy and power consumption per unit GDP, it adopts the price of 2005 for GDP.

2. As for the calculation of 2011 energy and power consumption per unit GDP, it adopts the price of 2010 for GDP.

3. Since 2011, the energy consumtions of Chongchuan, Gangzha and Development Zone have been calculated respectively.

9-3 规模以上工业企业分地区综合能耗(当量值)(2014年)

COMPREHENSIVE ENERGY CONSUMPTION OF INDUSTRIAL ENTERPRISES ABOVE DESIGNATED SIZE BY REGIONS (EQUIVALENT VALUE) 2014

地 区	Region	综合能源消费量(吨标准煤) Comprehensive Energy Consumption (ton of SCE)		产值能耗(吨标准煤/万元) Output Energy Consumption (ton of SCE/10,000 Yuan)	
		指标值(吨标准煤) Index Value(ton of SCE)	增幅(%) Increase(%)	指标值(吨标准煤/万元) Index Value(ton of SCE/10,000 Yuan)	增幅(%) Increase(%)
总 计	**Total**	**15016539**	**9.8**	**0.119**	**-1.3**
市 区	Urban Area	7369975	27.5	0.173	15.3
崇川区	Chongchuan	709795	-4.2	0.185	-7.1
港闸区	Gangzha	3858574	54.9	0.835	37.3
开发区	Developing Area	1889607	9.3	0.122	1.0
通州区	Tongzhou	911999	11.5	0.049	-2.0
海安县	Hai´an	1142220	2.7	0.064	-10.0
如东县	Rudong	1031304	4.5	0.060	-7.5
启东市	Qidong	2987275	-9.3	0.199	-17.7
如皋市	Rugao	1193112	-5.3	0.075	-14.8
海门市	Haimen	1292654	3.5	0.072	-5.5

9-4 规模以上工业企业分地区综合能耗(等价值)(2014年)

COMPREHENSIVE ENERGY CONSUMPTION OF INDUSTRIAL ENTERPRISES ABOVE DESIGNATED SIZE BY REGIONS (INDIFFERENCE VALUE) (2014)

地 区	Region	综合能源消费量(吨标准煤) Comprehensive Energy Consumption (ton of SCE)		产值能耗(吨标准煤/万元) Output Energy Consumption (ton of SCE/10,000 Yuan)	
		指标值(吨标准煤) Index Value(ton of SCE)	增幅(%) Increase(%)	指标值(吨标准煤/万元) Index Value(ton of SCE/10,000 Yuan)	增幅(%) Increase(%)
总 计	**Total**	**12662331**	**3.1**	**0.100**	**-7.3**
市 区	Urban Area	5320653	4.7	0.165	6.0
崇川区	Chongchuan	823826	-3.6	0.215	-6.5
港闸区	Gangzha	674309	15.8	0.146	2.7
开发区	Developing Zone	2451065	4.9	0.158	-3.0
通州区	Tongzhou	1371453	11.3	0.074	-2.3
海安县	Hai´an	1551866	3.3	0.876	-9.5
如东县	Rudong	1371056	3.9	0.080	-8.1
启东市	Qidong	1063190	-0.4	0.071	-9.6
如皋市	Rugao	1652248	-3.6	1.034	-13.3
海门市	Haimen	1703318	2.0	0.095	-6.9

9-5 规模以上工业企业分地区用水情况(2014年)

WATER CONSUMPTION OF INDUSTRIAL ENTERPRISES ABOVE DESIGNATED SIZE BY REGIONS(2014)

单位:万立方米 (Unit: 10,000 cubic meters)

地区	Region	取水总量 Total Water	陆地地表水 Land Surface Water	地下水 Underground Water	自来水 Tap Water	海水 Sea Water	雨水 Other Water	再生水 Recyclable Water	其他水 Other Water
总 计	**Total**	**78120**	**61799**	**1782**	**14127**	**2**	**5**	**18**	**387**
市 区	Urban Area	58797	51901	96	6549		1.84	18	231
崇川区	Chongchuan	45225	44121	5	1047		1.80		49
港闸区	Gangzha	1717	790	13	883				31
开发区	Developing Zone	9474	6571	53	2752			18	80
通州区	Tongzhou	2381	418	25	1867		0.04		71
海安县	Hai´an	3590	2382	368	839	0.29			0
如东县	Rudong	2476	391	154	1926	1.24	3.26		0
启东市	Qidong	2335	639	46	1650		0.18		0
如皋市	Rugao	2927	535	305	2083				3
海门市	Haimen	7995	5951	813	1079				152

9-5 续表

CONTINUED

单位:万立方米 (Unit: 10,000 cubic meters)

地区	Region	重复用水量 Recycled Water	直流冷却水量(河湖水) Cooling Water of River, Lake and Sea	直流冷却水量(海水) Cooling Water of River, Lake and Sea	废水排放量 Volume of Wastewater Discharging	污水处理企业污水处理量 Volume of Sewage Treatment Plants	外供自来水量 Tap Water for External Supply	净取水量 Net Water Withdrawal
总 计	**Total**	**95573**	**205476**	**139695**	**20168**	**2474**	**47769**	**30351**
市 区	Urban Area	85036	205449		10625		40671	18126
崇川区	Chongchuan	48527	2072		2350		40525	4700
港闸区	Gangzha	7385	200955		763		100	1617
开发区	Developing Zone	28876	2305		5664			9474
通州区	Tongzhou	249	117		1848		46	2335
海安县	Hai´an	127	21		1302	299	1896	1695
如东县	Rudong	2853			2697	1311		2476
启东市	Qidong	2759	5	139695	840			2335
如皋市	Rugao	3938			2852	864		2927
海门市	Haimen	860			1852		5202	2793

注:净取水量=取水总量-外供水量

Note: Net Water Withdrawal=Water Withdrawal-Water for External Supply

9-6 规模以上工业企业主要能源品种消费量(2014 年)

MAJOR ENERGY CONSUMPTION OF INDUSTRIAL PRODUCTS ABOVE DESIGNATED SIZE(2014)

指 标	Item	原煤（吨）Raw Coal (ton)	洗精煤（吨）Washing Coal (ton)	焦炭（吨）Coke (ton)	天然气（万立方米）Natural Gas ($10,000m^3$)
总 计	**Total**	**22301315**	**8**	**200273**	**14922**
按地区分	**Grouped by Regions**				
市 区	Urban Area	12296231		14371	8133
崇川区	Chongchuan	1036364		4	2807
港闸区	Gangzha	9042440		4008	1071
开发区	Development Zone	643073		10186	2008
通州区	Tongzhou	1574355		173	2246
海安县	Haian	1009206		7789	2197
如东县	Rudong	1059297		39359	1092
启东市	Qidong	6090373	8	172	519
如皋市	Rugao	787156		130935	2339
海门市	Haimen	1059051		7647	642
按行业分	**Grouped by Industries**				
农副食品加工业	Agrifood Processing	90710		3113	32
食品制造业	Food Production	9842			
酒、饮料和精制茶制造业	Alcohol, Beverage and Refined Tea Production	6692			
烟草制品业	Tobacco Industries				
纺织业	Textile	883393		376	1435
纺织服装、服饰业	Textile and Garment, Dress and Personal Adornment	99623		91	5
皮革、毛皮、羽毛及其制品和制鞋业	Leather, Fur, Feather(Fuzz) and Related Products	15590			
木材加工和木、竹、藤、棕、草制品业	Wood Processing and Industries of Wood, Bamboo, Rattan, Palm and Grass Products	138			
家具制造业	Furniture Manufacturing	191			
造纸及纸制品业	Paper Making and Industries of Paper Products	185980		916	811
印刷和记录媒介复制业	Printing and Record Medium Reproduction	4147			99
文教、工美、体育和娱乐用品制造业	Industries of Culture, Education, Arts, Sports and Recreational Products	172925		25830	448
石油加工、炼焦和核燃料加工业	Petroleum Processing, Coking and Nuclear Fuel Processing	1970			
化学原料和化学制品制造业	Production of Chemical Raw Materials and Chemical Products	1407246		4222	2828
医药制造业	Pharmaceutical Industry	64648			
化学纤维制造业	Chemical Fiber Manufacturing	785674			2613
橡胶和塑料制品业	Industry of Rubber and Plastic Products	194174			306
非金属矿物制品业	Industry of Nonmetallic Mineral Products	137956		8	1494
黑色金属冶炼和压延工业	Ferrous Metal Smelting and Pressing	248922		14267	729
有色金属冶炼和压延工业	Non-Ferrous Metal Smelting and Pressing	65784		5272	986
金属制品业	Manufacture of Metal Products	267043		1320	1037
通用设备制造业	Manufacture of General Purpose Machinery	51356	8	14348	537
专用设备制造业	Manufacture of Equipment for Special Purpose	34485		2500	5
汽车制造业	Automobile Industry	16347		243	543
铁路、船舶、航空航天和其他运输设备制造业	Manufacture of Railroad, Shipping, Aerospace and Other Transportation Equipments	8632		464	185
电气机械和器材制造业	Manufacture of Electrical Machinery and Equipments	204168		4415	313
计算机、通信和其他电子设备制造业	Manufacture of Computer, Communications and Other Electronic Products	29488		120179	143
仪器制造业	Instrument Manufacturing	56078		2710	90
其他制造业	Others	552			
废弃资源综合利用业	Comprehensive Utilization of Waste Resources				63
金属制品、机械和设备修理业	Metal Product, Machinery and Equipment Repair Industry	1408			
电力、热力的生产和供应	Generation and Supply of Electric Power and Heating Power	17256149			
燃气生产和供应业	Generation and Supply of Gas				221
水的生产和供应业	Generation and Supply of Water				

9-6 续表

指 标	Item	液化天然气（吨）Liquefied Natural Gas(ton)	汽油（吨）Gasoline (ton)
总 计	**Total**	**11355**	**118034**
按地区分	**Grouped by Regions**		
市 区	Urban Area	3696	46418
崇川区	Chongchuan	1219	1263
港闸区	Gangzha	99	2695
开发区	Development Zone	383	20142
通州区	Tongzhou	1995	22318
海安县	Haian	76	19647
如东县	Rudong	50	8253
启东市	Qidong	426	15931
如皋市	Rugao	566	7716
海门市	Haimen	6542	20068
按行业分	**Grouped by Industries**		
农副食品加工业	Agrifood Processing		2850
食品制造业	Food Production		291
酒、饮料和精制茶制造业	Alcohol, Beverage and Refined Tea Production		201
烟草制品业	Tobacco Industries		36
纺织业	Textile	912	18981
纺织服装、服饰业	Textile and Garment, Dress and Personal Adornment		6611
皮革、毛皮、羽毛及其制品和制鞋业	Leather, Fur, Feather(Fuzz) and Related Products		1016
木材加工和木、竹、藤、棕、草制品业	Wood Processing and Industries of Wood, Bamboo, Rattan, Palm and Grass Products		126
家具制造业	Furniture Manufacturing		109
造纸及纸制品业	Paper Making and Industries of Paper Products	2	363
印刷和记录媒介复制业	Printing and Record Medium Reproduction		517
文教、工美、体育和娱乐用品制造业	Industries of Culture, Education, Arts, Sports and Recreational Products	57	7516
石油加工、炼焦和核燃料加工业	Petroleum Processing, Coking and Nuclear Fuel Processing		80
化学原料和化学制品制造业	Production of Chemical Raw Materials and Chemical Products	744	11819
医药制造业	Pharmaceutical Industry	3	4428
化学纤维制造业	Chemical Fiber Manufacturing		1616
橡胶和塑料制品业	Industry of Rubber and Plastic Products		1797
非金属矿物制品业	Industry of Nonmetallic Mineral Products	380	3445
黑色金属冶炼和压延工业	Ferrous Metal Smelting and Pressing	1740	1761
有色金属冶炼和压延工业	Non-Ferrous Metal Smelting and Pressing		698
金属制品业	Manufacture of Metal Products	4540	6356
通用设备制造业	Manufacture of General Purpose Machinery	1487	11020
专用设备制造业	Manufacture of Equipment for Special Purpose	817	6257
汽车制造业	Automobile Industry		926
铁路、船舶、航空航天和其他运输设备制造业	Manufacture of Railroad, Shipping, Aerospace and Other Transportation Equipments	647	3001
电气机械和器材制造业	Manufacture of Electrical Machinery and Equipments	9	12859
计算机、通信和其他电子设备制造业	Manufacture of Computer, Communications and Other Electronic Products	17	7158
仪器制造业	Instrument Manufacturing		4945
其他制造业	Others		34
废弃资源综合利用业	Comprehensive Utilization of Waste Resources		8
金属制品、机械和设备修理业	Metal Product, Machinery and Equipment Repair Industry		35
电力、热力的生产和供应	Generation and Supply of Electric Power and Heating Power		730
燃气生产和供应业	Generation and Supply of Gas		65
水的生产和供应业	Generation and Supply of Water		380

CONTINUED

煤油 （吨） Kerosene (ton)	柴油 （吨） Diesel (ton)	燃料油 （吨） Fuel Oil (ton)	液化石油气 （吨） Liquefied Petroleum Gas (ton)	润滑油 （吨） Lubricant Oil (ton)	溶剂油 （吨） Solvent Oil (ton)	热力 （百万千焦） Heat (million kilo-joule)	电力 （万千瓦时） Electricity (10,000 kwh)	生物质废料 用于燃料（吨） Waste Biomass as Fuel (ton)
4151	**151315**	**34367**	**82448**	**941**	**699**	**51620540**	**2341628**	**521220**
2347	88084	30531	80162	56	448	29104961	988167	
19	10074	134	884		441	8597445	125884	
4	4972	9	29	26	7	1929864	192772	
2	22357	749	2756	30		2143690	284244	
2322	50681	29639	76493			16433962	385267	
93	20913		324	59		2591093	300444	29619
100	7227	1179	111	127	221	4717419	273628	196205
59	11880	2	150	81	30	7428367	195670	
144	11298	25	757	618		1904802	290291	
1407	11912	2630	944			5873898	293429	295396
	8603	740			441	1438057	30495	
	305					453298	11203	
	283					272404	2052	
	2						1195	
57	15769		7167	22		9505951	343540	29658
	5370	12	68	3		467023	46962	
	886				30	211575	9615	
	1051					156864	2500	
	299						2976	
	10526	35				1009038	36392	
	201	129					3950	
	2936		474			306213	58702	
	677						2144	
3550	12615	29646	64000		221	24371836	321164	
	1270					2871722	36834	250
0	2373		2452			8190464	149006	
	996	134	577	415		41731	59286	
127	24152		33	61		133697	91426	
88	2595	25				102933	128225	
3	1943	18	57	27			54179	
13	7625		3125	35		565787	209185	
181	12118	2	386	102		24883	93950	
4	12594	2570	891	33		16741	69196	
17	2071			103		27888	9651	
2	5910	9	730			96810	62113	
108	7785	1047	2483	103		644803	169761	
	3045		5			459772	93156	
	4029			34	7		42240	
	6						877	
							325	
	31						245	
	2993					101579	173442	491311
	22					149470	8219	
	236			3			17420	

9-7 规模以上工业企业能源购进、消费与库存(2014 年)

能源品种	Item	年初库存 Opening Balance	购进量 Purchases		消费量	
			实物量 Quantity	金额(万元) Amount of Money (10000 yuan)	合计 Total	工业生产消费 Consumption of Industrial Production
能源合计(吨标准煤)	**Total Energy (ton of SCE)**				**21367651**	**21292031**
原煤(吨)	Raw Coal (ton)	711320	22573698	1255133	22301315	22243991
#无烟煤	Anthracite	9805	183459	18304	180946	180544
#一般烟煤	General Bituminous Coal	692271	22371681	1235930	22096034	22039113
#褐煤	Brown Coal	9244	17160	759	24335	24335
洗精煤	Washing Coal		8	1	8	8
煤制品	Coal Products	5384	22026	1753	22473	22473
焦炭	Coke	1504	199948	49816	200273	200273
高炉煤气(万立方米)	Blast Furnace Gas(10,000 m^3)					
天然气	Natural Gas		14923	54878	14922	14859
液化天然气(吨)	Liquified Natural Gas (ton)		11335	5918	11355	11345
汽油	Gasoline	406	117400	101194	118034	116456
煤油	Karosene	12	4145	3256	4151	4137
柴油	Diesel	3784	149992	118579	151315	149609
燃料油	Fuel Oil	557	34304	15022	34367	34367
液化石油气	Liquified Petroleum Gas	168	82451	47671	82448	82235
润滑油	Lubricant Oil	30	934	982	941	939
溶剂油	Solvent Oil	261	626	547	699	699
石油焦	Petroleum Coke					
其它石油制品	Others		11	33.0	11	11
热力(百万千焦)	Heat (million kilo-joule)		38328880	335143	51620540	51536252
电力(万千瓦时)	Electricity(10,000 kwh)		2060255	1603724	2341628	2320036
生物质废料用于燃料(吨)	Waste Biomass as Fuel (ton)		521062	13341	521220	521220

ENERGY PURCHASE, CONSUMPTION AND INVENTORY OF INDUSTRIAL ENTERPRISES ABOVE DESIGNATED SIZE(2014)

Total Energy Consumption							年末库存 Closing Balance	能源加工转换产出 Output in Transformation	回收利用 Recycle
用于原材料 For Raw Materials	能源转换投入合计 Consumed in Transformation	火力发电 Power Generation	供热 Heating	炼焦 Coking	制气 Gas Production	非工业生产消费 Consumption of Non-Industrial Production			
	13104518	**11103599**	**2000919**			**75620**		**6275492**	
138323	18777968	15878981	2898987			57324	964617		
133166						402	12627		
5157	18771444	15876371	2895073			56921	949921		
	6524	2610	3914				2069		
							4871		
21							1104		
						63			
						11			
1401						1577	208		
121						14	13		
169						1706	2662		
							516		
287						214	164		
939						2	25		
699							188		
						84289		47881681	
						21593		3777646	
	431100	268169	162931						

9-8 规模以上工业企业分行业综合能耗(当量值)(2014 年)

指 标	Item
总 计	**Total**
按轻重工业分	**Grouped by Light and Heavy Industries**
轻工业	Light Industry
重工业	Heavy Industry
按行业分	**Grouped by Industries**
农副食品加工业	Agrifood Processing
食品制造业	Food Production
酒、饮料和精制茶制造业	Alcohol, Beverage and Refined Tea Production
烟草制品业	Tobacco Industries
纺织业	Textile
纺织服装、服饰业	Textile and Garment, Dress and Personal Adornment
皮革、毛皮、羽毛及其制品和制鞋业	Leather, Fur, Feather(Fuzz) and Related Products
木材加工和木、竹、藤、棕、草制品业	Wood Processing and Industries of Wood, Bamboo, Rattan, Palm and Grass Products
家具制造业	Furniture Manufacturing
造纸及纸制品业	Paper Making and Industries of Paper Products
印刷和记录媒介复制业	Printing and Record Medium Reproduction
文教、工美、体育和娱乐用品制造业	Industries of Culture, Education, Arts, Sports and Recreational Products
石油加工、炼焦和核燃料加工业	Petroleum Processing, Coking and Nuclear Fuel Processing
化学原料和化学制品制造业	Production of Chemical Raw Materials and Chemical Products
医药制造业	Pharmaceutical Industry
化学纤维制造业	Chemical Fiber Manufacturing
橡胶和塑料制品业	Industry of Rubber and Plastic Products
非金属矿物制品业	Industry of Nonmetallic Mineral Products
黑色金属冶炼和压延工业	Ferrous Metal Smelting and Pressing
有色金属冶炼和压延工业	Non-Ferrous Metal Smelting and Pressing
金属制品业	Manufacture of Metal Products
通用设备制造业	Manufacture of General Purpose Machinery
专用设备制造业	Manufacture of Equipment for Special Purpose
汽车制造业	Automobile Industry
铁路、船舶、航空航天和其他运输设备制造业	Manufacture of Railroad, Shipping, Aerospace and Other Transportation Equipments
电气机械和器材制造业	Manufacture of Electrical Machinery and Equipments
计算机、通信和其他电子设备制造业	Manufacture of Computer, Communications and Other Electronic Products
仪器制造业	Instrument Manufacturing
其他制造业	Others
废弃资源综合利用业	Comprehensive Utilization of Waste Resources
金属制品、机械和设备修理业	Metal Product, Machinery and Equipment Repair Industry
电力、热力的生产和供应	Generation and Supply of Electric Power and Heating Power
燃气生产和供应业	Generation and Supply of Gas
水的生产和供应业	Generation and Supply of Water

COMPREHENSIVE ENERGY CONSUMPTION OF INDUSTRIAL ENTERPRISES ABOVE DESIGNATED SIZE BY INDUSTRIES (EQUIVALENT VALUE)(2014)

综合能源消费量 Comprehensine Energy Consumption		万元产值能耗 Energy Consumption per 10,000 Yuan Output	
指标值(吨标准煤) Index Value(ton of SCE)	增幅(%) Increase(%)	指标值(吨标准煤/万元) Index Value (ton of size/10,000 yuan)	增幅(%) increase(%)
15016539	**9.8**	**0.119**	**-1.3**
3494241	5.2	0.087	-1.4
11522298	11.2	0.134	-2.0
173370	-0.9	0.040	-8.0
37194	20.1	0.112	-0.1
17299	1.7	0.092	-12.7
1469	73.2	0.013	56.7
1374087	1.8	0.104	-1.3
162224	0.2	0.033	-4.1
32952	-5.8	0.037	-8.8
10237	1.2	0.101	5.8
4321	20.1	0.020	5.2
190338	80.2	0.336	41.0
10340	18.4	0.051	17.9
257365	2.0	0.049	-6.0
5139	12.3	0.031	-3.1
2201849	-0.2	0.123	-8.7
197934	6.6	0.070	-5.6
746146	3.0	0.206	-4.0
190879	-5.2	0.106	-12.1
272625	-4.9	0.073	-12.5
371998	-0.3	0.160	-15.6
137315	17.5	0.082	3.3
514081	1.9	0.071	-3.0
209809	13.5	0.021	-3.9
146021	11.8	0.021	-14.3
38062	-4.2	0.030	-4.7
102368	6.9	0.023	3.0
442554	11.7	0.025	0.3
281747	12.0	0.041	-7.8
108722	17.3	0.019	-8.4
1532	77.1	0.024	73.4
1246	81.3	0.036	68.6
1393	21.0	0.034	1.7
6733392	18.6	4.088	8.2
18214	-40.2	0.064	-39.3
22316	1.2	0.155	-6.1

9-9 规模以上工业企业分行业综合能耗(等价值)(2014年)

指 标	Item
总 计	**Total**
按行业分	**Grouped by Industries**
农副食品加工业	Agrifood Processing
食品制造业	Food Production
酒、饮料和精制茶制造业	**Alcohol, Beverage and Refined Tea Production**
烟草制品业	Tobacco Industries
纺织业	Textile
纺织服装、服饰业	Textile and Garment, Dress and Personal Adornment
皮革、毛皮、羽毛及其制品和制鞋业	Leather, Fur, Feather(Fuzz) and Related Products
木材加工和木、竹、藤、棕、草制品业	Wood Processing and Industries of Wood, Bamboo, Rattan, Palm and Grass Products
家具制造业	Furniture Manufacturing
造纸及纸制品业	Paper Making and Industries of Paper Products
印刷和记录媒介复制业	Printing and Record Medium Reproduction
文教、工美、体育和娱乐用品制造业	Industries of Culture, Education, Arts, Sports and Recreational Products
石油加工、炼焦和核燃料加工业	Petroleum Processing, Coking and Nuclear Fuel Processing
化学原料和化学制品制造业	Production of Chemical Raw Materials and Chemical Products
医药制造业	Pharmaceutical Industry
化学纤维制造业	Chemical Fiber Manufacturing
橡胶和塑料制品业	Industry of Rubber and Plastic Products
非金属矿物制品业	Industry of Nonmetallic Mineral Products
黑色金属冶炼和压延工业	Ferrous Metal Smelting and Pressing
有色金属冶炼和压延工业	Non-Ferrous Metal Smelting and Pressing
金属制品业	Manufacture of Metal Products
通用设备制造业	Manufacture of General Purpose Machinery
专用设备制造业	Manufacture of Equipment for Special Purpose
汽车制造业	Automobile Industry
铁路、船舶、航空航天和其他运输设备制造业	Manufacture of Railroad, Shipping, Aerospace and Other Transportation Equipments
电气机械和器材制造业	Manufacture of Electrical Machinery and Equipments
计算机、通信和其他电子设备制造业	Manufacture of Computer, Communications and Other Electronic Products
仪器制造业	Instrument Manufacturing
其他制造业	Others
废弃资源综合利用业	Comprehensive Utilization of Waste Resources
金属制品、机械和设备修理业	Metal Product, Machinery and Equipment Repair Industry
电力、热力的生产和供应	Generation and Supply of Electric Power and Heating Power
燃气生产和供应业	Generation and Supply of Gas
水的生产和供应业	Generation and Supply of Water

COMPREHENSIVE ENERGY CONSUMPTION OF INDUSTRIAL ENTERPRISES ABOVE DESIGNATED SIZE BY INDUSTRIES (EQUIVALENT VALUE)(2014)

综合能源消费量 Comprehensine Energy Consumption		万元产值能耗 Energy Consumption per 10,000 Yuan Output	
指标值(吨标准煤) Index Value(ton of SCE)	增幅(%) Increase(%)	指标值(吨标准煤/万元) Index Value (ton of size/10,000 yuan)	增幅(%) Increase(%)
12661663	**3.1**	**0.100**	**-7.3**
225643	-0.8	0.052	-8.0
56355	21.2	0.169	0.8
20809	**4.1**	**0.110**	**-10.6**
3568	61.6	0.031	46.2
1937908	-0.3	0.147	-3.3
243629	-4.3	0.050	-8.4
49442	-8.7	0.056	-11.5
14512	2.9	0.143	7.6
9479	15.3	0.044	1.0
210155	69.5	0.371	32.6
17127	14.6	0.084	14.1
358017	1.4	0.069	-6.6
8814	10.2	0.053	-4.9
2716581	-0.6	0.152	-9.1
260961	11.6	0.093	-1.2
933952	5.8	0.258	-1.4
272017	-4.5	0.152	-11.6
429897	-4.4	0.115	-12.1
591357	-3.2	0.254	-18.1
230007	13.1	0.138	-0.6
873959	-1.2	0.121	-5.9
372973	13.8	0.037	-3.6
265379	13.5	0.039	-13.0
54723	-10.9	0.043	-11.5
210386	3.4	0.047	-0.4
733429	8.1	0.042	-2.9
444217	6.7	0.064	-12.2
181248	15.9	0.032	-9.6
3033	61.3	0.048	58.0
1802	32.7	0.053	23.4
1823	21.2	0.045	1.9
844035	12.7	0.512	2.9
32317	-22.7	0.113	-21.6
52110	-1.4	0.362	-8.5

9-10 规模以上工业企业用水情况(2014年)

单位:万立方米

指 标	Item	取水总量 Total Water
总 计	**Total**	**78120**
按轻重工业分	**Grouped by Light and Heavy Industries**	
轻工业	Light Industry	62579
重工业	Heavy Industry	15542
按行业分	**Grouped by Industries**	
农副食品加工业	Agrifood Processing	434
食品制造业	Food Production	155
酒、饮料和精制茶制造业	Alcohol, Beverage and Refined Tea Production	126
烟草制品业	Tobacco Industries	2
纺织业	Textile	4033
纺织服装、服饰业	Textile and Garment, Dress and Personal Adornment	615
皮革、毛皮、羽毛及其制品和制鞋业	Leather, Fur, Feather(Fuzz) and Related Products	138
木材加工和木、竹、藤、棕、草制品业	Wood Processing and Industries of Wood, Bamboo, Rattan, Palm and Grass Products	19
家具制造业	Furniture Manufacturing	31
造纸及纸制品业	Paper Making and Industries of Paper Products	846
印刷和记录媒介复制业	Printing and Record Medium Reproduction	27
文教、工美、体育和娱乐用品制造业	Industries of Culture, Education, Arts, Sports and Recreational Products	791
石油加工、炼焦和核燃料加工业	Petroleum Processing, Coking and Nuclear Fuel Processing	2
化学原料和化学制品制造业	Production of Chemical Raw Materials and Chemical Products	3960
医药制造业	Pharmaceutical Industry	393
化学纤维制造业	Chemical Fiber Manufacturing	2843
橡胶和塑料制品业	Industry of Rubber and Plastic Products	256
非金属矿物制品业	Industry of Nonmetallic Mineral Products	378
黑色金属冶炼和压延工业	Ferrous Metal Smelting and Pressing	367
有色金属冶炼和压延工业	Non-Ferrous Metal Smelting and Pressing	120
金属制品业	Manufacture of Metal Products	710
通用设备制造业	Manufacture of General Purpose Machinery	723
专用设备制造业	Manufacture of Equipment for Special Purpose	311
汽车制造业	Automobile Industry	57
铁路、船舶、航空航天和其他运输设备制造业	Manufacture of Railroad, Shipping, Aerospace and Other Transportation Equipments	532
电气机械和器材制造业	Manufacture of Electrical Machinery and Equipments	608
计算机、通信和其他电子设备制造业	Manufacture of Computer, Communications and Other Electronic Products	810
仪器制造业	Instrument Manufacturing	199
其他制造业	Others	9
废弃资源综合利用业	Comprehensive Utilization of Waste Resources	25
金属制品、机械和设备修理业	Metal Product, Machinery and Equipment Repair Industry	4
电力、热力的生产和供应	Generation and Supply of Electric Power and Heating Power	6806
燃气生产和供应业	Generation and Supply of Gas	10
水的生产和供应业	Generation and Supply of Water	51780

WATER CONSUMPTION OF INDUSTRIAL ENTERPRISES ABOVE DESIGNATED SIZE(2014)

(Unit: 10,000 cubic meters)

付费水 Paid Water	水费金额(万元) Amount of Water Pay (10,000 Yuan)	单价(元/立方米) Per Unit Price (Yuan/m³)	本年外供水量 Water for External Supply of the Year	净取水量 Net Water Withdrawal	地表水 Surface Water	付费水 Paid Water	水费金额(万元) Amount of Water Pay (10,000 Yuan)	单价(元/立方米) Per Unit Price (Yuan/m³)
47769	**30352**	**61799**	**1782**	**14127**	**95573**	**205476**	**139695**	**2474**
47481	15098	53667	931	7833	31617	2072		
288	15254	8132	851	6294	63956	203404	139695	2474
	434	51	101	279	28			
	155	25	50	67	17			
	126			117	2.16			
	2			2				
	4033	434	589	2917	1044			
	615	2	1	598	50			
	138	3		135	2			
	19			15				
	31			31				
	846	764	3	77	99			
	27			27	12			
	791	80	77	632	142			
	2			2	1			
	3960	1440	387	1904	36196			
	393	62	51	275	1645			
	2843	2479	32	330	28559	2072		
	256	2	4	249	12066			
	378	98	41	236	93			
	367	6	199	160	246	9		
	120	18	1	101	27			
	710	41	70	591	955			
	723	1	6	717	27			
	311	11	1	297	20			
	57	5	4	49	4			
	532	299		229	818			
	608	4	26	579	27			
	810		63	726	10456.26			
	199		13	186	6			
	9			9				
	25			25				
	4			4				
	6806	6215	63	527	3029	203394	139695	
	10			10	2			
47769	4011	49757		2022				2474

9-11 重点耗能工业企业能源购进、消费与库存(2014年)

能源品种	Item	年初库存 Opening Balance	购进量 Purchases 实物量 Quantity	金额(万元) Money (10000 yuan)	消费量 合计 Total	工业生产消费 Consumption of Industrial Production
能源合计(吨标准煤)	**Total Energy (ton of SCE)**				**18562538**	**18497491**
原煤(吨)	Raw Coal (ton)	675758	21453570	1161834	21181327	21125076
#无烟煤	Anthracite	9006	159097	16388	156294	156294
#一般烟煤	General Bituminous Coal	657590	21284373	1145088	21007771	20951520
#褐煤	Brown Coal	9162	10100	359	17262	17262
洗精煤	Washing Coal					
其它洗煤	Others					
焦炭	Coke	121	126347	35964	126055	126055
高炉煤气(万立方米)	Blast Furnace Gas(10,000m³)					
天然气	Natural Gas		11787	45814	11787	11768
液化天然气(吨)	Liquified Natural Gas (ton)		10560	5384	10560	10560
汽油	Gasoline	41	26299	22571	26340	25678
煤油	Karosene	9	3688	2875	3692	3684
柴油	Diesel	3130	66552	51638	67511	66468
燃料油	Fuel Oil	497	32388	13963	32385	32385
液化石油气	Liquified Petroleum Gas	162	78701	45197	78699	78535
润滑油	Lubricant Oil	29	467	455	475	473
溶剂油	Solvent Oil	261	369	327	441	441
石油焦	Petroleum Coke					
其它石油制品	Others					
热力(百万千焦)	Heat (million kilo-joule)		32078811	283652	45347747	45296347
电力(万千瓦时)	Electricity(10,000 kwh)		919570	686284	1199823	1182767
生物质废料用于燃料(吨)	Waste Biomass as Fuel (ton)		519862	13271	519862	519862

ENERGY PURCHASE, CONSUMPTION AND INVENTORY OF KEY ENERGY-CONSUMING INDUSTRIAL ENTERPRISES(2014)

Total Energy Consumption						非工业生产消费 Consumption of Non-Industrial Production	年末库存 Closing Balance	能源加工转换产出 Output in Transformation	回收利用 Recycle
用于原材料 For Raw Materials	能源转换投入合计 Consumed in Transformation	火力发电 Power Generation	供热 Heating	炼焦 Coking	制气 Gas Production				
	13104518	**11103599**	**2000919**			**65047**		**6275492**	
132003	18777968	15878981	2898987			56251	937173		
132003							11809		
	18771444	15876371	2895073			56251	923365		
	6524	2610	3914				2000		
							17		
						19			
17						662	9		
76						8	12		
						1043	2198		
							500		
						165	162		
473						2	22		
441							188		
						51400		47881681	
						17057		3777646	
	431100	268169	162931						

9-12 重点耗能工业企业分行业综合能耗(当量值)(2014年)

指　标	Item
总　计	**Total**
按轻重工业分	**Grouped by Light and Heavy Industries**
轻工业	Light Industry
重工业	Heavy Industry
按行业分	**Grouped by Industries**
农副食品加工业	Agrifood Processing
食品制造业	Food Production
酒、饮料和精制茶制造业	Alcohol, Beverage and Refined Tea Production
纺织业	Textile
纺织服装、服饰业	Textile and Garment, Dress and Personal Adornment
皮革、毛皮、羽毛及其制品和制鞋业	Leather, Fur, Feather(Fuzz) and Related Products
木材加工和木、竹、藤、棕、草制品业	Wood Processing and Industries of Wood, Bamboo, Rattan, Palm and Grass Products
造纸及纸制品业	Paper Making and Industries of Paper Products
文教、工美、体育和娱乐用品制造业	Industries of Culture, Education, Arts, Sports and Recreational Products
化学原料和化学制品制造业	Production of Chemical Raw Materials and Chemical Products
医药制造业	Pharmaceutical Industry
化学纤维制造业	Chemical Fiber Manufacturing
橡胶和塑料制品业	Industry of Rubber and Plastic Products
非金属矿物制品业	Industry of Nonmetallic Mineral Products
黑色金属冶炼和压延工业	Ferrous Metal Smelting and Pressing
有色金属冶炼和压延工业	Non-Ferrous Metal Smelting and Pressing
金属制品业	Manufacture of Metal Products
通用设备制造业	Manufacture of General Purpose Machinery
专用设备制造业	Manufacture of Equipment for Special Purpose
汽车制造业	Automobile Industry
铁路、船舶、航空航天和其他运输设备制造业	Manufacture of Railroad, Shipping, Aerospace and Other Transportation Equipments
电气机械和器材制造业	Manufacture of Electrical Machinery and Equipments
计算机、通信和其他电子设备制造业	Manufacture of Computer, Communications and Other Electronic Products
仪器制造业	Instrument Manufacturing
电力、热力的生产和供应	Generation and Supply of Electric Power and Heating Power
燃气生产和供应业	Generation and Supply of Gas
水的生产和供应业	Generation and Supply of Water
按地区分	**Grouped by Regions**
市　区	Urban Areas
崇川区	Chongchuan
港闸区	Gangzha
开发区	Developing Zone
通州区	Tongzhou
海安县	Hai´an
如东县	Rudong
启东市	Qidong
如皋市	Rugao
海门市	Haimen

COMPREHENSIVE ENERGY CONSUMPTION OF KEY ENERGY-CONSUMING INDUSTRIAL ENTERPRISES BY INDUSTRIES(EQUIVALENT VALUE)(2014)

单位数 Number of Units	综合能源消费量 Comprehensive Energy Consumption		万元产值能耗 Energy Consumption per 10,000 Yuan Output	
	指标值(吨标准煤) Index Value(ton of SCE)	增幅(%) Increase(%)	指标值(吨标准煤/万元) Index Value (ton of size/10,000 yuan)	增幅(%) Increase(%)
268	**12221999**	**11.2**	**0.309**	**3.0**
96	2290237	5.6	0.220	1.2
172	9931762	12.6	0.341	3.0
6	108175	−6.8	0.065	−6.4
1	18732	14.4	0.288	−11.9
1	11115	16.1	0.246	10.6
50	841955	1.7	0.242	−0.9
2	69627	−5.0	0.069	−6.2
2	13610	−9.3	0.069	−12.6
1	5624	6.2	0.230	0.4
2	144352	118.7	0.929	13.6
4	110816	3.0	0.322	−18.9
73	1858227	−0.8	0.204	−4.7
10	120929	8.3	0.206	11.7
11	687887	2.4	0.273	−2.9
4	115198	−4.4	0.211	−10.8
8	118799	8.3	0.183	−2.4
8	302685	−0.5	0.210	−19.8
6	99931	22.2	0.143	−3.8
19	209952	4.3	0.107	−0.9
3	31645	14.0	0.051	1.5
5	57105	3.9	0.033	1.8
2	22750	0.2	0.039	5.0
4	41446	1.7	0.018	1.1
14	260847	14.0	0.051	0.0
6	181166	13.6	0.101	−3.2
3	38686	16.6	0.030	−22.1
21	6730531	18.6	4.528	5.5
1	9900	−62.8	0.063	−55.0
1	10307	−3.3	0.276	−10.1
95	6462831	32.2	0.388	19.5
13	656346	−4.0	0.245	−6.1
12	3706633	58.6	3.373	34.7
46	1606125	10.7	0.191	2.9
24	493727	17.8	0.111	−2.9
29	756832	−2.8	0.115	−17.0
30	552930	8.3	0.113	−1.6
34	2767687	−9.8	0.921	−12.4
41	776991	−10.9	0.155	−9.5
39	904728	3.7	0.264	7.0

9-13 重点耗能工业企业主要工业产品单位产量能耗(2014年)

指 标	Item
吨锦纶综合能耗	Comprehensive Energy Consumption per ton of Chinlon
吨锦纶用电量	Power Consumption per ton of Chinlon
吨涤纶综合能耗(长丝)	Comprehensive Energy Consumption per ton of Dacron (long fiber)
吨涤纶用电量(长丝)	Power Consumption per ton of Dacron (long fiber)
吨纱(线)混合数综合能耗	Comprehensive Energy Consumption per ton of Yarn (line) Mixture
吨纱(线)混合数生产用电量	Power Consumption per ton of Yarn (line) Mixture
万米布混合数综合能耗	Comprehensive Energy Consumption per 10,000 m of Cloth Mixture
万米布混合数生产用电量	Power Consumption per 10,000 m of Cloth Mixture
万米印染布综合能耗	Comprehensive Energy Consumption per 10,000 m of Printed and Dyed Fabrics
吨桑蚕丝综合能耗	Comprehensive Energy Consumption per ton of Mulberry Silk
单位烧碱生产综合能耗(离子膜法 30%)	Comprehensive Energy Consumption per unit Caustic Soda Production (membrane process 3%)
单位烧碱生产耗交流电(离子膜法 30%)	Power Consumption per unit Caustic Soda Production (membrane process 3%)
单位合成氨生产综合能耗	Comprehensive Energy Consumption per unit Synthetic Ammonia
单位合成氨耗电	Power Consumption per unit Synthetic Ammonia
单位合成氨耗原料煤	Consumption of Raw Coal per unit Synthetic Ammonia
单位合成氨耗标准燃料煤	Consumption of SCE per unit Synthetic Ammonia
吨水泥综合能耗	Comprehensive Energy Consumption per ton of Cement
吨水泥综合电耗	Comprehensive Power Consumption per ton of Cement
机制纸及纸板综合能耗	Comprehensive Power Consumption of Machine-finished Paper and Cardboard
机制纸及纸板耗电	Power Consumption of Machine-finished Paper and Cardboard
电炉炼钢综合工序单位能耗	Per Unit Energy Consumption of Electric Steelmaking Comprehensive Procedure
电炉炼钢综合电力消耗	Comprehensive Power Consumption of Electric Steelmaking
轧钢工序单位能耗	Per Unit Energy Consumption of Steel Rolling
轧钢工序单位电力消耗	Per Unit Power Consumption of Steel Rolling
电厂火力发电标准煤耗	SCE Consumption of Power Plant´s Thermal Power Generation
电厂火力供电标准煤耗	SCE Consumption of Power Plant´s Thermal Power Generation
发电厂用电率	Auxiliary Power Rate of Power Plant

ENERGY CONSUMPTION PER UNIT OUTPUT OF MAIN INDUSTRIAL PRODUCTS OF MAJOR ENERGY-CONSUMPTIVE INDUSTRIAL ENTERPRISES(2014)

计量单位	Unit	2014 年	增速(%) Increase(%)
千克标准煤/吨	kg SCE/ton	244.8	-0.3
千瓦时/吨	Kwh/ton	1973.9	-0.3
千克标准煤/吨	kg SCE/ton	390.0	持平
千瓦时/吨	Kwh/ton	2082.2	持平
千克标准煤/吨	kg SCE/ton	262.4	-2.6
千瓦时/吨	Kwh/ton	2041.7	-3.6
千克标准煤/万米	kg SCE/10,000 m	1137.2	0.6
千瓦时/万米	Kwh/ton	870.6	-0.2
千克标准煤/万米	kg ce/10,000m	2408.3	-6.0
千克标准煤/吨	kg SCE/ton	4301.2	持平
千克标准煤/吨	kg SCE/ton	319.9	4.1
千瓦时/吨	Kwh/ton	2316.4	1.4
千克标准煤/吨	kg SCE/ton	1360.9	0.2
千瓦时/吨	Kwh/ton	1408.4	-0.8
千克标煤/吨	SCE/ton	1114.5	-0.5
千克标煤/吨	SCE/ton	90.7	-2.8
千克标准煤/吨	SCE/ton	4.9	3.8
千瓦时/吨	Kwh/ton	39.6	3.6
千克标准煤/吨	kg SCE/ton	507.0	持平
千瓦时/吨	Kwh/ton	851.7	持平
千克标准煤/吨	kg SCE/ton	141.0	0.1
千瓦时/吨	Kwh/ton	1147.2	0.1
千克标准煤/吨	kg SCE/ton	1226.9	-0.1
千瓦时/吨	Kwh/ton	12.8	-0.6
克标准煤/千瓦时	g SCE/Kwh	301.6	-0.1
克标准煤/千瓦时	g SCE/Kwh	316.4	持平
%	%	4.0	2.3

9-14 规模以上工业企业分地区发电量(2014年)

POWER GENERATION OF INDUSTRIAL ENTERPRISES ABOVE DESIGNATED SIZE BY REGIONS(2014)

地区	Region	指标值(万千瓦时) Index Value(10,000 Kwh)			增幅(%) Increase		
		发电量 Power Generation	火力发电量 Thermal	风力发电量 Wind	发电量 Power Generation	火力发电量 Thermal	风力发电量 Wind
总计	**Total**	**4030258**	**3735747**	**252612**	**22.4**	**24.4**	**0.6**
市区	Urban Area	2243615	2243615		66.8	66.8	
崇川区	Chongchuan	66637	66637		–4.2	–4.2	
港闸区	Gangzha	2088470	2088470		72.4	72.4	
开发区	Developing Zone	77845	77845		42.6	42.6	
通州区	Tongzhou	10663	10663		17.3	17.3	
海安县	Hai´an	42621	35571		–6.5	–10.8	
如东县	Rudong	244762	34957	191244	1.9	30.2	–1.6
启东市	Qidong	1457698	1396330	61368	–10.2	–10.9	7.9
如皋市	Rugao	10155	1511		–5.9	0.3	
海门市	Haimen	31407	23764		9.8	1.6	

9-15 南通市重点耗能工业企业名录(2014年末)

LIST OF NANTONG KEY ENERGY-CONSUMING INDUSTRIAL ENTERPRISES (END OF 2014)

序号 No.	地区 District	法人单位名称 Enterprise	序号 No.	地区 District	法人单位名称 Enterprise
1	启东市	江苏大唐国际吕四港发电有限责任公司	46	海安县	海安华新热电有限公司
2	港闸区	江苏南通发电有限公司	47	海门市	海门市化工原料厂有限公司
3	港闸区	华能国际电力股份有限公司南通电厂	48	开发区	先正达南通作物保护有限公司
4	港闸区	南通天生港发电有限公司	49	开发区	南通帝人有限公司
5	崇川区	南通醋酸纤维有限公司	50	海门市	南通海迪化工有限公司
6	开发区	南通江山农药化工股份有限公司	51	如皋市	上海电器环保热电(南通)有限公司
7	海安县	南通新正大特钢有限公司	52	开发区	东丽合成纤维(南通)有限公司
8	海安县	江苏联发纺织股份有限公司	53	启东市	江苏好收成韦恩农化股份有限公司
9	开发区	江苏王子制纸有限公司	54	启东市	国信启东热电有限公司
10	开发区	南通美亚热电有限公司	55	海门市	南通回力橡胶有限公司
11	开发区	南通星辰合成材料有限公司	56	开发区	江苏巨力钢绳有限公司
12	如皋市	南通华东液压铸业有限公司	57	如皋市	江苏南天化肥有限公司
13	海门市	江苏通海染整有限公司	58	启东市	江苏希迪制药有限公司
14	启东市	江苏海四达集团有限公司	59	海安县	鑫缘茧丝绸集团股份有限公司
15	开发区	三大雅精细化学品(南通)有限公司	60	如东县	南通泰禾化工有限公司
16	开发区	东丽酒伊织染(南通)有限公司	61	海门市	海门市环宇化工厂
17	通州区	江苏恒科新材料有限公司	62	海安县	江苏万力机械股份有限公司
18	开发区	台橡宇部(南通)化学工业有限公司	63	海安县	南通晓星变压器有限公司
19	海门市	海门鑫源环保热电有限公司	64	开发区	台橡(南通)实业有限公司
20	海门市	南通联海生物热电有限公司	65	海安县	海安天楹环保能源有限公司
21	如东县	江苏国信如东生物质发电有限公司	66	海门市	江苏黑鹰化学工业有限公司
22	开发区	凡特鲁斯特种化学品(南通)有限公司	67	海门市	泰山石膏(南通)有限公司
23	如东县	如东协鑫环保热电有限公司	68	如皋市	上海制皂集团(如皋)有限公司
24	如皋市	百川化工(如皋)有限公司	69	海门市	中兴能源装备股份有限公司
25	海安县	海安美亚热电有限公司	70	如东县	江苏九九久科技股份有限公司
26	通州区	江苏综艺集团	71	崇川区	南通来宝谷物蛋白有限公司
27	如皋市	江苏如皋钢铁有限公司	72	通州区	江苏甬金金属科技有限公司
28	如东县	南通东日钢铁有限公司	73	海安县	江苏文凤化纤集团有限公司
29	海门市	江苏联海生物科技有限公司	74	港闸区	江苏狼山钢绳股份有限公司
30	开发区	嘉吉粮油(南通)有限公司	75	海门市	海门市大千热电有限公司
31	海门市	江苏金雪集团有限公司	76	如皋市	如皋市中如化工有限公司
32	崇川区	南亚塑胶工业(南通)有限公司	77	崇川区	南通富士通微电子股份有限公司
33	港闸区	南通新兴热电有限公司	78	通州区	新建特阔漂整(南通)有限公司
34	开发区	宝泰菱工程塑料(南通)有限公司	79	如东县	南通大东有限公司
35	通州区	江苏亚伦集团股份有限公司	80	启东市	韩华新能源(启东)有限公司
36	如皋市	德源(中国)高科有限公司	81	海安县	江苏铁锚玻璃股份有限公司
37	通州区	南通紫鑫实业有限公司	82	如东县	江苏三美化工有限公司
38	如东县	如东洋口环保热电有限公司	83	开发区	南通衣依衬布有限公司
39	开发区	南通醋酸化工股份有限公司	84	海门市	南通东盛之花印染有限公司
40	海门市	南通新锦江印染有限公司	85	通州区	南通明德重工有限公司
41	开发区	申华化学工业有限公司	86	开发区	扬子高丽钢线(南通)有限公司
42	通州区	通州美亚热电有限公司	87	启东市	南通艾德旺化工有限公司
43	如皋市	如皋市双马化工有限公司	88	如东县	如东南天农科化工有限公司
44	如皋市	双钱集团(江苏)轮胎有限公司	89	海安县	江苏天成生化制品有限公司
45	崇川区	南通观音山环保热电有限公司	90	海安县	亚太轻合金(南通)科技有限公司

9-15 续表 1

CONTINUED 1

序号 No.	地区 District	法人单位名称 Enterprise	序号 No.	地区 District	法人单位名称 Enterprise
91	海门市	南通市常海食品添加剂有限公司	136	海门市	海门天尼电子有限公司
92	如皋市	江苏九鼎集团有限公司	137	崇川区	南通中远船务工程有限公司
93	如东县	南通立洋化学有限公司	138	海安县	南通市康桥油脂有限公司
94	如东县	南通辉煌彩色钢板有限公司	139	启东市	江苏正泰医药化工有限公司
95	通州区	江苏中联科技集团有限公司	140	崇川区	南通市自来水公司
96	如东县	中天科技集团有限公司	141	启东市	中远船务(启东)海洋工程有限公司
97	海安县	南通联荣集团有限公司	142	海门市	冠达尔钢结构(江苏)有限公司
98	如皋市	如皋市协和印染有限公司	143	如东县	中石油江苏液化天然气有限公司
99	开发区	三菱丽阳高分子材料(南通)有限公司	144	开发区	万洲石化(江苏)有限公司
100	如皋市	南通市振新精细化工有限公司	145	如东县	南通市天时化工有限公司
101	海门市	海门海螺水泥有限责任公司	146	海安县	海安县威仕重型机械有限公司
102	如皋市	江苏英田集团	147	如东县	江苏苏中电池科技发展有限公司
103	海门市	南通联普化学有限公司	148	如东县	如东富强针织印染有限公司
104	通州区	江苏韩通船舶重工有限公司	149	海安县	欧贝黎新能源科技股份有限公司
105	海安县	南通华强布业有限公司	150	如皋市	南通华东油压科技有限公司
106	如皋市	江苏意瑞达纺织科技有限公司	151	如皋市	南通中技桩业有限公司
107	崇川区	南通中远川崎船舶工程有限公司	152	海门市	南通四海植物精华有限公司
108	海安县	南通双弘纺织有限公司	153	通州区	江苏省银河面粉有限公司
109	启东市	南通柏盛化工有限公司	154	开发区	南通光明钢丝制品有限公司
110	如东县	江苏快达农化股份有限公司	155	海门市	海门市麒龙机械制造有限公司
111	港闸区	江苏大生集团有限公司	156	开发区	南通市帅龙钢绳有限公司
112	如皋市	南通长江镍矿精选有限公司	157	启东市	启东金美化学有限公司
113	如皋市	如皋市大行热电有限公司	158	通州区	南通鸿劲金属铝业有限公司
114	通州区	南通市通州区恒发印花有限责任公司	159	启东市	启东晋盛大公化工有限公司
115	如东县	南通强生轻工集团有限公司	160	海门市	南通欣昌家居饰品有限公司
116	海安县	卡姆丹克太阳能(江苏)有限公司	161	海门市	南通金秀铜材有限公司
117	开发区	南通振华重型装备制造有限公司	162	通州区	南通恒信铸锻有限公司
118	如皋市	如皋市宏茂铸钢有限公司	163	如皋市	江苏海纶染整有限公司
119	崇川区	江苏宏信化工有限公司	164	开发区	南通中集大型储罐有限公司
120	启东市	天同精细化工(南通)有限公司	165	崇川区	南通润达特阔染整有限公司
121	如皋市	南通宝众宝达药业有限公司	166	通州区	南通圣宝杰纺织印染有限公司
122	崇川区	南通佳禾染整有限公司	167	海门市	海门容汇通用锂业有限公司
123	如皋市	南通荣威娱乐用品有限公司	168	如皋市	如皋市泰尔特染整有限公司
124	海门市	海门市新龙锻压件有限公司	169	开发区	南通同方半导体有限公司
125	港闸区	江苏南通二棉有限公司	170	开发区	南通金利油脂工业有限公司
126	海门市	南通龙翔化工有限公司	171	如皋市	南通泰利达化工有限公司
127	开发区	江苏长江钢绳有限公司	172	海安县	海安县鹰球粉末冶金有限公司
128	开发区	迈图高新材料(南通)有限公司	173	启东市	江苏云帆化工有限公司
129	通州区	江苏大富豪酿酒科技发展有限公司	174	启东市	启东华拓药业有限公司
130	启东市	江苏科本医药化学有限公司	175	启东市	南通帝星化工有限公司
131	启东市	启东亚太化工厂有限公司	176	如皋市	如皋市五山漂染有限公司
132	通州区	南通云花色织有限公司	177	通州区	南通乐彩颜料化工有限公司
133	海门市	海门市声荣纺织印染有限公司	178	启东市	江苏启和化工有限公司
134	海安县	海安县中山合成纤维有限公司	179	如皋市	江苏熔盛重工有限公司
135	海门市	南通顾艺印染有限公司	180	如东县	如东县海宇纤维制品有限公司

9-15 续表 2

CONTINUED 2

序号 No.	地区 District	法人单位名称 Enterprise
181	启东市	启东市沪东化工有限公司
182	海安县	中平神马江苏新材料科技有限公司
183	启东市	南通协鑫热熔胶有限公司
184	港闸区	宝钢集团南通线材制品有限公司
185	启东市	南通远航医药化工有限公司
186	启东市	南通腾达服装粘合剂有限公司
187	启东市	江苏依柯化工有限公司
188	开发区	南通汇羽丰新材料有限公司
189	海安县	江苏鹏飞集团股份有限公司
190	开发区	南通东亚染整有限公司
191	如皋市	江苏威盛特钢铸锻有限公司
192	启东市	启东博文工程塑料有限公司
193	如东县	南通巴大饲料有限公司
194	开发区	马可迅(南通)车轮有限公司
195	如皋市	如皋市西东色织厂有限公司
196	海门市	南通市争妍颜料化工有限公司
197	如皋市	南通玉兔集团有限公司
198	如东县	英瑞纤维(南通)有限公司
199	如皋市	南通爱康太阳能器材有限公司
200	通州区	中纺国际(南通)实业有限公司
201	开发区	江苏泰力钢绳有限公司
202	如东县	南通昌邦手套有限公司
203	如皋市	江苏力星通用钢球股份有限公司
204	开发区	南通迪爱生色料有限公司
205	开发区	南通东星皮革有限公司
206	如东县	南通康福特纺织有限公司
207	海门市	金轮科创股份有限公司
208	崇川区	南通东邦纺织品有限公司
209	海门市	海门市海天纸业有限公司
210	如东县	爱德士鞋业江苏有限公司
211	如皋市	江苏长寿集团股份有限公司
212	通州区	南通博达特阔印染有限公司
213	海门市	南通大力神钢绳有限公司
214	港闸区	江苏永兴多媒体有限公司
215	开发区	江苏弘扬钢丝制品有限公司
216	开发区	南通南辉电子材料有限责任公司
217	开发区	东丽高新聚化(南通)有限公司
218	如东县	南通振新颜料有限公司
219	启东市	恒升化工(启东)有限公司
220	海安县	江苏省华强纺织有限公司
221	启东市	南通宝凯化工有限公司
222	开发区	南通开发区升阳金属制品有限公司
223	开发区	南通尼达威斯供热有限公司
224	开发区	中天科技光纤有限公司
225	海门市	龙舜印染(南通)有限公司
226	通州区	南通大来印染有限公司
227	启东市	启东东岳药业有限公司
228	启东市	启东市宝驹动力机械厂
229	开发区	南通江天化学品有限公司
230	如东县	如东振丰奕洋化工有限公司
231	海门市	海门瑞丰颜料有限公司
232	海安县	江苏海建股份有限公司
233	如东县	南通瑶华纤维有限公司
234	如皋市	南通市宇强金属制品有限公司
235	通州区	南通市禧瑞印染有限公司
236	开发区	南通市宇翔特种钢丝钢绳有限公司
237	如皋市	南通泰慕士服装有限公司
238	海门市	海门市利国玻璃制品有限责任公司
239	港闸区	南通中纺实业有限公司
240	如东县	江苏金太阳油脂有限责任公司
241	海门市	南通爱尔思轻合金精密成型有限公司
242	海安县	南通市京山锦纶有限公司
243	港闸区	南通新洋环保板业有限公司
244	如皋市	如皋市丹凤纺织有限公司
245	海安县	江苏双双布业有限公司
246	开发区	南通永高钢丝制品有限公司
247	如皋市	如皋市高诚化工有限公司
248	启东市	启东道达重工有限公司
249	如皋市	如皋市丁堰纺织有限公司
250	如东县	南通梦琦锐数码纺织有限公司
251	海门市	南通恒秀铝热传输材料有限公司
252	通州区	江苏大海塑料股份有限公司
253	启东市	南通莱嘉利化工有限公司
254	如皋市	南通天泽化工有限公司
255	开发区	南通市华星钢丝制品厂
256	启东市	启东市建国化纤纺织有限公司
257	港闸区	南通长扬建材有限责任公司
258	如东县	南通纬纶纺织有限公司
259	启东市	南通永安纺织有限公司
260	通州区	南通先盛宏针织品有限公司
261	如皋市	南通聚星铸锻有限公司
262	海安县	江苏飞亚化学工业有限责任公司
263	海门市	南通铭升印染有限公司
264	崇川区	南通纺织控股集团纺织染有限公司
265	如皋市	如皋市宏新医药原料有限公司
266	海安县	海安远东新材料有限公司
267	启东市	南通天恩化学科技有限公司
268	开发区	丸井织物(南通)有限公司

9-16 全社会用电情况(2014年)

单位:万千瓦时

指 标	Item	全市 Total
全社会用电总计	**Total**	**3332333**
全行业用电合计	**Farming, Forestry, Husbandry and Fishery**	**2895070**
第一产业	Mining	60022
第二产业	Manufacturing	2488788
第三产业	Production and Supply of Power, Heat, Gas and Water	346260
城乡居民生活用电合计	Construction	437263
城镇居民	Transportation, Storage and Postal Industry	159316
乡村居民	Information Transmission, Software and IT Service	277947
全行业用电分类	Wholesale and Retail	
农、林、牧、渔业	Accomodation and Catering Services	60022
工业	Banking	2428857
轻工业	Real Estate	988081
重工业	Leasing and Commercial Service	1440776
建筑业	S&T, Technic Services and Geological Survey	59931
交通运输、仓储和邮政业	Water, Environment and Public Facility Management	19924
信息传输、计算机服务和软件业	Service for Residents, Maintenance and Others	25769
商业、住宿和餐饮业	Education	111105
金融、房地产、商务及居民服务业	Health, Social Security and Social Welfare	83473
公共事业及管理组织	Culture, Sports and Entertainment	105989

TOTAL ELECTRICITY CONSUMPTION(2014)

(10000 kWh)

市区 Urban Area	通州区 Tongzhou	海安 Haian	如东 Rudong	启东 Qidong	如皋 Rugao	海门 Haimen
1368629	**476119**	**430136**	**419405**	**268669**	**457607**	**351180**
1206011	**406798**	**384783**	**369196**	**214689**	**386013**	**297671**
6788	5153	7656	25445	4812	6293	9028
1018490	366422	347670	318572	178985	336612	251751
180733	35223	29457	25179	30891	43108	36892
162618	69321	45353	50209	53980	71594	53509
86828	14140	12272	10323	17624	14888	17381
75790	55181	33081	39886	36356	56706	36128
6788	5153	7656	25445	4812	6293	9028
991734	356551	339608	313920	173500	327882	245506
425596	206136	140583	162993	56267	101994	88203
566138	150415	199025	150927	117233	225888	157303
26756	9871	8062	4652	5486	8730	6245
10702	1932	1422	2369	1511	2986	934
10569	3190	2414	2304	3356	3828	3298
45268	13721	13533	7920	10910	17028	16446
57220	4371	3817	4651	6628	4921	6236
56974	12009	8271	7935	8486	14345	9978

9-17 环境保护基本情况

指 标	Item
污染排放与处理利用情况	**Discharge and Utilization of Wastes**
废水	Waste Water
废水排放总量(万吨)	Total Discharge of Waster Water(10,000 ton)
工业废水排放量(万吨)	Discharge of Industial Waste Water(10,000 ton)
城镇生活污水排放量(万吨)	Discharge of Domestic Wastewater in Area(10,000 ton)
集中式治理设施污水排放量(万吨)	Discharge of Waste Water of Centralized Management Facilitles(10,000 ton)
化学需氧量排放量(吨)	Emission of Chemical Oxygen Demand(ton)
# 工业源	Industrial Source
农业源	Agrlcrltaral Source
城镇生活源	Urban Domestic Source
集中式治理设施	Centrallzed Management Facilities
氨氮排放量(吨)	Ammonia Nitrogen Emission
# 工业源	Industrial Source
农业源	Agricultaral Source
城镇生活源	Urban Domestic Source
集中式治理设施	Centrlized Management Facilities
废气	Waste Gas
二氧化硫排放量(吨)	SO_2 Emission(ton)
# 工业源	Industrial Source
城镇生活源	Urban Domestic Source
集中式治理设施	Centrlized Management Facilities
氮氧化物排放量(吨)	OXynitride Emission(tion)
# 工业源	Industrial Source
城镇生活源	Urban Domestic Source
机动车	Motorbike
集中式治理设施	Centrlized Management Facilities
烟(粉)尘排放量(吨)	Smoke(Dust) Emission
# 工业源	Industrial Source
城镇生活源	Urban Domestic Source
机动车	Motorbike
集中式治理设施	Centrlized Management Facilities
工业固体废物(万吨)	INdustrial Solicd Waste(10,000 ton)
一般工业固体废物产生量	General Industrial Solid Waste Generation
一般工业固体废物综合利用量	General Industrial Solid Waste Comprehensive Vtilization
# 综合利用往年贮存量	Comprehenslve Vtilization of Storage Capacity
一般工业固体废物综合利用率	Gentral Industrlal Solid Waste Comprehensive Utilization Rate
污染治理投资情况	**Investment in Pollution Abatement**
工业污染防治施工项目本年完成投资(万元)	Annual Investment of Industrial Pollution Prevention and Control Project
废水治理项目	Wastewater Treatment Project
废气治理项目	Wastegas Treatment Project
工业固体废物治理项目	Industrial Solid Waste Project
噪声治理项目	Noise Control Project
其它治理项目	Others
环保验收项目环保投资额	
废水治理设施运行费用	Operating Cost of Wastewater Thanagement Facility
废气治理设施运行费用	Operating Cost of Wastgas Mnangement Facility

BASIC SITUATION OF ENVIRONMENTAL PROTECTION

2010	2011	2012	2013	2014
46876	48457	47735	44478	46338
18884	19649	18200	14584	15809
27982	28798	29518	29877	30514
10.15	9.76	16.13	17.14	15.12
121622	119106	118909	112590	101060
27813	28075	27611	23954	23632
52948	51640	52344	51369	45624
40601	39131	38693	37014	31551
260.5	260.7	260.3	253.3	253.3
18236	18047	17648	16752	15752
1644	1666	1655	1094	982
7060	6985	6585	6497	6322
9501	9365	9376	9133	8420
31.3	31	31.3	28.5	28.5
69414	74271	72331	65145	64885
66808	71665	69821	63010	61812
2596	2596	2496	2121	3060
9	10	13	13	13
83047	84896	82830	71125	70949
66404	65807	64702	51706	50779
348	348	335	240	332
16251	18696	17748	19146	19804
45	45	45	33	33
54494	51586	37111	36439	43951
52116	49053	34652	33970	41362
1017	1017	978	978	1200
1353	1470	1434	1481	1379
8	46	47	10	10
344.94	464.95	447.48	438.52	507.56
301.34	453.23	438.86	429.61	499.05
0.01	0.01	0.08	0.01	0.01
87.36	97.48	98.06	97.97	98.32
11360	56927	43959	63219	79976
6515	19412	10045	24112	26227
1664	11056	21052	30346	52848
15	232	2087.5	544.91	210
1.5	6.2	52.3	7.8	0
3165	26221	10723	8208	691
—	124629	76073	216949	290412
33796	59437	62597	63382	69896
39262	64713	52805	58358	69857

9-18 分地区环境保护情况(2014 年)

指 标	Item	全市 Total
废水排放总量(万吨)	Total Discharge of Wastewater (10,000 tons)	46338
其中:工业	Of which: Industry	15809
化学需氧量排放量(吨)	Emission of Chemical Oxygen Demand (COD)	101060
单位 GDP 化学需氧量排放强度(千克/万元)	Per Unit GDP COD Emission Density (km/10,000 Yuan)	1.79
二氧化硫排放量(吨)	SO_2 Emission (ton)	64885
单位 GDP 二氧化硫排放强度(千克/万元)	Per Unit GDP SO_2 Emission Density (km/10,000 Yuan)	1.15
工业废气排放总量(亿标立方米)	Total Industrial Waste Gas Emission (10,000 million standard m^3)	2413
工业二氧化硫排放量(吨)	Industrial SO_2 Emission (ton)	61812
工业二氧化硫去除量	Industrial SO_2 Removal	183040
工业烟(粉)尘排放量(吨)	Industrial Smoke(Dust) Emission (ton)	41362
工业烟(粉)尘去除量	Industrial Smoke(Dust) Removal	2882921.06
工业固体废物产生量(万吨)	Industrial Solid Waste Generation (10,000 tons)	507.56
工业固体废物综合利用率(%)	Industrial Solid Waste Comprehensive Utilization Rate (%)	98.32
工业锅炉(台)	Industrial Boiler (set)	600.00
(蒸吨)	(ton vapor)	27940
工业窑炉(台)	Industrial Kiln (set)	523
空气质量达标天数(API<100)	Days with Standard Air Quality (API<100)	73
工业企业环境污染治理本年投资额(万元)	Annual Investment of Industrial Enterprises for Environmental Pollution Treatment (10,000 Yuan)	81755
三类以上地表水比例(%)	Above-Three-Level Surface Water Percentage (%)	73.50
自然保护区个数(个)	Natural Reserve Areas	1
自然保护区面积(百公顷)	Natural Researve Area (100 hectares)	215

注:城市空气质量优良以上天数。以 API 评价。市区空气质量优良天数包括崇川区、港闸区、开发区。

ENVIRONMENTAL PROTECTION BY REGION(2014)

市区 Urban Area	通州区 Tongzhou	海安 Haian	如东 Rudong	启东 Qidong	如皋 Rugao	海门 Haimen
23703	5119	3311	5078	4092	5892	4262
7529	2481	1107	1865	1468	2693	1147
25084	13739	17687	15705	10073	22312	10199
1.20	1.60	2.83	2.55	1.37	3.00	1.22
27198	5026	8111	5271	11100	7310	5894
1.30	0.58	1.30	0.86	1.51	0.98	0.70
1186	72	89	141	527	300	169
26173	4618	7295	5061	10282	7208	5792
125711	939	2566	7195	39643	3556	4368
12919	3590	3373	5531	5204	11067	3268
1538928.28	34186.01	59020.89	70208.03	1073751.89	42489.12	98522.87
249.82	20.17	22.03	26.97	136.05	56.17	16.52
98.40	97.50	96.14	98.83	98.05	99.01	99.09
174	83	52	119	50	122	83
16500	567	635	928	8439	788	649
185	79	58	101	45	102	32
71	68	70	77	81	73	73
52081	36	4570	12051	6991		6063
75.00	25.00	100.00	71.40	75.00	71.40	66.70
				1		
				215		

主要统计指标解释

能源消费量 指能源使用单位在报告期内实际消费的一次能源或二次能源的数量。就每种能源的实物消耗而言,是其消费量;如果将实际消费的各种能源折标准量相加所得到的能源消费量合计数据是企业投入消费的全部能源,没有扣除能源品种加工转换的重复因素。耗能工质(如水、氧气、压缩空气等),不论是外购的还是自产自用的,均不统计在能源消费量中。

工业生产能源消费 指工业企业为进行工业生产活动所消费的能源。主要包括:(1)用于本企业产品生产、工业性作业的能源,包括用作原料、材料、燃料、动力;作为能源加工转换企业,还包括用作加工转换的能源。(2)产品生产过程中作为辅助材料使用的能源。(3)生产工艺过程使用的能源。(4)新技术研究、新产品试制、科学试验使用的能源。(5)为了工业生产活动而在进行的各种修理过程中使用的能源。(6)生产区内的劳动保护用能等。

非工业生产能源消费 指在工业企业能源消费中,除"工业生产能源消费"以外的能源消费,即非工业生产用能和工业企业附属的不从事工业生产活动的非独立核算单位用能。比如本企业施工单位进行技术更新改造、维修等过程用能,非生产区的劳动保护用能,科研单位、农场、车队、学校、医院、食堂、托儿所等单位用能。但是必须注意,上述单位如果是独立核算的,其用能既不能包括在"工业企业能源消费"中,亦不能包括在"非工业生产能源消费"中。生产交通运输工具的企业(如造船厂、汽车制造厂),向成品轮船、汽车中添加动力用油,应算作企业的非工业生产消费。

能源加工、转换投入 能源加工、转换是为了特定的用途,将一种能源(一般为一次能源),经过一定的工艺,加工或转换成另外一种能源(二次能源)。

用作能源加工、转换的能源不能算作用于原材料。两者的区别是:用作加工、转换,投入的是能源,产出的主要产品还是能源,或产出的产品属于加工、转换过程中产生的不作能源使用的其他副产品和联产品。而用作原材料时,投入的是能源,产出的主要产品却是能源范畴以外的产品,包括产出的某种产品在广义上可以用作能源(比如可以燃烧以提供热量),但通常意义上不作能源使用的产品。

能源加工转换产出量 指经过能源加工转换装置产出的二次能源产品(包括不作能源使用的其他副产品和联产品),比如火力发电产出的电力,热电联产同时产出的电力、蒸汽、热水,洗煤产出的洗精煤、洗中煤、洗煤泥等,炼焦产出的焦炭、焦炉煤气和其他焦化产品,炼油产出的汽油、煤油、柴油、燃料油、液化石油气、炼厂干气和其他石油制品(石脑油、各种原料油、溶剂油、石蜡、润滑油、石油沥青等),制气产出的是焦炉煤气、其他煤气、焦炭和其他焦化产品(煤焦油、粗苯等)。

用作原材料的能源消费 指能源产品不作能源使用,即不作燃料、动力使用,而作为生产另外一种产品(非能源产品)的原料或作为辅助材料使用,作原料使用时通常构成这种产品的实体。它与用作加工、转换的区别是:用作加工、转换,投入的是能源,产出的主要产品还是能源(或产出的产品属于加工、转换过程中产生的不作能源使用的其他副产品和联产品)。而用作原材料时,投入的是能源,产出的主要产品却是能源范畴以外的产品,包括产出的某种产品在广义上可以用作能源(比如可以燃烧以提供热量),但通常意义上不作能源使用的产品。

综合能源消费量 指报告期内工业企业在工业生产活动中实际消费的各种能源的总和净值。计算综合能源消费量时,需要先将使用的各种能源折算成标准燃料后再进行计算。

综合能源消费量=工业生产消费的能源合计-加工转换产出能源合计 -回收利用能源合计。

终端能源消费量 是全国能源平衡表和地区能源平衡表中使用的概念,能源消费分两个部分,即加工转换消费和终端消费。终端能源消费,是在能源核算时,为反映能源的实际消费情况而设置的一个综合指标,它是指没有经过加工转换的一次能源或经过加工转换后的二次能源直接用作原料、材料、燃料、动力以及工艺性消费的数量,不包括用于加工转换的能源。

标准煤 亦称煤当量,指具有统一规定的标准热值的一种能源标准计量单位。我国规定每千克标准煤的热值为 7000 千卡。将不同品种、不同含量的能源按各自不同的热值,以 7000 千卡为一个计量单位换算成标准燃料,即为标准煤。

当量值 是指某种能源本身所含的热量,当量热值是固定不变的。

等价值 是指为了获得一个度量单位的某种二次能源(如汽油、柴油、电力、蒸气等)或耗能工质(如压缩空气、氧气、各种水等)所消耗的以热值表示的一次能源量。等价热值,实质上是除当量热值外,加上了能源转换过程中的能量损失,因此等价热值是个变动值,它与能源加工转换技术有关。随着技术水平的提高,等价值会不断降低,而趋向于二次能源所具有的能量。等价值可由下面的计算公式求得:等价热值当量热值/转化效率。

单位 GDP 能耗 是反映能源消费水平和节能降耗状况的主要指标,指一定时期内一个国家(地区)每生产一个单位的国内(地区)生产总值所消耗的能源。

计算公式为:单位 GDP 能耗=$\frac{\text{能源消费总量}}{\text{GDP}}$(注:十二五期间,GDP 均按 2010 年价格计算)

单位 GDP 能耗上升或下降(±%)=($\frac{\text{能源消费总量增长指数}}{\text{GDP 增长指数}}$-1)×100%

单位 GDP 电耗 是指一定期内一个国家(地区)每生产一个单位的国内(地区)生产总值所消耗的电力。

计算公式为:单位 GDP 电耗=$\frac{\text{全社会用电量}}{\text{GDP}}$(注:十二五期间,GDP 均按 2010 年价格计算)

单位 GDP 电耗上升或下降(±%)=($\frac{\text{全社会用电量增长指数}}{\text{GDP 增长指数}}$-1)×100%

取水量 指工业企业法人单位从各种水源实际提取的新水量。取水源包括地表水、地下水、自来水、污水处理达标水、未达标污水、收集雨水利用、以及企业从市场购得的其他水或水的产品(如纯净水、矿泉水等)。工业取水量包括采盐业所取的海水、汲取的地下卤水、盐湖水,包括海水淡化企业所取的海水,包括自来水生产企业所取的地表水和地下水,包括污水处理厂处理的污水。

取水量不包括重复用水量;不包括企业采自河流、水库、湖泊、海洋的水用于冷却,不重复使用,又排回到河流、水库、湖泊、海洋的水,我们称之为河湖海冷却水;不包括水力发电厂的发电动力用水量。

取水量按取水企业和供水单位商定的结算水表的流量计算。如没有水表,应按取水企业和供水单位商定的、或有关管理部门规定的计算方法计算取水量。

外供水量 指供水单位向用水单位提供的符合用水单位质量要求的水量。主要有自来水生产企业向城镇用户供应的自来水量;或者是纯净水、矿泉水生产企业向社会销售的产品水量;或者是污水处理厂将污水处理后得到的中水或符合用户要求标准的水质向用户单位提供的水量;或者是海水淡化水企业外供的淡化水量,或者是一些工业企业提取的低下水、地表水向外单位用户提供的水量。不包括向自然界直接排放的水量。

地表水 指河流、湖泊、水库、海洋等地表水源的水。地表水分为淡水和咸水。海水和内陆咸水湖的水为咸水。一般的河流、湖泊、水库的水是淡水。

地下水 指在地质岩层或土层中的水源,地下水的开采一般是通过钻井从地下抽取水量。地下水也分为淡水和咸水。

自来水 指地表水、地下水等经过供水企业加工处理,经认定达到自来水供水标准,通过城镇自来水管道网供应的水。

其他水 指上述水源没有涵盖的,或者界定不清的水。比如一些产品水,如纯净水、矿泉水、海水淡化水,或者污水处理厂处理的水等。其他水不应包括茶饮料、碳酸饮料、果汁饮料、酒类等大量用水的产品。

重复用水量 工业企业重复用水量就是指在企业内部,对生产和生活排放的废水直接或经过处理后回收再利用的水量,不包括企业从城市污水处理厂购买的中水或符合企业用水标准的水。企业废水在报告期每重复利用一次,计算一次重复用水量。重复用水量不包括河湖海冷却水用量。

河湖海冷却水用量 指企业采自河流、水库、湖泊、海洋的水用于冷却,不重复使用,又直接排回到的河流、水库、湖泊、海洋的水。河湖海冷却水用量是作为单独一项指标统计,不应包含在取水量的指标中。河湖海冷却水用量一般多见于发电厂。

废水排放量 指用水单位将所取水使用后,向本单位外排放的水量。废水排放可能经过本企业的净化处理,达到环保排放标准,也可能没有经过净化处理排放。废水排放量不包括河湖海冷却水。

废水排放量企业有计量装置的,按计量装置计量数据计算排放量。没有计量装置的,应依据有关管理部门规定的计算方法计算排水量,如没有具体的计算方法规定,可将取水量视为排水量填报。

废水处理达标水排放量 指用水单位所用的水,经过污水处理达到环保部门认可排放标准的水,向本单位外排放的水量。

废水未处理或未达标排放量 指用水单位所用的水,未经污水处理或经简单处理却没有达到环保部门认可排放标准的水,向本单位外排放的水量。

第十篇 农 业

Chapter 10

Agriculture

10-1 主要年份农村基本情况

BASIC STATISTICS ON RURAL AREAS IN MAIN YEARS

年份 Year	乡镇个数(个) Number of Villages and Towns	镇个数 Number of Towns	乡村从业人员 (万人) Rural Employment (10,000 persons)	农林牧渔业劳动力 Labors of Agriculture, Forestry, Husbandry and Fishery	工业劳动力 Labors of Industry	建筑业劳动力 Labors of Construction Industry
1949			227.75	217.39		
1952			246.12	236.14		
1957			264.21	250.13		
1962			249.67	232.03		
1965			277.00	266.43		
1970			331.83	325.86		
1975	300	21	344.44	328.87		
1978	300	21	353.51	306.22	25.78	
1980	301	21	363.10	300.59	33.33	
1985	293	31	395.00	242.80	70.64	33.13
1990	284	60	404.91	240.98	67.68	41.74
1991	285	62	408.48	248.72	63.98	42.16
1992	278	72	403.98	241.86	63.76	41.14
1993	276	74	391.85	230.83	62.26	41.96
1994	276	89	388.53	224.62	61.62	44.38
1995	255	94	383.33	210.54	62.23	48.76
1996	254	101	378.97	207.81	59.81	50.02
1997	254	101	376.24	204.70	56.72	51.80
1998	253	102	374.93	203.37	53.27	52.94
1999	253	105	371.94	201.74	50.48	53.74
2000	165	115	369.19	197.99	48.95	55.45
2001	145	133	368.11	193.47	51.24	57.60
2002	144	135	360.62	183.41	52.84	58.82
2003	139	130	357.89	170.50	60.25	61.96
2004	131	125	353.96	156.71	65.57	65.28
2005	125	121	350.59	131.59	68.45	64.95
2006	125	121	342.09	105.38	72.67	64.49
2007	122	118	340.20	94.49	78.75	65.54
2008	109	105	336.53	87.45	79.36	65.49
2009	104	102	333.94	82.21	82.28	65.67
2010	101	99	327.42	78.34	85.91	66.03
2011	95	93	317.41	74.20	82.01	62.31
2012	84	82	312.42	71.35	83.45	62.40
2013	75	73	306.30	68.84	82.19	62.98
2014	75	73	302.30	66.66	83.54	62.21

10-2 主要年份耕地、播种面积

ARABLE AND SOWN AREA IN MAIN YEARS

单位:千公顷 (Unit: 1000 hectares)

年份 Year	年末实有 耕地面积 Year-end Real Arable Land	农作物 总播种面积 Total Sown Area for Crops	经济作物 Cash Crops
1949	573.57	1114.82	
1952	578.94	1133.10	
1957	567.71	1083.77	
1962	505.08	1024.47	
1965	501.50	919.07	
1970	491.58	988.69	
1975	482.57	966.10	
1978	482.15	925.67	222.50
1980	480.47	918.78	226.50
1985	472.22	950.17	193.47
1990	471.10	935.37	211.06
1991	471.12	937.06	217.77
1992	470.55	932.54	219.46
1993	469.38	921.44	195.36
1994	468.67	907.96	192.29
1995	467.32	905.77	199.72
1996	466.41	910.26	194.72
1997	464.65	910.37	189.94
1998	464.09	902.24	179.38
1999	463.91	907.53	153.48
2000	482.83	902.76	167.99
2001	480.65	901.04	187.84
2002	480.13	891.45	176.20
2003	477.67	881.51	182.12
2004	475.07	876.21	189.08
2005	472.80	872.75	183.04
2006	470.11	857.58	179.23
2007	467.41	855.41	174.50
2008	465.98	851.96	178.31
2009	458.22	852.65	184.80
2010	446.10	854.96	184.43
2011	444.73	850.55	183.03
2012		846.98	177.54
2013		843.53	174.32
2014		835.55	166.57

10-3 主要年份粮、棉、油面积和产量

AREA AND OUTPUT OF GRAIN, COTTON AND OIL IN MAIN YEARS

年份 Year	粮食作物播种面积 (千公顷) Sown Area of Grain Crops (1000 hectares)	粮食产量 (万吨) Grain Output (10,000 tons)	棉花播种面积 (千公顷) Sown Area of Cotton (1000 hectares)	棉花产量 (吨) Cotton Output (Ton)	油料作物播种面积 (千公顷) Sown Area of Oil Crops (1000 hectares)	油料产量 (吨) Oil Output (Ton)
1949	933.39	84.49	104.57	10445	22.55	19776
1952	878.80	104.15	165.79	42365	24.33	30537
1957	758.75	110.95	218.78	65080	18.90	31594
1962	746.36	119.58	152.07	41405	13.78	19785
1965	627.57	178.63	198.00	152540	14.89	28273
1970	679.91	191.81	199.97	129805	11.21	19565
1975	631.66	211.60	199.71	183985	14.07	26028
1978	590.29	230.50	198.88	203160	14.77	43395
1980	578.20	219.82	197.71	129915	15.57	32359
1985	648.39	273.90	120.19	69392	37.05	91528
1990	628.18	300.73	118.63	91611	72.97	187780
1991	632.64	289.00	123.44	109996	75.84	187492
1992	627.82	317.40	125.77	121577	73.21	201823
1993	633.15	316.58	102.69	82201	81.81	192362
1994	624.30	317.70	99.35	89180	87.35	218234
1995	619.10	329.96	103.40	102800	91.89	248169
1996	629.02	349.48	98.06	115130	93.38	255738
1997	633.33	353.56	94.38	95294	92.32	241859
1998	629.27	326.36	81.34	73966	94.71	189034
1999	648.43	359.63	35.63	27372	113.60	328448
2000	606.07	340.60	30.13	32494	132.87	394091
2001	570.79	324.49	38.03	44782	145.08	361324
2002	563.32	309.53	27.19	33103	144.02	357099
2003	544.47	293.21	32.63	40759	144.74	405958
2004	535.00	302.70	39.70	52685	143.84	433999
2005	541.35	294.19	41.30	51115	137.60	406727
2006	544.71	302.65	53.53	68626	122.41	370582
2007	541.57	297.47	58.21	78399	114.55	347016
2008	535.88	319.12	48.52	67562	127.34	380659
2009	531.41	320.62	44.75	53091	137.46	425533
2010	528.78	324.94	44.04	59505	137.66	422056
2011	525.61	329.12	45.84	54395	134.65	399950
2012	522.23	332.97	42.82	55275	132.12	391950
2013	519.67	333.46	40.16	50657	131.53	408370
2014	515.56	334.02	37.21	43644	126.81	390637

10-4 主要年份畜禽、水果、水产品生产情况

PRODUCTION OF LIVESTOCK, FRUITS AND AQUATIC PRODUCTS IN MAIN YEARS

年份 Year	生猪出栏量 （万头） Pigs for Slaughter （10,000）	生猪存栏量 （万头） Pigs in Stock （10,000）	肉类产量 （万吨） Meat Production （10,000 tons）	禽蛋产量 （万吨） Egg Production （10,000 tons）	蚕茧产量 （吨） Silkworm Cocoon Production（ton）	水果产量 （吨） Fruit Production （ton）	水产品产量 （吨） Output of Aquatic Products（ton）
1949	48.08	59.70			65	3013	20800
1952	59.73	96.41			283	3956	40400
1957	73.82	107.31			549	4357	55000
1962	29.35	94.40			193	2576	45400
1965	116.54	186.78			465	2059	64700
1970	129.06	257.50			3052	5210	81300
1975	210.42	292.15			4719	6973	105600
1978	193.16	310.23	11.07	1.94	5807	8710	105200
1980	297.73	265.40	16.37	1.87	8795	10581	106800
1985	292.34	244.48	21.62	7.00	19603	28651	129000
1990	231.42	212.96	21.71	8.33	32594	44260	181800
1991	227.17	218.32	21.70	10.48	35914	37930	200700
1992	222.38	235.75	22.32	11.47	34908	51744	232800
1993	232.77	225.61	22.79	13.60	41459	56514	263200
1994	214.44	209.97	26.12	17.96	45909	69731	325200
1995	217.91	218.78	30.36	21.12	41866	91761	388300
1996	203.54	208.92	31.74	25.06	28122	110904	536200
1997	208.33	237.08	25.92	29.11	27008	110210	549400
1998	235.33	247.86	27.76	24.49	28496	106243	547900
1999	250.23	243.01	28.93	28.76	27483	118834	581487
2000	257.93	254.80	30.17	35.31	30253	120491	585557
2001	265.61	267.16	31.10	37.30	37048	130302	601834
2002	275.48	273.94	32.10	41.31	41076	131333	614805
2003	285.43	278.22	32.65	42.77	40905	139337	629950
2004	293.60	285.40	35.95	40.55	45192	104079	667583
2005	304.29	289.83	37.13	42.01	42625	102065	691597
2006	347.28	271.76	44.91	44.05	53360	116462	722763
2007	302.22	283.61	42.90	44.68	45924	118855	757956
2008	327.47	289.19	44.00	45.48	43371	110974	760205
2009	348.35	293.25	44.91	45.47	32632	173031	760002
2010	357.28	284.89	46.39	45.81	34383	173893	789225
2011	371.43	299.98	47.70	45.73	29100	184659	820850
2012	391.38	298.53	49.44	45.93	27229	189967	847774
2013	379.28	276.87	47.89	45.67	21175	193085	867147
2014	394.71	270.76	49.48	45.68	20008	193184	882069

10-5 蚕茧、水果生产情况(2014年)

PRODUCTION OF SILKWORM COCOON AND FRUITS(2014)

指 标	Item	全市 Whole City	市区 Urban Areas	通州区 Tongzhou	海安 Haian	如东 Rudong	启东 Qidong	如皋 Rugao	海门 Haimen
蚕桑	**Silkworm Cocoons**								
蚕茧产量(吨)	Output (ton)	20008	437	437	11228	1625	334	6216	168
年末实有桑园面积(公顷)	Actual Area of Mulberry Field(hectare)	12259	267	267	5933	1333	367	4059	300
水果产量(吨)	**Fruits (ton)**	**193184**	**74268**	**69689**	**13890**	**54440**	**23377**	**11493**	**15716**
#苹果	Apple (ton)								
梨	Pears (ton)	67677	3653	3499	6000	37520	17665	1800	1039
柑橘	Tangerines (ton)	13940	9927	9405	40	320	2230	35	1388
葡萄	Grapes (ton)	49045	23421	21587	3000	5100	2000	8000	7524
桃子	Peaches (ton)	29968	17612	16358	450	7550	1350	1600	1406
猕猴桃	Kiwi Fruirt (ton)	2201	179	179	50		12		1960
年末实有果园面积(公顷)	**Areas of Orchards (hectare)**	**9691.7**	**1513**	**1313**	**1110**	**2485**	**1380**	**1985**	**1219**
#苹果园	Apples								
梨园	Pears	3209.47	78	73	320	1720	863	90	138.47
柑橘园	Citrus	524.33	141	113	7	55	193	4	124
葡萄园	Grapes	2570.3	916	821	233	320	153	420	528
桃园	Peaches	1061.57	290	227	40	325	137	113	156
猕猴桃园	Kiwifruit	202.63	35	35	3		1		163

10-6 主要年份农林牧渔业总产值

TOTAL OUTPUT OF AGRICULTURE,FORESTRY,HUSBANDRY AND FISHERY

单位:亿元 (Unit: 100 million Yuan)

年份 Year	农林牧渔业总产值 Total Output of Agriculture, Forestry, Husbandry and Fishery	农业 Farming	林业 Forestry	牧业 Animal Husbandry	渔业 Fishery	农林牧渔服务业 Related Service Industry
1985	34.66	22.11	0.51	9.80	2.24	
1986	39.45	27.35	0.45	8.34	3.31	
1987	43.67	28.52	0.55	10.24	4.36	
1988	60.75	38.09	0.57	16.80	5.29	
1989	63.35	39.07	0.48	17.53	6.27	
1990	69.77	43.78	0.53	18.96	6.50	
1991	71.12	43.39	0.48	19.75	7.50	
1992	81.38	49.79	0.75	21.12	9.72	
1993	101.53	59.28	0.79	25.62	15.84	
1994	169.43	89.88	1.07	49.97	28.51	
1995	219.90	118.22	1.63	58.89	41.16	
1996	242.15	131.73	1.82	57.87	50.73	
1997	231.27	128.28	1.70	49.11	52.18	
1998	235.58	128.13	1.35	49.07	57.03	
1999	241.37	133.55	1.55	49.11	57.16	
2000	246.88	134.14	1.45	52.17	59.12	
2001	257.36	143.95	3.11	52.00	58.30	
2002	267.86	147.85	3.43	56.08	60.50	
2003	241.86	108.47	1.78	60.22	61.76	9.63
2004	277.56	122.88	1.78	73.97	68.27	10.66
2005	292.69	126.69	1.92	77.98	74.27	11.83
2006	305.41	129.58	2.33	83.19	77.80	12.51
2007	324.50	136.04	2.61	89.89	82.26	13.70
2008	395.10	162.56	2.89	112.11	97.71	19.83
2009	420.58	175.94	3.06	113.21	105.88	22.49
2010	467.11	207.46	3.00	118.99	113.10	24.56
2011	502.27	217.93	3.07	133.02	118.47	29.78
2012	548.86	243.71	3.38	130.48	131.00	40.29
2013	594.78	263.63	3.73	138.25	141.11	48.06
2014	631.88	278.94	4.07	145.07	147.83	55.97

注:本表按当年价格计算。

Note:Data in this table is calculated at current prices.

10-7 主要年份分地区农林牧渔业总产值

单位:亿元

年份 Year	全市 Whole City	市区 Urban Areas	通州区 Tongzhong
1985	34.66	8.81	8.20
1986	39.45	9.40	8.67
1987	43.67	9.12	8.31
1988	60.75	11.97	10.90
1989	63.35	11.98	10.75
1990	69.77	13.73	12.53
1991	71.12	14.38	12.32
1992	81.38	15.58	13.35
1993	101.53	18.46	15.92
1994	169.43	31.57	27.83
1995	219.90	41.56	36.61
1996	242.15	47.94	42.71
1997	231.27	43.23	37.65
1998	235.58	43.75	38.33
1999	241.37	45.61	40.00
2000	246.88	47.06	41.27
2001	257.36	48.68	38.24
2002	267.86	50.75	40.02
2003	241.86	36.89	30.71
2004	277.56	41.71	34.69
2005	292.69	44.31	36.93
2006	305.41	46.43	39.28
2007	324.50	49.44	41.70
2008	395.10	61.93	53.20
2009	420.58	65.29	56.91
2010	467.11	72.03	63.02
2011	502.27	77.56	68.67
2012	548.86	83.87	75.25
2013	594.78	90.06	81.97
2014	631.88	95.43	88.18

注:本表按当年价格计算。

Note:Data in this table is calculated at current prices.

REGIONAL TOTAL OUTPUT OF AGRICULTURE, FORESTRY, HUSBANDRY AND FISHERY IN MAIN YEARS

(Unit: 100 million Yuan)

海安 Haian	如东 Rudong	启东 Qidong	如皋 Rugao	海门 Haimen
4.79	6.68	5.04	5.32	4.02
5.07	7.49	6.62	6.29	4.58
5.43	9.59	7.34	6.89	5.30
8.09	14.52	9.83	8.79	7.55
7.83	14.66	11.39	9.12	8.37
9.61	15.13	12.09	10.68	8.53
9.62	16.34	12.29	11.17	7.32
11.03	18.05	15.94	12.61	8.17
11.66	22.66	22.53	14.51	11.71
23.70	34.99	36.16	25.02	17.99
28.68	44.40	49.69	30.30	25.27
31.54	49.23	53.67	32.90	26.87
31.77	46.30	50.24	30.60	29.13
32.56	46.86	51.78	30.31	30.32
33.24	47.51	52.91	31.01	31.09
33.82	47.69	54.79	31.06	32.46
35.19	50.00	56.89	32.37	34.23
36.55	52.30	58.11	33.99	36.16
38.64	50.10	50.85	34.04	31.34
46.05	57.04	57.27	39.95	35.54
47.73	58.98	61.22	42.38	38.07
50.82	62.28	62.43	43.74	39.71
52.98	65.91	68.18	47.05	40.94
62.58	79.52	82.26	58.70	50.11
65.51	85.27	88.39	61.86	54.26
71.75	93.80	97.15	68.59	59.99
80.84	100.77	99.93	77.13	66.04
87.57	109.79	108.91	85.02	73.70
95.71	120.51	115.71	92.36	80.43
102.71	126.86	121.52	98.98	86.38

10-8 主要年份农村基本情况

指 标	Item	1990
农村组织情况(个)	**Rural Units(unit)**	
乡镇个数	Number of Township	262
#镇个数	Of Which: Town	38
村民委员会	Village Committees	4778
村民小组	Village Groups	52022
乡村户数、人口	**Households, Rural Population**	
乡村户数(万户)	Households(10000 units)	222.17
劳动年龄内人口数	Laborers	
#劳动年龄内上学的学生数	Students of Labor Age	
乡村从业人员(万人)	**Rural Laborers (10000 persons)**	**404.91**
#劳动年龄内从业人员	Persons of Labor Age	
按性别分	Grouped by Sex	
男	Male	203.39
女	Female	201.52
按行业分	Grouped by Sector	
农林牧渔业	Farming, Forestry, Animal Husbandry and Fishery	240.98
#种植业	Planting	206.99
工业	Industry	67.68
建筑业	Construction	41.74
交通运输业.仓储业和邮政业	Transportation,Storage, Post and Telecommunication	7.25
信息传输、计算机服务和软件业	Information Transmission, Computer Service and Software Industries	
批发、零售贸易业	Wholesale and Retail Trade	4.73
住宿和餐饮业	Accommodation and Catering	
金融、保险业	Banking and Insurance	0.32
房地产、社会服务业	Real Estate,Social Services	2.84
卫生、体育和社会福利业	Healthcare, Sports,and Social Welfare	1.11
教育、文化、艺术和广播电视事业	Education,Culture,Art and Radio,Film and Television	1.81
科学研究和综合技术服务事业	Scientific Research and Polytechnical Services	0.21
乡经济组织管理	Rural Economic Management	1.69
其他非农行业	Other Non-agricultural Seetors	34.55

BASIC STATISTICS ON RURAL AREAS IN MAIN YEARS

2000	2005	2006	2007	2008	2009	2010	2013	2014
165	125	125	122	109	104	101	75	75
115	121	121	118	105	102	99	73	73
4313	1843	1824	1646	1446	1420	1382	1317	1316
51001	44522	44291	41185	41082	40942	40130	39472	39625
214.45	215.70	214.40	214.10	214.28	213.53	212.61	202.42	200.68
356.57	335.57	325.20	321.94	316.72	313.96	310.07	290.81	289.31
9.80	10.97	11.68	12.00	12.12	12.41	13.29	13.76	14.01
369.19	**350.59**	**342.09**	**340.20**	**336.53**	**333.94**	**327.42**	**306.30**	**302.30**
332.61	315.02	303.97	300.03	294.16	289.22	287.97	265.77	261.68
186.05	177.41	173.86	172.68	170.88	168.81	166.15	156.13	153.53
183.14	173.18	168.23	167.52	165.65	165.13	161.27	150.17	148.77
197.99	131.59	105.38	94.49	87.45	82.21	78.34	68.84	66.66
164.23	102.54	86.30	76.36	71.09	66.05	62.61	53.73	51.50
49.95	68.45	72.67	78.75	79.36	82.28	85.91	82.19	83.54
55.45	64.95	64.49	65.54	65.49	65.67	66.03	62.98	62.21
10.09	15.55	16.79	16.85	17.65	17.52	16.76	17.10	16.80
	0.64	0.84	0.94	0.99	1.10	1.20	2.44	2.58
13.75	21.63	25.51	27.82	28.43	29.35	28.15	29.17	28.54
	4.30	5.11	5.36	5.69	5.64	6.11	7.19	6.91
0.31	0.74	0.85	0.80	0.89	1.05	1.08	1.42	1.49
3.88	6.75	8.37	8.60	8.56	9.11	7.37	6.32	6.21
0.98	1.10	1.20	1.13	1.20	1.19	1.28	1.52	1.52
0.93	0.99	1.10	1.01	1.13	1.17	1.17	1.57	1.58
0.26	0.33	0.35	0.37	0.36	0.43	0.41	0.62	0.63
1.63	1.06	1.10	1.16	1.10	1.14	1.23	1.29	1.38
33.97	32.51	38.33	37.38	38.23	36.08	32.38	23.65	22.25

10-9 分地区农村基本情况(2014年)

指 标	Item	全市 Whole City
农村组织情况(个)	**Rural Units (unit)**	
乡镇个数	Number of Township	75
#镇个数	Of Which: Town	73
村民委员会	Village Committees	1316
村民小组	Village Groups	39625
乡村户数、人口	**Households, Rural Population**	
乡村户数(万户)	Households(10000 units)	200.68
劳动年龄内人口数	Laborers	289.31
#劳动年龄内上学的学生数	Students of Labor Age	14.01
乡村从业人员(万人)	**Rural Laborers(10000 persons)**	**302.30**
#劳动年龄内从业人员	Persons of Labor Age	261.68
按性别分	Grouped by Sex	
男	Male	153.53
女	Female	148.77
按行业分	Grouped by Sector	
农林牧渔业	Farming, Forestry, Animal Husbandry and Fishery	66.66
#种植业	Planting	51.50
工业	Industry	83.54
建筑业	Construction	62.21
交通运输业.仓储业和邮政业	Transportation,Storage, Post and Telecommunication	16.80
信息传输、计算机服务和软件业	Information Transmission, Computer Service and Software Industries	2.58
批发、零售贸易业	Wholesale,Retail Sales	28.54
住宿和餐饮业	Accommodation and Catering	6.91
金融、保险业	Banking and Insurance	1.49
房地产、社会服务业	Real Estate,Social Services	6.21
卫生、体育和社会福利业	Healthcare, Sports,and Social Welfare	1.52
教育、文化、艺术和广播电视事业	Education,Culture,Art and Radio,Film and Television	1.58
科学研究和综合技术服务事业	Scientific Research and Polytechnical Services	0.63
乡经济组织管理	Rural Economic Management	1.38
其他非农行业	Other Non-agricultural Sectors	22.25

STATISTICS ON RURAL AREAS BY REGION(2014)

市区 Urban Areas	通州区 Tongzhou	海安 Haian	如东 Rudong	启东 Qidong	如皋 Rugao	海门 Haimen
19	19	10	14	12	11	9
19	19	10	14	11	11	8
238	208	207	213	261	166	231
10065	9304	5097	5627	6319	4322	8195
41.27	37.10	24.84	30.62	38.68	35.40	29.87
57.86	52.88	33.90	45.77	49.92	57.30	44.56
2.82	2.57	1.60	1.82	2.15	3.10	2.52
57.75	**52.75**	**37.45**	**47.86**	**50.15**	**60.10**	**48.99**
52.74	48.18	31.23	40.62	44.91	52.10	40.08
29.54	26.99	18.97	24.45	25.15	30.10	25.32
28.21	25.76	18.48	23.41	25.00	30.00	23.67
12.43	11.45	7.19	8.62	12.81	13.90	11.71
9.55	8.77	4.77	6.90	10.57	10.50	9.21
15.28	13.09	11.03	16.27	12.26	17.30	11.40
11.92	11.56	8.38	10.12	9.64	10.70	11.45
3.79	3.57	3.11	2.57	2.55	2.50	2.28
0.47	0.40	0.09	0.28	0.36	0.90	0.48
6.68	6.32	3.41	2.74	5.49	3.50	6.72
1.56	1.43	1.04	0.71	1.27	1.10	1.23
0.25	0.20	0.15	0.21	0.27	0.40	0.21
1.10	1.05	0.65	0.59	1.15	0.90	1.82
0.20	0.17	0.18	0.18	0.31	0.40	0.25
0.19	0.16	0.14	0.13	0.29	0.60	0.23
0.09	0.08	0.05	0.03	0.18	0.20	0.08
0.26	0.24	0.16	0.12	0.16	0.50	0.18
3.53	3.03	1.87	5.29	3.41	7.20	0.95

10-10　分地区农林牧渔业总产值及增加值(2014 年)

单位:亿元

指　标	Item	全市 Whole City
农林牧渔业总产值(现价)	**Total Output of Farming, Forestry, Husbandry &Fishery (Current Price)**	**631.88**
农业	Farming	278.94
谷物及其他农作物	Grain and Other Crops	140.12
# 谷物	Grain	91.07
薯类	Tuber Crops	2.92
油料	Oil	20.86
豆类	Beans	11.12
棉花	Cotton	8.96
蔬菜园艺作物	Vegetables and Horticultural Crops	110.31
# 蔬菜(含果用瓜)	Vegetables (Including Melons)	95.40
水果、坚果、饮料和香料作物	Fruits, Nuts, Beverage and Spice Crops	24.24
中药材	Chinese Medicine	4.27
林业	Forestry	4.07
牧业	Animal Husbandry	145.07
牲畜饲养	Livestock Breeding	28.17
# 羊	Sheep	27.08
猪的饲养	Pig Breeding	47.75
家禽饲养	Poultry Breeding	59.18
# 肉禽	Meat Poultry	19.82
禽蛋	Poultry Egg	39.35
其他畜牧业	Other Breeding	9.98
# 蚕茧	Silkworm Cocoon	8.49
渔业	Fishery	147.83
海水产品	Sea Products	92.93
内陆水域水产品	Inland Water Products	54.90
农林牧渔服务业	Service Industry for Farming, Forestry, Husbandry and Fishery	55.97
农林牧渔业增加值	**Added Value of Farming, Forestry, Husbandry and Fishery**	**367.11**
农业	Farming	197.12
林业	Forestry	2.41
牧业	Husbandry	56.60
渔业	Fishery	83.44
农林牧渔服务业	Service Industry for Farming, Forestry, Husbandry and Fishery	27.53

TOTAL OUTPUT AND ADDED VALUE OF FARMING, FORESTRY, ANIMAL HUSBANDRY AND FISHERY BY REGIONS(2014)

(Unit: 100 million Yuan)

市区 Urban Areas	通州区 Tongzhou	海安 Haian	如东 Rudong	启东 Qidong	如皋 Rugao	海门 Haimen
95.43	**88.18**	**102.71**	**126.86**	**121.52**	**98.98**	**86.38**
50.65	45.76	41.36	48.46	40.58	55.10	42.78
25.26	23.27	21.66	33.18	17.17	26.30	16.55
15.72	14.48	18.60	25.99	4.28	21.85	4.64
0.18	0.18	0.09	0.12	0.65	0.39	1.49
5.67	5.28	0.73	2.39	4.80	2.18	5.08
1.98	1.68	0.65	1.74	4.11	1.03	1.61
1.40	1.38	0.00	2.19	2.39	0.02	2.96
18.84	16.54	16.10	9.61	20.30	25.24	20.22
18.08	16.00	10.83	9.58	19.86	17.35	19.70
6.09	5.49	1.60	5.67	3.10	3.49	4.29
0.47	0.47	2.00	0.00	0.02	0.07	1.72
1.16	1.08	0.31	0.97	0.63	0.23	0.72
14.50	13.21	44.45	29.78	12.55	32.14	11.64
3.40	2.95	7.60	3.18	3.35	6.43	4.20
3.03	2.82	7.48	3.09	3.23	6.22	4.03
5.84	5.23	10.23	14.51	3.68	11.79	1.70
5.02	4.80	21.53	11.45	4.69	11.26	5.24
2.22	2.11	3.02	5.11	2.97	4.49	2.02
2.81	2.69	18.50	6.34	1.72	6.76	3.22
0.25	0.22	5.09	0.65	0.83	2.66	0.50
0.16	0.16	4.80	0.62	0.13	2.55	0.24
15.09	14.49	8.31	40.53	57.40	5.41	21.09
3.15	3.15	1.90	26.21	46.67		15.00
11.93	11.33	6.41	14.32	10.74	5.41	6.09
14.03	13.64	8.28	7.12	10.29	6.10	10.15
61.57	**57.05**	**56.00**	**65.30**	**68.55**	**61.14**	**54.55**
39.03	35.60	28.20	29.43	27.42	42.12	30.93
0.80	0.75	0.17	0.55	0.30	0.12	0.46
6.34	5.88	17.44	11.32	4.74	12.44	4.34
10.37	10.02	5.45	20.87	30.48	2.92	13.34
5.03	4.81	4.73	3.13	5.62	3.54	5.48

10-11 主要农产品生产情况(2014年)

单位:千公顷、公斤/公顷、吨

指 标	Item	全市 Municipality
农作物总播种面积	**Total Sown Areas of Farm Crops**	
粮食作物	**Grain Crops**	**515.56**
单产	Per hectare Output	6479
总产	Total Output	3340163
夏收粮食:播种面积	Summer Grain: Sown Areas	230.59
单产	Per hectare Output	5189
总产	Total Output	1196595
夏收谷物:播种面积	Summer Millet:Sown Areas	187.02
单产	Per hectare Output	5877
总产	Total Output	1099077
小麦:播种面积	Wheat:Sown Areas	171.78
单产	Per hectare Output	5905
总产	Total Output	1014392
元麦:播种面积	Hull-less Barley:Sown Areas	0.80
单产	Per hectare Output	4309
总产	Total Output	3447
大麦:播种面积	Barley:Sown Areas	14.44
单产	Per hectare Output	5626
总产	Total Output	81238
蚕豌豆:播种面积	Broad and Dea Beans:Sown Areas	43.57
单产	Per hectare Output	2238
总产	Total Output	97518
秋收粮食:播种面积	Autumn Grain:Sown Areas	284.97
单产	Per hectare Output	7522
总产	Total Output	2143568
秋收谷物:播种面积	Autumn Millet:Sown Areas	222.07
单产	Per hectare Output	8807
总产	Total Output	1955661

STATISTICS ON MAIN AGRICULTURAL PRODUCTS(2014)

(Unit: thousands of hectares, kg/hectare, ton)

市区 Urban Areas	通州区 Tongzhou	海安 Haian	如东 Rudong	启东 Qidong	如皋 Rugao	海门 Haimen
88.54	**79.60**	**78.95**	**132.03**	**68.44**	**108.79**	**38.81**
6609	6718	8122	7024	3650	6865	4886
585176	534737	641249	927414	249825	746880	189619
36.04	32.47	37.08	66.67	25.86	49.96	14.98
5157	5159	6630	5585	3000	5394	3037
185873	167520	245832	372343	77590	269470	45487
28.99	26.13	36.76	59.51	7.78	48.65	5.33
5697	5694	6654	5899	5953	5462	4922
165167	148785	244585	351042	46312	265736	26235
27.98	25.13	36.63	48.47	7.58	46.69	4.43
5703	5700	6656	5910	6005	5490	5130
159571	143241	243791	286458	45518	256328	22726
0.21	0.20			0.09		0.50
4990	4980			4067		4066
1048	996			366		2033
0.80	0.80	0.13	11.04	0.11	1.96	0.40
5685	5685	6108	5850	3891	4800	3690
4548	4548	794	64584	428	9408	1476
7.05	6.34	0.32	7.16	18.03	1.31	9.65
2937	2955	3897	2975	1730	2850	1995
20706	18735	1247	21301	31278	3734	19252
52.50	47.13	41.87	65.36	42.58	58.83	23.83
7606	7792	9444	8493	4045	8115	6048
399303	367217	395417	555071	172235	477410	144132
41.34	37.82	39.39	58.59	17.19	50.96	14.60
8989	9110	9746	9093	6207	8929	7237
371606	344531	383882	532788	106699	455031	105655

10-11 续表 1

单位：千公顷、公斤/公顷、吨

指 标	Item	全市 Municipality
稻谷：播种面积	Rice:Sown Areas	172.22
单产	Per hectare Output	9478
总产	Total Output	1632307
#粳稻：播种面积	Nonglutinous Rice:Sown Areas	167.24
单产	Per hectare Output	9476
总产	Total Output	1584848
玉米：播种面积	Corn:Sown Areas	48.95
单产	Per hectare Output	6548
总产	Total Output	320518
其他谷物：播种面积	Others:Sown Areas	0.72
单产	Per hectare Output	3486
总产	Total Output	2510
秋收豆类：播种面积	Autumn Beans:Sown Areas	55.94
单产	Per hectare Output	2471
总产	Total Output	138255
大豆：播种面积	Soybeans:Sown Areas	53.33
单产	Per hectare Output	2483
总产	Total Output	132442
绿豆：播种面积	Greenbeans:Sown Areas	0.17
单产	Per hectare Output	2241
总产	Total Output	381
红小豆：播种面积	Redbean:Sown Areas	2.44
单产	Per hectare Output	2226
总产	Total Output	5432
油料合计：播种面积	**Oil-bearing Crops:Sown Areas**	**126.81**
单产	Per hectare Output	3080
总产	Total Output	390637

CONTINUED 1

(Unit: thousands of hectares, kg/hectare, ton)

市区 Urban Areas	通州区 Tongzhou	海安 Haian	如东 Rudong	启东 Qidong	如皋 Rugao	海门 Haimen
34.18	31.47	36.96	52.90		46.74	1.44
9335	9450	9908	9480		9255	8997
319057	297382	366214	501492	10	432579	12955
30.82	28.11	36.52	51.75		46.71	1.44
9314	9441	9910	9481		9255	8997
287053	265378	361906	490624	10	432300	12955
7.16	6.35	2.42	5.68	17.15	3.89	12.65
7339	7425	7278	5502	6210	5475	7218
52549	47149	17613	31251	106501	21297	91307
			0.01	0.04	0.33	0.34
			4500	4700	3500	3300
			45	188	1155	1122
10.33	8.50	2.30	6.33	23.70	6.21	7.07
2384	2313	4252	3187	2281	2401	2082
24624	19661	9780	20171	54054	14909	14717
10.16	8.40	2.28	6.28	21.84	6.16	6.61
2388	2310	4230	3197	2280	2400	2100
24264	19404	9644	20077	49792	14784	13881
0.07	0.07	0.01	0.02	0.03		0.04
2443	2443	2900	1850	2133		2000
171	171	29	37	64		80
0.10	0.03	0.01	0.03	1.83	0.05	0.42
1890	2867	10700	1900	2294	2500	1800
189	86	107	57	4198	125	756
32.65	**30.32**	**3.84**	**14.96**	**32.65**	**14.12**	**28.59**
3246	3253	3985	3099	2872	2706	3187
105992	98633	15301	46367	93783	38207	90987

10-11 续表 2

单位：千公顷、公斤/公顷、吨

指　标	Item	全市 Municipality
花生：播种面积	Peanuts:Sown Areas	24.6
单产	Per hectare Output	3007
总产	Total Output	73960
油菜籽：播种面积	Rapeseed:Sown Areas	100.71
单产	Per hectare Output	3120
总产	Total Output	314252
芝麻：播种面积	Sesame:Sown Areas	1.5
单产	Per hectare Output	1617
总产	Total Output	2425
棉花(皮棉)：播种面积	**Cotton Crops:Sown Areas**	**37.21**
单产	Per hectare Output	1173
总产	Total Output	43644
糖料：播种面积	**Sugar Crops:Sown Areas**	**1.04**
单产	Per hectare Output	68902
总产	Total Output	71658
药材类：播种面积	**Crude Drugs:Sown Areas**	**1.3**
蔬菜类播种面积	**Vegetable:Sown Areas**	**124.13**
单产	Per hectare Output	31074
总产	Total Output	3857223
瓜果类播种面积	**Melon and Fruits Crops:Sown Areas**	**14.98**
单产	Per hectare Output	35765
总产	Total Output	535757
# 西瓜：播种面积	# Watermelon:Sown Areas	10.54
单产	Per hectare Output	39139
总产	Total Output	412522
其他农作物：播种面积	**Others:Sown Areas**	**14.52**
附：常年种蔬菜面积	Sown Areas of Vegetables Year-Round	50.58

CONTINUED 2

(Unit: thousands of hectares, kg/hectare, ton)

市区 Urban Areas	通州区 Tongzhou	海安 Haian	如东 Rudong	启东 Qidong	如皋 Rugao	海门 Haimen
4.45	3.90	0.44	1.68	8.21	3.51	6.31
2924	2865	3916	2450	3015	2500	3420
13013	11174	1723	4116	24753	8775	21580
27.71	26.09	3.39	13.19	24.04	10.57	21.81
3324	3330	4003	3185	2850	2778	3150
92095	86880	13571	42010	68514	29360	68702
0.49	0.33	0.01	0.09	0.40	0.04	0.47
1804	1755	700	2678	1290	1800	1500
884	579	7	241	516	72	705
5.76	**5.71**	**0.01**	**10.49**	**11.68**	**0.12**	**9.15**
1290	1290	1200	1125	1165	975	1166
7429	7366	12	11801	13615	117	10669
0.18	**0.14**			**0.37**		**0.49**
74394	76950			82568		56565
13391	10773			30550		27717
0.37	**0.37**	**0.29**		**0.07**	**0.02**	**0.55**
25.78	**22.75**	**16.38**	**10.48**	**29.29**	**18.39**	**23.81**
29119	29423	36263	43000	26886	35344	26225
750698	669373	593988	450640	787500	649980	624417
3.12	**2.41**	**0.69**	**2.16**	**3.11**	**1.77**	**4.13**
35340	34304	49093	42861	28571	48492	30110
110262	82673	33874	92580	88857	85830	124354
2.29	1.67	0.57	1.95	1.92	0.95	2.86
40143	40680	54600	41923	38076	50000	30460
91928	67936	31122	81750	73106	47500	87116
0.50	**0.04**	**2.51**	**0.15**	**2.12**	**7.90**	**1.34**
10.88	10.60	5.06	9.80	9.80	5.96	9.08

10-12 畜牧业生产情况(2014 年)

指　标	Item	全市 Municipality
大牲畜年末头数(万头)	Livestock of Large Animals (Year-End) (10000 units)	1.10
奶牛	Cow	0.75
水牛	Buffalo	0.32
当年出栏大牲畜头数(万头)	Livestock of Large Animals for Slaughter(Year-End) (10000 units)	0.15
# 奶牛	Cattle	0.01
水牛	Buffalo	0.11
生猪年末存栏数(万头)	Hogs in Stock(Year-End) (10000 units)	270.76
当年出栏数猪	Hogs for Slaughter of the Year	394.71
羊年末存栏数(万只)	Sheep and Goats in Stock(Year-End) (10000 units)	227.33
当年羊出栏数	Sheep and Goats for Slaughter	279.43
家禽年末存栏数(万只)	Poultry in Stock(Year-End) (10000 units)	4780.86
当年家禽出栏数	Poultry for Slaughter	10920.05
兔年末存栏数(万只)	Rabbits in Stock(Year-End) (10000 units)	19.89
当年出栏兔只数	Rabbits for Slaughter	82.39
畜牧业产品产量(吨)	Output of Animal Husbandry (ton)	494805
牛肉产量	Beef	309
猪肉产量	Pork	280696
羊肉产量	Mutton	30410
禽肉产量	Poultry	177134
兔肉产量	Rabbit	875
其他肉产量	Others	5381
奶类产量	Milk	24548
蜂蜜产量	Honey	320
禽蛋产量	Poultry and Eggs	456830

STATISTICS ON LIVESTOCK(2014)

市区 Urban Areas	通州区 Tongzhou	海安 Haian	如东 Rudong	启东 Qidong	如皋 Rugao	海门 Haimen
0.32	0.15	0.08	0.17	0.20	0.13	0.20
0.26	0.11	0.07		0.11	0.12	0.19
0.04	0.04	0.01	0.17	0.09	0.01	
0.07	0.03	0.02	0.05		0.01	
0.01						
0.03	0.03	0.02	0.05		0.01	
31.63	27.99	50.10	82.93	15.67	80.52	9.91
62.93	55.70	76.67	99.09	28.90	113.06	14.06
26.76	25.59	47.81	28.86	53.86	23.21	46.83
35.25	33.82	59.62	24.74	64.01	46.05	49.76
472.62	435.12	1651.00	853.26	381.60	1081.79	340.59
1315.83	1235.73	1882.00	2548.30	1485.00	2309.50	1379.42
0.00		9.53	0.25	6.30	3.31	0.50
0.00		60.03	3.00	4.02	15.34	
75957	68728	93663	107215	58049	116537	43384
131	45	27	149		2	
47369	42000	57900	66400	21744	77109	10174
4251	4057	5995	2160	6949	4605	6450
23772	22193	28744	38192	25033	34633	26760
		778	30	57	10	
434	433	219	284	4266	178	
8275	3200	2622		3595	5456	4600
129	125	36	95	21	33	6
31220	28972	221947	65740	20545	71380	45998

10-13 渔业生产情况(2014年)

单位:吨

指 标	Item	全市 Municipality
水产品总产量	**Output of Aquatic Products**	**882069**
一、海洋产品产量	Total Output of Seawater Aquatic Products	638104
(一)海洋捕捞产量	Sea Fishery	287805
鱼类	Fish	204149
甲壳类	Shrimp,Prawn and Crab	47636
贝类	Shell-fish	18614
藻类	Algae	678
其他	Others	11407
(二)海水养殖产量	Seawater Aquatic Products	350299
鱼类	Fish	25042
甲壳类	Shrimp,Prawn and Crab	48127
贝类	Shell-fish	262852
藻类	Algae	10519
其他	Others	3,759
二、内陆产品产量	Fresh Water Aquatic Products	228901
(一)捕捞产量	Fishery	36135
鱼类	Fish	19826
甲壳类	Shrimp,Prawn and Crab	8956
贝类	Shell-fish	7259
藻类	Algae	
其他	Others	94
(二)养殖产量	Artificially Cultured	192766
鱼类	Fish	134883
甲壳类	Shrimp,Prawn and Crab	53525
贝类	Shell-fish	2945
藻类	Algae	
其他	Others	1413
渔业养殖面积(万亩)	**Aquatic Raised Areas (10000 mu)**	**203.46**
海水	SeaWater Aquatic Area	135.09
淡水	Fresh Water Aquatic Area	68.37

STATISTICS ON FISHERY(2014)

(Unit: ton)

市区 Urban Areas	通州区 Tongzhou	海安 Haian	如东 Rudong	启东 Qidong	如皋 Rugao	海门 Haimen
57674	**34989**	**34592**	**309703**	**360154**	**25932**	**94014**
8510	0	9801	243460	316451	0	59882
5496		7861	50406	194440		29602
2920		3374	40298	140503		17054
808		1380	6870	30321		8257
1688		830	846	14121		1129
0		0	0	673		0
19		2080	1904	5942		1462
3014		1940	193054	122011		30280
0		0	24078	765		199
459		0	36030	10860		778
2555		329	127572	103535		28861
0		1611	5320	3146		442
0		0	54	3,705		
40500	34989	24791	66243	43703	25932	27732
7551	6020	6090	7457	8161	5037	1839
4746	3678	3745	2586	3808	3631	1310
1035	837	1205	1803	3690	841	382
1765	1505	1130	3064	619	565	116
5		10	4	44		31
32949	28969	18701	58786	35542	20895	25893
24541	22253	15046	35067	25112	17608	17509
7895	6619	2516	23216	8676	3155	8067
413		744		1443	71	274
100	97	395	503	311	61	43
12.95	**8.37**	**24.38**	**86.29**	**56.30**	**8.87**	**14.67**
3.15	0.00	16.65	72.83	37.82	0.00	4.64
9.80	8.37	7.73	13.47	18.48	8.87	10.03

10-14 农业机械年末拥有量(2014年)

指 标	Item	全市 Municipality
农业机械总动力(千瓦)	**General Power of Agricultural Machines (kilowatt)**	**3870201**
柴油机	Diesel Engine	2201504
汽油机	Gasoline Engine	277313
电动机	Electromotor	1391384
耕种机械	Farm Machinery	
大中型拖拉机(台)	Large and Medium Size Tractors (set)	7869
(千瓦)	(kilowatt)	385225
小型拖拉机(台)	Small Size Tractors (set)	38780
(千瓦)	(kilowatt)	373459
农用排灌动力机械	Agricultural Irrigation and Drainage Machinery	81769
(千瓦)	(kilowatt)	441880
柴油机(台)	Diesel Engine (set)	8146
(千瓦)	(kilowatt)	45147
电动机(台)	Electromotor (set)	73526
(千瓦)	(kilowatt)	363354
农用水泵(台)	Agriculture Pump	81314
节水灌溉类机械(套)	Water-saving Irrigation Machinery (set)	2809
收获机械	Harvest Machinery	
联合收获机(台)	Combine-harvester (set)	6671
(千瓦)	(kilowatt)	257061
机动割晒机(台)	Motor Swather (set)	128
(千瓦)	(kilowatt)	656
机动脱粒机(台)	Power Thresher (set)	18575
(千瓦)	(kilowatt)	27052

YEAR-END POSSESSION OF AGRICULTURAL MACHINES (2014)

市区 Urban Areas	通州区 Tongzhou	海安 Hai´an	如东 Rudong	启东 Qidong	如皋 Rugao	海门 Haimen
629743	**512062**	**636500**	**875857**	**541327**	**838111**	**348663**
305486	243328	350000	539850	346663	447792	211713
30801	23769	28500	132862	29274	47764	8112
293456	244965	258000	203145	165390	342555	128838
1120	962	1043	1988	601	2302	815
61504	53654	46727	99110	23682	116367	37835
6815	5426	6691	12420	2648	7888	2318
63324	50746	64410	113920	23489	86207	22109
10840	5652	4404	3860	25261	4055	33349
80596	63901	77419	74119	97650	60821	51275
135	28	90	50	7131		740
1276	380	3400	441	33692		6338
10705	5624	4314	3810	18130	4055	32512
79320	63521	69837	73678	35199	60821	44499
10342	5624	5200	5450	23609	4029	32684
54	38	2100	120	225	150	160
1410	1320	1320	1928	263	1594	156
54263	49026	42516	70996	14103	66517	8666
38	38		74	10	2	4
208	208		340	80	7	21
2059	1946	6790	5256	383	3439	648
5263	5263	1981	6973	3481	4237	5117

10-14 续 表

指 标	Item	全市 Municipality
田间管理机械	Field Management Machinery	
机动喷雾(粉)机(台)	Motor Dusting Machine (set)	92633
(千瓦)	(kilowatt)	127756
畜牧养殖机械	Stockbreeding Machinery	
饲草料加工机械(台)	Forage Grass Processing Machine (set)	34227
(千瓦)	(kilowatt)	140327
渔业机械(台)	Fishery Machine (set)	43693
(千瓦)	(kilowatt)	150184
农产品初加工机械	Agrifood Processing Machine	
农产品初加工动力机械(台)	Agrifood Motor Processing Machine (set)	66734
(千瓦)	(kilowatt)	492351
柴油机(台)	Diesel Machine (set)	4758
(千瓦)	(kilowatt)	49794
电动机(台)	Electromotor (set)	59631
(千瓦)	(kilowatt)	426101
农产品初加工作业机械(台)	Agricultural Product Processing Machine (set)	58320
粮食加工机械	Grain Processing Machine	50336
棉花加工机械	Cotton Processing Machine	1970
油料加工机械	Oil Extracting and Processing Machine	4974
运输机械	Transportation Machinery	
农用运输车(辆)	Vehicle for Agricultural Transport (set)	14010
(千瓦)	(kilowatt)	313277
农田基本建设机械(台)	Farmland Fundamental Construction Machinery (set)	11327
(千瓦)	(kilowatt)	149399

CONTINUED

市区 Urban Areas	通州区 Tongzhou	海安 Haian	如东 Rudong	启东 Qidong	如皋 Rugao	海门 Haimen
10497	6851	12520	39258	15130	9050	6178
15459	10986	23217	52473	18281	11768	6558
0						
1133	1045	23969	4133	2404	569	2019
10820	9451	58445	37090	14955	7117	11900
1900	1221	7892	18033	10159	2024	3685
5252	3172	29420	32296	23619	5559	54038
4278	3420	5940	5890	7642	36120	6864
44759	36411	50166	70580	71247	198856	56743
384	121	640	750	1677	210	1097
3122	881	8150	5522	20466	2310	10224
3659	3299	5300	5140	5965	33800	5767
39287	35530	42016	65058	50781	182440	46519
3056	2258	5358	6050	7091	31494	5271
2304	1793	4230	5105	6025	28781	3891
474	239	36	200	576	199	485
166	114	1060	720	233	2496	299
2983	1817	2810	2850	1485	3687	194
58548	36928	65243	66348	28234	93726	1178
449	206	411	545	8990	234	698
21919	14436	21852	8175	52861	14080	30512

主要统计指标解释

农林牧渔业总产值 指以货币表现的农、林、牧、渔业全部产品和对农业生产进行各种支持性服务活动的总量，它反映一定时期内农业总规模和总成果。从2003年开始农林牧渔业总产值执行新的国民经济行业分类标准，包括农业、林业、牧业、渔业、农林牧渔服务业，不再包括包民家庭兼营商品性工业。农林牧渔业总产值中的农、林、牧、渔四业的计算方法通常是按农、林、牧、渔业产吕及其副产品的产量分别乘以各自单位产品价格求得，现行价格从2003年开始使用生产价格调查的价格；少数生产周期较长，当年没有产品或产品产量不易统计的，则采用间接方法匡算其产值；然后将四业产品产值与农林牧渔服务业产值相加即为农林牧渔业总产值。

粮食产量 指全社会的产量。包括国有经济经营的、集体统一经营的和农民家庭经营的粮食产量，还包括工矿企业办的农场和其他生产单位的产量。粮食除包括稻谷、小麦、玉米、高粱、谷子及其他杂粮外，还包括薯类和豆类。其产量计算方法，豆类按去豆荚后的干豆计算；薯类(包括甘薯和马铃薯，不包括芋头和木薯)按5公斤鲜薯折1公斤粮食计算。

棉花产量 指全社会的产量，产量按皮棉计算。

油料产量 指全部油料作物的生产量。包括花生、油菜籽、芝麻、向日葵籽、胡麻籽、(亚麻籽)和其他油料。不包括大豆、大本油料和野生油料。花生以带壳干花生计算。

水产品产量 指人工养殖的水产品和天然生长的水产品的捕捞量。包括海水的鱼类、虾蟹类、贝类和藻类以及内陆水域的鱼类、虾蟹类和贝类，不包括淡水水生植物。

猪、牛、羊肉产量 指当年出栏并已屠宰、除去头蹄下水后带骨肉(即胴体重)的重量。

期初(末)畜禽存栏头(只)数 指报告期初(末)农村各种合作经济组织和国营农场、农民个人、机关、团体、学校、工矿企业、部队等单位以及城镇居民饲养的大牲畜、猪、羊、家禽等畜的存栏数。

耕地面积 是指年初可用来种植农作物并经常进行耕种、能够正常收获土地。包括当年实际耕种的熟地、当年新开荒地、休闲不满三年随时可以复耕的地和当年休闲以及以种植农作物为主并附带种植桑树、茶树、果树和其他林木的土地、沿海、沿湖地区已围垦利用的"海涂"、"湖田"等面积。不包括临时种值农作物的坡度在25度以上的陡坡地、在河套、湖畔、库区临时开发的成片或零星土地，属于专业性的桑园、茶图、果园、果木苗圃、林地、芦苇地、天然或人工草地面积、也不包括已列为国家和省(区、市)退耕计划但临时耕种的土地。

农作物播种面积 指实际播种或移植有农作物的面积。凡是实际种植有农作物的面积，不论种植在耕地上还是种植在非耕地上，均包括在农作物播种面积中。在播种季节基本结束后，因遭灾而重新改种和补种的农作物面积，也包括在内。

有效灌溉面积 指具有一定的水源，地块比较平整，灌溉工程或设备已经配套，在一般年景下当年能够进行正常灌溉的耕地面积。在一般情况下，有效灌溉面积应等于灌溉工程或设备已经配备，能够进行正常灌溉的水男和水浇地面积之和。

农用化肥施用量 指本年内实际用于农业生产的化肥数量，包括氮肥、磷肥、钾肥和复合肥。化肥施用量要求按折纯量计算数量。折纯量是指把氮肥、磷肥、钾肥分别按含氮、含五氧化二磷、含氧化钾的百分之一百成份进行折算后的数量。复合肥按其所含主要成分析算。

农业机械总动力 指主要用于农、林、牧、渔业的各种动力机械的动力总和。包括耕地机械、排灌机械、收获机械、农用运输机械、植物保护机械、牧业机械、林业机械、渔业机械和其他农业机械(内燃机按引擎马力折成瓦(特)计算、电动机按功率折成瓦(特)计算)。不包括专门用于乡、镇、村、组办工业、基本建设、非农业运输、科学试验和教学等非农业生产方面用的动力机械与作业机械。

第十一篇

工　业

Chapter 11

Industry

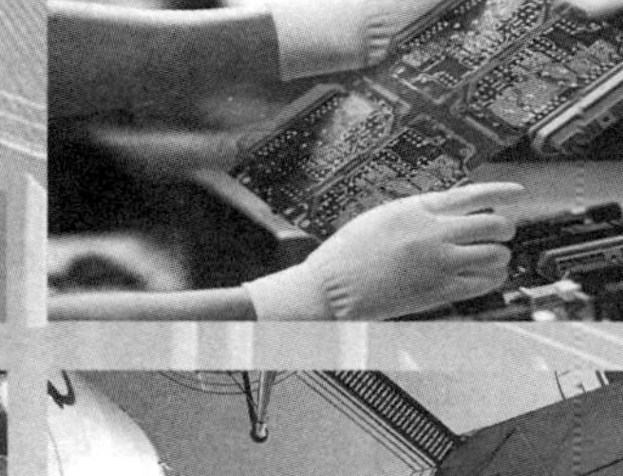

11-1 主要年份规模以上工业企业主要经济指标

MAJOR ECONOMIC INDICATORS OF INDUSTRIAL ENTERPRISES ABOVE DESIGNATED SIZE OVER THE YEARS

单位:万元 (Unit:10,000 Yuan)

年份 Years	从业人员平均人数(万人) Average Employees (10000 people)	工业总产值(现价) Total Industrial Output Value (Current Price)	固定资产原价 Original Value of Fixed Assets	固定资产净值平均余额 Average Balance of Net Fixed Assets	流动资产合计 Total Current Assets	流动资产年平均余额 Average Balance of Current Assets	主营业务收入 Main Business Revenue	利税总额 Total Profit and Tax
1978	40.08	299436	101526					50569
1979	48.16	364721	124536				310767	60630
1980	57.23	430807	151494	100977			378573	75154
1985	75.59	783510	313256	202271			668309	106969
1986	81.23	933874	384276	258418			787375	101529
1987	86.53	1183485	479497	322286	516382		1034714	121933
1988	88.60	1559194	595110	402274	640088	578235	1370909	155127
1989	86.64	1764804	700250	481988	778843	709466	1479247	127312
1990	85.10	1880087	790754	546307	918818	851737	1564795	120880
1991	87.60	2191814	1097278	685322	1126882	1061073	1968284	132466
1992	88.15	2824640	1267825	849217	1424011	1276651	2467038	182051
1993	87.97	4249780	1544321	1091857	1814639	1680758	3660856	238449
1994	84.43	5993966	2161538	1439070	2297681	2131815	4184861	312802
1995	79.58	5726932	2721978	1814940	2738461	2581672	5042275	264991
1996	72.83	5879907	3222093	2184126	2737782	2700648	4865042	257083
1997	66.56	6226126	3461787	2386933	2920914	2931203	5112937	344182
1998	45.99	5390233	3357584	2221223	2477632	2466143	4474245	298767
1999	43.68	5967097	3970653	2668736	2772752	2720526	4968059	348594
2000	41.58	6971002	4424811	3021209	3107796	3008559	6157226	572840
2001	41.48	7754374	4699362	3166928	3352059	3256304	6879964	570636
2002	41.02	8775490	5045044	3282384	3734070	3640180	7970462	676029
2003	43.97	11239072	5566275	3644598	4484577	4217089	10528746	904708
2004	53.27	15992862	5958619	3856939	5909011	5503478	15508804	1189377
2005	52.86	21433853	7224509	4537526	7095800	6552646	20811437	1626822
2006	57.01	29495274	8410173	5395787	8984804	8292925	29195581	2413168
2007	65.58	40294186	10042901	6451603	12723867	11792423	39911463	3771503
2008	89.86	52970751	17988442	9394476	16789416	16174620	52368258	6734044
2009	80.91	60948875	16124547	—	19960943	—	59578254	6257393
2010	90.84	73831630	20411642	—	24424508	—	72545588	8257860
2011	87.73	86798171	24483372	—	29043347	—	84325914	10175026
2012	93.62	98901246	29879982	—	33399793	—	96909539	11601534
2013	98.28	112539581	34503310	—	35605365	—	111958052	13310238
2014	98.83	124996978	40877622	—	36843108	—	123513619	14777086

注:1.1997年以前为乡及乡以上独立核算工业企业口径。2.2004年为全国第一次经济普查数据。3.2004年起不包括江苏省电力公司南通分公司数据。4.2008年为全国第二次经济普查数据。5.2013年为全国第三次经济普查数据。

Notes:1.The data before 1997 was based on the independant accounting of the Industrial enterprises of Township level or above. 2.The data of 2004 was from that of the first national economic survey. 3.The data from 2004 didn′t cover that of the Jiangsu Power Co.ltd, Nantong Branch. 4.The data of 2008 was from the second National Census. 5.The data of 2013 was from the third National Census.

11-2 主要年份国有工业企业主要财务指标

MAIN FINANCIAL INDICATORS OF STATE-OWNED ENTERPRISES OVER THE YEARS

单位：万元 (Unit:10,000 Yuan)

年份 Years	从业人员平均人数(万人) Average Employees (10000 people)	工业总产值(现价) Total Industrial Output Value (Current Price)	固定资产原价 Original Value of Fixed Assets	固定资产净值平均余额 Average Balance of Net Fixed Assets	流动资产合计 Total Current Assets	流动资产年平均余额 Average Balance of Current Assets	主营业务收入 Main Business Revenue	利税总额 Total Profit and Tax
1978	10.37	181080	59319	40660				28868
1979	10.57	218301	73970	45400			182493	35149
1980	11.90	231659	90706	57188			195336	42111
1985	15.17	327938	162068	103731			274056	46523
1986	16.09	362743	183443	123616			307891	44803
1987	17.22	426645	216857	143554	140235	129173	371921	51462
1988	17.84	527054	252847	168586	179217	156635	458231	61395
1989	18.11	600622	296534	197230	238303	206911	500943	55969
1990	18.40	649002	340208	228959	281345	259757	519391	48269
1991	19.14	677536	391052	261249	344168	320722	603590	37524
1992	19.36	798090	451091	303433	409672	378913	679886	45113
1993	19.35	968987	471807	391523	470791	446814	860115	39172
1994	18.62	1191725	658385	368373	494923	465413	825699	61233
1995	18.43	1141504	883842	509216	594962	558857	994278	25662
1996	16.59	1130549	1227288	851177	642123	652567	1016272	70776
1997	13.69	1013480	1184847	817772	566832	573031	914702	66681
1998	9.33	676555	668150	458710	357598	359242	584882	15682
1999	7.42	584290	607209	405006	317979	303972	437889	14857
2000	6.28	666557	855583	560393	396308	388112	545460	68252
2001	4.92	583988	807978	541281	340516	321162	423358	27323
2002	3.28	403545	841654	552548	295052	293880	279739	24220
2003	1.61	273444	708640	515316	245429	238401	146280	23056
2004	0.58	75451	142900	91580	63885	69024	83008	4892
2005	0.41	85894	137045	79712	55553	56060	85174	7398
2006	0.33	64782	140372	85054	50481	48401	67972	6480
2007	0.26	79091	149543	89665	66504	60754	81397	12687
2008	0.25	102678	194501	114264	73883	73416	101057	12951
2009	0.26	114893	208889	—	82009	—	113078	10547
2010	0.32	381921	318974	—	247632	—	364284	42571
2011	0.38	591134	448428	—	328941	—	570907	65898
2012	0.46	1237261	1729173	—	537266	—	1245645	109309
2013	0.13	117038	164183	—	234126	—	113039	16136
2014	0.12	118390	202834	—	274055	—	113608	16171

11-3　规模以上工业企业单位数(2014 年)

单位：个

指　标	Item	全市 Municipality
总计	**Total**	**5081**
# 亏损企业	Unprofitable Firm	307
# 国有控股企业	State-holding Enterprise	73
# 轻工业	Light Industry	2447
重工业	Heavy Industry	2634
# 大型企业	Large-scale Enterprise	110
中型企业	Medium-sized Enterprise	497
小微型企业	Micro Enterprise	4474
按登记注册类型分组	**Grouped by Registration Types**	
内资企业	Domestic Enterprise	3846
国有企业	State-owned Enterprise	5
集体企业	Collective Enterprise	13
股份合作企业	Joint Equity Cooperative Enterprise	15
联营企业	Joint Venture	1
有限责任公司	Limited Liability Company	619
股份有限公司	Limited Company	78
私营企业	Private Company	3111
其他企业	Others	4
港、澳、台商投资企业	HK, Macau or Taiwan Funded Enterprise	491
合资经营企业(港或澳、台资)	Joint Venture(HK, Macau or Taiwan)	182
合作经营企业(港或澳、台资)	Cooperative Enterprise(HK, Macau or Taiwan)	4
港澳台商独资经营企业	Sole Proprietorship(HK, Macau or Taiwan)	301
港澳台商投资股份有限公司	Shareholding Limited Company(HK, Macau or Taiwan)	3
其他港澳台商投资企业	Others	1
外商投资企业	Foreign Funded Enterprise	744
中外合资经营企业	Sino-foreign Joint Venture	327
中外合作经营企业	Sino-foreign Cooperative Enterprise	13
外资企业	Foreign-owned Enterprise	397
外商投资股份有限公司	Foreign Investment Joint Stock Company	7
按经济组织类型分组	**Grouped by Types of Ownership**	
独资企业	Sole Proprietorship	806
合作、合伙企业	Cooperative and Partnership Enterprises	59
股份有限公司	Joint Stock Company	146
有限责任公司	Limited Liability Company	4070

INDUSTRIAL ENTERPRISES ABOVE DESIGNATED SIZE(2014)

(Unit)

市区 Urban Areas	崇川区 Chongchuan	港闸区 Gangzha	开发区 Developing Zone	通州区 Tongzhou	海安 Haian	如东 Rudong	启东 Qidong	如皋 Rugao	海门 Haimen
1580	**100**	**245**	**471**	**764**	**863**	**658**	**512**	**820**	**648**
118	14	27	45	32	99	15	19	44	12
49	14	19	13	3	1	7	7	2	7
805	68	93	187	457	364	418	164	389	307
775	32	152	284	307	499	240	348	431	341
37	4	7	8	18	20	10	10	23	10
148	14	19	49	66	63	70	51	103	62
1395	82	219	414	680	780	578	451	694	576
1155	74	189	317	575	722	513	376	694	386
1		1				1	1		2
3	1			2	2	2		1	5
7	1	1	1	4	1	2			5
									1
260	26	65	47	122	138	32	41	97	51
24	6	8	4	6	20	12	6	8	8
859	39	114	265	441	558	464	328	588	314
1	1				3				
111	6	9	34	62	70	78	50	54	128
57	2	6	22	27	32	13	26	21	33
1				1		1	1		1
51	4	3	10	34	37	63	23	33	94
2			2		1				
						1			
314	20	47	120	127	71	67	86	72	134
132	14	29	33	56	36	28	48	38	45
8		3	1	4			1	4	
168	6	14	84	64	34	39	37	30	89
6		1	2	3	1				
237	12	19	97	109	85	120	69	93	202
23	2	4	3	14	7	7	7	4	11
39	7	10	10	12	43	16	18	13	17
1281	79	212	361	629	728	515	418	710	418

11-3 续表

单位:个

指 标	Item	全市 Municipality
按行业分	**Grouped by Industries**	
制造业	Manufacturing	5032
农副食品加工业	Agrifood Processing	175
食品制造业	Food Production	25
酒、饮料和精制茶制造业	Alcohol, Beverage and Refined Tea Production	7
烟草制品业	Tobacco Industries	1
纺织业	Textile	1019
纺织服装、服饰业	Textile and Garment, Dress and Personal Adornment	384
皮革、毛皮、羽毛(绒)及其制品业	Leather, Fur, Feather(Fuzz) and Related Products	64
木材加工及木、竹、藤、棕、草制品业	Wood Processing and Industries of Wood, Bamboo, Rattan, Palm and Grass Products	10
家具制造业	Furniture Manufacturing	24
造纸及纸制品业	Paper Making and Industries of Paper Products	45
印刷业和记录媒介的复制	Printing and Record Medium Reproduction	25
文教、工美、体育和娱乐用品制造业	Industries of Culture, Education, Arts, Sports and Recreational Products	327
石油加工、炼焦及核燃料加工业	Petroleum Processing, Coking and Nuclear Fuel Processing	9
化学原料及化学制品制造业	Production of Chemical Raw Materials and Chemical Products	423
医药制造业	Pharmaceutical Industry	77
化学纤维制造业	Chemical Fiber Manufacturing	70
橡胶和塑料制品业	Industry of Rubber and Plastic Products	131
非金属矿物制品业	Industry of Nonmetallic Mineral Products	230
黑色金属冶炼和压延加工业	Ferrous Metal Smelting and Pressing	85
有色金属冶炼及压延加工业	Non-Ferrous Metal Smelting and Pressing	66
金属制品业	Manufacture of Metal Products	357
通用设备制造业	Manufacture of General Purpose Machinery	484
专用设备制造业	Manufacture of Equipment for Special Purpose	211
汽车制造业	Automobile Industry	39
铁路、船舶、航空航天和其他运输设备制造业	Manufacture of Railroad, Shipping, Aerospace and Other Transportation Equipments	123
电气机械和器材制造业	Manufacture of Electrical Machinery and Equipments	316
计算机、通信和其他电子设备制造业	Manufacture of Computer, Communications and Other Electronic Products	163
仪器仪表制造业	Instrument Manufacturing	126
其他制造业	Others	6
废弃资源综合利用业	Comprehensive Utilization of Waste Resources	3
金属制品、机械和设备修理业	Metal Product, Machinery and Equipment Repair Industry	7
电力、热力和水供应业	Electric Power, Heating Power and Water Supply Industry	49
电力、热力生产和供应业	Generation and Supply of Electric Power and Heating Power	30
燃气生产和供应业	Generation and Supply of Gas	8
水的生产和供应业	Generation and Supply of Water	11

CONTINUED

(Unit)

市区 Urban Areas	崇川区 Chongchuan	港闸区 Gangzha	开发区 Developing Zone	通州区 Tongzhou	海安 Haian	如东 Rudong	启东 Qidong	如皋 Rugao	海门 Haimen
1567	97	240	469	761	857	646	504	815	643
20	3	2	3	12	47	44	21	34	9
4		2	1	1	5	3	4	6	3
1				1	1	2	1	2	
1	1								
408	32	27	106	243	154	177	35	109	136
162	19	26	36	81	35	48	22	89	28
17	3	1	4	9	6	4	9	12	16
4		1	1	2	2	1		1	2
8		1	2	5	3	4	2	5	2
14		1	3	10	4	12	2	7	6
11		5	1	5	2	2	2	5	3
65	3	14	6	42	42	73	26	65	56
3			2	1		2		4	
100	3	21	54	22	52	98	42	81	50
17	3	3	8	3	8	11	14	14	13
10	1	0	4	5	37	16	4	2	1
43	2	3	9	29	15	11	7	29	26
72	5	22	14	31	44	22	13	38	41
14	1	4	2	7	11	13	1	29	17
8			3	5	21	3	2	10	22
199	1	13	125	60	36	21	14	43	44
97	9	26	24	38	117	14	151	40	65
43	1	13	9	20	50	29	29	37	23
14	3	1	6	4	6	1	3	14	1
52	2	26	7	17	2	10	13	38	8
71	2	8	20	41	88	16	44	49	48
53	3	9	10	31	27	5	21	39	18
50		7	9	34	39	2	22	8	5
					2	2		2	
1				1				2	
5				1	1			1	
13	3	5	2	3	6	12	8	5	5
9	1	5	2	1	3	9	4	2	3
2	1			1	1	1	3		1
2	1			1	2	2	1	3	1

11-4 规模以上工业企业现价产值(2014年)

单位:万元

指 标	Item	全市 Municipality
总计	**Total**	**124996978**
# 亏损企业	Unprofitable Firm	4438757
# 国有控股企业	State-holding Enterprise	6949290
# 轻工业	Light Industry	39556445
重工业	Heavy Industry	85440533
# 大型企业	Large-scale Enterprise	31464816
中型企业	Medium-sized Enterprise	32761719
小微型企业	Micro Enterprise	60770443
按登记注册类型分组	**Grouped by Registration Types**	
内资企业	Domestic Enterprise	82339302
国有企业	State-owned Enterprise	118390
集体企业	Collective Enterprise	125967
股份合作企业	Joint Equity Cooperative Enterprise	355272
联营企业	Joint Venture	10009
有限责任公司	Limited Liability Company	13120265
股份有限公司	Limited Company	7769818
私营企业	Private Company	60790060
其他企业	Others	49521
港、澳、台商投资企业	HK, Macau or Taiwan Funded Enterprise	15631146
合资经营企业(港或澳、台资)	Joint Venture(HK, Macau or Taiwan)	5892762
合作经营企业(港或澳、台资)	Cooperative Enterprise(HK, Macau or Taiwan)	70948
港澳台商独资经营企业	Sole Proprietorship(HK, Macau or Taiwan)	9100713
港澳台商投资股份有限公司	Shareholding Limited Company(HK, Macau or Taiwan)	564390
其他港澳台商投资企业	Others	2335
外商投资企业	Foreign Funded Enterprise	27026530
中外合资经营企业	Sino-foreign Joint Venture	12709012
中外合作经营企业	Sino-foreign Cooperative Enterprise	412884
外资企业	Foreign-owned Enterprise	13250443
外商投资股份有限公司	Foreign Investment Joint Stock Company	654192
按经济组织类型分组	**Grouped by Types of Ownership**	
独资企业	Sole Proprietorship	23534239
合作、合伙企业	Cooperative and Partnership Enterprises	1119676
股份有限公司	Joint Stock Company	11964832
有限责任公司	Limited Liability Company	88378231

MARKET VALUE OF INDUSTRIAL ENTERPRISES ABOVE DESIGNATED SIZE(2014)

(Unit: 10,000 Yuan)

市区 Urban Areas					海安 Haian	如东 Rudong	启东 Qidong	如皋 Rugao	海门 Haimen
	崇川区 Chongchuan	港闸区 Gangzha	开发区 Developing Zone	通州区 Tongzhou					
42042108	**3817293**	**4401860**	**15268046**	**18554910**	**17899578**	**16709843**	**15084775**	**15897802**	**17362872**
1536073	147981	306254	798047	283791	612596	114227	824900	1250458	100503
5414126	1959687	882079	2510108	62252	15948	278540	859647	167360	213668
13562944	1561561	814641	3926082	7260660	6756296	7280087	3076362	4477938	4402819
28479164	2255732	3587219	11341963	11294251	11143282	9429756	12008413	11419864	12960053
11909395	1705243	1044361	2791693	6368099	5790714	3593422	2288850	4794467	3087968
12057867	1157259	810668	6562844	3527096	4057310	3274726	3609970	4470351	5291494
18074846	954791	2546832	5913509	8659715	8051554	9841696	9185955	6632984	8983409
22615238	1182032	2528800	6636588	12267818	14588980	11533818	10426448	12511479	10663339
2040		2040				19157	10159		87035
25567	5815			19752	32816	18761		8290	40533
61216	2844	2773	3300	52298	115555	27933			150567
									10009
6526564	596845	979966	2683212	2266542	1474927	618594	1380479	2241253	878448
2069450	175325	277217	642981	973928	3453357	531758	305869	707653	701730
13893059	363861	1266804	3307096	8955298	9500147	10317614	8729941	9554283	8795017
37343	37343				12179				
3876183	325067	473809	1382572	1694735	1641507	2965131	1591221	2227592	3329513
1198607	73541	110172	449654	565239	921985	510139	667271	1501118	1093643
35689				35689		29050	2751		3458
2082519	251526	363636	373549	1093808	714501	2423608	921198	726474	2232412
559369			559369		5021				
						2335			
15550688	2310194	1399251	7248886	4592357	1669091	2210894	3067106	1158732	3370020
7591693	2090271	574272	2018166	2908984	848168	1032916	1334013	540554	1361668
304588		188719	30020	85849			38181	70115	
7004431	219922	396968	4818477	1569064	816708	1177978	1694912	548063	2008351
649977		239293	382223	28461	4215				
9233240	480667	765608	5205941	2781025	1677883	3788698	2804503	1507354	4522561
500813	40187	191492	40751	228384	140394	93611	113619	70115	201125
4629730	185670	526573	1591032	2326454	3688342	751975	491732	880503	1522550
27678325	3110769	2918187	8430322	13219048	12392959	12075559	11674922	13439830	11116636

11-4 续表

单位：万元

指 标	Item	全市 Municipality
按行业分	**Grouped by Industries**	
制造业	Manufacturing	122940052
农副食品加工业	Agrifood Processing	4285813
食品制造业	Food Production	535695
酒、饮料和精制茶制造业	Alcohol, Beverage and Refined Tea Production	192326
烟草制品业	Tobacco Industries	116618
纺织业	Textile	13264531
纺织服装、服饰业	Textile and Garment, Dress and Personal Adornment	4818753
皮革、毛皮、羽毛及其制品和制鞋业	Leather, Fur, Feather(Fuzz) and Related Products	882634
木材加工及木、竹、藤、棕、草制品业	Wood Processing and Industries of Wood, Bamboo, Rattan, Palm and Grass Products	102429
家具制造业	Furniture Manufacturing	239224
造纸和纸制品业	Paper Making and Industries of Paper Products	540768
印刷和记录媒介复制业	Printing and Record Medium Reproduction	210936
文教、工美、体育和娱乐用品制造业	Industries of Culture, Education, Arts, Sports and Recreational Products	5093080
石油加工、炼焦和核燃料加工业	Petroleum Processing, Coking and Nuclear Fuel Processing	297943
化学原料和化学制品制造业	Production of Chemical Raw Materials and Chemical Products	17670567
医药制造业	Pharmaceutical Industry	2599756
化学纤维制造业	Chemical Fiber Manufacturing	2956099
橡胶和塑料制品业	Industry of Rubber and Plastic Products	1783219
非金属矿物制品业	Industry of Nonmetallic Mineral Products	3712930
黑色金属冶炼和压延加工业	Ferrous Metal Smelting and Pressing	2322327
有色金属冶炼和压延加工业	Non-Ferrous Metal Smelting and Pressing	1790575
金属制品业	Manufacture of Metal Products	7331579
通用设备制造业	Manufacture of General Purpose Machinery	10040227
专用设备制造业	Manufacture of Equipment for Special Purpose	6844578
汽车制造业	Automobile Industry	1239081
铁路、船舶、航空航天和其他运输设备制造业	Manufacture of Railroad, Shipping, Aerospace and Other Transportation Equipments	4402922
电气机械和器材制造业	Manufacture of Electrical Machinery and Equipments	17212040
计算机、通信和其他电子设备制造业	Manufacture of Computer, Communications and Other Electronic Products	6853649
仪器仪表制造业	Instrument Manufacturing	5460360
其他制造业	Others	60573
废弃资源综合利用业	Comprehensive Utilization of Waste Resources	38892
金属制品、机械和设备修理业	Metal Product, Machinery and Equipment Repair Industry	39930
电力、热力和水供应业	Electric Power, Heating Power and Water Supply Industry	2056926
电力、热力生产和供应业	Generation and Supply of Electric Power and Heating Power	1656037
燃气生产和供应业	Generation and Supply of Gas	253549
水的生产和供应业	Generation and Supply of Water	147340

CONTINUED

(10000 yuan)

市区 Urban Areas	崇川区 Chongchuan	港闸区 Gangzha	开发区 Developing Zone	通州区 Tongzhou	海安 Haian	如东 Rudong	启东 Qidong	如皋 Rugao	海门 Haimen
41054415	3708625	3633407	15208432	18503951	17841171	16365383	14522012	15847960	17309111
1416462	243605	36304	901699	234854	987870	836878	239900	551839	252865
41447		8586	4737	28124	39160	48212	267113	41379	98386
45238				45238	25073	15873	39429	66714	
116618	116618								
5353887	285283	296868	1957004	2814733	2771485	2357720	534447	909627	1337365
2315152	145921	163851	257213	1748167	213800	931605	237475	788643	332079
153716	15978	5538	65323	66877	25755	209955	43072	85529	364606
71417		24464	20806	26147	7012	14372		2658	6970
85249		6210	32896	46144	15032	87485	7946	38287	5225
218994		4529	115587	98878	46348	183550	7183	39450	45243
76624		30308	2341	43976	5923	14951	61492	25152	26794
972045	34416	97213	62831	777585	401448	1208969	242802	974634	1293182
62546			43213	19334		54074		181322	
6518392	87710	444441	5290490	695752	1218008	3217740	1308137	2913103	2495187
367052	14540	53829	91828	206856	562450	480542	637736	332148	219828
1293940	557830		240449	495661	1304296	282264	60494	4905	10201
780815	228467	36734	83987	431627	121920	104425	49947	399867	326246
1092732	135996	290740	259149	406846	538355	523768	255150	708540	594386
667529	2878	27034	58219	579398	607030	144559	52572	606499	244138
161904			40743	121161	250555	297057	30007	374425	676626
3632384	28173	781515	2122665	700032	417899	1437599	286130	514500	1043068
2350009	177257	380274	1228631	563847	1404040	320853	3997514	382718	1585093
2421828	459529	132526	414521	1415252	460905	626319	1512908	517390	1305228
184098	9294	17840	92689	64275	91896	205514	68070	678823	10680
2340075	548441	460285	206327	1125023	42960	133255	325458	1358231	202942
3288917	17265	104987	1206645	1960021	3824910	2355504	2564279	1195001	3983429
3084245	599424	100700	306118	2078004	540661	197095	718859	2000023	312765
1904498		98088	102325	1704086	1903159	42437	973892	99792	536583
					9819	32807		17948	
2002				2002				36890	
34601		30549		4053	3404			1925	
987694	108668	768452	59613	50960	58407	344460	562763	49842	53761
866557	26786	768452	59613	11705	28065	198137	501488	21755	40035
61051	44539			16512	10789	124123	51116		6470
60086	37343			22744	19553	22200	10159	28087	7255

11-5 规模以上工业企业销售产值(2014年)

单位:万元

指 标	Item	全市 Municipality
总计	**Total**	**123695124**
#亏损企业	Unprofitable Firm	4367702
#国有控股企业	State-holding Enterprise	6872628
#轻工业	Light Industry	39313969
重工业	Heavy Industry	84381156
#大型企业	Large-scale Enterprise	31207669
中型企业	Medium-sized Enterprise	32341413
小微型企业	Micro Enterprise	60146042
按登记注册类型分组	**Grouped by Registration Types**	
内资企业	Domestic Enterprise	81499261
国有企业	State-owned Enterprise	115131
集体企业	Collective Enterprise	125514
股份合作企业	Joint Equity Cooperative Enterprise	354317
联营企业	Joint Venture	10009
有限责任公司	Limited Liability Company	12948741
股份有限公司	Limited Company	7718095
私营企业	Private Company	60177966
其他企业	Others	49488
港、澳、台商投资企业	HK, Macau or Taiwan Funded Enterprise	15543563
合资经营企业(港或澳、台资)	Joint Venture(HK, Macau or Taiwan)	5832859
合作经营企业(港或澳、台资)	Cooperative Enterprise(HK, Macau or Taiwan)	70303
港澳台商独资经营企业	Sole Proprietorship(HK, Macau or Taiwan)	9033134
港澳台商投资股份有限公司	Shareholding Limited Company(HK, Macau or Taiwan)	604932
其他港澳台商投资企业	Others	2335
外商投资企业	Foreign Funded Enterprise	26652300
中外合资经营企业	Sino-foreign Joint Venture	12572515
中外合作经营企业	Sino-foreign Cooperative Enterprise	408667
外资企业	Foreign-owned Enterprise	13071455
外商投资股份有限公司	Foreign Investment Joint Stock Company	599663
按经济组织类型分组	**Grouped by Types of Ownership**	
独资企业	Sole Proprietorship	23279431
合作、合伙企业	Cooperative and Partnership Enterprises	1112372
股份有限公司	Joint Stock Company	11849849
有限责任公司	Limited Liability Company	87453473

SALES VALUE OF INDUSTRIAL ENTERPRISES ABOVE DESIGNATED SIZE(2014)

(10000 yuan)

市区 Urban Areas	崇川区 Chongchuan	港闸区 Gangzha	开发区 Developing Zone	通州区 Tongzhou	海安 Haian	如东 Rudong	启东 Qidong	如皋 Rugao	海门 Haimen
41383018	**3752736**	**4336100**	**14873018**	**18421165**	**17817327**	**16471753**	**14934362**	**15758619**	**17330044**
1484431	145236	303016	774194	261984	606835	110728	821489	1243230	100988
5347073	1954468	878157	2452612	61836	15948	278957	859647	167808	203196
13479632	1546163	808205	3903758	7221506	6722188	7210285	3048023	4459361	4394481
27903387	2206573	3527895	10969260	11199659	11095140	9261468	11886340	11299258	12935563
11821446	1658941	1028115	2790505	6343885	5792252	3515888	2253521	4736594	3087968
11781348	1135825	801792	6354342	3489389	4044850	3250836	3560624	4429449	5274306
17780224	957969	2506193	5728172	8587891	7980226	9705029	9120218	6592576	8967769
22244359	1157544	2484697	6448828	12153290	14502255	11369192	10353712	12385320	10644424
2040		2040				18716	10159		84216
25505	5800			19705	32604	18582		8290	40533
60848	2844	2773	3184	52047	115555	27347			150567
									10009
6401039	578738	971920	2633623	2216757	1465306	614516	1375622	2216897	875361
2042316	172454	274855	627781	967227	3450520	526022	321720	677460	700056
13675269	360365	1233109	3184240	8897554	9426123	10164009	8646211	9482673	8783681
37343	37343				12146				
3893824	314079	480691	1415544	1683510	1629160	2910689	1583787	2208868	3317237
1179814	73041	108657	443821	554296	919845	503308	658814	1484655	1086424
35689				35689		28406	2751		3458
2078410	241039	372034	371812	1093526	704294	2376641	922221	724213	2227355
599911			599911		5021				
						2335			
15244836	2281112	1370712	7008646	4584365	1685913	2191873	2996864	1164431	3368384
7486697	2049931	566603	1962477	2907687	846439	1018508	1321753	538663	1360454
301549		188719	29418	83413			38181	68937	
6861132	231182	376097	4689043	1564810	835268	1173364	1636930	556832	2007929
595457		239293	327709	28455	4206				
9084994	481387	753135	5074195	2776276	1684604	3735182	2747543	1513075	4514033
496782	40187	191492	39754	225350	140130	92781	112617	68937	201125
4568109	182736	524211	1561588	2299574	3680763	746337	499350	838318	1516972
27233133	3048425	2867262	8197481	13119965	12311830	11897453	11574853	13338289	11097915

11-5 续表

单位：万元

指 标	Item	全市 Municipality
按行业分	**Grouped by Industries**	
制造业	Manufacturing	121645022
农副食品加工业	Agrifood Processing	4289014
食品制造业	Food Production	530402
酒、饮料和精制茶制造业	Alcohol, Beverage and Refined Tea Production	190283
烟草制品业	Tobacco Industries	112532
纺织业	Textile	13182168
纺织服装、服饰业	Textile and Garment, Dress and Personal Adornment	4770791
皮革、毛皮、羽毛及其制品和制鞋业	Leather, Fur, Feather(Fuzz) and Related Products	878907
木材加工及木、竹、藤、棕、草制品业	Wood Processing and Industries of Wood, Bamboo, Rattan, Palm and Grass Products	97692
家具制造业	Furniture Manufacturing	234617
造纸和纸制品业	Paper Making and Industries of Paper Products	544755
印刷和记录媒介复制业	Printing and Record Medium Reproduction	210114
文教、工美、体育和娱乐用品制造业	Industries of Culture, Education, Arts, Sports and Recreational Products	5077911
石油加工、炼焦和核燃料加工业	Petroleum Processing, Coking and Nuclear Fuel Processing	298641
化学原料和化学制品制造业	Production of Chemical Raw Materials and Chemical Products	17376381
医药制造业	Pharmaceutical Industry	2575158
化学纤维制造业	Chemical Fiber Manufacturing	2940555
橡胶和塑料制品业	Industry of Rubber and Plastic Products	1746402
非金属矿物制品业	Industry of Nonmetallic Mineral Products	3675289
黑色金属冶炼和压延加工业	Ferrous Metal Smelting and Pressing	2303947
有色金属冶炼和压延加工业	Non-Ferrous Metal Smelting and Pressing	1745578
金属制品业	Manufacture of Metal Products	7218146
通用设备制造业	Manufacture of General Purpose Machinery	9946881
专用设备制造业	Manufacture of Equipment for Special Purpose	6816506
汽车制造业	Automobile Industry	1218934
铁路、船舶、航空航天和其他运输设备制造业	Manufacture of Railroad, Shipping, Aerospace and Other Transportation Equipments	4353944
电气机械和器材制造业	Manufacture of Electrical Machinery and Equipments	17001559
计算机、通信和其他电子设备制造业	Manufacture of Computer, Communications and Other Electronic Products	6747984
仪器仪表制造业	Instrument Manufacturing	5421584
其他制造业	Others	59674
废弃资源综合利用业	Comprehensive Utilization of Waste Resources	38892
金属制品、机械和设备修理业	Metal Product, Machinery and Equipment Repair Industry	39782
电力、热力和水供应业	Electric Power, Heating Power and Water Supply Industry	2050102
电力、热力生产和供应业	Generation and Supply of Electric Power and Heating Power	1651616
燃气生产和供应业	Generation and Supply of Gas	251587
水的生产和供应业	Generation and Supply of Water	146899

CONTINUED

(10000 yuan)

市区 Urban Areas	崇川区 Chongchuan	港闸区 Gangzha	开发区 Developing Zone	通州区 Tongzhou	海安 Haian	如东 Rudong	启东 Qidong	如皋 Rugao	海门 Haimen
40396654	3644068	3567648	14813669	18371269	17760923	16129689	14371935	15708777	17277045
1434591	254773	36251	908797	234769	983657	834297	239367	540982	256121
40832		7971	4737	28124	38871	47315	266316	40794	96275
44721				44721	25073	15714	38065	66712	
112532	112532								
5323247	282039	293327	1945813	2802068	2757508	2332008	528845	906547	1334012
2286782	145778	163642	247320	1730042	210866	916624	236595	788094	331830
151947	16135	5538	63864	66410	25623	209212	42557	85343	364225
67277		24464	16666	26147	6954	13834		2658	6970
82726		6210	32262	44255	15025	86053	7549	38039	5225
225526		4529	122392	98605	45956	181621	7010	39399	45243
76424		30308	2244	43872	5915	14817	61492	24673	26794
967115	34328	97421	59506	775861	394492	1206976	234795	984151	1290382
60735			41416	19319		54074		183831	
6302353	87294	426921	5103951	684188	1210757	3190385	1287692	2892263	2492931
361918	13399	51771	89892	206856	561807	467620	635624	329142	219048
1283690	553479		235314	494896	1300238	280660	60813	4954	10201
753350	218098	36656	68635	429961	115830	102636	48670	399671	326246
1084247	135878	288072	253944	406354	534766	523890	253645	685460	593280
659083	2878	27034	58195	570976	606710	140890	52572	604459	240233
149202			41301	107901	245769	276367	29135	372688	672418
3539441	28173	776425	2052396	682448	414234	1430439	281317	512987	1039727
2297598	175188	370356	1193647	558407	1393871	312345	3981932	376722	1584414
2412573	459266	130721	410502	1412084	454953	618703	1510386	515709	1304183
179949	9127	17840	90155	62827	93558	200838	67941	665969	10680
2313560	548842	442869	198919	1122930	42954	128256	324124	1349067	195983
3248158	16831	108334	1176753	1946240	3837988	2280779	2481183	1171238	3982213
3016902	550029	95266	295570	2076037	538817	191101	718171	1971164	311830
1883722		95324	99481	1688917	1885769	39955	976140	99416	536583
					9559	32283		17832	
2002				2002				36890	
34453		30400		4053	3404			1925	
986365	108668	768452	59349	49896	56404	342064	562428	49842	52999
865228	26786	768452	59349	10641	26075	197796	501488	21755	39274
61051	44539			16512	10776	122509	50781		6470
60086	37343			22744	19553	21759	10159	28087	7255

11-6 规模以上工业企业主要经济指标(2014年)

单位:万元

指标	Item	企业单位数(个) Number of Enterprises and Units
总 计	**Total**	**5081**
#亏损企业	Unprofitable Firm	307
#国有控股企业	State-holding Enterprise	73
#轻工业	Light Industry	2447
重工业	Heavy Industry	2634
#大型企业	Large-scale Enterprise	110
中型企业	Medium-sized Enterprise	497
小微型企业	Micro Enterprise	4474
按登记注册类型分组	**Grouped by Registration Types**	
内资企业	Domestic Enterprise	3846
国有企业	State-owned Enterprise	5
集体企业	Collective Enterprise	13
股份合作企业	Joint Equity Cooperative Enterprise	15
联营企业	Joint Venture	1
有限责任公司	Limited Liability Company	619
股份有限公司	Limited Company	78
私营企业	Private Company	3111
其他企业	Others	4
港、澳、台商投资企业	HK, Macau or Taiwan Funded Enterprise	491
合资经营企业(港或澳、台资)	Joint Venture(HK, Macau or Taiwan)	182
合作经营企业(港或澳、台资)	Cooperative Enterprise(HK, Macau or Taiwan)	4
港澳台商独资经营企业	Sole Proprietorship(HK, Macau or Taiwan)	301
港澳台商投资股份有限公司	Shareholding Limited Company(HK, Macau or Taiwan)	3
其他港澳台商投资企业	Others	1
外商投资企业	Foreign Funded Enterprise	744
中外合资经营企业	Sino-foreign Joint Venture	327
中外合作经营企业	Sino-foreign Cooperative Enterprise	13
外资企业	Foreign-owned Enterprise	397
外商投资股份有限公司	Foreign Investment Joint Stock Company	7

MAJOR ECONOMIC INDICATORS OF INDUSTRIAL ENTERPRISES ABOVE DESIGNATED SIZE(2014)

(Unit: 10,000 Yuan)

亏损企业 Unprofitable Firms	工业总产值（当年价格）Total Value of Industrial Output (Price of Current Year)	工业销售产值（当年价格）Industrial Sales Value (Price of Current Year)	出口交货值 Value of Export Delivery	资产总计 Total Assets	流动资产合计 Total Current Assets	应收账款 Accounts Receivable
307	**124996978**	**123695124**	**18805018**	**75587992**	**36843108**	**10651551**
307	4438757	4367702	1558829	9838749	4129132	1035499
15	6949290	6872628	1749279	12727758	4602999	1526122
137	39556445	39313969	7416522	21292052	10266474	2391585
170	85440533	84381156	11388496	54295940	26576634	8259966
5	31464816	31207669	8450351	23517307	11565025	3558099
28	32761719	32341413	5056631	20147774	8972990	2102069
274	60770443	60146042	5298037	31922911	16305093	4991383
200	82339302	81499261	7031119	45348994	22571372	6829227
2	118390	115131		508774	274055	52234
	125967	125514	4440	76404	37264	9396
	355272	354317	6946	87395	39376	10102
	10009	10009		3336	1319	295
61	13120265	12948741	1370769	12686934	5011821	1703655
6	7769818	7718095	1344406	5911117	3287864	756518
131	60790060	60177966	4304558	25858917	13900855	4286947
	49521	49488		216117	18818	10080
37	15631146	15543563	3430347	11688332	5589855	1399715
13	5892762	5832859	1451985	5718035	2224896	430742
	70948	70303	2835	34873	7768	2916
24	9100713	9033134	1946392	5626645	3174374	878465
	564390	604932	29134	306624	181809	87025
	2335	2335		2150	1009	567
70	27026530	26652300	8343552	18550665	8681881	2422608
26	12709012	12572515	4738986	9699158	4412001	1256145
1	412884	408667	30454	514581	108290	29062
42	13250443	13071455	3410497	7842651	3957743	1092711
1	654192	599663	163616	494276	203847	44689

11-6 续表 1

单位：万元

指 标	Item	企业单位数(个) Number of Enterprises and Units
按经济组织类型分组	**Grouped by Types of Ownership**	
独资企业	Sole Proprietorship	806
合作、合伙企业	Cooperative and Partnership Enterprises	59
股份有限公司	Joint Stock Company	146
有限责任公司	Limited Liability Company	4070
按地区分组	**Grouped by Regions**	
市 区	Urban Area	1580
崇川区	Chongchuan	100
港闸区	Gangzha	245
开发区	Development Zone	471
通州区	Tongzhou	764
海安县	Haian	863
如东县	Rudong	658
启东市	Qidong	512
如皋市	Rugao	820
海门市	Haimen	648
按行业分	**Grouped by Industries**	
制造业	Manufacturing	5032
农副食品加工业	Agrifood Processing	175
食品制造业	Food Production	25
酒、饮料和精制茶制造业	Alcohol, Beverage and Refined Tea Production	7
烟草制品业	Tobacco Industries	1
纺织业	Textile	1019
纺织服装、服饰业	Textile and Garment, Dress and Personal Adornment	384
皮革、毛皮、羽毛及其制品和制鞋业	Leather, Fur, Feather(Fuzz) and Related Products	64
木材加工及木、竹、藤、棕、草制品业	Wood Processing and Industries of Wood, Bamboo, Rattan, Palm and Grass Products	10
家具制造业	Furniture Manufacturing	24

CONTINUED 1

(Unit: 10,000 Yuan)

亏损企业 Unprofitable Firms	工业总产值（当年价格） Total Value of Industrial Output (Price of Current Year)	工业销售产值（当年价格） Industrial Sales Value (Price of Current Year)	出口交货值 Value of Export Delivery	资产总计 Total Assets	流动资产合计 Total Current Assets	应收账款 Accounts Receivable
69	23534239	23279431	5376339	14298816	7574972	2088717
1	1119676	1112372	43891	910499	207711	67645
10	11964832	11849849	1965850	9213048	4945637	1151838
227	88378231	87453473	11418937	51165629	24114787	7343351
118	42042108	41383018	9880154	31473685	14680114	3868576
14	3817293	3752736	1609594	4623280	2423345	990218
27	4401860	4336100	1002772	5124126	2578661	624211
45	15268046	14873018	2357225	12405648	5174142	1209337
32	18554910	18421165	4910563	9320630	4503966	1044809
99	17899578	17817327	1756867	8780933	4416737	1246785
15	16709843	16471753	1816331	7762555	3721166	1076323
19	15084775	14934362	1577883	9404288	4824984	1828585
44	15897802	15758619	2392197	9965759	5036077	1350014
12	17362872	17330044	1381587	8200772	4164030	1281268
306	122940052	121645022	18805018	69921821	35642264	10429268
14	4285813	4289014	194776	1583215	944509	167135
4	535695	530402	117118	293121	134254	41039
2	192326	190283		175528	87596	9271
	116618	112532		120935	63054	13250
38	13264531	13182168	2284870	6635095	3469535	945238
24	4818753	4770791	1789722	2874927	1484494	280325
3	882634	878907	451587	338308	189777	44352
	102429	97692	11462	68283	46890	11752
4	239224	234617	67662	226803	117324	21053

11-6 续表 2

单位：万元

指 标	Item	企业单位数(个) Number of Enterprises and Units
造纸和纸制品业	Paper Making and Industries of Paper Products	45
印刷和记录媒介复制业	Printing and Record Medium Reproduction	25
文教、工美、体育和娱乐用品制造业	Industries of Culture, Education, Arts, Sports and Recreational Products	327
石油加工、炼焦和核燃料加工业	Petroleum Processing, Coking and Nuclear Fuel Processing	9
化学原料和化学制品制造业	Production of Chemical Raw Materials and Chemical Products	423
医药制造业	Pharmaceutical Industry	77
化学纤维制造业	Chemical Fiber Manufacturing	70
橡胶和塑料制品业	Industry of Rubber and Plastic Products	131
非金属矿物制品业	Industry of Nonmetallic Mineral Products	230
黑色金属冶炼和压延加工业	Ferrous Metal Smelting and Pressing	85
有色金属冶炼和压延加工业	Non-Ferrous Metal Smelting and Pressing	66
金属制品业	Manufacture of Metal Products	357
通用设备制造业	Manufacture of General Purpose Machinery	484
专用设备制造业	Manufacture of Equipment for Special Purpose	211
汽车制造业	Automobile Industry	39
铁路、船舶、航空航天和其他运输设备制造业	Manufacture of Railroad, Shipping, Aerospace and Other Transportation Equipments	123
电气机械和器材制造业	Manufacture of Electrical Machinery and Equipments	316
计算机、通信和其他电子设备制造业	Manufacture of Computer, Communications and Other Electronic Products	163
仪器仪表制造业	Instrument Manufacturing	126
其他制造业	Others	6
废弃资源综合利用业	Comprehensive Utilization of Waste Resources	3
金属制品、机械和设备修理业	Metal Product, Machinery and Equipment Repair Industry	7
电力、热力和水供应业	Electric Power, Heating Power and Water Supply Industry	49
电力、热力生产和供应业	Generation and Supply of Electric Power and Heating Power	30
燃气生产和供应业	Generation and Supply of Gas	8
水的生产和供应业	Generation and Supply of Water	11

CONTINUED 2

(Unit: 10,000 Yuan)

亏损企业 Unprofitable Firms	工业总产值（当年价格） Total Value of Industrial Output (Price of Current Year)	工业销售产值（当年价格） Industrial Sales Value (Price of Current Year)	出口交货值 Value of Export Delivery	资产总计 Total Assets	流动资产合计 Total Current Assets	应收账款 Accounts Receivable
4	540768	544755	3227	1256567	204004	51270
4	210936	210114	9587	115860	66981	20457
12	5093080	5077911	1622920	2069429	1142523	278330
4	297943	298641		120625	51572	16588
36	17670567	17376381	2135778	8428075	4104903	1021660
7	2599756	2575158	283469	1368948	602452	141307
7	2956099	2940555	136051	1747017	569343	101765
9	1783219	1746402	144330	1280818	657067	214859
17	3712930	3675289	404382	2557785	1641472	644448
4	2322327	2303947	8914	759999	365773	96152
9	1790575	1745578	153988	859618	494752	139441
21	7331579	7218146	1021418	3879890	2114537	643908
31	10040227	9946881	597476	6680481	3213581	821431
18	6844578	6816506	1729211	6077495	3723400	1590804
3	1239081	1218934	76827	605071	249334	90845
10	4402922	4353944	2153889	5659400	2369778	348083
8	17212040	17001559	1344272	8673329	4859047	1819373
4	6853649	6747984	1301031	2941826	1349058	434497
4	5460360	5421584	749811	2404902	1261643	399518
2	60573	59674	10490	40981	25382	5037
2	38892	38892		35016	14115	3707
1	39930	39782	752	42474	24116	12374
1	2056926	2050102		5666171	1200844	222283
	1656037	1651616		4068141	795950	198871
	253549	251587		702013	77653	4534
1	147340	146899		896018	327241	18878

11-6 续表3

单位：万元

指 标	Item
总 计	**Total**
# 亏损企业	Unprofitable Firm
# 国有控股企业	State-holding Enterprise
# 轻工业	Light Industry
重工业	Heavy Industry
# 大型企业	Large-scale Enterprise
中型企业	Medium-sized Enterprise
小微型企业	Micro Enterprise
按登记注册类型分组	**Grouped by Registration Types**
内资企业	Domestic Enterprise
国有企业	State-owned Enterprise
集体企业	Collective Enterprise
股份合作企业	Joint Equity Cooperative Enterprise
联营企业	Joint Venture
有限责任公司	Limited Liability Company
股份有限公司	Limited Company
私营企业	Private Company
其他企业	Others
港、澳、台商投资企业	HK, Macau or Taiwan Funded Enterprise
合资经营企业(港或澳、台资)	Joint Venture(HK, Macau or Taiwan)
合作经营企业(港或澳、台资)	Cooperative Enterprise(HK, Macau or Taiwan)
港澳台商独资经营企业	Sole Proprietorship(HK, Macau or Taiwan)
港澳台商投资股份有限公司	Shareholding Limited Company(HK, Macau or Taiwan)
其他港澳台商投资企业	Others
外商投资企业	Foreign Funded Enterprise
中外合资经营企业	Sino-foreign Joint Venture
中外合作经营企业	Sino-foreign Cooperative Enterprise
外资企业	Foreign-owned Enterprise
外商投资股份有限公司	Foreign Investment Joint Stock Company

CONTINUED 3

(Unit: 10,000 Yuan)

资产总计 Total Assets						负债合计 Total Liability		
流动资产合计 Total Current Assets		固定资产合计	固定资产原价				流动负债合计	
存货 Stock	产成品 Finished Product	Total Fixed Assets	Original Value of Fixed Assets	累计折旧 Accumulated Depreciation	固定资产净值 Net Value of Fixed Assets		Total Current Liabilities	应付账款 Accounts Payable
8727829	**3339885**	**26341630**	**40877622**	**14738449**	**26139172**	**41769230**	**34885997**	**6923693**
1057140	213371	3952680	5038232	1170021	3868211	7341690	4943730	1048511
853496	355026	5718914	8171168	2511780	5659388	8327577	5780554	1793658
2616833	1127869	7628810	12023457	4466285	7557172	10924464	9364459	1519665
6110996	2212016	18712820	28854165	10272165	18582000	30844766	25521538	5404029
2618450	811766	7150577	11803798	4650094	7153704	14130579	11316325	2425586
2526877	1097137	7800536	12479992	4770877	7709115	10508222	8412369	1755019
3582502	1430982	11390517	16593832	5317479	11276353	17130429	15157304	2743089
4887880	2013516	15236223	22599375	7452308	15147067	25210916	21499428	4532847
22551	11897	149728	202834	53644	149190	420082	311124	46976
3770	520	20026	40060	20033	20026	47518	42561	7678
10087	4054	36506	56548	20256	36292	51133	39953	3109
49	32	1170	1817	647	1170	1621	1621	92
1091448	492645	5224474	7142215	1936595	5205620	7902970	5975762	1773705
687358	259721	1551406	2382213	828680	1553533	2992201	2550591	589646
3070931	1244643	8066933	12544337	4501457	8042881	13675868	12509414	2107437
1687	5	185979	229351	90995	138356	119524	68403	4204
1517921	396917	4115730	5868063	1761376	4106687	6993892	5730666	825902
803698	168782	2321726	3167171	845606	2321565	4019428	3028737	367560
1451	313	15758	24276	8518	15758	8404	7113	2564
686702	220529	1729583	2602922	882222	1720700	2918155	2648511	440491
26060	7294	47604	71276	23672	47604	47884	46282	15287
10		1059	2418	1359	1059	21	21	
2322028	929451	6989678	12410184	5524766	6885418	9564423	7655903	1564944
1091659	359727	3833475	6389976	2577628	3812348	5183077	3928617	847536
17100	3222	194544	406366	211822	194544	238434	181718	19589
1153786	536543	2696744	4883016	2192813	2690203	3966347	3471261	664777
59483	29960	264915	730826	542503	188323	176565	74307	33042

11-6 续表 4

单位：万元

指 标	Item
按经济组织类型分组	**Grouped by Types of Ownership**
独资企业	Sole Proprietorship
合作、合伙企业	Cooperative and Partnership Enterprises
股份有限公司	Joint Stock Company
有限责任公司	Limited Liability Company
按地区分组	**Grouped by Regions**
市 区	Municipality
崇川区	Chongchuan
港闸区	Gangzha
开发区	Development Zone
通州区	Tongzhou
海安县	Haian
如东县	Rudong
启东市	Qidong
如皋市	Rugao
海门市	Haimen
按行业分	**Grouped by Industries**
制造业	Manufacturing
农副食品加工业	Agrifood Processing
食品制造业	Food Production
酒、饮料和精制茶制造业	Alcohol, Beverage and Refined Tea Production
烟草制品业	Tobacco Industries
纺织业	Textile
纺织服装、服饰业	Textile and Garment, Dress and Personal Adornment
皮革、毛皮、羽毛及其制品和制鞋业	Leather, Fur, Feather(Fuzz) and Related Products
木材加工及木、竹、藤、棕、草制品业	Wood Processing and Industries of Wood, Bamboo, Rattan, Palm and Grass Products
家具制造业	Furniture Manufacturing

CONTINUED 4

(Unit: 10,000 Yuan)

资产总计 Total Assets						负债合计 Total Liability	流动负债合计 Total Current Liabilities	
流动资产合计 Total Current Assets		固定资产合计 Total Fixed Assets	固定资产原价 Original Value of Fixed Assets					应付账款 Accounts Payable
存货 Stock	产成品 Finished Product			累计折旧 Accumulated Depreciation	固定资产净值 Net Value of Fixed Assets			
1889744	779864	4680215	7853752	3189499	4664253	7471785	6587220	1179688
37938	10624	446177	743249	345048	398201	447916	327048	38001
1027840	437959	2496828	4269056	1846623	2422433	4646144	4008028	746428
5772308	2111438	18718410	28011564	9357279	18654285	29203385	23963702	4959576
3792901	1577874	11554484	20135078	8734247	11400831	17107444	14248134	3311071
513523	136364	1585216	2730094	1211514	1518580	2410444	1853182	660132
582207	166328	1783432	3073661	1290676	1782984	2898520	2213586	561772
1902833	994261	4665808	7815145	3225234	4589911	6697893	5640066	1376174
794338	280920	3520028	6516178	3006822	3509356	5100586	4541300	712994
888023	295652	2474228	3581608	1108798	2472810	4632478	4150095	668491
684101	327463	2803155	4147344	1345491	2801852	3803875	3246758	609963
955839	427792	3022530	4186855	1166700	3020155	5297693	3857454	830426
1516743	441070	3287136	4508182	1221046	3287136	6581880	5434680	874584
890222	270033	3200098	4318556	1162167	3156389	4345861	3948877	629157
8674325	3339627	22671564	35628618	13108394	22520224	38167810	32877180	6626020
402287	158523	500576	841497	341008	500490	887593	808034	149971
29848	14189	94956	138745	44353	94392	133182	121939	17617
21999	3822	75179	105119	29940	75179	91125	91052	8582
29215	5945	53404	60231	16879	43352	38578	38578	17810
910333	406575	2341777	3944247	1608800	2335447	3362182	2965795	525441
238828	127550	741217	1223137	482752	740385	1571894	1463753	147942
44147	14135	128708	182139	53635	128505	170021	159413	24277
13862	7953	13031	26015	12984	13031	46959	38428	8389
42171	16996	59878	76653	16803	59850	131041	98523	17399

11-6 续表5

单位：万元

指 标	Item
造纸和纸制品业	Paper Making and Industries of Paper Products
印刷和记录媒介复制业	Printing and Record Medium Reproduction
文教、工美、体育和娱乐用品制造业	Industries of Culture, Education, Arts, Sports and Recreational Products
石油加工、炼焦和核燃料加工业	Petroleum Processing, Coking and Nuclear Fuel Processing
化学原料和化学制品制造业	Production of Chemical Raw Materials and Chemical Products
医药制造业	Pharmaceutical Industry
化学纤维制造业	Chemical Fiber Manufacturing
橡胶和塑料制品业	Industry of Rubber and Plastic Products
非金属矿物制品业	Industry of Nonmetallic Mineral Products
黑色金属冶炼和压延加工业	Ferrous Metal Smelting and Pressing
有色金属冶炼和压延加工业	Non-Ferrous Metal Smelting and Pressing
金属制品业	Manufacture of Metal Products
通用设备制造业	Manufacture of General Purpose Machinery
专用设备制造业	Manufacture of Equipment for Special Purpose
汽车制造业	Automobile Industry
铁路、船舶、航空航天和其他运输设备制造业	Manufacture of Railroad, Shipping, Aerospace and Other Transportation Equipments
电气机械和器材制造业	Manufacture of Electrical Machinery and Equipments
计算机、通信和其他电子设备制造业	Manufacture of Computer, Communications and Other Electronic Products
仪器仪表制造业	Instrument Manufacturing
其他制造业	Others
废弃资源综合利用业	Comprehensive Utilization of Waste Resources
金属制品、机械和设备修理业	Metal Product, Machinery and Equipment Repair Industry
电力、热力和水供应业	Electric Power, Heating Power and Water Supply Industry
电力、热力生产和供应业	Generation and Supply of Electric Power and Heating Power
燃气生产和供应业	Generation and Supply of Gas
水的生产和供应业	Generation and Supply of Water

CONTINUED 5

(Unit: 10,000 Yuan)

资产总计 Total Assets						负债合计 Total Liability		
流动资产合计 Total Current Assets		固定资产合计 Total Fixed Assets	固定资产原价 Original Value of Fixed Assets				流动负债合计 Total Current Liabilities	应付账款 Accounts Payable
存货 Stock	产成品 Finished Product			累计折旧 Accumulated Depreciation	固定资产净值 Net Value of Fixed Assets			
53643	19774	789808	1043015	253214	789801	694874	317281	36567
14984	5743	42285	65589	23304	42285	59165	57267	9522
245091	96958	607404	942285	338779	603506	1138882	1098451	185802
11512	8891	19098	52059	32961	19098	73819	73819	24907
1244730	627868	3196673	5038633	1952440	3086194	4570478	4124585	656897
139335	62319	505435	716780	211345	505435	554770	457653	106711
202733	100977	810083	1459828	649744	810083	709057	554166	109930
152954	58668	487184	864177	378671	485506	602028	539762	77243
285945	68395	685870	1087470	402142	685328	1488019	1433114	287137
133666	52797	283827	415933	132106	283827	432342	376979	52627
129550	26794	248536	332261	85198	247063	531661	477214	40763
596627	245357	1125946	1747334	623462	1123872	1974033	1855448	319069
798697	309618	1926864	2851015	931245	1919771	3681124	3264169	1253674
501015	124433	1490900	2250979	760566	1490413	4079369	3037150	841542
71618	37156	280941	380026	100055	279971	299482	216613	86132
866392	72859	2109635	3040352	930744	2109608	4281493	3113362	346272
960609	462675	2211293	3469915	1259165	2210750	4075628	3865874	685558
269119	117399	1088048	2084382	998997	1085385	1393018	1163482	329640
249006	79022	717344	1141019	424984	716035	1020788	991209	238017
9743	5871	13993	17557	3564	13993	26668	26608	9793
1494	105	12093	14890	2797	12093	17189	17189	1699
3174	260	9577	15335	5758	9577	31352	30271	9092
53504	257	3670066	5249004	1630056	3618948	3601420	2008818	297674
43481	141	2759448	4097027	1340534	2756492	2711124	1314649	245693
5622	117	529837	658486	128649	529837	308602	308227	32907
4401		380781	493492	160873	332619	581695	385942	19074

11-6 续表 6

单位:万元

指 标	Item
总 计	**Total**
# 亏损企业	Unprofitable Firm
# 国有控股企业	State-holding Enterprise
# 轻工业	Light Industry
重工业	Heavy Industry
# 大型企业	Large-scale Enterprise
中型企业	Medium-sized Enterprise
小微型企业	Micro Enterprise
按登记注册类型分组	**Grouped by Registration Types**
内资企业	Domestic Enterprise
国有企业	State-owned Enterprise
集体企业	Collective Enterprise
股份合作企业	Joint Equity Cooperative Enterprise
联营企业	Joint Venture
有限责任公司	Limited Liability Company
股份有限公司	Limited Company
私营企业	Private Company
其他企业	Others
港、澳、台商投资企业	HK, Macau or Taiwan Funded Enterprise
合资经营企业(港或澳、台资)	Joint Venture(HK, Macau or Taiwan)
合作经营企业(港或澳、台资)	Cooperative Enterprise(HK, Macau or Taiwan)
港澳台商独资经营企业	Sole Proprietorship(HK, Macau or Taiwan)
港澳台商投资股份有限公司	Shareholding Limited Company(HK, Macau or Taiwan)
其他港澳台商投资企业	Others
外商投资企业	Foreign Funded Enterprise
中外合资经营企业	Sino-foreign Joint Venture
中外合作经营企业	Sino-foreign Cooperative Enterprise
外资企业	Foreign-owned Enterprise
外商投资股份有限公司	Foreign Investment Joint Stock Company

CONTINUED 6

(Unit: 10,000 Yuan)

非流动负债合计 Total Non-current Liabilities	所有者权益合计 Total Owners's Equity	实收资本 Paid-in Capital	国家资本 National Capital	集体资本 Collectively Owned Capital	法人资本 Corporate Capital	个人资本 Personal Capital	港澳台资本 Hong Kong, Macao and Taiwan capital	外商资本 Foreign Capital	主营业务收入 Main Business Revenue
6882167	**33818762**	**16477203**	**1129201**	**200789**	**3519234**	**5696591**	**1632504**	**4298883**	**123513619**
2397961	2497058	2995682	254301	55110	530562	314304	198823	1642582	4243916
2547023	4400181	2370030	832990	49022	891342	86295	317280	193101	6849475
1559250	10367587	4864169	235937	32604	775939	1636865	489925	1692899	39307339
5322916	23451174	11613034	893265	168185	2743295	4059726	1142579	2605984	84206281
2814254	9386728	3898766	410547	4026	452392	1190668	435078	1406055	31508784
2095278	9639552	4701950	361119	97640	1098399	1144316	386277	1614199	32334755
1972635	14792482	7876487	357536	99123	1968443	3361607	811149	1278629	59670080
3710422	20138078	8581911	637477	174369	2626896	4970413	98178	74578	81464433
108958	88693	79359	50859		28500				113608
4956	28887	4616	300	3704		612			124455
11180	36262	11470		325	6302	4843			352146
	1714	111			111				10008
1927082	4783964	2737176	435459	117312	1336957	823382	6076	17989	12869060
441610	2918916	756271	50219	588	230409	469195	2251	3610	7785381
1165514	12183049	4937004	46039	52126	1024617	3671393	89851	52979	60160287
51121	96593	55904	54601	315		988			49489
1263226	4694441	3008733	205987	1934	244428	424685	1343306	788394	15455722
990691	1698606	1364402	80653	1934	192411	123763	408441	557200	5721935
1291	26474	7871				1470	6401		69381
269643	2708491	1597758	125334		52016	297734	891479	231194	9048571
1601	258740	36984					36984		613501
	2128	1718				1718			2335
1908519	8986243	4886558	285737	24487	647911	301493	191020	3435911	26593464
1254459	4516082	2305096	254853	18554	500985	167964	175539	1187201	12528416
56716	276147	74056	30859	5869	973	2892	5762	27702	406484
495086	3876304	2441305	26	64	145953	129794	9600	2155870	13033332
102258	317710	66102				843	120	65138	625232

11-6 续表 7

单位：万元

指 标	Item
按经济组织类型分组	**Grouped by Types of Ownership**
独资企业	Sole Proprietorship
合作、合伙企业	Cooperative and Partnership Enterprises
股份有限公司	Joint Stock Company
有限责任公司	Limited Liability Company
按地区分组	**Grouped by Regions**
市 区	Urban Area
崇川区	Chongchuan
港闸区	Gangzha
开发区	Development Zone
通州区	Tongzhou
海安县	Haian
如东县	Rudong
启东市	Qidong
如皋市	Rugao
海门市	Haimen
按行业分	**Grouped by Industries**
制造业	Manufacturing
农副食品加工业	Agrifood Processing
食品制造业	Food Production
酒、饮料和精制茶制造业	Alcohol, Beverage and Refined Tea Production
烟草制品业	Tobacco Industries
纺织业	Textile
纺织服装、服饰业	Textile and Garment, Dress and Personal Adornment
皮革、毛皮、羽毛及其制品和制鞋业	Leather, Fur, Feather(Fuzz) and Related Products
木材加工及木、竹、藤、棕、草制品业	Wood Processing and Industries of Wood, Bamboo, Rattan, Palm and Grass Products
家具制造业	Furniture Manufacturing

CONTINUED 7

(Unit: 10,000 Yuan)

非流动负债合计 Total Non-current Liabilities	所有者权益合计 Total Owners´s Equity	实收资本 Paid-in Capital	国家资本 National Capital	集体资本 Collectively Owned Capital	法人资本 Corporate Capital	个人资本 Personal Capital	港澳台资本 Hong Kong, Macao and Taiwan capital	外商资本 Foreign Capital	主营业务收入 Main Business Revenue
884565	6827031	4153165	176747	3818	230398	454061	901079	2387064	23247807
120868	462583	153965	85460	6509	7386	14746	12163	27702	1104806
638116	4566904	1158544	50219	588	307642	691992	39356	68748	11968702
5238618	21962244	11011528	816776	189876	2973808	4535793	679906	1815369	87192304
2858873	14366242	6882913	575506	136614	1735724	1351715	448502	2634851	41045126
557215	2212836	1069415	158833	34717	387871	119819	189756	178419	3745983
684855	2225607	1033710	142043	14528	402473	238398	43948	192321	4280072
1057828	5707755	3302793	247124	46236	585118	222364	81147	2120805	14798829
558975	4220044	1476994	27506	41134	360263	771134	133652	143306	18220242
482382	4148455	1600529	3537	24158	219739	1188587	90532	73975	17863506
556488	3958680	2347318	131501	18056	389131	1088777	552889	166964	16626781
1440239	4106595	1890396	143724	2006	376555	756101	155350	456660	14862291
1147200	3383879	2158367	110311	18727	331398	803237	107064	787629	15810170
396984	3854911	1597680	164623	1228	466687	508174	278166	178804	17305745
5289564	31754011	15290724	848505	177784	3112543	5600649	1324668	4226575	121497202
79559	695623	339071	2168	50	39722	125812	75312	96007	4347227
11243	159940	54027		200	13328	17457	13295	9748	533091
72	84404	57098			15000	7066		35032	191317
	82356	22274	22274						112532
396332	3272913	1356866	27408	7153	206655	536431	175480	403739	13193805
108141	1303033	369730	2546	2108	82597	154937	48070	79473	4789959
10608	168287	69457		515	21310	22650	1465	23517	878089
8531	21325	16793				7787	5865	3140	99090
32518	95762	70269			6753	37389	5218	20908	234184

11-6 续表 8

单位：万元

指 标	Item
造纸和纸制品业	Paper Making and Industries of Paper Products
印刷和记录媒介复制业	Printing and Record Medium Reproduction
文教、工美、体育和娱乐用品制造业	Industries of Culture, Education, Arts, Sports and Recreational Products
石油加工、炼焦和核燃料加工业	Petroleum Processing, Coking and Nuclear Fuel Processing
化学原料和化学制品制造业	Production of Chemical Raw Materials and Chemical Products
医药制造业	Pharmaceutical Industry
化学纤维制造业	Chemical Fiber Manufacturing
橡胶和塑料制品业	Industry of Rubber and Plastic Products
非金属矿物制品业	Industry of Nonmetallic Mineral Products
黑色金属冶炼和压延加工业	Ferrous Metal Smelting and Pressing
有色金属冶炼和压延加工业	Non-Ferrous Metal Smelting and Pressing
金属制品业	Manufacture of Metal Products
通用设备制造业	Manufacture of General Purpose Machinery
专用设备制造业	Manufacture of Equipment for Special Purpose
汽车制造业	Automobile Industry
铁路、船舶、航空航天和其他运输设备制造业	Manufacture of Railroad, Shipping, Aerospace and Other Transportation Equipments
电气机械和器材制造业	Manufacture of Electrical Machinery and Equipments
计算机、通信和其他电子设备制造业	Manufacture of Computer, Communications and Other Electronic Products
仪器仪表制造业	Instrument Manufacturing
其他制造业	Others
废弃资源综合利用业	Comprehensive Utilization of Waste Resources
金属制品、机械和设备修理业	Metal Product, Machinery and Equipment Repair Industry
电力、热力和水供应业	Electric Power, Heating Power and Water Supply Industry
电力、热力生产和供应业	Generation and Supply of Electric Power and Heating Power
燃气生产和供应业	Generation and Supply of Gas
水的生产和供应业	Generation and Supply of Water

CONTINUED 8

(Unit: 10,000 Yuan)

非流动负债合计 Total Non-current Liabilities	所有者权益合计 Total Owners's Equity	实收资本 Paid-in Capital	国家资本 National Capital	集体资本 Collectively Owned Capital	法人资本 Corporate Capital	个人资本 Personal Capital	港澳台资本 Hong Kong, Macao and Taiwan capital	外商资本 Foreign Capital	主营业务收入 Main Business Revenue
377593	561694	704778	66943	338	1660	29443	1649	604745	508630
1898	56695	38513			3543	22280	2704	9986	204938
39855	930548	344826	40	8048	38010	169475	19601	109652	5064011
	46807	33000			904	7228	21651	3217	290773
445892	3857598	2007890	146191	12881	542444	475257	86612	744506	17334105
96991	814178	366936	10142	550	92703	122965	46442	94134	2565937
154891	1037960	504477		475	153734	208860	70819	70590	2912466
62266	678790	409157	46832	506	42577	102438	132785	84019	1724082
54594	1069767	510579	14782	15828	123113	302150	26858	27848	3646300
55363	327657	149383		21999	32322	75615	7928	11519	2238234
54447	327957	203820	30500		17207	51970	43073	61071	1760621
118585	1905856	890125	114799	200	184337	331552	141530	117708	7186752
416955	2999357	1300644	62884	43212	323667	657594	89860	123427	9914809
1042219	1998126	1146815	268969	19337	125268	420902	38565	273773	6828966
82869	305589	147202			41121	49193	8589	48299	1233815
1168131	1377907	1073097	21771	1842	173780	228201	26568	620935	4312907
209754	4597701	2186914	3440	29256	507398	1007651	167413	471755	17132397
229536	1548808	509185	5649	60	202316	199282	47891	53985	6702880
29579	1384113	370288		13225	115757	204046	16067	21194	5421930
60	14314	15405			5000	5378	3358	1668	55233
	17827	12804				12600		204	38886
1082	11122	9305	1167		318	7042		778	39237
1592603	2064751	1186479	280696	23006	406692	95942	307835	72308	2016417
1396475	1357017	723740	129166	11757	390652	74700	45158	72308	1627710
375	393411	319731	47640		14000	3393	254698		240522
195753	314323	143007	103890	11249	2040	17849	7979		148185

11-6 续表 9

单位：万元

指 标	Item	主营业务成本 Main Business Cost
总 计	**Total**	**107316216**
#亏损企业	Unprofitable Firm	4002938
#国有控股企业	State-holding Enterprise	5611843
#轻工业	Light Industry	34282585
重工业	Heavy Industry	73033631
#大型企业	Large-scale Enterprise	27336362
中型企业	Medium-sized Enterprise	27748540
小微型企业	Micro Enterprise	52231314
按登记注册类型分组	**Grouped by Registration Types**	
内资企业	Domestic Enterprise	71013269
国有企业	State-owned Enterprise	86961
集体企业	Collective Enterprise	110308
股份合作企业	Joint Equity Cooperative Enterprise	307358
联营企业	Joint Venture	9035
有限责任公司	Limited Liability Company	11350805
股份有限公司	Limited Company	6594344
私营企业	Private Company	52523161
其他企业	Others	31295
港、澳、台商投资企业	HK, Macau or Taiwan Funded Enterprise	13465490
合资经营企业(港或澳、台资)	Joint Venture(HK, Macau or Taiwan)	5025673
合作经营企业(港或澳、台资)	Cooperative Enterprise(HK, Macau or Taiwan)	59429
港澳台商独资经营企业	Sole Proprietorship(HK, Macau or Taiwan)	7867222
港澳台商投资股份有限公司	Shareholding Limited Company(HK, Macau or Taiwan)	511284
其他港澳台商投资企业	Others	1883
外商投资企业	Foreign Funded Enterprise	22837457
中外合资经营企业	Sino-foreign Joint Venture	10566540
中外合作经营企业	Sino-foreign Cooperative Enterprise	348227
外资企业	Foreign-owned Enterprise	11390494
外商投资股份有限公司	Foreign Investment Joint Stock Company	532196

CONTINUED 9

(Unit: 10,000 Yuan)

主营业务税金及附加 Tax and Extra Charges of Main Business	其他业务利润 Other Business Profit	销售费用 Selling Expenses	管理费用 Administrative Expenses	财务费用 Financial Cost			投资收益 Investment Income	营业利润 Operating Profit
					利息收入 Interest Income	利息支出 Interest Expenditure		
529051	**25612**	**1835439**	**3424385**	**1117229**	**121741**	**1194828**	**138906**	**9475706**
14088	5186	96517	306191	197997	7669	214444	9162	-324489
31687	17772	101145	299837	167831	28998	190376	50928	729959
179870	8885	589668	1062944	277560	41407	309690	60028	2977224
349181	16727	1245771	2361441	839669	80334	885138	78879	6498482
126225	12578	473423	830346	350416	59239	403968	88077	2491615
141270	12157	434150	937205	267780	35696	297029	26879	2854650
261557	877	927865	1656835	499033	26806	493831	23950	4129440
367522	15335	1230113	2174585	695069	41177	691251	81426	6090533
302	1441	6502	11524	4253	404	4620		5396
621		2810	3205	626	32	275	267	6970
1032		3208	5684	1544	3	1498		33320
104		89	105	25	3	27		651
42246	6237	170346	393455	202488	19349	205981	4861	739086
37743	3855	179371	281817	91145	8036	94741	29996	622935
285187	2099	857701	1473937	390832	13293	379901	44408	4679774
287	1704	10087	4859	4156	57	4208	1895	2403
53080	8402	205203	453963	208734	13913	224287	1699	1121502
20142	6863	65482	171902	138072	3939	151479	1306	331075
541		533	1585	1113		1113		6181
30188	1539	133901	274378	70875	7192	70274	393	706138
2198		5284	5798	-1319	2774	1421		77964
12		4	300	-7	7	1		143
108449	1874	400122	795838	213426	66651	279290	55782	2263671
57605	5430	179363	426198	99813	25107	131174	713	1185224
2105	149	1999	13365	6745	1152	7724	36393	69274
45735	3681	216674	348205	105966	39725	138898	18676	934417
3005	-7386	2087	8071	902	666	1494		74757

11-6 续表 10

单位:万元

指 标	Item	主营业务成本 Main Business Cost
按经济组织类型分组	**Grouped by Types of Ownership**	
独资企业	Sole Proprietorship	20269223
合作、合伙企业	Cooperative and Partnership Enterprises	945654
股份有限公司	Joint Stock Company	10125094
有限责任公司	Limited Liability Company	75976245
按地区分组	**Grouped by Regions**	
市 区	Urban Area	35646284
崇川区	Chongchuan	3011118
港闸区	Gangzha	3637017
开发区	Development Zone	13053821
通州区	Tongzhou	15944328
海安县	Haian	15558438
如东县	Rudong	14556608
启东市	Qidong	12784602
如皋市	Rugao	14103101
海门市	Haimen	14667183
按行业分	**Grouped by Industries**	
制造业	Manufacturing	105851688
农副食品加工业	Agrifood Processing	3960773
食品制造业	Food Production	453031
酒、饮料和精制茶制造业	Alcohol, Beverage and Refined Tea Production	157514
烟草制品业	Tobacco Industries	87500
纺织业	Textile	11688708
纺织服装、服饰业	Textile and Garment, Dress and Personal Adornment	4132951
皮革、毛皮、羽毛及其制品和制鞋业	Leather, Fur, Feather(Fuzz) and Related Products	777037
木材加工及木、竹、藤、棕、草制品业	Wood Processing and Industries of Wood, Bamboo, Rattan, Palm and Grass Products	88056
家具制造业	Furniture Manufacturing	200308

CONTINUED 10

(Unit: 10,000 Yuan)

主营业务税金及附加 Tax and Extra Charges of Main Business	其他业务利润 Other Business Profit	销售费用 Selling Expenses	管理费用 Administrative Expenses	财务费用 Financial Cost	利息收入 Interest Income	利息支出 Interest Expenditure	投资收益 Investment Income	营业利润 Operating Profit
83279	6661	371813	657250	186887	47364	218984	19335	1724988
5110	1853	19615	32075	14834	1233	15839	38288	126346
57310	−3420	237395	377295	136902	12496	143898	48985	1062283
383352	20518	1206617	2357765	778606	60648	816106	32299	6562089
172219	13689	570701	1380722	352745	84828	427666	87352	3014955
21228	12427	79408	218431	29937	18923	48416	18313	407014
22344	1712	87504	187396	62646	7127	66008	48180	342472
42751	−1471	177873	448109	96700	49690	147199	7654	971886
85895	1021	225917	526786	163462	9089	166043	13205	1293582
74286	521	305547	411334	189509	4417	187916	8684	1334770
67796	1096	211556	385966	117035	6577	116254	34916	1325389
85841	2931	307455	445836	176822	11839	181957	7771	1084851
57858	5081	237828	423955	196992	6444	196874	−16722	792055
71051	2294	202353	376571	84126	7636	84161	16907	1923686
516995	20324	1813587	3376631	994012	113742	1064275	98855	9069294
12746	1011	59538	65568	20670	23416	39919	18137	233008
3065		10415	14955	5445	532	5400	5	46208
5634		9048	11667	2109	91	2329		6179
488	61	1293	6804	−446	447	2		16954
57048	2169	168818	313467	88851	8709	93204	9143	897386
23714	1194	72881	153162	49263	1130	47902	16936	373114
5251	52	15008	20358	5187	212	5278	240	55481
558		2001	2491	1162	46	1006		5125
1160	146	4678	12952	2833	309	2958	201	13023

11-6 续表 11

单位：万元

指 标	Item	主营业务成本 Main Business Cost
造纸和纸制品业	Paper Making and Industries of Paper Products	465554
印刷和记录媒介复制业	Printing and Record Medium Reproduction	182091
文教、工美、体育和娱乐用品制造业	Industries of Culture, Education, Arts, Sports and Recreational Products	4347557
石油加工、炼焦和核燃料加工业	Petroleum Processing, Coking and Nuclear Fuel Processing	274990
化学原料和化学制品制造业	Production of Chemical Raw Materials and Chemical Products	15416961
医药制造业	Pharmaceutical Industry	2204098
化学纤维制造业	Chemical Fiber Manufacturing	2353532
橡胶和塑料制品业	Industry of Rubber and Plastic Products	1494504
非金属矿物制品业	Industry of Nonmetallic Mineral Products	3130436
黑色金属冶炼和压延加工业	Ferrous Metal Smelting and Pressing	2035718
有色金属冶炼和压延加工业	Non-Ferrous Metal Smelting and Pressing	1588477
金属制品业	Manufacture of Metal Products	6251338
通用设备制造业	Manufacture of General Purpose Machinery	8510693
专用设备制造业	Manufacture of Equipment for Special Purpose	5838908
汽车制造业	Automobile Industry	1064112
铁路、船舶、航空航天和其他运输设备制造业	Manufacture of Railroad, Shipping, Aerospace and Other Transportation Equipments	3769673
电气机械和器材制造业	Manufacture of Electrical Machinery and Equipments	14708334
计算机、通信和其他电子设备制造业	Manufacture of Computer, Communications and Other Electronic Products	5908789
仪器仪表制造业	Instrument Manufacturing	4644251
其他制造业	Others	48154
废弃资源综合利用业	Comprehensive Utilization of Waste Resources	32221
金属制品、机械和设备修理业	Metal Product, Machinery and Equipment Repair Industry	35423
电力、热力和水供应业	Electric Power, Heating Power and Water Supply Industry	1464527
电力、热力生产和供应业	Generation and Supply of Electric Power and Heating Power	1190262
燃气生产和供应业	Generation and Supply of Gas	181126
水的生产和供应业	Generation and Supply of Water	93139

CONTINUED 11

(Unit: 10,000 Yuan)

主营业务税金及附加 Tax and Extra Charges of Main Business	其他业务利润 Other Business Profit	销售费用 Selling Expenses	管理费用 Administrative Expenses	财务费用 Financial Cost			投资收益 Investment Income	营业利润 Operating Profit
					利息收入 Interest Income	利息支出 Interest Expenditure		
2542	3	12334	24303	4081	260	14348	20	−3854
1005	132	3869	6699	1805	41	1372	3	9586
23796	212	63751	132584	24173	677	22719	619	472041
466	−852	3958	5393	216	−14	224	419	5319
44145	−3940	206702	378080	109448	23618	120701	3975	1158984
11520	426	48966	97141	14071	1003	13173	6176	196856
14478	132	39936	86625	22460	2899	24548	134	398952
7558	5386	35526	65170	23151	3261	25513	−294	103623
19930	−65	76893	102324	44138	2164	43104	−161	270721
5830		16679	42022	14709	378	12830	13	124409
4067		18838	25260	16736	779	15603	158	109499
30511	1102	87984	187701	59498	5913	60380	1477	571988
55020	4890	216828	348547	65848	5355	70214	9829	729981
27898	3511	106260	294789	71578	16096	83136	376	518045
10961	73	24919	34989	10956	1317	12371	−18372	69622
17855	397	43006	165154	122357	3904	133917	−2418	203822
70967	679	277283	428001	139698	5802	138417	51196	1557388
34504	2536	90704	186194	40531	3032	39757	−945	447102
23875	938	92326	156682	32461	2288	33075	1800	473169
125		1257	2935	352	39	352		2381
33		1285	1453	346		163		3548
245	133	602	3162	327	40	366	191	−364
12057	5288	21852	47754	123217	7999	130553	40051	406412
9434	1154	316	23076	104928	7225	111645	36573	344903
1692	989	3724	9147	9432	275	9597	1532	44930
932	3145	17813	15532	8856	500	9312	1946	16579

11-6 续表12

单位：万元

指 标	Item	营业外收入 Non-business Income
总 计	**Total**	**175980**
#亏损企业	Unprofitable Firm	26475
#国有控股企业	State-holding Enterprise	31825
#轻工业	Light Industry	46444
重工业	Heavy Industry	129536
#大型企业	Large-scale Enterprise	57108
中型企业	Medium-sized Enterprise	43725
小微型企业	Micro Enterprise	75147
按登记注册类型分组	**Grouped by Registration Types**	
内资企业	Domestic Enterprise	104768
国有企业	State-owned Enterprise	4747
集体企业	Collective Enterprise	134
股份合作企业	Joint Equity Cooperative Enterprise	2
联营企业	Joint Venture	
有限责任公司	Limited Liability Company	31806
股份有限公司	Limited Company	24496
私营企业	Private Company	43415
其他企业	Others	169
港、澳、台商投资企业	HK, Macau or Taiwan Funded Enterprise	25920
合资经营企业(港或澳、台资)	Joint Venture(HK, Macau or Taiwan)	8004
合作经营企业(港或澳、台资)	Cooperative Enterprise(HK, Macau or Taiwan)	
港澳台商独资经营企业	Sole Proprietorship(HK, Macau or Taiwan)	17873
港澳台商投资股份有限公司	Shareholding Limited Company(HK, Macau or Taiwan)	
其他港澳台商投资企业	Others	44
外商投资企业	Foreign Funded Enterprise	45292
中外合资经营企业	Sino-foreign Joint Venture	26704
中外合作经营企业	Sino-foreign Cooperative Enterprise	1053
外资企业	Foreign-owned Enterprise	16002
外商投资股份有限公司	Foreign Investment Joint Stock Company	1532

CONTINUED 12

(Unit: 10,000 Yuan)

补贴收入 Subsidy Income	营业外支出 Non-business Expenditure	利润总额 Total Profit	应交所得税 Income Tax Payable	亏损企业亏损总额 Total Loss of Unprofitable Enterprises	利税总额 Total Profits and Taxes	本年应交增值税 Added Value Tax Payable of the Year	全部从业人员年平均人数(人) The Annual Number of All Employees(person)
61254	**274082**	**9378526**	**1865937**	**314359**	**14777086**	**4866370**	**988301**
7926	16347	-314359	1444	314359	-249600	50536	55205
10850	77506	684278	165299	71630	942218	225750	38246
8644	78491	2945630	592470	79045	4676497	1549822	432307
52610	195591	6432896	1273467	235314	10100589	3316548	555994
18946	135526	2413197	423329	100084	3949906	1410051	240642
11948	59959	2838587	605607	113345	4341753	1360589	267467
30359	78597	4126742	837001	100930	6485428	2095730	480192
32218	133923	6062209	1204607	126088	9690824	3259356	652767
107	939	9204	1756	1024	16171	6544	1201
	56	7048	1434		11260	3591	1540
	41	33281	6574		50176	15863	2520
		651	163		1208	454	91
11731	27678	743325	159428	72457	1139051	352647	98845
7298	16854	630577	117789	19068	995852	327484	63218
13045	88161	4635747	917277	33539	7472250	2550579	484716
38	196	2376	188		4856	2194	636
4329	15261	1132225	222414	91865	1792022	606426	132180
1097	5247	333853	79200	70907	585222	231100	53609
	243	5939	1010		10715	4236	1192
3232	9771	714284	131714	20958	1095581	351041	73653
		77964	10481		100306	20048	3702
	1	186	9		198		24
24707	124897	2184092	438916	96406	3294240	1000588	203354
19242	83439	1128489	238084	48289	1695015	508575	98710
15	1619	68708	6389	60	91838	21019	4093
4637	35951	914494	179078	42635	1409837	448870	98641
813	3889	72400	15366	5422	97549	22124	1910

11-6 续表 13

单位:万元

指 标	Item	营业外收入 Non-business Income
按经济组织类型分组	**Grouped by Types of Ownership**	
独资企业	Sole Proprietorship	38757
合作、合伙企业	Cooperative and Partnership Enterprises	1280
股份有限公司	Joint Stock Company	30323
有限责任公司	Limited Liability Company	105619
按地区分组	**Grouped by Regions**	
市 区	Urban Area	87005
崇川区	Chongchuan	21401
港闸区	Gangzha	24649
开发区	Development Zone	21279
通州区	Tongzhou	19676
海安县	Haian	16596
如东县	Rudong	24847
启东市	Qidong	6945
如皋市	Rugao	14259
海门市	Haimen	26328
按行业分	**Grouped by Industries**	
制造业	Manufacturing	161606
农副食品加工业	Agrifood Processing	1051
食品制造业	Food Production	625
酒、饮料和精制茶制造业	Alcohol, Beverage and Refined Tea Production	1639
烟草制品业	Tobacco Industries	266
纺织业	Textile	20376
纺织服装、服饰业	Textile and Garment, Dress and Personal Adornment	1008
皮革、毛皮、羽毛及其制品和制鞋业	Leather, Fur, Feather(Fuzz) and Related Products	48
木材加工及木、竹、藤、棕、草制品业	Wood Processing and Industries of Wood, Bamboo, Rattan, Palm and Grass Products	30
家具制造业	Furniture Manufacturing	150

CONTINUED 13

(Unit: 10,000 Yuan)

补贴收入 Subsidy Income	营业外支出 Non-business Expenditure	利润总额 Total Profit	应交所得税 Income Tax Payable	亏损企业亏损总额 Total Loss of Unprofitable Enterprises	利税总额 Total Profits and Taxes	本年应交增值税 Added Value Tax Payable of the Year	全部从业人员年平均人数(人) The Annual Number of All Employees(person)
7977	47808	1716008	328056	64637	2644020	843805	182913
52	2120	125505	16961	60	182882	52260	10309
9750	32020	1060586	186143	25049	1654192	536133	89289
43474	192134	6476427	1334777	224613	10295993	3434173	705790
35088	168742	2934076	566736	162864	4493129	1384549	336154
14681	61204	368032	87087	17281	478359	89001	30386
7426	9772	357349	67083	30524	501614	121676	44015
8690	45492	947676	229767	97772	1377788	385599	88470
4292	52275	1261020	182799	17289	2135368	788273	173283
3354	33843	1317523	287169	22658	2036370	644446	138367
11800	33212	1317025	260999	5333	2143550	758629	110213
2231	13250	1078546	192170	41073	1800093	635605	108652
6806	22045	784269	137416	75977	1368881	526315	175686
1976	2991	1947087	421447	6453	2935064	916826	119229
52600	266722	8965099	1777392	313798	14240237	4755125	980324
498	12967	221092	49083	4470	335098	101150	22624
58	48	46786	7733	1889	74259	24408	4511
	1	7818	1645	2289	19928	6476	2911
	4	17215	4304		21771	4068	587
4133	22836	895170	180443	10468	1459989	507220	154066
125	11781	362341	54875	2782	598154	212036	80573
17	301	55232	11352	218	100418	39935	14923
	71	5084	999		10755	5100	1607
	612	12560	3769	5161	24087	10337	4405

11-6 续表 14

单位：万元

指 标	Item	营业外收入 Non-business Income
造纸和纸制品业	Paper Making and Industries of Paper Products	239
印刷和记录媒介复制业	Printing and Record Medium Reproduction	39
文教、工美、体育和娱乐用品制造业	Industries of Culture, Education, Arts, Sports and Recreational Products	1491
石油加工、炼焦和核燃料加工业	Petroleum Processing, Coking and Nuclear Fuel Processing	32
化学原料和化学制品制造业	Production of Chemical Raw Materials and Chemical Products	14689
医药制造业	Pharmaceutical Industry	6680
化学纤维制造业	Chemical Fiber Manufacturing	7029
橡胶和塑料制品业	Industry of Rubber and Plastic Products	7334
非金属矿物制品业	Industry of Nonmetallic Mineral Products	5855
黑色金属冶炼和压延加工业	Ferrous Metal Smelting and Pressing	678
有色金属冶炼和压延加工业	Non-Ferrous Metal Smelting and Pressing	4342
金属制品业	Manufacture of Metal Products	7702
通用设备制造业	Manufacture of General Purpose Machinery	14957
专用设备制造业	Manufacture of Equipment for Special Purpose	13148
汽车制造业	Automobile Industry	4389
铁路、船舶、航空航天和其他运输设备制造业	Manufacture of Railroad, Shipping, Aerospace and Other Transportation Equipments	6939
电气机械和器材制造业	Manufacture of Electrical Machinery and Equipments	19164
计算机、通信和其他电子设备制造业	Manufacture of Computer, Communications and Other Electronic Products	17619
仪器仪表制造业	Instrument Manufacturing	3895
其他制造业	Others	2
废弃资源综合利用业	Comprehensive Utilization of Waste Resources	
金属制品、机械和设备修理业	Metal Product, Machinery and Equipment Repair Industry	191
电力、热力和水供应业	Electric Power, Heating Power and Water Supply Industry	14374
电力、热力生产和供应业	Generation and Supply of Electric Power and Heating Power	12032
燃气生产和供应业	Generation and Supply of Gas	1803
水的生产和供应业	Generation and Supply of Water	538

CONTINUED 14

(Unit: 10,000 Yuan)

补贴收入 Subsidy Income	营业外支出 Non-business Expenditure	利润总额 Total Profit	应交所得税 Income Tax Payable	亏损企业亏损总额 Total Loss of Unprofitable Enterprises	利税总额 Total Profits and Taxes	本年应交增值税 Added Value Tax Payable of the Year	全部从业人员年平均人数(人) The Annual Number of All Employees(person)
15	277	-3892	6911	34624	14617	15959	5637
	413	9212	1343	1010	16604	6375	2914
588	8715	465007	99353	3786	711279	222452	67724
	150	5201	2143	3484	8433	2766	833
4892	45822	1127892	239380	29814	1729406	556592	68864
1185	5331	198204	34778	4244	323961	114179	18703
224	7975	398006	94353	2118	545534	133004	15621
3907	1938	109019	24498	8894	185916	69293	21082
3447	4667	272205	46804	4654	437265	145039	30905
288	2406	122681	23012	188	202102	73558	12953
1438	464	113377	21775	4519	172778	55331	10153
1457	5616	574075	115767	6052	885011	280328	57029
6229	5761	739306	155469	50367	1166331	371803	80630
1177	69098	462097	93688	37900	747683	257570	51183
127	4155	69856	13805	2568	135462	54475	13180
1486	10714	200047	44321	69514	365047	146968	48118
7759	21698	1554868	307692	3531	2491489	865386	98488
12635	8410	456311	62133	9222	721080	230169	54151
917	14161	462904	74338	7111	724755	237955	33265
		2383	612	845	4766	2258	1092
		3548	816	430	4867	1287	484
	334	-507	199	1648	1393	1653	1108
8654	7360	413427	88545	561	536849	111245	7977
7732	6704	350231	75153		455303	95638	4987
815	136	46597	11450		56591	8302	967
107	519	16598	1943	561	24955	7305	2023

11-7　大中型工业企业主要经济指标(2014 年)

单位:万元

指　标	Item	企业单位数(个) Number of Enterprises(unit)
总　计	**Total**	**607**
# 亏损企业	Unprofitable Firm	33
# 国有控股企业	State-holding Enterprise	35
# 轻工业	Light Industry	275
重工业	Heavy Industry	332
# 大型企业	Large-scale Enterprise	110
中型企业	Medium-sized Enterprise	497
按登记注册类型分组	**Grouped by Registration Types**	
内资企业	Domestic Enterprise	379
国有企业	State-owned Enterprise	1
股份合作企业	Joint Equity Cooperative Enterprise	2
有限责任公司	Limited Liability Company	68
股份有限公司	Limited Company	43
私营企业	Private Company	264
其他企业	Others	1
港、澳、台商投资企业	HK, Macau or Taiwan Funded Enterprise	92
合资经营企业(港或澳、台资)	Joint Venture(HK, Macau or Taiwan)	36
合作经营企业(港或澳、台资)	Cooperative Enterprise(HK, Macau or Taiwan)	1
港澳台商独资经营企业	Sole Proprietorship(HK, Macau or Taiwan)	53
港澳台商投资股份有限公司	Shareholding Limited Company(HK, Macau or Taiwan)	2
外商投资企业	Foreign Funded Enterprise	136
中外合资经营企业	Sino-foreign Joint Venture	64
中外合作经营企业	Sino-foreign Cooperative Enterprise	5
外资企业	Foreign-owned Enterprise	66
外商投资股份有限公司	Foreign Investment Joint Stock Company	1
按地区分组	**Grouped by Regions**	
市　区	Urban Area	185
崇川区	Chongchuan	18
港闸区	Gangzha	26
开发区	Development Zone	57
通州区	Tongzhou	84
海安县	Haian	83
如东县	Rudong	80

MAJOR ECONOMIC INDICATORS OF LARGE AND MEDIUM SIZE INDUSTRIAL ENTERPRISES(2014)

(Unit: 10,000 Yuan)

亏损企业 Unprofitable Firms	工业总产值（当年价格） Total Industrial Output (Price of Current Year)	工业销售产值（当年价格） Industrial Sales Value (Price of Current Year)	出口交货值 Value of Export Delivery	资产总计 Total Assets	流动资产合计 Total Current Assets	应收账款 Accounts Receivable
33	**64226535**	**63549082**	**13506982**	**43665081**	**20538015**	**5660167**
33	2317145	2303577	1391366	7111610	2752427	641808
8	5769743	5704949	1733299	9252938	3692043	1340963
14	17765696	17679560	4101554	11934433	5154182	992238
19	46460839	45869522	9405427	31730648	15383832	4667929
5	31464816	31207669	8450351	23517307	11565025	3558099
28	32761719	32341413	5056631	20147774	8972990	2102069
18	39030040	38611670	4847056	24399203	11526212	3144301
1	10159	10159		146013	94912	1139
	133002	133002		46995	16892	3759
11	6595532	6496512	958627	6710610	2428203	866811
2	7133897	7086057	1319425	5335846	2984920	665235
4	25120107	24848598	2569004	11951375	5986962	1600281
	37343	37343		208364	14324	7077
4	9145962	9139456	2635272	7635886	3620119	871048
1	3305385	3272512	1135937	3764122	1402024	247388
	35689	35689	2835	23033	3479	1427
3	5245520	5231345	1472387	3544442	2034234	535400
	559369	599911	24114	304288	180383	86834
11	16050533	15797956	6024653	11629992	5391685	1644818
7	8277984	8146261	3940960	6533762	3063935	934240
	265308	263550	20144	459147	86929	21403
4	7267947	7148853	2063549	4396772	2163393	661960
	239293	239293		240311	77428	27215
19	23967262	23602794	7087089	20313371	9036765	2143296
2	2862502	2794767	1486491	3870945	1934001	828593
6	1855028	1829907	797162	2783618	1441593	250061
6	9354537	9144847	1519802	7769576	2890833	653964
5	9895196	9833274	3283633	5889233	2770338	410679
1	9848024	9837102	1428608	4203916	1971533	514783
	6868147	6766724	1211877	3238145	1804277	644313

11-7 续表1

单位：万元

指 标	Item	企业单位数(个) Number of Enterprises(unit)
启东市	Qidong	61
如皋市	Rugao	126
海门市	Haimen	72
按行业分组	**Grouped by Industries**	
农副食品加工业	Agrifood Processing	15
食品制造业	Food Production	6
酒、饮料和精制茶制造业	Alcohol, Beverage and Refined Tea Production	3
烟草制品业	Tobacco Industries	1
纺织业	Textile	75
纺织服装、服饰业	Textile and Garment, Dress and Personal Adornment	45
皮革、毛皮、羽毛及其制品和制鞋业	Leather, Fur, Feather(Fuzz) and Related Products	10
木材加工和木、竹、藤、棕、草制品业	Wood Processing and Industries of Wood, Bamboo, Rattan, Palm and Grass Products	1
家具制造业	Furniture Manufacturing	6
造纸和纸制品业	Paper Making and Industries of Paper Products	3
印刷和记录媒介复制业	Printing and Record Medium Reproduction	2
文教、工美、体育和娱乐用品制造业	Industries of Culture, Education, Arts, Sports and Recreational Products	50
化学原料和化学制品制造业	Production of Chemical Raw Materials and Chemical Products	49
医药制造业	Pharmaceutical Industry	19
化学纤维制造业	Chemical Fiber Manufacturing	12
橡胶和塑料制品业	Industry of Rubber and Plastic Products	9
非金属矿物制品业	Industry of Nonmetallic Mineral Products	11
黑色金属冶炼和压延加工业	Ferrous Metal Smelting and Pressing	8
有色金属冶炼和压延加工业	Non-Ferrous Metal Smelting and Pressing	6
金属制品业	Manufacture of Metal Products	29
通用设备制造业	Manufacture of General Purpose Machinery	45
专用设备制造业	Manufacture of Equipment for Special Purpose	28
汽车制造业	Automobile Industry	7
铁路、船舶、航空航天和其他运输设备制造业	Manufacture of Railroad, Shipping, Aerospace and Other Transportation Equipments	25
电气机械和器材制造业	Manufacture of Electrical Machinery and Equipments	67
计算机、通信和其他电子设备制造业	Manufacture of Computer, Communications and Other Electronic Products	39
仪器仪表制造业	Instrument Manufacturing	26
其他制造业	Others	2
金属制品、机械和设备修理业	Metal Product, Machinery and Equipment Repair Industry	1
电力、热力生产和供应业	Generation and Supply of Electric Power and Heating Power	3
燃气生产和供应业	Generation and Supply of Gas	1
水的生产和供应业	Generation and Supply of Water	3

CONTINUED 1

(Unit: 10,000 Yuan)

亏损企业 Unprofitable Firms	工业总产值 (当年价格) Total Industrial Output (Price of Current Year)	工业销售产值 (当年价格) Industrial Sales Value (Price of Current Year)	出口交货值 Value of Export Delivery	资产总计 Total Assets	流动资产合计 Total Current Assets	应收账款 Accounts Receivable
6	5898820	5814145	1251915	5843897	2911361	1185646
5	9264818	9166043	1935534	6456957	3039755	676576
2	8379463	8362275	591960	3608795	1774324	495554
	1976259	1977650	60312	716220	411486	73534
1	337124	334339	78102	177857	88167	27255
1	133986	133469		120032	54352	2654
	116618	112532		120935	63054	13250
2	5589342	5569550	1309721	3223251	1545139	339978
3	2313105	2287504	1101609	1925497	918474	136863
	470840	469096	296699	165773	90198	19853
	20806	16666	11462	22711	13256	1760
1	147957	143811	57749	163277	74614	12539
1	126366	133818		1081339	103784	10172
	59785	59785		7360	4103	1917
2	1863934	1865166	727827	979386	572212	102121
2	7870873	7725843	1301205	3763463	1837672	450059
1	1372580	1371913	211135	885997	377881	89901
	2017219	2006551	89288	1352905	384669	61209
	723395	706230	75314	623297	322647	94471
	838166	811234	248710	694184	380724	98007
	1485524	1473251	8232	442175	198003	41017
1	450748	443248	14902	297438	196039	58804
3	3136975	3105645	797085	1634943	837681	208327
7	3189802	3141885	363841	3769780	1661506	310985
3	4378284	4371592	1669701	4855083	3027318	1365263
1	897727	880823	21994	327167	117644	32912
1	3101543	3068780	2038155	4625785	1794329	185146
	12347631	12178657	1134679	6147021	3487522	1331906
1	4666383	4573159	1244884	2018318	831565	267220
1	3566179	3560025	634857	1449688	752103	205266
	32807	32283	9520	15406	8785	1596
	3987	3987		2094	1442	891
	875807	875807		1568569	243725	103650
	44539	44539		106719	16721	2776
1	70245	70245		381412	121198	8865

11-7 续表 2

单位：万元

指 标	Item
总 计	**Total**
#亏损企业	Unprofitable Firm
#国有控股企业	State-holding Enterprise
#轻工业	Light Industry
重工业	Heavy Industry
#大型企业	Large-scale Enterprise
中型企业	Medium-sized Enterprise
按登记注册类型分组	**Grouped by Registration Types**
内资企业	Domestic Enterprise
国有企业	State-owned Enterprise
股份合作企业	Joint Equity Cooperative Enterprise
有限责任公司	Limited Liability Company
股份有限公司	Limited Company
私营企业	Private Company
其他企业	Others
港、澳、台商投资企业	HK, Macau or Taiwan Funded Enterprise
合资经营企业(港或澳、台资)	Joint Venture(HK, Macau or Taiwan)
合作经营企业(港或澳、台资)	Cooperative Enterprise(HK, Macau or Taiwan)
港澳台商独资经营企业	Sole Proprietorship(HK, Macau or Taiwan)
港澳台商投资股份有限公司	Shareholding Limited Company(HK, Macau or Taiwan)
外商投资企业	Foreign Funded Enterprise
中外合资经营企业	Sino-foreign Joint Venture
中外合作经营企业	Sino-foreign Cooperative Enterprise
外资企业	Foreign-owned Enterprise
外商投资股份有限公司	Foreign Investment Joint Stock Company
按地区分组	**Grouped by Regions**
市 区	Urban Area
崇川区	Chongchuan
港闸区	Gangzha
开发区	Development Zone
通州区	Tongzhou
海安县	Haian
如东县	Rudong

CONTINUED 2

(Unit: 10,000 Yuan)

资产总计 Total Assets						负债合计 Total Liability		
流动资产合计 Total Current Assets		固定资产合计 Total Fixed Assets	固定资产原价 Original Value of Fixed Assets				流动负债合计 Total Current Liabilities	
存货 Stock	产成品 Finished Product			累计折旧 Accumulated Depreciation	固定资产净值 Net Value of Fixed Assets			应付账款 Accounts Payable
5145327	**1908903**	**14951113**	**24283790**	**9420971**	**14862819**	**24638801**	**19728694**	**4180604**
703984	99528	2911319	3790224	884099	2906125	5667200	3507636	718813
695657	265031	3615807	5564597	2008317	3556280	6070657	4121579	1594363
1420449	644404	4595656	7266120	2732350	4533771	5907625	4627868	750710
3724878	1264499	10355457	17017669	6688621	10329048	18731177	15100826	3429894
2618450	811766	7150577	11803798	4650094	7153704	14130579	11316325	2425586
2526877	1097137	7800536	12479992	4770877	7709115	10508222	8412369	1755019
2655838	1149760	8077312	12341754	4330312	8011442	13685016	11128551	2632518
1223		48022	66877	19393	47484	130580	40280	3860
6471	1956	20623	24615	3992	20623	31064	19911	-1090
640585	335697	2694718	3893642	1214397	2679244	4400522	3115219	1205319
625644	242025	1392961	2161368	764862	1396506	2702189	2293786	550725
1380485	570083	3736501	5970886	2240165	3730721	6303855	5593559	870565
1429		184488	224367	87503	136864	116806	65796	3141
1071588	215287	2545083	3600696	1056488	2544209	5044142	3903995	504983
592366	83760	1429082	1932676	503594	1429082	3022301	2123194	230872
422		9555	13952	4397	9555	3892	2725	2125
452784	124233	1059213	1583590	525252	1058338	1971720	1733449	256860
26017	7294	47234	70478	23245	47234	46229	44627	15125
1417901	543856	4328718	8341339	4034171	4307169	5909643	4696147	1043103
779749	209515	2535268	4490818	1976434	2514384	3409504	2526397	645786
13502	2076	163631	331015	167384	163631	217571	165224	17546
616530	332265	1480045	2878710	1399331	1479379	2240255	1971421	356489
8120		149775	640797	491022	149775	42313	33106	23283
2398069	1007455	7312475	13490487	6238577	7251910	10772797	8754551	2313873
375191	86358	1396530	2378847	1044851	1333997	1905556	1367189	509576
291161	88599	779641	1784163	1004421	779743	1427379	1100735	347787
1224005	646825	2985502	5269249	2280405	2988844	4150577	3444887	1052441
507712	185673	2150802	4058228	1908900	2149328	3289285	2841740	404070
467169	170811	1178155	1797928	619773	1178155	2235914	1924804	282612
348076	196108	798276	1321601	523639	797962	1447077	1358044	291414

11-7 续表 3

单位：万元

指 标	Item
启东市	Qidong
如皋市	Rugao
海门市	Haimen
按行业分组	**Grouped by Industries**
农副食品加工业	Agrifood Processing
食品制造业	Food Production
酒、饮料和精制茶制造业	Alcohol, Beverage and Refined Tea Production
烟草制品业	Tobacco Industries
纺织业	Textile
纺织服装、服饰业	Textile and Garment, Dress and Personal Adornment
皮革、毛皮、羽毛及其制品和制鞋业	Leather, Fur, Feather(Fuzz) and Related Products
木材加工和木、竹、藤、棕、草制品业	Wood Processing and Industries of Wood, Bamboo, Rattan, Palm and Grass Products
家具制造业	Furniture Manufacturing
造纸和纸制品业	Paper Making and Industries of Paper Products
印刷和记录媒介复制业	Printing and Record Medium Reproduction
文教、工美、体育和娱乐用品制造业	Industries of Culture, Education, Arts, Sports and Recreational Products
化学原料和化学制品制造业	Production of Chemical Raw Materials and Chemical Products
医药制造业	Pharmaceutical Industry
化学纤维制造业	Chemical Fiber Manufacturing
橡胶和塑料制品业	Industry of Rubber and Plastic Products
非金属矿物制品业	Industry of Nonmetallic Mineral Products
黑色金属冶炼和压延加工业	Ferrous Metal Smelting and Pressing
有色金属冶炼和压延加工业	Non-Ferrous Metal Smelting and Pressing
金属制品业	Manufacture of Metal Products
通用设备制造业	Manufacture of General Purpose Machinery
专用设备制造业	Manufacture of Equipment for Special Purpose
汽车制造业	Automobile Industry
铁路、船舶、航空航天和其他运输设备制造业	Manufacture of Railroad, Shipping, Aerospace and Other Transportation Equipments
电气机械和器材制造业	Manufacture of Electrical Machinery and Equipments
计算机、通信和其他电子设备制造业	Manufacture of Computer, Communications and Other Electronic Products
仪器仪表制造业	Instrument Manufacturing
其他制造业	Others
金属制品、机械和设备修理业	Metal Product, Machinery and Equipment Repair Industry
电力、热力生产和供应业	Generation and Supply of Electric Power and Heating Power
燃气生产和供应业	Generation and Supply of Gas
水的生产和供应业	Generation and Supply of Water

CONTINUED 3

(Unit: 10,000 Yuan)

资产总计 Total Assets						负债合计 Total Liability		
流动资产合计 Total Current Assets		固定资产合计 Total Fixed Assets	固定资产原价 Original Value of Fixed Assets				流动负债合计 Total Current Liabilities	
存货 Stock	产成品 Finished Product			累计折旧 Accumulated Depreciation	固定资产净值 Net Value of Fixed Assets			应付账款 Accounts Payable
487354	222764	1944851	2682751	738653	1944098	3643220	2385985	542448
1003666	223911	2268388	3078354	809966	2268388	4628705	3646587	540068
440993	87854	1448968	1912668	490363	1422305	1911089	1658722	210189
196620	80351	265789	511487	245698	265789	373709	319869	63022
18204	9161	47479	74871	27956	46916	88738	82248	11828
15342	435	64175	89837	25662	64175	77874	77874	2588
29215	5945	53404	60231	16879	43352	38578	38578	17810
455202	219544	1225336	2094199	869876	1224323	1437668	1142911	202117
127590	92637	455907	725717	269811	455907	1113959	1025319	66004
18506	5662	67681	96054	28459	67596	81435	75414	9184
7776	5725	2815	8597	5782	2815	19011	11470	4524
31971	13467	47899	57017	9118	47899	94375	63776	11669
35685	13363	730054	956692	226638	730054	587174	216923	20878
921	543	1521	3131	1610	1521	2978	2978	486
129281	52561	202880	325642	124664	200979	567564	560587	96226
567375	289197	1370649	2339072	987007	1352066	2022820	1845736	270796
75396	31344	347720	474918	127198	347720	365217	277416	76697
163450	81219	656153	1220141	563988	656153	486036	337848	80095
80716	27948	237757	517253	280311	236942	260285	238254	27017
134203	28424	214201	313644	99443	214201	353086	327084	43095
89203	30757	178158	263618	85460	178158	263377	219474	29821
56642	1514	79802	105633	25831	79802	200965	184524	12197
295093	129400	454420	712544	259903	452641	686039	650774	106861
406495	182922	1002195	1577911	580586	997325	2356496	2045163	972608
361766	63544	1127419	1717641	590153	1127489	3551128	2517323	749087
46182	23677	180981	234610	53629	180981	143471	108370	44172
703642	27938	1759914	2518239	758326	1759914	3670591	2611499	266388
738321	370032	1577682	2558373	981231	1577142	2938072	2807529	468965
170655	72395	801271	1618092	816821	801271	915087	718250	245057
160846	48571	400811	689924	289113	400811	602949	588792	128928
2619	626	6321	8075	1754	6321	7540	7480	1327
		652	1176	524	652	1041	1041	416
22528		1076110	2013351	937241	1076110	996301	434615	132358
1229		66378	85897	19519	66378	74590	74215	4141
2653		247582	310202	110782	199420	260650	115361	14243

11-7 续表4

单位：万元

指标	Item
总计	**Total**
#亏损企业	Unprofitable Firm
#国有控股企业	State-holding Enterprise
#轻工业	Light Industry
重工业	Heavy Industry
#大型企业	Large-scale Enterprise
中型企业	Medium-sized Enterprise
按登记注册类型分组	**Grouped by Registration Types**
内资企业	Domestic Enterprise
国有企业	State-owned Enterprise
股份合作企业	Joint Equity Cooperative Enterprise
有限责任公司	Limited Liability Company
股份有限公司	Limited Company
私营企业	Private Company
其他企业	Others
港、澳、台商投资企业	HK, Macau or Taiwan Funded Enterprise
合资经营企业(港或澳、台资)	Joint Venture(HK, Macau or Taiwan)
合作经营企业(港或澳、台资)	Cooperative Enterprise(HK, Macau or Taiwan)
港澳台商独资经营企业	Sole Proprietorship(HK, Macau or Taiwan)
港澳台商投资股份有限公司	Shareholding Limited Company(HK, Macau or Taiwan)
外商投资企业	Foreign Funded Enterprise
中外合资经营企业	Sino-foreign Joint Venture
中外合作经营企业	Sino-foreign Cooperative Enterprise
外资企业	Foreign-owned Enterprise
外商投资股份有限公司	Foreign Investment Joint Stock Company
按地区分组	**Grouped by Regions**
市区	Urban Area
崇川区	Chongchuan
港闸区	Gangzha
开发区	Development Zone
通州区	Tongzhou
海安县	Haian
如东县	Rudong

CONTINUED 4

(Unit: 10,000 Yuan)

非流动负债合计 Total Non-current Liabilities	所有者权益合计 Total Owners Equity	实收资本 Paid-in Capital	国家资本 National Capital	集体资本 Collectively Owned Capital	法人资本 Corporate Capital	个人资本 Personal Capital	港澳台资本 Hong Kong, Macao and Taiwan capital	外商资本 Foreign Capital	主营业务收入 Main Business Revenue
4909532	**19026280**	**8600716**	**771666**	**101666**	**1550792**	**2334984**	**821355**	**3020254**	**63843540**
2159564	1444410	1991080	228328	44100	217895	39505	103623	1357629	2202662
1949077	3182281	1508091	570310	37202	590369	75998	77851	156361	5718260
1279181	6026808	2793343	198699	10455	434858	680252	288511	1180569	17755636
3630351	12999471	5807373	572967	91211	1115934	1654732	532844	1839685	46087903
2814254	9386728	3898766	410547	4026	452392	1190668	435078	1406055	31508784
2095278	9639552	4701950	361119	97640	1098399	1144316	386277	1614199	32334755
2555889	10714187	3802906	450963	87886	1148578	1985972	90629	38878	38831750
90300	15433	15213	15213						10285
11153	15930	2859				2859			132479
1285303	2310087	1140000	330930	62201	597499	134871	2450	12049	6463515
408403	2633657	643019	50219	380	197825	388734	2251	3610	7153475
709720	5647521	1947214		25305	353254	1459508	85928	23219	25034653
51010	91558	54601	54601						37343
1140147	2591743	1755121	176163	909	66309	231815	584958	694968	9129926
899107	741821	778172	52585	909	60533	56098	74231	533816	3215802
1168	19141	2400					2400		34794
238271	1572722	938077	123577		5776	175718	471854	161152	5270850
1601	258059	36473					36473		608480
1213495	5720350	3042689	144540	12871	335905	117197	145768	2286408	15881864
883107	3124258	1639178	113740	12871	335905	73554	141438	961670	8173821
52347	241577	48256	30800			1475		15981	262543
268834	2156517	1355254				42167	4330	1308757	7206207
9207	197998								239293
2018246	9540574	4077905	451289	87653	811858	598146	310974	1817984	23515571
538367	1965389	885631	147733	30000	327498	64270	181183	134946	2779030
326644	1356239	472764	91136	6000	107846	83330	25258	159194	1819861
705691	3618999	2015235	189897	25452	208303	71377	36723	1483484	9222486
447545	2599948	704276	22523	26201	168212	379170	67811	40360	9694194
311110	1968002	554072		5864	63304	382804	39512	62588	9868188
88457	1791068	951978		7921	131923	577446	184172	50516	6984787

11-7 续表 5

单位：万元

指 标	Item
启东市	Qidong
如皋市	Rugao
海门市	Haimen
按行业分组	**Grouped by Industries**
农副食品加工业	Agrifood Processing
食品制造业	Food Production
酒、饮料和精制茶制造业	Alcohol, Beverage and Refined Tea Production
烟草制品业	Tobacco Industries
纺织业	Textile
纺织服装、服饰业	Textile and Garment, Dress and Personal Adornment
皮革、毛皮、羽毛及其制品和制鞋业	Leather, Fur, Feather(Fuzz) and Related Products
木材加工和木、竹、藤、棕、草制品业	Wood Processing and Industries of Wood, Bamboo, Rattan, Palm and Grass Products
家具制造业	Furniture Manufacturing
造纸和纸制品业	Paper Making and Industries of Paper Products
印刷和记录媒介复制业	Printing and Record Medium Reproduction
文教、工美、体育和娱乐用品制造业	Industries of Culture, Education, Arts, Sports and Recreational Products
化学原料和化学制品制造业	Production of Chemical Raw Materials and Chemical Products
医药制造业	Pharmaceutical Industry
化学纤维制造业	Chemical Fiber Manufacturing
橡胶和塑料制品业	Industry of Rubber and Plastic Products
非金属矿物制品业	Industry of Nonmetallic Mineral Products
黑色金属冶炼和压延加工业	Ferrous Metal Smelting and Pressing
有色金属冶炼和压延加工业	Non-Ferrous Metal Smelting and Pressing
金属制品业	Manufacture of Metal Products
通用设备制造业	Manufacture of General Purpose Machinery
专用设备制造业	Manufacture of Equipment for Special Purpose
汽车制造业	Automobile Industry
铁路、船舶、航空航天和其他运输设备制造业	Manufacture of Railroad, Shipping, Aerospace and Other Transportation Equipments
电气机械和器材制造业	Manufacture of Electrical Machinery and Equipments
计算机、通信和其他电子设备制造业	Manufacture of Computer, Communications and Other Electronic Products
仪器仪表制造业	Instrument Manufacturing
其他制造业	Others
金属制品、机械和设备修理业	Metal Product, Machinery and Equipment Repair Industry
电力、热力生产和供应业	Generation and Supply of Electric Power and Heating Power
燃气生产和供应业	Generation and Supply of Gas
水的生产和供应业	Generation and Supply of Water

CONTINUED 5

(Unit: 10,000 Yuan)

非流动负债合计 Total Non-current Liabilities	所有者权益合计 Total Owners Equity	实收资本 Paid-in Capital	国家资本 National Capital	集体资本 Collectively Owned Capital	法人资本 Corporate Capital	个人资本 Personal Capital	港澳台资本 Hong Kong, Macao and Taiwan capital	外商资本 Foreign Capital	主营业务收入 Main Business Revenue
1257235	2200678	1120009	115213		202578	320855	109764	371600	5809882
982118	1828252	1223630	48587	228	145819	285961	50141	692896	9243310
252367	1697706	673122	156577		195310	169772	126792	24671	8421803
53840	342512	144038	1820		14290	21676	48729	57524	2031927
6490	89119	25237			10000	2403	8442	4391	335739
	42158	18856			12000	6856			135093
	82356	22274	22274						112532
294757	1785583	682661	27408	3421	78137	198735	99369	275591	5607681
88640	811538	171241	600		58617	73799	21297	16929	2313994
6021	84339	28469			8445	2292		17733	470229
7541	3700	3140						3140	18313
30599	68903	50578				30921		19657	142899
370250	494166	670806	66943			580		603283	107373
	4382	826				826			59225
6401	411822	166380		5832	10351	83415	6433	60349	1854621
177084	1740643	810520	95170	8802	263185	134213	10423	298727	7823592
87800	520780	180599	9839		44555	75532	31068	19605	1373718
148188	866869	418970			147463	134107	68183	69217	1982068
22031	363013	198068	46767		2354	11192	122523	15233	695073
26002	341098	109873			54910	44910	10053		830213
43903	178798	84358		21999	26800	35559			1419436
16441	96472	65123	20000			2500	10015	32608	457904
35266	948903	308132	35735		38138	61083	94591	78586	3083058
311332	1413285	558046	60932	36000	128893	178866	62906	90449	3144420
1033805	1303956	767350	267041	3000	17410	201779	17566	260555	4400099
35101	183696	57854			10258	25800		21796	895703
1059092	955194	834468			108061	97493	23369	605546	3041250
130543	3208949	1451137	2523	21150	185793	689267	146377	406027	12346695
196837	1103231	335622		60	148280	113167	34664	39451	4542695
14157	846739	179562		200	58834	107014	5349	8165	3583036
60	7866	6668			5000			1668	31980
	1052	1000				1000			3987
561685	572269	149843	30800		105019			14025	875807
375	32130	28000	14000		14000				52633
145289	120762	71017	69814	1202					70548

11-7 续表 6

单位：万元

指 标	Item	主营业务成本 Main Business Cost
总 计	**Total**	**55084902**
#亏损企业	Unprofitable Firm	2068289
#国有控股企业	State-holding Enterprise	4773305
#轻工业	Light Industry	15278806
重工业	Heavy Industry	39806096
#大型企业	Large-scale Enterprise	27336362
中型企业	Medium-sized Enterprise	27748540
按登记注册类型分组	**Grouped by Registration Types**	
内资企业	Domestic Enterprise	33595521
国有企业	State-owned Enterprise	8429
股份合作企业	Joint Equity Cooperative Enterprise	111718
有限责任公司	Limited Liability Company	5821592
股份有限公司	Limited Company	6065579
私营企业	Private Company	21567742
其他企业	Others	20461
港、澳、台商投资企业	HK, Macau or Taiwan Funded Enterprise	7944694
合资经营企业(港或澳、台资)	Joint Venture(HK, Macau or Taiwan)	2844641
合作经营企业(港或澳、台资)	Cooperative Enterprise(HK, Macau or Taiwan)	31166
港澳台商独资经营企业	Sole Proprietorship(HK, Macau or Taiwan)	4562177
港澳台商投资股份有限公司	Shareholding Limited Company(HK, Macau or Taiwan)	506710
外商投资企业	Foreign Funded Enterprise	13544687
中外合资经营企业	Sino-foreign Joint Venture	6844664
中外合作经营企业	Sino-foreign Cooperative Enterprise	221901
外资企业	Foreign-owned Enterprise	6303971
外商投资股份有限公司	Foreign Investment Joint Stock Company	174151
按地区分组	**Grouped by Regions**	
市 区	Urban Area	20281257
崇川区	Chongchuan	2127664
港闸区	Gangzha	1539684
开发区	Development Zone	8187847
通州区	Tongzhou	8426062
海安县	Haian	8491889
如东县	Rudong	6004631

CONTINUED 6

(Unit: 10,000 Yuan)

主营业务税金及附加 Tax and Extra Charges of Main Business	其他业务利润 Other Business Profit	销售费用 Selling Expenses	管理费用 Administrative Expenses	财务费用 Financial Cost	利息收入 Interest Income	利息支出 Interest Expenditure	投资收益 Investment Income	营业利润 Operating Profit
267494	**24735**	**907574**	**1767550**	**618196**	**94935**	**700997**	**114956**	**5346266**
7436	4040	44903	181168	158716	5916	176598	8883	−212100
26797	15842	80763	249214	109864	23601	128096	50790	560712
85368	4665	275800	480187	137079	34230	172679	43962	1533742
182127	20070	631773	1287363	481116	60705	528318	70994	3812523
126225	12578	473423	830346	350416	59239	403968	88077	2491615
141270	12157	434150	937205	267780	35696	297029	26879	2854650
171921	12360	582045	1027231	337018	30098	347564	72879	3222225
45	736	1524	1752	−31	55	24		−698
326		1426	2087	1169		1169		15754
16553	5398	56936	176877	99604	15638	105522	2377	319593
33589	3506	164107	257873	82015	7958	86450	25953	568057
121212	1016	348108	584257	150157	6391	150243	42655	2317670
195	1704	9945	4384	4105	56	4156	1895	1851
28258	6119	105108	277594	153666	11416	167523	1476	657703
9938	5643	30729	101339	110112	2878	120831	1242	134620
142		199	518	119		119		2650
15999	475	68942	169978	44771	5764	45169	234	442795
2179		5238	5759	−1336	2774	1404		77638
67316	6256	220420	462726	127512	53421	185910	40602	1466338
38063	4966	102551	285823	54836	18912	84591	−2354	832795
1510	149	1148	7776	6495	1053	7468	36493	58798
25809	1142	116722	163472	66025	33454	93695	6463	514156
1934			5655	155	2	156		60590
99936	15414	309183	802917	198918	71040	267970	69026	1895015
17603	10582	57239	179113	19324	16095	36763	2267	384157
13062	1041	39838	88531	21513	5718	26806	46895	173417
20664	3088	92811	261609	53659	43387	96656	6672	595825
48606	703	119295	273665	104423	5840	107745	13193	741617
37975	−13	160145	204925	96684	3399	97460	7522	882386
28665	228	92010	182173	38577	1355	36792	35110	671034

11-7 续表 7

单位:万元

指 标	Item	主营业务成本 Main Business Cost
启东市	Qidong	4938043
如皋市	Rugao	8220717
海门市	Haimen	7148365
按行业分组	**Grouped by Industries**	
农副食品加工业	Agrifood Processing	1839531
食品制造业	Food Production	283232
酒、饮料和精制茶制造业	Alcohol, Beverage and Refined Tea Production	106052
烟草制品业	Tobacco Industries	87500
纺织业	Textile	4921221
纺织服装、服饰业	Textile and Garment, Dress and Personal Adornment	1955654
皮革、毛皮、羽毛及其制品和制鞋业	Leather, Fur, Feather(Fuzz) and Related Products	411092
木材加工和木、竹、藤、棕、草制品业	Wood Processing and Industries of Wood, Bamboo, Rattan, Palm and Grass Products	15344
家具制造业	Furniture Manufacturing	120570
造纸和纸制品业	Paper Making and Industries of Paper Products	116299
印刷和记录媒介复制业	Printing and Record Medium Reproduction	54813
文教、工美、体育和娱乐用品制造业	Industries of Culture, Education, Arts, Sports and Recreational Products	1597155
化学原料和化学制品制造业	Production of Chemical Raw Materials and Chemical Products	6875950
医药制造业	Pharmaceutical Industry	1174233
化学纤维制造业	Chemical Fiber Manufacturing	1553968
橡胶和塑料制品业	Industry of Rubber and Plastic Products	585789
非金属矿物制品业	Industry of Nonmetallic Mineral Products	689209
黑色金属冶炼和压延加工业	Ferrous Metal Smelting and Pressing	1310511
有色金属冶炼和压延加工业	Non-Ferrous Metal Smelting and Pressing	421125
金属制品业	Manufacture of Metal Products	2658474
通用设备制造业	Manufacture of General Purpose Machinery	2724022
专用设备制造业	Manufacture of Equipment for Special Purpose	3754712
汽车制造业	Automobile Industry	781159
铁路、船舶、航空航天和其他运输设备制造业	Manufacture of Railroad, Shipping, Aerospace and Other Transportation Equipments	2646700
电气机械和器材制造业	Manufacture of Electrical Machinery and Equipments	10528471
计算机、通信和其他电子设备制造业	Manufacture of Computer, Communications and Other Electronic Products	4027583
仪器仪表制造业	Instrument Manufacturing	3034179
其他制造业	Others	26672
金属制品、机械和设备修理业	Metal Product, Machinery and Equipment Repair Industry	3685
电力、热力生产和供应业	Generation and Supply of Electric Power and Heating Power	683651
燃气生产和供应业	Generation and Supply of Gas	47684
水的生产和供应业	Generation and Supply of Water	48664

CONTINUED 7

(Unit: 10,000 Yuan)

主营业务税金及附加 Tax and Extra Charges of Main Business	其他业务利润 Other Business Profit	销售费用 Selling Expenses	管理费用 Administrative Expenses	财务费用 Financial Cost	利息收入 Interest Income	利息支出 Interest Expenditure	投资收益 Investment Income	营业利润 Operating Profit
32858	2869	122323	183080	112705	9857	117345	8265	444010
35533	5536	136187	243922	146528	4591	154269	−17514	462231
32528	700	87727	150534	24784	4694	27160	12547	991591
5240	82	31364	28786	2715	21997	22321	6308	119673
1917		6041	9251	3957	462	4027		31364
5415		8445	8621	1916	50	2094		5478
488	61	1293	6804	−446	447	2		16954
24531	1160	73448	131154	41141	6193	44398	8676	426153
12463	611	31371	64827	36529	492	36615	14043	225297
3019		9896	11334	2862	59	2947		32027
164		446	773	295	27	299		1594
759	146	3096	9394	2351	56	2335	201	7530
301	−163	4839	12230	1226	168	11503		−31745
380		900	931	219	1	218		1982
8636	144	26008	43971	11580	187	11334	473	166924
17462	1958	82112	148443	44630	19879	56966	2355	635473
6552	74	26558	45622	8677	358	7883	6275	118183
9905		23083	63624	9523	2786	11982	52	325268
3040	5385	15462	32286	12430	2867	15017		51452
5058		16116	26917	13407	929	13586	−44	79213
3022		8222	28468	9372	113	7802	3	60035
582		8533	8690	2781	600	2048		18810
13312	838	38127	77067	17140	2560	17036	1478	284815
12976	4613	69656	129772	24714	4398	30104	9815	194142
14316	3442	51413	210813	55328	15359	68108	159	341339
9340		14099	18796	7899	1172	9396	−18372	45789
12866	34	29361	116886	112483	3638	124941	−2582	131495
50680	496	197531	294448	102897	4538	103884	46448	1216726
23512	2397	56180	117759	20828	2215	20408	−1042	302104
14284	874	61562	98986	20332	2072	21165	834	355372
48		539	1824	154	21	161		2743
60			136	8		8		99
6756			9290	47102	1060	48079	36493	173239
58	141	108	2422	−18	96	62	1487	4030
353	2440	11765	7227	4164	138	4270	1895	2709

11-7 续表 8

单位：万元

指 标	Item	营业外收入 Non-business Income
总 计	**Total**	**100833**
#亏损企业	Unprofitable Firm	10990
#国有控股企业	State-holding Enterprise	19644
#轻工业	Light Industry	33586
重工业	Heavy Industry	67247
#大型企业	Large-scale Enterprise	57108
中型企业	Medium-sized Enterprise	43725
按登记注册类型分组	**Grouped by Registration Types**	
内资企业	Domestic Enterprise	66540
国有企业	State-owned Enterprise	138
股份合作企业	Joint Equity Cooperative Enterprise	
有限责任公司	Limited Liability Company	14626
股份有限公司	Limited Company	22719
私营企业	Private Company	28930
其他企业	Others	128
港、澳、台商投资企业	HK, Macau or Taiwan Funded Enterprise	11902
合资经营企业(港或澳、台资)	Joint Venture(HK, Macau or Taiwan)	3407
合作经营企业(港或澳、台资)	Cooperative Enterprise(HK, Macau or Taiwan)	
港澳台商独资经营企业	Sole Proprietorship(HK, Macau or Taiwan)	8495
港澳台商投资股份有限公司	Shareholding Limited Company(HK, Macau or Taiwan)	
外商投资企业	Foreign Funded Enterprise	22391
中外合资经营企业	Sino-foreign Joint Venture	15865
中外合作经营企业	Sino-foreign Cooperative Enterprise	869
外资企业	Foreign-owned Enterprise	4132
外商投资股份有限公司	Foreign Investment Joint Stock Company	1525
按地区分组	**Grouped by Regions**	
市 区	Urban Area	56069
崇川区	Chongchuan	19750
港闸区	Gangzha	15059
开发区	Development Zone	6280
通州区	Tongzhou	14980
海安县	Haian	8432
如东县	Rudong	14745

CONTINUED 8

(Unit: 10,000 Yuan)

补贴收入 Subsidy Income	营业外支出 Non-business Expenditure	利润总额 Total Profit	应交所得税 Income Tax Payable	亏损企业亏损总额 Total Loss of Unprofitable Enterprises	利税总额 Total Profits and Taxes	本年应交增值税 Added Value Tax Payable of the Year	全部从业人员年平均人数(人) The Annual Number of All Employees(person)
30895	**195485**	**5251784**	**1028936**	**213429**	**8291658**	**2770640**	**508109**
2792	12320	-213429	577	213429	-177527	28429	29693
6404	74874	505482	121559	65243	705391	172744	33007
5490	41482	1526016	304158	46928	2363344	751345	197036
25405	154003	3725768	724778	166501	5923314	2019295	311073
18946	135526	2413197	423329	100084	3949906	1410051	240642
11948	59959	2838587	605607	113345	4341753	1360589	267467
16944	78799	3210137	623377	79051	5149615	1766647	304921
		-561		561	208	723	354
		15754	3827		22906	6826	915
3435	16978	317240	69775	54262	489339	155046	45581
6517	16754	574022	106089	18131	914320	306661	58224
6992	44908	2301862	443685	6098	3718908	1295472	199371
	158	1821			3935	1920	476
1621	9757	659848	125271	76928	1066258	377990	81501
165	3089	134937	36931	64175	280293	135390	33697
	243	2407	125		4134	1584	703
1456	6424	444866	77816	12753	681947	221043	43506
		77638	10400		99885	19973	3595
12330	106929	1381799	280288	57449	2075786	626003	121687
11188	75865	772795	164381	40965	1147196	336198	62834
11	1354	58313	4048		74703	14873	3081
319	25832	492456	97131	16484	777976	259190	54917
813	3879	58236	14729		75911	15742	855
21852	134719	1816535	336504	108408	2701395	783565	174989
13651	60053	344023	81472	13277	433552	71841	19873
4644	5812	182664	30080	22770	242950	47222	22618
1452	34637	567468	139793	61998	809609	220358	47293
2104	34217	722380	85159	10364	1215283	444145	85205
1276	24644	866174	179041	1829	1359494	455338	76431
4722	8696	677082	127822		1103484	397737	53562

11-7 续表 9

单位：万元

指 标	Item	营业外收入 Non-business Income
启东市	Qidong	4663
如皋市	Rugao	5679
海门市	Haimen	11245
按行业分组	**Grouped by Industries**	
农副食品加工业	Agrifood Processing	187
食品制造业	Food Production	543
酒、饮料和精制茶制造业	Alcohol, Beverage and Refined Tea Production	1639
烟草制品业	Tobacco Industries	266
纺织业	Textile	14992
纺织服装、服饰业	Textile and Garment, Dress and Personal Adornment	533
皮革、毛皮、羽毛及其制品和制鞋业	Leather, Fur, Feather(Fuzz) and Related Products	
木材加工和木、竹、藤、棕、草制品业	Wood Processing and Industries of Wood, Bamboo, Rattan, Palm and Grass Products	
家具制造业	Furniture Manufacturing	148
造纸和纸制品业	Paper Making and Industries of Paper Products	146
印刷和记录媒介复制业	Printing and Record Medium Reproduction	
文教、工美、体育和娱乐用品制造业	Industries of Culture, Education, Arts, Sports and Recreational Products	461
化学原料和化学制品制造业	Production of Chemical Raw Materials and Chemical Products	8510
医药制造业	Pharmaceutical Industry	2909
化学纤维制造业	Chemical Fiber Manufacturing	6644
橡胶和塑料制品业	Industry of Rubber and Plastic Products	1813
非金属矿物制品业	Industry of Nonmetallic Mineral Products	1059
黑色金属冶炼和压延加工业	Ferrous Metal Smelting and Pressing	568
有色金属冶炼和压延加工业	Non-Ferrous Metal Smelting and Pressing	301
金属制品业	Manufacture of Metal Products	2086
通用设备制造业	Manufacture of General Purpose Machinery	8206
专用设备制造业	Manufacture of Equipment for Special Purpose	9728
汽车制造业	Automobile Industry	3074
铁路、船舶、航空航天和其他运输设备制造业	Manufacture of Railroad, Shipping, Aerospace and Other Transportation Equipments	5833
电气机械和器材制造业	Manufacture of Electrical Machinery and Equipments	12824
计算机、通信和其他电子设备制造业	Manufacture of Computer, Communications and Other Electronic Products	12662
仪器仪表制造业	Instrument Manufacturing	1818
其他制造业	Others	
金属制品、机械和设备修理业	Metal Product, Machinery and Equipment Repair Industry	
电力、热力生产和供应业	Generation and Supply of Electric Power and Heating Power	2685
燃气生产和供应业	Generation and Supply of Gas	933
水的生产和供应业	Generation and Supply of Water	265

CONTINUED 9

(Unit: 10,000 Yuan)

补贴收入 Subsidy Income	营业外支出 Non-business Expenditure	利润总额 Total Profit	应交所得税 Income Tax Payable	亏损企业亏损总额 Total Loss of Unprofitable Enterprises	利税总额 Total Profits and Taxes	本年应交增值税 Added Value Tax Payable of the Year	全部从业人员年平均人数(人) The Annual Number of All Employees(person)
1708	12370	436302	86550	35626	725355	256195	47830
1087	12981	454929	76609	65722	837755	346919	105330
250	2075	1000762	222410	1844	1564176	530886	49967
177	9951	109909	22941		165639	50382	10833
15	41	31866	5448	100	50048	16266	2631
		7117	1504	1514	18117	5585	2491
	4	17215	4304		21771	4068	587
2181	9824	431321	87370	1096	692904	236581	63425
73	8940	216889	29267	581	339964	110605	32506
		32027	6692		60704	25658	8188
	70	1525	350		3608	1906	620
	600	7078	2541	4487	15114	7265	2581
8	99	-31698	872	34130	-30041	1353	1608
		1982	82		5480	3118	887
417	2581	164974	34028	1998	259857	86247	33572
3546	28250	615733	133001	5491	935222	301614	35088
935	3047	118046	21618	2303	188604	64005	11319
79	5492	326419	77286		431677	95338	9744
	1464	51802	11553		87456	32615	9138
687	878	79394	8494		118275	33824	9887
250	746	59858	10358		108562	45683	6612
4	208	18904	4585	2978	44548	25062	4763
980	1670	285231	54780	2706	428825	130215	22519
3956	3074	199275	49335	43269	310084	97660	29762
439	64008	287058	58299	35153	463909	162470	31301
	3646	45217	9582	2090	97064	42495	9459
677	9979	127350	27647	64175	239954	99617	35652
5009	15235	1214315	240932		1972016	706845	69505
9338	7289	307476	35707	6617	476644	145572	36956
496	12811	344379	55217	4181	531796	173134	21207
		2743	504		4306	1515	763
	1	98	20		209	51	409
813	5188	170735	33667		237678	60187	2475
815	34	4929	879		4987		437
	355	2620	75	561	6679	3706	1184

11-8 规模以上工业企业主要产品产量(2014年)

产品名称	Product	全市 Total	市区 Urban Area
小麦粉(吨)	Wheat Flour(ton)	694764	562881
大米(吨)	Rice(ton)	214218	21516
饲料(吨)	Forage (ton)	571317	7753
#配合饲料	Formula Feed	475797	
混合饲料	Mixed Feed	76473	
精制食用植物油(吨)	Refined Edible Vegetable Oil (ton)	1020608	875836
鲜、冷藏肉(吨)	Fresh and Frozen Meat(ton)	41152	1249
冷冻水产品(吨)	Frozen Aquatic Products(ton)	96314	
速冻食品(吨)	Quick-Frozen Rice Flour Food(ton)	2153	
#速冻米面食品	Quick-frozen Rice Flour Food	2153	
乳制品(吨)	Dairy Products(ton)	4517	4517
液体乳	Liquid Milk	4125	4125
固体及半固体乳制品	Solid and walf-solid Dairy Products	392	392
罐头(吨)	Can(ton)	10441	
酱油(吨)	Soy Sauce(ton)	879	879
食品添加剂(吨)	Food Addctives(ton)	213525	6261
发酵酒精(折96度,商品量)(千升)	Fermentation Alcohol(96 degree,commodity), (kiloliter)	49663	
饮料酒(千升)	Alcohol Beverage(kiloliter)	283496	255904
#白酒(折65度,商品量)	White Spirit (65 degree, commodity)	4183	
啤酒	Beer	255904	255904
软饮料(千升)	Soft Drinks (Kiloliter)	37974	
包装饮用水	Packaged Drinking water	37974	
纱(吨)	Yarn (ton)	627145	225453
棉纱	Cotton Yarn	413080	160288
棉混纺纱	Cotton Blended Yarn	120749	15218
化学纤维纱	Chemical Fiber Yarn	93316	49947
布(万米)	Cloth (10,000 meters)	326433	129914
#色织布(含牛仔布)	Yarn-dyed Cloth (including denim)	49221	14303
#棉布	Cotton Cloth	219255	87541
棉混纺布	Cotton Blended Cloth	30650	10349
化学纤维布	Chemical Fiber Cloth	76528	32024
印染布(万米)	Printed and Dyed Fabrics (10,000 meters)	305065	119204
绒线(俗称毛线)(吨)	Wool (hand-knitting wool)(ton)	4194	3893
蚕丝(吨)	Silk(ton)	5431	
蚕丝及交织机织物(含蚕丝≥50%)(万米)	Silk and Loom Fabrics(including silk≥50%)(10,000 meters)	4129	183
化纤长丝机织物(万米)	Chemical Fiber Filament Loom Fabrics(10,000 meters)	2998	
蚕丝被(万条)	Silk Quilt(10,000 pieces)	80	56
无纺布(无纺织物)(吨)	Non-woven Cloth(fabrics) (ton)	77786	70522
帘子布(吨)	Tyre Fabrics(ton)	2408	115

OUTPUT OF PRODUCTS IN INDUSTRIAL ENTERPRISES ABOVE DESIGNATED SIZE(2014)

崇川区 Chongchuan	港闸区 Gangzha	开发区 Developing Zone	通州区 Tongzhou	海安 Hai'an	如东 Rudong	启东 Qidong	如皋 Rugao	海门 Haimen
90884			471997	58184	61248		12451	
			21516	89457	90714		12531	
7753				262043	200402		101119	
				250749	142859		82189	
					57543		18930	
119264		754792	1780	23159	121612			
			1249	21903			18000	
					13885	81369		1060
								2153
								2153
	4517							
	4125							
	392							
							3973	6468
			879					
		6261		1463		189494	12904	3404
								49663
			255904	2282			25310	
				2282			1901	
			255904					
					37974			
					37974			
25560	27813	26173	145907	125528	83721	70152	70289	52001
16621	2739	22176	118752	56440	54143	68306	36809	37095
3364	3525	3997	4332	56923	28878	1846	15523	2361
5574	21550		22823	12166	700		17958	12545
18310	11461	37558	62585	42082	104411	6402	36803	6821
8166		2699	3439	34233			684	
16950	6451	29209	34931	37539	67141	4122	22499	414
811	1299	656	7584	4365	3923	721	5104	6187
550	3711	7693	20071	178	33347	1559	9199	220
1761	7538	42538	67367	18346	14277	6346	14776	132116
2716	1177						301	
				4120	777		533	
			183	3620	322		4	
				124		2874		
		34	22	17	5			3
2280		47996	20246			5628	1636	
		115			2293			

11-8 续表 1

产品名称	Product	全市 Total	市区 Urban Area
服装(万件)	Clothing (10,000 pieces)	76328	36822
梭织服装	Woven Garments	56696	32450
# 羽绒服装	Down Clothes	27	1
西服套装	Suits	1780	161
衬衫	Shirts	1488	209
针织服装	Knitwear	19632	4372
轻革(平方米)	Light Leather (㎡)	2279458	1492424
皮革服装(件)	Leather Clothes (piece)	40	1
手提包(袋)、背包(万个)	Handbag and Packsack(10,000)	92	27
鞋(万双)	Shoes (10,000 pairs)	4741	1473
# 纺织面鞋	Textile Fabric Shoes	1364	1364
皮革鞋靴	Leather Shoes and Boots (10,000 pairs)	3377	109
人造板(立方米)	Artificial Board (㎥)	19117	
# 胶合板	Plywood	19117	
复合木地板(平方米)	Composite Wood Floor(㎡)	1205427	1205427
家具(件)	Furniture (piece)	436821	202718
# 木质家具	Wood Furniture	371537	168236
金属家具	Metal Furniture	34798	34482
软体家具	Upholstered Furniture	30486	
纸浆(原生浆及废纸浆)(吨)	Paper Pulp (Virgin fiber and waste Paper pulp)(ton)	101257	101257
机制纸及纸板(外购原纸加工除外)(吨)	Machine-made Paper and Cardboard (excluding oursourcing base paper processing)(ton)	362299	240967
# 未涂布印刷书写用纸	Uncoated Printing and Writing Paper	31866	31866
涂布类印刷用纸	Coated Printing and Writing Paper	178384	178384
包装用纸及纸板	Packing Paper and Paperboard	87803	30717
# 箱纸板	Case Board	87803	30717
纸制品(吨)	Paper Products (ton)	421556	68717
# 瓦楞纸箱(吨)	Corrugated Paper Container (ton)	281603	68717
卫生用纸制品	Sanitary Paper Products	48159	
单色印刷品(令)	Monochrome Printing Product (ream)	46941	31229
多色印刷品(对开色令)	Multi-color Printing Product (split color ream)	165417	145177
盐酸(氯化氢,含量 31%)(吨)	Hydrochloric Acid (31%) (ton)	90016	90016
烧碱(折 100%)(吨)	Caustic Soda (100%) (ton)	180624	180624
# 离子膜法烧碱(折 100%)	Ion-exchange Membrane Caustic Soda (100%)	180624	180624
合成氨(无水氨)(吨)	Synthesis Ammonia (anhydrous ammonia) (ton)	99970	
农用氮、磷、钾化学肥料总计(折纯)(吨)	Agricultural Nitrogen, Phosphorus and Potassium Fertilizer (pure) (ton)	17404	
氮肥(折含 N100%)	Nitrogen Fertilizer (100%N)	17404	
化学农药原药(折有效成分 100%)(吨)	Chemical Pesticide Technical(100% active ingredient) (ton)	189503	113098
# 杀虫剂原药	Pesticide Technical	27742	15297
杀菌剂原药	Bactericide Technical	9915	7989
除草剂原药	Herbicide Technical	150591	89812
涂料(吨)	Coating (ton)	86359	20556

CONTINUED 1

崇川区 Chongchuan	港闸区 Gangzha	开发区 Developing Zone	通州区 Tongzhou	海安 Hai´an	如东 Rudong	启东 Qidong	如皋 Rugao	海门 Haimen
1753	2346	4724	28000	4546	16491	2369	13438	2661
1101	2089	2410	26851	4546	7660	1310	9344	1385
			1	13			13	
62	52		46	87	502		297	734
	193		16	729	192		53	305
652	256	2314	1149		8831	1059	4094	1276
		1492424					787034	
			1			31	8	
			27			65		
384		109	980		1160			2108
384			980					
		109			1160			2108
				19117				
				19117				
		1205427						
	17949	113192	71577		210575	13606	9671	251
	17949	113192	37095		179773	13606	9671	251
			34482		316			
					30486			
		101257						
		210250	30717	4984	96536	142	19670	
		31866						
		178384						
			30717		37416		19670	
			30717		37416		19670	
		2675	66042	63582	226669	13012	24808	24768
		2675	66042	63582	86716	13012	24808	24768
					48159			
	31229					15712		
	145177			19890				350
		90016						
		180624						
		180624						
						75924	24046	
						9097	8307	
						9097	8307	
	8052	105045		1255	24788	50363		
		15297			12445			
	7195	794			1926			
	857	88954			10417	50363		
	834	5583	14139	10944	51635		2604	620

11-8 续表 2

产品名称	Product	全市 Total	市区 Urban Area
初级形态的塑料(吨)	Primary Forms of Plastic (ton)	259200	235364
聚丙烯树脂	Polypropylene Resin	749	16
聚氯乙烯树脂	PVC	8296	6564
合成橡胶(吨)	Synthetic Rubber (ton)	533461	298378
合成纤维单体(吨)	Synthetic Fiber Monomer(ton)	1047	
合成纤维聚合物(吨)	Synthetic Polymers (ton)	111619	111619
#聚酯	Polyster	110730	110730
化学试剂(吨)	Chemical Reagent (ton)	9859	9859
单晶硅(千克)	Monocrystal Silicon(kg)	11616	
合成洗涤剂(吨)	Synthetic Detergent (ton)	18327	
液体洗涤剂	Liquid Detergent	17227	
化学药品原药(吨)	Chemical Technical (ton)	13954	11609
中成药(吨)	Chinese Patent Drugs (ton)	3010	679
化学纤维(吨)	Chemical Fiber (ton)	1303311	779236
#人造纤维(纤维素纤维)	Artificial Fiber (cellulosic fiber)	387157	288836
#粘胶短纤维	Viscose Fibre	113962	15641
醋酸纤维长丝	Acetate Filaments	273195	273195
#合成纤维	Synthetic Fiber	916155	490400
#锦纶纤维	Polyamide Fiber	357603	4159
涤纶纤维	Polyester Fiber	543579	480007
丙纶纤维	Polypropylene Fibre	6235	6235
氨纶纤维	Spandex Fiber	8727	
橡胶轮胎外胎(条)	Rubber Tire	1146938	
子午线轮胎外胎	Meridian Tire	1146938	
塑料制品(吨)	Plastic Products (ton)	432477	338321
#塑料薄膜	Plastic Membrane	210783	197159
泡沫塑料	Foamed Plastic (ton)	62150	17707
塑料人造革、合成革	Plastic Leatheroid and Synthetic Leather	35309	29942
日用塑料制品	Daily-use Plastic Products	63497	48491
水泥(吨)	Cement (ton)	11108480	1904556
商品混凝土(立方米)	Commercial Concrete (cubic meter)	20413772	10214378
水泥混凝土电杆(根)	Cement Concrete Pole	316850	
预应力混凝土桩(米)	Prestressed Concrete Pile (meter)	2687911	1459718
砖(万块)	Brick (10,000 pieces)	31136	5231
瓦(万片)	Tile (10,000 pieces)	305	
钢化玻璃(平方米)	Tempered glass(m^2)	1547324	
夹层玻璃(平方米)	Sandwich glass(m^2)	186108	
日用玻璃制品(吨)	Daily-use Glass Products (ton)	54240	5793
玻璃包装容器(吨)	Glass Packaging Container (ton)	38708	36849
玻璃保温容器(万个)	Insulated Glass Container (10,000)	134	134
玻璃纤维纱(吨)	Glass Fiber Yarn (ton)	25518	
纤维增强塑料制品(吨)	Fiber-reinforced Plastics (ton)	18800	
卫生陶瓷制品(件)	Sanitary wares	8529	8529
耐火材料制品(吨)	Fire-resistant Products (ton)	79891	

CONTINUED 2

崇川区 Chongchuan	港闸区 Gangzha	开发区 Developing Zone	通州区 Tongzhou	海安 Hai´an	如东 Rudong	启东 Qidong	如皋 Rugao	海门 Haimen
	65701	163099	6564	7792	7117	2138	3840	2950
		16		733				
			6564					1732
		298378						235083
				1047				
889		110730						
		110730						
		9144	715					
				11616				
					17227		1100	
					17227			
		11609		236	1991			119
202	477							2331
273195	16833	82934	406274	390286	22835	25354		85600
273195	11984		3657	23428	4			74888
	11984		3657	23428	4			74888
273195								
	4849	82934	402617	366858	22830	25354		10712
		4159		349802	3642			
		78775	401231	17046	10460	25354		10712
	4849		1386					
					8727			
							1146938	
							1146938	
99325		34580	204416	5296	58126	7790	3021	19924
73471		14691	108997	1220				12404
			17707		38913		1688	3842
25637			4305			1689		3678
		3332	45159		15006			
1001615	902941			1232078	1803361	2214004	530641	3423840
3251221	1116109	3275089	2571959	2481699	1951862	581501	2858860	2325472
					273275	14253	29322	
			1459718	500828	727365			
	3918		1313	2986	4908	5639	7760	4612
								305
				1026369				520955
				186108				
			5793		13163			35284
			36849					1859
			134					
				862	7155		17500	
							18800	
			8529					
				72799			7092	

11-8 续表 3

产品名称	Product	全市 Total	市区 Urban Area
石墨及炭素制品(吨)	Graphite and Carbon Products (ton)	142548	39202
粗钢(吨)	Crude Steel (ton)	527017	
铸铁件(吨)	Iron Casting (ton)	123282	12662
铸钢件(吨)	Steel Casting (ton)	172323	
钢材(吨)	Steels (ton)	1066818	376142
#棒材	Bar	161723	
钢筋	Concrete Iron	510887	
线材(盘条)	Wire Rod (wire rod)	64430	64430
冷轧薄板	Cold-rolled Sheet	304084	304084
镀层板(带)	Coating Plate	1936	
涂层板(带)	Coated Plate	7628	7628
无缝钢管	Seamless Steel Tube	16130	
用外购国产钢材再加工生产的钢材	Steels Reprocessed from Outsourcing Domestic Steels	501143	337484
用进口钢材再加工生产钢材	Steels Reprocessed from Imported Steels	38658	38658
用外购钢材再加工生产钢材(吨)	Steels Reporcessed from Outsourcing Steels(ton)	539801	376142
铝合金(吨)	Aluminium Auoy(ton)	3682	
铜材(吨)	Copper Product(ton)	96152	1832
铝材(吨)	Aluminium Product (ton)	16721	2502
钢结构(吨)	SteelWork(ton)	51059	49001
金属集装箱(立方米)	Metal Container (cubic meter)	4207018	4194617
钢丝(吨)	Steel Wire (ton)	468036	467811
钢丝绳(吨)	Steel Wire Rope (ton)	2384229	2336208
钢绞线(吨)	Steel Strand (ton)	176020	176020
不锈钢日用制品(吨)	Stainless Steel Household Product (ton)	6755	1332
锻件(吨)	Forging (ton)	14830	
粉末冶金零件(吨)	Powdermetal Part (ton)	21509	
电站锅炉(蒸发量吨)	Power Station Boiler (evaporation ton)	7125	7125
工业锅炉(蒸发量吨)	Industrial Boiler (evaporation ton)	1132	1132
发动机(千瓦)	Engine (kilowatt)	4336797	633854
#汽车用发动机	Automobile Engine	3702943	
金属切削机床(台)	Metal-cutting Machine (set)	12142	3833
#数控金属切削机床	CNC Metal-cutting Machine	464	464
金属成形机床(台)	Metal Forming Machine	13814	2576
#数控金属成形机床(数控锻压设备)	CNS Metal Forming Machine (CNC forging equipment)	3583	2445
铸造机械(台)	Foundry Machine	29685	29685
电焊机(台)	Electric Welder	97966	97700
起重机(吨)	Crane (ton)	91335	88132
输送机械(输送机和提升机)(吨)	Conveying Machinery (Conveyor and Hoister) (ton)	211282	140
电梯、自动扶梯及升降机(台)	Elevator, Escalator and Lifter	138	
升降机	Lifter	138	
泵(台)	Pump	886969	441797
#真空泵	Vacuum Pump	434775	434442
真空应用设备(台)	Vacuum Equipment	45769	

CONTINUED 3

崇川区 Chongchuan	港闸区 Gangzha	开发区 Developing Zone	通州区 Tongzhou	海安 Hai´an	如东 Rudong	启东 Qidong	如皋 Rugao	海门 Haimen
	19993	16401	2808	3646		5993	91060	2646
							510887	16130
	6963	1002	4697	2116			50011	58493
							121843	50480
		64430	311712	1936			510887	177853
								161723
							510887	
		64430						
			304084					
				1936				
			7628					
								16130
		25772	311712	1936				161723
		38658						
		64430	311712	1936				161723
								3682
			1832	18156				76164
			2502	4805	5752	2979		683
		2372	46629	2059				
	4194617					12401		
		423017	44794					225
	271860	1945767	118581					48021
			176020					
			1332				1701	3721
								14830
								21509
7125								
1132								
633854							3702943	
							3702943	
	3833			1763				6546
	464							
	131		2445	7179	215	339	1820	1685
			2445	923	215			
		1284	28401					
97700								266
	35526	10633	41972	3203				
			140	5476		205666		
					138			
					138			
		434442	7355	10903	2406	422823	23	9017
		434442					23	310
						45769		

11-8 续表 4

产品名称	Product	全市 Total	市区 Urban Area
气体压缩机(台)	Gas Compressor	403493	
制冷设备用压缩机(台)	Refrigeration Compressor	20	
非制冷设备用压缩机(台)	Non-refrigeration Compressor	403473	
阀门(吨)	Valve (ton)	73743	8545
液压元件(件)	Hydraulic Component (piece)	501559	9849
气动元件(件)	Pneumatic Component(piece)	4226	4226
滚动轴承(万套)	Roll Bearing (10,000 sets)	20449	
齿轮(吨)	Gear (ton)	35497	35497
钢铁铰接链(工业链条)(吨)	Steel Link Chain (Industrial Chain) (ton)	29755	29755
工业电炉(台)	Electric Stoue	184	
风机(台)	Draught Fan	1147639	26074
#鼓风机	Air Blower	11814	1765
气体分离及液化设备(台)	Gas Seperotion and Liquifaction Equipment	993	993
工商用制冷、空调设备(台(套)	Commercial Refrigeration and Air-conditioning Equipment(set)	830	325
#工商用空调设备	Commericial Air-conditioning Equipment	505	
电动手提式工具(台)	Electric Portable Tool	91810184	
包装专用设备(台)	Packaging Equipment	547	547
复印和胶版印制设备(台)	Copy and Offset Printing Equipment	262	
金属密封件(万件)	Metallic Seal(10,000)	361	361
金属紧固件(吨)	Metal Fastenings (ton)	68848	
弹簧(吨)	Spring (ton)	92572	
减速机(台)	Reducer	1531	
矿山专用设备(吨)	Special Equipment for Mining (ton)	3966	2190
石油钻井设备(台(套))	Oil Drilling Equipment (set)		
水泥专用设备(吨)	Special Equipment for Cement (ton)	249116	
混凝土机械(台)	Concrete Machinery	961	961
炼油、化工生产专用设备(吨)	Special Equipments for Oil Refining and Chemical Industry Production (ton)	24647	14875
塑料加工专用设备(台)	Special Equipments for Plastic Processing	146	
模具(套)	Mould (set)	44907	9648
电子工业专用设备(台)	Special Equipments for Electronic Industry	38940	
机械化农业及园艺机具(台)	Mechanized Farming and Gardening Equipment	3238	
环境污染防治专用设备(台(套))	Special Equipment for Environment Pollution Treatment (set)	15609	11533
大气污染防治设备	Equipment for Gas Pollution Treatment	15280	11530
固体废弃物处理设备	Equipment for Solid Waste Treatment	145	3
噪音与振动控制设备	Equipment for Noise and Vibration Control	184	
汽车(辆)	Vehicle	29536	
载货汽车	Truck	29536	
改装汽车(辆)	Modified Vehicle	312	312
民用钢质船舶(载重吨)	Civil Steel Ship(DWT)	4853807	2796539
钢质机动货船	Steel motor Cargo Boat	4378261	2342493
#散货船	Bulk Freighter	940332	940332
钢质机动非货船	Steel Motor Non-cargo Boat	454046	454046
钢质非机动船	Steel Non-motor Boat	21500	

CONTINUED 4

崇川区 Chongchuan	港闸区 Gangzha	开发区 Developing Zone	通州区 Tongzhou	海安 Hai'an	如东 Rudong	启东 Qidong	如皋 Rugao	海门 Haimen
							20	403473
							20	
								403473
4669	2840	1036		16977		43202	5020	
			9849			36564		455146
			4226					
				7104	164	12554	627	
		3937	31560					
		29755						
				184				
1478	1829	1765	21002			1110233		11332
		1765						10049
			993					
			325	505				
				505				
						91187903		622281
	184		363					
							262	
			361					
					35703	9013		24132
				1134		91438		
							1531	
			2190	224			234	1318
				249116				
	961							
			14875		268	9504		
					146			
	697	8951			35259			
				2514		36426		
				3238				
	3		11530	142		3744	190	
			11530			3560	190	
	3			142				
						184		
							29536	
							29536	
	312							
1175000	459351	1227	1160962			191528	1865740	
1175000	400505	1227	765762			191528	1844240	
	400505	1227	538600					
	58846		395200					
							21500	

11-8 续表 5

产品名称	Product	全市 Total	市区 Urban Area
两轮脚踏自行车(辆)	Bicycle	256811	256811
电动自行车(辆)	Electric Bicycle	133793	133793
发电机组(发电设备)(千瓦)	Power Set(equipment)(Kilowatt)	51256	
风力发电机组	Wind Power Set	51256	
电动机(千瓦)	Electromotor (Kilowatt)	1300545	1288102
交流电动机	Alternating Current Motor	798584	787836
变压器(千伏安)	Transformer (KVA)	48603952	10475039
互感器(台)	Mutual Inductor	31021	31021
电力电容器(千乏)	Power Capacitor(10,000 farah)	109620	109620
高压开关板(面)	High-tension Switchboard	15775	15497
低压开关板(面)	Low-tension Switchboard	13890	12368
高压开关设备(11 万伏以上)(台)	High-voltage Switchgear (above 110,000 voltage)	15245	15011
通信及电子网络用电缆(对千米)	Cable for Communications and Electric Network (pair km)	88156	86412
电力电缆(千米)	Power Cable (km)	368527	113507
光纤(千米)	Optical Cable(km)	19603210	15649449
光缆(芯千米)	Optical Cable (core km)	8416268	
原电池及原电池组(非扣式)(万只)	Primary Battery and Pack (R20 standard) (10,000)	6313	
太阳能电池(光伏电池)(千瓦)	Solar Cell (kilowatt)	1286189	35900
电饭锅(个)	Electric Cooker	155521	
家用燃气灶具(台)	Household Gas Cooker(Set)	1207228	
太阳能热水器(平方米)	Solar Water Heater (square meters)	640499	604514
电光源(万只)	Electric Light Source (10,000)	79493	76938
#荧光灯	Florescent Lamp	1185	921
灯具及照明装置(套(台、个))	Lamps and Lighting Equipment (set)	517283	
电子计算机整机(台)	Electronic Computer Machine(set)	197559	
彩色电视机(台)	Color TV Set	232437	
液晶(LCD)电视机	LCD TV Set	232437	
电视接收机顶盒(台)	RF Component	6118732	6118732
半导体分立器件(万只)	Discrete Semiconductor Devices (10,000)	801051	166414
集成电路(万块)	Integrated Circuit (10,000 pieces)	993246	993246
电子元件(万只)	Electronic Component (10,000 pieces)	520107	285220
射频元器件	Analytical Instrument(set)	9270	6442
工业自动调节仪表与控制系统(台(套))	Industrial Automatic Control Instrument and Control System (set)	2352824	1382463
电工仪器仪表(台)	Electrical Instrument	2004227	132360
分析仪器及装置(台(套))		74	
试验机(台)	Test Machine	5972	
环境监测专用仪器仪表(台)	Special Equipment for Environment Monitoring	109522	98982
光学仪器(台(个))	Optical Instrument	8932348	8932348
船舶修理(载重吨)	Ship Repair (DWT)	5842967	5842967
自来水生产量(万立方米)	Tap Water Production (10,000 cubic meters)	52431	36476

CONTINUED 5

崇川区 Chongchuan	港闸区 Gangzha	开发区 Developing Zone	通州区 Tongzhou	海安 Hai´an	如东 Rudong	启东 Qidong	如皋 Rugao	海门 Haimen
		256811						
			133793					
					51256			
					51256			
	291020	496816	500266	1695		10748		
	291020	496816				10748		
			10475039	32475743		5653170		
			31021					
109620								
1552	376	8844	4725	278				
2894	364		9110	1522				
			15011					234
			86412			1744		
		43670	69838	14199	230781	6233	3806	
		15649449						3953761
					7499078			917190
								6313
			35900	586607	24953	638729		
						155521		
						1207228		
			604514	35985				
			76938	264	1960	331		
			921	264				
					460000	57283		
				197559				
							232437	
							232437	
6118732								
166414							634637	
991931			1315					
	1118		284102	226761		1882	3080	3165
			6442					2828
		91	1382372	389607		580686	68	
			132360			1871867		
				74				
						4701		1271
		73	98909	6992	3548			
	450545		8481803					
5798940	44027							
36476				4961	3144		2700	5150

11-9 规模以上民营工业企业主要经济指标(2014 年)

单位:万元

指标	Item	企业单位数(个) Number of Enterprises and Units
总计	**Total**	**3790**
#亏损企业	Unprofitable Firm	187
#轻工业	Light Industry	1735
重工业	Heavy Industry	2055
#大型企业	Large-scale Enterprise	63
中型企业	Medium-sized Enterprise	288
小微型企业	Micro Enterprise	3439
按登记注册类型分组	**Grouped by Registration Types**	
内资企业	Domestic Enterprise	3790
集体企业	Collective Enterprise	13
股份合作企业	Joint Equity Cooperative Enterprise	15
联营企业	Joint Venture	1
有限责任公司	Limited Liability Company	577
股份有限公司	Limited Company	70
私营企业	Private Company	3111
其他企业	Others	3
按地区分组	**Grouped by Regions**	
市区	Urban Area	1117
崇川区	Chongchuan	64
港闸区	Gangzha	175
开发区	Development Zone	306
通州区	Tongzhou	572
海安县	Haian	721
如东县	Rudong	509
启东市	Qidong	370
如皋市	Rugao	693
海门市	Haimen	380

MAIN INDICES ON ECONOMIC BENEFIT OF INDUSTRIAL ENTERPRISES ABOVE DESIGNATED SIZE(2014)

(Unit: 10,000 Yuan)

亏损企业 Unprofitable Firms	工业总产值（当年价格） Total Value of Industrial Output (Price of Current Year)	工业销售产值（当年价格） Industrial Sales Value (Price of Current Year)	出口交货值 Value of Export Delivery	资产总计 Total Assets	流动资产合计 Total Current Assets	应收账款 Accounts Receivable
187	**77704862**	**76926481**	**6292497**	**36741131**	**19572564**	**5934081**
187	1376677	1342269	92656	1752561	962504	300756
80	24014770	23805674	3233611	11706123	5967635	1471346
107	53690092	53120806	3058886	25035008	13604929	4462734
1	17672426	17489796	2272431	9694325	4975283	1335003
9	17569941	17389608	1838562	8108182	4159673	1072181
177	42462495	42047077	2181505	18938624	10437609	3526896
187	77704862	76926481	6292497	36741131	19572564	5934081
	125967	125514	4440	76404	37264	9396
	355272	354317	6946	87395	39376	10102
	10009	10009		3336	1319	295
51	9356696	9223339	847896	6327709	3134170	936734
5	7054680	7023190	1128658	4379617	2455085	687603
131	60790060	60177966	4304558	25858917	13900855	4286947
	12179	12146		7753	4495	3003
46	19135493	18825687	2572711	10796096	5861076	1631983
7	831644	809948	107009	932991	544483	236645
9	1850835	1809697	275441	1246733	816874	263781
5	4247447	4114588	251748	2138158	1392115	380546
25	12205566	12091454	1938513	6478214	3107604	751012
82	14573032	14486306	1252674	6952420	3495914	1023286
10	11421263	11254157	735649	5025882	2664910	886212
11	9576009	9503273	302279	4223996	2337365	755816
30	12506751	12380145	936592	5531508	3191983	1009408
8	10492315	10476912	492593	4211229	2021318	627376

11-9 续表1

单位：万元

指标	Item	企业单位数(个) Number of Enterprises and Units
按行业分组	**Grouped by Industries**	
农副食品加工业	Agrifood Processing	129
食品制造业	Food Production	19
酒、饮料和精制茶制造业	Alcohol, Beverage and Refined Tea Production	5
纺织业	Textile	807
纺织服装、服饰业	Textile and Garment, Dress and Personal Adornment	203
皮革、毛皮、羽毛及其制品和制鞋业	Leather, Fur, Feather(Fuzz) and Related Products	38
木材加工及木、竹、藤、棕、草制品业	Wood Processing and Industries of Wood, Bamboo, Rattan, Palm and Grass Products	6
家具制造业	Furniture Manufacturing	16
造纸和纸制品业	Paper Making and Industries of Paper Products	40
印刷和记录媒介复制业	Printing and Record Medium Reproduction	18
文教、工美、体育和娱乐用品制造业	Industries of Culture, Education, Arts, Sports and Recreational Products	217
石油加工、炼焦和核燃料加工业	Petroleum Processing, Coking and Nuclear Fuel Processing Industries	7
化学原料和化学制品制造业	Production of Chemical Raw Materials and Chemical Products	302
医药制造业	Pharmaceutical Industry	43
化学纤维制造业	Chemical Fiber Manufacturing	60
橡胶和塑料制品业	Industry of Rubber and Plastic Products	96
非金属矿物制品业	Industry of Nonmetallic Mineral Products	194
黑色金属冶炼和压延加工业	Ferrous Metal Smelting and Pressing	74
有色金属冶炼和压延加工业	Non-Ferrous Metal Smelting and Pressing	52
金属制品业	Manufacture of Metal Products	300
通用设备制造业	Manufacture of General Purpose Machinery	380
专用设备制造业	Manufacture of Equipment for Special Purpose	168
汽车制造业	Automobile Industry	31
铁路、船舶、航空航天和其他运输设备制造业	Manufacture of Railroad, Shipping, Aerospace and Other Transportation Equipments	97
电气机械和器材制造业	Manufacture of Electrical Machinery and Equipments	248
计算机、通信和其他电子设备制造业	Manufacture of Computer, Communications and Other Electronic Products	116
仪器仪表制造业	Instrument Manufacturing	102
其他制造业	Others	4
废弃资源综合利用业	Comprehensive Utilization of Waste Resources	1
金属制品、机械和设备修理业	Metal Product, Machinery and Equipment Repair Industry	5
电力、热力生产和供应业	Generation and Supply of Electric Power and Heating Power	7
燃气生产和供应业	Generation and Supply of Gas	2
水的生产和供应业	Generation and Supply of Water	3

CONTINUED 1

(Unit: 10,000 Yuan)

亏损企业 Unprofitable Firms	工业总产值（当年价格） Total Value of Industrial Output (Price of Current Year)	工业销售产值（当年价格） Industrial Sales Value (Price of Current Year)	出口交货值 Value of Export Delivery	资产总计 Total Assets	流动资产合计 Total Current Assets	应收账款 Accounts Receivable
10	2391773	2377715	82079	836626	478633	96952
1	431397	426830	81310	228771	102591	32074
1	146030	145352		129066	57624	2667
26	8399366	8326153	1154284	3845500	2093087	579016
9	2647913	2618463	811496	2001137	1012617	172916
3	312404	309964	33758	142739	83391	20933
	50576	49979		18125	11384	3006
2	157377	154623	8487	134807	85710	16060
2	375692	372469	136	169595	100541	38638
2	167110	167025	1758	87673	47386	14850
6	2945526	2930971	692531	1212491	686514	165766
2	154920	156144		60818	31509	6902
20	9446244	9368916	538731	3626132	1940844	513111
6	1430412	1411562	88528	657387	284479	86581
6	2016817	2010663	50158	1085997	299461	52852
3	996908	986818	54530	467127	273550	98677
13	2868214	2839135	279069	1900813	1228488	519637
4	2174897	2158233	8582	683442	312131	78474
7	988489	968279	43249	317843	176798	46938
16	4408663	4313443	242769	1983042	1151148	369183
21	6854775	6800718	326720	3124463	1736034	540674
12	3230318	3208037	125260	1524684	838937	271163
	1136978	1120650	44156	425104	197134	77463
5	1666545	1640517	131887	1492625	727831	189022
5	12942149	12788023	565004	6159360	3477945	1273526
	4732127	4680883	466823	1579907	821202	262560
3	4402934	4367292	450921	2058727	1122488	372116
1	36014	35115	9520	30528	20029	4579
1	2002	2002		14432	3925	
	15518	15369	752	26029	9998	3170
	125907	126605		592116	133165	19117
	20215	19880		12397	5767	165
	28653	28653		111632	20224	5293

11-9 续表 2

单位：万元

指 标	Item
总计	**Total**
# 亏损企业	Unprofitable Firm
# 轻工业	Light Industry
重工业	Heavy Industry
# 大型企业	Large-scale Enterprise
中型企业	Medium-sized Enterprise
小微型企业	Micro Enterprise
按登记注册类型分组	**Grouped by Registration Types**
内资企业	Domestic Enterprise
集体企业	Collective Enterprise
股份合作企业	Joint Equity Cooperative Enterprise
联营企业	Joint Venture
有限责任公司	Limited Liability Company
股份有限公司	Limited Company
私营企业	Private Company
其他企业	Others
按地区分组	**Grouped by Regions**
市 区	Urban Area
崇川区	Chongchuan
港闸区	Gangzha
开发区	Development Zone
通州区	Tongzhou
海安县	Haian
如东县	Rudong
启东市	Qidong
如皋市	Rugao
海门市	Haimen

CONTINUED 2

(Unit: 10,000 Yuan)

资产总计 Total Assets						负债合计 Total Liability		
流动资产合计 Total Current Assets		固定资产合计 Total Fixed Assets	固定资产原价 Original Cost of Fixed Assets	累计折旧 Accumulated Depreciation	固定资产净值 Net Value of Fixed Assets		流动负债合计 Total Current Liabilities	应付账款 Accounts Payable
存货 Stock	产成品 Finished Product							
4374216	**1782035**	**11374320**	**17353434**	**6008742**	**11344691**	**19219096**	**17461434**	**3176545**
269291	66218	591827	771411	180310	591101	1103424	1047271	238053
1374332	628341	3779388	5694560	1923462	3771097	6524634	5894591	902596
2999884	1153694	7594932	11658874	4085280	7573594	12694462	11566843	2273949
1071428	423951	2805050	4512063	1707227	2804836	4947553	4263537	739786
1143661	518177	2539308	3930647	1397468	2533179	4098257	3746539	645015
2159127	839906	6029962	8910724	2904047	6006677	10173287	9451358	1791743
4374216	1782035	11374320	17353434	6008742	11344691	19219096	17461434	3176545
3770	520	20026	40060	20033	20026	47518	42561	7678
10087	4054	36506	56548	20256	36292	51133	39953	3109
49	32	1170	1817	647	1170	1621	1621	92
753472	341492	2149953	3013777	867769	2146009	3426769	3081846	687761
535650	191289	1098240	1691910	595089	1096822	2013469	1783432	369405
3070931	1244643	8066933	12544337	4501457	8042881	13675868	12509414	2107437
258	5	1492	4984	3492	1492	2718	2607	1063
1338562	613835	3317150	5871823	2565319	3306504	5929189	5409396	887746
112559	46986	179252	300474	125299	175175	536574	495552	162859
233240	61380	286699	497183	210780	286404	673570	654736	127303
432112	265128	518075	928638	411180	517458	1085175	1032600	147489
560652	240341	2333124	4145528	1818060	2327468	3633870	3226508	450095
686233	233007	1945056	2805453	861815	1943638	3628444	3211086	531662
474280	236487	1523493	2307626	785436	1522191	2395175	2194041	465217
608387	237928	1215626	1683577	468162	1215415	2034863	1753855	389942
770269	313586	1687191	2373396	686205	1687192	3130167	2925595	579558
496486	147193	1685804	2311559	641806	1669752	2101259	1967462	322421

11-9 续表 3

单位:万元

指 标	Item
按行业分组	**Grouped by Industries**
农副食品加工业	Agrifood Processing
食品制造业	Food Production
酒、饮料和精制茶制造业	Alcohol, Beverage and Refined Tea Production
纺织业	Textile
纺织服装、服饰业	Textile and Garment, Dress and Personal Adornment
皮革、毛皮、羽毛及其制品和制鞋业	Leather, Fur, Feather(Fuzz) and Related Products
木材加工及木、竹、藤、棕、草制品业	Wood Processing and Industries of Wood, Bamboo, Rattan, Palm and Grass Products
家具制造业	Furniture Manufacturing
造纸和纸制品业	Paper Making and Industries of Paper Products
印刷和记录媒介复制业	Printing and Record Medium Reproduction
文教、工美、体育和娱乐用品制造业	Industries of Culture, Education, Arts, Sports and Recreational Products
石油加工、炼焦和核燃料加工业	Petroleum Processing, Coking and Nuclear Fuel Processing Industries
化学原料和化学制品制造业	Production of Chemical Raw Materials and Chemical Products
医药制造业	Pharmaceutical Industry
化学纤维制造业	Chemical Fiber Manufacturing
橡胶和塑料制品业	Industry of Rubber and Plastic Products
非金属矿物制品业	Industry of Nonmetallic Mineral Products
黑色金属冶炼和压延加工业	Ferrous Metal Smelting and Pressing
有色金属冶炼和压延加工业	Non-Ferrous Metal Smelting and Pressing
金属制品业	Manufacture of Metal Products
通用设备制造业	Manufacture of General Purpose Machinery
专用设备制造业	Manufacture of Equipment for Special Purpose
汽车制造业	Automobile Industry
铁路、船舶、航空航天和其他运输设备制造业	Manufacture of Railroad, Shipping, Aerospace and Other Transportation Equipments
电气机械和器材制造业	Manufacture of Electrical Machinery and Equipments
计算机、通信和其他电子设备制造业	Manufacture of Computer, Communications and Other Electronic Products
仪器仪表制造业	Instrument Manufacturing
其他制造业	Others
废弃资源综合利用业	Comprehensive Utilization of Waste Resources
金属制品、机械和设备修理业	Metal Product, Machinery and Equipment Repair Industry
电力、热力生产和供应业	Generation and Supply of Electric Power and Heating Power
燃气生产和供应业	Generation and Supply of Gas
水的生产和供应业	Generation and Supply of Water

CONTINUED 3

(Unit: 10,000 Yuan)

资产总计 Total Assets						负债合计 Total Liability		
流动资产合计 Total Current Assets		固定资产合计 Total Fixed Assets	固定资产原价 Original Cost of Fixed Assets				流动负债合计 Total Current Liabilities	
存货 Stock	产成品 Finished Product			累计折旧 Accumulated Depreciation	固定资产净值 Net Value of Fixed Assets			应付账款 Accounts Payable
137546	59342	263690	409098	145453	28656	470306	433082	70125
25797	11898	75074	109994	35483	8799	115572	105125	16971
18021	2716	69565	96916	27350	6678	82862	82790	4609
488134	229849	1363816	2143674	783935	175232	2120251	1916452	316248
157560	109051	443219	730387	288000	69303	1201671	1122958	85435
21007	7728	48493	65148	16773	4409	82179	77672	11685
1729	497	5335	9381	4046	694	9876	8886	1673
26469	11020	25153	36318	11194	1936	67040	64578	10047
19251	6615	55405	82021	26616	5898	99861	92670	14820
10685	4229	34337	50193	15856	3253	43290	41855	7968
129557	47153	303601	468723	166750	35046	724980	701503	101101
6488	4383	15787	46862	31075	3801	38809	38809	2394
410081	179116	1245827	1770504	536697	132522	1912851	1791145	278443
69110	27678	264217	369146	104929	31637	304643	261781	71552
92282	43053	502611	647931	145321	52322	559312	404453	79554
53024	17554	122886	190180	68968	14041	260666	255959	36414
222270	44719	513173	827825	315195	71493	1108336	1055285	224673
116477	44974	268399	382376	113977	32195	388399	339250	42079
46886	12144	87153	119752	32599	6972	184980	167839	17722
263075	123415	584735	933406	350679	70898	1108005	1070937	147920
444894	150941	940012	1303100	365420	83317	1442421	1276951	343320
186862	64316	460969	730674	270026	58034	721584	648944	115322
57750	32182	177881	247934	71023	15550	185549	167474	56827
237561	61071	599782	872850	273096	70960	991711	753128	93522
741162	340396	1533384	2436539	903698	219746	2742450	2593037	546083
159465	70683	456703	1026215	569512	97370	805233	723846	165801
219176	69183	547408	833344	287144	65600	916032	895511	221567
7869	5622	9006	11251	2245	1157	21220	21160	9280
221	105	8495	9882	1388	400	4098	4098	
483	254	7686	9482	1796	515	15495	14807	892
2778	141	302183	336311	34819	11045	406012	277381	79337
68	10	5990	6689	699	381	8105	8105	2231
480		32349	39331	6982	572	75298	43964	931

11-9 续表4

单位：万元

指　标	Item
总计	**Total**
#亏损企业	Unprofitable Firm
#轻工业	Light Industry
重工业	Heavy Industry
#大型企业	Large-scale Enterprise
中型企业	Medium-sized Enterprise
小微型企业	Micro Enterprise
按登记注册类型分组	**Grouped by Registration Types**
内资企业	Domestic Enterprise
集体企业	Collective Enterprise
股份合作企业	Joint Equity Cooperative Enterprise
联营企业	Joint Venture
有限责任公司	Limited Liability Company
股份有限公司	Limited Company
私营企业	Private Company
其他企业	Others
按地区分组	**Grouped by Regions**
市　区	Urban Area
崇川区	Chongchuan
港闸区	Gangzha
开发区	Development Zone
通州区	Tongzhou
海安县	Haian
如东县	Rudong
启东市	Qidong
如皋市	Rugao
海门市	Haimen

CONTINUED 4

(Unit: 10,000 Yuan)

非流动负债合计 Total Non-current Liabilities	所有者权益合计 Total Owners´s Equity	实收资本 Paid-in Capital	国家资本 National Capital	集体资本 Collectively Owned Capital	法人资本 Corporate Capital	个人资本 Personal Capital	港澳台资本 Hong Kong, Macao and Taiwan capital	外商资本 Foreign Capital	主营业务收入 Main Business Revenue
1756597	**17522035**	**7200309**	**60477**	**125347**	**1968141**	**4884118**	**98178**	**64048**	**76859375**
56152	649137	540459	1735	9547	263384	265391		403	1328507
629289	5181489	1890912	3000	8294	440857	1396914	14639	27209	23796653
1127308	12340546	5309396	57476	117053	1527284	3487205	83539	36840	53062722
684015	4746772	1427037	1820	605	235989	1103568	79127	5928	17681776
351142	4009926	1447732	5682	50079	551642	806406	11502	22422	17378556
721439	8765337	4325540	52975	74663	1180510	2974144	7549	35699	41799043
1756597	17522035	7200309	60477	125347	1968141	4884118	98178	64048	76859375
4956	28887	4616	300	3704		612			124455
11180	36262	11470		325	6302	4843			352146
	1714	111			111				10008
344798	2900940	1691024	9159	68290	804510	795529	6076	7460	9102925
230037	2366148	554781	4979	588	132600	410753	2251	3610	7097409
1165514	12183049	4937004	46039	52126	1024617	3671393	89851	52979	60160287
111	5035	1303		315		988			12146
519356	4866907	1951093	11940	82407	672809	1164354	9014	10571	18585906
40975	396417	187611		1470	92719	91049		2373	815482
18756	573163	280947	1585	6218	102936	168972		1237	1763414
52575	1052983	448226	5074	36544	212655	193550		403	4062069
407051	2844345	1034310	5281	38175	264499	710784	9014	6558	11944940
417358	3323976	1223979	3472	10558	201001	999958	6259	2731	14528197
200505	2630707	1449492		14635	327792	1020234	68633	18198	11347190
281008	2189133	778099	2750	1506	191463	557137	6620	18623	9458698
204572	2401341	1074886	42120	15013	270281	738242	2615	6615	12452013
133797	2109971	722760	195	1228	304797	404193	5037	7310	10487371

11-9　续表 5

单位：万元

指　标	Item
按行业分组	**Grouped by Industries**
农副食品加工业	Agrifood Processing
食品制造业	Food Production
酒、饮料和精制茶制造业	Alcohol, Beverage and Refined Tea Production
纺织业	Textile
纺织服装、服饰业	Textile and Garment, Dress and Personal Adornment
皮革、毛皮、羽毛及其制品和制鞋业	Leather, Fur, Feather(Fuzz) and Related Products
木材加工及木、竹、藤、棕、草制品业	Wood Processing and Industries of Wood, Bamboo, Rattan, Palm and Grass Products
家具制造业	Furniture Manufacturing
造纸和纸制品业	Paper Making and Industries of Paper Products
印刷和记录媒介复制业	Printing and Record Medium Reproduction
文教、工美、体育和娱乐用品制造业	Industries of Culture, Education, Arts, Sports and Recreational Products
石油加工、炼焦和核燃料加工业	Petroleum Processing, Coking and Nuclear Fuel Processing Industries
化学原料和化学制品制造业	Production of Chemical Raw Materials and Chemical Products
医药制造业	Pharmaceutical Industry
化学纤维制造业	Chemical Fiber Manufacturing
橡胶和塑料制品业	Industry of Rubber and Plastic Products
非金属矿物制品业	Industry of Nonmetallic Mineral Products
黑色金属冶炼和压延加工业	Ferrous Metal Smelting and Pressing
有色金属冶炼和压延加工业	Non-Ferrous Metal Smelting and Pressing
金属制品业	Manufacture of Metal Products
通用设备制造业	Manufacture of General Purpose Machinery
专用设备制造业	Manufacture of Equipment for Special Purpose
汽车制造业	Automobile Industry
铁路、船舶、航空航天和其他运输设备制造业	Manufacture of Railroad, Shipping, Aerospace and Other Transportation Equipments
电气机械和器材制造业	Manufacture of Electrical Machinery and Equipments
计算机、通信和其他电子设备制造业	Manufacture of Computer, Communications and Other Electronic Products
仪器仪表制造业	Instrument Manufacturing
其他制造业	Others
废弃资源综合利用业	Comprehensive Utilization of Waste Resources
金属制品、机械和设备修理业	Metal Product, Machinery and Equipment Repair Industry
电力、热力生产和供应业	Generation and Supply of Electric Power and Heating Power
燃气生产和供应业	Generation and Supply of Gas
水的生产和供应业	Generation and Supply of Water

CONTINUED 5

(Unit: 10,000 Yuan)

非流动负债合计 Total Non-current Liabilities	所有者权益合计 Total Owners's Equity	实收资本 Paid-in Capital	国家资本 National Capital	集体资本 Collectively Owned Capital	法人资本 Corporate Capital	个人资本 Personal Capital	港澳台资本 Hong Kong, Macao and Taiwan capital	外商资本 Foreign Capital	主营业务收入 Main Business Revenue
37223	366321	140527	2168	50	33130	105180			2392557
10447	113199	29384		200	11728	17457			428727
72	46204	22066			15000	7066			146956
203745	1725249	580788		2193	127086	438953	6783	5773	8310850
78713	799466	188337	50	1440	64589	117626	2127	2504	2639944
4507	60560	33291			15620	17672			309036
990	8249	5911				5911			49730
2462	67767	42389			4134	36889	1366		153007
7192	69734	30132		338	1660	28133			362527
1435	44384	25181			3543	21638			162583
22901	487510	182539		569	32202	147039	165	2564	2940931
	22009	8132			904	7228			150186
121706	1713281	816028	8219	7750	361414	413733	500	24412	9324751
42737	352743	169530		550	62752	93485	350	12394	1409190
154859	526685	215736			8376	203512	3848		1974288
4707	206461	90055	66	250	8561	81176	2		979776
52741	792477	362887	482	12508	76819	272678	400		2807783
49149	295043	124106		21999	31760	69777		569	2100040
17142	132862	60957			8607	51970	380		971751
37068	875037	410223	41585	200	77771	290667			4319416
165471	1682041	768253	81	7212	217885	537041		6034	6760945
72639	803101	378248	1885	19337	67537	289189		300	3202408
18075	239555	89141			39948	49193			1140306
238583	500914	261174		1842	53453	202193	2450	1237	1645195
149412	3416911	1452807	2733	25163	414579	932801	73387	4144	12918222
81387	774674	223842	2908		63184	147777	6000	3973	4659152
20521	1142695	305973		12200	112543	180666	420	145	4375844
60	9307	10378			5000	5378			31527
	10334	10600				10600			2002
688	10535	7360			318	7042			14969
128631	186104	129700		9500	46000	74200			126319
	4292	2400				2400			19805
31335	36334	22236	300	2047	2040	17849			28653

11-9 续表 6

单位：万元

指 标	Item	主营业务成本 Main Business Cost
总计	**Total**	**67054223**
# 亏损企业	Unprofitable Firm	1225600
# 轻工业	Light Industry	20945830
重工业	Heavy Industry	46108393
# 大型企业	Large-scale Enterprise	15228058
中型企业	Medium-sized Enterprise	15021529
小微型企业	Micro Enterprise	36804636
按登记注册类型分组	**Grouped by Registration Types**	
内资企业	Domestic Enterprise	67054223
集体企业	Collective Enterprise	110308
股份合作企业	Joint Equity Cooperative Enterprise	307358
联营企业	Joint Venture	9035
有限责任公司	Limited Liability Company	8065765
股份有限公司	Limited Company	6027762
私营企业	Private Company	52523161
其他企业	Others	10834
按地区分组	**Grouped by Regions**	
市 区	Urban Area	16261577
崇川区	Chongchuan	721860
港闸区	Gangzha	1548679
开发区	Development Zone	3548391
通州区	Tongzhou	10442647
海安县	Haian	12690575
如东县	Rudong	9908757
启东市	Qidong	8169055
如皋市	Rugao	11134125
海门市	Haimen	8890134

CONTINUED 6

(Unit: 10,000 Yuan)

主营业务税金及附加 Tax and Extra Charges of Main Business	其他业务利润 Other Business Profit	销售费用 Selling Expenses	管理费用 Administrative Expenses	财务费用 Financial Cost	利息收入 Interest Income	利息支出 Interest Expenditure	投资收益 Investment Income	营业利润 Operating Profit
353799	**6965**	**1160162**	**2002520**	**560418**	**29027**	**551655**	**65635**	**5794839**
9233	530	40905	87187	33885	1119	29563	653	-64874
115158	1917	334615	594155	197361	7212	192400	34071	1646404
238641	5048	825546	1408365	363057	21815	359256	31564	4148435
82233	1149	283069	419896	130534	10040	137631	46810	1584941
79130	3790	246513	473123	112701	9327	112231	10370	1463198
192436	2026	630579	1109501	317183	9660	301793	8455	2746701
353799	6965	1160162	2002520	560418	29027	551655	65635	5794839
621		2810	3205	626	32	275	267	6970
1032		3208	5684	1544	3	1498		33320
104		89	105	25	3	27		651
31268	2068	135952	286750	94121	8384	93162	1769	489522
35495	2798	160260	232365	73219	7311	76741	19192	584051
285187	2099	857701	1473937	390832	13293	379901	44408	4679774
92		142	475	51	2	52		552
90174	5608	261197	606225	157602	15007	160837	16314	1223035
3374	2555	22903	42946	13842	1302	12871	1141	10122
9349	505	32916	81833	11970	2728	11887	1878	81638
18308	1716	42778	127996	23326	3855	26080	176	294260
59144	832	162601	353450	108464	7122	110000	13119	837015
62050	67	235749	330852	151052	3708	150512	8437	1067634
50908	159	142935	278785	71354	2035	70191	34292	924453
55894	1416	189945	280354	54815	2470	53930	8043	718618
48146	-457	195061	294413	76228	3299	68555	-17241	691171
46628	174	135275	211892	49368	2507	47630	15791	1169930

11-9 续表 7

单位:万元

指 标	Item	主营 业务成本 Main Business Cost
按行业分组	**Grouped by Industries**	
农副食品加工业	Agrifood Processing	2177315
食品制造业	Food Production	363786
酒、饮料和精制茶制造业	Alcohol, Beverage and Refined Tea Production	116774
纺织业	Textile	7384988
纺织服装、服饰业	Textile and Garment, Dress and Personal Adornment	2286861
皮革、毛皮、羽毛及其制品和制鞋业	Leather, Fur, Feather(Fuzz) and Related Products	271974
木材加工及木、竹、藤、棕、草制品业	Wood Processing and Industries of Wood, Bamboo, Rattan, Palm and Grass Products	44543
家具制造业	Furniture Manufacturing	124233
造纸和纸制品业	Paper Making and Industries of Paper Products	311069
印刷和记录媒介复制业	Printing and Record Medium Reproduction	143899
文教、工美、体育和娱乐用品制造业	Industries of Culture, Education, Arts, Sports and Recreational Products	2567075
石油加工、炼焦和核燃料加工业	Petroleum Processing, Coking and Nuclear Fuel Processing Industries	136967
化学原料和化学制品制造业	Production of Chemical Raw Materials and Chemical Products	8352421
医药制造业	Pharmaceutical Industry	1220691
化学纤维制造业	Chemical Fiber Manufacturing	1735130
橡胶和塑料制品业	Industry of Rubber and Plastic Products	852747
非金属矿物制品业	Industry of Nonmetallic Mineral Products	2420077
黑色金属冶炼和压延加工业	Ferrous Metal Smelting and Pressing	1913869
有色金属冶炼和压延加工业	Non-Ferrous Metal Smelting and Pressing	886911
金属制品业	Manufacture of Metal Products	3735771
通用设备制造业	Manufacture of General Purpose Machinery	5754629
专用设备制造业	Manufacture of Equipment for Special Purpose	2732275
汽车制造业	Automobile Industry	980056
铁路、船舶、航空航天和其他运输设备制造业	Manufacture of Railroad, Shipping, Aerospace and Other Transportation Equipments	1451925
电气机械和器材制造业	Manufacture of Electrical Machinery and Equipments	11124831
计算机、通信和其他电子设备制造业	Manufacture of Computer, Communications and Other Electronic Products	4092277
仪器仪表制造业	Instrument Manufacturing	3717877
其他制造业	Others	27625
废弃资源综合利用业	Comprehensive Utilization of Waste Resources	1802
金属制品、机械和设备修理业	Metal Product, Machinery and Equipment Repair Industry	12500
电力、热力生产和供应业	Generation and Supply of Electric Power and Heating Power	79766
燃气生产和供应业	Generation and Supply of Gas	17234
水的生产和供应业	Generation and Supply of Water	14328

CONTINUED 7

(Unit: 10,000 Yuan)

主营业务税金及附加 Sales Tax and Extra Charges	其他业务利润 Profits of Other Business	销售费用 Sales Expenditure	管理费用 Management Expenditure	财务费用 Accounting Expenditure	利息收入 Interest Income	利息支出 Interest Expenditure	投资收益 Investment Income	营业利润 Operating Profit
8924		29057	33743	16544	136	14743	-253	126749
2523		8253	11902	4805	532	4859	4	37487
5462		8735	8993	1927	50	2105		5899
40830	224	96671	200896	61758	3833	61370	7660	532491
13048	910	35144	74680	37616	481	36878	13993	204412
2105	52	5297	7593	2556	62	2537	200	19762
267		500	984	226	1	227		3210
871	146	4029	9175	827	286	981	201	14677
2251	167	7795	12730	2943	23	2891	20	26292
870	132	3434	5708	1181	19	1075	3	7629
14253	165	36277	66592	15786	203	14726	277	241391
348	-852	2248	4392	228	-26	224	419	5572
22399	1255	101833	198021	52927	5080	52777	2038	596347
5672	13	27451	53055	7652	188	7288	5514	100456
7218		27278	39017	20357	315	20018	85	147987
3769		17149	30123	11912	479	11859		64070
16321	58	60314	76181	34692	1154	33511	-112	199725
5572		14773	39443	13068	372	11299	13	113833
3250		5891	11042	8373	83	8288	115	58319
21442	499	46926	129431	37732	2871	38113	426	344702
42735	812	158622	225537	42964	2629	42150	472	537922
17906	470	68082	106812	17240	768	16518	356	260601
10757	69	23453	30118	8749	851	9100	-18372	68907
6952	397	17168	50402	13542	428	12923	164	105839
51724	386	194960	317298	74103	4990	73984	51184	1203530
26313	1192	72801	111566	25872	886	25803	-683	334297
19295	872	83442	137574	28209	2252	28786	1709	392225
89		612	2218	173	21	178		811
		6	511	79				-396
153		260	1189	247	34	276	191	811
193		43	2098	12717	15	12745		31481
43		309	694	258		258		1266
246		1353	2806	3156	12	3168	13	6536

11-9 续表 8

单位：万元

指 标	Item	营业外收入 Non-business Income
总计	**Total**	**83025**
# 亏损企业	Unprofitable Firm	10595
# 轻工业	Light Industry	26883
重工业	Heavy Industry	56142
# 大型企业	Large-scale Enterprise	29191
中型企业	Medium-sized Enterprise	23704
小微型企业	Micro Enterprise	30130
按登记注册类型分组	**Grouped by Registration Types**	
内资企业	Domestic Enterprise	83025
集体企业	Collective Enterprise	134
股份合作企业	Joint Equity Cooperative Enterprise	2
联营企业	Joint Venture	
有限责任公司	Limited Liability Company	20256
股份有限公司	Limited Company	19178
私营企业	Private Company	43415
其他企业	Others	41
按地区分组	**Grouped by Regions**	
市 区	Urban Area	33905
崇川区	Chongchuan	3949
港闸区	Gangzha	6684
开发区	Development Zone	5594
通州区	Tongzhou	17677
海安县	Haian	13270
如东县	Rudong	15435
启东市	Qidong	3168
如皋市	Rugao	7831
海门市	Haimen	9416

CONTINUED 8

(Unit: 10,000 Yuan)

补贴收入 Subsidy Income	营业外支出 Non-business Expenditure	利润总额 Total Profit	应交所得税 Income Tax Payable	亏损企业亏损总额 Total Loss of Unprofitable Enterprises	利税总额 Total Profits and Taxes	本年应交增值税 Added Value Tax Payable of the Year	全部从业人员年平均人数(人) The Annual Number of All Employees(person)
24722	**115302**	**5763393**	**1121066**	**56116**	**9237657**	**3119133**	**625229**
3229	1838	-56116	667	56116	-29789	17073	20231
4620	48760	1624934	306433	17872	2647687	907146	264507
20102	66542	4138459	814633	38244	6589971	2211987	360722
6556	42704	1571427	278997	1514	2582271	928592	128313
5075	19465	1467607	291196	12295	2287414	740070	153248
13090	53133	2724359	550873	42308	4367972	1450471	343668
24722	115302	5763393	1121066	56116	9237657	3119133	625229
	56	7048	1434		11260	3591	1540
	41	33281	6574		50176	15863	2520
		651	163		1208	454	91
7202	11321	498569	89088	20337	763592	233205	80332
4437	15687	587542	106342	2240	938250	315167	55870
13045	88161	4635747	917277	33539	7472250	2550579	484716
38	38	555	188		921	274	160
12502	34186	1223567	213975	14427	1993711	679262	174501
2680	2114	12754	4428	4506	31759	15618	11573
3209	1620	86702	12827	1455	143045	46755	19780
2451	4323	295531	69399	1488	455264	141145	35470
4163	26129	828579	127321	6978	1363644	475743	107678
2703	30160	1050744	230253	17371	1632868	519959	111407
4351	29514	910374	174503	2529	1461200	499839	75077
1950	1164	720622	126990	10096	1161492	384977	68878
1396	18987	680014	111576	8502	1139228	410640	130372
1819	1291	1178074	263770	3191	1849158	624457	64994

11-9 续表 9

单位：万元

指 标	Item	营业外收入 Non-business Income
按行业分组	**Grouped by Industries**	
农副食品加工业	Agrifood Processing	521
食品制造业	Food Production	598
酒、饮料和精制茶制造业	Alcohol, Beverage and Refined Tea Production	1639
纺织业	Textile	10470
纺织服装、服饰业	Textile and Garment, Dress and Personal Adornment	503
皮革、毛皮、羽毛及其制品和制鞋业	Leather, Fur, Feather(Fuzz) and Related Products	48
木材加工及木、竹、藤、棕、草制品业	Wood Processing and Industries of Wood, Bamboo, Rattan, Palm and Grass Products	
家具制造业	Furniture Manufacturing	62
造纸和纸制品业	Paper Making and Industries of Paper Products	79
印刷和记录媒介复制业	Printing and Record Medium Reproduction	38
文教、工美、体育和娱乐用品制造业	Industries of Culture, Education, Arts, Sports and Recreational Products	543
石油加工、炼焦和核燃料加工业	Petroleum Processing, Coking and Nuclear Fuel Processing Industries	29
化学原料和化学制品制造业	Production of Chemical Raw Materials and Chemical Products	7314
医药制造业	Pharmaceutical Industry	3387
化学纤维制造业	Chemical Fiber Manufacturing	5844
橡胶和塑料制品业	Industry of Rubber and Plastic Products	797
非金属矿物制品业	Industry of Nonmetallic Mineral Products	4217
黑色金属冶炼和压延加工业	Ferrous Metal Smelting and Pressing	675
有色金属冶炼和压延加工业	Non-Ferrous Metal Smelting and Pressing	2223
金属制品业	Manufacture of Metal Products	1437
通用设备制造业	Manufacture of General Purpose Machinery	7589
专用设备制造业	Manufacture of Equipment for Special Purpose	6613
汽车制造业	Automobile Industry	2820
铁路、船舶、航空航天和其他运输设备制造业	Manufacture of Railroad, Shipping, Aerospace and Other Transportation Equipments	1336
电气机械和器材制造业	Manufacture of Electrical Machinery and Equipments	17075
计算机、通信和其他电子设备制造业	Manufacture of Computer, Communications and Other Electronic Products	4610
仪器仪表制造业	Instrument Manufacturing	2539
其他制造业	Others	
废弃资源综合利用业	Comprehensive Utilization of Waste Resources	
金属制品、机械和设备修理业	Metal Product, Machinery and Equipment Repair Industry	
电力、热力生产和供应业	Generation and Supply of Electric Power and Heating Power	20
燃气生产和供应业	Generation and Supply of Gas	1
水的生产和供应业	Generation and Supply of Water	

CONTINUED 9

(Unit: 10,000 Yuan)

补贴收入 Subsidy Income	营业外支出 Non-business Expenditure	利润总额 Total Profit	应交所得税 Income Tax Payable	亏损企业亏损总额 Total Loss of Unprofitable Enterprises	利税总额 Total Profits and Taxes	本年应交增值税 Added Value Tax Payable of the Year	全部从业人员年平均人数(人) The Annual Number of All Employees(person)
244	6065	121205	24396	1334	189933	59804	13987
58	42	38043	7268	1365	60429	19863	3354
		7537	1526	1514	18695	5695	2698
1881	11255	531925	105763	4719	888012	314915	101767
15	8936	195979	24314	1329	319922	110874	42303
17	50	19764	3715	218	33401	11531	5324
	1	3209	597		5569	2092	627
	565	14174	3008	211	21425	6353	3080
6	146	26225	5947	484	42258	13777	4037
	374	7293	850	15	13997	5825	2380
323	5871	236233	50222	568	382536	132150	38530
	149	5452	2120	3233	8396	2295	563
1544	18656	585022	123395	7131	946470	338744	43249
270	3467	100376	21126	2900	164564	58500	10224
146	6077	147754	32059	1551	223151	68151	11327
704	653	64214	14687	1770	108357	40334	12355
3123	3945	200293	36129	2197	328842	112196	24230
288	1705	112803	20803	188	188252	69848	11933
10	349	60193	13258	833	88909	25464	5517
10	3493	342646	77590	4130	538511	174399	39189
4731	1683	543936	106794	7246	853951	267262	55863
779	7004	260213	51827	2792	417971	139825	26982
123	4051	67676	12633		131702	53111	11947
520	816	106358	19488	1597	176059	62707	21789
7607	17722	1202896	240488	1179	1925593	670792	70545
1491	3229	335677	48604		523356	161346	32695
830	8722	386042	66685	6565	592625	187284	25999
		811	322	653	1466	565	695
		–396		396	–396		102
	5	806	135		1746	787	923
4	271	31230	4758		32493	1070	650
	1	1266	252		1750	441	97
		6536	310		7915	1133	268

11-10 规模以上高新技术企业主要经济指标(2014年)

单位:万元

指标	Item	企业单位数(个) Number of Enterprises and Units
总计	**Total**	**1393**
#亏损企业	Unprofitable Firm	76
#国有控股企业	State-holding Enterprise	28
#轻工业	Light Industry	150
重工业	Heavy Industry	1243
#大型企业	Large-scale Enterprise	57
中型企业	Medium-sized Enterprise	189
小微型企业	Micro Enterprise	1147
按登记注册类型分组	**Grouped by Registration Types**	
内资企业	Domestic Enterprise	1094
国有企业	State-owned Enterprise	1
集体企业	Collective Enterprise	3
股份合作企业	Joint Equity Cooperative Enterprise	5
有限责任公司	Limited Liability Company	163
股份有限公司	Limited Company	39
私营企业	Private Company	881
其他企业	Others	2
港、澳、台商投资企业	HK, Macau or Taiwan Funded Enterprise	141
合资经营企业(港或澳、台资)	Joint Venture(HK, Macau or Taiwan)	65
合作经营企业(港或澳、台资)	Cooperative Enterprise(HK, Macau or Taiwan)	1
港澳台商独资经营企业	Sole Proprietorship(HK, Macau or Taiwan)	74
港澳台商投资股份有限公司	Shareholding Limited Company(HK, Macau or Taiwan)	1

MAJOR ECONOMIC INDICATORS OF HI-TECH ENTERPRISES ABOVE DESIGNATED SIZE(2014)

(Unit: 10,000 Yuan)

亏损企业 Unprofitable Firms	工业总产值 (当年价格) Total Value of Industrial Output (Price of Current Year)	工业销售产值 (当年价格) Industrial Sales Value (Price of Current Year)	出口交货值 Value of Export Delivery	资产总计 Total Assets	流动资产合计 Total Current Assets	应收账款 Accounts Receivable
76	**53129264**	**52505981**	**6687807**	**30275194**	**15210883**	**4837776**
76	1665083	1642625	583140	3570139	1969788	682531
9	3356209	3304640	744212	6597575	2640255	944460
9	5736154	5682746	666408	2819564	1204841	271497
67	47393110	46823236	6021399	27455629	14006042	4566280
3	15093499	14891346	3195245	10552284	5400822	2233244
8	15528768	15378767	2068048	9249260	4567437	1053129
65	22506997	22235869	1424514	10473650	5242625	1551403
58	38340346	37869610	3004520	20549744	10498430	3330763
1	2040	2040		4443	1867	415
	40621	40565	4440	19374	12602	5027
	258576	257874		63496	27011	4225
21	5745527	5638448	573820	5806509	2490536	954707
3	4732381	4700736	659627	3768390	2087050	480800
33	27551655	27220428	1766633	10881081	5875868	1883329
	9546	9520		6452	3495	2260
7	5970172	5920571	1050727	3731233	1743013	498478
2	2688793	2648673	253072	1603910	664912	212427
	3458	3458		5883	2920	1176
5	3166773	3159477	787267	2066498	1039292	272911
	111149	108963	10389	54942	35890	11964

11-10 续表 1

单位：万元

指 标	Item	企业单位数(个) Number of Enterprises(unit)
外商投资企业	Foreign Funded Enterprise	158
中外合资经营企业	Sino-foreign Joint Venture	79
中外合作经营企业	Sino-foreign Cooperative Enterprise	4
外资企业	Foreign-owned Enterprise	73
外商投资股份有限公司	Foreign Investment Joint Stock Company	2
按经济组织类型分组	**Grouped by Types of Ownership**	
独资企业	Sole Proprietorship	165
合作、合伙企业	Cooperative and Partnership Enterprises	17
股份有限公司	Joint Stock Company	65
有限责任公司	Limited Liability Company	1146
按地区分组	**Grouped by Regions**	
市 区	Urban Area	460
崇川区	Chongchuan	18
港闸区	Gangzha	70
开发区	Development Zone	193
通州区	Tongzhou	179
海安县	Haian	290
如东县	Rudong	139
启东市	Qidong	144
如皋市	Rugao	205
海门市	Haimen	155

CONTINUED 1

(Unit: 10,000 Yuan)

亏损企业 Unprofitable Firms	工业总产值（当年价格）Total Value of Industrial Output (Price of Current Year)	工业销售产值（当年价格）Industrial Sales Value (Price of Current Year)	出口交货值 Value of Export Delivery	资产总计 Total Assets	流动资产合计 Total Current Assets	应收账款 Accounts Receivable
11	8818746	8715801	2632560	5994218	2969441	1008535
5	4587684	4559580	1555842	3373589	1538547	540856
1	86572	86549	5110	20561	7788	2447
5	4122073	4047264	1058957	2594333	1420241	464529
	22417	22408	12651	5734	2866	703
11	7641987	7558799	1850663	4741145	2501210	752383
1	400973	399875	5110	103964	45202	12339
4	6326433	6276537	801501	4520165	2498862	614884
60	38759872	38270769	4030534	20909919	10165609	3458170
27	17072404	16756471	3536241	12279886	5588402	1434375
4	1596347	1539865	652396	1887754	944820	433400
8	1530115	1489522	284968	2124571	1353427	238839
6	6089470	5943622	864881	5243830	1999007	452646
9	7856472	7783463	1733996	3023732	1291147	309490
26	8216189	8204513	834231	3699452	1863076	565717
3	6782104	6653981	581747	3798597	1888386	697204
7	6615205	6543437	1049229	4448670	2573962	1169426
10	6618250	6529689	470865	2937034	1732833	507736
3	7825110	7817890	215494	3111554	1564225	463318

11-10　续表 2

单位：万元

指　标	Item
总计	**Total**
# 亏损企业	Unprofitable Firm
# 国有控股企业	State-holding Enterprise
# 轻工业	Light Industry
重工业	Heavy Industry
# 大型企业	Large-scale Enterprise
中型企业	Medium-sized Enterprise
小微型企业	Micro Enterprise
按登记注册类型分组	**Grouped by Registration Types**
内资企业	Domestic Enterprise
国有企业	State-owned Enterprise
集体企业	Collective Enterprise
股份合作企业	Joint Equity Cooperative Enterprise
有限责任公司	Limited Liability Company
股份有限公司	Limited Company
私营企业	Private Company
其他企业	Others
港、澳、台商投资企业	HK, Macau or Taiwan Funded Enterprise
合资经营企业(港或澳、台资)	Joint Venture(HK, Macau or Taiwan)
合作经营企业(港或澳、台资)	Cooperative Enterprise(HK, Macau or Taiwan)
港澳台商独资经营企业	Sole Proprietorship(HK, Macau or Taiwan)
港澳台商投资股份有限公司	Shareholding Limited Company(HK, Macau or Taiwan)

CONTINUED 2

(Unit: 10,000 Yuan)

资产总计 Total Assets						负债合计 Total Liability		
流动资产合计 Total Current Assets		固定资产合计 Total Fixed Assets	固定资产原价 Original Cost of Fixed Assets				流动负债合计 Total Current Liabilities	
存货 Stock	产成品 Finished Product			累计折旧 Accumulated Depreciation	固定资产净值 Net Value of Fixed Assets			应付账款 Accounts Payable
3186298	**1383189**	**9748383**	**15478202**	**5770030**	**9708172**	**15879596**	**13879833**	**3361415**
261069	69673	1185150	1600996	420980	1180015	2611284	1816302	635414
502671	252196	2410538	3668301	1259076	2409225	4294057	3307485	1332199
322175	150050	1055164	1702116	647744	1054372	1120428	948921	216542
2864123	1233139	8693219	13776086	5122286	8653800	14759168	12930911	3144874
902901	376442	3006697	5106088	2096049	3010039	6045317	4941699	1621538
1123232	523666	3040754	4927502	1913127	3014375	4697121	4123934	854492
1160165	483082	3700932	5444613	1760854	3683759	5137159	4814199	885386
2147654	936029	6135680	9606930	3486892	6120038	10885466	9412649	2525569
1029	555	2296	5847	3551	2296	13610	13610	3185
2600	186	3218	6464	3246	3218	5225	4389	390
7522	2586	26123	31756	5842	25914	38746	27565	-1010
568587	320688	1791185	2628967	844291	1784676	3581320	2884954	1142124
419278	167449	926206	1450602	520851	929751	1390059	1602377	418336
1148498	444560	3385454	5479106	2106122	3372984	5354376	4877724	961624
139	5	1198	4187	2989	1198	2130	2030	919
348555	130770	1404410	1962810	561884	1400926	1792186	1662625	292827
166652	73052	720778	962770	242145	720625	690128	664677	128251
596	115	1630	1936	305	1630	1693	1693	271
170297	54470	671969	974840	306202	668638	1076688	974179	162651
11011	3134	10033	23265	13232	10033	23678	22076	1655

11-10 续表 3

单位：万元

指 标	Item
外商投资企业	Foreign Funded Enterprise
中外合资经营企业	Sino-foreign Joint Venture
中外合作经营企业	Sino-foreign Cooperative Enterprise
外资企业	Foreign-owned Enterprise
外商投资股份有限公司	Foreign Investment Joint Stock Company
按经济组织类型分组	**Grouped by Types of Ownership**
独资企业	Sole Proprietorship
合作、合伙企业	Cooperative and Partnership Enterprises
股份有限公司	Joint Stock Company
有限责任公司	Limited Liability Company
按地区分组	**Grouped by Regions**
市 区	Urban Area
崇川区	Chongchuan
港闸区	Gangzha
开发区	Development Zone
通州区	Tongzhou
海安县	Haian
如东县	Rudong
启东市	Qidong
如皋市	Rugao
海门市	Haimen

CONTINUED 3

(Unit: 10,000 Yuan)

资产总计 Total Assets						负债合计 Total Liability		
流动资产合计 Total Current Assets		固定资产合计 Total Fixed Assets	固定资产原价 Original Cost of Fixed Assets				流动负债合计 Total Current Liabilities	
存货 Stock	产成品 Finished Product			累计折旧 Accumulated Depreciation	固定资产净值 Net Value of Fixed Assets			应付账款 Accounts Payable
690089	316390	2208293	3908462	1721254	2187208	3201944	2804559	543019
372229	153902	1338970	2422714	1104628	1318086	1731229	1465518	375627
2035	970	12073	17388	5315	12073	6863	6863	157
314617	161174	854382	1463202	609021	854181	1460094	1329122	165937
1208	346	2868	5159	2291	2868	3758	3056	1298
492828	217626	1551882	2481553	933204	1548349	2584995	2347042	337849
10986	4077	43392	59722	16539	43183	53657	42377	1643
517029	197889	1169918	1922867	749334	1173533	2253241	1943829	492128
2165456	963599	6983191	11014061	4070954	6943108	10987703	9546586	2529795
1423951	707886	4382927	7898497	3523728	4374770	6678877	5778245	1712047
172495	60876	675625	1232436	563261	669175	897866	628809	272310
261126	81324	470146	818396	348301	470096	1197131	943679	329063
725503	471309	1894741	3241480	1344463	1897017	3253924	3099144	874176
264826	94377	1342416	2606185	1267703	1338482	1329956	1106612	236499
343446	82993	974796	1386131	411335	974796	1956199	1733780	302131
302015	175760	1268769	1936769	668574	1268195	1634220	1560787	326489
372001	156437	994192	1377049	382857	994192	2462120	1927977	462667
391565	169451	908988	1283595	374608	908988	1588894	1462078	325583
353320	90664	1218712	1596161	408928	1187233	1559285	1416965	232499

11-10 续表 4

单位：万元

指 标	Item
总计	**Total**
# 亏损企业	Unprofitable Firm
# 国有控股企业	State-holding Enterprise
# 轻工业	Light Industry
重工业	Heavy Industry
# 大型企业	Large-scale Enterprise
中型企业	Medium-sized Enterprise
小微型企业	Micro Enterprise
按登记注册类型分组	**Grouped by Registration Types**
内资企业	Domestic Enterprise
国有企业	State-owned Enterprise
集体企业	Collective Enterprise
股份合作企业	Joint Equity Cooperative Enterprise
有限责任公司	Limited Liability Company
股份有限公司	Limited Company
私营企业	Private Company
其他企业	Others
港、澳、台商投资企业	HK, Macau or Taiwan Funded Enterprise
合资经营企业(港或澳、台资)	Joint Venture(HK, Macau or Taiwan)
合作经营企业(港或澳、台资)	Cooperative Enterprise(HK, Macau or Taiwan)
港澳台商独资经营企业	Sole Proprietorship(HK, Macau or Taiwan)
港澳台商投资股份有限公司	Shareholding Limited Company(HK, Macau or Taiwan)

CONTINUED 4

(Unit: 10,000 Yuan)

非流动负债合计 Total Non-current Liabilities	所有者权益合计 Total Owners Equity	实收资本 Paid-in Capital	国家资本 National Capital	集体资本 Collectively Owned Capital	法人资本 Corporate Capital	个人资本 Personal Capital	港澳台资本 Hong Kong, Macao and Taiwan capital	外商资本 Foreign Capital	主营业务收入 Main Business Revenue
1999638	**14395598**	**6520675**	**482892**	**93720**	**1564163**	**2569450**	**726382**	**1084068**	**52382049**
794982	958855	847782	171202	45843	239914	132256	77951	180617	1643994
986573	2303517	1201555	416953	36000	325098	76295	302897	44312	3300364
171382	1699136	827019	31776	1559	254205	295107	125383	118989	5668488
1828256	12696462	5693656	451117	92161	1309958	2274343	600998	965079	46713560
1103618	4506968	1784021	235653	60	228857	802777	169397	347277	15044666
573187	4552139	2016236	107429	61890	639122	644746	174493	388557	15344374
322834	5336492	2720417	139811	31770	696183	1121927	382492	348234	21993009
1472692	9664278	3966688	349127	87533	1164321	2229886	78797	57025	37867217
	–9167	1871	1871						2113
837	14148	901		641		260			40124
11180	24751	8445			5401	3044			255949
696241	2225188	1220201	296337	42500	590630	278989		11745	5635305
287683	1878330	444304	48399	240	119582	275342		742	4726579
476652	5526705	2289979	2521	44152	448708	1671264	78797	44537	27197627
100	4322	988				988			9520
129562	1939047	1034054	77695	1835	51367	236012	543982	123163	5856300
25451	913782	455599	26508	1835	45683	60670	314164	6740	2611745
	4191	4001					4001		3458
102509	989810	566053	51187		5683	175342	217418	116423	3134219
1601	31265	8400					8400		106878

11-10 续表 5

单位：万元

指 标	Item
外商投资企业	Foreign Funded Enterprise
中外合资经营企业	Sino-foreign Joint Venture
中外合作经营企业	Sino-foreign Cooperative Enterprise
外资企业	Foreign-owned Enterprise
外商投资股份有限公司	Foreign Investment Joint Stock Company
按经济组织类型分组	**Grouped by Types of Ownership**
独资企业	Sole Proprietorship
合作、合伙企业	Cooperative and Partnership Enterprises
股份有限公司	Joint Stock Company
有限责任公司	Limited Liability Company
按地区分组	**Grouped by Regions**
市 区	Urban Area
崇川区	Chongchuan
港闸区	Gangzha
开发区	Development Zone
通州区	Tongzhou
海安县	Haian
如东县	Rudong
启东市	Qidong
如皋市	Rugao
海门市	Haimen

CONTINUED 5

(Unit: 10,000 Yuan)

非流动负债合计 Total Non-current Liabilities	所有者权益合计 Total Owners Equity	实收资本 Paid-in Capital	国家资本 National Capital	集体资本 Collectively Owned Capital	法人资本 Corporate Capital	个人资本 Personal Capital	港澳台资本 Hong Kong, Macao and Taiwan capital	外商资本 Foreign Capital	主营业务收入 Main Business Revenue
397384	2792274	1519933	56070	4352	348476	103553	103603	903880	8658532
265711	1642360	709079	56070	239	270581	63486	102786	215917	4515806
	13698	9047		4113		564		4371	86220
130972	1134239	800964			77895	38660	816	683593	4034403
702	1976	843				843			22104
237953	2156150	1379476	53058	641	83593	223934	218234	800015	7518240
11280	50307	23114		4113	5401	5228	4001	4371	397403
309412	2266924	591824	48399	240	133902	400142	8400	742	6294010
1440992	9922216	4526261	381436	88727	1341267	1940146	495747	278939	38172396
900507	5601009	2427299	248052	71275	813778	575590	159094	559511	16598898
269010	989888	432319	30228	30151	227334	40936	64336	39335	1545288
253373	927440	496289	100121	6770	109473	122614	17855	139457	1473953
154780	1989906	891367	94515	22354	284063	130102	27699	332634	5889255
223344	1693776	607324	23188	12000	192908	281939	49205	48084	7690402
222419	1743253	703516	2526	8473	62623	557629	26097	46169	8223537
73432	2164378	1229411	26508	4500	124611	685988	344060	43744	6642641
534143	1986549	888552	101757	1500	136148	272251	86448	290448	6530585
126817	1348140	594214	21424	7423	168118	266747	37295	93207	6558932
142320	1552270	677683	82626	550	258885	211245	73387	50990	7827454

11-10 续表6

单位：万元

指 标	Item	主营业务成本 Main Business Cost
总计	**Total**	**45318366**
# 亏损企业	Unprofitable Firm	1539951
# 国有控股企业	State-holding Enterprise	2702964
# 轻工业	Light Industry	4730026
重工业	Heavy Industry	40588340
# 大型企业	Large-scale Enterprise	13002256
中型企业	Medium-sized Enterprise	13004323
小微型企业	Micro Enterprise	19311788
按登记注册类型分组	**Grouped by Registration Types**	
内资企业	Domestic Enterprise	33016682
国有企业	State-owned Enterprise	2268
集体企业	Collective Enterprise	35278
股份合作企业	Joint Equity Cooperative Enterprise	221718
有限责任公司	Limited Liability Company	5093028
股份有限公司	Limited Company	3979683
私营企业	Private Company	23676194
其他企业	Others	8513
港、澳、台商投资企业	HK, Macau or Taiwan Funded Enterprise	5045371
合资经营企业(港或澳、台资)	Joint Venture(HK, Macau or Taiwan)	2238604
合作经营企业(港或澳、台资)	Cooperative Enterprise(HK, Macau or Taiwan)	3033
港澳台商独资经营企业	Sole Proprietorship(HK, Macau or Taiwan)	2715476
港澳台商投资股份有限公司	Shareholding Limited Company(HK, Macau or Taiwan)	88258

CONTINUED 6

(Unit: 10,000 Yuan)

主营业务税金及附加 Tax and Extra Charges of Main Business	其他业务利润 Other Business Profit	销售费用 Selling Expenses	管理费用 Administrative Expenses	财务费用 Financial Cost	利息收入 Interest Income	利息支出 Interest Expenditure	投资收益 Investment Income	营业利润 Operating Profit
220455	**12705**	**791884**	**1560607**	**400846**	**38716**	**411989**	**66230**	**4197592**
3601	2399	40295	136216	71398	5690	68291	9542	−109255
13579	6945	48396	179468	55549	12470	63552	12498	328402
28201	526	95851	199130	32661	3356	33400	7890	593943
192254	12179	696033	1361477	368184	35360	378589	58340	3603649
56040	4686	239983	422867	122285	17376	132632	40742	1253416
72248	6663	214788	521144	119840	14004	125512	19484	1455706
92167	1357	337114	616596	158721	7336	153845	6004	1488470
157108	8452	580642	1061592	257252	24328	262430	66190	2864757
12		67	2181	25	1	25		−2365
106		949	1356	132	2	71	8	2312
638		2055	3903	1325		1325		26310
13064	4477	71749	180908	55699	12237	59821	2293	228112
19607	2782	114663	185815	58168	4463	60385	22723	387920
123601	1193	391073	687143	141900	7623	140799	41167	2221918
81		86	286	4	2	5		550
21574	1538	79254	205388	54878	3229	54494	315	484221
10349	1170	36923	66209	20189	1979	21417	68	248668
11		37	235	74		75		67
10762	368	42104	138179	34346	1012	32529	248	219899
452		190	765	269	238	474		15587

11-10 续表 7

单位：万元

指 标	Item	主营业务成本 Main Business Cost
外商投资企业	Foreign Funded Enterprise	7256313
中外合资经营企业	Sino-foreign Joint Venture	3704044
中外合作经营企业	Sino-foreign Cooperative Enterprise	75625
外资企业	Foreign-owned Enterprise	3457772
外商投资股份有限公司	Foreign Investment Joint Stock Company	18872
按经济组织类型分组	**Grouped by Types of Ownership**	
独资企业	Sole Proprietorship	6473902
合作、合伙企业	Cooperative and Partnership Enterprises	347495
股份有限公司	Joint Stock Company	5321423
有限责任公司	Limited Liability Company	33175546
按地区分组	**Grouped by Regions**	
市 区	Urban Area	14307307
崇川区	Chongchuan	1148120
港闸区	Gangzha	1284259
开发区	Development Zone	5125888
通州区	Tongzhou	6749041
海安县	Haian	7114246
如东县	Rudong	5734169
启东市	Qidong	5667552
如皋市	Rugao	5834446
海门市	Haimen	6660647

CONTINUED 7

(Unit: 10,000 Yuan)

主营业务税金及附加 Tax and Extra Charges of Main Business	其他业务利润 Other Business Profit	销售费用 Selling Expenses	管理费用 Administrative Expenses	财务费用 Financial Cost	利息收入 Interest Income	利息支出 Interest Expenditure	投资收益 Investment Income	营业利润 Operating Profit
41773	2716	131988	293627	88715	11159	95065	−276	848614
24151	2712	57527	183030	34854	7703	40939	−379	513828
502		531	3521	93	3	66	−100	5849
16945	3	73550	106245	53558	3452	53849	203	327302
175		380	830	210	1	210		1636
30145	371	121190	254004	89542	4468	87938	458	577056
1321		2906	8879	1591	10	1571	−100	35110
26984	2789	138831	228797	66328	5343	68953	28029	538001
162006	9545	528958	1068926	243384	28894	253527	37843	3047426
75126	10079	214106	651067	132556	21926	144558	13803	1260616
9135	6531	17274	109693	16184	7078	23324	793	247733
7891	744	44623	89370	17946	3346	21344	11316	44167
18847	2545	57077	249066	57290	5457	55099	700	402447
39253	259	95131	202938	41135	6045	44792	994	566269
29800	32	155298	174083	87817	341	85962	−500	661865
27941	854	84036	193777	42923	1336	41722	34526	597053
35394	1260	131937	215433	72858	8718	77061	3689	418026
21892	301	121073	170969	36868	3941	34981	−380	377237
30302	180	85435	155278	27824	2454	27705	15092	882794

11-10 续表8

单位：万元

指 标	Item	营业外收入 Non-business Income
总计	**Total**	**81915**
#亏损企业	Unprofitable Firm	11432
#国有控股企业	State-holding Enterprise	16852
#轻工业	Light Industry	16044
重工业	Heavy Industry	65870
#大型企业	Large-scale Enterprise	35007
中型企业	Medium-sized Enterprise	23346
小微型企业	Micro Enterprise	23561
按登记注册类型分组	**Grouped by Registration Types**	
内资企业	Domestic Enterprise	57553
国有企业	State-owned Enterprise	2702
集体企业	Collective Enterprise	16
股份合作企业	Joint Equity Cooperative Enterprise	
有限责任公司	Limited Liability Company	16256
股份有限公司	Limited Company	14745
私营企业	Private Company	23831
其他企业	Others	3
港、澳、台商投资企业	HK, Macau or Taiwan Funded Enterprise	8637
合资经营企业(港或澳、台资)	Joint Venture(HK, Macau or Taiwan)	2461
合作经营企业(港或澳、台资)	Cooperative Enterprise(HK, Macau or Taiwan)	
港澳台商独资经营企业	Sole Proprietorship(HK, Macau or Taiwan)	6176
港澳台商投资股份有限公司	Shareholding Limited Company(HK, Macau or Taiwan)	

CONTINUED 8

(Unit: 10,000 Yuan)

补贴收入 Subsidy Income	营业外支出 Non-business Expenditure	利润总额 Total Profit	应交所得税 Income Tax Payable	亏损企业亏损总额 Total Loss of Unprofitable Enterprises	利税总额 Total Profits and Taxes	本年应交增值税 Added Value Tax Payable of the Year	全部从业人员年平均人数(人) The Annual Number of All Employees(person)
26609	**114855**	**4164813**	**814732**	**110834**	**6506339**	**2120133**	**329071**
3271	13011	–110834	760	110834	–97483	9721	16796
5271	40916	304338	89604	68142	408346	90235	20600
1956	13620	596380	125106	2560	891605	266941	36980
24654	101234	3568433	689626	108274	5614734	1853192	292091
15124	68834	1219589	218482	34395	1977272	701526	99708
7061	17644	1461408	302742	51126	2203108	668946	103511
4425	28377	1483815	293509	25313	2325959	749660	125852
15623	64840	2857610	572650	88547	4544601	1529198	237317
	801	–463		463	–256	195	219
	20	2307	380		3089	676	426
		26310	4988		37829	10881	1252
4760	16546	227931	54677	60322	358501	117042	36045
5540	10619	392046	72537	18388	606981	195280	33876
5323	36853	2208927	439881	9373	3537568	1204868	165397
		553	188		890	256	102
1054	6782	486097	87102	13790	739368	231515	38403
255	1532	249618	49691	190	380628	120579	16619
		67	18		178	100	88
800	5250	220825	36300	13600	340938	109313	20946
		15587	1092		17623	1524	750

11-10 续表 9

单位：万元

指 标	Item	营业外收入 Non-business Income
外商投资企业	Foreign Funded Enterprise	15725
中外合资经营企业	Sino-foreign Joint Venture	12355
中外合作经营企业	Sino-foreign Cooperative Enterprise	
外资企业	Foreign-owned Enterprise	3367
外商投资股份有限公司	Foreign Investment Joint Stock Company	4
按经济组织类型分组	**Grouped by Types of Ownership**	
独资企业	Sole Proprietorship	12260
合作、合伙企业	Cooperative and Partnership Enterprises	3
股份有限公司	Joint Stock Company	17121
有限责任公司	Limited Liability Company	52530
按地区分组	**Grouped by Regions**	
市 区	Urban Area	44783
崇川区	Chongchuan	14625
港闸区	Gangzha	16363
开发区	Development Zone	6607
通州区	Tongzhou	7188
海安县	Haian	5029
如东县	Rudong	14851
启东市	Qidong	3777
如皋市	Rugao	4899
海门市	Haimen	8576

CONTINUED 9

(Unit: 10,000 Yuan)

补贴收入 Subsidy Income	营业外支出 Non-business Expenditure	利润总额 Total Profit	应交所得税 Income Tax Payable	亏损企业亏损总额 Total Loss of Unprofitable Enterprises	利税总额 Total Profits and Taxes	本年应交增值税 Added Value Tax Payable of the Year	全部从业人员年平均人数(人) The Annual Number of All Employees(person)
9933	43233	821105	154980	8497	1222370	359420	53351
9749	34034	492148	100841	6619	712238	195913	27587
	241	5608	1604	60	10391	4282	421
184	8954	321714	52313	1818	497144	158439	25118
	4	1636	224		2597	786	225
983	15124	574192	95952	15881	883459	279039	48102
	241	34872	7245	60	52839	16646	2296
5561	13999	541123	99437	18520	854526	286311	43416
20066	85490	3014626	612098	76373	4715515	1538137	235257
18824	61347	1244174	232753	59378	1902609	582507	123700
11636	26541	235925	60398	14801	301266	56203	10976
4149	2741	57789	10280	22646	89752	23984	15882
2143	8164	400890	90536	17523	578291	157994	38349
896	23901	549570	71539	4409	933300	344326	58493
1123	15445	651449	146661	8175	998185	316923	47780
3736	15183	596721	116283	2782	925455	300749	33116
1365	11907	409896	65410	34734	717890	272600	38015
1520	9731	372405	60646	2602	605210	210835	51232
42	1241	890168	192979	3162	1356989	436519	35228

11-11 规模以上工业企业主要效益指标(2014年)

单位:%

指标	Item	企业亏损面 Enterprise Deficit Scale
总 计	**Total**	**6.04**
#亏损企业	Unprofitable Firm	100.00
#国有控股企业	State-holding Enterprise	20.55
#轻工业	Light Industry	5.60
重工业	Heavy Industry	6.45
#大型企业	Large-scale Enterprise	4.55
中型企业	Medium-sized Enterprise	5.63
小微型企业	Micro Enterprise	6.12
按登记注册类型分组	**Grouped by Registration Types**	
内资企业	Domestic Enterprise	5.20
国有企业	Collective Enterprise	40.00
集体企业	State-owned Enterprise	
股份合作企业	Joint Equity Cooperative Enterprise	
联营企业	Joint Venture	
有限责任公司	Limited Liability Company	9.85
股份有限公司	Limited Company	7.69
私营企业	Private Company	4.21
其他企业	Others	
港、澳、台商投资企业	HK, Macau or Taiwan Funded Enterprise	7.54
合资经营企业(港或澳、台资)	Joint Venture(HK, Macau or Taiwan)	7.14
合作经营企业(港或澳、台资)	Cooperative Enterprise(HK, Macau or Taiwan)	
港澳台商独资经营企业	Sole Proprietorship(HK, Macau or Taiwan)	7.97
港澳台商投资股份有限公司	Shareholding Limited Company(HK, Macau or Taiwan)	
其他港澳台商投资企业	Others	

MAJOR PERFORMANCE INDICATORS OF INDUSTRIAL ENTERPRISES ABOVE DESIGNATED SIZE(2014)

(Unit: %)

产值利税率 Ratio of Output to Profit & Tax	销售利税率 Ratio of Sales to Profit & Tax	总资产贡献率 Total Asset-Contribution Ratio	资产负债率 Asset-Liability Ratio	成本费用利润率 Profits to Cost Ratio	产销率 Output to Sales Ratio
11.82	**11.96**	**20.97**	**55.26**	**8.18**	**98.96**
-5.62	-5.88	-0.44	74.62	-6.69	98.40
13.56	13.76	8.67	65.43	10.82	98.90
11.82	11.90	23.22	51.31	8.08	99.39
11.82	12.00	20.09	56.81	8.23	98.76
12.55	12.54	18.26	60.09	8.26	99.18
13.25	13.43	22.85	52.16	9.52	98.72
10.67	10.87	21.78	53.66	7.43	98.97
11.77	11.90	22.80	55.59	8.03	98.98
13.66	14.23	4.01	82.57	7.99	97.25
8.94	9.05	15.06	62.19	6.02	99.64
14.12	14.25	59.12	58.51	10.47	99.73
12.07	12.07	36.96	48.61	7.03	100.00
8.68	8.85	10.45	62.29	6.05	98.69
12.82	12.79	18.31	50.62	8.77	99.33
12.29	12.42	30.31	52.89	8.37	98.99
9.81	9.81	4.17	55.31	4.11	99.93
11.46	11.59	17.13	59.84	7.82	99.44
9.93	10.23	12.81	70.29	6.09	98.98
15.10	15.44	33.91	24.10	9.48	99.09
12.04	12.11	20.59	51.86	8.53	99.26
17.77	16.35	32.27	15.62	14.06	107.18
8.49	8.49	8.90	0.99	8.54	100.00

11-11 续表 1

单位:%

指 标	Item	企业亏损面 Enterprise Deficit Scale
外商投资企业	Foreign Funded Enterprise	9.41
中外合资经营企业	Sino-foreign Joint Venture	7.95
中外合作经营企业	Sino-foreign Cooperative Enterprise	7.69
外资企业	Foreign-owned Enterprise	10.58
外商投资股份有限公司	Foreign Investment Joint Stock Company	14.29
按经济组织类型分组	**Grouped by Types of Ownership**	
独资企业	Sole Proprietorship	8.56
合作、合伙企业	Cooperative and Partnership Enterprises	1.69
股份有限公司	Joint Stock Company	6.85
有限责任公司	Limited Liability Company	5.58
按行业分	**Grouped by Industries**	
农副食品加工业	Agrifood Processing	8.00
食品制造业	Food Production	16.00
酒、饮料和精制茶制造业	Alcohol, Beverage and Refined Tea Production	28.57
烟草制品业	Tobacco Industries	
纺织业	Textile	3.73
纺织服装、服饰业	Textile and Garment, Dress and Personal Adornment	6.25
皮革、毛皮、羽毛及其制品和制鞋业	Leather, Fur, Feather(Fuzz) and Related Products	4.69
木材加工及木、竹、藤、棕、草制品业	Wood Processing and Industries of Wood, Bamboo, Rattan, Palm and Grass Products	
家具制造业	Furniture Manufacturing	16.67
造纸和纸制品业	Paper Making and Industries of Paper Products	8.89
印刷和记录媒介复制业	Printing and Record Medium Reproduction	16.00
文教、工美、体育和娱乐用品制造业	Industries of Culture, Education, Arts, Sports and Recreational Products	3.67

CONTINUED 1

(Unit: %)

产值利税率 Ratio of Output to Profit & Tax	销售利税率 Ratio of Sales to Profit & Tax	总资产贡献率 Total Asset-Contribution Ratio	资产负债率 Asset-Liability Ratio	成本费用利润率 Profits to Cost Ratio	产销率 Output to Sales Ratio
12.19	12.39	18.90	51.56	8.86	98.62
13.34	13.53	18.57	53.44	9.91	98.93
22.24	22.59	19.12	46.34	18.50	98.98
10.64	10.82	19.24	50.57	7.42	98.65
14.91	15.60	19.90	35.72	12.97	91.66
11.23	11.37	19.69	52.25	7.88	98.92
16.33	16.55	21.69	49.19	12.30	99.35
13.83	13.82	19.38	50.43	9.67	99.04
11.65	11.81	21.60	57.08	8.01	98.95
7.82	7.71	22.21	56.06	5.33	100.07
13.86	13.93	26.99	45.44	9.65	99.01
10.36	10.42	12.63	51.91	4.31	98.94
18.67	19.35	17.63	31.90	18.09	96.50
11.01	11.07	23.28	50.67	7.23	99.38
12.41	12.49	22.43	54.68	8.20	99.00
11.38	11.44	31.18	50.26	6.75	99.58
10.50	10.85	17.16	68.77	5.36	95.38
10.07	10.29	11.79	57.78	5.65	98.07
2.70	2.87	2.28	55.30	–0.76	100.74
7.87	8.10	15.48	51.07	4.70	99.61
13.97	14.05	35.44	55.03	10.15	99.70

11-11 续表 2

单位:%

指 标	Item	企业亏损面 Enterprise Deficit Scale
石油加工、炼焦和核燃料加工业	Petroleum Processing, Coking and Nuclear Fuel Processing Industries	44.44
化学原料和化学制品制造业	Production of Chemical Raw Materials and Chemical Products	8.51
医药制造业	Pharmaceutical Industry	9.09
化学纤维制造业	Chemical Fiber Manufacturing	10.00
橡胶和塑料制品业	Industry of Rubber and Plastic Products	6.87
非金属矿物制品业	Industry of Nonmetallic Mineral Products	7.39
黑色金属冶炼和压延加工业	Ferrous Metal Smelting and Pressing	4.71
有色金属冶炼和压延加工业	Non-Ferrous Metal Smelting and Pressing	13.64
金属制品业	Manufacture of Metal Products	5.88
通用设备制造业	Manufacture of General Purpose Machinery	6.40
专用设备制造业	Manufacture of Equipment for Special Purpose	8.53
汽车制造业	Automobile Industry	7.69
铁路、船舶、航空航天和其他运输设备制造业	Manufacture of Railroad, Shipping, Aerospace and Other Transportation Equipments	8.13
电气机械和器材制造业	Manufacture of Electrical Machinery and Equipments	2.53
计算机、通信和其他电子设备制造业	Manufacture of Computer, Communications and Other Electronic Products	2.45
仪器仪表制造业	Instrument Manufacturing	3.17
其他制造业	Others	33.33
废弃资源综合利用业	Comprehensive Utilization of Waste Resources	66.67
金属制品、机械和设备修理业	Metal Product, Machinery and Equipment Repair Industry	14.29
电力、热力生产和供应业	Generation and Supply of Electric Power and Heating Power	
燃气生产和供应业	Generation and Supply of Gas	
水的生产和供应业	Generation and Supply of Water	9.09

CONTINUED 2

(Unit: %)

产值利税率 Ratio of Output to Profit & Tax	销售利税率 Ratio of Sales to Profit & Tax	总资产贡献率 Total Asset-Contribution Ratio	资产负债率 Asset-Liability Ratio	成本费用利润率 Profits to Cost Ratio	产销率 Output to Sales Ratio
2.83	2.90	7.19	61.20	1.80	100.23
9.79	9.98	21.67	54.23	6.86	98.34
12.46	12.63	24.55	40.53	8.37	99.05
18.45	18.73	32.47	40.59	15.74	99.47
10.43	10.78	16.25	47.00	6.65	97.94
11.78	11.99	18.70	58.18	8.09	98.99
8.70	9.03	28.23	56.89	5.79	99.21
9.65	9.81	21.82	61.85	6.85	97.49
12.07	12.31	24.21	50.88	8.65	98.45
11.62	11.76	18.43	55.10	8.04	99.07
10.92	10.95	13.41	67.12	7.29	99.59
10.93	10.98	24.21	49.50	6.11	98.37
8.29	8.46	8.75	75.65	4.83	98.89
14.48	14.54	30.25	46.99	9.94	98.78
10.52	10.76	25.76	47.35	7.31	98.46
13.27	13.37	31.42	42.45	9.38	99.29
7.87	8.63	12.40	65.07	4.52	98.52
12.51	12.52	14.37	49.09	10.05	100.00
3.49	3.55	4.05	73.82	-1.28	99.63
27.49	26.62	13.76	66.64	26.52	99.73
22.32	27.97	9.39	43.96	22.67	99.23
16.94	23.53	3.77	64.92	11.17	99.70

11-12　工业企业现价产值100强(2014年)

TOP 100 INDUSTIAL ENTERPRISES OF OUTPUT VALUE(2014)

序号 No.	企业名称 Names	序号 No.	企业名称 Names
1	中天科技集团有限公司	26	南通富士通微电子股份有限公司
2	嘉吉粮油(南通)有限公司	27	江苏大唐国际吕四港发电有限责任公司
3	申华化学工业有限公司	28	江苏中联科技集团有限公司
4	江苏熔盛重工有限公司	29	三菱丽阳高分子材料(南通)有限公司
5	江苏综艺集团	30	南通中远船务工程有限公司
6	南通明德重工有限公司	31	南通新正大特钢有限公司
7	南通辉煌彩色钢板有限公司	32	罗莱家纺股份有限公司
8	欧贝黎新能源科技股份有限公司	33	三大雅精细化学品(南通)有限公司
9	江苏韩通船舶重工有限公司	34	海门市鑫源新材料有限公司
10	韩华新能源(启东)有限公司	35	江苏海峰电力机械集团股份有限公司
11	南通星辰合成材料有限公司	36	江苏海建股份有限公司
12	南通华东液压铸业有限公司	37	江苏文凤化纤集团有限公司
13	江苏东源电器集团股份有限公司	38	南通回力橡胶有限公司
14	江苏通光光缆有限公司	39	南通晓星变压器有限公司
15	江苏鹏飞集团股份有限公司	40	上海振华重工集团(南通)有限公司
16	招商局重工(江苏)有限公司	41	江苏恒科新材料有限公司
17	江苏通能信息有限公司	42	鑫缘茧丝绸集团股份有限公司
18	南通醋酸纤维有限公司	43	台橡宇部(南通)化学工业有限公司
19	南通中远川崎船舶工程有限公司	44	南通天泽化工有限公司
20	江苏英田集团	45	南通中集罐式储运设备制造有限公司
21	江苏联发纺织股份有限公司	46	江苏中联风能机械有限公司
22	南通江海电容器股份有限公司	47	江苏南通发电有限公司
23	创斯达科技集团(中国)有限责任公司	48	江苏天成科技集团有限公司
24	江苏甬金金属科技有限公司	49	中远船务(启东)海洋工程有限公司
25	南通振华重型装备制造有限公司	50	南通东泰新能源设备有限公司

11-12 续表
CONTINUED

序号 No.	企业名称 Names of the Enterprises	序号 No.	企业名称 Names of the Enterprises
51	富加宜电子(南通)有限公司	76	江苏海迅实业集团股份有限公司
52	江苏雄风科技有限公司	77	江苏黄海汽配股份有限公司
53	南通江山农药化工股份有限公司	78	南通市康桥油脂有限公司
54	南通振康焊接机电有限公司	79	江苏恒康家居科技有限公司
55	中天科技光纤有限公司	80	南通来宝谷物蛋白有限公司
56	江苏黑鹰化学工业有限公司	81	上海振华重工集团(南通)传动机械有限公司
57	海门市森达装饰材料有限公司	82	中天科技海缆有限公司
58	江苏万力机械股份有限公司	83	江苏双林海洋生物药业有限公司
59	海安县申菱电器制造有限公司	84	江苏三通科技有限公司
60	凡特鲁斯特种化学品(南通)有限公司	85	江苏哥尔德贵金属有限公司
61	东丽酒伊织染(南通)有限公司	86	如皋市双马化工有限公司
62	江苏大岛机械集团有限公司	87	江苏林洋电子股份有限公司
63	南通双弘纺织有限公司	88	南通天和树脂有限公司
64	华能国际电力股份有限公司南通电厂	89	东丽合成纤维(南通)有限公司
65	东丽高新聚化(南通)有限公司	90	南通东日钢铁有限公司
66	江苏宏强船舶重工有限公司	91	旭有机材树脂(南通)有限公司
67	江苏飞亚化学工业有限责任公司	92	南通迪皮茜电子有限公司
68	江苏通达动力科技股份有限公司	93	南通利比特电子电器有限公司
69	江苏福克斯新能源科技有限公司	94	南通蛟龙重工发展有限公司
70	江苏九鼎集团有限公司	95	江苏铁锚玻璃股份有限公司
71	惠生(南通)重工有限公司	96	南通家惠油脂发展有限公司
72	南通海迪化工有限公司	97	一亿贵金属如皋有限公司
73	江苏如皋钢铁有限公司	98	雄邦压铸(南通)有限公司
74	江苏东成机电工具有限公司	99	卡姆丹克太阳能(江苏)有限公司
75	南亚塑胶工业(南通)有限公司	100	陶氏益农农业科技(中国)有限公司

11-13 工业企业主营业务收入100强(2014年)
TOP 100 INDUSTRIAL ENTERPRISES OF SALES INCOME(2014)

序号 No.	企业名称 Names	序号 No.	企业名称 Names
1	中天科技集团有限公司	26	江苏大唐国际吕四港发电有限责任公司
2	嘉吉粮油(南通)有限公司	27	江苏中联科技集团有限公司
3	中华化学工业有限公司	28	南通中远船务工程有限公司
4	江苏综艺集团	29	三菱丽阳高分子材料(南通)有限公司
5	南通辉煌彩色钢板有限公司	30	南通新正大特钢有限公司
6	南通明德重工有限公司	31	南通富士通微电子股份有限公司
7	江苏熔盛重工有限公司	32	海门市鑫源新材料有限公司
8	欧贝黎新能源科技股份有限公司	33	江苏甬金金属科技有限公司
9	江苏韩通船舶重工有限公司	34	江苏海峰电力机械集团股份有限公司
10	南通星辰合成材料有限公司	35	南通晓星变压器有限公司
11	韩华新能源(启东)有限公司	36	南通回力橡胶有限公司
12	江苏鹏飞集团股份有限公司	37	三大雅精细化学品(南通)有限公司
13	南通华东液压铸业有限公司	38	江苏海建股份有限公司
14	江苏通光光缆有限公司	39	江苏文凤化纤集团有限公司
15	江苏东源电器集团股份有限公司	40	鑫缘茧丝绸集团股份有限公司
16	招商局重工(江苏)有限公司	41	上海振华重工集团(南通)有限公司
17	江苏通能信息有限公司	42	江苏中联风能机械有限公司
18	南通醋酸纤维有限公司	43	南通天泽化工有限公司
19	南通中远川崎船舶工程有限公司	44	江苏南通发电有限公司
20	江苏英田集团	45	南通中集罐式储运设备制造有限公司
21	江苏联发纺织股份有限公司	46	江苏恒科新材料有限公司
22	南通江海电容器股份有限公司	47	江苏天成科技集团有限公司
23	南通振华重型装备制造有限公司	48	中远船务(启东)海洋工程有限公司
24	罗莱家纺股份有限公司	49	台橡宇部(南通)化学工业有限公司
25	创斯达科技集团(中国)有限责任公司	50	南通东泰新能源设备有限公司

11-13 续表
CONTINUED

序号 No.	企业名称 Names	序号 No.	企业名称 Names
51	江苏雄风科技有限公司	76	江苏恒康家居科技有限公司
52	富加宜电子(南通)有限公司	77	江苏九鼎集团有限公司
53	江苏黑鹰化学工业有限公司	78	江苏海迅实业集团股份有限公司
54	南通振康焊接机电有限公司	79	南亚塑胶工业(南通)有限公司
55	中天科技光纤有限公司	80	江苏林洋电子股份有限公司
56	南通江山农药化工股份有限公司	81	南通市康桥油脂有限公司
57	海门市森达装饰材料有限公司	82	江苏三通科技有限公司
58	江苏万力机械股份有限公司	83	江苏双林海洋生物药业有限公司
59	海安县申菱电器制造有限公司	84	江苏哥尔德贵金属有限公司
60	东丽酒伊织染(南通)有限公司	85	东丽合成纤维(南通)有限公司
61	江苏大岛机械集团有限公司	86	南通东日钢铁有限公司
62	凡特鲁斯特种化学品(南通)有限公司	87	中天科技海缆有限公司
63	东丽高新聚化(南通)有限公司	88	旭有机材树脂(南通)有限公司
64	江苏飞亚化学工业有限责任公司	89	上海振华重工集团(南通)传动机械有限公司
65	华能国际电力股份有限公司南通电厂	90	南通天和树脂有限公司
66	南通双弘纺织有限公司	91	南通利比特电子电器有限公司
67	江苏宏强船舶重工有限公司	92	江苏铁锚玻璃股份有限公司
68	江苏通达动力科技股份有限公司	93	南通家惠油脂发展有限公司
69	江苏如皋钢铁有限公司	94	南通蛟龙重工发展有限公司
70	惠生(南通)重工有限公司	95	南通迪皮茜电子有限公司
71	江苏福克斯新能源科技有限公司	96	江苏华灿电讯股份有限公司
72	南通海迪化工有限公司	97	上海制皂集团(如皋)有限公司
73	江苏东成机电工具有限公司	98	卡姆丹克太阳能(江苏)有限公司
74	南通来宝谷物蛋白有限公司	99	南通永安纺织有限公司
75	江苏黄海汽配股份有限公司	100	南通天生港发电有限公司

11-14　工业企业利税100强(2014年)

TOP 100 INDUSTRIAL ENTERPRISES OF PRE-TAX PROFITS(2014)

序号 No.	企业名称 Names	序号 No.	企业名称 Names
1	中天科技集团有限公司	26	江苏中联科技集团有限公司
2	南通醋酸纤维有限公司	27	江苏林洋电子股份有限公司
3	江苏通能信息有限公司	28	南通中远川崎船舶工程有限公司
4	江苏通光光缆有限公司	29	嘉吉粮油(南通)有限公司
5	江苏综艺集团	30	江苏雄风科技有限公司
6	江苏韩通船舶重工有限公司	31	南通振康焊接机电有限公司
7	江苏南通发电有限公司	32	江苏黑鹰化学工业有限公司
8	南通辉煌彩色钢板有限公司	33	江苏大岛机械集团有限公司
9	江苏大唐国际吕四港发电有限责任公司	34	江苏英田集团
10	南通回力橡胶有限公司	35	南通天生港发电有限公司
11	申华化学工业有限公司	36	南通天泽化工有限公司
12	招商局重工(江苏)有限公司	37	江苏海建股份有限公司
13	韩华新能源(启东)有限公司	38	海门市鑫源新材料有限公司
14	南通明德重工有限公司	39	南通星辰合成材料有限公司
15	江苏东源电器集团股份有限公司	40	江苏飞亚化学工业有限责任公司
16	罗莱家纺股份有限公司	41	南通中集罐式储运设备制造有限公司
17	欧贝黎新能源科技股份有限公司	42	江苏万力机械股份有限公司
18	海门市森达装饰材料有限公司	43	江苏文凤化纤集团有限公司
19	华能国际电力股份有限公司南通电厂	44	南通新正大特钢有限公司
20	南通江海电容器股份有限公司	45	中石油江苏液化天然气有限公司
21	江苏海峰电力机械集团股份有限公司	46	海安县申菱电器制造有限公司
22	江苏联发纺织股份有限公司	47	江苏天成科技集团有限公司
23	江苏鹏飞集团股份有限公司	48	南通晓星变压器有限公司
24	创斯达科技集团(中国)有限责任公司	49	江苏铁锚玻璃股份有限公司
25	江苏中联风能机械有限公司	50	富加宜电子(南通)有限公司

11-14 续表

CONTINUED

序号 No.	企业名称 Names	序号 No.	企业名称 Names
51	江苏宏强船舶重工有限公司	76	江苏福克斯新能源科技有限公司
52	江苏双林海洋生物药业有限公司	77	德尔福连接器系统(南通)有限公司
53	江苏恒康家居科技有限公司	78	南通华东液压铸业有限公司
54	江苏黄海汽配股份有限公司	79	中兴能源装备有限公司
55	三大雅精细化学品(南通)有限公司	80	上海振华重工集团(南通)传动机械有限公司
56	鑫缘茧丝绸集团股份有限公司	81	江苏三通科技有限公司
57	江苏海迅实业集团股份有限公司	82	南通大东有限公司
58	南通海迪化工有限公司	83	燕达(海门)重型装备制造有限公司
59	上海振华重工集团(南通)有限公司	84	南通蛟龙重工发展有限公司
60	南通汤始建华管桩有限公司	85	江苏省华强纺织有限公司
61	中天科技光纤有限公司	86	南通奥贝尔工程技术有限公司
62	南通利比特电子电器有限公司	87	海安县鹰球粉末冶金有限公司
63	南通江山农药化工股份有限公司	88	南通东日钢铁有限公司
64	江苏东成机电工具有限公司	89	南通迪皮茜电子有限公司
65	南通亿能彩钢板有限公司	90	台橡宇部(南通)化学工业有限公司
66	南亚塑胶工业(南通)有限公司	91	绿洲生物技术(南通)有限公司
67	三菱丽阳高分子材料(南通)有限公司	92	南通延锋江森座椅面套有限公司
68	迈图高新材料(南通)有限公司	93	江苏世纪燎原针织有限公司
69	先正达南通作物保护有限公司	94	南通昌邦手套有限公司
70	南通双弘纺织有限公司	95	南通宝石服装有限公司
71	南通市康桥油脂有限公司	96	台橡(南通)实业有限公司
72	江苏通达动力科技股份有限公司	97	江苏西欧电子有限公司
73	南通恒秀铝热传输材料有限公司	98	江苏戴园建材集团有限公司
74	江苏省如高高压电器有限公司	99	江苏远威重工有限公司
75	南通太平洋海洋工程有限公司	100	海门市液压件厂有限责任公司

11-15 民营工业企业主营业务收入100强(2014年)

TOP 100 PRIVATE INDUSTRIAL ENTERPRISES OF SALES REVENUE(2014)

序号 No.	企业名称 Names	序号 No.	企业名称 Names
1	中天科技集团有限公司	26	江苏雄风科技有限公司
2	江苏综艺集团	27	中天科技光纤有限公司
3	欧贝黎新能源科技股份有限公司	28	海门市森达装饰材料有限公司
4	江苏鹏飞集团股份有限公司	29	江苏万力机械股份有限公司
5	南通华东液压铸业有限公司	30	海安县申菱电器制造有限公司
6	江苏通光光缆有限公司	31	江苏大岛机械集团有限公司
7	江苏东源电器集团股份有限公司	32	南通双弘纺织有限公司
8	江苏通能信息有限公司	33	江苏宏强船舶重工有限公司
9	江苏英田集团	34	江苏通达动力科技股份有限公司
10	江苏联发纺织股份有限公司	35	江苏如皋钢铁有限公司
11	南通江海电容器股份有限公司	36	江苏福克斯新能源科技有限公司
12	江苏中联科技集团有限公司	37	南通海迪化工有限公司
13	南通新正大特钢有限公司	38	江苏东成机电工具有限公司
14	海门市鑫源新材料有限公司	39	江苏黄海汽配股份有限公司
15	江苏甬金金属科技有限公司	40	江苏恒康家居科技有限公司
16	江苏海峰电力机械集团股份有限公司	41	江苏九鼎集团有限公司
17	南通回力橡胶有限公司	42	江苏海迅实业集团股份有限公司
18	江苏海建股份有限公司	43	江苏林洋电子股份有限公司
19	江苏文凤化纤集团有限公司	44	江苏三通科技有限公司
20	鑫缘茧丝绸集团股份有限公司	45	江苏双林海洋生物药业有限公司
21	江苏中联风能机械有限公司	46	江苏哥尔德贵金属有限公司
22	南通天泽化工有限公司	47	中天科技海缆有限公司
23	江苏恒科新材料有限公司	48	南通天和树脂有限公司
24	江苏天成科技集团有限公司	49	南通利比特电子电器有限公司
25	南通东泰新能源设备有限公司	50	江苏铁锚玻璃股份有限公司

11-15 续表
CONTINUED

序号 No.	企业名称 Names	序号 No.	企业名称 Names
51	南通家惠油脂发展有限公司	76	江苏苏中电池科技发展有限公司
52	南通蛟龙重工发展有限公司	77	江苏恒源丝绸集团有限公司
53	江苏华灿电讯股份有限公司	78	江苏天成生化制品有限公司
54	上海制皂集团(如皋)有限公司	79	江苏隆昌化工有限公司
55	南通永安纺织有限公司	80	江苏巨力钢绳有限公司
56	江苏通海染整有限公司	81	江苏长寿集团股份有限公司
57	中平神马江苏新材料科技有限公司	82	南通巴大饲料有限公司
58	江苏省银河面粉有限公司	83	江苏东泰薄板科技有限公司
59	江苏省如高高压电器有限公司	84	中天合金技术有限公司
60	如皋市双马化工有限公司	85	江苏亚伦集团股份有限公司
61	一亿贵金属如皋有限公司	86	南通华纶化纤有限公司
62	江苏江海机床集团有限公司	87	江苏涤诺日化集团有限公司
63	江苏金洲粮油食品有限公司	88	江苏金呢工程织物股份有限公司
64	海安县鹰球粉末冶金有限公司	89	江苏省海安石油化工厂
65	江苏省华强纺织有限公司	90	南通英菲新能源有限公司
66	南通亚华船舶制造集团有限公司	91	南通利华农化有限公司
67	海门市化工原料厂有限公司	92	南通永大管业股份有限公司
68	江苏戴园建材集团有限公司	93	海门市油威力液压工业有限责任公司
69	南通奥贝尔工程技术有限公司	94	江苏金太阳油脂有限责任公司
70	百川化工(如皋)有限公司	95	江苏中新资源集团有限公司
71	江苏远威重工有限公司	96	南通醋酸化工股份有限公司
72	江苏西欧电子有限公司	97	江苏力星通用钢球股份有限公司
73	江苏铭安电气有限公司	98	南通鸿瑞金业有限公司
74	海安县中山合成纤维有限公司	99	江苏九九久科技股份有限公司
75	江苏瑞安特机械集团有限公司	100	江苏世泰实验器材有限公司

11-16　民营工业企业利税100强(2014年)

TOP 100 PRIVATE INDUSTRIAL ENTERPRISES OF PRE-TAX PROFITS(2014)

序号 No.	企业名称 Names	序号 No.	企业名称 Names
1	中天科技集团有限公司	26	江苏天成科技集团有限公司
2	江苏通能信息有限公司	27	江苏铁锚玻璃股份有限公司
3	江苏通光光缆有限公司	28	江苏宏强船舶重工有限公司
4	江苏综艺集团	29	江苏双林海洋生物药业有限公司
5	南通回力橡胶有限公司	30	江苏恒康家居科技有限公司
6	江苏东源电器集团股份有限公司	31	江苏黄海汽配股份有限公司
7	欧贝黎新能源科技股份有限公司	32	鑫缘茧丝绸集团股份有限公司
8	海门市森达装饰材料有限公司	33	江苏海迅实业集团股份有限公司
9	南通江海电容器股份有限公司	34	南通海迪化工有限公司
10	江苏海峰电力机械集团股份有限公司	35	中天科技光纤有限公司
11	江苏联发纺织股份有限公司	36	南通利比特电子电器有限公司
12	江苏鹏飞集团股份有限公司	37	江苏东成机电工具有限公司
13	江苏中联风能机械有限公司	38	南通双弘纺织有限公司
14	江苏中联科技集团有限公司	39	江苏通达动力科技股份有限公司
15	江苏林洋电子股份有限公司	40	江苏省如高高压电器有限公司
16	江苏雄风科技有限公司	41	江苏福克斯新能源科技有限公司
17	江苏大岛机械集团有限公司	42	南通华东液压铸业有限公司
18	江苏英田集团	43	中兴能源装备有限公司
19	南通天泽化工有限公司	44	江苏三通科技有限公司
20	江苏海建股份有限公司	45	南通蛟龙重工发展有限公司
21	海门市鑫源新材料有限公司	46	江苏省华强纺织有限公司
22	江苏万力机械股份有限公司	47	南通奥贝尔工程技术有限公司
23	江苏文凤化纤集团有限公司	48	海安县鹰球粉末冶金有限公司
24	南通新正大特钢有限公司	49	江苏西欧电子有限公司
25	海安县申菱电器制造有限公司	50	江苏戴园建材集团有限公司

11-16 续表
CONTINUED

序号 No.	企业名称 Names	序号 No.	企业名称 Names
51	江苏远威重工有限公司	76	南通天和树脂有限公司
52	海门市化工原料厂有限公司	77	江苏威尔曼科技股份有限公司
53	江苏金呢工程织物股份有限公司	78	南通德玛瑞机械制造有限公司
54	中平神马江苏新材料科技有限公司	79	江苏江海机床集团有限公司
55	江苏铭安电气有限公司	80	南通祥峰电子有限公司
56	江苏省海安石油化工厂	81	南通天蓝环保能源成套设备有限公司
57	上海制皂集团(如皋)有限公司	82	人民电器集团江苏斯诺成套设备工程有限公司
58	海门市石油机械厂有限公司	83	金轮科创股份有限公司
59	江苏晨牌药业集团股份有限公司	84	海门市常乐粉末冶金厂
60	南通华纶化纤有限公司	85	江苏海四达集团有限公司
61	江苏瑞安特机械集团有限公司	86	江苏世泰实验器材有限公司
62	江苏哥尔德贵金属有限公司	87	南通市恒荣机泵厂有限公司
63	江苏省银河面粉有限公司	88	南通东泰新能源设备有限公司
64	南通英菲新能源有限公司	89	江苏华灿电讯股份有限公司
65	海安县中山合成纤维有限公司	90	江苏亚伦集团股份有限公司
66	南通亚华船舶制造集团有限公司	91	江苏九鼎集团有限公司
67	南通永大管业股份有限公司	92	南通市帅龙钢绳有限公司
68	江苏恒源丝绸集团有限公司	93	南通市德心食品有限公司
69	海门市海四达电子有限公司	94	中天科技装备电缆有限公司
70	一亿贵金属如皋有限公司	95	海门市油威力液压工业有限责任公司
71	南通家惠油脂发展有限公司	96	海门市荣鑫铜业有限公司
72	南通永安纺织有限公司	97	江苏中新资源集团有限公司
73	江苏天成生化制品有限公司	98	南通米兰特电气有限公司
74	南通巴大饲料有限公司	99	江苏万鹏机电有限公司
75	江苏巨力钢绳有限公司	100	中天科技海缆有限公司

11-17 大中型工业企业名录(2014 年末)

LIST OF LARGE AND MEDIUM SIZED INDUSTRIAL ENTERPRISE(END OF 2014)

企业名称 Names	企业规模 Scale	法人代表 Legal representatives	企 业 地 址 Addresses
南通中远船务工程有限公司	大型	梁岩峰	崇川区中远路 1 号
南通中远川崎船舶工程有限公司	大型	神林伸光	崇川区临江路 117 号
南亚塑胶工业(南通)有限公司	大型	吴嘉昭	崇川区通京大道 101 号
南通富士通微电子股份有限公司	大型	石明达	崇川区崇川路 288 号
江苏大生集团有限公司	大型	沈健宏	港闸区唐闸南市街 14 号
南通天生港发电有限公司	大型	孙宏宁	港闸区天生港镇大达街 87 号
南通中集顺达集装箱有限公司	大型	张宝清	港闸区城港路 159 号
南通中集特种运输设备制造有限公司	大型	张宝清	港闸区港闸经济开发区芦径港村一组
南通中集罐式储运设备制造有限公司	大型	高翔	港闸区城港路 155 号
南通亚华船舶制造集团有限公司	大型	赵建飞	港闸区九圩港虹闸路 1 号
南通润邦重机有限公司	大型	吴建	港闸区船舶配套工业集中区沿港路 88 号
南通江山农药化工股份有限公司	大型	李大军	开发区江山路 998 号
南通同方半导体有限公司	大型	陆致成	开发区东方大道 999 号
东丽酒伊织染(南通)有限公司	大型	丁野良助	开发区瑞兴路 301 号
南通帝人有限公司	大型	唐泽佳长	开发区中央路 19 号
罗莱家纺股份有限公司	大型	薛伟成	开发区星湖大道 1699 号
江苏润邦重工股份有限公司	大型	吴建	开发区振兴路 9 号
嘉吉粮油(南通)有限公司	大型	陈立新	开发区同兴路 1 号
南通振华重型装备制造有限公司	大型	曹伟忠	开发区江海路 169 号
江苏东源电器集团股份有限公司	大型	孙益源	通州区十总镇振兴北路
江苏帝奥服装集团股份有限公司	大型	王进飞	通州区金沙镇新金西路 66 号
江苏综艺集团	大型	昝瑞林	通州区兴东镇孙李桥村
江苏亚伦集团股份有限公司	大型	刘伯香	通州区川姜镇斜桥村
江苏省银河面粉有限公司	大型	蔡飞	通州区余北居通吕公路 1888 号
江苏大富豪酿酒科技发展有限公司	大型	易昕	通州区朝霞路 666 号
南通江海电容器股份有限公司	大型	陈卫东	通州区通扬南路 79 号
江苏通达动力科技股份有限公司	大型	姜煜峰	通州区四安镇庵东村
江苏南明集团有限公司	大型	钱志林	通州区平潮镇三官殿村
江苏恒科新材料有限公司	大型	陈建华	通州区五接镇恒力纺织新材料产业园
富加宜电子(南通)有限公司	大型	罗汉	通州区经济开发区青岛路 990 号
南通华盛新材料股份有限公司	大型	张春华	通州区杏园路 289 号
江苏中联科技集团有限公司	大型	严季新	通州区通扬南路 519 号

11-17 续表 1

CONTINUED 1

企业名称 Names of the Enterprises	企业规模 Scale	法人代表 Legal representatives	企业地址 Addresses
南通明德重工有限公司	大型	季风华	通州区五接镇天后宫村
江苏韩通船舶重工有限公司	大型	孟成君	通州区五接镇天后宫村
南通蛟龙重工发展有限公司	大型	徐建	通州区平潮镇云台山村
创斯达科技集团(中国)有限责任公司	大型	刘佳炎	通州区经济开发区金通大道 1888 号
雄邦压铸(南通)有限公司	大型	唐亚雄	通州区朝霞西路北
鑫缘茧丝绸集团股份有限公司	大型	储呈平	海安县海安镇曙光西路 20 号
江苏万力机械股份有限公司	大型	徐希才	海安县海安镇江海西路 168 号
南通双弘纺织有限公司	大型	杨广泽	海安县曲塘镇双楼路 191 号
海安县申菱电器制造有限公司	大型	李春涛	海安县海安镇海南路 88 号
南通联荣集团有限公司	大型	于永进	海安县曲塘镇双工路 1 号
江苏恒源丝绸集团有限公司	大型	毛兆清	海安县黄海大道(西)198 号
海安县鹰球粉末冶金有限公司	大型	申承秀	海安县工业园区海南路 8 号
江苏省华强纺织有限公司	大型	卞童	海安县开发区鑫来路 79 号
江苏鹏飞集团股份有限公司	大型	王家安	海安县北郊贲家集
江苏联发纺织股份有限公司	大型	薛庆龙	海安县城东镇恒联路 88 号
西蒙电气(中国)有限公司	大型	朱建国	海安县海安开发区西蒙路 1 号
南通新正大特钢有限公司	大型	陈玉霖	海安县海安工业园区 88 号
欧贝黎新能源科技股份有限公司	大型	费建明	海安县海安镇黄海西路 188 号
江苏海建股份有限公司	大型	顾正义	海安县曲塘镇双楼路 198 号
南通晓星变压器有限公司	大型	赵显文	海安县开发区晓星大道 88 号
江苏双双布业有限公司	大型	王勇	海安县海安镇江海西路 188 号
江苏文凤化纤集团有限公司	大型	陈文凤	海安县海安镇长江西路 105 号
南通市苏中纺织有限公司	大型	黄立勇	海安县墩头镇墩西村 6 组
江苏海迅实业集团股份有限公司	大型	仲跻和	海安县城东镇东海大道(东)18 号
江苏铁锚玻璃股份有限公司	大型	吴贲华	海安县海安镇长江西路 128 号
江苏黄海汽配股份有限公司	大型	刘振声	如东县人民南路 203 号
南通市燎原针织有限公司	大型	黄继石	如东县兵房镇健康路 88 号
南通强生轻工集团有限公司	大型	沙晓林	如东县经济开发区嘉陵江路
江苏九九久科技股份有限公司	大型	周新基	如东县马塘镇建设路
爱德士鞋业江苏有限公司	大型	朱建琪	如东县掘港镇掘西村
中天科技集团有限公司	大型	薛济萍	如东县河口镇中天工业园区
南通大东有限公司	大型	吴兆显	如东县富春江西路 168 号

11-17 续表 2

CONTINUED 2

企业名称 Names	企业规模 Scale	法人代表 Legal representatives	企业地址 Addresses
江苏世纪燎原针织有限公司	大型	黄麓瑜	如东县掘港镇芳泉路
江苏苏中电池科技发展有限公司	大型	沈维新	如东县经济开发区鸭绿江路 1 号
南通辉煌彩色钢板有限公司	大型	刘允华	如东县经济开发区通达路
江苏林洋电子股份有限公司	大型	陆永华	启东市经济开发区林洋路 666 号
上海振华重工启东海洋工程股份有限公司	大型	李爱东	启东市海工船舶工业园
中远船务(启东)海洋工程有限公司	大型	梁岩峰	启东市寅阳镇中远路 1 号
南通永安纺织有限公司	大型	陈旭东	启东市经济开发区南苑西路 899 号
江苏海四达集团有限公司	大型	沈涛	启东市经济开发区南苑西路 899 号
韩华新能源(启东)有限公司	大型	KI JOON HONG	启东市开发区林洋路 888 号
启东乾朔电子有限公司	大型	王涧鸣	启东市华石南路 688 号
江苏宏强船舶重工有限公司	大型	左志健	启东市惠萍镇宏强大道 1 号
启东胜狮能源装备有限公司	大型	赵春崦	启东市海工船舶工业园
江苏东成机电工具有限公司	大型	施新平	启东市天汾电动工具产业园
江苏九鼎集团有限公司	大型	顾清波	如皋市如城镇中山路 5 号
江苏省如高高压电器有限公司	大型	董增平	如皋市经济开发区惠民西路
南通汤始建华管桩有限公司	大型	郑赛荣	如皋市郭园镇车马湖社区
南通泰慕士服装有限公司	大型	吴兆显	如皋市开发区益寿路 666 号
江苏瑞晨化学有限公司	大型	张勇	如皋市长江镇头案居
南通华东液压铸业有限公司	大型	丁先华	如皋市白蒲镇蒲西村
江苏英田集团	大型	张英田	如皋市如城镇陆桥村 22 组
江苏恒康家居科技有限公司	大型	倪张根	如皋市丁堰镇鞠庄社区 31 组
双钱集团(江苏)轮胎有限公司	大型	王文浩	如皋市益寿北路 888 号
江苏熔盛重工有限公司	大型	陈强	如皋市长江镇船舶园区
华泰重工(南通)有限公司	大型	朱红兵	如皋市长江镇钢贸园区
南通荣威娱乐用品有限公司	大型	王海青	如皋市经济开发区鹿门居委会
一亿贵金属如皋有限公司	大型	陆曾荣	如皋市高新技术产业开发区
江苏天海服饰有限公司	大型	徐卫民	如皋市长江镇郭园工业园区
南通长江镍矿精选有限公司	大型	姜笃簱	如皋市长江镇长青居委会
南通玉兔集团有限公司	大型	黄奎生	如皋市江安镇玉兔路
江苏长寿集团股份有限公司	大型	魏祝明	如皋市仁寿路 216 号
南通爱康金属科技有限公司	大型	邹承慧	如皋市经济开发区鹿门居委会
上海制皂集团(如皋)有限公司	大型	张亚明	如皋市丁堰镇丁新东路 1 号

11-17 续表 3

CONTINUED 3

企业名称 Names of the Enterprises	企业规模 Scale	法人代表 Legal representatives	企业地址 Addresses
江苏海通海洋工程装备有限公司	大型	金淑英	如皋市长江镇长青居委会
江苏华灿电讯股份有限公司	大型	吴灿华	如皋市长江镇三洞口社区
江苏哥尔德贵金属有限公司	大型	周小银	如皋市柴湾镇街道邓园社区 15 组
南通天泽化工有限公司	大型	谭建平	如皋市石庄镇永兴居委会
南通回力橡胶有限公司	大型	倪雪文	海门市包场镇通光大街 8 号
南通健林鞋业有限公司	大型	季建忠	海门市六匡镇三条桥
江苏泰森食品有限公司	大型	李益铭	海门市东灶港镇港西大道 999 号
江苏黑鹰化学工业有限公司	大型	郭建华	海门市常乐镇工业园区
江苏通能信息有限公司	大型	陆兵	海门市包场镇海门港新区
南通市冠东模塑科技有限公司	大型	郑新平	海门市海门港福州路 388 号
江苏通光光缆有限公司	大型	张忠	海门市大生路 3966 号中 2 号
海门市鑫源新材料有限公司	大型	陆兵	海门市包场镇通光大街 88 号
金轮科创股份有限公司	大型	陆挺	海门市四甲镇富强路 86 号
招商局重工(江苏)有限公司	大型	周志禹	海门市滨江街道新安江路 1 号
江苏新生服饰有限公司	中型	戴国牛	崇川区濠东路 258 号
南通市自来水公司	中型	顾宇人	崇川区工农路 221 号
南通华达微电子集团有限公司	中型	石明达	崇川区紫琅路 99 号
南通烟滤嘴有限责任公司	中型	黄彪	崇川区孩儿巷北路 73 号
南通柴油机股份有限公司	中型	胡曰明	崇川区任港路 46 号
江苏金通灵流体机械科技股份有限公司	中型	季伟	崇川区钟秀东路 666 号
江苏三友集团股份有限公司	中型	陆尔穗	崇川区人民东路 218 号
南通醋酸纤维有限公司	中型	孙桂泉	崇川区钟秀东路 27 号
南通同洲电子有限责任公司	中型	袁明	崇川区观音山街道新胜路 188 号
南通通能精机热加工有限责任公司	中型	武立新	崇川区观音山街道钟秀东路 333 号
南通万达锅炉股份有限公司	中型	张奇	崇川区外环西路 151 号
南通铁人运动用品有限公司	中型	黄承斌	崇川区崇川路 21 号
南通纺织控股集团纺织染有限公司	中型	陈忠	崇川区五一路 99 号
南通大众燃气有限公司	中型	柯品剑	崇川区百花路 11 号
江苏狼山钢绳股份有限公司	中型	顾其林	港闸区天生港镇街道福利村
精华制药集团股份有限公司	中型	朱春林	港闸区兴泰路 9 号
江苏南通二棉有限公司	中型	沈健宏	港闸区港闸经济开发区大生路 1 号
南通科技投资集团股份有限公司	中型	王建华	港闸区永和路 1 号

11-17 续表 4

CONTINUED 4

企业名称 Names	企业规模 Scale	法人代表 Legal representatives	企业地址 Addresses
江苏赛奥生化有限公司	中型	陈剑慧	港闸区越江路 98 号
江苏政田重工股份有限公司	中型	单幼华	港闸区黄海路 118 号
南通扬子碳素股份有限公司	中型	刘明	港闸区唐闸西市街 208 号
南通光明服装有限公司	中型	孙倩	港闸区国强路 298 号
南通大生西尔克纺织有限公司	中型	马晓辉	港闸区唐闸镇南市街 14 号
华能国际电力股份有限公司南通电厂	中型	曹学高	港闸区天生港镇街道爱国村
吉宝(南通)重工有限公司	中型	陆惠聪	港闸区沿江路 9 号
江苏永兴多媒体有限公司	中型	萧英怡	港闸区城港路 136 号
南通富士美帽业有限公司	中型	孙建华	港闸区富美路 11 号
南通大地电气有限公司	中型	蒋明泉	港闸区外环北路 188 号
南通机床有限责任公司	中型	沈春华	港闸区天生港镇街道龙潭村
南通顺友船舶工程有限公司	中型	时守丰	港闸区天生路 1118 号
江苏现代电力科技股份有限公司	中型	施博一	港闸区现代电力路 1 号
南通万德科技有限公司科	中型	顾成华	港闸区永兴街道通港路北侧
中润(南通)家用纺织品有限公司	中型	吴志均	港闸区唐闸镇街道都市产业园区 1 号路
丝路咖精机(南通)有限公司	中型	冈本道明	开发区通达路 100 号
南通醋酸化工股份有限公司	中型	顾清泉	开发区江山路 968 号
南通市帅龙钢绳有限公司	中型	杨伟	开发区小海街道朝阳港村
南通长江电器实业有限公司	中型	张耀东	开发区民兴路 2 号
南通远洋船舶配套有限公司	中型	张明华	开发区狼山军用码头东首
南通力峰钢绳有限公司	中型	吴金池	开发区小海街道庙桥村
江苏弘扬钢丝制品有限公司	中型	杨兵	开发区小海街道庙桥村
江苏尚约服装有限公司	中型	景爱梅	开发区清风创业园
广岛铝工业(南通)有限公司	中型	冈茂宪三	开发区苏通科技产业园海伦路 108 号
上海振华重工集团(南通)有限公司	中型	曹伟忠	开发区振华路 1 号
上海振华重工集团(南通)传动机械有限公司	中型	张建勇	开发区团结东路 1 号
美利达自行车(江苏)有限公司	中型	曾崧柱	开发区新兴东路 11 号
江苏宝灵化工股份有限公司	中型	朱文新	开发区红星社区居委会六组
南通东星皮革有限公司	中型	朴春绪	开发区振兴路 36 号
东丽合成纤维(南通)有限公司	中型	福田康男	开发区新开南路 58 号
申华化学工业有限公司	中型	涂伟华	开发区申华路 1 号
南通爱慕希机械有限公司	中型	汪昕	开发区星湖大道 1692 号

11-17 续表 5

CONTINUED 5

企业名称 Names of the Enterprises	企业规模 Scale	法人代表 Legal representatives	企业地址 Addresses
先正达南通作物保护有限公司	中型	贝士祺	开发区中央路 1 号
南通中集大型储罐有限公司	中型	赵庆生	开发区国营南通农场
南通凯瑞德机械有限公司	中型	小克劳斯	开发区国营南通农场
南通月星家具制造有限公司	中型	丁佐龙	开发区通州路 18 号
台因光电科技(南通)有限公司	中型	许泽生	开发区江韵路 291 号
南通市起帆钢绳有限公司	中型	赵非非	开发区小海街道庙桥村
江苏巨力钢绳有限公司	中型	施聪	开发区小海街道庙桥村
南通星辰合成材料有限公司	中型	季钢	开发区江港路 118 号
南通瑞升机械有限公司	中型	钱林	开发区五步口社区居委会二组
万高(南通)电机制造有限公司	中型	哈利 史麦尔泽	开发区新开南路 128 号
南通南辉电子材料有限责任公司	中型	林炯阳	开发区剑新路 128 号
南通佳可服饰有限公司	中型	林敏	开发区通富南路 15 号
南通衣依衬布有限公司	中型	唐新东	开发区定海街道定港村
三林合板(南通)有限公司	中型	翟麟	开发区广州路 38 号
南通江东碳素股份有限公司	中型	朱浩明	开发区中兴街道通富南路 9 号
三菱丽阳高分子材料(南通)有限公司	中型	小白井厚典	开发区广州路 6 号
南通友星线束有限公司	中型	潘晓林	开发区星湖大道 1692 号 9 号 10 号厂房
中天科技光纤有限公司	中型	朱兆章	开发区中天路 6 号
南通市华东热处理有限公司	中型	吴金池	开发区小海街道朝阳港村
三大雅精细化学品(南通)有限公司	中型	黑田照	开发区新开南路 5 号
南通开发区精技电子有限公司	中型	林国财	开发区中央路 62 号
百灵达刺绣机械(南通)有限公司	中型	山上哲司	开发区中天路 18 号
江苏王子制纸有限公司	中型	渡边正	开发区通达路 18 号
扬子高丽钢线(南通)有限公司	中型	韩相德	开发区中央路 45 号
惠生(南通)重工有限公司	中型	华邦嵩	开发区江海路 189 号
中天科技海缆有限公司	中型	薛济萍	开发区新开南路 1 号
南通大通宝富风机有限公司	中型	张立新	开发区通盛大道 88 号
台橡(南通)实业有限公司	中型	涂伟华	开发区通旺路 22 号
富士新能源(南通)有限公司	中型	大林证	开发区复兴路 33 号
东丽高新聚化(南通)有限公司	中型	李泳官	开发区新开南路 56 号
马可迅(南通)车轮有限公司	中型	朱尼奥	开发区通盛南路 89 号
南通延锋江森座椅面套有限公司	中型	叶思豪	开发区中兴街道

11-17 续表 6

CONTINUED 6

企业名称 Names	企业规模 Scale	法人代表 Legal representatives	企 业 地 址 Addresses
南通棉花机械有限公司	中型	王颐	通州区锦绣路北、希望大道西
南通市通州区南洋灯泡有限公司	中型	王永祥	通州区税务新村 3 号
南通虹波机械有限公司	中型	沙明军	通州区兴仁镇孙家桥村一组
江苏华宇印涂设备集团有限公司	中型	沈惠峰	通州区二甲镇袁南居 32 组
南通宏德机电有限公司	中型	杨金德	通州区四安镇戚家桥村
江苏蛟龙重工集团有限公司	中型	徐国华	通州区平潮镇新坝村
南通同源环保科技有限公司	中型	葛兴元	通州区先锋镇十六里墩村
江苏新中酿造有限责任公司	中型	吴之纲	通州区石港镇广济桥居
南通海浪玻璃制品厂	中型	曹建	通州区二甲镇交通街 5 号
南通恒信铸锻有限公司	中型	印栋林	通州区石港镇石东村 1 组
南通市通州区自来水有限公司	中型	孙雪梅	通州区金通路 18 号
南通四方冷链装备股份有限公司	中型	黄杰	通州区兴仁镇金通公路 3888 号
南通第十二棉纺织有限公司	中型	朱卫强	通州区草市桥居米市桥中路 129 号
南通市通州区兴达制线有限公司	中型	赵剑	通州区新联居刘家桥 19 组
江苏大海塑料股份有限公司	中型	沈祁峰	通州区川姜镇三圩埭村
桑夏太阳能股份有限公司	中型	赵峰	通州区西亭镇工业园区 1 号
南通综艺新材料有限公司	中型	昝瑞林	通州区青岛路 168 号
紫罗兰家纺科技股份有限公司	中型	陈永兵	通州区张芝山镇塘坊村
江苏甬金金属科技有限公司	中型	虞纪群	通州区鹏程大道 999 号
南通新恒祥纺织服装有限公司	中型	曹晨曦	通州区二甲镇光明路 33 号
广东鸿图南通压铸有限公司	中型	张国光	通州区杏园西路 777 号
宜家环保木业制造(南通)有限公司	中型	WieslawMotylinski	通州区高新技术产业开发区希望大道 001 号
德尔福连接器系统(南通)有限公司	中型	利亚姆大卫巴特沃思	通州区河滨路 9 号
南通华新环保设备工程有限公司	中型	包宏明	通州区五甲镇庆丰居
南通四方罐式储运设备制造有限公司	中型	黄杰	通州区兴仁镇金通公路 3888 号
中航虹波风电设备有限公司	中型	陈钢	通州区兴仁镇孙家桥村 3 组
南通大富豪纺织科技有限公司	中型	易昕	通州区金沙镇朝霞西路 668 号
南通中汇重工有限公司	中型	蔡勇	通州区五接镇韩通路 28 号
江苏乔德福莱蒙德家居股份有限公司	中型	杭卫平	通州区高新技术产业开发区狮子桥村 2 组
江苏宝缦卧室用品有限公司	中型	陆维祖	通州区川姜镇川港工业园区 F 区
南通金创针织有限公司	中型	张奇秀	通州区高新技术产业开发区通掘路
南通华伟运动服饰有限公司	中型	张华伟	通州区世纪大道 188 号

11-17 续表 7

CONTINUED 7

企业名称 Names of the Enterprises	企业规模 Scale	法人代表 Legal representatives	企业地址 Addresses
江苏凯瑞家用纺织品有限公司	中型	吴卫兵	通州区川姜镇姜川村
南通海立电子有限公司	中型	黑木铁也	通州区平潮镇平西村
南通艺源家用纺织品有限公司	中型	孙平	通州区川姜镇望海台村 16 组
江苏蓝丝羽家用纺织品有限公司	中型	俞建辉	通州区川姜镇志南村
江苏通塑科技集团有限公司	中型	孙月柏	通州区先锋镇三圩头村
南通海声电子有限公司	中型	顾洪钟	通州区通扬南路 79 号
南通中瑾服饰有限公司	中型	毛金中	通州区世纪大道 188 号
精源(南通)化纤制品有限公司	中型	李琨世	通州区杏园路 288 号
南通星维海威精密机械有限公司	中型	刘斌	通州区碧华路西首
南通金驰机电有限公司	中型	褚惠南	通州区高新技术产业开发区狮子桥村
江苏中新资源集团有限公司	中型	朱卫强	通州区先锋镇苏家埭村
丽王化工(南通)有限公司	中型	张晓明	通州区通灵桥村 24 组
南通市丰杰印染有限公司	中型	洪丽霞	通州区通灵桥村二组
南通信一服饰有限公司	中型	顾有智	通州区十总镇十总居
南通环球光学仪器有限公司	中型	张宜南	通州区平潮镇九圩港村
南通通州海通船舶修造有限公司	中型	金星	通州区平东镇新三十里居 10 组
南通金翔服装有限公司	中型	沈世军	通州区高新技术产业开发区碧堂庙社区
南通市通州区大达麻纺织有限公司	中型	野建军	通州区通刘路 4 号
南通诚信氨基酸有限公司	中型	邢将军	通州区碧华路 86 号
南通迪美纺织品有限公司	中型	蔡振发	通州区川姜镇姜川村
南通唐盛纺织有限公司	中型	唐建新	通州区川姜镇姜川村
南通居梦莱家用纺织品有限公司	中型	顾平	通州区兴仁镇孙家桥村
新东海(南通)纺织有限公司	中型	徐聪	通州区金通大道 1688 号
南通牧野织物有限公司	中型	葛翠英	通州区高新技术产业开发区花家渡村三组
江苏宝达纺织有限公司	中型	吴江榕	通州区兴仁镇居委会
南通中润照明电器有限公司	中型	沈锦华	通州区平潮镇三官殿村
南通全技纺织涂层有限公司	中型	蔡俊	通州区先锋镇三圩头村
南通星维油泵油嘴有限公司	中型	陈平	通州区工农街 40 号
江苏格雷特起重机械有限公司	中型	王建春	通州区平潮镇九圩港村
南通中瑞重工科技有限公司	中型	殷建明	通州区平潮镇云台山村
新建特阔漂整(南通)有限公司	中型	周建	通州区先锋镇双盟村 37 组
南通思恩电子有限责任公司	中型	李思恩	通州区高新技术产业开发区华山社区

11-17 续表 8

CONTINUED 8

企业名称 Names	企业规模 Scale	法人代表 Legal representatives	企 业 地 址 Addresses
南通海星顺达船舶工程有限公司	中型	钱志兵	通州区平潮镇九圩港村
科维(南通)机械有限公司	中型	刘斌	通州区通州经济开发区青岛路888号
南通联发领才织染有限公司	中型	陈建发	海安县海安镇永安南路299号
海安县东华纺织印染有限公司	中型	张玉华	海安县海安镇河滨东路30号
江苏瑞安特机械集团有限公司	中型	周建伟	海安县海安镇长江西路118号
南通中邦丝织有限公司	中型	刘佩云	海安县开发区东湖路9号
江苏兴华胶带股份有限公司	中型	魏昌林	海安县海安镇河滨西路7号
江苏省海安石油化工厂	中型	王加国	海安县海安镇海化路28号
海安县恒业制丝有限公司	中型	杨宏旺	海安县墩头镇仇湖村33组
江苏飞亚化学工业有限责任公司	中型	曹宏生	海安县精细化工园区南海大道(中)226号
南通江中光电有限公司	中型	许应龙	海安县海安镇海北村8组
海安县兰波实业有限公司	中型	李海波	海安县老坝港北凌新闸西首
海安县中山合成纤维有限公司	中型	杨忠国	海安县墩头镇吉庆村8组
海安县中祥线业有限公司	中型	卢崇国	海安县墩头镇吉庆村十组
江苏菱安光电科技有限公司	中型	严圣军	海安县海安镇黄海大道(西)268号
卡姆丹克太阳能(江苏)有限公司	中型	JOHN ZHANG	海安县海安开发区黄海大道
人民电器集团江苏斯诺成套设备工程有限公司	中型	王小飞	海安县城南工业集中区(陈港村十三组)
浚丰太阳能(江苏)有限公司	中型	徐文燕	海安县海安工业园区(谭港村20、21组)
南通美铭锦纶有限公司	中型	田永圣	海安县墩头镇吉庆工业集中区
江苏骆氏减震件有限公司	中型	骆联盟	海安县城东镇221省道与和谐路交汇处
上海水星家纺海安有限公司	中型	李裕杰	海安县城东镇东海大道(东)109号
南通鑫来丝绸制衣有限公司	中型	储呈平	海安县开发区鑫来路69号
南通鑫平制衣有限公司	中型	王海宏	海安县开发区宁海南路148号
南通中尧机电制造有限公司	中型	曹中	海安县海安镇长江西路88-89号
海安县联发制衣有限公司	中型	薛庆龙	海安县联发工业园
南通永大管业股份有限公司	中型	陈文凤	海安县海安镇开元大道111号
南通米兰特电气有限公司	中型	王杰	海安县工业园区西园大道88号
南通三恩时装有限公司	中型	张宏德	海安县城东镇中坝南路185号
江苏福克斯新能源科技有限公司	中型	袁正	海安县城东镇南玻路10号2幢
上海爱登堡电梯江苏有限公司	中型	李绥	海安县开发区南海大道
南通华纶化纤有限公司	中型	顾玲	海安县海安镇朝阳路9号
亚太轻合金(南通)科技有限公司	中型	周福海	海安县开发区海防路29号

11-17 续表 9

CONTINUED 9

企业名称 Names of the Enterprises	企业规模 Scale	法人代表 Legal representatives	企业地址 Addresses
江苏天成科技集团有限公司	中型	陈正荣	海安县开发区长江东路 29 号
南通保来利轴承有限公司	中型	周园园	海安县开发区通榆中路 203 号
南通双弘制线有限公司	中型	王瑞根	海安县双楼镇双楼路 191 号
南通市德心食品有限公司	中型	景素兵	海安县曲塘镇人民东路 25 号
江苏品王酒业集团股份有限公司	中型	陈永康	海安县海安镇长江西路 98 号
江苏鑫港企业有限公司	中型	王正春	海安县开发区通榆路
海安县联发张氏色织有限公司	中型	张宏德	海安县开发区宁海南路 162 号
南通恒力重工机械有限公司	中型	吴桂林	海安县胡集镇人民路 7 号
海安县通源纱线有限公司	中型	周国银	海安县墩头镇双新村十组
江苏铭安电气有限公司	中型	曹洪新	海安县海安工业园区
南通中邦纺织有限公司	中型	刘佩云	海安县开发区东湖路
江苏华艺服饰有限公司	中型	郃卫国	海安镇长江西路 88-1 号
南通普乐工具有限公司	中型	翁少波	海安县海安镇长江西路 88-6 号
江苏通海线业有限公司	中型	顾华来	海安县墩头镇毛庄村六组
江苏天成保健品有限公司	中型	魏剑鹏	海安县海安镇林桥村
南通华银毛绒制品有限公司	中型	王丽	海安县开发区通榆中路 188 号
南通飞日电子有限公司	中型	孙秀芳	海安县开发区黄海大道(东)2 号
海安县兄弟合成纤维有限公司	中型	何咸稳	海安县墩头镇工业园区
南通华强布业有限公司	中型	卞童	海安县海安镇中坝南路 188 号
南通启领纺织制衣有限公司	中型	王孟晋	海安县海安镇长江西路 88 号
南通联发印染有限公司	中型	黄长根	海安县城东镇恒联路 88 号
南通弘联服饰有限公司	中型	夏常评	海安县曲塘镇刘圩工业园区双楼路 9 号
海安联发棉纺有限公司	中型	崔恒富	海安县城东镇联发工业园
江苏广达医材集团有限公司	中型	冯大云	海安县李堡镇包场北路 18 号
南通通洋机电制造有限公司	中型	王应才	海安县海安镇平桥村 18 组
南通顺裕工艺品有限公司	中型	张秀光	海安县胡集镇谢河村 8 组
南通众润混凝土有限公司	中型	张宏明	海安县高新技术产业开发区花园大道 88 号
江苏威尔曼科技股份有限公司	中型	周经成	海安县海安镇园庄居委会
江苏晨朗电子集团有限公司	中型	陈栋	海安县城东镇东海大道(中)18 号
南通奥特机械设备有限公司	中型	陈金生	海安县曲塘镇刘圩村一组
南通万宝实业有限公司	中型	周连明	海安县海安镇黄海西大道 88 号
南通市京山锦纶有限公司	中型	王义军	海安县墩头镇吉庆工业集中区(办公场所)

11-17　续表 10
CONTINUED 10

企业名称 Names	企业规模 Scale	法人代表 Legal representatives	企业地址 Addresses
江苏江海机床集团有限公司	中型	江琳	海安县李堡工业园区
精华制药集团南通有限公司	中型	朱春林	如东县洋口化工园区
江苏新象股份有限公司	中型	虞天笔	如东县建设路 42 号
江苏快达农化股份有限公司	中型	施永平	如东县建设路 2 号
江苏如通石油机械股份有限公司	中型	曹彩红	如东县开发区淮河路 33 号
南通联发手套针织有限公司	中型	王校尉	如东县曹埠镇上漫村
南通巴大饲料有限公司	中型	缪淑华	如东县岔河镇银河路 66 号
南通万隆纺织有限公司	中型	万群山	如东县河口镇花园头
南通利华农化有限公司	中型	黄桂泉	如东县沿海经济开发区
如东县铁链厂有限公司	中型	马陈	如东县岔河镇力神路 88 号
如东通园化工有限公司	中型	万玉霜	如东县新店镇汤园人民路 18 号
南通振新颜料有限公司	中型	费洁云	如东县新店镇新店社区
江东金具设备有限公司	中型	薛驰	如东县河口镇中天村
江苏宇迪光学股份有限公司	中型	吴迪富	如东县双甸镇工业园区
江苏金太阳油脂有限责任公司	中型	陈曙燕	如东县交通东路 33 号
南通志兴服饰有限公司	中型	解小燕	如东县青园社区居委会
江苏三美化工有限公司	中型	李献荣	如东县洋口镇化学工业园区
江苏伊贝实业有限公司	中型	徐明	如东县曹埠镇上漫社区十组
江苏长青农化南通有限公司	中型	赵河	如东县洋口镇沿海经济开发区
江苏辉腾休闲用品有限公司	中型	罗雄	如东县开发区金沙江路 69 号
南通正大有限公司	中型	鲍国余	如东县掘港镇友谊西路 32 号
南通海达水产食品有限公司	中型	蔡守清	如东县掘港镇富春江路 588 号
南通天天肠衣食品有限公司	中型	王正建	如东县掘港镇范堤社区
南通楠桥纹织有限公司	中型	市川隆史	如东县掘港镇江海西路
霍尼韦尔安全防护产品(南通)有限公司	中型	李宁	如东县开发区振新社区
南通水鑫织造有限公司	中型	李琰	如东县河口镇中天村
思妍时装(南通)有限公司	中型	萧玉妍	如东县沿海经济开发区
南通苏信电气有限公司	中型	陈洁	如东县掘港镇掘西村
南通纬纶纺织有限公司	中型	冒国平	如东县河口镇中天村
南通祥峰电子有限公司	中型	康宜峰	如东县河口镇中天工业园区
南通市东昌化工有限公司	中型	陶坤山	如东县建设路 40-1 号
南通利奥纱线有限公司	中型	金根中	如东县河口镇花园头 20 组

11-17 续表 11

CONTINUED 11

企业名称 Names of the Enterprises	企业规模 Scale	法人代表 Legal representatives	企 业 地 址 Addresses
江苏南黄海实业股份有限公司	中型	吴希鹏	如东县马塘镇仁和南路 86 号
东海(南通)冷冻食品有限公司	中型	黄廖美淑	如东县东海路 8 号
江苏瑞邦农药厂有限公司	中型	景伟平	如东沿海经济开发区
如东县海宇纤维制品有限公司	中型	钱春梅	如东县河口镇立新桥 6 组
亚振家具股份有限公司	中型	高伟	如东县曹埠镇亚振桥
江苏祥盛倍得满家具有限公司	中型	周炳祥	如东县友谊西路 29 号
江苏盾王劳保用品有限公司	中型	王志雄	如东县兵房镇工业集中区
如东县振兴机床有限公司	中型	徐安平	如东县大豫镇各平路 49 号
南通建民丝绸有限公司	中型	施崇高	如东县马塘镇市河西路 108 号
南通威尔斯服装有限公司	中型	徐建泉	如东县掘港镇通海路 27 号
如东县沪马福利针织机械有限公司	中型	王登如	如东县掘港镇陈高村工业园
南通华亮健身器材有限公司	中型	祁琴	如东县新店镇孙桥村一组
江苏苏通茧丝绸有限公司	中型	徐金海	如东县岔河镇西大街 21 号
如东县明珠织造有限公司	中型	韩宗秀	如东县掘港镇陈高村
南通天鑫健身器材有限公司	中型	王霞	如东县掘港镇宾东村
江苏如石机械有限公司	中型	刘志刚	如东县卫海北路 888 号
南通世纪天虹纺织有限公司	中型	汤道平	如东县江海西路 2 号
南通辉煌彩色钢板有限公司	中型	刘允华	如东县经济开发区通达路
如东双马针业有限公司	中型	奚金明	如东县掘港镇虹元村
南通东洋时装有限公司	中型	陈霞光	如东县新店社区五组
南通环宇手套有限公司	中型	管永喜	如东县曹埠镇上漫社区
南通东日钢铁有限公司	中型	李忠乐	如东县开发区牡丹江路
南通昌邦手套有限公司	中型	陈智荣	如东县曹埠镇埠中路 100 号
南通万誉服饰有限公司	中型	徐冬元	如东县双甸镇高前村工业园区
南通大江灯饰有限公司	中型	汤炳林	如东县大豫镇工业集中区
南通锐阳纺织有限公司	中型	丁居兵	如东县掘港镇城南工业园区
恒辉(南通)安全防护用品有限公司	中型	王咸华	如东县开发区黄山路西侧金沙江路
南通泰禾化工有限公司	中型	田晓宏	如东县洋口化工园区
如东富强针织印染有限公司	中型	张国强	如东县曹埠镇孙窑针织工业园区
南通康福特纺织有限公司	中型	马勤	如东县掘港镇掘西村工业新区
如东县银鑫制衣厂	中型	夏卫华	如东县掘港镇潮墩村三组
南通世川时装有限公司	中型	李世军	如东县新店镇胡港村二组

11-17　续表 12
CONTINUED 12

企业名称 Names	企业规模 Scale	法人代表 Legal representatives	企业地址 Addresses
南通滨江船舶修造工程有限公司	中型	李兵	如东县袁庄镇赵港村六组
南通日盛五金制刷有限公司	中型	林少廷	如东县开发区黄河路
南通市光阳针业有限公司	中型	崔永青	如东县双甸镇高前村
赛立特(南通)安全用品有限公司	中型	赵卫	如东县掘港镇友谊西路 198
汇鸿(南通)安全用品有限公司	中型	林栋梁	如东县开发区新区淮河路 98 号
南通万通食品科技有限公司	中型	张京京	如东县开发区新区湘江路北侧
南通亿能彩钢板有限公司	中型	黄卫平	如东县开发区新区天山路
江苏林洋光伏科技有限公司	中型	陆永华	启东市汇龙镇华石路 612 号
江苏双林海洋生物药业有限公司	中型	梁双林	启东市吕四港镇吕东街 40 号
江苏捷捷微电子股份有限公司	中型	黄善兵	启东市科技创业园兴龙路 8 号
启东市南方润滑液压设备有限公司	中型	张超	启东市惠萍镇工业园区
启东市自来水厂	中型	张熹	启东市汇龙镇花园路 802 号
江苏澳兴服装集团有限公司	中型	季冬冬	启东市惠萍镇振兴街
启东市胶鞋厂有限公司	中型	汤建忠	启东市向阳镇东进村
江苏诚信药业有限公司	中型	邢将军	启东市滨江精细化工园区上海路 338 号
南通润邦海洋工程装备有限公司	中型	吴建	启东市海工大道 3333 号
江苏龙腾鹏达机电有限公司	中型	毛鹏飞	启东市吕四港镇兆明工业园区 88 号
启东太平物流装备有限公司	中型	赵春崦	启东市惠萍镇白港村 1 组
启东市盖天力药业有限公司	中型	徐无为	启东市开发区城西村和平南路 88 号
南通迪皮茜电子有限公司	中型	丁海松	启东市惠丰镇双庆村
启东上拓船务工程有限公司	中型	谌炯	启东市滨海工业园汇海路
宏华海洋油气装备(江苏)有限公司	中型	张弭	启东市寅阳镇戤效港
南通市南方润滑液压设备有限公司	中型	张爱东	启东市开发区纬二路 236-238 号
江苏国强工具有限公司	中型	张国强	启东市天汾科技五金工业园
南通申东冶金机械有限公司	中型	黄新标	启东市民主镇工业集中区 118 号
江苏西欧电子有限公司	中型	沈忠彬	启东市开发区南区(西欧科技园)
南通成生齿轮厂	中型	潘成生	启东市吕四港镇天汾居委会
启东润滑设备有限公司	中型	张标	启东市汇龙镇城河村和平中路 360 号
江苏神通阀门股份有限公司	中型	吴建新	启东市南阳镇南阳村
江苏三上机电制造股份有限公司	中型	高飞	启东市城北工业园青年路 333 号
江苏恒通电气仪表有限公司	中型	尹宇	启东市开发区人民西路 1999 号
启东吉莱电子有限公司	中型	李建新	启东市汇龙镇公园北路 1261 号

11–17 续表 13
CONTINUED 13

企业名称 Names	企业规模 Scale	法人代表 Legal representatives	企业地址 Addresses
江苏好收成韦恩农化股份有限公司	中型	江连	启东市北新镇三和村
南通山本电动工具有限公司	中型	陈三海	启东市天汾镇工业园区
南通利比特电子电器有限公司	中型	卢美娟	启东市吕四港镇茅家港工业区
江苏索利得电器有限公司	中型	李洪昌	启东市天汾科技五金工业园
江苏飞虎针业有限公司	中型	薛宏飞	启东市日新河镇人民街 116 号
启东市生力电动工具厂	中型	钱杨生	启东市天汾科技五金工业园
启东新盛电动工具有限公司	中型	周建新	启东市天汾镇周街村 12 组
启东兴隆园瑞孚铸造有限公司	中型	刘勇	启东市启隆生态科技产业园
启东市华泰陶瓷制品有限公司	中型	林永欣	启东市开发区南苑西路 1199 号
南通国立箱包有限公司	中型	庄善家	启东市寅阳镇和合镇村
启东东岳药业有限公司	中型	蔡水洪	启东市寅阳镇和合镇村
江苏大唐国际吕四港发电有限责任公司	中型	王宪周	启东市吕四港镇秦潭村
南通瑞泰纺织有限公司	中型	陈旭东	启东市汇龙镇建都新村
南通东华服装有限公司	中型	邢福海	启东市寅阳镇和合镇村
启东市宏威针织有限公司	中型	陆志鹏	启东市王鲍镇久西村
南通艾德旺化工有限公司	中型	林澄茂	启东市北新镇精细化工园区
江苏希迪制药有限公司	中型	刘蔚	启东市开发区滨江精细化工园江风路 3 号
南通春秋时装有限公司	中型	陈正岳	启东市开发区人民西路 3333 号
南通东泰新能源设备有限公司	中型	吴杨建	启东市开发区南苑西路 1300 号
江苏科本医药化学有限公司	中型	蒋善会	启东市沿江精细化工园区
启东金美化学有限公司	中型	潘行平	启东市滨江精细化工园上海路
南通太平洋海洋工程有限公司	中型	梁小雷	启东市和合镇裕丰村
江苏百特电器有限公司	中型	虞智武	启东市滨海工业园汇海路
江苏嘉盟电力设备有限公司	中型	施希锋	启东市滨海工业园临海村
启东姚记扑克实业有限公司	中型	姚朔斌	启东市开发区银河路
江苏康耐特光学有限公司	中型	费铮翔	启东滨海工业园江枫路
江苏昌昇集团股份有限公司	中型	沙晓明	如皋市如城镇福寿路 68 号
江苏南天化肥有限公司	中型	吴克祥	如皋市白蒲镇文峰居 5 组
江苏陆地方舟新能源电动汽车有限公司	中型	刘晓静	如皋市柴湾镇镇南村戴营路口
南通亮典彩印包装有限公司	中型	秦海亮	如皋市九华镇杨码村 26 组
江苏神马电力股份有限公司	中型	马斌	如皋市如城镇贺洋社区
如皋市中如化工有限公司	中型	蔡可建	如皋市吴窑镇迎宾路 1 号

11-17 续表 14
CONTINUED 14

企业名称 Names	企业规模 Scale	法人代表 Legal representatives	企业地址 Addresses
如皋市长江食品有限公司	中型	陈建坤	如皋市长江镇二案居
如皋市双马化工有限公司	中型	冒建兰	如皋市东陈镇南东陈
江苏涤诺日化集团有限公司	中型	张春林	如皋市丁堰镇丁新东路 1 号
南通永林船舶配套有限公司	中型	赵宏军	如皋市石庄镇石南村
江苏里高家具有限公司	中型	倪贵平	如皋市丁堰镇皋南路 999 号
如皋市鑫泰特钢铸锻有限公司	中型	叶化勇	如皋市长江镇创业路 1 号
江苏长寿大红门食品有限公司	中型	魏祝明	如皋市开发区仁寿路 216 号
南通伟越电器有限公司	中型	徐正鱼	如皋市九华镇郑甸居
瑞声科技(如皋)有限公司	中型	张爱明	如皋市桃园镇新桃路 8 号
南通茂鑫工艺品有限公司	中型	王芸芸	如皋市白浦镇松杨村
如皋市易达电子有限责任公司	中型	胡忠军	如皋市搬经镇群岸居
如皋市大昌电子有限公司	中型	王志敏	如皋市柴湾镇镇南 13 组
南通明龙时装有限公司	中型	石亚明	如皋市如城镇李渔路 18 号
南通市利信德海制衣有限公司	中型	张如芳	如皋市郭元镇郭元居
南通华凯船舶设备有限公司	中型	秦利明	如皋市长江镇二案居
南通市腾跃晟业通讯设备有限公司	中型	王兵	如皋市长江镇粮棉原种场部
江苏如皋钢铁有限公司	中型	杨效仙	如皋市蒲港村十九组
江苏意瑞达纺织科技有限公司	中型	陈耀良	如皋市柴湾镇镇南社区
如皋市海华毛纺织品有限公司	中型	陈德明	如皋市长江镇二百亩社区
南通睿鑫钢结构工程有限公司	中型	周银树	如皋市长江镇长新街 50 号
森松(江苏)重工有限公司	中型	松久信夫	如皋市长江镇长青居
江苏瀚艺商用空调有限公司	中型	甘泉	如皋市开发区起凤西路 88 号
如皋市逸人服饰有限公司	中型	李季	如皋市林梓镇林梓村 15 组
南通百正电子新材料有限公司	中型	徐明强	如皋市经济开发区太平居委会
南通金帝贵金属有限公司	中型	马荣萍	如皋市桃园镇天堡村
江苏永大化工机械有限公司	中型	李进	如皋市九华镇华兴路 9 号
如皋华澜船务有限公司	中型	张年华	如皋市长江镇长青居委会
如皋市润林船务有限公司	中型	邵炎林	如皋市长江镇长青居委会
南通市泰尔佳针织制衣有限公司	中型	钱德平	如皋市城西大道 1 号
如皋市丁堰纺织有限公司	中型	陈坚	如皋市丁堰镇茄儿园居委会
如皋市伟业合金厂	中型	吴宏伟	如皋市吴窑镇吴窑居 4 组
南通华东油压科技有限公司	中型	丁洋	如皋市白蒲镇邓杨村

11-17　续表 15
CONTINUED 15

企业名称 Names	企业规模 Scale	法人代表 Legal representatives	企业地址 Addresses
江苏力星通用钢球股份有限公司	中型	施祥贵	如皋市如城镇大殷社区兴源大道
南通市鑫华有色材料有限公司	中型	张勇华	如皋市九华镇景泰路 8 号
江苏隆昌化工有限公司	中型	佘道才	如皋市丁堰镇皋南社区
南通锻压设备有限公司	中型	郭庆	如皋市柴湾镇镇南居二组
南通绅宝利工艺服饰有限公司	中型	朱济华	如皋市石庄镇板桥北路 28 号
南通天龙畜产品有限公司	中型	许春龙	如皋市丁堰镇茄儿园居委会
如皋市亚雅油脂化工有限公司	中型	金茂圣	如皋市丁堰镇丁新东路 1 号
南通泰利达化工有限公司	中型	徐拥军	如皋市丁堰镇凤山社区 3 组
如皋市双龙健制衣有限公司	中型	邵海建	如皋市开发区东风路 8 号
南通金久服饰有限公司	中型	吴丽霞	如皋市白蒲镇康庄村七组
如皋市光华橡胶厂	中型	石征才	如皋市吴窑镇人民北路 60 号
南通蓝星装饰工程有限公司	中型	徐华	如皋市如城镇福寿西路 230 号
如皋市大生线路器材有限公司	中型	征大生	如皋市如城镇陆桥村 9 组
如皋市宏茂铸钢有限公司	中型	偶洪元	如皋市长江镇永丰社区
江苏万达特种轴承有限公司	中型	徐群生	如皋市如城镇纪庄 5 组
南通市燕南工艺品有限公司	中型	李进	如皋市丁堰镇堰南社区
南通市星球石墨设备有限公司	中型	张艺	如皋市九华镇九华居委会
如皋市旭日时装有限责任公司	中型	朱美如	如皋市吴窑镇迎宾路 6 号
南通康比电子有限公司	中型	张春来	如皋市如城镇纪庄兴园路 8 号
南通针王工艺品有限公司	中型	周秀云	如皋市白蒲镇松杨村
如皋市飞鹏纺织有限公司	中型	许映飞	如皋市江安镇宁通 7 组
南通白蒲黄酒有限公司	中型	张斌	如皋市白蒲镇光明居市河路 155 号
南通市华燕照明电器有限公司	中型	姚桂华	如皋市九华镇小马桥村 10 组
如皋市天马棉毛纺织公司	中型	黄勇风	如皋市江安镇中心居
如皋市丹凤纺织有限公司	中型	吴训华	如皋市吴窑镇吴窑居
南通恒一钢结构有限公司	中型	陈永昌	如皋市吴窑镇吴窑居
帕瓦服饰(南通)有限公司	中型	家山英夫	如皋市开发区香江路
南通润泉服饰有限公司	中型	杨巧英	如皋市白蒲镇康庄村 7 组
如皋市东祥色织有限公司	中型	沈梅	如皋市吴窑镇迎宾东路 1 号
南通三荣实业有限公司	中型	王建华	如皋市九华工业园区
江苏金元亚麻有限公司	中型	沈跃明	如皋市开发区鹿门社区
南通沪港装饰有限公司	中型	周国建	如皋市石庄镇新生港村 17 组

11-17 续表 16

CONTINUED 16

企业名称 Names	企业规模 Scale	法人代表 Legal representatives	企业地址 Addresses
南通小樱时装有限公司	中型	殷志祥	如皋市石庄镇石南村
南通东润实业有限公司	中型	龙继东	如皋市九华工业园区
南通三润时装有限公司	中型	景爱梅	如皋市九华镇郭李社区
顺帆家庭用品(南通)有限公司	中型	汤鸿光	如皋市搬经镇群岸居
南通川邻铸造技术有限公司	中型	陆炳林	如皋市长江镇中心沙社区
南通方正海洋工程科技有限公司	中型	秦利明	如皋市长江镇文晋路
华泰(南通)船务有限公司	中型	秦丽	如皋市长江镇中小船舶园区
江苏思源赫兹互感器有限公司	中型	陈邦栋	如皋市开发区惠民西路
南通三喜名星服装有限公司	中型	陈振平	如皋市石庄镇草张庄居委会
南通康盛时装有限公司	中型	尹美华	如皋市九华镇杨码村 8 组
南通市新空间幕墙材料制造有限公司	中型	曹建国	如皋市东陈工业区
南通雷成运动休闲服饰有限公司	中型	陈进	如皋市开发区泰宁路 68 号
南通市康瑞汽车附件制造有限公司	中型	毛平西	如皋市江安镇宁通居 2 组
南通金华府服饰有限公司	中型	冯德明	如皋市林梓镇蒋殿村 4 组
南通泛成纺织品有限公司	中型	闻凤珍	如皋市郭园镇薛窑村
南通超达机械科技有限公司	中型	冯建军	如皋市桃园镇申徐村 1 组
南通佳特盛机械制造有限公司	中型	杜世荣	如皋市江安镇宁通居 9 组
南通长青沙船舶工程有限公司	中型	王志南	如皋市长江镇知青村
如皋市天鹏冶金有限公司	中型	周平	如皋市长江镇钱江路
南通宝众宝达药业有限公司	中型	陈金根	如皋市长江镇粤江路
南通亨得利高分子材料科技有限公司	中型	王燃	如皋市长江镇滨江路 6 号
如皋市百瑞服装有限公司	中型	纪广祥	如皋市九华镇营防村 6 组
江苏长寿如皋广兴米业有限公司	中型	姚广圣	如皋市白蒲镇松杨村
如皋市三源电器设备有限公司	中型	沈建高	如皋市吴窑镇吴窑居 9 组
南通德玛瑞机械制造有限公司	中型	邓珊	如皋市郭园镇天海路 88 号
南通思英船务工程有限公司	中型	徐建成	如皋市长江镇长江村
江苏意隆机械制造有限公司	中型	杜世荣	如皋市江安镇宁通居 6 组
南通润创时装有限公司	中型	洪大维	如皋市九华镇杨码村 29 组
国鼎(南通)管桩有限公司	中型	姜平平	如皋市长江镇钢贸园区
善龙食品(南通)有限公司	中型	李永东	如皋市长江镇二百亩社区
如皋市儒马纺织品有限公司	中型	周焕	如皋市吴窑镇鲁班路 19 号
江苏国泰(集团)如皋服装有限公司	中型	王炜	如皋市袁桥镇何庄村

11-17　续表 17
CONTINUED 17

企业名称 Names	企业规模 Scale	法人代表 Legal representatives	企业地址 Addresses
百川化工(如皋)有限公司	中型	郑铁江	如皋长江镇香江路 6 号
南通之禾时装有限公司	中型	叶寿增	海门市海门镇通源路 631 号
江苏海峰电力机械集团股份有限公司	中型	张雪峰	海门市正余镇青正村
江苏白兔纺织集团股份有限公司	中型	成伯新	海门市开发区秀山东路 677 号
海门市常乐粉末冶金厂	中型	陆洲	海门市常乐镇工业园区
南通市恒荣机泵厂有限公司	中型	曹彭年	海门市三厂镇中华西路 297 号
中兴能源装备股份有限公司	中型	仇云龙	海门市三厂镇中兴村
江苏晨牌药业集团股份有限公司	中型	李建新	海门市人民中路 172 号
海门市海天纸业有限公司	中型	张家斌	海门市天补镇陶港村海天西路东侧 300 米
南通海林汽车橡塑制品有限公司	中型	张禹林	海门市正余镇双烈村
凯盛家纺股份有限公司	中型	顾萍	海门市海门镇人民西路 858 号
上海现代制药海门有限公司	中型	王国平	海门市临江镇灵甸工业集中东区 3 号
江苏景越塑料科技有限公司	中型	江凌	海门市滨海新区港西大道 999 号
燕达(海门)重型装备制造有限公司	中型	雷建民	海门市滨海新区港西大道 999 号
江苏宝钢精密钢丝有限公司	中型	吴文华	海门市海门镇解放东路电视塔东
海科工程股份有限公司	中型	徐建	海门开发区海门港大兴路 8 号
南通中远重工有限公司	中型	张明华	海门市海门港长春路 2 号
南通维达鞋业有限公司	中型	季建忠	海门市六匡镇三条桥
南通宝石服装有限公司	中型	张新	海门市悦来镇三条桥东首
江苏通海染整有限公司	中型	王庆杰	海门市三阳镇友爱村 10 组
江苏希诺实业有限公司	中型	黄伟军	海门市树勋镇工业园区希诺路 1 号
路特利举升机(海门)有限公司	中型	JAMES LOUIS WYSINSKI	海门市开发区秀山东路 1388 号
江苏联海生物科技有限公司	中型	陈玉和	海门市灵甸工业集中区纬四路
海科工业有限公司	中型	钱胜华	海门市滨江街道珠海路 1 号内 1 号房
江苏金呢工程织物股份有限公司	中型	陆平	海门市六匡镇三条桥
江苏铁锚工具有限公司	中型	周海春	海门市滨海新区铁锚路 88 号
南通奥贝尔工程技术有限公司	中型	凌美琴	海门市滨海新区广东路 9 号
浩博(海门)机械制造有限公司	中型	陈淑惠	海门市麒麟镇常久公路 888 号
海门市森达装饰材料有限公司	中型	朱善忠	海门市天补镇通启路 23 号
江苏英力科技发展有限公司	中型	马士新	海门市三厂镇大庆路 18 号
南通海迪化工有限公司	中型	倪海平	海门市汤家镇西首
海门泰森禽业发展有限公司	中型	李益铭	海门市东灶港镇西首(海门盐场内)

11-17　续表 18

CONTINUED 18

企业名称 Names	企业规模 Scale	法人代表 Legal representatives	企业地址 Addresses
南通凯旋体育用品有限公司	中型	毛志荣	海门市四甲镇二桥路
南通爱尔思轻合金精密成型有限公司	中型	翟春江	海门市货隆镇工业园区
南通市申海工业技术科技有限公司	中型	仇士学	海门市青龙港大庆路 27 号
海门市利国玻璃制品有限责任公司	中型	蔡建国	海门市瑞祥大桥处
南通东盛之花印染有限公司	中型	施亚斐	海门经济开发区青龙化工园区
海门市晋帛家用纺织品有限公司	中型	仇前斌	海门市三星工贸园区 B 区(三星镇镇南村 7 组)
南通喜洋洋家用纺织品有限公司	中型	袁仲石	海门市三星镇太阳村七组
南通市争妍颜料化工有限公司	中型	赵觉新	海门市临江新区临江工业园
南通三星健身器材有限公司	中型	傅军华	海门市悦来镇悦来村 14 组
江苏世泰实验器材有限公司	中型	王忠	海门市海门镇新秀路 48 号
南通振康焊接机电有限公司	中型	汤子康	海门市正余镇双烈村
南通大力神钢绳有限公司	中型	顾其林	海门市三厂镇大生路 128 号
江苏大岛机械集团有限公司	中型	施潜新	海门市三星工业园区
南通华润大生纺织有限公司	中型	向明	海门市三厂镇中华中路 269 号
南通八津谷服装有限公司	中型	张新	海门市悦来镇三条桥东首
江苏三通科技有限公司	中型	施善国	海门市三厂镇望江路 100 号
紫琅衬布(南通)有限公司	中型	沈荣	海门市三厂镇中华西路 353 号
南通新锦江印染有限公司	中型	施洪生	海门市三厂镇丁陆村
江苏雄风科技有限公司	中型	沈哲昊	海门市正余镇科技工业园区
东辰塑胶(南通)有限公司	中型	俞军	海门市开发区北海路北侧
南通市常海食品添加剂有限公司	中型	庄俊	海门市开发区青龙化工园区大庆路南侧
南通四海植物精华有限公司	中型	倪继达	海门市常乐镇工业集中区(常中村)
江苏中兴精密机械有限公司	中型	江義福	海门市货隆镇工业园区
南通玉灿鞋业有限公司	中型	宋加升	海门市三厂镇新东街
南通奥斯特鞋业有限公司	中型	袁建新	海门市余东镇凤城南路 288 号
海门市新鑫船舶工程有限公司	中型	江国新	海门市滨海新区闸中村 2 组
海门市沪海有色铸造有限公司	中型	翟峰	海门市货隆镇新街村二组
南通海易瓶盖有限公司	中型	陈晓平	海门市海门镇城兴村 1 组
江苏中兴创元高压电气有限公司	中型	江义福	海门市货隆镇工业园区
江苏中联风能机械有限公司	中型	花世华	海门市正余镇工业集中区西区
南通飞鹰电子有限公司	中型	俞豪	海门市开发区北海路 9 号

主要统计指标解释

工业 指从事自然资源的开采,对采掘品和农产品进行加工和再加工的物质生产部门。具体包括:(1)对自然资源的开采,如采矿、晒盐等(但不包括禽兽捕猎和水产捕捞);(2)对农副产品的加工、再加工,如粮油加工、食品加工、缫丝、纺织、制革等;(3)对采掘品的加工、再加工,如炼铁、炼钢、化工生产、石油加工、机器制造、木材加工等,以及电力、自来水、煤气的生产和供应等;(4)对工业品的修理、翻新,如机器设备的修理、交通运输工具(如汽车)的修理等。

工业统计调查单位为独立核算法人工业企业。

独立核算法人工业企业指从事工业生产经营活动的单位。独立核算法人工业企业应同时具备以下条件:①依法成立,有自己的名称、组织机构和场所,能够承担民事责任;②独立拥有和使用资产,承担负债,有权与其他单位签订合同;③独立核算盈亏,并能够编制资产负债表。

国有及国有控股企业 指国有企业加上国有控股企业。国有企业(即原全民所有制工业或国营工业)指企业全部资产归国家所有,并按《中华人民共和国企业法人登记管理条例》规定登记注册的非公司制的经济组织。包括国有企业、国有独资公司和国有联营企业。1957年以前的公私合营和私营工业,后均改造为国营工业,1992年改为国有工业,这部分工业的资料不单独分列时,均包括在国有企业内。国有控股企业是对混合所有制经济的企业进行的"国有控股"分类。它是指这些企业的全部资产中国有资产(股份)相对其他所有者中的任何一个所有者占资(股)最多的企业。该分组反映了国有经济控股情况。

本篇涉及的其他企业登记注册类型的解释详见综合篇。

轻工业 指主要提供生活消费品和制作手工工具的工业。按其所使用的原料不同,可分为两大类:(1)以农产品为原料的轻工业,是指直接或间接以农产品为基本原料的轻工业。主要包括食品制造、饮料制造、烟草加工、纺织、缝纫、皮革和毛皮制作、造纸以及印刷等工业;(2)以非农产品为原料的轻工业,是指以工业品为原料的轻工业。主要包括文教体育用品、化学药品制造、合成纤维制造、日用化学制品、日用玻璃制品、日用金属制品、手工工具制造、医疗器械制造、文化和办公用机械制造等工业。

重工业 指为国民经济各部门提供物质技术基础的主要生产资料的工业。按其生产性质和产品用途, 可以分为下列三类:(1)采掘(伐)工业,是指对自然资源的开采,包括石油开采、煤炭开采、金属矿开采、非金属矿开采等工业;(2)原材料工业,指向国民经济各部门提供基本材料、动力和燃料的工业。包括金属冶炼及加工、炼焦及焦炭、化学、化工原料、水泥、人造板以及电力、石油和煤炭加工等工业;(3)加工工业,是指对工业原材料进行再加工制造的工业。包括装备国民经济各部门的机械设备制造工业、金属结构、水泥制品等工业,以及为农业提供的生产资料如化肥、农药等工业。

根据上述划分原则,修理业中以重工业产品为修理作业对象的划为重工业,反之划为轻工业。

资产总计 指企业过去的交易或者事项形成的、由企业拥有或者控制的、预期会给企业带来经济利益的资源。资产一般按流动性分为流动资产和非流动资产。其中流动资产可分为货币资金、交易性金融资产、应收票据、应收账款、预付款项、其他应收款、存货等;非流动资产可分为长期股权投资、固定资产、无形资产及其他非流动资产等。根据会计"资产负债表"中"资产总计"项目的期末余额数填报。

流动资产合计 资产满足以下条件之一应归为流动资产:(1)预计在一个正常营业周期中变现、出售或耗用,主要包括存货、应收账款等;(2)主要为交易目的而持有;(3)预计在资产负债表日起一年内(含一年)变现 (4)自资产负债日起一年内,交换其他资产或清偿负债的能力不受限制的现金或现金等价物。包括货币资金、应收票据、应收账款、存货等项目。根据会计"资产负债表"中"流动资产合计"项目的期末余额数填报。

固定资产原价 指固定资产的成本,包括企业在购置、自行建造、安装、改建、扩建、技术改造某项固定资产时所发生的全部支出总额。根据会计"固定资产"科目的期末借方余额填报。

累计折旧 指企业在报告期末提取的历年固定资产折旧累计数。根据会计"累计折旧"科目的期末贷方余额填报。

负债合计 指企业过去的交易或者事项形成的,预期会导致经济利益流出企业的现时义务。负债一般按偿还期长短分为流动负债和非流动负债。根据会计"资产负债表"中"负债合计"项目的期末余额数填报。

流动负债合计 负债满足下列条件之一的应归为流动负债:(1)预计在一个正常营业周期中清偿;(2)主要为交易目的而持

有;(3)自资产负债表日起一年内到期应予清偿;(4)企业无权自主地将清偿推迟至资产负债表日后一年以上。包括短期借款、应付票据、应付账款、应付职工薪酬、应交税费等项目。根据会计“资产负债表”中“流动负债合计”项目的期末余额数填报。

所有者权益合计 指企业资产扣除负债后由所有者享有的剩余权益。公司的所有者权益又称股东权益。包括实收资本、资本公积、盈余公积、未分配利润等。根据会计“资产负债表”中“所有者权益合计”项目的期末余额数填报。

主营业务收入 指企业确认的销售商品、提供劳务等主营业务的收入。根据会计“主营业务收入”科目的期末贷方余额填报。

主营业务成本 指企业经营主要业务所发生的成本总额。根据会计“主营业务成本”科目的期末借方余额填报。

主营业务税金及附加 指企业经营主要业务应负担的营业税、消费税、城市维护建设税、教育费附加等。根据会计“主营业务税金及附加”科目的期末借方余额填报。

利润总额 指企业在一定会计期间的经营成果,是生产经营过程中各种收入扣除各种耗费后的盈余,反映企业在报告期内实现的盈亏总额。根据会计“利润表”中“利润总额”项目的本期金额数填报。

应交增值税 指企业按税法规定,从事货物销售或提供加工、修理修配劳务等增加货物价值的活动本期应交纳的税金。计算公式为:

应交增值税=销项税额-(进项税额-进项税额转出)-出口抵减内销产品应纳税额-减免税款+出口退税

进项税额指企业在报告期内购入货物或接受应税劳务而支付的、准予从销项税额中抵扣的增值税额。

销项税额指企业在报告期内销售货物或提供应税劳务应收取的增值税额。

总资产贡献率 反映企业全部资产的获利能力,是企业经营业绩和管理水平的集中体现,是评价和考核企业盈利能力的核心指标。计算公式为:

$$总资产贡献率(\%)=\frac{利润总额+税金总额+利息支出}{平均资产总额}\times 100\%$$

公式中:税金总额为主营业务税金及附加与应交增值税之和;平均资产总额为期初期末资产之和的算术平均值。

资产负债率 该指标既反映企业经营风险的大小,也反映企业利用债权人提供的资金从事经营活动的能力。计算公式为:

$$资产贡献率(\%)=\frac{负债总额}{资产总额}\times 100\%$$

资产与负债均为报告期期末数。

成本费用利润率 反映企业投入的生产成本及费用的经济效益,同时也反映企业降低成本所取得的经济效益。计算公式为:

$$成本费用利润率(\%)=\frac{利润总额}{成本费用总额}\times 100\%$$

公式中:成本费用总额为主营业务成本、销售费用、管理费用、财务费用之和。

产品销售率 该指标反映工业产品已实现销售的程度,是分析工业产销衔接情况,研究工业产品满足社会需求的指标。计算公式为:

$$产品销售率(\%)=\frac{工业销售产值}{工业总产值}\times 100\%$$

第十二篇 建筑业

Chapter 12 Construction

12-1 分地区建筑业生产情况(2014 年)

指　标	Item	全市 Municipality	市区 Urban Areas (Tongzhou Excluded)
企业单位数(个)	Number of Enterprises	892	373
#亏损企业	Nonprofitable Enterprises	29	22
建筑业企业合同情况(万元)	Contract of Construction Enterprises (10,000Yuan)		
签订的合同额	Signed Contract Amount	92073361	26384650
上年结转合同额	Contract Amount Carried Forward from Last Year	42468974	10900194
本年新签合同额	Contract Amount Newly Signed this Year	49604387	15484456
承包工程完成情况(万元)	Completion of Contracted Project (10,000 Yuan)		
直接从建设单位承揽工程完成的产值	Output by Undertaking Project from Construction Owner Directly	58809383	17023211
自行完成施工产值	Output by Completing Construction on Its Own	58799123	17019978
分包出去工程的产值	Output by Outsourcing Contruction Project	10260	3235
从建设单位以外承揽工程完成的产值	Output by Undertaking Project From Party other than Construction Owner	4012943	1022915
建筑业总产值(万元)	Total Output of Construction Industry (10,000 Yuan)	62812065	18042892
#装饰装修产值	Decoration Output	2196155	1078629
#在外省完成的产值	Output Completed in other Provinces	34994186	6377217
建筑工程产值	Output of Construction Project	60363160	16778552
安装工程产值	Output of Installation Project	2229266	1194469
其他产值	Others	219640	69871
竣工产值(万元)	Output of Completed Buildings (10,000 Yuan)	44401490	13904947
房屋建筑施工面积(万平方米)	Contruction Area of the Building (10,000 m^2)	68201	15900
#本年新开工面积	Newly-begun Construction Area of the Year	23438	6285
#实行投标承包面积	Construction Area by Bidding	64517	15207
#本年新开工	Newly-begun Construction of the Year	22205	6012

STATISTICS ON CONSTRUCTION INDUSTRY BY REGIONS(2014)

崇川区 Chongchuan	港闸区 Gangzha	开发区 Developing Zone	通州区 Tongzhou	海安 Hai´an	如东 Rudong	启东 Qidong	如皋 Rugao	海门 Haimen
112	64	47	135	94	69	89	122	145
9	4		9	1		3	1	2
2328643	2466264	540245	18877094	14079863	6583325	13260723	11854391	19910410
751469	811280	219134	8195335	6375017	3288767	5440363	4700981	11763651
1577174	1654984	321111	10681760	7704846	3294557	7820360	7153410	8146758
1547959	1808602	401967	11920051	8424059	4467997	7334219	7782582	13777314
1547377	1806163	401967	11919840	8417604	4467996	7334219	7782137	13777189
582	2439		211	6455			445	125
151396	86500	24573	705407	763382	167121	476558	453026	1129941
1698773	1892664	426539	12625247	9180986	4635117	7810777	8235163	14907131
55302	67712	26336	867434	117921	41449	222109	139396	596651
376953	416645	32890	4794399	6471166	1209604	4815651	5345049	10775500
1625475	1839379	405746	11641721	9115245	4611233	7291477	8045036	14521617
58299	40348	12594	950384	60148	9428	474278	168137	322804
14999	12936	8200	33143	5592	14455	45022	21990	62709
1381906	1649202	289162	9765851	6312090	4376990	5619414	6264974	7923076
1008	1541	264	11656	13739	4973	8280	11534	13774
449	776	115	4459	4815	1821	2874	3624	4019
858	1461	235	11230	13602	4788	8061	9725	13135
384	735	105	4303	4761	1730	2794	3104	3804

12-2 分经济类型、资质等级建筑业生产情况(2014 年)

指 标	Item	总计 Total
企业单位数(个)	Number of Enterprises	892
# 亏损企业	Nonprofitable Enterprises	28
建筑业企业合同情况(万元)	Contract of Construction Enterprises (10,000Yuan)	
签订的合同额	Signed Contract Amount	92073361
上年结转合同额	Contract Amount Carried Forward from Last Year	42468974
本年新签合同额	Contract Amount Newly Signed this Year	49604387
承包工程完成情况(万元)	Completion of Contracted Project (10,000 Yuan)	
直接从建设单位承揽工程完成的产值	Output by Undertaking Project from Construction Owner Directly	58809383
自行完成施工产值	Output by Completing Construction on Its Own	58799123
分包出去工程的产值	Output by Outsourcing Contruction Project	10260
从建设单位以外承揽工程完成的产值	Output by Undertaking Project From Party other than Construction Owner	4012943
建筑业总产值(万元)	Total Output of Construction Industry (10,000 Yuan)	62812065
# 装饰装修产值	Decoration Output	2196155
# 在外省完成的产值	Output Completed in other Provinces	34994186
建筑工程产值	Output of Construction Project	60363160
安装工程产值	Output of Installation Project	2229266
其他产值	Others	219640
竣工产值(万元)	Output of Completed Buildings (10,000 Yuan)	44401490
房屋建筑施工面积(万平方米)	Contruction Area of the Building (10,000 m²)	68201
# 本年新开工面积	Newly-begun Construction Area of the Year	23438
# 实行投标承包面积	Construction Area by Bidding	64517
# 本年新开工	Newly-begun Construction of the Year	22205

STATISTICS ON CONSTRUCTION INDUSTRIES CATEGORIZED BY ECONOMIC TYPES AND GRADES OF QUALIFICATION(2014)

内资企业 Domestic Enterprises	港、澳、台商投资企业 HK, Macau or Taiwan Invested Enterprises	外商投资企业 Foreign Invested Enterprises	特级 Special Grade	一级 First Grade	二级 Second Grade	三级 Third Grade
881	2	9	15	120	303	454
27		1		1	1	26
91971105	17038	85218	51023008	29296057	8853983	2899018
42392792	5739	70444	26173909	11716975	3567831	1010259
49578313	11300	14774	24849099	17579082	5286152	1888759
58753244	14854	41285	32237453	18858718	5606232	2105685
58742983	14854	41285	32237453	18858705	5603761	2097909
10260				13	2472	7775
3970490	4703	37750	899052	1680111	915969	517725
62713473	19557	79035	33136505	20538816	6519730	2615634
2196155			497292	1472451	131279	95134
34958208	1545	34433	20714587	11696589	1913705	669305
60266455	19557	77148	32692680	18867451	6357845	2443804
2227379		1887	342794	1617575	133531	135366
219640			101031	53790	28354	36465
44308193	20775	72522	21876193	15311213	5282922	1929781
68112	7	81	38314	21419	6369	2098
23419	7	12	12187	8027	2399	825
64434	7	76	37086	20128	5642	1661
22190	7	8	11863	7613	2105	618

12-3 分行业建筑业生产情况(2014年)

指 标	Item	总计 Total
企业单位数(个)	Number of Enterprises	892
#亏损企业	Nonprofitable Enterprises	28
建筑业企业合同情况(万元)	Contract of Construction Enterprises (10,000Yuan)	
签订的合同额	Signed Contract Amount	92073361
上年结转合同额	Contract Amount Carried Forward from Last Year	42468974
本年新签合同额	Contract Amount Newly Signed this Year	49604387
承包工程完成情况(万元)	Completion of Contracted Project (10,000 Yuan)	
直接从建设单位承揽工程完成的产值	Output by Undertaking Project from Construction Owner Directly	58809383
自行完成施工产值	Output by Completing Construction on Its Own	58799123
分包出去工程的产值	Output by Outsourcing Contruction Project	10260
从建设单位以外承揽工程完成的产值	Output by Undertaking Project From Party other than Construction Owner	4012943
建筑业总产值(万元)	Total Output of Construction Industry (10,000 Yuan)	62812065
#装饰装修产值	Decoration Output	2196155
#在外省完成的产值	Output Completed in other Provinces	34994186
建筑工程产值	Output of Construction Project	60363160
安装工程产值	Output of Installation Project	2229266
其他产值	Others	219640
竣工产值(万元)	Output of Completed Buildings (10,000 Yuan)	44401490
房屋建筑施工面积(万平方米)	Contruction Area of the Building (10,000 m²)	682005
#本年新开工面积	Newly-begun Construction Area of the Year	234378
#实行投标承包面积	Construction Area by Bidding	645169
#本年新开工	Newly-begun Construction of the Year	222046

STATISTICS ON CONSTRUCTION BY INDUSTRIES(2014)

房屋建筑业 House Building Industry	土木工程建筑业 Civil Engineering Construction	建筑安装业 Construction and Installation	建筑装饰和其他建筑业 Architectural Ornament and Others
398	203	128	163
6	4	8	10
84568847	3130699	2860428	1513387
40330356	1044450	885396	208772
44238491	2086249	1975032	1304616
53446281	2223592	1961652	1177858
53445535	2217152	1959249	1177186
746	6439	2403	672
2592779	396346	540584	483134
56038313	2613498	2499934	1660321
863369	32863	10341	1289582
32794093	250880	1212636	736577
55352983	2556832	823061	1630284
493111	43104	1667095	25956
192220	13562	9778	4080
39123050	2244803	1667348	1366289
674294	1781	5193	737
231356	633	2390	
638719	1391	4745	315
219193	524	2329	

12-4 分地区建筑业企业产品产量(2014年)

指 标	Item	全市 Municipality	市区 Urban Areas
合计(万平方米)	**Total (10,000 m^2)**	**20199.21**	**5580.45**
住宅房屋	Residential Building	15834.67	3922.46
商业及服务用房屋	Commercial Building and House for Service	762.03	281.91
商厦房屋(批发和零售用房)	Mall Building (for wholesale and retails)	337.62	91.76
宾馆用房屋(住宿用房)	Hotel Building (for accommodation)	133.74	58.17
餐饮用房屋(餐饮用房)	Catering Building (for catering)	103.33	59.33
商务会展用房屋	Building for Commercial Exhibitions	90.18	50.42
其他商业及服务用房屋(居民服务业用房)	Others	97.16	22.23
办公用房屋	Office Building	1001.82	509.73
科研、教育、医疗用房屋	Buildings for Scientific Research, Education and Medical Care	529.27	237.51
科学研究用房屋	Building for Scientific Research	61.49	36.74
教育用房屋	Building for Education	277.95	104.80
医疗用房屋(卫生医疗用房)	Building for Medical Care (Health Care)	189.84	95.97
文化、体育、娱乐用房屋	Building for Culture, Sports and Recreations	95.74	43.57
厂房及建筑物	Workshop and Factory Buildings	1737.25	509.92
厂房	Workshop	1384.02	413.49
仓库	Warehouse	65.56	29.62
其他未列明的房屋建筑物 *	Others	172.90	45.73

PRODUCTION OF CONSTRUCTION ENTERPRISES BY REGIONS(2014)

崇川区 Chongchuan	港闸区 Gangzha	开发区 Developing Zone	通州区 Tongzhou	海安 Hai´an	如东 Rudong	启东 Qidong	如皋 Rugao	海门 Haimen
380.58	**872.71**	**67.53**	**3966.42**	**3916.17**	**1925.70**	**2195.34**	**3719.66**	**2861.89**
259.84	673.10	45.08	2768.30	3387.62	1442.41	1508.67	3048.03	2525.48
5.01	53.12	0.40	210.42	171.72	37.64	95.13	92.26	83.37
4.50	25.46	0.40	60.30	126.46	4.62	51.83	28.15	34.80
	4.88		53.29	26.14	9.75	5.65	26.89	7.16
	10.41		48.92	5.94	10.41	26.37	1.23	0.05
	8.98		41.44	2.40	4.46	4.17	9.35	19.37
0.51	3.39		6.46	10.78	8.41	7.12	26.64	21.99
22.63	56.69	1.71	385.53	92.25	97.59	82.18	149.05	71.02
9.79	20.81	0.00	203.62	81.25	56.52	60.34	73.21	20.45
			34.94	16.71	1.21	0.18	6.02	0.62
6.59	20.03		76.69	42.06	23.17	49.63	52.58	5.71
3.20	0.78		91.99	22.47	32.14	10.53	14.60	14.12
1.96	7.79	1.55	17.90	15.60		9.22	7.18	20.17
81.22	54.59	18.80	312.01	150.37	246.91	373.25	332.86	123.93
39.88	52.59	17.95	265.23	82.44	178.52	312.92	282.26	114.39
	6.58		23.03	2.26	22.02	5.90	4.49	1.27
0.11	0.01		45.61	15.09	22.61	60.66	12.60	16.21

12-5　分经济类型、资质等级建筑业企业产品产量(2014 年)

指　标	Item	总计 Total
合计(万平方米)	**Total (10,000 m2)**	**20199.21**
住宅房屋	Residential Building	15834.67
商业及服务用房屋	Commercial Building and House for Service	762.03
商厦房屋(批发和零售用房)	Mall Building (for wholesale and retails)	337.62
宾馆用房屋(住宿用房)	Hotel Building (for accommodation)	133.74
餐饮用房屋(餐饮用房)	Catering Building (for catering)	103.33
商务会展用房屋	Building for Commercial Exhibitions	90.18
其他商业及服务用房屋(居民服务业用房)	Others	97.16
办公用房屋	Office Building	1001.82
科研、教育、医疗用房屋	Buildings for Scientific Research, Education and Medical Care	529.27
科学研究用房屋	Building for Scientific Research	61.49
教育用房屋	Building for Education	277.95
医疗用房屋(卫生医疗用房)	Building for Medical Care (Health Care)	189.84
文化、体育、娱乐用房屋	Building for Culture, Sports and Recreations	95.74
厂房及建筑物	Workshop and Factory Buildings	1737.25
厂房	Workshop	1384.02
仓库	Warehouse	65.56
其他未列明的房屋建筑物 *	Others	172.90

12-6　分行业建筑业企业产品产量情况(2014 年)

指　标	Item	总计 Total
合计(万平方米)	**Total (10,000 m2)**	**20199.21**
住宅房屋	Residential Building	15834.67
商业及服务用房屋	Commercial Building and House for Service	762.03
商厦房屋(批发和零售用房)	Mall Building (for wholesale and retails)	337.62
宾馆用房屋(住宿用房)	Hotel Building (for accommodation)	133.74
餐饮用房屋(餐饮用房)	Catering Building (for catering)	103.33
商务会展用房屋	Building for Commercial Exhibitions	90.18
其他商业及服务用房屋(居民服务业用房)	Others	97.16
办公用房屋	Office Building	1001.82
科研、教育、医疗用房屋	Buildings for Scientific Research, Education and Medical Care	529.27
科学研究用房屋	Building for Scientific Research	61.49
教育用房屋	Building for Education	277.95
医疗用房屋(卫生医疗用房)	Building for Medical Care (Health Care)	189.84
文化、体育、娱乐用房屋	Building for Culture, Sports and Recreations	95.74
厂房及建筑物	Workshop and Factory Buildings	1737.25
厂房	Workshop	1384.02
仓库	Warehouse	65.56
其他未列明的房屋建筑物 *	Others	172.90

PRODUCTION OF CONSTRUCTION INDUSTRIES CATEGORIZED BY ECONOMIC TYPES AND GRADES OF QUALIFICATION(2014)

内资企业 Domestic Enterprises	港、澳、台商投资企业 HK, Macau or Taiwan Invested Enterprises	外商投资企业 Foreign Invested Enterprises	特级 Special Grade	一级 First Grade	二级 Second Grade	三级 Third Grade
20189.22	**0.35**	**9.64**	**10357.34**	**6947.81**	**2201.95**	**692.11**
15832.20		2.46	7939.73	5735.89	1707.99	451.06
761.97		0.05	501.14	185.95	57.54	17.40
337.62			264.97	56.54	11.61	4.50
133.74			109.02	8.73	14.59	1.40
103.27		0.05	32.97	54.18	8.65	7.53
90.18			47.61	34.73	6.54	1.29
97.16			46.57	31.76	16.15	2.67
1001.25		0.57	670.03	203.72	66.94	61.12
528.65		0.62	349.09	140.90	36.59	2.69
60.87		0.62	53.26	6.40	1.21	0.62
277.95			176.61	82.14	17.18	2.02
189.84			119.22	52.36	18.20	0.05
95.74			65.90	24.22	3.30	2.31
1733.07		4.18	731.72	578.02	297.17	130.33
1379.84		4.18	634.25	464.98	171.00	113.79
65.56			42.12	13.90	3.16	6.37
170.78	0.35	1.77	57.61	65.19	29.26	20.83

PRODUCTION OF CONSTRUCTION ENTERPRISES BY INDUSTRIES(2014)

房屋建筑业 House Building Industry	土木工程建筑业 Civil Engineering Construction	建筑安装业 Construction and Installation	建筑装饰和其他建筑业 Architectural Ornament and Others
19929.11	**93.20**	**156.06**	**20.84**
15639.61	81.50	92.72	20.84
757.00	1.68	3.35	
337.22	0.40		
132.47	1.28		
103.33			
90.18			
93.82		3.35	
988.61	2.92	10.28	
528.49	0.75	0.03	
61.49			
277.20	0.75		
189.81		0.03	
90.14	1.68	3.92	
1696.25	4.33	36.67	
1347.72	3.72	32.58	
60.84		4.72	
168.16	0.35	4.38	

12-7 分地区建筑业出省生产情况(2014年)

单位:万元

指 标	Item	全市 Municipality	市区 Urban Areas
北 京	Beijing	2379.54	675.80
天 津	Tianjin	2167.94	271.15
河 北	Hebei	4923.60	410.46
山 西	Shanxi	1580.03	176.02
内蒙古	Inner Mogolia	1412.58	343.38
辽 宁	Liaoning	2219.35	130.68
吉 林	Jilin	1209.14	268.98
黑龙江	Heilongjiang	1565.50	367.86
上 海	Shanghai	3062.01	744.26
浙 江	Zhejiang	496.17	190.53
安 徽	Anhui	2238.59	639.21
福 建	Fujian	223.22	90.17
江 西	Jiangxi	131.08	52.06
山 东	Shandong	5198.62	576.14
河 南	Henan	623.00	92.93
湖 北	Hubei	591.22	112.33
湖 南	Hunan	239.10	39.50
广 东	Guangdong	748.96	506.83
广 西	Guangxi	245.56	41.93
海 南	Hainan	498.54	137.48
重 庆	Chongqing	92.80	4.58
四 川	Sichuan	340.42	60.51
贵 州	Guizhou	93.74	8.40
云 南	Yunnan	78.01	21.89
西 藏	Xizang	19.22	
陕 西	Shaanxi	890.92	140.94
甘 肃	Gansu	113.58	11.97
青 海	Qinghai	143.97	
宁 夏	Ningxia	319.19	11.51
新 疆	Xinjiang	1148.60	249.70

CONSTRUCTION IN OTHER PROVINCES BY REGIONS(2014)

(10000 yuan)

崇川区 Chongchuan	港闸区 Gangzha	开发区 Developing Zone	通州区 Tongzhou	海安 Haian	如东 Rudong	启东 Qidong	如皋 Rugao	海门 Haimen
147.28	22.40	0.07	506.05	242.97	17.99	297.83	54.43	1090.51
38.65		0.43	232.08	329.53	84.22	445.75	42.14	995.15
120.33	17.60		272.53	1682.53	28.22	423.95	958.49	1419.95
2.50	11.82	0.74	160.96	86.05		149.89	1087.15	80.92
68.57	88.95	1.47	184.39	604.57	9.71	61.61	221.39	171.93
7.43	2.15	0.63	120.47	499.31	146.26	592.80	178.70	671.59
11.92			257.06	106.41	0.14	143.54	690.06	
49.89			317.97	435.12	11.96	131.50	414.88	204.18
192.42	9.78	4.88	537.19	311.51	383.53	454.98	62.18	1105.54
11.70	5.00	0.55	173.28	0.00	23.26	141.79	55.32	85.28
127.98	35.24	8.18	467.82	374.35	95.91	379.57	377.16	372.39
5.96	33.03		51.19	0.95	0.15	33.27	54.27	44.41
1.31	2.37		48.37	0.90	0.20	35.37	34.80	7.75
28.77	54.22	18.34	474.80	516.95	143.27	672.85	594.40	2695.03
34.14	4.05	0.50	54.25	230.53	8.29	35.70	82.51	173.04
8.87	73.95		29.51	12.18	89.37	70.89	132.76	173.70
33.21	0.06		6.23	11.88	23.99	9.11		154.62
74.21	42.72	3.80	386.10	0.25	47.53	27.98	18.88	147.49
4.78	0.15		37.00	1.63	2.18	1.42	1.37	197.04
74.06		0.83	62.58	54.74	5.48	53.18	5.35	242.31
1.59			2.99	46.20		7.46	3.93	30.62
16.90	3.31		40.30	51.87	3.87	53.10	66.91	104.16
8.40				10.44		40.78	1.30	32.82
0.88			21.02	21.48		13.23	14.53	6.88
						19.22		
8.35	3.10		129.50	160.64	48.30	47.57	30.17	463.29
1.10			10.87	14.63		69.62	8.19	9.17
				4.04		98.80		41.14
0.12			11.39	183.61		81.30	6.87	35.91
35.14	14.13	1.87	198.56	475.90	35.78	221.60	146.93	18.68

12-8 分经济类型、资质等级劳务分包建筑企业生产经营情况(2014 年)

单位:万元

指 标	Item
产值情况	Output Value Completed
建筑业总产值	Total Output Value of the Construction Industry
装饰装修产值	Of which: the Output of Decoration
财务状况	Financial Status
本年折旧	Depreciation of the Year
营业收入	Operating Revenue
主营业务收入	Main Business Income
营业成本	Operating Costs
主营业务成本	Main Business Cost
营业税金及附加	Business Tax and Surcharges
主营业务税金及附加	Main Business Tax and Surcharges
销售费用	Selling Expense
管理费用	Management Expense
管理费用中的税金	Taxes of Management Expense
财务费用	Financial Expense
营业利润	Operating Profits
利润总额	Total Profits
本年应付职工薪酬	Payable Staff Salary of the Year

PRODUCTION AND OPERATION OF LABOR-OUTSOURCING CONSTRUCTION ENTERPRISES CATEGORIZED BY ECONOMIC TYPES AND GRADES OF QUALIFICATION(2014)

(10000 yuan)

总计 Total	内资企业 Domestic Enterprises	一级 First Grade	二级 Second Grade	其他 Others
548241	548241	543960	1230	3051
27664	27664	26223	248	1193
6442	6442	6384	15	42
519213	519213	515025	1121	3068
518696	518696	514514	1121	3061
478703	478703	475367	931	2405
476559	476559	473230	931	2398
15453	15453	15272	43	138
15296	15296	15121	43	132
220	220	207	13	
9703	9703	9341	63	300
465	465	441		24
672	672	666	-1	7
15608	15608	15289	88	231
15231	15231	14924	88	219
271597	271597	269586	759	1252

12-9　分地区劳务分包建筑企业生产经营情况(2014年)

单位：万元

指　标	Item
产值情况	Output Value Completed
建筑业总产值	Total Output Value of the Construction Industry
装饰装修产值	Of which: the Output of Decoration
财务状况	Financial Status
本年折旧	Depreciation of the Year
营业收入	Operating Revenue
主营业务收入	Main Business Income
营业成本	Operating Costs
主营业务成本	Main Business Cost
营业税金及附加	Business Tax and Surcharges
主营业务税金及附加	Main Business Tax and Surcharges
销售费用	Selling Expense
管理费用	Management Expense
管理费用中的税金	Taxes of Management Expense
财务费用	Financial Expense
营业利润	Operating Profits
利润总额	Total Profits
本年应付职工薪酬	Payable Staff Salary of the Year

PRODUCTION AND OPERATION OF LABOR-OUTSOURCING CONSTRUCTION ENTERPRISES BY REGIONS(2014)

(10000 yuan)

全市 Municipality	市区 Urban Areas	崇川区 Chongchuan	港闸区 Gangzha	通州区 Tongzhou	海安 Haian	如东 Rudong	启东 Qidong	如皋 Rugao	海门 Haimen
548241	155543		6256	80588	176555	11695	14384	52447	137617
27664	6273		682	5591	14653	67	6301	168	203
6442	211		44	79	445	58	143	363	5222
519213	153816		6256	78861	160404	11313	14384	49932	129363
518696	153621		6253	78854	160404	11309	14384	49932	129045
478703	143326		5658	73117	151126	10217	12669	42917	118448
476559	143317		5657	73109	151126	10202	12669	42817	116428
15453	5288		225	2727	4573	401	552	1795	2845
15296	5282		225	2721	4573	401	552	1795	2693
220	65			54	8			89	57
9703	1604		245	1009	2658	347	509	2874	1711
465	132		5	37	18	2	22	64	227
672	45		2	39	32	2	5	102	487
15608	3319		148	1949	2917	320	649	2386	6018
15231	3283		131	2000	2828	306	649	2264	5902
271597	104806		2479	36503	76732	8594	10347	19145	51974

12–10　建筑业企业资产排名 50 强

TOP 50 CONSTRUCTION ENTERPRISES OF ASSETS

序号 No.	企业名称 Names of the Enterprises	序号 No.	企业名称 Names of the Enterprises
1	江苏中南建筑产业集团有限责任公司	26	江苏中信建设集团有限公司
2	江苏南通二建集团有限公司	27	南通启益建设集团有限公司
3	江苏南通三建集团有限公司	28	江苏信拓建设(集团)股份有限公司
4	江苏省苏中建设集团股份有限公司	29	南通市裕成建设有限公司
5	龙信建设集团有限公司	30	江苏海宏建设工程有限公司
6	南通四建集团有限公司	31	苏通建设集团有限公司
7	启东建筑集团有限公司	32	南通市常青建筑安装工程有限公司
8	南通五建宏业建设工程有限公司	33	江苏新龙兴建设发展有限公司
9	江苏南通六建建设集团有限公司	34	江苏弘霖建设集团有限公司
10	江苏南通三建集团第三建筑安装工程有限公司	35	南通通宇建设工程有限公司
11	中联世纪建设集团有限公司	36	南通华荣建设集团有限公司
12	南通海洲建设集团有限公司	37	南通通明投资实业有限公司
13	南通新华建筑集团有限公司	38	江苏隆辉建设股份有限公司
14	南通建工集团股份有限公司	39	南通市戴庄建筑安装工程有限公司
15	南通五建建设工程有限公司	40	南通市金磊建设工程有限责任公司
16	南通华新建工集团有限公司	41	万通建设集团有限公司
17	南通市达欣工程股份有限公司	42	江苏通州四建集团有限公司
18	江苏江中集团有限公司	43	南通长城建筑安装工程有限公司
19	江苏启安建设集团有限公司	44	南通市通盛建筑安装工程有限公司
20	江苏顺通建设集团有限公司	45	江苏巨业建设集团有限公司
21	通州建总集团有限公司	46	南通一建集团有限公司
22	江苏润宇建设有限公司	47	江苏辉业集团有限公司
23	南通路桥工程有限公司	48	南通卓强建设工程有限公司
24	南通英雄建设集团有限公司	49	江苏华东工业设备安装股份有限公司
25	江苏宏景集团有限公司	50	江苏昌盛建设集团有限公司

12-11 建筑业企业总产值排名50强

TOP 50 CONSTRUCTION ENTERPRISES OF TOTAL OUTPUT VALUE

序号 No.	企业名称 Names of the Enterprises	序号 No.	企业名称 Names of the Enterprises
1	江苏南通三建集团有限公司	26	南通华荣建设集团有限公司
2	江苏南通二建集团有限公司	27	南通市达欣工程股份有限公司
3	江苏省苏中建设集团股份有限公司	28	江苏信拓建设(集团)股份有限公司
4	南通四建集团有限公司	29	南通海洲建设集团有限公司
5	江苏南通六建建设集团有限公司	30	南通苏中建设有限公司
6	通州建总集团有限公司	31	南通永峰建筑安装工程有限公司
7	龙信建设集团有限公司	32	江苏新龙兴建设发展有限公司
8	江苏江中集团有限公司	33	南通八建集团有限公司
9	南通五建建设工程有限公司	34	江苏弘霖建设集团有限公司
10	南通华新建工集团有限公司	35	江苏华东工业设备安装股份有限公司
11	江苏中信建设集团有限公司	36	南通大辰建设集团股份有限公司
12	南通新华建筑集团有限公司	37	江苏巨业建设集团有限公司
13	南通建工集团股份有限公司	38	江苏宏景集团有限公司
14	江苏顺通建设集团有限公司	39	江苏昌盛建设集团有限公司
15	南通建工集团股份有限公司	40	南通四建装饰工程有限公司
16	启东建筑集团有限公司	41	南通扬子设备安装有限公司
17	南通英雄建设集团有限公司	42	南通华鼎建设工程有限公司
18	南通长城建筑安装工程有限公司	43	江苏润宇建设有限公司
19	南通卓强建设工程有限公司	44	江苏金轮装饰集团股份有限公司
20	江苏通州二建建设工程有限公司	45	江苏竑成建设集团有限公司
21	江苏通州四建集团有限公司	46	南通市常青建筑安装工程有限公司
22	江苏启安建设集团有限公司	47	南通一建集团有限公司
23	苏通建设有限公司	48	南通市裕成建设有限公司
24	中联世纪建设集团有限公司	49	江苏南通三建集团第三建筑安装工程有限公司
25	南通启益建设集团有限公司	50	江苏紫浪装饰装潢有限公司

主要统计指标解释

建筑业总产值　建筑业总产值是以货币表现的建筑安装企业在一定时期内生产的建筑业产品的总和。建筑业总产值包括三部分内容：

① 建筑工程产值：指列入建筑工程预算内的各种工程价值。

② 设备安装工程产值：指设备安装工程价值。

③ 其他产值：包括房层构筑物修理产值、非标准设备制造产值、总包企业向分包企业收取的管理费以及不能明确划分的施工活动所完成的产值。

竣工产值　指在报告期内，按照设计所规定的工程内容全部完成，达到了设计规定的交工条件，经有关部门检查验收鉴定合格的单位工程价值之和。

房屋建筑施工面积　指在报告期内施工的全部房层建筑面积。包括本期内新开工的；上期施工跨入本期继续施工、上期停建本期复工的房屋建筑面积；不包括上期开工后又停工，本期未施工的房层建筑面积。

房屋建筑竣工面积　指在报告期内，按照设计所规定的工程内容全部完成，达到了设计规定的交工条件，经有关部门检查验收鉴定合格的房屋建筑面积。

住宅竣工面积　指房层建筑竣工面积中供居住用的房层建筑竣工面积。

自有机械设备年末总台数　指归本企业（或单位）所有，属于本企业固定资产的生产性机械设备年末总台数。包括施工机械、生产设备、运输设备以及其他设备。

自有机械设备年末总功率　指本企业（或单位）自有施工机构、生产设备、运输设备以及其他设备等列为在册固定资产的生产性机械设备年末总功率、按设定能力或查定能力计算。包括机械本身的动力和为该机械服务的单独动力设备，如电动机等。计量单位用千瓦，动力换算可按 1 马力=0.735 千瓦折合成千瓦数。电焊、变压器、锅炉不计算动力。

工程结算收入　指企业（或单位）按工程的分部分项自行完成的建筑产品价值并已与甲方在报告期内办理结算手续的工程价款收入，以及向甲方收取的除工程价款以外的按规定列作营业收入的各种款项，如临时施费、劳动保险费、施工机械调迁费等以及向甲方收取的各种索赔款。

工程结算利润　指已结算工程实现的利润。如亏损以"—"号表示。

计算公式为：工程结算利润=工程结算收入-工程结算成本-工程结算税金及附加

劳务收入　指劳务分包企业与总承包企业或专业承包企业签定劳务合同后，按照合同规定应收取的各项收入。

第十三篇 交通 邮电

Chapter 13 Transportaion and Post

13-1 全社会车辆拥有量(2014年)

CIVIL MOTOR VEHICLES(2014)

单位:辆 (coach)

指 标	Item	机动车保有量 Motor Vehicles				其中:营运 of which:in Operation			
		总计 Total	# 进口 Import	# 个人 Private	# 新注册 New Registrition	合计 Total	# 公路 Highway	# 公交 Public Traffic	# 货运 Freight Transports
年末车辆数	**Motor Vehicles at the end of the Year**	**1949486**	**37714**	**1816068**	**196049**	**65880**	**1172**	**2249**	**52964**
汽车	Total Vehicles	996593	37593	869429	173109	57673	1131	2239	45908
1.载客汽车	Passenger Vehicles	918370	37444	832403	161342	9574	1131	2239	
大型	Large Scale	4812	75	12	806	3423	1129	2106	
中型	Medium Scale	5771	194	3025	262	159	2	133	
小型	Small Scale	893893	36150	816037	159751	5992			
微型	Mini Scale	13894	1025	13329	523				
2.载货汽车	Trucks	70943	136	33349	10757	45885			43701
重型	Heavy Scale	24114	93	8508	3603	20206			18377
中型	Medium Scale	11016	2	4552	1207	7198			6908
轻型	Light Scale	35781	41	20267	5947	18462			18397
微型	Mini Scale	32		22		19			19
摩托车	Motorcycles	947951	120	945600	22351				
普通	Ordinary Motors	925170	120	922821	22074				
轻便	Light Motors	22781		22779	277				

13-2　公路、航道基本情况(2014 年)

指　标	Item	全市 Total
公路总里程(公里)	**Highway Total Distance(km)**	**18094**
按等级分	Grouped by Grades	
高速	High Speed	298
一级	First Grade	1336
二级	Second Grade	1461
三级	Third Grade	1642
四级	Fourth Grade	13294
等外	Substandard	63
按行政等级分	Grouped by Administrative Standards	
国道	National Road	585
省道	Provincial Road	618
县道	County Road	2298
乡道	Township Road	5514
专用公路	Accomodation Highway	2
村道	Village Road	9077
按路面标准分	Grouped by Road Surface Standards	
高级	High Level	18031
其它	Others	63
公路桥梁(座)	**Highway Bridge**	**7954**
公路桥梁长度(米)	Total Length (meter)	314099
内河航道总里程(公里)	**Inland Waterway Total Distance (km)**	**3522**
# 水深 1 米以上里程	With Depth of More Than 1 meter	3260
船闸(座)	**Navigation Lock**	**14**
# 交通部门管理	Administered by Transportation Department	5

HIGHWAY AND WATERWAY(2014)

市区 Urban Area	通州区 Tongzhou	海安 Haian	如东 Rudong	启东 Qidong	如皋 Rugao	海门 Haimen
3922	**3432**	**2355**	**2534**	**3576**	**3219**	**2488**
103	66	42		40	72	40
236	114	203	202	233	180	282
393	348	236	224	144	311	154
274	216	240	274	301	338	215
2903	2679	1613	1829	2847	2318	1784
13	10	21	4	10		14
131	77	115	76	102	107	54
186	134	30	128	97	80	97
470	370	321	386	377	435	309
1011	898	887	933	954	903	825
2						
2121	1954	1002	1011	2045	1695	1203
3909	3423	2334	2529	3566	3219	2474
13	10	21	4	10		14
1544	**1363**	**1627**	**1352**	**1310**	**1012**	**1109**
73683	48688	64625	45492	38459	56280	35561
717	**570**	**574**	**779**	**649**	**455**	**348**
541	441	574	701	647	455	343
6		**3**		**1**	**2**	**2**
2		1		1	1	

13-3 历年客运量

PASSENGER TRAFFIC OVER THE YEARS

单位：万人、万人公里 (Unit: 10,000 people, 10,000 people km)

年份 Year	总计 Total	铁路 Railway	公路 Highway	水运 Waterway	航空 Aviation
1985	4387		3947	440	
1990	4355		4115	240	
1991	4795		4529	266	
1992	4901		4612	289	
1993	7001		6732	269	1.8
1994	5447		5231	216	9.0
1995	8303		8090	213	12.5
1996	6506		6381	125	14.5
1997	6390		6317	73	12.6
1998	6813		6770	43	9.8
1999	7000		6954	46	8.8
2000	7654		7628	26	8.7
2001	7912		7886	26	7.4
2002	7940		7936	4	6.9
2003	8059		8050	3	6.4
2004	8860	34	8815	3	8.2
2005	9319	88	9220	3	8.4
2006	10092	103	9978		11.3
2007	11719	207	11495		16.8
2008	13672	267	13389		16.1
2009	14099	253	13824		22.0
2010	16715	263	16425		27.1
2011	19851	221	19605		25.0
2012	21621	232	21350		38.6
2013	22421	235	22119		67.6
2014	10345	253	9998		93.2

13–4 历年货运量

FREIGHT TRAFFIC OVER THE YEARS

单位：万吨、万吨公里 (Unit: 10,000 tons, 10,000 ton km)

年份 Year	总计 Total	铁路 Railway	公路 Highway	水运 Waterway	航空 Aviation
1985	3393		1150	2243	
1990	2601		1180	1421	
1991	2451		1151	1300	
1992	2794		1320	1474	
1993	4755		3354	1401	0.02
1994	5364		4020	1344	0.14
1995	5836		4417	1419	0.20
1996	6113		4312	1801	0.22
1997	5788		4078	1710	0.21
1998	5260		3899	1361	0.15
1999	6349		5093	1256	0.15
2000	6678		5314	1364	0.18
2001	7019		5643	1376	0.15
2002	7073		5728	1345	0.13
2003	7293		5885	1408	0.11
2004	7859	26	6296	1537	0.13
2005	8650	23	6957	1670	0.16
2006	10574	34	8670	1870	0.21
2007	12027	69	9823	2132	0.27
2008	12307	110	10099	2098	0.15
2009	15942	106	12336	3500	0.31
2010	20301	92	15392	4817	0.59
2011	24213	115	18181	5917	0.77
2012	26815	94	20199	6521	1.32
2013	30347	87	22782	7476	2.46
2014	18558	91	11279	7185	3.19

注：2014 年交通部门调整旅客、货物运输量口径。

13-5 全行业客货运输量(2014年)

TOTAL PASSENGER TRAFFIC(2014)

指 标	Item	公路运输 Highway Transport				水路运输 Waterway Transport	
		旅客运输量（万人）Passenger Traffic (10,000 people)	旅客周转量（万人公里）Passenger Turnover (10,000 people km)	货物运输量（万吨）Freight Volume (10,000 tons)	货物周转量（万吨公里）Freight Turnover (10,000 ton km)	货物运输量（万吨）Freight Volume (10,000 tons)	货物周转量（万吨公里）Freight Turnover (10,000 ton km)
全市	**Total**	**9998**	**703594**	**11279**	**1687202**	**7185**	**5020328**
市区	Urban Area	6702	470388	5320	796410	5267	4587776
#通州区	Tongzhou	1260	88401	964	143229	187	39856
海安	Haian	841	59411	1830	272595	645	144864
如东	Rudong	418	30013	1121	166573	325	71612
启东	Qidong	891	62272	816	123226	172	39557
如皋	Rugao	441	31389	1552	232279	761	173611
海门	Haimen	705	50121	640	96119	15	2908

13-6 历年南通港吞吐量

VOLUME OF CARGO HANDLED OF NANTONG PORT OVER THE YEARS

年份 Year	货物吞吐量 (万吨) Freight (10000 tons)		集装箱吞吐量 (标箱) Container Throughput (TEU)
		外贸吞吐量 Foreign Trade Throughput	
1978	301.6		
1979	285.1		
1980	293.4		
1985	1013.2	171.0	2566
1990	1042.7	145.8	10915
1991	1060.6	181.8	20009
1992	1246.1	284.4	30046
1993	1326.7	289.3	46534
1994	1487.8	236.8	65899
1995	1609.6	276.4	87179
1996	1711.2	319.9	93077
1997	1910.0	344.0	121591
1998	2017.1	363.8	130326
1999	2277.3	370.6	158131
2000	2747.8	490.8	182441
2001	3510.8	418.0	183546
2002	3746.4	404.2	205097
2003	5009.9	490.5	246588
2004	7218.2	694.2	287382
2005	8326.9	776.1	301156
2006	10386.2	966.1	360730
2007	12339.0	1882.3	428046
2008	13214.4	2439.5	443328
2009	13641.4	2860.0	350579
2010	15069.8	2961.2	462322
2011	17330.6	3114.0	539812
2012	18526.4	3867.3	504306
2013	20494.5	4056.2	600559
2014	22019.4	4813.6	711043

13-7 南通港基本情况(2014 年)

BASIC CONDITIONS OF NANTONG PORT(2014)

指 标	Item	数值 Number	指 标	Item	数值 Number
一、码头泊位	Quay Berth		3.堆场(万平方米)	Yard (10,000 m²)	208.7
1.生产用码头	For Production		(万吨)	(10,000 tons)	891.3
总延长(米)	Total Length (m)	17540	# 煤场(万平方米)	Coal Yard (10,000 m²)	36.1
泊位(个)	Berths	99	(万吨)	(10,000 tons)	125.6
# 万吨级	10,000 ton Class	51	三、工作船(艘)	Working Ship (set)	32
2.非生产用码头	Not for Production		拖轮	Tugboat	22
总延长(米)	Total Length (m)	555	供应船	Supply Ship	2
泊位(个)	Berths	6	交通船	Accomodation Ship	4
3.浮筒泊位(个)	Buoy Berth	10	驳船	Barge	4
# 万吨级	10,000 ton Class	5	四、装卸机械(台)	Loading &Unloading Machine (set)	934
二、仓库堆场	Storage Yard		起重机械(台)	Hoisting Machinery (set)	311
1.仓库(万平方米)	Warehouse (10,000 m²)	37.2	输送机械(台)	Conveying Machinery(set)	225
2.仓库(万立方米)	Warehouse (10,000 m³)	401.7	(米)	(m)	92351
			装卸搬运机械(台)	Handling Machineries (set)	248
			专用机械(台)	Special-purpose Machinery (set)	150

13-8 南通港集装箱吞吐量(2014)

VOLUME OF CONTAINER HANDLED OF NANTONG PORT(2014)

单位:万标箱 (TEU)

指 标	Item	合计 Total	进港 In-Port	出港 Out-Port
合 计	**Total**	**71.10**	**24.91**	**46.20**
1.国际航线	International Airline	1.13	0.24	0.90
# 韩国	Korea	0.00	0.00	0.00
日本	Japan	0.68	0.16	0.53
2.内支线	Feeder Line	30.51	14.68	15.83
# 上海	Shanghai	28.06	13.57	14.49
3.国内航线	Domestic Airline	39.47	10.00	29.47
# 上海	Shanghai	26.13	2.92	23.21
南京	Nanjing	0.14	0.02	0.12
苏州	Suzhou	4.71	0.69	4.02
宁波	Ningbo	0.31	0.01	0.30
广州	Guangzhou	2.91	2.90	0.00

13-9 南通港货物吞吐量(2014年)

VOLUME OF CARGO HANDLED OF NANTONG PORT(2014)

单位:万吨 (10000 tons)

指 标	Item	总计 Total	按进出港分 Grouped by In-and-out Port		按内外贸分 Grouped by Foreign-and-Domestic Trade	
			进港 In-Port	出港 Out-Port	外贸 Foreign Trade	内贸 Domestic Trade
总 计	**Total**	**12889.3**	**8710.1**		**4813.6**	**16785.8**
1.煤炭	Coal	3561.7	1686.0		415.0	4832.6
2.石油	Oil	883.8	389.8		407.8	865.9
3.金属矿石	Metallic Mineral	3077.7	3056.0		2149.2	3984.4
4.钢铁	Steel	176.2	100.4		93.0	183.6
5.矿建材料	Mine Construction Materials	2366.7	1260.9			3627.6
6.水泥	Cement	762.6	385.6		385.6	762.6
7.木材	Wood	25.6	0.9		24.9	1.5
8.非金属矿石	Non-metallic Mineral	269.9	255.9		224.3	301.4
9.化肥和农药	Fertilizer and Pesticide	116.6	153.6		132.5	137.8
10.盐	Salt	27.4	4.9		3.6	28.6
11.粮食	Grain	599.5	281.5		431.3	449.7
12.机械电器设备	Machinery and Electric Equipments	13.4	16.0		18.0	11.4
13.化工原料及制品	Chemical Raw Material and Products	210.7	124.5		142.4	192.8
15.轻工医药产品	Light Industry Pharmaceutical Products	10.6	4.5		8.0	7.2
16.农林牧渔产品	Agriculture, Forestry, Husbandry and Fishery Products	24.1	69.3		29.3	64.1
17.其他	Others	762.9	920.2		348.7	1334.4

13-10　邮电通讯业基本情况(2014年)

指 标	Item	全市 Total
邮政局 (处)	Number of Post&Telecommunications Offices(unit)	312
邮电业务收入(万元)	Business Volume of Post&Telecommunications (10000 yuan)	761720
#函件 (万件)	Letters(10000 pcs)	3341
机要文件(万件)	Confidentials (10000 pcs)	3.48
包件 (万件)	Pieces of Courier Services (10000 pcs)	7.28
特快专递(万件)	Special Express (10000 pcs)	33.59
汇票 (万张)	Bill of Exchange (10000 pcs)	69.58
报纸累计份数(万份)	Newspapers Circulation(10000 pcs)	15990
杂志累计份数 (万份)	Magzines Circulation(10000 copies)	860.04
邮政储蓄余额 (亿元)	Savings Balance (100 million yuan)	528.31
集邮 (万枚)	Philately (10000 pcs)	357.20
邮路长度(公里)	Length of Postal Routes(km)	5472
农村投递线路(公里)	Length of Rural Delivery Routes(km)	42782
长途电话通话量(万分钟)	Long Distance Telephone Calls(10,000 minutes)	53949
移动短信业务量(亿条)	Mobile SMS Traffic(100 million)	34.37
年末固定电话用户 (万户)	Year-end Number of Fixed Phone Users(10,000 households)	256.13
#城市	Urban Area	134.88
乡村	Rural Area	121.25
#住宅电话用户 (万户)	Home Phone Users(10,000 Households)	156.48
城市	Urban Area	69.63
乡村	Rural Area	86.85
年末移动电话用户(万户)	Year-end Number of Mobile Phone Users(10,000 households)	864.00
固定宽带接入用户(万户)	Fixed Borad Band Users	182.97
局用电话交换机容量(万门)	Capacity of Office Telephone Exchanges(10,000 line)	248.63
移动电话交换机容量(万门)	Capacity of Mobile Phone Exchanges(10,000 line)	942.80

POSTS AND TELECOMMUNICATIONS(2014)

市区 Urban Area	通州区 Tongzhou	海安 Haian	如东 Rudong	启东 Qidong	如皋 Rugao	海门 Haimen
75	47	45	47	50	57	38
315970	111905	74784	76881	101573	105940	86572
2120	136	140	135	140	634	172
2.83	0.07	0.08	0.09	0.15	0.16	0.10
3.42	0.99	0.44	0.37	1.02	0.63	1.40
13.50	4.57	4.97	3.16	3.80	4.28	3.88
20.34	8.97	8.42	8.68	5.93	15.81	10.40
4683	1420	1938	2302	1830	2409	2828
364.29	89.24	59.48	99.63	100.39	134.49	101.76
126.07	85.05	70.84	78.59	72.55	111.32	68.94
170.90	37.96	33.18	28.50	31.71	57.49	35.44
1975	670	674	902	664	737	520
8012	5848	5204	5919	7720	9242	6685
25947	7050	4968	3391	6515	5560	7568
15.60	4.48	3.66	3.24	3.75	4.53	3.59
87.19	35.59	34.09	28.25	36.12	36.56	33.93
64.90	17.05	13.84	11.54	15.66	14.24	15.52
22.29	18.54	20.26	16.71	20.46	22.32	18.41
30.27	27.89	24.08	21.83	27.00	27.86	25.44
27.18	8.88	8.19	6.92	8.84	9.47	9.04
3.09	19.01	15.89	14.91	18.16	18.39	16.40
387.83	113.35	87.67	86.91	113.72	105.30	82.58
69.42	24.86	21.86	19.71	23.10	30.73	18.16
99.82	27.78	27.50	24.77	33.84	33.02	29.68
357.20	135.20	109.00	117.00	126.00	116.60	117.00

主要统计指标解释

公路里程 指一定时期内实际达到《公路工程技术标准 JTJ01—88》规定的等级公路，并经公路主管部门正式验收交付使用的公路里程数。其计算单位为 km。它包括大中城市的郊区公路以及通过小城镇街道部分的公里里程，也包括桥梁、渡口的长度，但不包括大中城市的街道、厂矿、林区生产用道和农业生产用道的里程。两条或多条公路共同经由同一路段，只计算一次，不得重复计算里程长度，公路里程是反映公路建设发展规模的重要指标，也是计算运输网密度等指标的基础资料。

内河航道里程 也称"内河通航里程"，是反映内河水运网规模、水平和发展情况的主要指标，是指在一定时期内，能通航运输船舶及排筏的天然河流、湖泊水库、运河及通航渠道的长度。包括全年季节性通航累计三个月以上的航道，但不包括仅供零散流放竹、木排的河道。

货(客)运量 指在一定时期内，各运输部门实际运送的货物(旅客)数量。是反映运输业为国民经济和人民生活服务的数量指标，也是制定和检查运输生产计划，研究运输发展规模和速度的重要指标。货运按吨计算，客运按人计算。货物不论运输距离长短，货物类别，均按实际重量统计；旅客不论行程远近或票价多少，均按一人一次作为客运量统计。半价票、小孩票也按一人统计。

货物(旅客)周转量 指在一定时期内，由各种运输工具运送的货物(旅客)数量与其相应运输距离的乘积之总和，是反映运输业生产总成果的重要指标，也是编制和检查运输生产计划，计算运输效率、劳动生产率以及核算运输单位成本的主要基础资料。通常以吨公里和人公里为计算单位、计算货物周转量通常接发出站与到达站之间最短距离，也就是计验距离计算。

邮电业务总量 指以货币表现的邮电部门用于传递信息和提供其他邮电服务的总数量。它综合反映了一定时期邮电工作的总成果，是研究邮电业务量构成和发展趋势的重要指标。根据邮电管理体制不同，分为中央国营业务总量和地方国营业务总量。它用各种邮电分类业务量，如函件件数、电报价数、长话次数、市内电话和农村电话的年均户数、订销报刊累计份数等，分别乘以相应的平均单价(不变价)，加总后再加上出租电路和设备的收入、代用户维护电话交换机和线路等设备的收入、其他业务收人求得。

移动电话用户 指在邮电部门登记，通过移动电话交换机进入移动电话网，占有移动电话号码的电话用户。用户数量以实际办理登记手续进入邮电部门移动电话网的户数进行计算，一部或一台移动电话统计为一户。

第十四篇 国内贸易

Chapter 14

Domestic Trade

14-1 主要年份社会消费品零售总额

TOTAL RETAIL PRICE OF CONSUMMER GOODS OVER THE YEARS

单位:万元 (10,000 Yuan)

年份 Year	全市 Whole Municipality	市区 Urban Area	通州区 Tongzhou	海安 Haian	如东 Rudong	启东 Qidong	如皋 Rugao	海门 Haimen
1952	19101	7010	2699	1354	2259	3029	2657	2792
1957	27901	9259	5112	2835	3767	4175	3883	3982
1962	34241	12057	5946	3767	4432	4824	4946	4215
1965	47545	15270	8417	4977	6234	7859	6650	6555
1970	50429	16234	9019	5523	6823	8025	7845	5979
1975	72564	23794	12913	7916	9230	11433	10931	9260
1978	81894	27517	14818	9376	10509	11920	11890	10682
1980	135585	44255	24132	14940	17470	20879	19857	18184
1985	258575	86372	40854	30750	32553	41509	36036	31355
1986	313344	100563	46989	38919	42053	49549	44315	37945
1987	366587	117377	54957	46772	47295	58385	52702	44056
1988	487339	159347	71193	63583	59665	74780	71197	58767
1989	523965	174503	77117	66957	68194	80033	72864	61414
1990	524540	174629	79490	65107	72587	76507	72029	63681
1991	574653	198331	88434	70259	78406	80402	76540	70715
1992	697964	246324	111202	80705	96297	96270	92337	86031
1993	919992	324609	139568	112823	107690	144593	121924	108353
1994	1283075	453369	180332	145374	155237	224417	161736	142942
1995	1714933	641792	252812	181441	205297	259770	198375	228258
1996	1945178	744243	295748	175189	227606	282110	240489	275541
1997	2047931	767140	309490	177763	235893	313315	243724	310096
1998	2133735	809119	331591	172169	244227	330164	247169	330887
1999	2298177	887585	360405	180243	259612	355005	259010	356722
2000	2501140	983732	388186	194408	276486	384550	275786	386178
2001	2709821	1057738	362035	211841	303536	419013	294511	423182
2002	2971353	1139748	402187	235187	334472	460600	330726	470620
2003	3312757	1281049	450609	264398	368012	502690	373554	523054
2004	4615444	1698475	643990	479902	542442	625600	618325	650700
2005	5374082	1978688	750900	562002	631950	725800	723442	752200
2006	6242708	2303379	872053	652891	733911	841636	839813	871078
2007	7406381	2778344	1028266	767369	861773	988291	986062	1024542
2008	9219000	3445704	1294188	963768	1075141	1228932	1237310	1268145
2009	10804538	4027693	1513823	1137317	1266847	1439374	1450034	1483273
2010	12763399	4770795	1782952	1341526	1493084	1696449	1711883	1749662
2011	14975547	5638700	2084760	1570008	1745783	1985277	1986459	2049320
2012	17218115	6419478	2371813	1819796	2021796	2287279	2298544	2371222
2013	19383381	7701049	2499371	1969203	2302580	2380768	2505869	2523911
2014	21660973	8566028	2798796	2219489	2578890	2664104	2807701	2824761

14–2 分地区社会消费品零售总额(2014 年)

单位:万元

指 标	Item	全市 Whole Municipality	市区 Urban Area
社会消费品零售总额	Total Retail of Consuming Goods	21660973	8566028
按地区分	Grouped By Region		
城镇	Cities and Towns	15884812	7254320
# 城区	Urban Area	12166388	6616151
乡村	Coutryside	5776161	1311708
按行业分	Grouped By Sector		
批发零售贸易业	Wholesale and Retail Sales	19828834	7928355
批发业	Wholesale	2816805	1182401
零售业	Retail Sales	17012029	6745954
住宿餐饮业	Accommodation and Catering Industry	1832139	637673
住宿业	Accommodation Industry	97470	41336
餐饮业	Catering Industry	1734669	596337

14–3 分地区批发零售业、住宿餐饮业经营情况(2014 年)

单位:万元

指 标	Item	全市 Whole Municipality	市区 Urban Area
一、批发零售业销售总额	Total Sales of Consuming Goods	79311771	37810637
批发业销售总额	Total Wholesales	55267785	27095408
零售业销售总额	Total Retail Sales	24043986	10715229
二、住宿餐饮业营业额	Turnover of Accommodation and Catering	2260041	797816
住宿业营业额	Turnover of Accommodation	268021	107810
餐饮业营业额	Turnover of Catering	1992020	690007

TOTAL RETAIL SALES OF CONSUMMER GOODS BY REGION(2014)

(10,000 Yuan)

崇川区 Chongchuan District	港闸区 Gangzha District	开发区 Developing Zone	通州区 Tongzhou District	海安 Haian	如东 Rudong	启东 Qidong	如皋 Rugao	海门 Haimen
3346423	1119115	1301695	2798796	2219489	2578890	2664104	2807701	2824761
3346423	834235	1171525	1902137	1467438	1642082	1817137	1802073	1901762
3346423	834042	1171525	1264161	877653	887959	1289238	1162742	1332645
	284880	130170	896659	752051	936808	846967	1005628	923000
3032236	1065240	1249153	2581726	1919919	2433667	2434356	2507137	2605399
569275	73584	57254	482288	201156	629180	116046	208090	479933
2462961	991656	1191899	2099438	1718764	1804488	2318310	2299047	2125466
314187	53875	52542	217070	299570	145223	229747	300564	219362
20180	2504	4565	14087	10813	13512	10657	10491	10662
294007	51371	47977	202983	288757	131711	219091	290073	208700

OPERATION OF RETAIL SALES & WHOLESALE , ACCOMMODATION AND CATERING BY REGIONS(2014)

(10,000 Yuan)

崇川区 Chongchuan District	港闸区 Gangzha District	开发区 Developing Zone	通州区 Tongzhou District	海安 Haian	如东 Rudong	启东 Qidong	如皋 Rugao	海门 Haimen
17337110	4584753	5841476	10047297	6544973	8849482	6444841	9845436	9816402
13077394	3463396	3148166	7406453	4371771	6164310	3583237	6850217	7202843
4259717	1121357	2693311	2640845	2173202	2685172	2861605	2995219	2613559
398588	65116	65306	268807	338796	193288	286731	368859	274550
58879	6820	11560	30551	29883	34588	35081	30441	30219
339708	58296	53746	238256	308913	158700	251651	338419	244332

14-4 分地区限额以上批发和零售业分类销售额(2014年)

单位:万元

指标	Item	全市 Whole Municipality	市区 Urban Areas
商品销售额合计	**Total Sales of Goods**	**25330177**	**14925023**
粮油、食品、饮料、烟酒类		2715870	1145930
粮油食品类		1483882	653212
粮油类	Grain and Oil	492263	176221
肉禽蛋类	Meat,Poultry and Eggs	213517	52763
水产品类	Aquatic Products	120466	19763
蔬菜类	Vegetables	96245	21327
干鲜果品类	Fresh and Dried Furits	107323	49045
饮料类	Beverage	148274	72353
烟酒类	Tobacco and Alcohol	1083714	420365
服装、鞋帽、针纺织品类	Garments,Shoes&Hats and Textiles	2547852	1568454
服装类	Garments	946529	724290
鞋帽类	Shoes&Hats	160238	105792
针、纺织品类	Textiles	1441085	738371
化妆品类	Cosmetics	118820	71026
金银珠宝类	Treasures	342559	227964
日用品类	Articles for Daily Use	449117	299849
洗涤用品类	Detergent	148893	95092
儿童玩具类	Children´s Toys	54020	33788
五金、电料类	Hardware Materials	306006	164930
体育、娱乐用品类	Sports and Recreation Articles	106687	86323
书报杂志类	Books,Newspapers,Magazines	73491	28389
电子出版物和音像制品类	Electronic Moviolas Products	8233	3374
家用电器和音像器材类	Household Facilities and Moviolas	731775	392657
中西药品类	Chinese and Western Medicines	928304	533612
# 西药	Western Medicines	738543	460111
中草药及中成药类	Chinese Medicine and Chinese Patent Medicine	169208	73493
文化办公用品类	Cultural and Office Articles	335324	213675
家俱类	Furniture	70221	17821
通讯器材类	Communications tools	83431	33025
煤炭及制品类	Coal and Its Products	1632820	1069867
木材及制品类	Wood and Its Products	95307	27094
石油及制品类	Oil and Its Products	3593323	2370000
化工材料及制品类	Chemical Material and Products	4271912	3354689
# 化肥类	Fertilizer	95832	40785
金属材料类	Metal Materials	2481599	1030535
建筑及装潢材料类	Construction and Decoration Materials	752508	210582
机电产品及设备类	Mechanical and Electrical Equipments	339144	93659
# 农机类	Agricultural Machinery	25441	8486
汽车类	Auto Mobile	2725430	1875004
种子饲料类	Seeds and Feed	100725	21574
棉麻类	Cotton and Hemp	235095	3735
其他类	Others	284627	81255

注:以上数据是快报数据。

TOTAL RETAIL PRICE OF CONSUMMER GOODS BY REGION(2014)

(10,000 Yuan)

崇川区 Chongchuan District	港闸区 Gangzha District	开发区 Developing Zone	通州区 Tongzhou District	海安 Haian	如东 Rudong	启东 Qidong	如皋 Rugao	海门 Haimen
7000990	**2828568**	**3212391**	**1883074**	**2675091**	**2078347**	**1189511**	**2522486**	**1939719**
518287	68993	355976	202675	306316	431912	225881	335191	270640
235898	39953	326210	51152	181637	265169	91874	172244	119746
85771	8267	62720	19463	33632	99969	23701	119509	39232
16701	1638	26757	7667	81435	41054	7114	15472	15678
5394	635	9458	4276	8694	55365	24182	7208	5255
8489	695	8509	3635	19306	41396	2358	5744	6116
14938	4562	26748	2797	7315	10966	9313	5483	25200
23423	24611	14718	9601	7054	15105	12158	18112	23492
258966	4429	15048	141922	117625	151638	121849	144836	127402
606988	126527	276820	558119	165139	148265	70396	91089	504510
409049	75274	195346	44621	47549	32878	45715	49024	47073
80193	9559	10239	5801	6770	13793	9283	7848	16752
117746	41693	71235	507697	110819	101594	15398	34218	440685
64833	2111	52	4030	4124	4752	16123	13788	9006
214360	255		13349	21778	11593	18424	25800	37000
126201	10138	142547	20963	20494	28975	46983	19174	33643
28694	4596	56959	4842	5072	8282	16671	8531	15246
3338	2200	26196	2054	1261	1842	9726	1663	5741
25672	880	117793	20585	45257	26270	31446	19737	18367
77079	1479	1811	5955	1164	7657	2317	1952	7274
9513	9625	603	8648	10443	7751	4976	12879	9053
2139	200	77	959	529	95	1118	1879	1239
292276	6846	21767	71768	68154	75203	56003	70948	68809
496010	2502	7444	27655	129823	163321	26572	48715	26261
430914	2087	7430	19681	100138	106106	14594	37678	19917
65096	415	14	7968	19774	56193	7682	6573	5493
78949	14918	112170	7639	13549	39787	22965	36723	8624
3594	12540		1687	4722	14039	6711	5511	21417
27890	1278	261	3596	5112	7433	19607	11001	7253
49714	723872	186927	109353	79457	81654	32905	311598	57339
	21360		5734	9813	3333		54576	491
1150620	583714	430847	204819	153588	294512	190064	404378	180782
2406396	47115	848144	53034	90096	196327	29316	498408	103077
16888		2916	20981	19897	21472	12037		1641
179322	433140	136210	281862	1130357	28567	34424	116369	141349
7953	17591	270	184769	84070	95129	133259	67004	162463
37523	27795	11909	16431	53858	77915	58854	41845	13013
		5853	2633	3023	3424	5735	4774	
600480	702400	542253	29871	130596	132817	124171	255504	207338
3881		17694		16952	37610	3490	16296	4803
			3735	49807	139602	31031	7866	3054
21312	13289	816	45838	79894	23829	2478	54256	42916

Note:Above are express statistics

14-5 限额以上批发零售贸易业、住宿餐饮业基本情况(2014年)

单位:个

指 标	Item
总计	**Total**
批发和零售业小计	**Subtotal of Wholesale and Retails**
批发业	**Wholesale**
#国有控股	State-owned Holding
按登记注册类型分组	**Grouped by Registration Types**
内资企业	Domestic Funded
国有企业	State-owned Enterprise
集体企业	Collective Enterprise
股份合作企业	Joint Equity Cooperative Enterprise
联营企业	Joint Venture
有限责任公司	Limited Liability Company
股份有限公司	Limited Company
私营企业	Private Company
其他企业	Others
港、澳、台商投资企业	HK, Macau or Taiwan Funded Enterprise
外商投资企业	Foreign Funded Enterprise
按国民经济行业分组	**Grouped by National Economy Sectors**
农畜产品批发	Agricultural &Husbandry Products
食品、饮料及烟草制品批发	Food, Beverage and Tobacco Products
纺织、服装及日用品批发	Textile, Garments and Goods for Daily Use
文化、体育用品及器材批发	Culture and Sports Products
医药及医疗器材批发	Medicine and Medical Equipments
矿产品、建材及化工产品批发	Mineral Products, Construction Materials and Chemical Products
机械设备、五金交电及电子产品批发	Machinery Equipments, Hardware Material and Electronic Products
贸易经纪与代理	Trade Agency
其他批发	Others
按经营方式分组	**Grouped by Ways of Operation**
独立门店	Independent Store
连锁总店(总部)	Chain Store (Headquarter)
连锁门店	Chain Store
其他	Others

BASIC CONDITIONS OF ENTERPRISES ABOVE DESIGNATED SIZE IN WHOLESALE AND RETAIL SALES TRADE AND CATERING TRADE(2014)

(unit)

限额以上法人企业 Enterprise Above Designated Size	所属全部贸易住餐活动单位 All Units of Trading, Accommodation and Catering	非贸易住餐法人所属限上贸易餐饮活动单位 Units of Non Corporate Enterprise Above Designated Size of Trading, Accommodation and Catering	营业面积（平方米） Floor Space of Business (sq·m)	从业人员（人） Employees (person)
2299	**3713**	**61**	**2887343**	**88829**
2057	**3451**	**35**	**2438351**	**73915**
1239	**1772**	**7**	**198721**	**29310**
43	70	1	13746	1808
1219	1748	6	195449	28699
19	28		1201	720
3	3		93	28
1	1			11
377	451	2	94192	9049
6	6	1	560	407
751	1197	3	97256	16168
62	62	0	2147	2316
9	10		3001	203
11	14	1	271	408
64	64	1	4265	2046
115	141	2	30375	4415
298	300		30943	7948
38	41		4648	1013
23	25		35653	1577
514	1005	1	70941	8110
138	141	3	19427	3506
11	11		418	145
38	44		2051	550
1097	1258	5	177842	25630
5	360		5072	464
1	1	1		107
136	153	1	15807	3109

14-5 续表 1

单位：个

指 标	Item
零售业	**Retail Sales**
# 国有控股	State-owned Holding
按经济注册类型分组	**Grouped by Registration Types**
内资企业	Domestic Funded
国有企业	State-owned Enterprise
集体企业	Collective Enterprise
股份合作企业	Joint Equity Cooperative Enterprise
联营企业	Joint Venture
有限责任公司	Limited Liability Company
股份有限公司	Limited Company
私营企业	Private Company
其他企业	Others
港、澳、台商投资企业	HK, Macau or Taiwan Funded Enterprise
外商投资企业	Foreign Funded Enterprise
按国民经济行业分组	**Grouped by National Economy Sectors**
综合零售	General Retail
食品、饮料及烟草制品专门零售	Food, Beverage and Tobacco Products
纺织、服装及日用品专门零售	Textile, Garments and Goods for Daily Use
文化、体育用品及器材专门零售	Culture and Sports Products
医药及医疗器材专门零售	Medicine and Medical Equipments
汽车、摩托车、燃料及零配件专门零售	Automobile, Motorbike, Fuel and Spare Part
家用电器及电子产品专门零售	Household Appliances and Electronic Products
五金、家具及室内装修材料专门零售	Hardware, Furniture and Interior Decoration Material
货摊、无店铺及其他零售业	Stand, Non-store and Others
按经营方式分组	**Grouped by Ways of Operation**
独立门店	Independent Store
连锁总店(总部)	General Chain Store (Headquarter)
连锁门店	Chain Store
其他	Others
按零售业态分组	**Grouped by Retail Formats**
有店铺零售	Store-based Retailing
食杂店	Grocery Store
便利店	Convenience Store
超市	Supermarket
大型超市	Hypermarket
仓储会员店	Warehouse Club
百货店	Department Store
专业店	Professional Store
专卖店	Monopoly Store
家居建材店	Store of Home Building Materials
厂家直销中心	Factory Outlet Center
无店铺零售	Non-store Retailing

CONTINUED 1

(unit)

限额以上法人企业 Enterprise Above Designated Size	所属全部贸易住餐活动单位 All Units of Trading, Accommodation and Catering	非贸易住餐法人所属限上贸易餐饮活动单位 Units of Non Corporate Enterprise Above Designated Size of Trading, Accommodation and Catering	营业面积（平方米） Floor Space of Business (sq·m)	从业人员（人） Employees (person)
818	**1679**	**28**	**2239630**	**44605**
22	360		116888	1866
794	1580	17	1689608	32483
7	66	4	6949	505
6	6		3520	46
1	1		80	15
217	571	7	705042	14032
6	230		129470	1007
553	702	6	836397	16813
4	4		8150	65
11	86	1	496581	10986
13	13	10	53441	1136
90	242	4	1131957	20859
70	111	5	58038	1860
46	50	9	44585	1243
43	146	2	55332	1550
42	251		45425	2235
338	625	2	656393	12155
90	152	5	147365	3008
47	47		24127	718
52	55	1	76408	977
747	1101	16	1270864	24294
21	325		596722	12883
37	207	11	329676	6589
13	46	1	42368	839
813	1674	27	2238548	44379
1	1		360	35
		1	800	147
50	90	1	71635	1782
21	133	1	681955	14894
1	1		4067	10
24	24	2	389743	4428
576	1253	6	749035	15454
132	163	16	319393	7518
6	6		4960	63
2	3		16600	48
5	5	1	1082	226

14-5 续表 2

单位：个

指 标	Item
住宿和餐饮业小计	**Accommodation and Catering Industry**
住宿业	**Accommodation**
# 国有控股	State-owned Holding
按登记注册类型分组	**Grouped by Registration Types**
内资企业	Domestic Funded
国有企业	State-owned Enterprise
集体企业	Collective Enterprise
股份合作企业	Joint Equity Cooperative Enterprise
联营企业	Joint Venture
有限责任公司	Limited Liability Company
股份有限公司	Limited Company
私营企业	Private Company
其他企业	Others
港、澳、台商投资企业	HK, Macau or Taiwan Funded Enterprise
外商投资企业	Foreign Funded Enterprise
按国民经济行业分组	**Grouped by National Economy Sectors**
旅游饭店	Tourist Hotel
一般旅馆	General Hotel
按星级等级分组	**Grouped by Star Levels**
二星	Two Star
三星	Three Star
四星	Four Star
五星	Five Star
其他	Others
按经营方式分组	**Grouped by Ways of Operation**
独立门店	Independent Store
连锁总店（总部）	General Chain Store (Headquarter)
连锁门店	Chain Store
其他	Others

CONTINUED 2

(unit)

限额以上法人企业 Enterprise Above Designated Size	所属全部贸易住餐活动单位 All Units of Trading, Accommodation and Catering	非贸易住餐法人所属限上贸易餐饮活动单位 Units of Non Corporate Enterprise Above Designated Size of Trading, Accommodation and Catering	营业面积（平方米） Floor Space of Business (sq·m)	从业人员（人） Employees (person)
242	**262**	**26**	**448992**	**14914**
47	**48**	**4**	**71107**	**3043**
1	1		4000	138
41	42	3	47647	2270
11	12	1	22454	1205
30	30	2	25193	1065
2	2	1	8800	369
4	4		14660	404
17	17	1	59514	1918
30	31	3	11593	1125
3	3		545	74
9	9		5980	269
5	5		22150	881
30	31	4	42432	1819
41	41	2	70453	2831
6	7	2	654	212

14-5 续表 3

单位：个

指 标	Item
餐饮业	**Catering Industry**
# 国有控股	State-owned Holding
按登记注册类型分组	**Grouped by Registration Types**
内资企业	Domestic Funded
国有企业	State-owned Enterprise
集体企业	Collective Enterprise
股份合作企业	Joint Equity Cooperative Enterprise
联营企业	Joint Venture
有限责任公司	Limited Liability Company
股份有限公司	Limited Company
私营企业	Private Company
其他企业	Others
港、澳、台商投资企业	HK, Macau or Taiwan Funded Enterprise
外商投资企业	Foreign Funded Enterprise
按国民经济行业分组	**Grouped by National Economy Sectors**
正餐服务	Diner Services
快餐服务	Fast Food Services
饮料及冷饮服务	Beverage and Cold Drinks Services
其他餐饮服务	Others
按经营方式分组	**Grouped by Ways of Operation**
独立门店	Independent Store
连锁总店(总部)	General Chain Store (Headquarter)
连锁门店	Chain Store
其他	Others

CONTINUED 3

(unit)

限额以上法人企业 Enterprise Above Designated Size	所属全部贸易住餐活动单位 All Units of Trading, Accommodation and Catering	非贸易住餐法人所属限上贸易餐饮活动单位 Units of Non Corporate Enterprise Above Designated Size of Trading, Accommodation and Catering	营业面积（平方米） Floor Space of Business (sq·m)	从业人员（人） Employees (person)
195	**214**	**22**	**377885**	**11871**
4	4		4250	297
191	210	15	345557	11253
3	3	10	19161	485
1	1		450	22
24	34	2	62375	2799
161	170	3	259971	7894
2	2		3600	53
3	3	3	27580	410
1	1	4	4748	208
191	202	15	372735	11542
3	11	3	3860	229
		4	890	90
1	1		400	10
188	192	15	358098	10861
1	7		1800	306
3	11	7	10337	463
3	4		7650	241

14-6 限额以上批发零售贸易业商品购进、销售、库存总额(2014年)

单位:万元

指标	Item
总计	**Total**
批发业	**Wholesale**
#国有控股	State-owned Holding
按登记注册类型分组	**Grouped by Registration Types**
内资企业	Domestic Funded
国有企业	State-owned Enterprise
集体企业	Collective Enterprise
股份合作企业	Joint Equity Cooperative Enterprise
联营企业	Joint Venture
有限责任公司	Limited Liability Company
股份有限公司	Limited Company
私营企业	Private Company
其他企业	Others
港、澳、台商投资企业	HK, Macau or Taiwan Funded Enterprise
外商投资企业	Foreign Funded Enterprise
按国民经济行业分组	**Grouped by National Economy Sectors**
农畜产品批发	Agricultural &Husbandry Wholesale
食品、饮料及烟草制品批发	Food, Beverage and Tobacco Products
纺织、服装及日用品批发	Textile, Garments and Goods for Daily Use
文化、体育用品及器材批发	Culture and Sports Products
医药及医疗器材批发	Medicine and Medical Equipments
矿产品、建材及化工产品批发	Mineral Products, Construction Materials and Chemical Products
机械设备、五金交电及电子产品批发	Machinery Equipments, Hardware Material and Electronic Products
贸易经纪与代理	Trade Agency
其他批发	Others
按经营方式分组	**Grouped by Ways of Operation**
独立门店	Independent Store
连锁总店(总部)	Chain Store (Headquarter)
连锁门店	Chain Store
其他	Others

CONDITIONS ON COMMODITY PURCHASE, SALES AND STORAGE OF ENTERPRISE ABOVE DESIGNATED SIZE IN WHOLESALE AND RETAIL SALES TRADE(2014)

(10,000 Yuan)

购进总额 Total Purchase	进口 Imports	销售总额 Total Sales	批发额 Wholesale	出口 Exports	零售额 Retail Sales	年末库存总额 Total Storage (Year End)
23354985	**513046**	**25392022**	**18408246**	**865188**	**6983776**	**1449083**
16341145	**249647**	**17718870**	**17251274**	**865166**	**467595**	**876176**
2263716	1398	2683415	2681236	22860	2179	334900
15709129	243559	17053495	16588078	857101	465417	865336
652025		966674	966014		660	280873
7381		7318	7318			385
4135		4278	4278			408
5642765	84155	6042323	5854116	385972	188208	201815
2127146	405	2100091	2089543	58098	10548	59035
7070593	158999	7710352	7460700	413031	249653	316226
205084		222458	206110		16348	6594
467018	817	469791	469791	1817		3302
164998	5270	195584	193406	6248	2179	7538
517010	47	581172	567985		13187	45210
1071415	10944	1456369	1402769	4598	53600	290959
1916920	33185	2306719	2206477	581677	100242	83132
268305	265	320828	307110	66072	13718	14333
781192		774753	652710		122044	54151
10486223	175822	10923767	10807598	54134	116168	297631
1036988	29274	1042867	999365	142706	43502	86419
46808	110	56143	56138	15979	5	512
216282		256252	251122		5130	3830
14369902	223672	15664019	15206979	710045	457040	805062
55689		67436	67436			6273
17822		17787	17787			43
1897731	25975	1969628	1959072	155121	10556	64798

14-6 续表

单位：万元

指 标	Item
零售业	**Retail Sales**
# 国有控股	State-owned Holding
按经济注册类型分组	**Grouped by Registration Types**
内资企业	Domestic Funded
国有企业	State-owned Enterprise
集体企业	Collective Enterprise
股份合作企业	Joint Equity Cooperative Enterprise
联营企业	Joint Venture
有限责任公司	Limited Liability Company
股份有限公司	Limited Company
私营企业	Private Company
其他企业	Others
港、澳、台商投资企业	HK, Macau or Taiwan Funded Enterprise
外商投资企业	Foreign Funded Enterprise
按国民经济行业分组	**Grouped by National Economy Sectors**
综合零售	Comprehensive Retail Sales
食品、饮料及烟草制品专门零售	Food, Beverage and Tobacco Products
纺织、服装及日用品专门零售	Textile, Garments and Goods for Daily Use
文化、体育用品及器材专门零售	Culture and Sports Products
医药及医疗器材专门零售	Medicine and Medical Equipments
汽车、摩托车、燃料及零配件专门零售	Automobile, Motocycle, Fuel and Spare Parts
家用电器及电子产品专门零售	Household Appliances and Electronic Products
五金、家具及室内装修材料专门零售	Hardware, Furniture and Indoor Decoration Materials
货摊、无店铺及其他零售业	Stall, Non-store Retaling, etc.
按经营方式分组	**Grouped by Ways of Operation**
独立门店	Independent Store
连锁总店(总部)	Chain Store (Headquarter)
连锁门店	Chain Store
其他	Others
按零售业态分组	**Grouped by Retail Formats**
有店铺零售	Store-based Retailing
食杂店	Grocery Store
便利店	Convenience Store
折扣店	Discount Store
超市	Supermarket
大型超市	Hypermarket
仓储会员店	Warehouse Club
百货店	Department Store
专业店	Professional Store
专卖店	Monopoly Store
家居建材店	Store of Home Building Materials
厂家直销中心	Factory Outlet Center
无店铺零售	Non-store Retailing

CONTINUED

(10,000 Yuan)

购进总额 Total Purchase	进口 Imports	销售总额 Total Sales	批发额 Wholesale	出口 Exports	零售额 Retail Sales	年末库存总额 Total Storage (Year End)
7013840	**263399**	**7673152**	**1156971**	**22**	**6516181**	**572907**
1058409		1077746	376751		700995	28918
5643847	211071	6172277	644335	22	5527942	463502
28649		33008	442		32567	3364
9108		18000	4270		13731	315
5160		5578			5578	206
1996613	94703	2194504	153377		2041128	183884
1000284		1015525	373245		642280	15225
2598576	116368	2900082	112782	22	2787301	260192
5456		5579	221		5358	318
1177654	43886	1281317	512636		768681	103908
192340	8442	219558			219558	5497
2072790	8469	2329034	544210		1784824	149678
109111		125578	17889		107689	6319
89686		107575	4289		103286	9735
131014		143249	15367		127882	27133
158523	1719	170489	6403		164086	16818
3856466	253211	4118603	503939	22	3614664	307691
417608		460568	35072		425496	46672
56438		74875	20426		54450	4891
122204		143181	9377		133804	3970
4705891	254930	5160098	634849	22	4525249	381037
1440629		1567952	513070		1054882	123170
689908	8469	759862	6262		753601	52327
177413		185241	2791		182449	16374
7005647	263399	7663394	1156971	22	6506423	572535
3941		3933	3933			8
		4850			4850	6
152426	1	174366	16222		158144	13756
1385907	8442	1512231	512636		999594	126391
1348		1303			1303	113
557916	26	677111	22292		654818	13788
3186231	149226	3402972	577829	22	2825143	228678
1702839	105704	1869702	20389		1849313	188702
9733		10902	512		10390	786
5307		6025	3157		2868	308
8193		9758			9758	372

14-7 限额以上批发零售贸易企业财务状况(2014年)

单位:万元

指 标	Item	流动资产 Circulating Assets
总计	**Total**	**6464295**
批发业	**Wholesale**	**4448659**
# 国有控股	State-owned Holding	782864
按登记注册类型分组	**Grouped by Registration Types**	
内资企业	Domestic Funded	4220751
国有企业	State-owned Enterprise	530371
集体企业	Collective Enterprise	1765
股份合作企业	Joint Equity Cooperative Enterprise	572
联营企业	Joint Venture	
有限责任公司	Limited Liability Company	1533417
股份有限公司	Limited Company	161402
私营企业	Private Company	1973058
其他企业	Others	20168
港、澳、台商投资企业	HK, Macau or Taiwan Funded Enterprise	179249
外商投资企业	Foreign Funded Enterprise	48659
按国民经济行业分组	**Grouped by National Economy Sectors**	
农畜产品批发	Agricultural &Husbandry Products	107873
食品、饮料及烟草制品批发	Food, Beverage and Tobacco Products	611563
纺织、服装及日用品批发	Textile, Garments and Goods for Daily Use	522734
文化、体育用品及器材批发	Culture and Sports Products	110609
医药及医疗器材批发	Medicine and Medical Equipments	256748
矿产品、建材及化工产品批发	Mineral Products, Construction Materials and Chemical Products	2380515
机械设备、五金交电及电子产品批发	Machinery Equipments, Hardware Material and Electronic Products	352746
贸易经纪与代理	Trade Agency	8269
其他批发	Others	97604
按经营方式分组	**Grouped by Ways of Operation**	
独立门店	Independent Store	3833828
连锁总店(总部)	Chain Store (Headquarter)	22146
连锁门店	Chain Store	353
其他	Others	592332

FINANCIAL CONDITIONS OF ENTERPRISES ABOVE DESIGNATED SIZE IN WHOLESALE AND RETAIL SALES TRADE(2014)

(10,000 Yuan)

固定资产原价 Original Price of Fixed Assets	累计折旧 Accumulated Depreciation	资产 Assets	负债 Liability	所有者权益 Ownership	实收资本 Actually Utilized Assets	国家资本 State-Owned Assets	集体资本 Collective Assets	法人资本 Personal Assets	个人资本 Foreign Assets
1580529	**467469**	**8832992**	**5784264**	**3291047**	**3228305**	**77367**	**14298**	**469712**	**2416015**
648896	**198200**	**5471368**	**3465385**	**2005984**	**1043773**	**44914**	**11783**	**242615**	**606438**
107062	42854	880271	342281	537990	60972	44751	240	13900	2081
596282	189884	5184906	3349069	1835837	897446	44914	11783	234418	606069
67271	26007	583414	136045	447369	14394	12814		1580	
1264	386	2643	1047	1596	197		147	50	
29	29	572	327	245	300			300	
194422	57915	1883558	1293671	589888	376678	32087	5538	167287	171503
21973	7446	253313	141405	111907	21246			12548	8698
269932	92025	2401224	1758007	643217	460953	13	288	43480	417172
41392	6076	60183	18567	41616	23679		5810	9173	8696
39604	6655	225242	79294	145948	121758			1128	
13010	1662	61220	37022	24199	24569			7069	369
61161	13997	176161	92839	83322	57561	9220	1980	9479	36882
120956	37587	717614	197949	519665	63173	3637	3830	18805	30031
84692	29786	638632	370861	267771	118124	868	137	37200	79621
21370	6314	138604	88681	49924	22972			2254	11340
45815	8603	306825	239936	66890	32938	5110	4778	10551	12499
264387	85074	2946892	2092661	854231	611604	20079	732	127277	337072
35977	12656	404728	298729	105999	76581	1000	276	21175	54096
2919	1344	12531	7033	5498	1738			350	1388
11620	2841	129382	76697	52685	59083		50	15524	43509
548609	172385	4711747	2905135	1806612	870109	39419	5733	166034	539472
13563	2986	39951	12548	27403	20228			16060	4168
496	15	835	290	545	159				159
86228	22815	718836	547413	171424	153278	5494	6050	60521	62639

14-7 续表 1

单位：万元

指 标	Item	流动资产 Circulating Assets
零售业	**Retail Sales**	**2015637**
#国有控股	State-owned Holding	84620
按经济注册类型分组	**Grouped by Registration Types**	
内资企业	Domestic Funded	1702608
国有企业	State-owned Enterprise	16542
集体企业	Collective Enterprise	1498
股份合作企业	Joint Equity Cooperative Enterprise	758
联营企业	Joint Venture	
有限责任公司	Limited Liability Company	536647
股份有限公司	Limited Company	41967
私营企业	Private Company	1102369
其他企业	Others	2828
港、澳、台商投资企业	HK, Macau or Taiwan Funded Enterprise	298432
外商投资企业	Foreign Funded Enterprise	14596
按国民经济行业分组	**Grouped by National Economy Sectors**	
综合零售	Comprehensive Retail Sales	763219
食品、饮料及烟草制品专门零售	Food, Beverage and Tobacco Products	31590
纺织、服装及日用品专门零售	Textile, Garments and Goods for Daily Use	19594
文化、体育用品及器材专门零售	Culture and Sports Products	70338
医药及医疗器材专门零售	Medicine and Medical Equipments	66267
汽车、摩托车、燃料及零配件专门零售	Automobile, Motocycle, Fuel and Spare Parts	922254
家用电器及电子产品专门零售	Household Appliances and Electronic Products	74597
五金、家具及室内装修材料专门零售	Hardware, Furniture and Indoor Decoration Materials	20771
货摊、无店铺及其他零售业	Stall, Non-store Retaling, etc.	47007
按经营方式分组	**Grouped by Ways of Operation**	
独立门店	Independent Store	1240471
连锁总店(总部)	Chain Store (Headquarter)	591608
连锁门店	Chain Store	137686
其他	Others	45872
按零售业态分组	**Grouped by Retail Formats**	
有店铺零售	Store-based Retailing	2013165
食杂店	Grocery Store	504
便利店	Convenience Store	
折扣店	Discount Store	
超市	Supermarket	30327
大型超市	Hypermarket	338195
仓储会员店	Warehouse Club	481
百货店	Department Store	402075
专业店	Professional Store	645166
专卖店	Monopoly Store	586915
家居建材店	Store of Home Building Materials	1732
厂家直销中心	Factory Outlet Center	7770
无店铺零售	Non-store Retailing	2471

CONTINUED 1

(10,000 Yuan)

固定资产原价 Original Price of Fixed Assets	累计折旧 Accumulated Depreciation	资 产 Assets	负 债 Liability	所有者权益 Ownership	实收资本 Actually Utilized Assets	国家资本 State-Owned Assets	集体资本 Collective Assets	法人资本 Personal Assets	个人资本 Foreign Assets
931633	**269269**	**3361624**	**2318879**	**1285063**	**2184532**	**32953**	**2515**	**227097**	**1809578**
98468	38612	185766	147239	280845	64472	31095		9509	732
735740	206445	2828844	1837862	1233300	2039175	8873	2515	217897	1809578
5554	2663	20482	12859	7623	1462	1462			
1456	173	2832	1700	1132	271		150	122	
164	77	982	602	381	3				3
267286	70840	928880	694837	234043	195229	6138	1110	129526	58455
98261	38058	153894	112444	283768	10794	400		2062	8332
361610	94491	1717344	1014292	703052	1828672	873	1255	86150	1740082
1409	143	4430	1128	3302	2743			37	2706
157896	52592	477164	446234	30930	83827			8653	
37997	10232	55616	34783	20833	61531	24080		547	
435172	123370	1418676	924458	494217	241016	840	1419	117739	58374
20704	4731	79155	46776	32380	26527	932		4530	21065
14696	1809	33521	10348	23173	15582			4120	11312
26935	10502	96186	55774	40411	18105	2063		40	12959
10442	3221	83088	59035	24053	14087	995		1068	12024
334695	100861	1388723	1067595	563446	1791499	25394	1096	78169	1649531
16654	6050	120084	77821	42262	35016			15564	19452
10601	2151	33957	17910	16047	11831			645	11186
61734	16575	108235	59162	49073	30870	2730		5222	13675
535511	158474	1949421	1425894	765845	1960125	28628	1135	106482	1766608
174685	69422	973563	569483	404080	145919	985		68324	24754
205255	37254	372676	285391	87285	63338	2703	1380	43895	12100
16181	4119	65964	38111	27853	15149	637		8396	6116
925548	267346	3354922	2317878	1279362	2180213	32953	2515	227097	1808805
3531	42	4641	1151	3490	3400				3400
17857	6317	49266	31727	17539	17644		25	1098	16521
179519	68214	530267	541702	-11435	76319	840	1380	9676	1780
19	2	590	457	133	100				100
241006	50046	849289	358906	490383	149096		14	107563	41519
350334	103117	1096409	721049	617678	284540	30973	646	59234	148187
131555	39125	812448	661177	151271	1640359	1140	450	49521	1588548
1371	356	3878	1462	2415	1985			5	1980
356	127	8135	247	7888	6770				6770
6085	1923	6702	1001	5701	4319				773

14-7 续表 2

单位:万元

指 标	Item	主营业务收入 Main Operation Revenue
总计	**Total**	**23012706**
批发业	**Wholesale**	**16407429**
#国有控股	State-owned Holding	2392169
按登记注册类型分组	**Grouped by Registration Types**	
内资企业	Domestic Funded	15823468
国有企业	State-owned Enterprise	789098
集体企业	Collective Enterprise	6875
股份合作企业	Joint Equity Cooperative Enterprise	3656
联营企业	Joint Venture	
有限责任公司	Limited Liability Company	5647092
股份有限公司	Limited Company	2381766
私营企业	Private Company	6800672
其他企业	Others	194309
港、澳、台商投资企业	HK, Macau or Taiwan Funded Enterprise	429995
外商投资企业	Foreign Funded Enterprise	153966
按国民经济行业分组	**Grouped by National Economy Sectors**	
农畜产品批发	Agricultural &Husbandry Products	509023
食品、饮料及烟草制品批发	Food, Beverage and Tobacco Products	1185275
纺织、服装及日用品批发	Textile, Garments and Goods for Daily Use	2115374
文化、体育用品及器材批发	Culture and Sports Products	300356
医药及医疗器材批发	Medicine and Medical Equipments	665301
矿产品、建材及化工产品批发	Mineral Products, Construction Materials and Chemical Products	10443718
机械设备、五金交电及电子产品批发	Machinery Equipments, Hardware Material and Electronic Products	934035
贸易经纪与代理	Trade Agency	54986
其他批发	Others	199361
按经营方式分组	**Grouped by Ways of Operation**	
独立门店	Independent Store	14549640
连锁总店(总部)	Chain Store (Headquarter)	64994
连锁门店	Chain Store	1416
其他	Others	1791379

CONTINUED 2

(10,000 Yuan)

主营业务成本 Cost of Main Operation	主营业务税金及附加 Taxes and Extra Charges of Main Business	销售费用 Operation Fees	管理费用 Management Expenditures	财务费用 Financial Expenditures	营业利润 Operating Profit	利润总额 Total Profits	应付工资总额 Total Wages Payable	本年应交增值税额 Income Taxes Payable
21003844	**124031**	**621253**	**388202**	**121834**	**673981**	**614048**	**327169**	**537418**
15050832	**90263**	**229732**	**213353**	**71637**	**527463**	**491856**	**147294**	**407623**
2203664	43398	25831	34591	−8162	101271	98871	15365	242158
14487573	89141	226110	208684	70087	518111	489296	143658	404731
646634	42596	11085	21418	−10152	81188	83647	5067	236190
6185	6	297	186		201	201	136	15
3561	2	43	51			−2	31	19
5079437	14111	83912	62645	28764	149156	129994	46511	50224
2349933	427	13213	9853	1405	8555	13278	4909	879
6239312	27760	112580	108065	48237	264789	248298	77404	115474
162512	4238	4981	6466	1833	14223	13880	9598	1931
418676	585	1425	2232	1291	5789	−1010	1226	1456
144583	537	2197	2437	259	3562	3570	2410	1436
469877	2521	9588	9356	4349	14103	13726	6993	2312
972944	48083	24652	37513	−7611	113486	115321	20509	244288
1830376	9592	47001	55908	9110	170167	165847	44656	33782
263028	1545	8810	7876	1528	18768	13312	6044	4219
625951	820	10766	8085	2748	22797	17919	7161	7524
9805292	19737	96059	73519	56781	146742	128074	43293	78575
851689	5308	28419	16285	2859	32690	30296	15025	10478
50207	95	1355	1323	95	1949	1107	738	1896
181468	2562	3081	3488	1779	6762	6255	2876	24550
13282521	85964	196315	190598	57040	512228	478788	129245	392091
54512	334	3731	1607	178	4615	4561	2033	950
1251		12	145		8	8	171	
1712547	3965	29674	21003	14419	10612	8498	15845	14582

14-7 续表 3

单位：万元

指 标	Item	主营业务收入 Main Operation Revenue
零售业	**Retail Sales**	**6605277**
#国有控股	State-owned Holding	935166
按经济注册类型分组	**Grouped by Registration Types**	
内资企业	Domestic Funded	5369746
国有企业	State-owned Enterprise	26746
集体企业	Collective Enterprise	12043
股份合作企业	Joint Equity Cooperative Enterprise	4768
联营企业	Joint Venture	
有限责任公司	Limited Liability Company	1900062
股份有限公司	Limited Company	870193
私营企业	Private Company	2552229
其他企业	Others	3705
港、澳、台商投资企业	HK, Macau or Taiwan Funded Enterprise	1122049
外商投资企业	Foreign Funded Enterprise	113482
按国民经济行业分组	**Grouped by National Economy Sectors**	
综合零售	Comprehensive Retail Sales	1991364
食品、饮料及烟草制品专门零售	Food, Beverage and Tobacco Products	93011
纺织、服装及日用品专门零售	Textile, Garments and Goods for Daily Use	50164
文化、体育用品及器材专门零售	Culture and Sports Products	123848
医药及医疗器材专门零售	Medicine and Medical Equipments	141012
汽车、摩托车、燃料及零配件专门零售	Automobile, Motocycle, Fuel and Spare Parts	3639855
家用电器及电子产品专门零售	Household Appliances and Electronic Products	374806
五金、家具及室内装修材料专门零售	Hardware, Furniture and Indoor Decoration Materials	68934
货摊、无店铺及其他零售业	Stall, Non-store Retaling, etc.	122282
按经营方式分组	**Grouped by Ways of Operation**	
独立门店	Independent Store	4458948
连锁总店(总部)	Chain Store (Headquarter)	1380621
连锁门店	Chain Store	597893
其他	Others	167815
按零售业态分组	**Grouped by Retail Formats**	
有店铺零售	Store-based Retailing	6598308
食杂店	Grocery Store	3933
便利店	Convenience Store	
折扣店	Discount Store	
超市	Supermarket	136017
大型超市	Hypermarket	1285110
仓储会员店	Warehouse Club	1303
百货店	Department Store	587961
专业店	Professional Store	2976612
专卖店	Monopoly Store	1591815
家居建材店	Store of Home Building Materials	9607
厂家直销中心	Factory Outlet Center	5950
无店铺零售	Non-store Retailing	6969

CONTINUED 3

(10000 yuan)

主营业务成本 Cost of Main Operation	主营业务税金及附加 Taxes and Extra Charges of Main Business	销售费用 Operation Fees	管理费用 Management Expenditures	财务费用 Financial Expenditures	营业利润 Operating Profit	利润总额 Total Profits	应付工资总额 Total Wages Payable	本年应交增值税额 Income Taxes Payable
5953012	**33768**	**391521**	**174850**	**50197**	**146518**	**122192**	**179875**	**129795**
842063	1001	34952	15739	879	43579	44796	11040	6412
4804764	32118	236532	146021	45595	185993	176524	135385	119580
21277	58	1947	2394	–194	1312	2059	1659	162
10223	142	391	400	150	736	736	249	66
4410	6	96	155	14	88	91	60	47
1707675	9716	121792	55636	15555	20465	19050	58432	59664
785220	2514	27325	13275	342	44705	44028	5995	6187
2273577	19384	84851	73813	29627	118242	110115	68786	53427
2382	298	130	350	101	445	445	205	27
1050004	1191	142797	27743	4181	–44267	–59131	39596	6830
98244	459	12193	1085	420	4792	4799	4894	3386
1793192	13273	210569	61427	5848	18059	–1217	77161	50835
75603	1224	4219	3694	787	6504	6419	5374	1666
39508	362	3379	2123	152	4767	4673	2893	1362
97922	2060	8899	8524	16	7378	8788	7785	1678
119975	1051	8195	6473	1236	4297	4166	7502	1998
3346632	11268	114839	73085	38613	74397	71795	59870	57796
325096	2276	33438	11111	1687	10864	7082	11322	8821
56312	1056	2075	2684	807	6104	5625	2901	1195
98773	1199	5908	5729	1051	14149	14863	5068	4446
4016908	24240	170743	120424	43746	124339	118146	100685	87494
1278805	4617	156168	35431	2714	4943	–11823	48371	14751
505566	4742	59347	14738	1271	13155	11523	27211	26728
151734	169	5263	4257	2466	4082	4346	3608	822
5948436	33564	390278	174558	50176	145862	121534	179416	129356
3749	10	54	78	58	–16	–16	96	1
112658	1417	9645	5496	763	6581	6243	5934	7976
1182029	1958	178867	30423	4509	–50885	–68862	53915	10167
1197	4	45	29	0	27	27	44	13
512813	9980	23062	26464	958	63337	62367	18049	34151
2656144	16409	123849	71811	20956	109316	103901	66714	47412
1468241	3585	54238	39758	22729	14973	15351	34191	29479
6684	153	480	409	198	1684	1676	280	94
4923	49	38	91	3	846	846	193	63
4575	204	1243	291	21	656	658	459	439

14-8 限额以上住宿餐饮企业财务状况(2014年)

单位:万元

指 标	Item	流动资产 Circulating Assets	固定资产原价 Original Price of Fixed Assets
总计	**Total**	**211756**	**412149**
住宿业	**Accommodation**	**67237**	**142528**
#国有控股	State-owned Holding	25447	17270
按登记注册类型分组	**Grouped by Registration Types**		
内资企业	Domestic Funded	48276	104570
国有企业	State-owned Enterprise		
集体企业	Collective Enterprise		
股份合作企业	Joint Equity Cooperative Enterprise		
联营企业	Joint Venture		
有限责任公司	Limited Liability Company	33284	89867
股份有限公司	Limited Company		
私营企业	Private Company	14993	14703
其他企业	Others		
港、澳、台商投资企业	HK, Macau or Taiwan Funded Enterprise	5267	16551
外商投资企业	Foreign Funded Enterprise	13693	21408
按国民经济行业分组	**Grouped by National Economy Sectors**		
旅游饭店	Tourist Hotel	59222	132150
一般旅馆	General Hotel	8014	10378
按星级等级分组	**Grouped by Star Levels**		
二星	Two Star	2113	843
三星	Three Star	5750	8801
四星	Four Star	33743	79709
五星	Five Star		
其他	Others	25631	53175
按经营方式分组	**Grouped by Ways of Operation**		
独立门店	Independent Store	65369	141339
连锁总店(总部)	General Chain Store (Headquarter)		
连锁门店	Chain Store	1868	1189
其他	Others		

FINANCIAL CONDITIONS OF ENTERPRISES ABOVE DESIGNATED SIZE IN HOTEL AND CATERING TRADE(2014)

(10,000 Yuan)

累计折旧 Accumulated Depreciation	资产 Assets	负债 Liability	所有者权益 Ownership	实收资本 Actually Utilized Assets	国家资本 State-Owned Capital	法人资本 Collective Capital	个人资本 Personal Assets
123587	**635686**	**388332**	**247354**	**242034**	**18090**	**48269**	**126019**
39972	**206638**	**144693**	**61945**	**80298**	**16570**	**15560**	**20184**
3691	39030	28165	10866	15343	15343		
22472	163436	139777	23660	39599	16570	13520	9509
17017	127547	115853	11694	30122	16270	13443	409
5454	35890	23924	11966	9476	300	77	9100
5358	16616	1113	15503	16912			
12142	26586	3804	22782	23787		2040	10675
35638	189077	132039	57038	72382	16570	13727	14951
4334	17561	12654	4907	7916		1832	5233
505	2452	1518	934	1151			850
3695	17316	14774	2572	3326		543	2710
18826	116346	88896	27450	31234	15643	12294	2700
16946	70525	39535	30990	44587	927	2723	13924
39131	204172	142776	61397	78268	16570	14528	19734
841	2466	1917	548	2030		1031	449

14-8 续表1

单位:万元

指 标	Item	流动资产 Circulating Assets	固定资产原价 Original Price of Fixed Assets
餐饮业	**Catering Industry**	**144520**	**269621**
#国有控股	State-owned Holding	9522	10285
按登记注册类型分组	**Grouped by Registration Types**		
内资企业	Domestic Funded	140607	242969
国有企业	State-owned Enterprise	3678	9871
集体企业	Collective Enterprise	106	219
股份合作企业	Joint Equity Cooperative Enterprise		
联营企业	Joint Venture		
有限责任公司	Limited Liability Company	37840	99555
股份有限公司	Limited Company		
私营企业	Private Company	98881	133129
其他企业	Others	103	196
港、澳、台商投资企业	HK, Macau or Taiwan Funded Enterprise	3627	13027
外商投资企业	Foreign Funded Enterprise	285	13626
按国民经济行业分组	**Grouped by National Economy Sectors**		
正餐服务	Diner Services	143960	269367
快餐服务	Fast Food Services	555	249
饮料及冷饮服务	Beverage and Cold Drinks Services		
其他餐饮服务	Others	5	5
按经营方式分组	**Grouped by Ways of Operation**		
独立门店	Independent Store	126744	265272
连锁总店(总部)	General Chain Store (Headquarter)	4599	665
连锁门店	Chain Store	9009	2477
其他	Others	4168	1208

CONTINUED 1

(10,000 Yuan)

累计折旧 Accumulated Depreciation	资产 Assets	负债 Liability	所有者权益 Ownership	实收资本 Actually Utilized Assets	国家资本 State-Owned Capital	法人资本 Collective Capital	个人资本 Personal Assets
83616	**429048**	**243639**	**185410**	**161737**	**1521**	**32709**	**105836**
2962	21245	12948	8297	1520	1520		
73692	397510	231487	166023	138357	1521	32709	103792
2870	14940	7569	7371	520	520		
17	345	90	255	12			
30863	128591	77551	51040	37811	1000	28780	7831
39842	253437	146145	107291	99963		3929	95911
102	198	133	65	51			50
2789	15981	7259	8722	9748			2044
7134	15558	4893	10665	13632			
83483	425231	242540	182691	159527	1521	31539	104796
130	3741	1096	2645	2160		1120	1040
3	76	3	73	50		50	
81802	392409	215745	176664	147757	1520	32679	91886
179	5226	5461	–235	500			500
1174	26488	20577	5911	8080		30	8050
461	4925	1855	3070	5400			5400

14-8 续表 2

单位:万元

指 标	Item	营业收入 Operation Revenue	主营业务收入 Main Business Income	营业务成本 Business Cost
总计	**Total**	**275890**	**274191**	**143943**
住宿业	**Accommodation**	**50500**	**49643**	**21628**
#国有控股	State-owned Holding	1788	1788	337
按登记注册类型分组	**Grouped by Registration Types**			
内资企业	Domestic Funded	39548	38826	16450
国有企业	State-owned Enterprise			
集体企业	Collective Enterprise			
股份合作企业	Joint Equity Cooperative Enterprise			
联营企业	Joint Venture			
有限责任公司	Limited Liability Company	21789	21604	6017
股份有限公司	Limited Company			
私营企业	Private Company	17759	17222	10433
其他企业	Others			
港、澳、台商投资企业	HK, Macau or Taiwan Funded Enterprise	4691	4691	2053
外商投资企业	Foreign Funded Enterprise	6262	6127	3125
按国民经济行业分组	**Grouped by National Economy Sectors**			
旅游饭店	Tourist Hotel	35223	34502	12442
一般旅馆	General Hotel	15277	15141	9186
按星级等级分组	**Grouped by Star Levels**			
二星	Two Star	1475	1475	867
三星	Three Star	4134	3952	2226
四星	Four Star	20245	19841	5948
五星	Five Star			
其他	Others	24646	24375	12587
按经营方式分组	**Grouped by Ways of Operation**			
独立门店	Independent Store	46596	45883	19927
连锁总店(总部)	General Chain Store (Headquarter)			
连锁门店	Chain Store	3905	3760	1701
其他	Others			

CONTINUED 2

(10,000 Yuan)

主营业务成本 Cost of Main Operation	营业业务税金及附加 Taxes and Surcharges of Business	主营业务税金及附加 Taxes and Surcharges of Main Business	销售费用 Operation Fees	管理费用 Management Expenditures	财务费用 Financial Expenditures	营业利润 Operating Profit	利润总额 Total Profits	应付职工薪酬 Total Wages Payable
143350	**13198**	**12635**	**55826**	**50559**	**11560**	**5259**	**8453**	**52963**
21623	**2579**	**2564**	**11318**	**14492**	**4830**	**–4153**	**–5309**	**10029**
337	102	102	653	1665	17	–986	–975	462
16445	1971	1956	9053	10543	4743	–3021	–4144	7474
6017	1202	1201	7018	7840	4017	–4120	–4171	4793
10428	770	755	2036	2703	727	1099	27	2681
2053	260	260	485	2602	–10	–699	–608	1154
3125	348	348	1780	1348	96	–433	–557	1401
12442	1894	1879	9401	11786	4383	–4491	–4675	7089
9181	685	684	1917	2706	447	338	–633	2940
867	75	75	233	437	156	–292	–287	271
2226	186	186	1578	451	129	–391	–531	753
5948	1122	1107	4176	7846	3060	–1760	–1896	3425
12583	1196	1196	5331	5759	1485	–1710	–2595	5580
19927	2354	2340	10275	13702	4676	–4148	–5174	9481
1696	224	223	1043	790	153	–5	–135	548

14-8 续表 3

单位:万元

指 标	Item	营业收入 Operation Revenue	主营业务收入 Main Business Income	营业务成本 Business Cost
餐饮业	**Catering Industry**	**225390**	**224548**	**122315**
#国有控股	State-owned Holding	3026	2508	1206
按登记注册类型分组	**Grouped by Registration Types**			
内资企业	Domestic Funded	217397	216648	119120
国有企业	State-owned Enterprise	1999	1848	948
集体企业	Collective Enterprise	396	396	225
股份合作企业	Joint Equity Cooperative Enterprise			
联营企业	Joint Venture			
有限责任公司	Limited Liability Company	56927	56561	23765
股份有限公司	Limited Company			
私营企业	Private Company	157452	157240	93828
其他企业	Others	624	604	354
港、澳、台商投资企业	HK, Macau or Taiwan Funded Enterprise	6142	6079	2864
外商投资企业	Foreign Funded Enterprise	1851	1821	332
按国民经济行业分组	**Grouped by National Economy Sectors**			
正餐服务	Diner Services	220538	219696	119850
快餐服务	Fast Food Services	4424	4424	2430
饮料及冷饮服务	Beverage and Cold Drinks Services			
其他餐饮服务	Others	428	428	35
按经营方式分组	**Grouped by Ways of Operation**			
独立门店	Independent Store	209593	209008	115909
连锁总店(总部)	General Chain Store (Headquarter)	4229	4229	1836
连锁门店	Chain Store	7164	7059	2174
其他	Others	4404	4253	2397

CONTINUED 4

(10,000 Yuan)

主营业务成本 Cost of Main Operation	营业务税金及附加 Taxes and Surcharges of Business	主营业务税金及附加 Taxes and Surcharges of Main Business	销售费用 Operation Fees	管理费用 Management Expenditures	财务费用 Financial Expenditures	营业利润 Operating Profit	利润总额 Total Profits	应付职工薪酬 Total Wages Payable
121727	**10619**	**10072**	**44508**	**36067**	**6730**	**9412**	**13762**	**42934**
1206	114	114	608	2215	554	–1671	–899	1395
118531	10263	9716	41370	34061	6493	10353	13997	41065
948	78	78	123	1773	191	–1114	–929	867
225	39	39		71	5	56	56	61
23757	3819	3290	18121	12773	1417	973	3715	11131
93257	6307	6288	23114	19282	4874	10367	11153	28766
344	21	21	12	162	6	71	2	241
2864	253	253	1559	1486	217	–236	–235	1419
332	104	104	1580	520	20	–705		450
119262	10439	9892	43649	35805	6730	8664	13560	42180
2430	178	178	859	219		739	200	708
35	2	2		44		10	2	46
115320	9758	9216	39098	31111	6446	11535	16175	39053
1836	241	241	1963	829	14	–654	–648	1350
2174	404	398	2637	1833	156	–40	–43	1695
2397	216	216	810	2294	115	–1428	–1723	836

14-9 限额以上住宿和餐饮业经营情况(2014年)

OPERATION OF ACCOMMODATION AND CATERING INDUSTRIES ABOVE DESIGNATED SIZE(2013)

指标	Item	营业额(万元) Operation Revenue (10000 yuan)	零售额 Total Retail Sales	年末拥有床位数(个) Beds Possessed (Year End)(unit)	年末拥有餐位数(位) Seats Possessed (Year End)(unit)
总计	**Total**	**311796**	**10767**	**21395**	**115394**
住宿业	**Accommodation**	**55403**	**546**	**9002**	**10500**
#国有控股	State-owned Holding	1788	64	123	500
按登记注册类型分组	**Grouped by Registration Types**				
内资企业	Domestic Funded	42375	401	7045	6316
国有企业	State-owned Enterprise				
集体企业	Collective Enterprise				
股份合作企业	Joint Equity Cooperative Enterprise				
联营企业	Joint Venture				
有限责任公司	Limited Liability Company	22217	228	2839	2589
股份有限公司	Limited Company				
私营企业	Private Company	20158	173	4206	3727
其他企业	Others				
港、澳、台商投资企业	HK, Macau or Taiwan Funded Enterprise	6553		759	1960
外商投资企业	Foreign Funded Enterprise	6475	145	1198	2224
按国民经济行业分组	**Grouped by National Economy Sectors**				
旅游饭店	Diner Services	37462	301	4830	7782
一般旅馆	Fast Food Services	17941	245	4172	2718
按星级等级分组	**Beverage and Cold Drinks Services**				
二星	Two Star	1475	3	238	154
三星	Three Star	4555	72	1121	244
四星	Four Star	20245	182	1963	3174
五星	Five Star				
其他	Others	29128	289	5680	6928
按经营方式分组	**Grouped by Ways of Operation**				
独立门店	Independent Store	50688	444	7552	10249
连锁总店(总部)	General Chain Store (Headquarter)				
连锁门店	Chain Store	4716	102	1450	251
其他	Others				

14-9 续表

CONTINUED

指 标	Item	营业额(万元) Operation Revenue (10000 yuan)	零售额 Total Retail Sales	年末拥有床位数(个) Beds Possessed (Year End) (unit)	年末拥有餐位数(位) Seats Possessed (Year End) (unit)
餐饮业	**Catering**	**256393**	**10221**	**12393**	**104894**
# 国有控股	State-owned Holding	3199	40	277	1520
按登记注册类型分组	**Grouped by Registration Types**				
内资企业	Domestic Funded	238527	9586	11542	101063
国有企业	State-owned Enterprise	8921	158	214	14850
集体企业	Collective Enterprise	456	144		80
股份合作企业	Joint Equity Cooperative Enterprise				
联营企业	Joint Venture				
有限责任公司	Limited Liability Company	58684	1211	3761	16930
股份有限公司	Limited Company				
私营企业	Private Company	169842	8074	7567	68673
其他企业	Others	624			530
港、澳、台商投资企业	HK, Macau or Taiwan Funded Enterprise	11688	39	508	2485
外商投资企业	Foreign Funded Enterprise	6178	595	343	1346
按国民经济行业分组	**Grouped by National Economy Sectors**				
正餐服务	Dinner Services	242060	9625	12393	103295
快餐服务	Fast Food Services	9578			1199
饮料及冷饮服务	Beverage and Cold Drinks Services	4327	595		380
其他餐饮服务	Others	428			20
按经营方式分组	**Grouped by Ways of Operation**				
独立门店	Independent Store	230728	9543	11606	98697
连锁总店(总部)	General Chain Store (Headquarter)	4229			1600
连锁门店	Chain Store	16932	599	208	3539
其他	Others	4505	78	579	1058

14-10 连锁总店(公司)经营情况(2014年)

单位:万元

指标	Item	连锁总店数(个) Number of Chain Store General (unit)	连锁门店数(个) Number of Chain Store Branch (unit)
总计	**Total**	**23**	**1976**
#内资企业	Domestic Funded Enterprise	20	1906
港澳台投资企业	HK, Macau or Taiwan Funded Enterprise	2	69
外商投资企业	Foreign Funded Enterprise	1	1
按零售业态分	**Grouped By Operating Situation**		
#超市	Supermarkets	2	213
大型超市	Hypermarkets	3	70
百货店	Department Stores	1	879
专业店	Professional Store	16	808
其他	Others	1	6

14-10 续表

单位:万元

指标	Item	通过非自有配送中心配送商品购进额 Non-Private Rationing Center Admeasurement
总计	**Total**	**5475.1**
#内资企业	Domestic Funded Enterprise	5475.1
港澳台投资企业	HK, Macau or Taiwan Funded Enterprise	
外商投资企业	Foreign Funded Enterprise	
按零售业态分	**Grouped By Operating Situation**	
#超市	Supermarkets	
大型超市	Hypermarkets	
百货店	Department Stores	
专业店	Professional Store	5475.1
其他	Others	

14-11 连锁分店经营情况(2014年)

单位:万元

指标	Item	连锁门店数(个) Number of Chain Stores (unit)	直营店(个) Direct Operated
总计	**Total**	**20**	**17**
批发业		1	1
零售业	Wholesale and Retail Sales	16	14
#内资企业	Domestic Funded Enterprise	9	7
外商投资企业	Foreign Funded Enterprise	6	6
按零售业态分	**Grouped By Operating Situation**		
#超市	Supermarkets	3	2
大型超市	Hypermarkets	5	4
专业店	Professional Store	4	4
专卖店		3	3
其它	Others	1	1
住宿业	Hotels	1	1
餐饮业	Catering Trade	2	1
#快餐	Fastfood	1	
饮料及冷饮服务		1	1

OPERATION OF GENERAL CHAIN STORE(ENTERPRISE)(2014)

(10,000 Yuan)

直营店 Direct-Sale Store	加盟店 Franchise Store	连锁门店商品购进额 Chain Store Commodity Purchase	通过统一配送金额 Total Rationing Amount	通过自有配送中心配送商品购进额 Private Rationing Center Admeasurement
703	**1273**	**2573089**	**2541248**	**2523974**
633	1273	2006095	1974255	1956980
69		521905	521905	521905
1		45089	45089	45089
45	168	32299	28690	25090
70		566994	566994	566994
47	832	1771333	1771333	1771333
535	273	202263	174232	160557
6		200		

CONTINUED

(10,000 Yuan)

连锁门店商品销售额 Commodity Sales of Chain Stores	零售额 Retail Sales	批发和零售业总店在省外设立的分店实现的商品销售额 Commodity Sales of Chain Store Branches out of the Province	零售额 Retail Sales	营业面积(平方米) Operation Space (sq·m)	年末从业人员(人) Year-end Employees (person)
3576235	**2407537**	**85510**	**81273**	**1329937**	**34021**
2407664	1751601	4237		869123	23532
1119079	606444	81273	81273	452277	9652
49492	49492			8537	837
21351	21351			76056	1612
1168571	655937	81273	81273	460814	10489
2170675	1584626			678000	19281
215638	145624	4237		115067	2333
					306

OPERATION OF BRANCH CHAIN STORE(2014)

(10,000 Yuan)

加盟店(个) Franchise Store	商品购进总额 Total Commodity Purchased	接受统一配送商品金额 Total Rationing	商品销售总额(或营业总收入) Total Sales	商品零售额 Total Retail Sales	从业人员(人) Employees (person)
3	**185594**	**183993**	**189295**	**189295**	**2094**
	16412	16412	16371	16371	10
2	165624	164724	172924	172924	1885
2	110863	109963	109725	109725	1623
	54182	54182	62277	62277	248
1	4507	3607	6546	6546	226
1	117998	117998	119059	119059	1144
	29833	29833	28634	28634	434
	11852	11852	15570	15570	49
	1433	1433	3115	3115	32
	11	2			31
1	3547	2856			168
1	2518	1827			116
	1029	1029			52

14-12 亿元以上商品交易市场成交情况(2014 年)

单位:万元

指 标	Item	市场个数 Number of Markets
总 计	**Total**	**88**
按经营环境分	**Grouped By Forms of Operation Environment**	
露天式	Open Air	5
封闭式	Enclosed	70
其他	Others	13
按经营方式分	**Grouped By Forms of Operation**	
批发	Wholesale	32
零售	Retail Sales	56
按市场类别分	**Grouped By Market Category**	
综合市场	Comprehensive Market	34
综合贸易市场	Comprehensive Trade Market	34
工业消费品综合市场	Comprehensive Market for Industrial Consumption Goods	5
农副产品综合市场	Comprehensive Market for Agriculture and Side-line Products	24
其他综合市场	Others	5
专业市场	Special Market	54
生产资料市场	Market for Factors of Production	8
农用生产资料市场	Market for Agricultural Production Goods	1
木材市场	Wood Market	1
建材市场	Construction Material Market	3
金属材料市场	Metal Material Market	2
机械设备市场	Mechanical Equipment Market	1
其他生产资料市场	Others	
农产品市场	Market for Agricultural Products	16
粮油市场	Market for Grain and Oil	
肉禽蛋市场	Market for Meat,Poultry and Eggs	12
水产品市场	Market for Aquatic Products	2
蔬菜市场	Market for Vegetables	1
干鲜果品市场	Market for Dried and Fresh Fruits	
其他农产品市场	Market for Other Agricultural Products	1
食品、饮料及烟酒市场	Market for Food, Beverage, Tobacco and Alcohol	4
食品饮料市场	Market for Food and Beverage	1
其他食品、饮料及烟酒市场	Others	3
纺织品服装鞋帽市场	Market for Garments,Shoes&Hats and Textiles	5
布料及纺织品市场	Market for Clothing and Textile Products	2
服装市场	Market for Garments	1
其他纺织服装鞋帽市场	Others	2
日用品及文化用品市场	Market for Daily Necessities and Cultural Articles	2
小商品市场	Small Commodity Market	2
家具、五金及装饰材料市场	Market for Furniture, Hardware and Decoration Materials	16
家具市场	Market for Furniture	5
装饰材料市场	Market for Decoration Materials	7
灯具市场	Lighting Market	1
五金材料市场	Hardware Market	2
其他装修市场	Others	1
汽车、摩托车及零配件市场	Market for Automobile, Motocycle and Spare Parts	2
汽车市场	Automobile Market	2
花、鸟、鱼、虫市场	Market of Flowers, Birds, Fish and Insects	1
花卉市场	Flower Market	1

BUSINESS CONDITIONS OF TRANSACTION MARKETS WITH TRANSACTION VALUE EACH MORE THAN 100 MILLION YUAN(2014)

(10,000 Yuan)

市场摊位总量(个) Year End Number of Rented Stands	年末已出租摊位(个) Rented To Individuals	商品成交额 Business Revenue	商品零售额 Total Retail Sales	税金总额 Total Tax	摊位租金总额 Total Rentage	从业人员 Employees	营业面积 Floor Space of Business
48896	**44606**	**16708092**	**5455966**	**103279**	**53327**	**117768**	**3352611**
1591	1587	1026273	141983	350	3296	2569	51460
41970	38445	14803783	4903735	100988	43711	106956	3039551
5335	4574	878036	410248	1941	6320	8243	261600
23555	21795	14629484	4016350	86972	16228	79266	2205581
25341	22811	2078608	1439616	16307	37099	38502	1147030
20394	19009	2811243	898479	8972	18360	31012	490761
20394	19009	2811243	898479	8972	18360	31012	490761
3538	3138	708370	110450	1454	6111	8585	208564
11732	11251	1913919	629905	4201	10067	17210	176725
5124	4620	188954	158124	3317	2182	5217	105472
28502	25597	13896849	4557487	94307	34967	86756	2861850
1397	860	273942	39614	19282	1239	2605	216703
130	120	13240			65	245	9250
120	116	12654	5983	75	68	397	6660
719	349	136119	33108	17680	616	738	87833
128	105	60729	523	1317	295	775	73000
300	170	51200		210	195	450	39960
5552	4559	803692	423788	1245	3313	19787	161684
4022	3036	471923	334585	456	2815	5323	103184
1130	1124	293510	68510	175	360	13351	40000
350	349	20659	10133	86	93	1108	15000
50	50	17600	10560	528	45	5	3500
1153	899	130693	53385	688	1120	874	115492
150	30	12140	1008	296	90	12	50692
1003	869	118553	52377	392	1030	862	64800
11813	11766	11353668	3539720	57924	7818	48546	1060650
9920	9880	11303693	3493527	57387	5148	45934	1000000
317	317	15471	15469	103	732	743	15000
1576	1569	34504	30724	434	1938	1869	45650
798	586	33429	17651	582	732	1423	92000
798	586	33429	17651	582	732	1423	92000
6195	5501	749615	288231	10344	19844	11138	986721
1440	1065	133420	84188	218	12617	1716	278863
3451	3379	504071	114305	8879	5729	7465	615400
100	86	30250	25000	16	350	300	7458
1008	775	52868	35738	531	348	1203	45000
196	196	29006	29000	700	800	454	40000
574	414	199400	185030	3742	340	1783	93600
574	414	199400	185030	3742	340	1783	93600
1020	1012	352410	10068	500	561	600	135000
1020	1012	352410	10068	500	561	600	135000

14-13 限额以上批发企业销售总额50强(2014年)

TOP 50 WHOLESALE ENTERPRISES ABOVE DESIGNATED SIZE OF SALES VOLUME(2014)

序号 No.	企业名称 Enterprise	地址 Address
1	南通化工轻工股份有限公司	南通市崇川区南大街28号
2	江苏省烟草公司南通市公司	南通市崇川区工农南路66号
3	江苏金荣金属材料有限公司	海安县城东镇界墩村14组
4	南通东海石油化工有限公司	江苏省国营南通农场
5	南通川东石油公司	南通市崇川区姚港路6号8楼
6	好盈(南通)实业有限公司	南通市港闸区永兴大道388号
7	南通文峰商贸采购批发有限公司	南通市南大街3-21号
8	南通绿洲电力能源有限公司	南通市港闸区秦灶新村二期55幢三、四层
9	南通宏川化工有限公司	南通市如皋市长江镇疏港路10号
10	南通长江石油化工有限公司	南通市崇川区通盛南路16号
11	海门叠石桥叠龙纺织品贸易有限公司	海门市三星镇大岛路188号
12	百川化工销售如皋有限公司	如皋市长江镇香江路6号
13	南通天诚石油化工有限公司	江苏省国营南通农场
14	海安酒钢商贸有限责任公司	海安商贸物流产业开发区核心区界墩村14组
15	国药控股南通有限公司	南通市崇川区人民西路附90号
16	江苏江盛燃料物资有限公司	如皋市长江镇知青居委会疏港路6号
17	南通明润燃料有限公司	南通市港闸区天生港镇街道龙潭村
18	南通长江油品销售有限公司	如皋市长江镇海坝村
19	江苏瑞华燃料集团有限公司	南通市外环北路650号
20	南通中天恒利达煤炭贸易有限公司	南通苏通科技产业园纬14路9号
21	华润南通医药有限公司	南通市崇川区人民西路499号1楼4楼
22	南通多川博国际贸易有限公司	海安县城东镇界墩村14组
23	江苏海钰金属材料有限公司	海门市悦来镇工业集中区新城西路76号附1号
24	中天世贸有限公司	南通经济技术开发区中天路6号
25	江苏文峰电器有限公司	南通开发区通富北路81-1号

14-13 续表
CONTINUED

序号 No.	企业名称 Enterprise	地址 Address
26	王子制纸商贸(中国)有限公司	南通市崇川区经济技术开发区通达路 18 号
27	江苏大世界服饰有限公司	南通市崇川区南大街 3-21 号
28	江苏润富新能源发展有限公司	南通市港闸区永兴大道 388 号
29	南京医药南通健桥有限公司	如东县掘港镇友谊西路 84 号
30	南通燃料股份有限公司	南通市崇川路 88 号南通国贸中心 2001 室
31	江苏华港燃气有限公司	如东县长沙镇洋口港综合商务大厦
32	南通开发区炜赋对外贸易有限公司	南通市崇川区工农路 228 号银星大厦
33	南通苏中医药物流有限公司	海安县海安镇凤山北路 28 号
34	南通华氏佳源医药有限公司	南通市校北路 5 号
35	江苏金太阳纺织科技有限公司	通州区川港镇志浩工业园区
36	如皋市丰瀛贸易有限公司	如皋市长江镇(如皋港区)疏港路 6 号
37	南通舜僖们实业有限公司	南通市港闸区横河村四组
38	南通宝嘉石油化工有限公司	南通市港闸区唐闸镇街道尖沟头村 8 组
39	南通中昱建材有限公司	海门市常乐镇常青路 188 号
40	南通恒谊金属材料有限公司	南通市港闸区横河村五组
41	华发投资股份公司	如东县掘港镇友谊西路 22 号
42	南通礼安医药有限公司	南通市崇川区人民西路 499 号
43	如东泰邦化工有限公司	如东县沿海经济开发区
44	南通巨丰金属材料有限公司	通州区世纪大道金桥路口
45	南通通诚金属材料有限公司	南通市港闸区外环北路 206 号
46	南通苏润实业集团有限公司	南通市开发区上海路 9 号
47	南通市石油有限公司	南通市王府大厦 B 座 7 楼
48	南通苏润燃料有限公司	南通市开发区区星海商贸中心内
49	江苏三润服装集团股份有限公司	南通市永和路 496 号
50	南通纪氏金属材料有限公司	通州区兴仁镇孙家桥村

14-14 限额以上零售企业销售总额50强(2014年)

TOP 50 RETAIL ENTERPRISES ABOVE DESIGNATED SIZE OF SALES VOLUME(2014)

序号 No.	企业名称 Enterprise	地址 Address
1	江苏乐天玛特商业有限公司	南通市开发区上海路
2	中国石化销售有限公司江苏南通石油分公司	南通市崇川区青年中路309号
3	中国石油天然气股份有限公司江苏南通销售分公司	南通市工农路6号华丽大厦13楼
4	文峰大世界连锁发展股份有限公司南通文峰大世界	南通市南大街3-21号
5	南通文峰电器销售有限公司	南通工农南路999号和平桥街
6	南通润宝行汽车销售服务有限公司	南通开发区中央路东、上海路北
7	南通苏宁云商销售有限公司	南通市南大街2号
8	南通银奥汽车销售服务有限公司	南通开发区星湖大道1085号
9	南通益昌汽车销售服务有限公司	南通市崇川区观音山街道山港桥社区(号)
10	南通文峰伟恒汽车销售服务有限公司	南通市崇川区山港桥社区二组
11	南通之星汽车维修服务有限公司	南通经济技术开发区星湖大道1051号
12	南通八佰伴商贸股份有限公司	南通市人民中路47号
13	南通长江汽车贸易有限公司	南通市港闸区城港路166号
14	南通福联汽车贸易有限公司	南通市城港路150号
15	南通宝诚汽车销售服务有限公司	南通市青年东路277号
16	南通通润发超市有限公司	南通市崇川区人民中路29号
17	如皋文峰大世界有限公司	如皋市如城镇中山路418号
18	南通欧尚超市有限公司	海门市海门镇长江路东、黄海路南侧
19	南通通州润泰商业有限公司	通州区金沙镇建设路18号
20	如东文峰大世界有限公司	如东县掘港镇青园北路19号
21	南通东城悦起贸易有限公司	南通市开发区区星湖大道1075号
22	如皋市大润发商业有限公司	如皋市如城镇福寿路199号
23	南通长江五菱汽车销售服务有限公司	南通市港闸区城港路166号
24	南通文峰伟嘉汽车销售服务有限公司	南通市港闸区秦灶街道秦北村委会
25	南通东方永达佳晨汽车销售服务有限公司	南通市崇川区啬园路136号

14-14 续表
CONTINUED

序号 No.	企业名称 Enterprise	地址 Address
26	南通东方鼎辰汽车销售服务有限公司	南通市啬园路 138 号
27	海安县文峰大世界有限公司	海安县海安镇宁海南路 2 号
28	通州文峰大世界有限公司	通州区金沙镇建设路 76 号
29	启东文峰大世界有限公司	启东市汇龙镇人民中路 650 号
30	海门市金天众达汽车销售服务有限公司	海门市海门镇人民西路 1716 号
31	南通长江上通汽车销售服务有限公司	南通市崇川区工农南路 110 号
32	中海油销售南通有限公司	南通开发区中央路 8 号
33	南通嘉华汽车销售服务有限公司	南通市港闸区城港路 150 号
34	海门文峰大世界有限公司	海门市海门镇江海路 115 号
35	南通德立汽车销售服务有限公司	南通开发区中央路 52 号福星楼
36	南通鑫湖汽车贸易服务有限公司	南通市开发区星湖大道 1075 号
37	如东众驰汽车销售服务有限公司	如东县掘港芳泉村四组
38	无锡商业大厦大东方海门百货有限公司	海门市海门镇解放中路 369 号
39	南通庆堂春医药有限公司	如东县掘港镇通洋南路 11 号
40	如皋长江汽车销售服务有限公司	南通市如皋市如城街道惠政西路 16 号
41	上海永达启东汽车销售服务有限公司	启东市汇龙镇台角村
42	南通宝腾汽车销售服务有限公司	南通市崇川区长江中路 129 号
43	南通文峰恒润汽车销售有限公司	南通市崇川区工农南路 28 号
44	南通中油燃气有限责任公司	如皋市长江镇沿江公路 99 吃
45	南通文峰千家惠超市有限公司	南通市崇川区青年西路 16 号
46	如皋长江汽车贸易有限公司	如皋市如城街道惠政西路 12 号
47	南通大生丰田汽车销售服务有限公司	南通市城港路 187 号
48	江苏太平洋汽车集团有限公司	南通市城港路 136 号
49	江苏大生润达车业有限公司	南通市港闸区大生路 1 号
50	苏果超市(海安)有限公司	海安县海安镇长江中路 93 号(贵都广场)

14-15 限额以上住宿和餐饮业营业收入 50 强(2014 年)

TOP 50 ACCOMMODATION AND CATERING ENTERPRISES ABOVE DESIGNATED SIZE OF SALES REVENUE(2014)

序号 No.	企 业 名 称 Enterprise	地 址 Address
1	南通大饭店有限公司	南通市崇川区青年东路 81 号
2	南通市文峰饭店有限公司	南通市崇川区青年东路 1 号
3	南通中南新世界中心开发有限公司金石国际大酒店	南通市崇川路 85 号中南汇泉国际广场
4	海门东恒盛国际大酒店有限公司	海门市海门镇北京中路 777 号
5	南通市骏莱投资发展有限公司	启东市开发区人民西路 1188 号
6	启东宾馆有限公司	启东市汇龙镇民乐中路 490 号
7	南通速堡餐饮有限公司	南通市崇川区桃园路 12 号(第 L5012-5015 单元)
8	南通市崇川区时尚豆捞火锅城	南通市崇川区工农路 111 号
9	南通北山饭店有限公司	通州区金沙镇北山路 20 号
10	启东先豪国际酒店有限公司	启东市开发区人民西路 1888 号
11	南通光华国际大酒店有限公司	海门市海门镇南海东路 1 号
12	南通浅水湾大酒店有限公司	如东县掘港镇钟山路 111 号新光村委会
13	江苏雅成品尚餐饮发展有限公司	南通市通州区先锋镇秦家埭村十二组 1 幢
14	南通绿洲国际大酒店有限公司	南通市港闸区北大街 199 号
15	如东中天黄海大酒店有限公司	如东县掘港镇日晖西路 8 号
16	如皋市金鼎酒店管理有限公司	如皋市如城镇解放中路(新市政府北侧)
17	海门市三厂镇鼎鑫酒店	海门市中华中路 10 号
18	南通新有斐大酒店有限公司	南通市崇川区濠南路 8 号
19	如东海洲大饭店有限公司	如东县掘港镇友谊东路 1 号
20	海安锦龙国际大酒店有限公司	海安县海安镇长江中路 99-1 号
21	启东市海鲨岛商务咨询服务部	启东市经济开发区人民西路 1668 号
22	南通文景国际大酒店有限公司	南通市崇川区世纪大道 55 号
23	海安县正通假日酒店	海安县城东镇泰宁村
24	如东迎驾商务酒店	如东县洋口镇斜港村村委会
25	南通华通大酒店有限公司	南通市青年中路 88 号

14-15　续表

CONTINUED

序号 No.	企　业　名　称 Enterprise	地　址 Address
26	如皋永林国际大酒店有限公司	如皋市石庄镇石南居委会 16 组
27	如东县龙腾宾馆	如东县洋口镇斜港村村委会
28	启东市博圣酒店有限公司	启东市汇龙镇人民中路 669 号江海路口西南侧
29	海门市正余镇菜根香酒楼	海门市正余镇新桥村 23 组
30	如东印象南海假日酒店管理有限公司	如东县金蛤大道西侧如东沿海经济开发区
31	江苏中洋酒店有限公司	海安县海安镇中坝南路 100 号
32	海安县王府大酒店	海安经济技术开发区通榆中路 98 号
33	南通宇龙大酒店有限公司	如东县洋口镇斜港村
34	海门市金美酒店	海门市长桥村 32 组
35	南通金陵华侨饭店有限公司	南通市崇川区濠西路 39 号
36	海门市东方雁大饭店有限责任公司	海门市海门镇解放东路 2 号
37	南通四季资产投资管理有限公司	南通市濠西路 1 号
38	如东状元阁大酒店有限公司	如东县洋口镇斜港村委会海力路 146 号
39	南通大娘水饺餐饮有限公司	南通市十字街百货大楼底楼
40	南通王府花园酒店有限公司	海门市海门镇秀山西路 888 号
41	海门市凤岛休闲农庄	海门市余东镇八一村 35 组
42	南通宏海实业有限公司金海安大酒店分公司	海安县海安镇长江东路 2 号
43	南通市崇川区濠河八号大酒店	南通市崇川区濠南路 1 号
44	南通鹏欣投资发展有限公司花园国宾酒店	南通市崇川区山水路 1 号
45	南通宙辉实业有限公司丽辉国际酒店分公司	南通市通州区世纪大道 268 号
46	南通三德大酒店有限公司	南通市崇川区段家坝路 1 号
47	海门市赛城阳光商务酒店	海门市大岛路 88 号
48	如东华诚大酒店有限公司	如东县洋口镇斜港村
49	春林美食城	海门市叠三路 112 号
50	南通市通州区亚细亚大酒店有限公司	南通市通州区金沙镇银河路 66 号

主要统计指标解释

商品购进总额 指从本企业以外的单位和个人购进（包括从国外直接进品）作为转卖或加工后转卖的商品金额（含增值税）。本指标反映批发和零售业从国内外市场上购进商品的总价。

商品购进包括：(1)从工农业生产者、批发和零售业企业、住宿和餐饮企业、出版社或报社的出版发行部门和其他服务业企业购进的商口；(2)从机关团体、事业单位购进的商口；(3)从海关、市场管理部门购进的缉私和没收的商品；(4)从居民收购的废旧商品等。

不包括：(1)企业为本单位自身经营用，不是作为转卖而购进的商品，如材料物资、包装物、低值易耗品、办公用品等；(2)未通过买卖行为而收入的商品，如接受其他部门移交的商品、借入的商品、收入代其他单位保管的商品、其他单位赠送的样品、加工回收的成品等；(3)经本单位介绍，由买卖双方直接结算，本单位只收取手续费的业务；(4)销售退回和买方拒付货款的商品；(5)商品溢余。

商品销售额 指对本单位以外的单位和个人出售的商品金额(包括售给本单位消费用的商品，含增值税)，本指标反映批发和零售业在国内市场上销售商品的总量。

商品销售包括：(1)售给城乡居民和社会集团消费用的商品；(2)售给农业、工业、建筑业、运输邮电业、服务业、公用事业等国民经济各行业用于生产、经营用的商品，包括售予批发和零售业作为转卖或加工后转卖的商品；(3)对国(境)外直接出口的商品。

商品销售不包括：(1)未通过买卖行为付出的商品，如随机构变动移交给其他企业单位的商品、借出的商品、归还受其他单位委托代保管的商品、付出的加工原料和赠给其他单位的样品等；(2)经本单位介绍，由买卖双方直接结算，本单位只收取手续费的业务；(3)购货退回的商品；(4)商品损耗和损失；(5)出售本单位自用的废旧物资。

期末商品库存额 对于批发和零售业法人企业和个体经营户，是指取得所有权的全部商品金额(含增值税)；对于批发和零售业产业活动单位，是指期末实际在库且归属法人具有所有权的全部商品金额(含增值税)。这个指标反映批发和零售业的商品库存情况，以及对市场商口供应的保证程度。

库存商品包括：(1)存放在本单位(如门市部、批发部、采购站、经营处)的仓库、货场、货柜和货架中的商口；(2)挑选、整理、包装中的商品；(3)已记入购进而尚未运到本单位的商品，即发货单或银行承况凭证已到而货未到的商品；(4)寄放他处的商品，如因购货方拒绝付款而暂时存在购货方的商品；(5)委托其他单位代销(未作销售或调出)尚未售出的商品；(6)代其他单位购进尚未交付的商品。库存商品不包括：(1)所有权不属于本单位的商品，如商品已作销售但买方尚未取走的商品，代替他人保管、运输、加工的商品，代其他单位销售(未做购进或调入)而未售出的商品；(2)委托外单位加工的商品(包括本单位所属加工厂和其他生产单位加工生产尚未收回成品的商品)；(3)外贸企业代理其他单位从国外进口，尚未付给订货单位的商品；(4)代国家储备部门保管的商品。

社会消费品零售总额 指批发和零售业、住宿和餐饮业以及其他行业直接售给城乡居民和社会集团的消费品零售额。

批发和零售业零售额 指售给城乡居民用于生活消费和社会集团用于公共消费的商品金额。

住宿和餐饮业零售额 是指专门从事提供食宿服务、进行食品烹饪调制的住宿和餐饮业企业、产业活动单位和个体户，直接向居民和社会集团出售主食、菜肴、烟酒饮料和其他商品取得的餐费收入和商品销售额，包括各行业企业或单位附设的对外营业的旅馆、火车餐车、轮船餐车、轮船餐厅、机场餐厅的零售额，不包括机关、团体、学校、企事业单位不对外营业的职工食堂所出售的餐费收入。

其它行业零售额 是指批发和零售业、住宿和餐饮业以外的其他行业的单位和个体户，从事生活消费用品零售活动或者提供住宿服务所取得的商品销售额和餐费收入。

批发和零售业营业面积 指批发和零售企业或产业活动单位按建筑面积计算的直接对顾客销售商品的固定场地的面积，不包括办公室、仓库、加工场地等面积。

批发和零售企业从业人员 指在批发和零售企业工作并取得劳动报酬的全部人员数。包括在岗职工、再就业的离退休人员、在该企业(单位)工作的外方人员、港澳台方人员、兼职人员、借用的外单位人员和第二职业者。不包括离开本单位但仍保留劳动关系的职工。

批发、零售、住宿、餐饮企业统计限额标准(外贸企业一律包括在批发企业中,其年销售额以外币计量的,应折合人民币)

行业类别	统计指标	单位	限额标准
批发业	年主营业务收入	万元	2000及以上
零售业	年主营业务收入	万元	500及以上
住宿业	年主营业务收入	万元	200及以上
餐饮业	年主营业务收入	万元	200及以上

经营网点 指批发和零售企业设立的从事经营业务的自然单位数。凡具有独立固定的营业场所,配备一定的业务人员,不论单位大小,不论是否单独核算,按自然点计算。

零售网点 指批发和零售企业单位从事商品零售业务的自然单位数。凡具有独立固定的营业场所,配备一定的业务人员,不论单位大小,不论是否单独核算,按自然点计算。包括固定的售货亭。不包括同一营业场所内柜组以及临时或经常性的流动推销小组、流动售货车等。

独立商店 指独立经营,未与其他商业单位建立连锁关系的商店。

连锁企业 指在核心企业或总店的领导下,由分散的、经营同类商品或服务的企业或产业活动单位,通过规范化经营,实现规模效益的经济联合组织形式。一般连锁店应由若干个分店组成。其经营特征:(1)经营同类商品;(2)使用统一商号;(3)统一采购配送,采购与销售相分离(部分商品可根据物流合理和保质保鲜原则由供应商直接送货到门店,其余均由总部统一配送)。

直营连锁 也叫正规连锁。连锁门店均由总部独资或控股开设,在总部的直接领导下统一经营。

加盟连锁 也叫特许连锁。各连锁门店(被特许人)通过合同形式,取得使用总部(特许人)商标、商号、经营技术和销售总部开发的商品的特许权。各连锁门店大多为独立法人(不排除一些产业活动单位和个体经营户),但无自主经营权,统一接受总部指导。

连锁总店 负责连锁企业资源(商号、商誉、经营模式、服务标准、管理模式等等)的开发、配置、控制或使用等功能的企业核心管理机构。

连锁分店 指连锁总店所属各分散经营的企业或活动单位。

便利店 位于商业中心区、交通要道理以及车站、医院、学校、娱乐场所、办公楼、加油站等公共活动区;商圈范围小,顾客步行5分钟内到达,目标顾客主要为单身者、年轻人、顾客多为有目的的购买;营业面积一般在100平方米左右,利用率高;以即时食品、日用小百货为主,有即时消费性、小容量、应急性等特点,商品品种在3000种左右,售价一般高于市场平均水平;商品销售方式以开架自选为主,结算在收银处统一进行;营业时间一般在16小时以上,提供即时性食品的辅助设施,开设多项服务项目;信息管理系统程度较高。

折扣店 位于居民区、交通要道等租金相对便宜的地区;辐射半径2公里左右,目标顾客主要为商圈内的居民;自有晶牌占有较大的比例,商品平均价格低于市场平均水平;以开架自选方式进行商品销售,并统一结算;用工精简,为顾客提供有限的服务;信息管理系统程度一般。

超市 位于市、区商业中心、居住区;辐射半径2公里左右,目标顾客以居民为主;营业面积在6000平方米以下;经营包装食品、生鲜食品和日用品。食品超市与综合超市商品结构有所不同;采用自选销售,出入口分设,在收银台统一结算;营业时间12小时以上;信息管理系统程度较高。

大型超市 位于市、区商业中心、城郊结合部、交通要道及大型居住区;辐射半径2公里以上,目标顾客以居民、流动顾客为主;实际营业面积在6000平方米以上;以大众化衣、食、日用品为主,品种齐全,注重自有品牌开发;采用自选销售方式,出入口分设,在收银台统一结算;设不低于营业面积40%的停车场;信息管理系统程度较高。

仓储会员店 位于城乡结合部的交通要道;辐射半径5公里以上,目标顾客以中小零售店、餐饮店、集团购买和流动顾客为主;营业面积一般在6000平方米以上;以大众化衣、食、日用品为主,自有品牌占相当部分,商品在4000种左右,实行低价、批量销售;采用自选销售,出入口分设,在收银台统一结算;设相当于营业面积的停车场;信息管理系统程度较高并对顾客实行会员制管理。

百货店 位于市、区级商业中心、历史形成的商业集聚地;目标顾客以追求时尚和品味的流动顾客为主;营业面积一般在6000平方米以上;综合性商品结构,门类齐全,以服饰、鞋类、箱包、化妆品、家庭用品、家用电器为主;采取柜台销售和开架面售相结合方式进行商品销售;注重服务,设餐饮、娱乐等服务项目和设施;信息管理系统程度较高。

专业店 位于市、区级商业中心以及百货店、购物中心内;目标顾客以有目的选购某类商品的流动顾客为主;营业面积根据商品特点而定;以销售某类商品为主,体现专业性、深度性、品种丰富,选择余地大;采取柜台销售或开架面售方式进行商品销售;从业人员具有丰富的专业知识;信息管理系统程度较高。

专卖店 一般位于市\区级商业中心;专业街以及百货店、购物中心内;目标顾客以中高档消费者和追求时尚的年轻人为主;以销售某一品牌系列商品为主,具有销售量少、质优、高毛利等特点;采取柜台销售或开架面售方式进行商品销售,商店陈列、照明、包装、广告讲究;注重品牌声誉,从业人员具备丰富的专业知识,提供专业性服务;信息管理系统程度一般。

家居建材商店 位于城乡结合部、交通要道或消费者自有房产比较高的地区;目标顾客以拥有自有房产的顾客为主;营业面积一般在6000平方米以上;经营商品以改善、建设家庭居住环境有关的装饰、装修等用品、日用杂品、技术及服务为主;采取开架自选方式销售商品;提供一站式购足和一条龙服务,停车位一般在300个以上;信息管理系统程度较高。

厂家直销中心 一般远离市区;目标顾客多为重视品牌的有目的的购买;单个建筑面积在100-200平方米左右;品牌商品生产商直接设立,商品均为本企业的品牌;采用自选式售货方式进行商品销售;各个租赁店使用各自的信息管理系统。

门店总数 指该连锁企业所拥有的全部门店(包括直营店和加盟店,下同)数量。其中,总店(如总公司有门店的话)作为一个直营店处理。此外,有的地区分出控股店,控股店按直营店统计。

直营店 由连锁企业总部投资开设,按连锁经营管理模式,由总部统一管理的店铺。

加盟店 特许连锁中,被特许人获得特许人授权后,使用其商标、商号、经营模式、专利和专有技术等经营资源建立的店铺。也包括自愿连锁的成员店。系统内企业,如新华书店、烟草公司、石油公司等,应注意是否具备连锁经营特征,如果不具备连锁经营特征,则不能纳入连锁统计范畴。

正餐 指提供各种中西式炒菜和主食,并由服务员送餐上桌的餐饮服务。包括各种中式正餐和西式正餐。

快餐 指服务员不送餐上桌,由顾客自己领取食物的一种自我服务的餐饮活动。包括各种中式快餐和西式快餐。

茶馆 以现场提供现场消费茶饮料为主,兼卖各式点心和小食品。包括各种茶艺馆、茶楼、茶铺等。

咖啡馆 指现场制作现场消费咖啡饮料为主,兼卖各式点心和小食品。包括各种咖啡馆、咖啡厅、咖啡屋等。

酒吧 以出售各种酒及酒精饮料为主,兼卖各式点心和小食品。

餐饮业营业面积 指餐饮企业(单位)按建筑面积计算的直接供顾客用餐的餐厅营业面积及从事食品加工、烹饪、调制的厨房面积,不包括办公用房、仓库等面积。

餐饮业营业总收入 指餐饮业和从事餐饮活动的单位的全部营业收入,包括商品零售额、服务费、卡拉OK收入等。

餐饮业商品零售额 指餐饮企业直接对居民和社会集团零售的各种商品。包括:经烹饪、调制加工后出售的各种食品、不经加工直接转卖的各种外购商品,附设非独立核算的专门销售商品的小卖部出售的各种食品及其他商品。

餐饮业网点数 指住宿和餐饮企业设立的从事餐饮业务的自然单位数(包括本企业自身)。凡具有固定的营业场所,配备一定的业务人员,不论单位大小,不论是否单独核算,均按自然点计算,即有一个营业点就算一个网点。不包括派出的流动饮料、流动饮食货车等,不论临时性还是经常性的均不作为网点统计(固定的饮食售货亭应作为网点统计)。

餐饮业从业人员数 指在该餐饮企业(单位)工作并取得劳动报酬的全部人员数。包括在岗职工、再就业的离退休人员、在该企业(单位)工作的外方人员、港、澳、台方人员、兼职人员、借用的外单位人员和第二职业者。不包括离开本单位但仍保留劳动关系的职工。

配送中心 是连锁企业的物流机构,承担着各门店所需商品的进货、库存、分货、加工、集配、运输、送货等任务。配送中心主要为本连锁企业服务,也可面向社会。

统一配送比重 指统一配送的商品金额(按购进价计算)与全部商品购进总额之比。

配送中心面积 指配送中心的仓库面积和操作场的建筑面积,不包括办公区面积。

运输车辆 指该配送中心拥有的机动车数量,不包括平板车、人力三轮车等非机动车辆。

门店数 指该连锁店所拥有的全部连锁门店数量,包括总店(如果总公司有门店的话)和全部直营分店、加盟分店数。其中,总店作为一个直营店处理。

亿元以上商品交易市场 指年成交额在亿元及以上的商品交易市场。商品交易市场是指经有关部门和组织批准设立,有固定场所、设施,有经营管理部门和监管人员,若干市场经营者入内,常年或实际开业三个月以上,集中、公开、独立地进行生活消费品、生产资料等现货商品交易以及提供相关服务的交易场所,包括各类消费品市场、生产资料市场等。

市场成交总额 指商品交易市场所有摊位商品交易总额之和。

市场管理费总额 指市场管理部门收取的各种管理费金额合计数。包括向工商管理部门缴纳的工商管理费、向摊主收取的水、电、卫生、治安等费用。

市场营业面积 指市场营业用场地、仓库等营业性建筑面积。不包括为市场经营服务的办公室和附设的旅馆、招待所、餐馆、停车场的面积。

摊位出租率 为实际出租摊位数占全部摊位数的比率。

摊位租金总额 指市场出租场地或摊位而得到的租金收入。

税金总额 指摊主向当地税务部门缴纳的税金。

市场累计固定资产投资额 指市场建立之日至今,累计专门用于市场建设的固定资产投资总额,不含用于市场附属设施(如附设的旅馆、招待所、餐馆、停车场等)的投资额。

第十五篇 15

教育 科技 Chapter

Education, Science and Technology

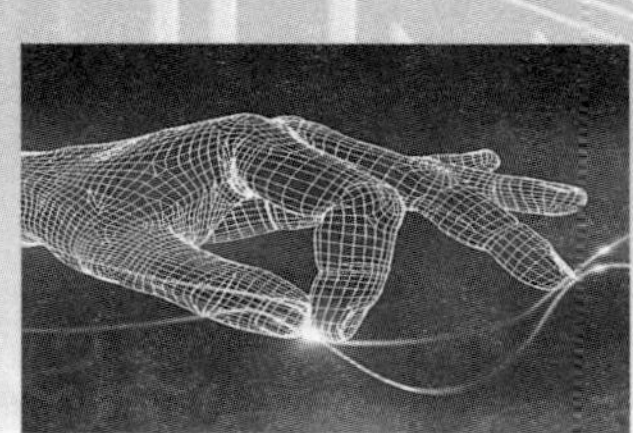

15-1 历年在校学生数和毕业生数

NUMBER OF STUDENT ENROLLMENT AND GRADUATES OVER THE YEARS

单位:万人 (10,000 person)

年份 Year	在校学生数 Student Enrollment			毕业生数 Graduates		
	中学 Secondary Schools	初中 Junior High School	小学 Primary Schools	中学 Secondary Schools	初中 Junior High School	小学 Primary Schools
1978	50.88	35.79	97.95	23.81	17.07	18.18
1979	43.25	32.06	93.10	21.67	14.78	16.76
1980	40.23	35.15	87.72	11.79	6.07	15.60
1985	32.55	27.23	61.29	9.72	8.25	10.29
1990	28.24	23.66	55.82	8.04	6.38	8.70
1991	28.50	23.77	54.21	8.56	7.11	8.59
1992	29.66	24.64	52.91	8.79	7.41	9.64
1993	30.09	25.16	53.54	9.01	7.44	9.29
1994	31.03	26.03	55.01	9.12	7.54	9.46
1995	31.42	25.91	57.45	10.02	8.40	9.08
1996	31.26	25.05	61.25	9.62	8.08	7.90
1997	30.41	23.88	64.38	10.35	8.63	7.43
1998	30.41	22.84	65.36	10.61	8.52	8.64
1999	32.96	25.12	63.96	9.48	7.27	10.15
2000	37.14	28.89	61.74	9.35	6.78	11.07
2001	41.83	32.28	58.78	10.59	7.97	11.87
2002	45.63	34.28	54.38	12.16	9.59	12.01
2003	47.26	34.28	50.01	13.44	10.52	10.92
2004	46.41	32.28	47.05	16.03	11.62	8.90
2005	44.13	29.40	43.53	15.82	11.48	8.89
2006	42.48	27.42	40.15	15.41	10.82	8.94
2007	41.23	26.82	36.79	14.33	9.37	8.72
2008	39.67	25.71	34.36	13.65	8.86	7.65
2009	36.70	23.37	32.81	13.89	9.00	6.72
2010	33.65	20.59	32.32	13.21	8.81	6.14
2011	30.52	18.29	32.22	12.13	7.71	5.49
2012	27.96	16.94	31.76	11.05	6.66	5.41
2013	28.25	16.00	31.82	11.38	6.12	5.26
2014	25.60	15.65	32.04	10.02	5.37	5.02

15-2 各级各类学校基本情况(2014年)

单位:人

指 标	Item	全市 Whole Municipality	市区 Urban Area
学校数(所)	**Number of Schools(unit)**	**578**	**34**
普通高等学校	Regular Institutions of Higher Education	8	8
普通中等专业学校	Regular Specialized Secondary Schools	5	5
技工学校	Technical Schools	9	3
职业中学	Vocational Schools	11	1
普通中学	Regular Secondary Schools	215	11
#高中	Senior	52	8
小学	Primary Schools	321	6
特殊教育学校	Special Education Schools	9	
教职工数	**Staff and Teachers**	**63723**	**11423**
普通高等学校	Regular Institutions of Higher Education	7294	7294
普通中等专业学校	Regular Specialized Secondary Schools	891	891
技工学校	Technical Schools	1503	572
职业中学	Vocational Schools	3934	102
普通中学	Regular Secondary Schools	28883	2350
小学	Primary Schools	20840	214
特殊教育学校	Special Education Schools	378	
专任教师数	**Number of Full-time Teachers**	**53397**	**8196**
普通高等学校	Regular Institutions of Higher Education	4902	4902
普通中等专业学校	Regular Specialized Secondary Schools	643	643
技工学校	Technical Schools	833	417
职业中学	Vocational Schools	3019	83
普通中学	Regular Secondary Schools	24956	1959
#高中	Senior	9783	1079
小学	Primary Schools	18741	192
特殊教育学校	Special Education Schools	303	

BASIC CONDITIONS OF SCHOOLS BY CATEGORY(2014)

(person)

崇川区 Chongchuan	港闸区 Gangzha	开发区	通州区 Tongzhou	海安 Haian	如东 Rudong	启东 Qidong	如皋 Rugao	海门 Haimen
35	**18**	**9**	**74**	**82**	**74**	**81**	**90**	**81**
				2	1		2	1
			2	2	1	2	2	1
8	7	4	30	31	26	29	31	38
		1	8	6	7	6	8	8
24	11	5	41	46	45	49	54	40
3			1	1	1	1	1	1
2937	**1119**	**1030**	**7847**	**7925**	**7244**	**6997**	**9409**	**7792**
				247	460		133	91
			508	963	440	549	748	624
776	472	471	4247	3940	3513	3755	5191	4168
2054	647	559	3044	2717	2782	2657	3298	2868
107			48	58	49	36	39	41
2708	**1020**	**976**	**6663**	**6027**	**5545**	**6441**	**8763**	**7058**
				207	23		105	81
			402	444	368	496	685	541
676	416	437	3484	3186	2952	3370	4774	3702
		157	1349	1359	1252	1228	1932	1427
1933	604	539	2742	2160	2162	2539	3168	2702
99			35	30	40	36	31	32

15-2 续表

单位:人

指 标	Item	全市 Whole Municipality	市区 Urban Area
在校学生数(人)	**Student Enrollment**	**732745**	**145762**
普通高等学校	Regular Institutions of Higher Education	87410	87410
普通中等专业学校	Regular Specialized Secondary Schools	53394	21801
技工学校	Technical Schools	14609	8504
职业中学	Vocational Schools	8520	
普通中学	Regular Secondary Schools	247432	24876
#高中	Senior	90933	12346
小学	Primary Schools	320425	3171
特殊教育学校	Special Education Schools	955	
毕业生数(人)	**Graduates**	**196652**	**45564**
普通高等学校	Regular Institutions of Higher Education	25739	25739
普通中等专业学校	Regular Specialized Secondary Schools	15566	7863
技工学校	Technical Schools	4779	3145
职业中学	Vocational Schools	9798	
普通中学	Regular Secondary Schools	90408	8277
#高中	Senior	36718	4320
小学	Primary Schools	50226	540
特殊教育学校	Special Education Schools	136	
招生人数(人)	**New Student Enrollment**	**181871**	**46286**
普通高等学校	Regular Institutions of Higher Education	28441	28441
普通中等专业学校	Regular Specialized Secondary Schools	17411	7013
技工学校	Technical Schools	4590	2431
职业中学	Vocational Schools	2976	
普通中学	Regular Secondary Schools	77057	7911
#高中	Senior	26741	3883
小学	Primary Schools	51286	490
特殊教育学校	Special Education Schools	110	

CONTINUED

(person)

崇川区 Chongchuan	港闸区 Gangzha	开发区	通州区 Tongzhou	海安 Haian	如东 Rudong	启东 Qidong	如皋 Rugao	海门 Haimen
46371	**15505**	**15999**	**86996**	**75826**	**64230**	**74065**	**119977**	**88014**
			3915	357	5446	5789	9271	6815
				4226	54		1518	307
				8520				
6766	4159	5404	36224	28755	28531	30606	47617	34494
		1793	13796	10769	11169	10982	17277	12801
39355	11346	10595	46734	33835	30089	37557	61471	46272
250			123	133	110	113	100	126
7853	**2665**	**3070**	**22653**	**21181**	**19193**	**20024**	**32111**	**22338**
			1674	139	2547	2286	100	957
				1294	98		242	
				3912			4525	1361
2188	1225	1576	13891	10052	11179	11600	17439	12981
		588	5474	4273	4954	4448	7303	5358
5599	1440	1494	7085	5769	5357	6128	9794	7020
66			3	15	12	10	11	19
8650	**3799**	**3983**	**19770**	**18242**	**14897**	**17135**	**28270**	**20839**
			1517	135	1386	2043	2957	2360
				1317			842	
				2976				
2195	1442	1916	11033	8736	8456	9263	15312	10793
		595	3944	2998	2999	3140	5449	3733
6417	2357	2067	7208	5069	5045	5822	9147	7664
38			12	9	10	7	12	22

15-3 普通高等学校基本情况(2014年)

BASIC CONDITIONS ON HIGHER EDUCATION INSTITUTES(2014)

单位:人 (person)

学校名称	Schools	学校数(个) Number of Institutions (unit)	在校研究生 Postgraduates Registered	本专科学生			
				毕业生数 Graduate	招生数 Student Enrollment	在校学生数 Students Registered	毕业班学生数 Graduating Class Students
合 计	**Total**	**8**	**1918**	**25182**	**27759**	**85492**	**26212**
南通大学	Nantong Univeristy	1	1918	8002	8717	33846	8017
南通职业大学	Nantong Vocational University	1		3383	3782	11078	3651
江苏工程职业技术学院	Jangsu College of Engineering and Technolgy	1		2901	3305	9530	3058
南通航运职业技术学院	Nantong Shipping College	1		2766	2892	8654	2868
南通农业职业技术学院	Nantong Farming Vocational College	1		2149	1883	5987	2183
南通理工学院	Nantong Polytechnic College,NPC	1		1444	2089	5756	2145
江苏商贸职业学院	Jiangsu Vocational College of Commevce and Trade	1			544	1055	
南通师范高等专科学校	Nantong Normal College	1		1569	1712	3071	1359
南通市开放大学	Nantong Open University			1152	884	2386	1108
南通卫生高等职业技术学校	Nantong Hdvanced Vocational and Technical Schoo of Health			891	897	1815	896
南通中等专业学校	Nantong Specialized Secondary School			227	271	497	224
通州职业教育中心	Tongzhou Vocational Education Center			367	334	675	369
海门中等专业学校	Haimen Specialized Secondary School			331	379	1072	334
如皋中等专业学校	Rugao Specialized Secondary School				70	70	

注:本表含职业技术学院或高等师范学校招收的五年制高职后两年学生。

Note:The graph includs the last-two year students of Vocational College or Normal College.

15-3 续表

CONTINUED

单位:人 (person)

学校名称	Schools	合计 Total	教职工数 Staffs and Teachers 专任教师数 Number of Full-time Teachers	正高级 High Degree	副高级 Vice-high Degree	中级 Medium Degree	初级 Junior Degree	未定级 Not Grading
合 计	**Total**	**7294**	**4902**	**456**	**1734**	**2083**	**516**	**113**
南通大学	Nantong Univeristy	3311	2113	327	872	758	124	32
南通职业大学	Nantong Vocational University	822	533	23	214	259	28	9
江苏工程职业技术学院	Jangsu college of Engineering and Technology	626	384	16	111	210	40	7
南通航运职业技术学院	Nantong Shipping College	654	462	25	159	220	53	5
南通农业职业技术学院	Nantong Farming Vocational College	390	315	13	72	162	68	
南通理工学院	Nantong Polytechnic College, NPC	489	307	36	70	131	56	14
江苏商贸职业学院	Jiangsu Vocational College of Commevce and Trade	406	322	2	72	108	94	46
南通师范高等专科学校	Nantong Normal College	596	466	14	164	235	53	

15-4 中等职业学校基本情况(2014 年)

BASIC CONDITIONS OF SPECIALZED SECONDARY SCHOOLS(2014)

单位:人(person)

学校名称	学校数(所) Number of Schools	毕业生数 Students Graduating	招生数 Students Enrollede	在校学生数 Students Registered	教职工数 Staff and Workers	专任教师 Full TimeTeach-ers
合 计	**21**	**26031**	**20818**	**64082**	**4648**	**3802**
南通市旅游中等专业学校	1	296	344	1601	102	83
南通中等专业学校	1	1410	1266	3444	265	187
南通高等师范学校		733				
如皋高等师范学校	1	522	543	1619	207	171
南通纵横国际职业技术学校	1	260		122	36	29
南通建筑职业技术学校	1	350	148	595	53	27
南通市体育运动学校	1	301	237	1049	79	55
南通体臣卫生学校	1	1149	1571	4160	304	201
南通市广播电视大学中职院	1	859	653	2310		
南通农业职业技术学院		146	377	971		
江苏商贸职业学院		1909	1121	4067		
南通师范高等专科学校			559	2169		
南通市工人业余大学		19	223	300		
江苏省通州中等专业学校(江苏电大通州学院)	1	1206	1359	3548	429	329
南通市通州区农业综合技术学校	1	468	158	367	79	73
南通市通州区建筑职工中等专业学校	1	421	240	956	72	40
南通市通州卫生职工中等专业学校	1	88	162	437	24	16
江苏省海安中等专业学校	1	2481	2620	7417	321	269
江苏省海安双楼中等专业学校	1	730	491	1460	198	175
海安县艺术学校	1	840			98	49
如东第一职业教育中心校	1	2547	1386	5446	440	368
启东市第二中等专业学校	1	1114	1092	3094	230	217
江苏省启东市中等专业学校	1	1172	951	2695	319	279
江苏省如皋中等专业学校	1	1853	1492	5197	504	454
江苏省如皋第一中等专业学校	1	2772	1465	4074	244	231
江苏省海门中等专业学校	1	2318	2360	6815	624	541
南通市海门卫生职工中等专业学校		67		169	20	8

注:此表仅含五年制高职前三年学生,后两年学生数统计在高校数据中。

15-5 技工学校基本情况(2014年)

BASIC CONDITIONS OF TECHNICAL SCHOOLS(2014)

单位:人 (person)

学校名称	School Name	学校数(所) Number of Schools	毕业生数 Graduates	招生数 Students Enrollment	在校学生数 Students Registered	教职工数 Teaching and Administrative Staff	专任教师 Full Time Teachers
合 计	**Total**	**9**	**5672**	**7770**	**18744**	**1308**	**1041**
南通市技师学院	Nantong Technician College	1	1244	1870	4624	247	195
南通市工贸技校	Nantong Industry &Trade Technical School	1	1800	2370	5355	260	230
南通蓝领技工学校	Nantong Blue-collar Technical School	1	735	444	1352	68	52
海安县技校	Haian Technical School	1	393	600	1326	68	52
海安县海陵技校	Haian Hailing Technical School	1	1011	1317	3467	185	163
如皋市技校	Rugao Technical School	1		594	1124	99	56
如皋市江海技校	Rugao River&Sea Technical School	1	98	50	138	21	17
如东县技校	Rudong Technical School	1	242	525	983	57	49
海门市技校	Haimen Technical School	1	149		375	112	74

15-6 幼儿园基本情况(2014年)

BASIC STATISTICS ON KINDERGARDENS(2014)

单位:人 (person)

地 区	Region	园数(个) Number (unit)	班数(个) Classes (unit)	在园幼儿数 Registered School-Age Children	教职工数 Teaching and Administrative Staff	专任教师 Full- Time Teachers	保健员 Health Worker
全 市	**Total**	**396**	**4326**	**153528**	**11806**	**7044**	**274**
市 区	Urban Area	144	1600	55802	5806	3227	148
#通州区	Tongzhou	53	599	22796	1969	1180	38
海 安	Haian	47	486	15665	472	364	4
如 东	Rudong	44	393	15177	1227	746	35
启 东	Qidong	61	554	18015	713	299	17
如 皋	Rugao	57	772	29867	2485	1597	55
海 门	Haimen	43	521	19002	1103	811	15

15-7 县级以上政府部门所属科研机构(2014年)

SCIENTIFIC REASEARCH INSTITUTION OF GOVERNMENT DEPARTMENT ABOVE THE COUNTY LEVEL(2014)

指 标	Item	机构数（个）Number of Institutions (unit)	职工人数（人）Number of Employees (person)	专业技术干部（人）Professional Technology Cadres(person)	从事科技活动人员（人）People engaged in Scientific and Technological Activities(person)		
						高级职称 Senior Professional Title	中级职称 Medium-grade Professional Title
合计	**Total**	**11**	**366**	**80**	**246**	**98**	**68**
省属	Departments of Province	1	116	16	90	47	19
市属	Departments of City	5	144	53	89	37	27
县属	Departments of County	5	106	11	67	14	22

15-8 科技成果获奖数(2014年)

SCIENTIFIC AND TECHNOLOGICAL ACHIEVEMENTS(2014)

单位：项 (item)

指 标	Item	全市 Municipality	市区 Urban Area		海安 Haian	如东 Rudong	启东 Qidong	如皋 Rugao	海门 Haimen
				通州区 Tongzhou					
合计	**Total**	**188**	**88**	**26**	**12**	**16**	**20**	**17**	**9**
国家科技进步奖	National Award for Science and Techology Progress	2	2						
一等奖	First Award								
二等奖	Second Award	2	2						
三等奖	Third Award								
省级科技进步奖	Provincial Prizes for S&T Progress	16	6		2	2	2	2	2
一等奖	First Award	0							
二等奖	Second Award	1	1						
三等奖	Third Award	15	5		2	2	2	2	2
市级科技进步奖	City Prizes for S&T Progress	170	80	26	10	14	18	15	7
特等奖	Special Award	0							
一等奖	First Award	10	5	2		1	2		
二等奖	Second Award	60	34	5	6	4	4	4	3
三等奖	Third Award	100	41	19	4	9	12	11	4
中国专利金奖		1	1						
中国专利优秀奖		2	1					1	

15-9 部分年份专利申请与授权数

PATENT APPLICATION AND AUTHORIZATION IN SOME YEARS

单位：件 (unit)

年份 Year	指标	Item	全市 Whole Municipality	市区 Urban Area	通州 Tongzhou	海安 Haian	如东 Rudong	启东 Qidong	如皋 Rugao	海门 Haimen
2000	申请	Applications Examined	623	359	90	78	46	50	59	31
	授权	Applications Granted	391	226	53	58	35	29	27	16
2001	申请	Applications Examined	844	425	126	86	45	99	131	58
	授权	Applications Granted	478	271	65	48	38	59	33	29
2002	申请	Applications Examined	1146	460	224	113	83	117	184	174
	授权	Applications Granted	422	242	67	39	25	58	15	31
2003	申请	Applications Examined	1431	447	183	210	209	178	184	203
	授权	Applications Granted	538	247	78	90	43	75	45	38
2004	申请	Applications Examined	1859	610	276	289	194	275	308	183
	授权	Applications Granted	612	213	62	153	59	88	42	57
2005	申请	Applications Examined	3120	1192	273	521	295	357	510	245
	授权	Applications Granted	792	239	53	218	76	105	97	57
2006	申请	Applications Examined	5342	1926	700	715	507	573	882	739
	授权	Applications Granted	1709	471	109	412	165	240	143	278
2007	申请	Applications Examined	9067	3475	1126	1182	695	844	1487	1384
	授权	Applications Granted	3756	1443	334	643	261	580	318	511
2008	申请	Applications Examined	14106	4258	1654	2942	1033	1616	2357	1900
	授权	Applications Granted	4102	1377	488	454	178	503	658	932
2009	申请	Applications Examined	21904	7319	2294	3709	1712	2790	3817	2557
	授权	Applications Granted	10722	3385	1408	1853	831	1202	1943	1508
2010	申请	Applications Examined	38707	13695	4046	5399	2113	4566	5588	7346
	授权	Applications Granted	22644	8115	2121	2310	1622	2533	3540	4524
2011	申请	Applications Examined	56421	20152	6488	6791	3250	7521	6549	12158
	授权	Applications Granted	31335	11344	3898	2434	1684	3424	2550	9899
2012	申请	Applications Examined	49924	19766	7515	5979	7983	2076	5248	8872
	授权	Applications Granted	36247	14351	3344	5179	5054	1975	3562	6126
2013	申请	Applications Examined	40771	19463	3549	7202	7115	620	4671	1700
	授权	Applications Granted	22086	9654	1471	5519	3559	315	2047	992
2014	申请	Applications Examined	27692	14118	3596	4245	1049	3676	2890	1714
	授权	Applications Granted	12391	6204	2141	2313	581	1378	1288	627

15-10 历年大中型工业企业研究与发展活动企业数

NUMBER OF RESEARCH AND DEVELOPMENT INSTITUTIONS OF LARGE AND MEDIUM-SIZED ENTERPRISES OVER THE YEARS

单位：个 (unit)

年份 Year	全市 Whole Municipality	市区 Urban Areas	通州 Tongzhou	海安 Haian	如东 Rudong	启东 Qidong	如皋 Rugao	海门 Haimen
1994	12	4			3			5
1996	35	20		1	5	8	1	
1997	39	30			3	3	3	
1998	53	31	4		8	4	4	6
1999	56	33	2	1	5	7	6	4
2000	62	37	5		6	5	7	7
2001	84	43	11	1	9	6	11	14
2002	85	56	14	1	7	6	7	8
2003	109	57	17	9	10	8	7	18
2004	82							
2005	91	34	11	11	12	10	9	15
2006	132	50	18	27	13	12	12	18
2007	137	48	17	28	11	12	17	21
2008	146	45	17	32	16	13	24	16
2009	167	64	26	28	20	16	24	15
2010	212	78	37	38	22	24	30	20
2011	237	101	40	26	19	28	44	19
2012	375	151	72	59	44	31	67	23
2013	463	169	76	61	48	60	85	40
2014	472	156	73	73	49	55	87	52

15-11 历年大中型工业企业研究与发展人员数

NUMBER OF RESEARCH AND DEVELOPMENT PERSONNEL OF LARGE AND MEDIUM-SIZED ENTERPRISES OVER THE YEARS

单位:人　　(person)

年份 Year	全市 Whole Municipality	市区 Urban Areas	通州 Tongzhou	海安 Haian	如东 Rudong	启东 Qidong	如皋 Rugao	海门 Haimen
1994	292	127			33			132
1995								
1996	882	462		6	164	151	99	
1997	1663	1364			135	45	119	
1998	2296	1610	58		431	81	83	91
1999	2288	1300	33	13	495	205	175	100
2000	3336	2621	131		188	103	331	93
2001	3241	1869	215	12	646	114	420	180
2002	4172	2500	228	18	695	193	575	191
2003	4469	2280	254	326	689	269	487	418
2004	4621	2453	602	480	504	145	761	278
2005	5260	1984	335	717	655	542	903	459
2006	7140	2939	1188	1019	1029	663	857	633
2007	8811	3618	1615	1071	1282	751	907	1182
2008	9680	3707	861	1245	1425	847	1549	907
2009	13570	6191	2090	2077	1526	1240	1756	780
2010	16037	7136	2280	1985	3139	1480	1447	850
2011	20004	8511	3185	2166	3404	2478	2189	1256
2012	22211	10903	3387	1627	2780	2307	2870	1724
2013	24225	9710	3802	3360	2921	3423	2698	2113
2014	24438	9575	4050	3442	2815	3640	2698	2268

15-12 历年大中型工业企业研究与发展经费支出总额

EXPENDITURES OF RESEARCH AND DEVELOPMENT FUNDS OF LARGE AND MEDIUM-SIZED ENTERPRISES OVER THE YEARS

单位:个 (unit)

年份 Year	全市 Whole Municipality	市区 Urban Areas	通州 Tongzhou	海安 Haian	如东 Rudong	启东 Qidong	如皋 Rugao	海门 Haimen
1994	541	212			258			72
1995	663	257			17	335	54	
1996	2049	750		5	348	600	347	
1997	4581	3259			727	353	243	
1998	8578	6165	172		1721	256	284	152
1999	8977	5306	55	25	1518	1087	691	350
2000	15545	11682	1651		1540	427	875	1021
2001	25559	11712	993	120	6491	819	4124	2292
2002	29535	18005	1734	117	3052	2129	3766	2467
2003	40743	22117	4566	2555	2483	3326	3623	6640
2004	69225	35428	10388	9283	3050	3437	7443	10585
2005	85867	34821	9271	13459	6201	8089	10264	13034
2006	144589	54305	24638	16818	9491	24330	15486	24159
2007	232139	93016	38572	31556	18981	28783	24890	34913
2008	275793	101812	41287	26603	23330	40535	34677	48836
2009	314343	137861	53111	37615	32665	44571	35887	25744
2010	407438	175095	54319	43402	41311	66405	44930	36295
2011	485740	220980	79796	60924	55319	72292	37953	38272
2012	599887	291049	111309	62302	63554	77440	53222	52321
2013	733020	345803	142350	73087	66214	96796	80463	70657
2014	824933	378450	155599	79755	95384	93041	97874	80429

注:2006年起,研究与试验发展内部经费支出总额包含科研基建经费支出。

Note: The expenditure of scientific research and infrastructure funds has been included in that of scientific research and experimental development funds.

15-13 历年大中型工业企业新产品开发项目数

NUMBER OF NEW PRODUCTS DEVELOPMENT PROJECTS OF LARGE AND MEDIUM-SIZED ENTERPRISES OVER THE YEARS

单位：个 (unit)

年份 Year	全市 Whole Municipality	市区 Urban Areas	通州 Tongzhou	海安 Haian	如东 Rudong	启东 Qidong	如皋 Rugao	海门 Haimen
1995	622	416	64	19	51	28	93	15
1996	405	250	67	33	19	42	41	20
1997	524	413	72	14	22	37	29	9
1998	565	446	43	13	18	26	25	37
1999	367	245	41	13	18	11	38	42
2000	367	241	20	49	22	13	31	11
2001	345	205	18	42	23	12	24	39
2002	311	170	20	43	25	14	26	33
2003	707	184	21	359	36	14	57	57
2004	401	188	36	59	56	31	39	28
2005	666	233	45	246	56	37	37	57
2006	1370	707	66	395	71	45	76	76
2007	934	246	76	354	129	50	86	69
2008	1360	359	174	716	94	45	103	43
2009	876	376	126	127	144	76	99	54
2010	1504	604	244	261	165	141	231	102
2011	1366	609	228	157	135	199	169	97
2012	2282	829	277	368	461	219	230	175
2013	2365	1044	474	305	263	266	251	236
2014	2289	909	372	286	284	311	269	230

15-14 历年大中型工业企业科技开发机构数

NUMBER OF SCIENTIFIC AND TECHNICAL RESEARCH INSTITUTIONS OF LARGE AND MEDIUM-SIZED ENTERPRISES OVER THE YEARS

单位:个 (unit)

年份 Year	全市 Whole Municipality	市区 Urban Areas	通州 Tongzhou	海安 Haian	如东 Rudong	启东 Qidong	如皋 Rugao	海门 Haimen
1994	131	70	15	12	12	8	22	7
1995	129	83	14	9	13	7	14	3
1996	118	67	13	10	9	11	10	11
1997	115	70	13	5	8	11	12	9
1998	114	65	11	9	9	15	12	4
1999	112	69	13	9	7	10	14	3
2000	72	42	10	9	6	6	7	2
2001	87	48	10	9	7	8	8	7
2002	73	41	14	8	6	5	6	7
2003	90	40	11	15	10	9	7	9
2004	143	49	14	21	15	34	13	11
2005	119	43	14	26	15	9	15	11
2006	134	53	21	26	14	8	19	14
2007	157	54	21	31	17	13	25	17
2008	154	62	27	29	19	13	20	11
2009	215	78	34	37	34	17	34	15
2010	269	92	42	49	31	23	51	23
2011	314	113	51	52	32	28	63	26
2012	605	222	99	101	73	41	115	53
2013	685	243	109	81	104	75	124	58
2014	736	230	101	104	115	65	142	80

15-15 历年大中型工业企业科技开发机构人员数

NUMBER OF PERSONNEL IN SCIENCE AND TECHNOLOGY DEVELOPMENT INSTITUTIONS OF LARGE AND MEDIUM-SIZED ENTERPRISES OVER THE YEARS

单位:人 (person)

年份 Year	全市 Whole Municipality	市区 Urban Areas	通州 Tongzhou	海安 Haian	如东 Rudong	启东 Qidong	如皋 Rugao	海门 Haimen
1994	2799	1927	149	217	138	61	364	92
1995	2023	1459	176	84	148	87	236	9
1996	1936	1274	150	91	158	126	214	73
1997	2298	1541	148	53	264	127	249	64
1998	2097	1226	156	146	218	259	192	56
1999	2223	1321	151	156	211	214	263	58
2000	2081	1178	152	274	218	124	237	50
2001	2734	1393	116	335	353	140	350	163
2002	2782	1582	188	432	244	120	235	169
2003	4246	1776	177	801	485	494	263	427
2004	3859	1660	303	690	341	416	409	343
2005	4187	1579	304	741	478	293	648	448
2006	5766	2000	429	1342	585	341	987	511
2007	7070	2483	514	1603	801	416	1108	659
2008	7188	3185	853	1309	663	335	1286	410
2009	10779	5050	2100	2158	905	477	1612	577
2010	12352	5506	1972	2106	918	871	2053	898
2011	16323	6744	2859	2395	2064	1264	2877	979
2012	25113	9262	3099	3118	3412	2042	4775	2504
2013	29855	10084	3975	4411	4995	2448	4210	3707
2014	33308	10770	4574	4703	5314	2811	4896	4814

15-16 历年大中型工业企业技术改造支出

EXPENDITURES ON TECHNICAL UPDATING OF LARGE AND MEDIUM-SIZED ENTERPRISES OVER THE YEARS

单位:万元 (10000 yuan)

年份 Year	全市 Whole Municipality	市区 Urban Areas	通州 Tongzhou	海安 Haian	如东 Rudong	启东 Qidong	如皋 Rugao	海门 Haimen
1994	47615	36576	3979	538	2156	3327	4089	930
1995	52827	32094	2944	4802	6288	3463	6158	22
1996	49088	33871	6928	1416	4429	2715	5722	935
1997	38316	24298	12328	271	2583	4802	5297	1065
1998	30089	21783	9629	438	3853	223	3778	14
1999	31654	23824	10307	103	3031	2500	1967	229
2000	64165	50862	9036	3834	3078	640	5201	550
2001	119266	94569	3919	4546	7202	233	4024	8693
2002	89910	68421	2458	2928	6418	1018	5938	5187
2003	100608	68547	1051	8517	4167	3304	10954	5119
2004	213702	140209	42403	18085	12567	5634	23829	13378
2005	211191	116384	35739	26771	16676	7202	28840	15318
2006	179144	87069	17299	29684	16522	23161	12833	9875
2007	278663	141266	18799	41348	18277	37931	23052	16789
2008	287112	160440	12652	40928	12046	26611	14855	32232
2009	259340	163431	23797	15198	7837	34428	17084	21362
2010	402977	224427	2768	21356	51019	47401	25025	33749
2011	253878	134027	10859	21893	5637	31112	18427	42782
2012	198325	65936	7230	8891	75117	18321	15697	14363
2013	282856	149606	11593	7185	72996	25584	16247	11238
2014	283866	124947	16629	11470	67118	27195	45876	7260

15-17 历年大中型工业企业技术引进支出

EXPENDITURES ON TECHNOLOGY INTRODUCTION OF LARGE AND MEDIUM-SIZED ENTERPRISES OVER THE YEARS

单位：万元 (10000 yuan)

年份 Year	全市 Whole Municipality	市区 Urban Areas	通州 Tongzhou	海安 Haian	如东 Rudong	启东 Qidong	如皋 Rugao	海门 Haimen
1994	7894	6970		780		15	99	30
1995								
1996	9865	5943	130	163	171	3236		352
1997	7235	6845	3916	223	127			40
1998	2577	2065	65	47	122	64	64	215
1999	8587	8092	322	51		80	180	185
2000	17845	15350	216	1017	160	400	744	175
2001	19183	16341	289	1800	160	516	202	164
2002	24042	21660	1114	960	707	8	120	587
2003	27459	17668	396	3309	3425	628	1422	1007
2004	24563	22497	692		1916	150		
2005	21251	18328	69	20	320	485	1998	100
2006	24840	21977	506	1433	420	500	490	20
2007	35947	29148	1648	1671	958	500	470	3200
2008	53199	24506	1678	1837	1026	15000	3730	7100
2009	29539	13091	2693	2207	217	5911	2840	5273
2010	36240	8342	1132	2218	825	6853	5576	12426
2011	37126	10206	3245	798	345	6805	72	18900
2012	13782	9695	5475	554	768		27	2738
2013	41106	23518	486	3892	1361			12335
2014	12706	8258	496	3047	1030		371	

15-18 规模以上工业法人单位R&D活动及相关情况

指 标	Item	法人单位数(个) Number of Legal Entites	# 有R&D活动(个) With R&D Activities	# 有科技机构(个) With S&T Institntion
总计	**Total**	**5081**	**1705**	**1763**
一、按企业规模分组	Grouped by Enterprise Size			
大型	Large	110	95	110
中型	Medium	497	377	474
小型	Small	4364	1220	1164
微型	Micro	110	13	15
二、按隶属关系分组	Grouped by Relationship of Administrative Subordination			
中央	Central	10	5	5
省(自治区、直辖市)	Province(Antonamous Region, Direct-controled Municipality)	7	2	3
地(区、市、州、盟)	Prefecture(District, City, State, League)	18	8	9
县(区、市、旗)	County(District, City, Banner)	15	9	8
街道	Snb-district	23	13	14
镇	Twon	11	4	3
乡				
社区(居委会)	Community	7		
村委会	Neighborhood Committee	12	3	4
其他	Others	4978	1661	1717
三、按登记注册类型分组	Grouped by Registered Type			
内资企业	Domestic Funded	3846	1228	1251
国有企业	State-owned Enterprise	5	2	2
集体企业	Collective Enterprise	13	2	
股份合作企业	Joint Equity Cooperative Enterprise	15	3	6
联营企业	Joint Venture	1	1	1
国有联营企业				
集体联营企业	Collective Joint Ownership	1	1	1
国有与集体联营企业				
其他联营企业				
有限责任公司		619	218	223
国有独资公司	Wholly State-owned Company	9	4	5
其他有限责任公司	Other Limited Liability Company	610	214	218
股份有限公司	Limited Company	78	52	59
私营企业	Private Enterprise	3111	949	959
私营独资企业	Sole Proprietorship	90	12	16
私营合伙企业	Private Partnership Enterprise	21	3	5
私营有限责任公司	Private Limited Liabiliy Company	2942	905	909
私营股份有限公司	Private Limied Company	58	29	29
其他企业	Others	4	1	1

R&D AND RLATED CONDITIONS OF LEGAL ENTITIESABOVE DESIGCOTED SIZE

R&D 活动人员情况 R&D Personnel		R&D 活动经费支出情况 R&D Expenditure		全部 R&D 项目情况 All R&D Projeets		
R&D 人员合计(人) Total Number of R&D Personnel	R&D 人员折合全时当量合计(人年) R&D Personnel FTE	R&D 经费内部支出合计(万元) Total R&D Internal Expenditure	R&D 经费外部支出合计(万元) Total R&D Exterral Expenditure	项目数(项) Number of Prejects	项目人员折合全时当量(人年) Personal FIE	项目经费内部支出(万元) Total Project Internal Experdiure
55175	**41448**	**1349998**	**12224**	**4659**	**38027**	**1229909**
15773	12321	421785	4443	808	11262	391473
16471	12116	403148	4383	1206	11162	362061
22838	16935	523695	3398	2630	15541	475125
93	75	1370		15	62	1251
931	667	30502		45	649	29617
78	28	1417		13	27	1242
516	239	12049	121	29	222	9829
380	272	7695	1	20	207	6533
1048	975	10116	16	47	929	9365
63	27	1247		14	25	1152
45	45	768	13	6	41	670
52114	39196	1286205	12074	4485	35929	1171502
37751	28104	870212	9090	3319	25916	791518
68	43	1996		6	42	1981
50	42	436		4	39	436
53	37	2405		5	34	2216
32	32	479		2	30	378
32	32	479		2	30	378
7292	5698	171123	1634	691	5304	155764
131	54	5190	29	20	51	4964
7161	5644	165933	1605	671	5253	150800
5278	3852	112219	1504	341	3640	103704
24945	18398	581055	5953	2269	16826	526539
182	145	6511		19	129	5452
27	17	701		3	16	618
23158	17227	542841	5749	2149	15766	492960
1578	1009	31002	204	98	915	27509
33	4	500		1	2	500

15-18 续表1

指 标	Item	法人单位数(个) Number of Legal Entites	# 有R&D活动(个) With R&D Activities	# 有科技机构(个) With S&T Institntion
港、澳、台商投资企业	HK, Macou and Taiwan Funded Enterprise	491	196	222
与港澳台商合资经营企业	Joint Venture With HK, Macau and Taiwan Enterprise	182	80	83
与港澳台商合作经营企业	Coperatve Enterprise With HK, Macan and Taiwan Enterprise	4	2	2
港澳台商独资经营企业	HK, Macau and Taiwan Sole Proprietorship	301	112	135
港澳台商投资股份有限公司	HK, Macau and Taiwan Funded Limited Company	3	2	2
其他港澳台投资企业		1		
外商投资企业	Foreign Funded Erterprlse	744	281	290
中外合资经营企业	Chinses Forecgn Joint Venture	327	146	140
中外合作经营企业	Chinese Foreign Cooperative Enterprise	13	6	9
外资企业	Foreign Funded Enterprise	397	128	139
外商投资股份有限公司	Foreigh Funded Limited Company	7	1	2
其他外商投资企业				
四、按国民经济行业大类分组 Grouped by National Ecnomic Sector				
制造业	Manufacturing	5032	1690	1746
农副食品加工业	Agrifood Processing	175	48	44
食品制造业	Food Production	25	12	11
酒、饮料和精制茶制造业	Alcohol, Beverage and Refined Tealeave	7	4	4
烟草制品业	Tobacco	1	1	1
纺织业	Textile	1019	164	182
纺织服装、服饰业	Garment & Textile	384	94	103
皮革、毛皮、羽毛及其制品和制鞋业	Leather, Fur, Feather and Others and Shoe	64	18	22
木材加工和木、竹、藤、棕、草制品业	Timber Processing and Woord, Bamboo, Rattan and Grass Produts	10	4	5
家具制造业	Furniture Manufacturing	24	6	6
造纸和纸制品业	Paper-malcing and Parper Products	45	7	11
印刷和记录媒介复制业	Printing and Record Media Dupbcate	25	7	8
文教、工美、体育和娱乐用品制造业	Cultvre and Education, Art and Recveatonal Products	327	104	116
石油加工、炼焦和核燃料加工业	Petroleum Processing, Coking and Nuclear Fuel Processing	9	1	1
化学原料和化学制品制造业	Chemical Raw Morferial & Chemical Products	423	162	175
医药制造业	Pharmaceatical Manufacturing	77	54	50
化学纤维制造业	Chemical Fibre Manufacturing	70	23	29
橡胶和塑料制品业	Rubber and Plastic Products	131	37	45
非金属矿物制品业	Non-metallic Mineral Products	230	64	72
黑色金属冶炼和压延加工业	Ferrons Metal Melting and Processing	85	23	26
有色金属冶炼和压延加工业	Non Ferrous Metal Melting and Processing	66	28	26
金属制品业	Manufacture of Metal Products	357	87	85

CONTINUED 1

R&D 活动人员情况 R&D Personnel		R&D 活动经费支出情况 R&D Expenditure		全部 R&D 项目情况 All R&D Projeets		
R&D 人员合计(人) Total Number of R&D Personnel	R&D 人员折合全时当量合计(人年) R&D Personnel FTE	R&D 经费内部支出合计(万元) Total R&D Internal Expenditure	R&D 经费外部支出合计(万元) Total R&D Exterral Expenditure	项目数(项) Number of Prejects	项目人员折合全时当量(人年) Personal FIE	项目经费内部支出(万元) Total Project Internal Experdiure
6612	**4988**	**151863**	**1474**	**567**	**4364**	**140247**
2701	1735	68076	185	233	1541	62849
46	28	1199		3	27	1019
3293	2657	73078	1286	301	2441	66936
572	568	9510	4	30	356	9443
10812	8356	327923	1659	773	7747	298144
5637	4269	208044	1452	456	3967	188865
183	90	2649	5	14	85	2594
4938	3983	116329	202	302	3682	105784
54	14	901		1	13	901
54635	41003	1343110	12224	4622	37597	1223359
1229	969	27109	84	82	891	24500
212	165	6447	35	18	150	6127
174	146	2582		13	134	2396
47	11	1107		10	10	932
5210	4209	85665	557	344	3715	77418
1829	1443	30091	117	145	1331	25892
367	264	5384	23	25	232	4587
49	46	1545		6	45	1376
220	169	3742		12	163	3714
71	50	2250		13	48	2190
56	35	741		10	31	655
2430	1720	49856	64	183	1598	43375
16	7	804		10	6	607
4742	3048	146242	1530	499	2811	135515
2337	1729	44012	356	217	1570	39296
871	613	46108	608	53	587	40555
1050	733	19398	16	147	661	17241
1202	951	29688	95	119	860	27786
748	525	17843	92	54	497	15398
691	486	17352	234	64	444	13988
2535	1866	64856	31	225	1760	60159

15-18 续表 2

指 标	Item	法人单位数(个) Number of Legal Entites	# 有 R&D 活动(个) With R&D Activities	# 有科技机构(个) With S&T Instittntion
通用设备制造业	Manufacture of General Equipment	484	220	185
专用设备制造业	Manufacture of Speclaized Eqwpment	211	122	126
汽车制造业	Autombile	39	20	18
铁路、船舶、航空航天和其他运输设备制造业	Manufacture of Rail Road, Ship Aeroplome and Others	123	32	45
电气机械和器材制造业	Manufacture of Electrical Machinery and Equipment	316	171	166
计算机、通信和其他电子设备制造业	PC, Telecomunication and Other Electronic Equipment	163	89	97
仪器仪表制造业	Manufacture of Instrument	126	82	79
其他制造业	Othrs	6	1	3
废弃资源综合利用业	Comprehnive Utilization of Waste Rosurce	3	2	1
金属制品、机械和设备修理业	Metal Products, Machine and Equipment Maintennce	7	3	4
电力、热力、燃气及水生产和供应业	Generation and Supply of Power, Heat, Gas and Water	49	15	17
电力、热力生产和供应业	Generation and Supply of Power & Heat	30	9	10
燃气生产和供应业	Generation and Supply of Gas	8	1	3
水的生产和供应业	Generation and Supply of Water	11	5	4
五、按企业控股情况分组	Gnuped by Holding			
国有控股	State Holding	73	40	47
集体控股	Collective Holding	41	16	16
私人控股	Private Holding	3894	1242	1260
港澳台商控股	HK, Mucau and Taiwan Holding	415	165	192
外商控股	Foreign Holding	566	192	200
其他	Others	92	50	48
六、按地区分组	Grouped by Region			
崇川区	ChongChuan	100	24	29
港闸区	Gangzha	245	87	99
开发区	Kaifa	471	95	100
通州区	Tongzhou	747	186	199
海安县	Haian	863	320	305
如东县	Rudong	654	128	162
启东市	Qidong	512	204	163
如皋市	Rugao	820	391	396
海门市	Haimen	648	268	309

CONTINUED 2

R&D 活动人员情况 R&D Personnel		R&D 活动经费支出情况 R&D Expenditure		全部 R&D 项目情况 All R&D Projeets		
R&D 人员合计(人) Total Number of R&D Personnel	R&D 人员折合全时当量合计(人年) R&D Personnel FTE	R&D 经费内部支出合计(万元) Total R&D Internal Expenditure	R&D 经费外部支出合计(万元) Total R&D Exterral Expenditure	项目数(项) Number of Prejects	项目人员折合全时当量(人年) Personal FIE	项目经费内部支出(万元) Total Project Internal Experdiure
5891	**4369**	**129377**	**1627**	**636**	**4062**	**119187**
5598	3815	141158	749	387	3537	130012
626	513	11459	853	53	481	10737
1469	1046	49500	583	96	974	45528
8582	7015	248455	2692	635	6283	230988
3836	3019	87251	1486	292	2839	76360
2459	1973	71036	339	263	1822	65024
18	9	139		1	8	134
31	19	1023	50	3	16	1013
39	39	892	5	6	35	670
540	444	6889		37	430	6551
445	396	3931		26	385	3600
20	14	2178		6	13	2173
75	35	780		5	31	778
4277	3012	142137	1016	271	2863	133119
992	854	33005	665	84	825	25464
34895	26033	813532	8457	3161	23956	741881
5738	4424	130195	1304	467	3859	120281
6888	5487	172849	240	475	5034	156990
2385	1638	58281	541	201	1490	52175
2568	1872	108272	1685	182	1812	96148
3590	3402	68947	704	331	3210	64072
4414	2288	107907	609	343	1907	97844
7011	5766	211130	1591	668	5514	194003
7345	6269	151444	1294	679	5784	144625
6026	4121	140310	3513	465	3587	123685
6859	5748	177848	277	658	5308	172138
8364	6266	181324	2073	736	5711	157956
8955	5684	202101	477	591	5163	178756

15-18 续表 3

指 标	Item	企业办科技机构情况 R&D Institutes by Enterprises		
		机构数(个) Institues	机构人员合计(人) Total Personnel	机构经费支出(万元) Expendiure
总计	**Total**	**1981**	**55175**	**1331145**
一、按企业规模分组	Grouped by Enterprise Size			
大型	Large	187	14482	465426
中型	Medium	549	18826	420056
小型	Small	1229	21737	439564
微型	Micro	16	130	6099
二、按隶属关系分组	Grouped by Relationship of Administrative Subordination			
中央	Central	6	458	11484
省(自治区、直辖市)	Province(Antonamous Region, Direct-controled Municipality)	3	74	2796
地(区、市、州、盟)	Prefecture(District, City, State, League)	14	349	7475
县(区、市、旗)	County(District, City, Banner)	9	389	2469
街道	Snb-district	21	625	5654
镇	Twon	5	84	1356
乡				
社区(居委会)	Community			
村委会	Neighborhood Committee	4	67	2099
其他	Others	1919	53129	1297812
三、按登记注册类型分组	Grouped by Registered Type			
内资企业	Domestic Funded	1419	37154	835855
国有企业	State-owned Enterprise	3	86	845
集体企业	Collective Enterprise			
股份合作企业	Joint Equity Cooperative Enterprise	6	145	4359
联营企业	Joint Venture	1	33	416
国有联营企业				
集体联营企业	Collective Joint Ownership	1	33	416
国有与集体联营企业				
其他联营企业				
有限责任公司		260	6117	132278
国有独资公司	Wholly State-owned Company	5	114	3273
其他有限责任公司	Other Limited Liability Company	255	6003	129005
股份有限公司	Limited Company	98	4838	87514
私营企业	Private Enterprise	1050	25921	610355
私营独资企业	Sole Proprietorship	16	285	7495
私营合伙企业	Private Partnership Enterprise	5	38	941
私营有限责任公司	Private Limited Liabiliy Company	991	24316	573531
私营股份有限公司	Private Limied Company	38	1282	28387
其他企业	Others	1	14	88

CONTINUED 3

科技活动产出及相关情况 R&D Output					
机构仪器和设备原价(万元) Original Price of Instruments and Equipments	进口(万元) Imports	专利申请数(件) Patent Application	发明专利(件) Patent for Invention	有效发明专利数(件) Validpatent for Invention	境外授权(件) Overseas Authorized
565588	**94614**	**10739**	**3818**	**3742**	**62**
171674	53905	1706	601	751	38
216495	30531	3057	1047	1162	4
176889	10178	5947	2164	1827	19
530		29	6	2	1
1841		18	7	42	
2685		23	10	11	
6575	1781	57	32	38	1
4716		71	32	18	
7405	2901	96	57	40	
412	135	106	19	14	
245		20	8	8	
541710	89797	10348	3653	3571	61
366173	67374	7259	2657	2670	23
321		12	5		
		1			
1149		14	12	2	
160					
160					
86035	9296	1530	686	601	6
3045	103	29	16	45	
82991	9193	1501	670	556	6
55349	7573	637	253	494	10
223134	50505	5065	1701	1573	7
2381		50	18	7	
172	7	6	1		
207171	47160	4827	1630	1440	7
13409	3338	182	52	126	
25					

15-18 续表 4

指 标	Item	企业办科技机构情况 R&D Institutes by Enterprises 机构数(个) Institues	机构人员合计(人) Total Personnel	机构经费支出(万元) Expendiure
港、澳、台商投资企业	HK, Macou and Taiwan Funded Enterprise	244	7896	191593
与港澳台商合资经营企业	Joint Venture With HK, Macau and Taiwan Enterprise	97	3332	103798
与港澳台商合作经营企业	Coperatve Enterprise With HK, Macan and Taiwan Enterprise	2	44	897
港澳台商独资经营企业	HK, Macau and Taiwan Sole Proprietorship	143	4097	77464
港澳台商投资股份有限公司	HK, Macau and Taiwan Funded Limited Company	2	423	9434
其他港澳台投资企业				
外商投资企业	Foreign Funded Erterprlse	318	10125	303697
中外合资经营企业	Chinses Forecgn Joint Venture	156	5168	175617
中外合作经营企业	Chinese Foreign Cooperative Enterprise	9	193	2723
外资企业	Foreign Funded Enterprise	151	4633	122796
外商投资股份有限公司	Foreigh Funded Limited Company	2	131	2561
其他外商投资企业				
四、按国民经济行业大类分组	Grouped by National Ecnomic Sector			
制造业	Manufacturing	1963	54846	1322689
农副食品加工业	Agrifood Processing	45	1258	26084
食品制造业	Food Production	11	290	7382
酒、饮料和精制茶制造业	Alcohol, Beverage and Refined Tealeave	4	164	2342
烟草制品业	Tobacco	1	51	2142
纺织业	Textile	205	5138	84736
纺织服装、服饰业	Garment & Textile	109	2371	30372
皮革、毛皮、羽毛及其制品和制鞋业	Leather, Fur, Feather and Others and Shoe	22	602	7590
木材加工和木、竹、藤、棕、草制品业	Timber Processing and Woord, Bamboo, Rattan and Grass Produts	5	55	1473
家具制造业	Furniture Manufacturing	8	222	2114
造纸和纸制品业	Paper-malcing and Parper Products	11	108	3195
印刷和记录媒介复制业	Printing and Record Media Dupbcate	8	59	912
文教、工美、体育和娱乐用品制造业	Cultvre and Education, Art and Recveatonal Products	119	2924	64186
石油加工、炼焦和核燃料加工业	Petroleum Processing, Coking and Nuclear Fuel Processing	1	17	11
化学原料和化学制品制造业	Chemical Raw Morferial & Chemical Products	203	5089	159169
医药制造业	Pharmaceatical Manufacturing	65	2455	51696
化学纤维制造业	Chemical Fibre Manufacturing	32	983	32396
橡胶和塑料制品业	Rubber and Plastic Products	55	1201	24531
非金属矿物制品业	Non-metallic Mineral Products	77	1580	38608
黑色金属冶炼和压延加工业	Ferrons Metal Melting and Processing	30	662	17832
有色金属冶炼和压延加工业	Non Ferrous Metal Melting and Processing	28	515	8654
金属制品业	Manufacture of Metal Products	90	2238	53866

CONTINUED 4

科技活动产出及相关情况 R&D Output					
机构仪器和设备原价(万元) Original Price of Instruments and Equipments	进口(万元) Imports	专利申请数(件) Patent Application	发明专利(件) Patent for Invention	有效发明专利数(件) Validpatent for Invention	境外授权(件) Overseas Authorized
80611	**4163**	**1586**	**451**	**448**	**20**
37209	3552	906	237	235	14
818	14				
40359	500	371	203	202	6
2226	97	309	11	11	
118804	23077	1894	710	624	19
68519	20065	1026	455	419	15
1126	155	197	93	77	
42839	2857	671	162	128	4
6320					
547154	94614	10701	3804	3727	62
6740	14	154	47	38	
3273	300	35	19	9	
638		45	11	3	
2462		20	7	11	
38613	8046	1768	221	268	1
10052	299	228	69	31	
3070		13	2	1	
779		3	2		
217	45	3	1	1	
4939		15	10	1	
332		7	3	3	
14003	2096	1191	117	71	
10		9	9	2	
60265	2337	783	448	486	5
21056	1676	480	297	278	10
24088	17801	138	71	31	1
7437	652	250	139	70	
11966	384	305	153	98	
7269	852	81	32	32	
2504	100	54	26	16	
22306	490	378	130	216	13

15-18 续表 5

指 标	Item	企业办科技机构情况 R&D Institutes by Enterprises		
		机构数(个) Institues	机构人员合计(人) Total Personnel	机构经费支出(万元) Expendiure
通用设备制造业	Manufacture of General Equipment	195	4864	89908
专用设备制造业	Manufacture of Speclaized Eqwpment	137	4837	108836
汽车制造业	Autombile	21	502	8334
铁路、船舶、航空航天和其他运输设备制造业	Manufacture of Rail Road, Ship Aeroplome and Others	51	2147	90554
电气机械和器材制造业	Manufacture of Electrical Machinery and Equipment	228	8243	232364
计算机、通信和其他电子设备制造业	PC, Telecomunication and Other Electronic Equipment	106	3442	94989
仪器仪表制造业	Manufacture of Instrument	88	2727	76636
其他制造业	Othrs	3	54	299
废弃资源综合利用业	Comprehnive Utilization of Waste Rosurce	1	12	604
金属制品、机械和设备修理业	Metal Products, Machine and Equipment Maintennce	4	36	875
电力、热力、燃气及水生产和供应业	Generation and Supply of Power, Heat, Gas and Water	18	329	8456
电力、热力生产和供应业	Generation and Supply of Power & Heat	10	241	5510
燃气生产和供应业	Generation and Supply of Gas	4	54	2721
水的生产和供应业	Generation and Supply of Water	4	34	225
五、按企业控股情况分组	Gnuped by Holding			
国有控股	State Holding	67	3070	67863
集体控股	Collective Holding	25	713	35350
私人控股	Private Holding	1399	35754	818364
港澳台商控股	HK, Mucau and Taiwan Holding	212	6707	157815
外商控股	Foreign Holding	215	6729	207714
其他	Others	63	2202	44039
六、按地区分组	Grouped by Region			
崇川区	ChongChuan	42	2073	60005
港闸区	Gangzha	110	3375	64993
开发区	Kaifa	124	3702	88355
通州区	Tongzhou	219	6688	210987
海安县	Haian	346	7953	168457
如东县	Rudong	212	7582	148318
启东市	Qidong	171	4376	123666
如皋市	Rugao	421	8894	247549
海门市	Haimen	335	10495	218615

CONTINUED 5

科技活动产出及相关情况 R&D Output					
机构仪器和设备原价(万元) Original Price of Instruments and Equipments	进口(万元) Imports	专利申请数(件) Patent Application	发明专利(件) Patent for Invention	有效发明专利数(件) Validpatent for Invention	境外授权(件) Overseas Authorized
43128	**4053**	**912**	**453**	**443**	**3**
42655	699	769	294	339	
7630	190	158	52	18	
14648		247	93	146	14
119205	32816	1310	544	580	7
43784	19355	762	347	330	1
32980	2409	523	187	197	7
432		13	1	2	
410		22	12	4	
261		25	7	2	
18434		38	14	15	
17826		33	13	15	
546					
62		5	1		
40229	7793	341	146	215	2
22886	15995	358	198	158	2
320896	61287	7769	2682	2522	14
66983	3034	1014	358	310	20
72138	3185	966	303	375	17
42455	3319	291	131	162	7
45778	24209	1072	205	205	2
45714	3693	688	287	338	14
60129	11288	1136	392	391	3
71056	16886	2171	690	622	1
22137	1828	1679	678	395	3
89357	20419	665	305	355	3
68383	2777	609	239	268	10
80011	5372	2071	787	854	21
82494	7884	642	233	311	5

15-18 续表 6

指 标	Item	专利所有权转让及许可数(件) Patent Transfer and License	专利所有权转让及许可收入(万元) Income of Paent Transfer and License	新产品开发项目数(项) Scinetifrce Essay Issued
总计	**Total**	**179**	**272**	**5259**
一、按企业规模分组	Grouped by Enterprise Size			
大型	Large	28	7	932
中型	Medium	40	4	1357
小型	Small	111	260	2951
微型	Micro			19
二、按隶属关系分组	Grouped by Relationship of Administrative Subordination			
中央	Central			44
省(自治区、直辖市)	Province(Antonamous Region, Direct-controled Municipality)			14
地(区、市、州、盟)	Prefecture(District, City, State, League)			33
县(区、市、旗)	County(District, City, Banner)	19		22
街道	Snb-district	1	2	48
镇	Twon			14
乡				
社区(居委会)	Community			
村委会	Neighborhood Committee			9
其他	Others	159	270	5075
三、按登记注册类型分组	Grouped by Registered Type			
内资企业	Domestic Funded	135	7	3594
国有企业	State-owned Enterprise			8
集体企业	Collective Enterprise			4
股份合作企业	Joint Equity Cooperative Enterprise			2
联营企业	Joint Venture			2
国有联营企业				
集体联营企业	Collective Joint Ownership			2
国有与集体联营企业				
其他联营企业				
有限责任公司		21	2	705
国有独资公司	Wholly State-owned Company			24
其他有限责任公司	Other Limited Liability Company	21	2	681
股份有限公司	Limited Company	26		335
私营企业	Private Enterprise	88	5	2538
私营独资企业	Sole Proprietorship			37
私营合伙企业	Private Partnership Enterprise			6
私营有限责任公司	Private Limited Liabiliy Company	82	5	2387
私营股份有限公司	Private Limied Company	6		108
其他企业	Others			

CONTINUED 6

新产品开发经费支出(万元) New Produet Develo Pment EXpenditure	新产品产值(万元) Product Value	新产品销售收入(万元) New Product Sales	出口(万元) Exports	发表科技论文(篇) Scientifice Essay Issued	拥有注册商标(件) Registered Trademark	境外注册(件) Oversea Registered	形成国家或行业标准(项) National or Industrial Standards
1748282	**21440239**	**20477383**	**2406715**	**608**	**3458**	**270**	**307**
620312	9391920	9349543	1447727	274	448	90	106
520162	7064616	6612767	727335	166	2013	75	103
601238	4969597	4501382	231654	168	989	105	97
6570	14106	13691			8		1
31403	415231	415231	303515	62			
1699	26649	25569	38	4	3		2
16711	101516	102260	12677	2	24	6	8
8083	78564	63155	20991	2	9		2
10542	147813	172085	24198	9	29	1	8
1585	34973	35423	82	2	17	9	
2357	15387	14362	153		1		1
1675902	20620106	19649299	2045062	527	3375	254	286
1064755	13637734	13054572	1329929	449	1978	207	236
2669							
477	8085	8001					
1025	68517	66426					
479	2305	5205					
479	2305	5205					
195318	1746765	1538125	350155	123	337	57	32
8322	53527	51337	38	4	3		2
186996	1693238	1486788	350117	119	334	57	30
117708	2017410	2020288	396066	70	362	37	41
747079	9794652	9416526	583708	256	1279	113	163
9541	50692	49992	1216		2		
1750	597	565	255				
700438	8202272	7832513	556394	242	921	109	157
35350	1541090	1533456	25844	14	356	4	6

15-18 续表 7

指 标	Item	专利所有权转让及许可数(件) Patent Transfer and License	专利所有权转让及许可收入(万元) Income of Paent Transfer and License	新产品开发项目数(项) Scinetifrce Essay Issued
港、澳、台商投资企业	HK, Macou and Taiwan Funded Enterprise	16	4	714
与港澳台商合资经营企业	Joint Venture With HK, Macau and Taiwan Enterprise	16	4	293
与港澳台商合作经营企业	Coperatve Enterprise With HK, Macan and Taiwan Enterprise			3
港澳台商独资经营企业	HK, Macau and Taiwan Sole Proprietorship			388
港澳台商投资股份有限公司	HK, Macau and Taiwan Funded Limited Company			30
其他港澳台投资企业				
外商投资企业	Foreign Funded Erterprlse	28	260	951
中外合资经营企业	Chinses Forecgn Joint Venture	27		547
中外合作经营企业	Chinese Foreign Cooperative Enterprise			20
外资企业	Foreign Funded Enterprise	1	260	383
外商投资股份有限公司	Foreigh Funded Limited Company			1
其他外商投资企业				
四、按国民经济行业大类分组 Grouped by National Ecnomic Sector				
制造业	Manufacturing	177	272	5222
农副食品加工业	Agrifood Processing			85
食品制造业	Food Production			18
酒、饮料和精制茶制造业	Alcohol, Beverage and Refined Tealeave			13
烟草制品业	Tobacco			11
纺织业	Textile	20	12	382
纺织服装、服饰业	Garment & Textile			151
皮革、毛皮、羽毛及其制品和制鞋业	Leather, Fur, Feather and Others and Shoe			41
木材加工和木、竹、藤、棕、草制品业	Timber Processing and Woord, Bamboo, Rattan and Grass Produts			10
家具制造业	Furniture Manufacturing			11
造纸和纸制品业	Paper-malcing and Parper Products			15
印刷和记录媒介复制业	Printing and Record Media Dupbcate			12
文教、工美、体育和娱乐用品制造业	Cultvre and Education, Art and Recveatonal Products		260	271
石油加工、炼焦和核燃料加工业	Petroleum Processing, Coking and Nuclear Fuel Processing			11
化学原料和化学制品制造业	Chemical Raw Morferial & Chemical Products	13		521
医药制造业	Pharmaceatical Manufacturing	3		237
化学纤维制造业	Chemical Fibre Manufacturing	5		72
橡胶和塑料制品业	Rubber and Plastic Products			136
非金属矿物制品业	Non-metallic Mineral Products	5		128
黑色金属冶炼和压延加工业	Ferrons Metal Melting and Processing			61
有色金属冶炼和压延加工业	Non Ferrous Metal Melting and Processing			75
金属制品业	Manufacture of Metal Products	11		270

CONTINUED 7

新产品开发经费支出(万元) New Produet Develo Pment EXpenditure	新产品产值(万元) Product Value	新产品销售收入(万元) New Product Sales	出口(万元) Exports	发表科技论文(篇) Scientifice Essay Issued	拥有注册商标(件) Registered Trademark	境外注册(件) Oversea Registered	形成国家或行业标准(项) National or Industrial Standards
250265	**2903141**	**2711465**	**356198**	**99**	**1035**	**11**	**47**
134687	1108531	997656	105707	86	1049	9	43
1199	4373	3978	1200				
104679	1631823	1473767	244650	13	35	2	4
9701	158413	236064	4641		1		
433262	4899364	4711346	720588	60	395	52	24
264009	3232832	3174356	625559	41	222	21	18
10781	21026	20866	5542	1	2	1	
157571	1506344	1376961	89488	7	171	30	6
901	139162	139162		11			
1733581	21435256	20472400	2406715	545	3457	270	306
26728	498817	502818	2247		21	3	1
6538	55793	48756	20074		2		
2582	42375	42253			52		
1388	23793	22793	38	3	1		2
95857	1702706	1816983	518709	71	501	33	30
30381	1056197	1037422	99691	7	157	6	4
8971	147984	147180	5610				1
2108	8698	8647			1		
3529	1210	1405					
5110	4176	4134			1		
1508	10252	10129			1		
86102	367348	368555	95192	18	140	9	12
809	13200	12104			2		
189372	2465199	2221761	234644	40	483	29	24
62427	507454	422216	50117	14	228	70	16
52397	313850	294371	475	9	4		
25582	155482	150928	1630	6	59		8
31055	395647	382901	10719	21	31		1
21241	111644	102376	2909	2	5		5
25130	325584	312223	3428		6		
77266	951407	942883	250004	13	33	3	

15-18 续表 8

指 标	Item	专利所有权转让及许可数(件) Patent Transfer and License	专利所有权转让及许可收入(万元) Income of Paent Transfer and License	新产品开发项目数(项) Scinetifrce Essay Issued
通用设备制造业	Manufacture of General Equipment	17		712
专用设备制造业	Manufacture of Speclaized Eqwpment	22		426
汽车制造业	Autombile			59
铁路、船舶、航空航天和其他运输设备制造业	Manufacture of Rail Road, Ship Aeroplome and Others	5		151
电气机械和器材制造业	Manufacture of Electrical Machinery and Equipment	18		747
计算机、通信和其他电子设备制造业	PC, Telecomunication and Other Electronic Equipment	24		305
仪器仪表制造业	Manufacture of Instrument	34		280
其他制造业	Othrs			1
废弃资源综合利用业	Comprehnive Utilization of Waste Rosurce			1
金属制品、机械和设备修理业	Metal Products, Machine and Equipment Maintennce			9
电力、热力、燃气及水生产和供应业	Generation and Supply of Power, Heat, Gas and Water	2		37
电力、热力生产和供应业	Generation and Supply of Power & Heat	2		25
燃气生产和供应业	Generation and Supply of Gas			10
水的生产和供应业	Generation and Supply of Water			2
五、按企业控股情况分组	Gnuped by Holding			
国有控股	State Holding	1	2	271
集体控股	Collective Holding	1	4	105
私人控股	Private Holding	129	6	3483
港澳台商控股	HK, Mucau and Taiwan Holding	13	0	598
外商控股	Foreign Holding	25	260	595
其他	Others	10		207
六、按地区分组	Grouped by Region			
崇川区	ChongChuan			198
港闸区	Gangzha	23	2	345
开发区	Kaifa	1		441
通州区	Tongzhou	24		638
海安县	Haian	72	10	699
如东县	Rudong	4		520
启东市	Qidong	22		758
如皋市	Rugao	29	260	768
海门市	Haimen	4		887

CONTINUED 8

新产品开发经费支出(万元) New Produet Develo Pment EXpenditure	新产品产值(万元) Product Value	新产品销售收入(万元) New Product Sales	出口(万元) Exports	发表科技论文(篇) Scientifice Essay Issued	拥有注册商标(件) Registered Trademark	境外注册(件) Oversea Registered	形成国家或行业标准(项) National or Industrial Standards
160341	**1245535**	**1042063**	**53821**	**47**	**71**	**1**	**41**
167721	1994257	1933777	643411	36	148	22	35
11775	108519	50789	7837	5	9		1
123190	1112913	1103108	30290	49	13		2
332300	5465836	5236966	90028	183	1329	89	103
108068	1023773	982287	166466	14	45	1	8
72234	1309295	1254224	114931	6	113	4	12
139	4770	4805	4445				
630	5000	5000		1			
1104	6543	6543			1		
14701	4983	4983		63	1		1
11853	4144	4144		63			1
2726							
122	839	839			1		
184180	1639765	1549962	547804	98	131	7	18
49234	480690	469481	143879	27	10		6
994353	12862405	12363317	869189	346	1967	213	212
214654	2984539	2802426	291483	84	1069	11	46
249254	2595341	2454279	205526	24	188	33	11
56607	877499	837918	348835	29	93	6	14
119899	1469085	1431108	469399	49	42	1	4
93925	798220	820290	290716	43	79	3	31
156104	2537479	2516294	177546	49	466	104	28
231164	2325488	2205499	274167	22	749	60	28
155961	2838049	2406108	314560	43	142	27	31
200753	2613514	2596703	128604	137	283	39	89
200584	1849072	1718380	217198	75	235	13	31
265313	2255364	2132739	236234	169	380	20	36
324221	4746492	4642794	295355	21	1080	2	27

15-18 续表 9

指 标	Item	来自政府部门的科技活动资金(万元) S&T Fund From Government(10,000 Yuan)	研究开发费用加计扣除减免税(万元) Total R&D Fund Catx-reliefo exchuded(10,000 Yuan)
总计	**Total**	**27121**	**24333**
一、按企业规模分组	Grouped by Enterprise Size		
大型	Large	12529	9756
中型	Medium	7712	7860
小型	Small	6880	6717
微型	Micro		
二、按隶属关系分组	Grouped by Relationship of Administrative Subordination		
中央	Central	1134	1364
省(自治区、直辖市)	Province(Antonamous Region, Direct-controled Municipality)		4
地(区、市、州、盟)	Prefecture(District, City, State, League)	784	436
县(区、市、旗)	County(District, City, Banner)	320	
街道	Snb-district	156	162
镇	Twon	23	48
乡			
社区(居委会)	Community		
村委会	Neighborhood Committee	4	
其他	Others	24700	22318
三、按登记注册类型分组	Grouped by Registered Type		
内资企业	Domestic Funded	14686	15751
国有企业	State-owned Enterprise		
集体企业	Collective Enterprise		
股份合作企业	Joint Equity Cooperative Enterprise		
联营企业	Joint Venture		
国有联营企业			
集体联营企业	Collective Joint Ownership		
国有与集体联营企业			
其他联营企业			
有限责任公司		4153	4169
国有独资公司	Wholly State-owned Company		4
其他有限责任公司	Other Limited Liability Company	4153	4165
股份有限公司	Limited Company	3010	2963
私营企业	Private Enterprise	7523	8618
私营独资企业	Sole Proprietorship		
私营合伙企业	Private Partnership Enterprise		
私营有限责任公司	Private Limited Liabiliy Company	6346	8134
私营股份有限公司	Private Limied Company	1177	485
其他企业	Others		

CONTINUED 9

其他相关情况 Others				
高新技术企业减免税(万元) High & New Techonology Enterprise tax Perliefs (10,000 Yuan)	引进技术经费支出(万元) Expenditure for Acquisitonof Technology (10,000 Yuan)	消化吸收经费支出(万元) Expenditure for Assimiation of Technology	购买境内技术经费支出(万元) Expenditure for Domestic Technology	技术改造经费支出(万元) Technology Upgrading Experditure (10,000 Yuan)
69787	**13364**	**3629**	**7374**	**311294**
38908	7006	1681	3350	217183
16542	5700	1337	1067	66683
14337	658	612	2957	27426
				2
295			569	
				40
453			297	21035
2				183
122			10	3426
228				212
68688	13364	3629	6498	286398
37672	7455	2636	5012	216085
6614		29	274	33810
				40
6614		29	274	33770
9436	4253	916	2714	33697
21622	3202	1691	1824	148578
				139
19880	3202	1691	1595	144773
1742			229	3666
			200	

15-18 续表 10

指 标	Item	来自政府部门的科技活动资金(万元) S&T Fund From Government(10,000 Yuan)	研究开发费用加计扣除减免税(万元) Total R&D Fund Catx-reliefo exchuded(10,000 Yuan)
港、澳、台商投资企业	HK, Macou and Taiwan Funded Enterprise	1547	2425
与港澳台商合资经营企业	Joint Venture With HK, Macau and Taiwan Enterprise	950	535
与港澳台商合作经营企业	Coperatve Enterprise With HK, Macan and Taiwan Enterprise		
港澳台商独资经营企业	HK, Macau and Taiwan Sole Proprietorship	569	1410
港澳台商投资股份有限公司	HK, Macau and Taiwan Funded Limited Company	28	481
其他港澳台投资企业			
外商投资企业	Foreign Funded Erterprlse	10888	6156
中外合资经营企业	Chinses Forecgn Joint Venture	7950	4214
中外合作经营企业	Chinese Foreign Cooperative Enterprise	110	15
外资企业	Foreign Funded Enterprise	2828	1927
外商投资股份有限公司	Foreigh Funded Limited Company		
其他外商投资企业			
四、按国民经济行业大类分组	Grouped by National Ecnomic Sector		
制造业	Manufacturing	27109	24333
农副食品加工业	Agrifood Processing	186	
食品制造业	Food Production	32	
酒、饮料和精制茶制造业	Alcohol, Beverage and Refined Tealeave		
烟草制品业	Tobacco		4
纺织业	Textile	1513	2078
纺织服装、服饰业	Garment & Textile	20	
皮革、毛皮、羽毛及其制品和制鞋业	Leather, Fur, Feather and Others and Shoe	80	
木材加工和木、竹、藤、棕、草制品业	Timber Processing and Woord, Bamboo, Rattan and Grass Produts		
家具制造业	Furniture Manufacturing		
造纸和纸制品业	Paper-malcing and Parper Products		
印刷和记录媒介复制业	Printing and Record Media Dupbcate		
文教、工美、体育和娱乐用品制造业	Cultvre and Education, Art and Recveatonal Products	585	181
石油加工、炼焦和核燃料加工业	Petroleum Processing, Coking and Nuclear Fuel Processing	120	
化学原料和化学制品制造业	Chemical Raw Morferial & Chemical Products	1994	1360
医药制造业	Pharmaceatical Manufacturing	1389	1060
化学纤维制造业	Chemical Fibre Manufacturing	78	
橡胶和塑料制品业	Rubber and Plastic Products	198	145
非金属矿物制品业	Non-metallic Mineral Products	251	436
黑色金属冶炼和压延加工业	Ferrons Metal Melting and Processing	300	386
有色金属冶炼和压延加工业	Non Ferrous Metal Melting and Processing	317	151
金属制品业	Manufacture of Metal Products	308	1136

CONTINUED 10

其他相关情况 Others				
高新技术企业减免税(万元) High & New Techonology Enterprise tax Perliefs (10,000 Yuan)	引进技术经费支出(万元) Expenditure for Acquisitonof Technology (10,000 Yuan)	消化吸收经费支出(万元) Expenditure for Assimiation of Technology	购买境内技术经费支出(万元) Expenditure for Domestic Technology	技术改造经费支出(万元) Technology Upgrading Experditure (10,000 Yuan)
13728	**993**	**88**	**1063**	**17969**
1718	958	18	574	10050
6613	35	70	490	5487
5397				2432
18387	4917	905	1299	77240
15579	4809	830	1288	73208
123				2513
2685	108	75	11	1520
69787	13364	3629	5992	311294
				870
				1400
				46
6200	3418	305	2419	23642
15		47	132	1248
		80	13	684
				100
112	57	497	101	1713
44				
7549	101	45	609	62980
3232		22	341	1322
			1	826
356				5767
1722			116	416
498			7	574
223				5437
6104	110	53	182	7150

15-18 续表11

指 标	Item	来自政府部门的科技活动资金(万元) S&T Fund From Government(10,000 Yuan)	研究开发费用加计扣除减免税(万元) Total R&D Fund Catx-reliefo exchuded(10,000 Yuan)
通用设备制造业	Manufacture of General Equipment	2372	2943
专用设备制造业	Manufacture of Speclaized Eqwpment	1770	3127
汽车制造业	Autombile	64	1155
铁路、船舶、航空航天和其他运输设备制造业	Manufacture of Rail Road, Ship Aeroplome and Others	1190	1341
电气机械和器材制造业	Manufacture of Electrical Machinery and Equipment	4673	3193
计算机、通信和其他电子设备制造业	PC, Telecomunication and Other Electronic Equipment	6674	3241
仪器仪表制造业	Manufacture of Instrument	2869	2398
其他制造业	Othrs	8	
废弃资源综合利用业	Comprehnive Utilization of Waste Rosurce		
金属制品、机械和设备修理业	Metal Products, Machine and Equipment Maintennce	118	
电力、热力、燃气及水生产和供应业	Generation and Supply of Power, Heat, Gas and Water	12	
电力、热力生产和供应业	Generation and Supply of Power & Heat	12	
燃气生产和供应业	Generation and Supply of Gas		
水的生产和供应业	Generation and Supply of Water		
五、按企业控股情况分组	Gnuped by Holding		
国有控股	State Holding	2106	2332
集体控股	Collective Holding	5722	1160
私人控股	Private Holding	12422	13724
港澳台商控股	HK, Mucau and Taiwan Holding	1611	2632
外商控股	Foreign Holding	3580	3513
其他	Others	1680	972
六、按地区分组	Grouped by Region		
崇川区	ChongChuan	7256	2392
港闸区	Gangzha	1997	1181
开发区	Kaifa	3943	1525
通州区	Tongzhou	6183	7575
海安县	Haian	2372	4073
如东县	Rudong	1533	1794
启东市	Qidong	718	1472
如皋市	Rugao	1885	3256
海门市	Haimen	1149	1066

CONTINUED 11

其他相关情况 Others				
高新技术企业减免税(万元) High & New Techonology Enterprise tax Perliefs (10,000 Yuan)	引进技术经费支出(万元) Expenditure for Acquisitonof Technology (10,000 Yuan)	消化吸收经费支出(万元) Expenditure for Assimiation of Technology	购买境内技术经费支出(万元) Expenditure for Domestic Technology	技术改造经费支出(万元) Technology Upgrading Experditure (10,000 Yuan)
3028	**4263**	**535**	**884**	**31057**
7628	35	29	736	3532
123		44	13	266
8174	553	200		9465
12512	1173	770	299	78417
5085	3640	875	45	69061
7182	15	128	95	5111
				13
				200
			1382	
			613	
			569	
			200	
6937			1153	37688
1520	4598	668		65261
30857	8054	2696	5073	176929
13409	35	70	495	13173
10866	678	175	441	5812
6198		20	212	12432
7651	7361	1145	359	80007
7495	310	253	233	9122
12024	92	20	280	23935
13086	496	65	271	24241
4178	3070	304	2465	11862
12641	1030	687	1639	69931
7435	93		893	30063
2885	371	73	189	48739
2269	542	1083	1047	13321

15-19　高新技术企业名录(2014年末)

BUSINESS DIRECTORY OF HIGH AND NEW TECHNOLOGY ENTERPRISES(YEAR-END OF 2014)

序号 sequence number	企业名称 Company Name	序号 sequence number	企业名称 Names of the Enterprises
1	太平洋水处理工程有限公司	41	南通友星线束有限公司
2	南通华达微电子集团有限公司	42	南通奥凯生物技术开发有限公司
3	江苏金通灵流体机械科技股份有限公司	43	中天科技海缆有限公司
4	南通通机股份有限公司	44	江苏汇动汽车电子有限公司
5	江苏现代电力科技股份有限公司	45	江苏好收成韦恩农化股份有限公司
6	南通大地电气有限公司	46	江苏恒源液压有限公司
7	南通新帝克单丝科技股份有限公司	47	南通市南方润滑液压设备有限公司
8	南通中集特种运输设备制造有限公司	48	启东市冶金机械有限公司
9	江苏苏通碳纤维有限公司	49	江苏三上机电制造股份有限公司
10	南通高欣耐磨科技股份有限公司	50	南通秋之友生物科技有限公司
11	南通国盛机电集团有限公司	51	南通三信塑胶装备科技股份有限公司
12	南通中集罐式储运设备制造有限公司	52	江苏双林海洋生物药业有限公司
13	江苏狼山钢绳股份有限公司	53	启东市联通测功器有限公司
14	江苏铁锚玻璃股份有限公司	54	南通市东昌化工有限公司
15	江苏晨朗电子集团有限公司	55	南通泰禾化工有限公司
16	江苏飞亚化学工业有限责任公司	56	中天日立光缆有限公司
17	江苏江海机床集团有限公司	57	江苏昌昇集团股份有限公司
18	江苏联发纺织股份有限公司	58	江苏德峰药业有限公司
19	江苏鹏飞集团股份有限公司	59	江苏华灿电讯股份有限公司
20	南通大东电子有限公司	60	江苏隆昌化工有限公司
21	南通双弘纺织有限公司	61	江苏南天农科化工有限公司
22	江苏威尔曼科技股份有限公司	62	南通超达机械科技有限公司
23	江苏恩达通用设备有限公司	63	南通皋液液压机有限公司
24	江苏天成生化制品有限公司	64	南通恒康数控机械有限公司
25	南通那芙尔服饰有限公司	65	南通力威机械有限公司
26	南通升辉建材科技有限公司	66	南通市电站阀门有限公司
27	南通丝乡丝绸有限公司	67	如皋市大生线路器材有限公司
28	南通市冠东模塑科技有限公司	68	如皋市非标轴承有限公司
29	江苏晨牌药业集团股份有限公司	69	如皋透平叶片制造有限公司
30	江苏通光光缆有限公司	70	江苏祥源电气设备有限公司
31	江苏万高药业有限公司	71	南通锻压设备股份有限公司
32	南通回力橡胶有限公司	72	南通天泽化工有限公司
33	南通克莱克莱空气处理设备有限公司	73	南通宏德机电有限公司
34	南通泰格动力机械有限公司	74	江苏通达动力科技有限公司
35	南通振康焊接机电有限公司	75	南通东帝纺织品有限公司
36	海门市沪海有色铸造有限公司	76	南通海星电子有限公司
37	江苏通能信息有限公司	77	南通华新环保设备工程有限公司
38	中兴能源装备有限公司	78	南通山口精工机电有限公司
39	江苏宝灵化工股份有限公司	79	南通泰富电器制造有限公司
40	江苏安惠生物科技有限公司	80	南通御丰塑钢包装有限公司

15-19 续表 1

CONTINUED 1

序号 sequence number	企业名称 Company Name	序号 sequence number	企业名称 Names of the Enterprises
81	南通海狮船舶机械有限公司	121	江苏鹿得医疗电子股份有限公司
82	南通星维油泵油嘴有限公司	122	南通中船机械制造有限公司
83	江苏久泰电缆有限公司	123	南通汇羽丰新材料有限公司
84	南通明德重工有限公司	124	东英(江苏)药业有限公司
85	南通诚信氨基酸有限公司	125	南通金仕达超微阻燃材料有限公司
86	南通市红星空压机配件制造有限公司	126	南通汉瑞新材料股份有限公司
87	江苏金太阳纺织科技有限公司	127	南通新三能电子有限公司
88	南通棉花机械有限公司	128	江苏韩通船舶重工有限公司
89	南通中远船务工程有限公司	129	南通福乐达汽车配件有限公司
90	南通醋酸化工股份有限公司	130	江苏新象股份有限公司
91	江苏铭安电气有限公司	131	如东县太极化纤纺织器材有限公司
92	南通亚威机械制造有限公司	132	江苏天恒纳米科技股份有限公司
93	江苏华艺服饰有限公司	133	南通奥普机械工程有限公司
94	江苏英力科技发展有限公司	134	南通通洋机电制造有限公司
95	南通市申海工业技术科技有限公司	135	江苏中威重工机械有限公司
96	南通市伊士生物技术有限责任公司	136	南通明诺机械有限公司
97	罗莱家纺股份有限公司	137	江苏四新界面剂科技有限公司
98	中天日立射频电缆有限公司	138	南通康比电子有限公司
99	启东市恒安防爆通信设备有限公司	139	南通中铁华宇电气有限公司
100	南通海尔斯医药有限公司	140	南通华东油压科技有限公司
101	双钱集团(江苏)轮胎有限公司	141	江苏瑞帆环保装备股份有限公司
102	如皋市日鑫电子有限公司	142	江苏捷捷微电子股份有限公司
103	江苏松野数控科技有限公司	143	江苏国莱特空调设备有限公司
104	江苏汤臣汽车零部件有限公司	144	江苏依柯化工有限公司
105	江苏天南电力器材有限公司	145	江苏昂彼特堡散热器有限公司
106	森松(江苏)海油工程装备有限公司	146	南通柏盛化工有限公司
107	江苏恒康家居科技有限公司	147	南通南辉电子材料股份有限公司
108	南通高盛机械制造有限公司	148	江苏元升太阳能集团有限公司
109	南通威明精工机械有限公司	149	江苏联海生物科技有限公司
110	南通海立电子有限公司	150	中广核中科海维科技发展有限公司
111	南通江华热动力机械有限公司	151	启东高压油泵有限公司
112	南通金驰机电有限公司	152	南通亚泰船舶工程有限公司
113	南通医疗器械有限公司	153	江苏瑞邦农药厂有限公司
114	南通晨曦焊业有限公司	154	南通通轮模具有限公司
115	江苏力普电子科技有限公司	155	江苏通光电子线缆股份有限公司
116	南通一品机械电子有限公司	156	南通爱尔思轻合金精密成型有限公司
117	南通华信中央空调有限公司	157	江苏京海禽业集团有限公司
118	南通中远川崎船舶有限公司	158	南通海林汽车橡塑制品有限公司
119	南通润邦重机有限公司	159	海安县石油科研仪器有限公司
120	江苏同康特种活性炭纤维面料有限公司	160	江苏海迅铁路器材集团股份有限公司

15-19　续表 2

CONTINUED 2

序号 sequence number	企业名称 Company Name	序号 sequence number	企业名称 Names of the Enterprises
161	江苏天鹏机电制造有限公司	201	南通爱普医疗器械有限公司
162	南通市恒达机械制造有限公司	202	中天宽带技术有限公司
163	南通昌荣机电有限公司	203	江东金具设备有限公司
164	海安联科汽车零部件有限公司	204	南通大东有限公司
165	南通超力卷板机制造有限公司	205	东瑞(南通)医药科技有限公司
166	南通明芯微电子有限公司	206	国能子金电缆南通有限公司
167	江苏奎泽机械工业有限公司	207	江苏如东金友机械有限公司
168	江苏双能太阳能有限公司	208	南通香地生物有限公司
169	南通万宝实业有限公司	209	海门市油威力液压工业有限责任公司
170	南通特力锻压机床有限公司	210	南通市争妍颜料化工有限公司
171	江苏金晟元特种阀门有限公司	211	南通恒秀铝热传输材料有限公司
172	江苏合海机械制造有限公司	212	江苏汉晨药业有限公司
173	南通曙光机电工程有限公司	213	海门容汇通用锂业有限公司
174	南通市康桥油脂有限公司	214	南通龙翔化工有限公司
175	南通奥特机械设备有限公司	215	江苏永和制药机械有限公司
176	南通东海机床制造有限公司	216	南通市金锐高技术陶瓷有限公司
177	南通市中矿水泥成套设备有限公司	217	南通路博石英材料股份有限公司
178	江苏晨日环保科技有限公司	218	江苏凌志环保设备有限公司
179	海安华达石油仪器有限公司	219	南通海鹰机电集团有限公司
180	南通永大管业股份有限公司	220	江苏希迪制药有限公司
181	南通国谊锻压机床有限公司有限公司	221	江苏道达海上风电工程科技有限公司
182	如皋市易达电子有限责任公司	222	启东吉莱电子有限公司
183	江苏康恒化工有限公司	223	江苏嘉盟电力设备有限公司
184	江苏中伟业通讯设备有限公司	224	博顿液压股份有限公司
185	南通康鑫药业有限公司	225	启东大同电机有限公司
186	南通赛孚机械设备有限公司	226	启东华拓药业有限公司
187	江苏环洋组合机床有限公司	227	南通安捷机械有限公司
188	南通星球石墨设备有限公司	228	南通通利智能化系统工程股份有限公司
189	如皋市大昌电子有限公司	229	南通市万帝来机电有限公司
190	威世药业(如皋)有限公司	230	江苏启尖丝杠制造有限公司
191	江苏东旭科技有限公司	231	南通力达环保设备有限公司
192	南通龙源电站阀门有限公司	232	南通东泰新能源设备有限公司
193	江苏熔盛重工有限公司	233	南通太平洋海洋工程有限公司
194	南通市力沛流体阀业有限公司	234	江苏风神空调集团股份有限公司
195	南通曼特威金属材料有限公司	235	江苏欧盛液压科技有限公司
196	南通泰利达化工有限公司	236	启东市南方润滑液压设备有限公司
197	江苏宝众宝达药业有限公司	237	启东金匙环保科技有限公司
198	如皋市金陵化工有限公司	238	上海振华重工启东海洋工程有限公司
199	江苏海力风电设备科技有限公司	239	江苏江海润液设备有限公司
200	迈克斯(如东)化工有限公司	240	南通四方罐式储运设备制造有限公司

15-19 续表 3

CONTINUED 3

序号 sequence number	企业名称 Company Name	序号 sequence number	企业名称 Names of the Enterprises
241	江苏达海智能系统股份有限公司	281	江苏绿源新材料有限公司
242	紫罗兰家纺科技股份有限公司	282	南通星诺冷冻设备有限公司
243	南通贝特医药机械有限公司	283	南通晨光石墨设备有限公司
244	南通市海鸥救生防护用品有限公司	284	江苏省勤奋药业有限公司
245	丽王化工(南通)有限公司	285	南通弘扬金属制品有限公司
246	江苏中科宇泰光能科技有限公司	286	南通惠康国际企业有限公司
247	南通晶鑫光学玻璃有限公司	287	江苏人先医疗科技有限公司
248	南通华鑫传质设备科技有限公司	288	南通环球转向器制造有限公司
249	南通瑞达电子材料有限公司	289	江苏汇环环保科技有限公司
250	南通凯迪自动机械有限公司	290	亚美滤膜(南通)有限公司
251	江苏蒙哥马利电梯有限公司	291	南通同方半导体有限公司
252	南通国盛精密机械有限公司	292	南通大通宝富风机有限公司
253	南通蛟龙重工发展有限公司	293	连邦软件(南通)有限公司
254	南通四通林业机械制造安装有限公司	294	中格复合材料(南通)有限公司
255	中航虹波风电设备有限公司	295	飞立股份有限公司
256	江苏腾通包装机械有限公司	296	江苏海建股份有限公司
257	南通华盛高聚物科技发展有限公司	297	亚太轻合金(南通)科技有限公司
258	雄邦压铸(南通)有限公司	298	南通天蓝环保能源成套设备有限公司
259	南通环球光学仪器有限公司	299	江苏浴普太阳能有限公司
260	南通水山环保设备有限公司	300	百川化工(如皋)有限公司
261	南通森蓝环保科技有限公司	301	南通中技桩业有限公司
262	南通金泰科技有限公司	302	南通百正电子新材料有限公司
263	南通威英软件有限公司	303	江苏瀚艺商用空调有限公司
264	南通必优信息系统有限公司	304	东力(南通)化工有限公司
265	南通科尔纺织服饰有限公司	305	江苏苏中电池科技发展有限公司
266	江苏磐宇科技有限公司	306	江苏天泽环保科技有限公司
267	南通瑞普埃尔生物工程有限公司	307	南通海迪化工有限公司
268	南通恺誉照明科技有限公司	308	江苏欧瑞防爆电气有限公司
269	南通海汇科技发展有限公司	309	江苏宏强船舶重工有限公司
270	江苏精一电气科技有限公司	310	启东市海信机械有限公司
271	江苏金冠停车产业股份有限公司	311	南通康盛医疗器械有限公司
272	江苏奥蓝工程玻璃有限公司	312	南通市飞宇精细化学品有限公司
273	南通国全木工机械制造有限公司	313	江苏吉星管业科技有限公司
274	南通斯得福纺织装饰有限公司	314	江苏辰星海洋生物科技有限公司
275	江苏中科机械有限公司	315	南通苏通分离工程科技有限公司
276	江苏大生集团有限公司	316	南通东南公路工程有限公司
277	南通澳兰德复合材料有限公司	317	江苏海湾电气科技有限公司
278	南通贝斯特船舶与海洋工程设计有限公司	318	南通钰成光电科技有限公司
279	南通市东方塑胶有限公司	319	江苏京源环保股份有限公司
280	南通福通机床有限公司	320	南通趣易信息技术有限公司

15-19 续表 4

CONTINUED 4

序号 sequence number	企业名称 Company Name	序号 sequence number	企业名称 Names of the Enterprises
321	南通华冈计算机系统有限公司	361	广东鸿图南通压铸有限公司
322	南通普力马弹性体技术有限公司	362	南通耀龙金属制造有限公司
323	南通中远船务自动化有限公司	363	南通京通石墨设备有限公司
324	上海振华重工集团(南通)传动机械有限公司	364	南通亿仕得医疗器械有限公司
325	南通富来威农业装备有限公司	365	南通红石科技发展有限公司
326	中江机电科技江苏有限公司	366	南通紫鑫实业有限公司
327	江苏紫石机械制造有限公司	367	南通华特铝热传输材料有限公司
328	南通江中光电有限公司	368	南通金兰数码打印材料有限公司
329	江苏亚星波纹管有限公司	369	南通久盛新材料科技有限公司
330	卡姆丹克太阳能(江苏)有限公司	370	南通好的防腐装备有限公司
331	南通太和机械集团有限公司	371	南通东源互感器制造有限公司
332	如皋市华阳铝制品有限公司	372	江苏中威科技软件系统有限公司
333	如皋市凯凯电信器材有限公司	373	南通伊诺精密塑胶导管有限公司
334	江苏中硅工程材料有限公司	374	南通斯恩特纺织科技有限公司
335	南通功成精细化工有限公司	375	江苏唐工纺实业有限公司
336	南通高盟新材料有限公司	376	江苏道达海洋装备技术有限公司
337	赛立特(南通)安全用品有限公司	377	安客诚全球信息服务(南通)有限公司
338	南通沃斯得医药化工有限公司	378	江苏龙源振华海洋工程有限公司
339	南通和泰通讯器材有限公司	379	南通久信石墨科技开发限公司
340	海门通能通讯科技有限公司	380	南通新洋环保板业有限公司
341	南通三鑫电子科技股份有限公司	381	南通山剑石墨设备有限公司
342	江苏海隆重机有限公司	382	江苏政田重工股份有限公司
343	江苏亨通电子线缆科技有限公司	383	南通万德科技有限公司
344	海门瑞一医药科技有限公司	384	中天科技精密材料有限公司
345	南通海发水处理工程有限公司	385	南通江天化学股份有限公司
346	南通新兴特种金属材料有限公司	386	南通联亚药业有限公司
347	南通亚浦照明电器制造有限公司	387	南通中集大型储罐有限公司
348	南通汇丰电子科技有限公司	388	南通众诚生物技术有限公司
349	开美化学科技(南通)有限公司	389	领新(南通)重工有限公司
350	金轮橡胶(海门)有限公司	390	南通通镭软件有限公司
351	江苏希诺实业有限公司	391	精华制药集团股份有限公司
352	江苏景越塑料科技有限公司	392	南通友联数码技术开发有限公司
353	南通正拓气体有限公司	393	江苏赛奥生化有限公司
354	南通合硕电子有限公司	394	中天科技装备电缆有限公司
355	南通市煌埔机械制造有限公司	395	南通爱慕希机械有限公司
356	江苏碧松照明股份有限公司	396	江苏普腾停车设备有限公司
357	江苏索利得电器有限公司	397	南通瑞翔新材料有限公司
358	南通柯瑞特机械制造有限公司	398	中天科技光纤有限公司
359	江苏甬金金属科技有限公司	399	江苏天舒电器有限公司
360	南通亿华塑胶有限公司	400	江苏格美高科技发展有限公司

15-19 续表 5

CONTINUED 5

序号 sequence number	企业名称 Company Name	序号 sequence number	企业名称 Names of the Enterprises
401	江苏优远生物科技有限公司	441	江苏星瑞化工工程科技有限公司
402	江苏埃尔贝勒汽车电子有限公司	442	森松(江苏)重工有限公司
403	江苏泰洁检测技术有限公司	443	江苏神马电力股份有限公司
404	中天合金技术有限公司	444	南通江森电子科技有限公司
405	江苏达成生物科技有限公司	445	开源塑业科技(南通)有限公司
406	南通三圣石墨设备科技股份有限公司	446	南通明德塑胶有限公司
407	南通昱品通信科技有限公司	447	南通国电电站阀门有限公司
408	江苏康非特动力科技有限公司	448	海迪科(南通)光电科技有限公司
409	江苏东源电器集团股份有限公司	449	启东尤希路化学工业有限公司
410	桑夏太阳能股份有限公司	450	江苏海四达电源股份有限公司
411	南通东方科技有限公司	451	江苏神通阀门股份有限公司
412	南通东源电力智能设备有限公司	452	启东鑫业网络科技有限公司
413	江苏中天科技股份有限公司	453	南通富莱克流体装备有限公司
414	江苏九九久科技股份有限公司	454	启东市巨龙石油化工装备有限公司
415	南通市天时化工有限公司	455	启东市爱普电器有限公司
416	江苏快达农化股份有限公司	456	江苏恒丰电动工具有限公司
417	如东县宇迪光学仪器厂有限公司	457	江苏大岛机械集团有限公司
418	江苏如石机械有限公司	458	南通富力机电设备有限责任公司
419	江苏如通石油机械股份有限公司	459	南通万达锅炉有限公司
420	江苏利田科技股份有限公司	460	南通易实工业制造有限公司
421	南通瑶华纤维有限公司	461	江苏吉泰科电气股份有限公司
422	江苏黄海汽配股份有限公司	462	南通同洲电子有限责任公司
423	南通保来利轴承有限公司	463	江苏天联信息科技发展有限公司
424	南通黄海药械有限公司	464	南通清波环保科技有限公司
425	南通市通润汽车零部件有限公司	465	南通牧井微电科技发展有限公司
426	西蒙电气(中国)有限公司	466	南通中集交通储运装备制造有限公司
427	海安县鹰球粉末冶金有限公司	467	山姆电器(南通)有限公司
428	南通市广益机电有限责任公司	468	南通科技投资集团股份有限公司
429	江苏明江阀业有限公司	469	南通明兴科技开发有限公司
430	江苏兴华胶带股份有限公司	470	南通京鼎数控设备有限公司
431	江苏瑞安特机械集团有限公司	471	南通时瑞塑胶制品有限公司
432	海安纺织机械有限公司	472	南通透明度动画设计有限公司
433	海安县申菱电器制造有限公司	473	南通永创航海机械有限公司
434	南通跃通数控设备有限公司	474	江苏力德尔电子信息技术有限公司
435	江苏文凤化纤集团有限公司	475	南通联农佳田作物科技有限公司
436	南通恒力重工机械有限公司	476	南通星辰合成材料有限公司
437	南通金亿达门业有限公司	477	江苏中天科技软件技术有限公司
438	欧贝黎新能源科技股份有限公司	478	南通海珥玛植物油脂有限公司
439	南通向阳光学元件有限公司	479	三德管业(南通)有限公司
440	南通新昱化工有限公司	480	江苏海纳精密装备有限公司

15-19 续表 6

CONTINUED 6

序号 sequence number	企业名称 Company Name	序号 sequence number	企业名称 Names of the Enterprises
481	南通居梦莱家用纺织品有限公司	521	南通常佑药业科技有限公司
482	南通华隆微电子有限公司	522	如东南天农科化工有限公司
483	江苏华宇印涂设备集团有限公司	523	江苏绿叶机械有限公司
484	南通瑞泰电子有限公司	524	江苏恒炫电气有限公司
485	江苏蓝天彩涂薄板科技有限公司	525	南通恒鼎重型机床有限公司
486	南通神华电气有限公司	526	江苏万力机械股份有限公司
487	南通惠得成包装材料有限公司	527	江苏华安科研仪器有限公司
488	南通华铮隆钢业制造有限公司	528	艾能赛克机械设备(江苏)有限公司
489	南通沪望塑料科技发展有限公司	529	南通华兴石油仪器有限公司
490	南通南洋照明科技有限公司	530	南通中尧特雷卡电梯产品有限公司
491	南通庞源机械工程有限公司	531	南通市飞宇石油科技开发有限公司
492	南通晋弘钢结构工程有限公司	532	南通欧特建材设备有限公司
493	南通华夏航空工程技术有限公司	533	江苏瑞恩电气股份有限公司
494	南通江海电容器股份有限公司	534	南通润德机械科技有限公司
495	南通市嘉诚机械有限公司	535	如皋市包装食品机械有限公司
496	南通苏宝建筑节能科技有限公司	536	如皋市图腾电力科技有限公司
497	江苏格雷特起重机械有限公司	537	江苏融达新材料股份有限公司
498	南通广兴气动设备有限公司	538	江苏曜彰体育用品有限公司
499	江苏旭田环保机械有限公司	539	江苏万达特种轴承有限公司
500	南通综艺新材料有限公司	540	江苏泰仓农化有限公司
501	南通阿斯通电器制造有限公司	541	江苏顺远纺织科技有限公司
502	江苏圣夫岛纺织生物科技有限公司	542	江苏思源赫兹互感器有限公司
503	南通星源仪器设备制造有限公司	543	江苏省如高高压电器有限公司
504	南通准信自动化科技有限公司	544	江苏永大化工机械有限公司
505	江苏华洋水箱给水设备有限公司	545	江苏力星通用钢球股份有限公司
506	南通凯赛生化工程设备有限公司	546	江苏恒祥化工有限责任公司
507	南通弘峰机电有限公司	547	南通思瑞机器制造有限公司
508	南通海一电子有限公司	548	江苏九鼎新材料股份有限公司
509	创斯达科技集团(中国)有限责任公司	549	江苏力沛电力工程技术服务有限公司
510	江苏博悦物联网技术有限公司	550	南通市振兴精细化工有限公司
511	南通大任永磁电机制造有限公司	551	如皋市万通防腐有限公司
512	南通四方冷链装备股份有限公司	552	南通皋鑫电子股份有限公司
513	南通巴大饲料有限公司	553	如皋市中罗印刷机械有限公司
514	南通市鸿鑫纤维有限公司	554	江苏阿尔法电梯有限公司
515	南通万达包装有限公司	555	南通欧意姆制冷设备有限公司
516	江苏赛孚石油机械有限公司	556	江苏顺达工程科技有限公司
517	南通诺德电子有限公司	557	江苏三科安全科技有限公司
518	江苏三旗线缆有限公司	558	南通鸿志化工有限公司
519	江苏科净炭纤维有限公司	559	江苏海纳空调净化设备有限公司
520	南通大力化工设备有限公司	560	江苏飞尔机电科技有限公司

15-19 续表 7

CONTINUED 7

序号 sequence number	企业名称 Company Name	序号 sequence number	企业名称 Names of the Enterprises
561	展志电子科技(南通)有限公司	601	巴塞利亚药业(中国)有限公司
562	江苏永佳电子材料有限公司	602	江苏金呢工程织物股份有限公司
563	江苏医邦医疗器械有限公司	603	南通麦隆能源设备有限公司
564	南通市华峰化工有限责任公司	604	海门市森达装饰材料有限公司
565	如皋市万利化工有限责任公司	605	招商局重工(江苏)有限公司
566	如皋市天元服饰印业有限公司	606	南通宏通生物科技有限公司
567	南通盛达铸造有限公司	607	南通捷科软件技术有限公司
568	江苏长寿集团南山饲料有限公司	608	南通春晖软件有限公司
569	南通明辉信息科技有限公司	609	江苏丽洋新材料股份有限公司
570	江苏锐聘信息科技有限公司	610	南通卓锐激光科技有限公司
571	南通希尔顿博世流体设备有限公司	611	南通德祺五金机械有限公司
572	南通东之杰电气有限公司	612	南通富士通微电子股份有限公司
573	南通申东冶金机械有限公司	613	江苏南通申通机械有限公司
574	启东万惠机械制造有限公司	614	南通联鑫机械制造有限公司
575	启东混合器厂有限公司	615	南通迪施有限公司
576	江苏天宇石化冶金设备有限公司	616	南通天工深冷新材料强化有限公司
577	南通鑫磁机械制造有限公司	617	南通市建筑科学研究院有限公司
578	江苏澳瑞思液压润滑设备有限公司	618	南通密炼捏合机械有限公司
579	南通恒立机械设备有限公司	619	南通天源气体有限公司
580	江苏克莱斯克能源装备有限公司	620	江苏远中电机股份有限公司
581	南通仟得电动工具有限公司	621	南通长江电器实业有限公司
582	江苏韦欧机械有限公司	622	江苏飞马药业有限公司
583	江苏林洋电子股份有限公司	623	晟大科技(南通)有限公司
584	启东东岳药业有限公司	624	南通帝诚华信实业有限公司
585	宏华海洋油气装备(江苏)有限公司	625	南通虹波机械有限公司
586	江苏汉盛海洋装备技术有限公司	626	南通亿能彩钢板有限公司
587	江苏康耐特光学有限公司	627	南通科赛尔机械有限公司
588	南通倍佳机械科技有限公司	628	南通正大有限公司
589	孚创动力控制技术(启东)有限公司	629	江苏天楹之光光电科技有限公司
590	启东市美迅机械有限公司	630	海安县兰菱机电设备有限公司
591	恒升化工有限公司	631	海安县联源机械制造有限公司
592	启东优思电子有限公司	632	江苏新旭磁电科技有限公司
593	南通东泰电工器材有限公司	633	海安县巨力磁材有限责任公司
594	江苏鸿得利机械有限公司	634	江苏中海重型机床有限公司
595	南通东利德工具有限公司	635	南通中菱绝缘材料有限公司
596	美通重工有限公司	636	南通贝思特机械工程有限公司
597	冠达尔钢结构(江苏)有限公司	637	南通万达摩擦材料有限公司
598	江苏宝钢精密钢丝有限公司	638	江苏新业重工股份有限公司
599	江苏中联风能机械有限公司	639	凯迈(江苏)机电有限公司
600	海门慧聚药业有限公司	640	江苏国能仪表科技有限公司

15-19 续表 9

CONTINUED 9

序号 sequence number	企业名称 Company Name	序号 sequence number	企业名称 Names of the Enterprises
641	南通市喜利得润滑设备有限公司	653	江苏环宇建筑设备制造有限公司
642	启东锦桥轴承有限公司	654	南通奥斯特鞋业有限公司
643	韩华新能源(启东)有限公司	655	海门市金昊自动化科技有限公司
644	江苏浙南装备技术有限公司	656	江苏永生电气有限公司
645	启东中冶润滑液压设备有限公司	657	江苏卡帕电气科技有限公司
646	江苏云帆化工有限公司	658	南通市威士真空设备有限公司
647	南通市海圣药业有限公司	659	南通金坤机械设备有限公司
648	南通嘉禾化工有限公司	660	南通中远重工有限公司
649	江苏通光强能输电线科技有限公司	661	海门市五洋化工有限公司
650	南通美固复合材料有限公司	662	金轮科创股份有限公司
651	江苏恒丰强生物技术有限公司	663	维柏思特衬布(南通)有限公司
652	江苏铁锚工具有限公司		

主要统计指标解释

科技活动 指在自然科学、农业科学、医药科学、工程与技术科学、人文对社会科学领域(简称科学技术领域)中,与科技知识的产生、发展、传播和应用密切相关的有组织的活动。为核算科技投入的需要,科技活动可分为科学研究与试验发展(R&D)、科学研究与试验发展成果应用及相关的科技服务三类活动。本报表制度规定,工业企业只统计科学研究与试验发展(R&D)及其成果应用两类活动,即通常讲的技术开发活动。

科学研究与试验发展 指在科学技术领域,为增加知识总量、以及运用这些知识去创造新的应用进行的系统的创造性的活动,包括基础研究、应用研究、试验发展三类活动。在工业企业开展的科学研究与试验发展(R&D)活动中,较为普遍的和大量的活动属于试验发展活动。

基础研究 指为了获得关于现象和可观察事实的基本原理的新知识(揭示客观事物的本质、运动规律,获得新发展、新学说)而进行的实验性或理论性研究,它不以任何专门或特定的应用或使用为目的。其成果以科学论文和科学著作为主要形式。

应用研究 指为获得新知识而进行的创造性研究,主要针对某一特定的目的或目标。应用研究是为了确定基础研究成果可能的用途,或是为达到预定的目标探索应采取的新方法(原理性)或新途径。其成果形式以科学论文、专著、原理性模型或发明专利为主。

试验发展 指利用从基础研究、应用研究和实际经验所获得的现有知识,为产生新的产品、材料和装置,建立新的工艺、系统和服务,以及对已产生和建立的上述各项作实质性的改进而进行的系统性工作。其成果形式主要是专利、专有技术、新产品原型或样机样件等。

科学研究与试验发展成果应用 指为使试验发展阶段产生的新产品、材料和装置,建立的新工艺、系统和服务以及实质性改进后的上述各项能够投人生产或实际应用,解决所存在的技术问题而进行的系统性的工作。这类活动的成果形式大多是可供生产和实际操作的带有技术和工艺参数的图纸、技术标准和操作规范。

微电子控制机器设备原价 指企业在年末拥有的、利用微电子技术(包括电子计算机、集成电路等)对生产过程进行控制、观察测量、测试等生产机器设备的原价。

科技活动人员 指工业企业在报告年度直接从事(或参与)科技活动、以及专门从事科技活动管理和为科技活动提供直接服务的人员。累计从事科技活动的时间占制度工作时间10%(不含)以下的人员不统计在内。

科技活动全时人员 指企业科技活动人员中在报告年度实际从事科技活动的时间占制度工作时间90%以上(含90%)的人员。在企业科技管理部门(科研管理处、部、科等)专职从事科技管理工作的人员、企业所属常年有开发任务的科技机构中专职从事科技活动及其管理和直接服务的人员,以及上述人员以外在报告年度实际从事科技活动开发的人员可视作科技活动全时人员。

科技活动非全时人员 指企业科技活动人员中在报告年度实际从事科技活动的时间占制度工作时间在10%(含10%)-90%(不含)的人员。科技活动非全时人员一般指在报告年度兼职或部分时间从事科技活动的人员。

科技活动经费筹集总额 指企业在报告年度从各种渠道筹集到的计划用于科技活动的经费,包括企业资金、金融机构贷款、政府资金、事业单位资金、国外资金、其他资金等。

科技活动经费支出总额 指企业在报告年度实际支出的费用,包括列入技术开发的经费支出以及技措技改等资金实际用于科技活动的支出。不包括生产性支出和归还贷款支出。科技活动经费支出总额分为内部支出和外部支出。

科技活动经费内部支出 指企业在报告年度用于内部开展科技活动实际支出的费用,包括外协加工费。不包括委托研制或合作研制而支付外单位的经费。科技活动经费内部支出按用途分为科技活动人员劳务费、原材料费、购买与自制设备支出、其他支出。

新产品开发经费支出 指报告年度内企业用于新产品研究开发的的经费支出。包括研究、设计、模型研制、测试、试验等费用支出。

科技活动经费外部支出 指企业在报告年度委托其他单位或与其合作开展科技活动而支付给其他单位的经费。不包括外协加工费。

用于科研的基建经费支出 指企业报告年度为改善科研条件，提高研制开发能力，使用基本建设资金、技措技改等资金进行新建、改建、扩建、购置、安装科研用固定资产、以及进行科研设备改造及大修理等的实际支出。科研与生产共用的基建项目，按企业计划和生产使用安排进行分摊。

科研土建工程支出 指企业用于科研的基建经费支出中购置土地、建造科研楼、中试车间和试验场地，或对有科研用房和固定设施进行更新改造等的经费支出。

全部科技项目数 指企业在报告年度当年立项并开展研制工作、以前年份立项仍继续进行研制的科技项目数，包括当年完成和年内研制已告失败的科技项目，但不包括委托外单位进行研制的科技项目。

新产品开发项目数 指企业在报告年度进行的全部科技项目中，属于新产品研制开发的项目数。

研究与试验发展项目数 指企业在报告年度进行的全部科技项目中，属于研究与试验发展的项目数。

科技项目参加人员合计 指企业在报告年度编人各个科技项目组的人员总数。报告年度一人参加两个及以上科技项目的人员，只能按一个人统计，不能重复计算。

专利申请数 指企业在报告年度内向专利行政部门提出专利申请并被受理的件数。

发明专利申请数 指企业在报告年度内向专利行政部门提出发明专利申请并受理的件数。

拥有发明专利数 指企业作为专利权人在报告年度拥有的、经国内外专利行政部门授权且在有效期内的发明专利件数。

技术改进 指企业在坚持科技进步的前提下，将科技成果应用于生产的各个领域(产品、设备、工艺等)，用先进技术改造落后技术，用先进工艺代替落后工艺、设备，实现以内涵为主的扩大再生产，从而提高产品质量、促进产品更新换代、节约能源、降低消耗，全面提高综合经济效益。

技术改造经费支出 指本企业在报告年度进行技术改造而发生的费用支出。在技术改造经费支出中，属于研究与试验发展的经费支出，除了包含在技术改造经费支出中，还要计人企业研究与试验发展经费支出中。

技术引进经费支出 指企业在报告年度用于购买国外技术，包括产品设计、工艺流程、图纸、配方、专利等技术资料的费用支出，以及购买关键设备、仪器、样机和样件等的费用支出。

引进技术资料及关键设备等的支出 指企业在报告年度用于购买国外产品设计、工艺流程、图纸、配方、专利、技术诀窍及关键设备的费用支出。

消化吸收的经费支出 指本企业在报告年度对国外引进项目进行消化吸收所支付的经费总额。包括：人员培训费、测绘费、参加消化吸收人员的工资、工装、工艺开发费、必备的配套设备费、翻版费等。引进技术的消化吸收指对引进技术的掌握、应用、复制而开展的工作，以及在此基础上的创新。通过消化吸收国外技术，达到掌握引进技术，提高自我创新能力的目的。

第十六篇 文化 卫生 体育

Chapter 16

Culture and Health , Sport

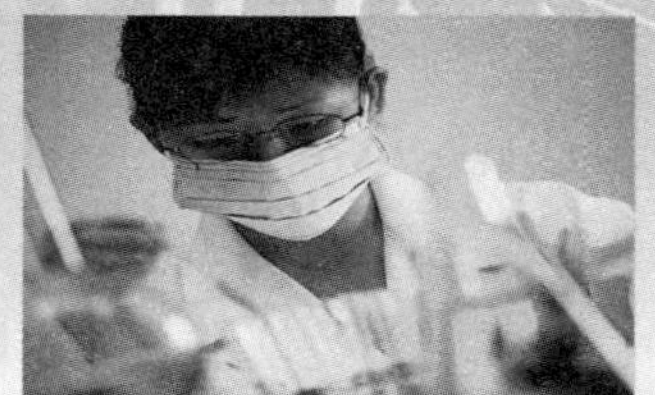

16-1　公有制艺术表演团体基本情况(2014年)
BASIC STATISTICS ON ART TROUPES(2014)

指　标	Item	全市 Total	市区 Urban Area	通州区 Tongzhou	海安 Haian	如东 Rudong	启东 Qidong	如皋 Rugao	海门 Haimen
从业人员数(人)	Employees	414	238	54	30	40	37	37	32
# 高级职称	Personnel With Higher Titles	39	36	1		1			2
中级职称	Personnel With Medium Titles	125	86	16	1	6	10	8	14
本团创作首演剧目(个)	Initial Programs	11	1				9	1	
演出场次(场次)	Times of Performance	3494	600	250	178	101	2080	305	230
# 国内演出场次	Domestic Performance	3449	600	250	178	56	2080	305	230
观众人数(千人次)	Audiences (1000 person-times)	1214	394	144	89	29	320	198	184
剧团数(个)	Troupes	8	2	1	1	1	2	1	1
艺术剧院	Art Theatre	1	1						
歌舞团	Song and Dance Assembles	2	1	1	1				
越剧团	YueDrama Troupe	1					1		
评弹团	Pingtan Troupe	1					1		
杂技团	Acrobatics Troupe	1				1			
木偶艺术团	Puppet Show Art Circus	1						1	
山歌剧团	Folk Song Troupe	1							1
共用房屋建筑面积(平方米)	Shared Housing Area (m^2)	19848	9649	584	1200	6861	460	870	808
# 排练练功用房	Room for Rehearsal	3448	1198	198	1200	480	90	300	180

16-2 文化馆基本情况(2014年)

BASIC CONDITIONS OF CULTURAL INSTITUTES(2014)

指 标	Item	全市 Total	市区 Urban Area	通州区 Tongzhou	海安 Haian	如东 Rudong	启东 Qidong	如皋 Rugao	海门 Haimen
机构数(个)	Institutions	9	4	1	1	1	1	1	1
职工人数(人)	Staff and Workers	191	89	17	25	18	15	26	18
举办展览个数(个)	Exhibitions	125	52	8	20	22	15	12	4
组织文化活动次数(次)	Cultural Activities	740	203	30	190	185	105	45	12
举办训练班结业人数(人次)	Graduates From Training Class	48343	16743	12000	1500	2800	800	26000	500
藏书(万册)	Books Collected(Unit:10,000)	36521	27371	3000		2000	2150	2000	3000

16-3 博物馆基本情况(2014年)

BASIC STATISTICS ON MUSEUMS(2014)

指 标	Item	全市 Total	市区 Urban Area	海安 Haian	如皋 Rugao	海门 Haimen	启东 Qidong
机构数(个)	Institutions	21	13	2	1	4	1
职工人数(人)	Staff and Workers	303	175	23	5	86	14
#高级职称	Personnel With High Title	24	19			5	
中级职称	Personnel With Medium Title	50	43	2	1	4	
文物藏品(件)	Collection of Cultural Relics	176471	159878	3192		4877	8524
#一级品	First Class	53	48	1		4	
二级品	Second Class	697	613	8		63	8
举办展览(个)	Exhibitions	169	126	12		29	2
参观人数(万人次)	Audiences (1000 person-times)	4022	2152	726		844	300
#未成年人参观人次	Youngsters	944	602	97		227	18
公用房屋建筑面积(万平方米)	Shared Housing Area (m^2)	113999	52434	13700		27835	19980
#陈列展览用房	Display Room	46120	22715	4000		18205	1200
文物库房	Storeroom of Cultural Relics	7205	5312	180		1513	200

16-4 电视台及节目制作情况(2014年)

BASIC STATISTICS ON TV STATION AND PROGRAM(2014)

指 标	Item	全市 Total	市区 Urban Area	通州区 Tongzhou	海安 Haian	如东 Rudong	启东 Qidong	如皋 Rugao	海门 Haimen
电视台(座)	TV Station	7	2	1	1	1	1	1	1
节目(套)	Programs	10	5	1	1	1	1	1	1
平均每周播出时间(小时)	Broadcasting Hours per Week	1077	532	120	81	116	155	110	83
电视人口覆盖率(%)	Coverage Rate of TV Program	100	100	100	100	100	100	100	100
有线电视入户率(%)	Cable TV Penetration	96.9	115.5	93.6	90.3	98.1	95.9	93.4	95.8
全年制作节目时间(小时)	Annual Program Hours	8552.33	3872.33	1127.33	500	765	702	837	1876
# 新闻节目	News	2830	1578.5	182.5	187	205.5	172	194	493
文艺节目	Entertainment	847	560.5	304.5	40	11.5		90	145

16-5 电台及节目制作情况(2014年)

BASIC STATISTICS ON BROADCASTING STATION AND PROGRAM MAKING(2014)

指 标	Item	全市 Total	市区 Urban Area	通州区 Tongzhou	海安 Haian	如东 Rudong	启东 Qidong	如皋 Rugao	海门 Haimen
电台(座)	Broadcasting Station	7	2	1	1	1	1	1	1
节目(套)	Programs	8	3	1	1	1	1	1	1
平均每日播音时间(小时)	Broadcasting Time Per day (Hour)	132	55	14	13	16	22	17	8
广播人口覆盖率(%)	Coverage Rate (%)	100	100	100	100	100	100	100	100
全年制作节目时间(小时)	Annual Program Time	27941	16274	1959	1470	3991	2050	1570	2587
# 新闻节目	News	9197	6406	421	185	1326	103	420	757
文艺节目	Entertainment	5934	3579	618	720	231	380	476	548

16-6 历年卫生机构、人员数
NUMBER OF HEALTH CARE INSTITUTIONS AND PERSONS OVER THE YEARS

年份 Year	机构数(个) Institutions (unit)	医院卫生院 Hospitals	卫生技术人员数(万人) Medical Technical Personnel(person)	医生 Doctors	床位数(万张) Beds(10000 unit)
1978	898	327	1.47	0.60	1.55
1979	829	321	1.53	0.63	1.59
1980	849	378	1.52	0.64	1.71
1985	1081	351	1.90	0.86	1.70
1990	1368	344	2.21	1.05	1.84
1991	1352	345	2.30	1.08	1.89
1992	1337	345	2.35	1.09	1.93
1993	1318	337	2.41	1.14	1.87
1994	1317	351	2.46	1.16	1.88
1995	1301	335	2.53	1.20	1.86
1996	1255	329	2.61	1.26	1.88
1997	2091	328	2.64	1.29	1.86
1998	2093	329	2.67	1.32	1.89
1999	1871	324	2.63	1.30	1.88
2000	1855	303	2.61	1.30	1.87
2001	1682	317	2.56	1.27	1.97
2002	1448	317	2.40	1.10	2.00
2003	1358	314	2.38	1.09	2.00
2004	1674	313	2.40	1.09	2.05
2005	1810	319	2.44	1.10	2.12
2006	1931	316	2.51	1.13	2.21
2007	3601	333	2.75	1.29	2.29
2008	1784	331	2.80	1.25	2.42
2009	1816	333	2.96	1.27	2.49
2010	1667	333	3.06	1.32	2.63
2011	1664	328	3.19	1.34	2.91
2012	1641	327	3.47	1.48	3.15
2013	1592	310	3.65	1.56	3.32
2014	1621	304	3.95	1.64	3.51

注:卫生机构个数不含村卫生室

Notes:The number of institutions does not include that of village clinics.

16-7 公共图书馆基本情况(2014年)

指 标	Item	全市 Total
机构数(个)	Number of Institutions	11
职工人数(人)	Staff and Workers	200
#高级职称	Personnel With Higher Titles	12
中级职称	Personnel With Medium Titles	55
总藏量(万册)	Book Collected	445.48
#图书	Books	382.94
#古籍	Ancient Books	22.44
报刊	Newspapers	32.66
#开架书刊	Periodicals	235.28
发放有效借书证数(万个)	Library Card Issued	20.03
总流通人次(千人次)	Circulation (1000 person-times)	2520
#书刊文献外借人次	Lending Person-Times	1181
书刊外借册次(千册次)	Times of Lending (1000 times)	2657
为读者举办各种活动(次)	Activities for Audiences	228
参加人次(人次)	Persons Involved (person-time)	43853
公用房屋建筑面积(平方米)	Shared Housing Area (m2)	82183
#书库	Book Storage	9635
阅览室	Reading Rooms	14135
阅览室座位(个)	Seats of Reading Rooms	2752

BASIC STATISTICS ON PUBLIC LIBRARIES(2014)

市区 Urban Area	通州区 Tongzhou	海安 Haian	如东 Rudong	启东 Qidong	如皋 Rugao	海门 Haimen
5	1	1	1	1	2	1
85	11	12	18	24	48	13
9	2	1				2
30	5	5	4	5	5	6
183.82	40.72	42.92	40.36	41.72	85.55	51.11
149.57	35.20	34.82	36.63	38.24	76.92	46.75
17.39	0.37	0.57	0.26	0.69	3.07	0.47
15.82	4.65	7.12	3.15	1.91	2.07	2.58
100.05	14.76	9.42	18.43	15.59	81.78	10.00
11.19	3.63	0.98	1.81	1.53	3.67	0.85
847	326	298	418	157	619	180
441	106	86	257	103	144	150
1048	378	258	268	618	330	135
98	6	15	7	66	24	18
10770	1500	14980	6283	1560	4060	6200
45700	8812	4080	4000	7864	17519	3020
4252	832	800	1100	509	1974	1000
6819	2496	800	2400	1503	1413	1200
1031	351	436	240	400	590	55

16-8 分地区卫生机构和人员(2014年)

指 标	Item	全市 Total
卫生机构数(个)	**Number of Health Care Institutions**	**3262**
医院	Hospital	201
#综合性医院	Comprehensive Hospital	162
中医院	Hospital of Traditional Chinese Medicine	8
疗养院	Sanatorium	1
社区卫生服务中心(站)	Community Health Service Center (Station)	157
卫生院	Health Center	103
街道卫生院	Sub-district Health Center	
中心卫生院	Central Health Center	34
乡卫生院	Country Health Center	69
村卫生室	Village Health Center	1641
门诊部、诊所、卫生所	Out-patient Department and Clinics	1082
门诊部	Out-patient Department	53
诊所卫生所医务室	Clinic, Health Center and Infirmary	1029
急救中心(站)	Emergency Center (Station)	2
采供血机构	Blood Bank	3
妇幼保健院(所站)	Maternity and Child Care Center	7
专科疾病防治院(所站)	Specialized Hospital for Disease Prevention and Control	3
疾病预防控制中心(防疫站)	Disease Prevention and Control Center	9
卫生监督所	Health Supervision Institute	8
医学科学研究机构	Medical Science Research Institute	
医学在职培训机构	Medical On-job Training Institute	5
其他卫生机构	Others	38
卫生工作人员(人)	**Health Workers(person)**	**50373**
卫生技术人员	Health Technician	39481
#医院、卫生院	Hospital and Health Center	11810
执业(助理)医师	Practicing Physician (Assistant)	16366
执业医师	Practicing Physician	14215
#医院、卫生院	Hospital and Health Center	11068
执业助理医师	Practicing Physician (Assistant)	2151
#医院、卫生院	Hospital and Health Center	742
注册护士	Registered Nurse	15637
#医院、卫生院	Hospital and Health Center	14121
药剂人员	Pharmaceutical Personnel	2618
检验人员	Inspection Personnel	1463
其他卫技人员	Others	2975
其他技术人员	Other Technicians	730
管理人员	Management Personnel	2636
工勤人员	Logistic Personnel	3540
卫生机构床位数(张)	**Beds of Health Care Institutions**	**35136**
#医院	Hospital	26865
卫生院	Health Center	7311

NUMBER OF HEALTH CARE INSTITUTIONS AND PERSONS ENGAGED BY REGION(2014)

市区 Urban Area	通州区 Tongzhou	海安 Haian	如东 Rudong	启东 Qidong	如皋 Rugao	海门 Haimen
1058	**505**	**401**	**461**	**426**	**511**	**405**
34	6	48	45	6	60	8
12	1	44	43	2	55	6
3	1	1	1	1	1	1
1						
114	13	10		19		14
31	27	10	9	35	2	16
6	6	7	8	6	2	5
25	21	3	1	29		11
316	308	217	241	281	366	220
547	142	101	147	80	75	142
40		5	5		2	1
497	142	96	142	80	73	141
1		1				
2	1				1	
2	1	1	1	1	1	1
2					1	
4	1	1	1	1	1	1
3	1	1	1	1	1	1
2	1		1	1		1
7	4	11	15	1	3	1
22644	**7041**	**5247**	**5194**	**5057**	**7254**	**4977**
18487	5480	4153	3780	3721	5540	3800
5043	1795	1357	1128	1343	1654	1285
7128	2406	1869	1608	1555	2533	1673
6640	2079	1585	1323	1407	1793	1467
4901	1680	1263	1023	1240	1455	1186
488	327	284	285	148	740	206
142	115	94	105	103	199	99
8300	2128	1538	1285	1378	1833	1303
7205	1959	1427	1164	1331	1751	1243
1115	365	312	317	273	375	226
633	191	174	161	154	194	147
1134	338	213	362	328	545	393
493	23	12	4	83	37	101
1375	348	251	298	182	353	177
1447	352	286	337	283	815	372
15134	**5671**	**4232**	**3286**	**3815**	**5189**	**3480**
12218	3315	3615	2612	1921	4838	1661
2321	2181	617	674	1844	271	1584

16-9 卫生事业基本情况(2014年)

BASIC STATISTICS ON HEALTH CARE(2014)

指 标	Item	机构数(个) Number of Institutions (unit)	床位数(张) Number of Beds (unit)	卫生工作人员(人) Health Workers (person)	卫生技术人员 Health Technician	执业(助理)医师 Practicing Physician (Assistant)	注册护士 Registered Nurse
总计	**Total**	**3262**	**35136**	**50373**	**39481**	**16366**	**15637**
医院	Hospital	201	26865	29467	24870	8544	11777
#综合医院	Comprehensive Hospital	162	17162	18640	15698	5450	7291
中医医院	Hospital of Traditional Chinese Medicine	8	3991	4588	4014	1488	1811
疗养院	Sanatorium	1		114	63	24	25
社区卫生服务中心(站)	Community Health Service Center (Station)	157	800	1952	1659	817	470
卫生院	Health Center	103	7311	8254	7174	3266	2344
中心卫生院	Central Health Center	34	4203	5306	4628	1912	1780
乡卫生院	Country Health Center	69	3108	2948	2546	1354	564
村卫生室	Village Health Center	1641		5195	1209	1127	82
门诊部、诊所、卫生所	Out-patient Department and Clinics	1082		2749	2632	1755	621
门诊部	Out-patient Department	53		349	311	137	126
诊所卫生所医务室	Clinic, Health Center and Infirmary	1029		2400	2321	1618	495
急救中心(站)	Emergency Center (Station)	2		84	37	20	12
采供血机构	Blood Bank	3		162	121	18	71
妇幼保健院(所、站)	Maternity and Child Care Center	7		240	199	134	20
专科疾病防治院(所、站)	Specialized Hospital for Disease Prevention and Control	3		130	82	35	28
疾病预防控制中心(防疫站)	Disease Prevention and Control Center	9		615	463	271	31
卫生监督所	Health Supervision Institute	8		289	265		
医学在职培训机构	Medical On-job Training Institute	5		387	148	61	32
其他卫生机构	Others	38		427	296	190	35

16-10 卫生机构诊治情况(2014年)

SITUATION OF HOSPITAL PATIENT SERVICE OF HEALTH INSTITUTES(2014)

指 标	Item	合计 Total	医院 Hospital	综合医院 Comprehensive Hospital	中医院 Hospital of Traditional Chinese Medicine	中心卫生院 Health Center	乡卫生院 Country Health Center
诊疗人次数(万人次)	Number of Dignosis (10,000 person-times)	3935.66	1594.69	1077.38	279.12	296.99	414.72
#门、急诊人次数	As for Out-patient and Emergency	3843.35	1572.74	1069.55	275.85	287.25	410.71
观察室收容病人数(万人)	Patients of Observance Room (10,000 persons)	4.25	2.00	1.87	0.04	0.18	2.04
健康检查人数(万人)	Number of Health Check People (10,000 persons)	203.94	112.31	63.71	19.16	20.55	27.31
出院人数(万人)	Number of Discharged Patients (10,000 persons)	106.97	84.11	58.74	13.73	15.36	6.33
住院病人手术人次数(万人次)	Number of Impatient Surgery (10,000 person-times)	23.39	23.36	16.48	3.68		
出院者平均住院日数(日)	Average Length of Hospital Stay (day)	9.80	10.40	9.40	10.30	8.00	7.50
病床周转次数(次)	Turnover of Hospital Beds	30.80	31.70	34.20	34.90	36.50	20.40
病床使用率(%)	Utilization Rate of Hospital Beds(%)	84.41	91.71	89.43	98.99	81.22	42.77

16-11 前十位疾病死因及比重(2014年)

DEATH RATE OF 10 MAJOR DISEASES IN WHOLE MUNICIPALITY(2014)

位次 No.	死 因	Cause of Death	占全部死因比重(%) As % of Total Deaths
1	恶性肿瘤	Malignant Tumor	30.33
2	脑血管病	Cerebrovascular Disease	22.87
3	呼吸系统疾病	Respiratory Disease	15.05
4	心脏病	Heart Disease	12.83
5	损伤和中毒	Trauma and Toxicosis	6.59
7	内分泌营养代谢疾病	Endocrine Nutrition Metabolic Disease	2.65
6	消化系统疾病	Digestive System Disease	2.01
8	神经系统疾病	Nervous System Disease	1.90
9	精神障碍	Mental Disorders	0.96
10	泌尿生殖系统疾病	Disease of Genitourinary System	0.85

注:平均期望寿命:81.36岁,其中男性78.85岁,女性83.93岁。

Note: The average life expectancy is 81.36. For man, it is 78.85 and for woman, it is 83.93.

16-12 体育事业
SPORTS

指 标	Item	2014 年	2013 年
体育场(个)	Sports Field	13	13
体育馆(个)	Stadium	16	15
游泳池馆(个)	Swimming Pool	15	14
教练员(人)	Coach	189	185
等级裁判员(人)	Referee	614	411
等级运动员(人)	Athlete	137	197
运动员获奖牌数(枚)	Number of Medals	152	143
举办体育竞赛表演次数(次)	Number of Sports Competition Performance	625	540
全民健身活动设施数(个)	Infrastructure for Whole People Fitness	8037	7978
参加体育人口数(万人次)	Participation in Sports (10,000 person-times)	385	356
体育彩票销售点个数(个)	Selling Sites of Sports Lottery	978	1212
体育彩票发行额(万元)	Issued Amount of Sports Lottery (10,000 Yuan)	133600	119000

第十七篇 17

其他社会事业 Chapter

Other Social Activities

17-1 历年社会福利事业基本情况

BASIC STATISTICS ON SOCIAL WELFARE OVER THE YEARS

指　标	Item	2005	2010	2011	2012	2013	2014
社会福利院	**Social Welfare Institute**						
院数(个)	Institute	5	6	8	8	8	8
职工人数(人)	Employees	150	224	230	467	486	354
年末床位(张)	Year-end Number of Beds	708	1141	1768	2127	2521	2754
年末在院人数(人)	Year-end Number of Inpatients	506	743	890	1217	1458	1366
精神病人福利院	**Welfare Institute of Mental Patients**						
院数(个)	Institute	2	2	2	2	2	2
职工人数(人)	Employees	203	209	209	229	231	253
年末床位(张)	Year-end Number of Beds	410	850	850	600	600	850
年末在院人数(人)	Year-end Number of Inpatients	405	700	710	456	471	686
#老人	The Aged	98	400	192	340	368	281
敬老院	**Seniors´ Home**						
院数(个)	Number of Seniors´ Home	165	145	131	128	97	96
职工人数(人)	Employees	908	1513	1519	1466	1357	1396
年末床位(张)	Year-end Number of Beds	8936	19991	20357	21809	21772	22760
年末在院人数(人)	Year-end Number of Inpatients	7400	14679	19888	15972	16922	13988
#五保老人	"Five Guarantee" Elders	7245	20240	19888	14760	13325	11769

注:社会福利院口径为国办养老机构。

Note:The calibre for social welfare institute is the state-run pension institution.

17-2 分地区民政事业基本情况(2014年)

BASIC STATISTICS ON CIVIL ADMINISTRATION BY REGION(2014)

指　标	Item	全市 Whole Municipality	市区 Urban Area	通州区 Tongzhou	海安 Haian	如东 Rudong	启东 Qidong	如皋 Rugao	海门 Haimen
社会福利院	**Social Welfare Institute**								
院数(个)	Institute	8	3	1	1	1	1	1	1
职工人数(人)	Employees	354	242	24	24	23	20	22	23
床位数(张)	Year-end Number of Beds	2754	1369	172	380	330	277	330	68
在院人数(人)	Year-end Number of Inpatients	1366	800	145	83		221	194	68
# 老人	The Aged	1251	706	137	83		221	189	52
精神病人福利院	**Welfare Institute of Mental Patients**								
院数(个)	Institute	2	1					1	
职工人数(人)	Employees	253	211					42	
床位数(张)	Year-end Number of Beds	850	350					500	
在院人数(人)	Year-end Number of Inpatients	686	394					292	
# 老人	The Aged	281	121					160	
敬老院	**Seniors´ Home**								
院数(个)	Number of Seniors´ Home	96	27	20	22	14	8	14	11
职工人数(人)	Employees	1396	288	193	345	310	147	150	156
年末床位(张)	Year-end Number of Beds	22760	5033	3942	4693	4292	1768	4214	2760
年末在院人数(人)	Year-end Number of Inpatients	13988	3378	2752	3390	3349	1213	1410	1248
# 五保老人	“Five Guarantee” Elders	11769	1504	1279	3390	3349	1054	1410	1062

17-3 社会救济和城镇居民最低生活保障情况(2014 年)

STATISTICS ON SOCIAL RELIEF AND URBAN& RURAL RESIDENTS´ SUBSISTANCE ALLOWANCES(2014)

指 标	Item	全市 Whole Municipality	市区 Urban Area	通州区 Tongzhou	海安 Haian	如东 Rudong	启东 Qidong	如皋 Rugao	海门 Haimen
城乡居民最低生活保障人数(人)	Urban & Rural Residents of Subsistance Allowances	8804	4814	1160	1006	582	550	931	921
#在职人员	In-service Staff	109	75	6	3	4	5	2	20
失业人员	Unemployed Person	4223	2407	452	420	335	249	434	378
“三无”人员	Three Non Personnel	127	65	42	6	11	6	9	30
其他人员	Others	729	576	8	18	22	16		97
#农村居民最低生活保障人数	Rural People of Subsistance Allowances	88563	19741	18155	14523	8715	13173	22643	9768
城乡居民最低生活保障情况(万元)	Urban&Rural Residents´ Subsistance Allowance (10,000 Yuan)	32067	10610	6241	4174	3289	4778	5724	3492
城镇保障资金	Urban Security Funds	5147	3365	495	384	309	299	378	412
农村保障资金	Rural Security Funds	26920	7245	5746	3790	2980	4479	5346	3080

17–4 婚姻登记情况(2014年)

STATISTICS ON MARRIAGE REGISTRATION(2014)

地 区	Region	结婚(对) Married (couple)	协议离婚(对) Divorced(couple)	判决离婚(对) Judicial Diorce(couple)
全 市	Whole Municipality	67617	12881	842
市 区	Urban Area	21795	4400	222
崇川区	Chongchuan District	6049	1996	48
港闸区	Gangzha District	2365	395	21
开发区	Development Zone	2846	473	7
通州区	Tongzhou District	10535	1536	146
海 安	Haian	8012	1325	93
如 东	Rudong	7783	1340	142
启 东	Qidong	9912	2557	97
如 皋	Rugao	11743	1686	225
海 门	Haimen	8372	1573	63

17–5 计划生育情况(2014年)

STATISTICS ON FAMILY PLANNING(2014)

地 区	Region	计划生育率(%) Birth Control Rate (%)	育龄妇女人数(万人) Women of Childbearing Age (10,000 Persons)	已婚育龄妇女人数 Married Women of Childbearing Age	领证率(%) Registration Rate (%)	节育率(%) Birth Control Rate (%)
全 市	Whole Municipality	99.2	188.7	142.1	26.6	87.3
市 区	Urban Area	99.4	59.7	45.2	44.5	88.7
崇川区	Chongchuan District	99.4	15.7	11.0	53.9	84.7
港闸区	Gangzha District	100.0	4.2	3.3	44.2	85.3
开发区	Kaifa District	100.0	3.8	2.9	59.0	92.0
通州区	Tongzhou District	99.2	35.9	28.0	39.2	90.4
海 安	Haian	99.5	21.8	16.7	21.0	85.4
如 东	Rudong	99.4	24.4	18.7	7.3	83.6
启 东	Qidong	98.8	25.7	18.6	25.3	86.3
如 皋	Rugao	98.8	35.2	27.2	18.4	87.1
海 门	Haimen	99.5	21.9	15.7	10.6	91.2

17-6　分地区道路交通事故情况(2014年)

ROAD TRAFFIC ACCIDENTS BY REGIONS(2014)

指　标	Item	全市 Whole Municipality	市区 Urban Area	通州区 Tongzhou	海安 Haian	如东 Rudong	启东 Qidong	如皋 Rugao	海门 Haimen
道路交通事故	Road Traffic Accidents								
事故数(件)	Number of Accidents	1280	209	141	157	43	208	546	117
死亡(人)	Death (person)	437	35	27	70	39	82	147	64
伤人(人)	Hurt People (person)	1168	208	138	128	15	223	517	77
损失折款(万元)	Losses Converted into Cash (10,000 Yuan)	295.7	58.7	46.4	14.7	6.7	32.0	169.0	14.5

17-7　道路交通事故情况(2014年)

ROAD TRAFFIC ACCIDENTS(2014)

指标	Item	总计 Total	重大事故 Major Accidents	机动车 Motor Vehicle	汽车 Automobile	摩托车 Motorcycle	非机动车 Non-motor Vehicle	自行车 Bicycle	行人乘车人 Pedestrian & Passenger
事故数(件)	Number of Accidents	1280	437	1115	853	205	189	9	7
死亡(人)	Death (person)	437	437	404	330	48	28		4
伤人(人)	Hurt People (person)	1168	154	969	677	248	233	12	3
损失折款(万元)	Losses Converted into Cash (10,000 Yuan)	295.7	111.0	262.2	193.5	36.4	38.0	0.7	0.9

17-8 分地区火灾综合情况(2014年)

COMPREHENSIVE STATISTICS ON FIRE DISASTERS(2014)

指 标	Item	全市 Whole Municipality	市区 Urban Area	通州区 Tongzhou	海安 Haian	如东 Rudong	启东 Qidong	如皋 Rugao	海门 Haimen
火灾次数(次)	Fire Cases	3237	1228	553	302	172	371	650	514
死亡(人)	Death (person)	20	6	4		1		4	9
伤人(人)	Hurt People (person)	20	10	4		3		1	6
直接财产损失(万元)	Direct Property Loss (10,000 Yuan)	1883.7	788.0	611.0	61.7	74.4	103.1	172.6	684.0

17-9 律师工作情况(2014年)

STATISTICS ON LAWYERS(2014)

指 标	Item	全市 Whole Municipality	市区 Urban Area	通州区 Tongzhou	海安 Haian	如东 Rudong	启东 Qidong	如皋 Rugao	海门 Haimen
律师事务所(家)	Law Firm	89	46	4	10	8	6	11	8
律师人员(人)	Lawyers	860	507	32	85	50	63	93	62
#女律师	Female Lawyers	248	158	12	18	14	11	28	19
义务法律咨询服务件数(件)	Compulsory Legal Consulting Services(case)	11558	2541	89	179	261	2291	6188	98
参加义务法律咨询律师(人次)	Lawyers Providing Compulsory Legal Consulting(person-time)	3749	1697	44	196	304	831	549	172
担任法律顾问(家)	Legal Advisor (law firm)	10480	7619	109	492	317	203	1475	374
刑事诉讼辩护及代理(件)	Criminal Litigation Defense and Agent (case)	2932	1948	65	90	115	107	490	182
民事案件诉讼代理	Civil Litigation Agent	25078	18742	621	787	1219	2171	845	1314
经济案件诉讼代理	Economic Case Litigation Agent	18123	17158	174	68	314	120	366	97
非诉讼法律事务	Non-litigation Legal Affairs	3837	3088	24	156	71	18	467	37

17-10　公证工作情况(2014 年)

STATISTICS OF NOTARIZATION WORK(2014)

指　标	Item	全市 Whole Municipality	市区 Urban Area		海安 Haian	如东 Rudong	启东 Qidong	如皋 Rugao	海门 Haimen
				通州区 Tongzhou					
公证处(个)	Notarization Office	9	4	1	1	1	1	1	1
公证处人员(人)	Notarization Personnel	111	67	11	7	8	12	10	7
# 公证员	Notary	47	26	5	3	5	5	4	4
办理公证总数(件)	Number of Notarization Case	68150	37689	3411	9843	3795	6050	6011	4762
国内公证	Domestic Notarization	46307	28918	1175	4301	2799	4244	4318	1727
涉外及涉港澳台	Foreign and HK, Macau& Taiwan Affairs	21843	8771	2236	5542	996	1806	1693	3035

17-11　基层人民调解工作情况(2014 年)

STATISTICS OF GRASSROOTS PEOPLE MEDIATION WORK(2014)

指　标	Item	全市 Whole Municipality	市区 Urban Area		海安 Haian	如东 Rudong	启东 Qidong	如皋 Rugao	海门 Haimen
				通州区 Tongzhou					
人民调解委员会(个)	People´s Mediation Committee	3652	818	341	688	581	439	675	451
调解人数(人)	People Mediated (person)	151533	88873	9196	15441	16226	11231	11069	8693
调解纠纷总数(件)	Total Number of Dispute Resolution(case)	60753	36567	4182	6618	6233	3601	4243	3491
调解纠纷成功数(件)	Successful Mediation Cases	59914	36066	4162	6471	6137	3571	4178	3491
# 婚姻家庭	Cases of Marriage and Family	7106	3144	857	1054	1019	545	750	594
# 防止民间纠纷引起自杀	Prevention of Suicides Caused by Civil Disputes	26	2		22			2	
# 防止民间纠纷转化为刑事案件	Prevention of Criminal Cases Caused by Civil Disputes	80	17	11	28	12	11	12	

17-12 基层法律服务所工作情况(2014年)

STATISTICS ON WORK OF GRASSROOTS LEGAL SERVICE STATIONS(2014)

指 标	Item	全市 Whole Municipality	市区 Urban Area	通州区 Tongzhou	海安 Haian	如东 Rudong	启东 Qidong	如皋 Rugao	海门 Haimen
基层法律服务所(家)	Grassroots Legal Service Station	138	40	26	18	19	21	20	20
基层法律工作者(人)	Grassroots Legal Workers (person)	593	174	96	80	82	84	105	68
民事诉讼代理(件)	Civil Litigation Agent (case)	13040	5270	3005	1668	1974	1724	2272	1856
民事非诉讼代理(件)	Civil Non-litigation Agent (case)	4133	1088	928	824	316	729	960	216
担任法律顾问(家)	Legal Advisor (law firm)	4346	1023	771	536	393	145	1806	443

17-13 法律援助工作情况(2014年)

STATISTICS ON LEGAL AID WORK(2014)

指 标	Item	全市 Whole Municipality	市区 Urban Area	通州区 Tongzhou	海安 Haian	如东 Rudong	启东 Qidong	如皋 Rugao	海门 Haimen
法律援助中心(个)	Legal Aid Center	9	4	1	1	1	1	1	1
民事法律援助(起)	Civil Legal Aid(case)	8374	1582	602	1347	780	1496	1403	1766
刑事法律援助(起)	Criminal Legal Aid (case)	867	331	100	77	43	146	176	94
接待来访咨询(件)	Visit Reception and Consultation (case)	63306	19243	11943	8715	10374	11152	9751	4071
“148”来电接待(件)	148 Telephone Reception (case)	8539	5052	395	457	656	1038	523	813

17-14 档案机构人员情况(2014 年)

STATISTICS ON ARCHIVE INSTITUTION PERSONNEL(2014)

单位:人 (person)

指标	Item	机构数(个) Number of Institutes	人员数 Number of Employees	专业人员 Professionals	# 高级 High Degree	中级 Medium Degree	初级 Junior Degree
总　计	**Total**	**159**	**334**	**261**	**28**	**115**	**44**
一、国家综合档案馆(局)	National Comprehensive Archive (Bureau)	10	106	67	9	47	2
南通市档案馆(局)	Nantong Archive (Bureau)	1	38	17	3	11	
海安县档案馆(局)	Haian Archive (Bureau)	1	6	6	3	5	
如东县档案馆(局)	Rudong Archive (Bureau)	1	8	7		1	1
启东市档案馆(局)	Qidong Archive (Bureau)	1	13	6		6	
如皋市档案馆(局)	Rugao Archive (Bureau)	1	15	7	3	4	
通州市档案馆(局)	Tongzhou Archive (Bureau)	1	10	10		7	
海门市档案馆(局)	Haimen Archive (Bureau)	1	3	3		7	
崇川区档案馆	Chongchuan Archive	1	3	1			1
港闸区档案馆	Gangzha Archive	1	5	5		4	
开发区档案馆	Development Zone Archive	1	5	5		2	
二、专门档案馆	Specialized Archive						
城建档案馆	Urban Construction Archive	7	31	31	5	25	1
三、部门档案馆	Deparment Archive						
农业科技档案馆	Agricultural S&T Archive	1	9	4		1	
房地产档案馆	Real Estate Archive	1	15	13	1	1	4
四、大型企业档案室	Large&Medium Enterprise Archive	25	33	33	1	5	12
五、中型企业档案室	Medium Enterprise Archive	6	9	9		2	6
六、机关事业单位档案室	Archive Room of Government Organizations And Institutions	109	131	104	12	34	19

17-15 档案馆藏及利用情况(2014 年)

COLLECTION AND UTILIZATION OF ARCHIVES(2014)

指标	Item	保存档案 Archives in Storage				开放档案(卷) Open Archives (volume)	利用档案情况 Utilization of Archives	
		全宗(个) General Archive (unit)	案卷(万卷) Files (10,000)	录音、录像、照片(张) Audio & Video Records and Pictures (piece)	底图(张) Base Map (piece)		人次 Person-time	卷次(卷件册) Volume
总　计	**Total**	**2478**	**1072.02**	**302555**	**259615**	**165305**	**170733**	**267402**
一、国家综合档案馆(局)	National Comprehensive Archive (Bureau)							
南通市档案馆(局)	Nantong Archive (Bureau)	876	106.51	32383		47293	2983	8623
海安县档案馆(局)	Haian Archive (Bureau)	214	21.52	1923	39	29388	9874	65318
如东县档案馆(局)	Rudong Archive (Bureau)	232	14.81	8227		10368	4181	8479
启东市档案馆(局)	Qidong Archive (Bureau)	221	8.63	5968	1354	4240	4138	2425
如皋市档案馆(局)	Rugao Archive (Bureau)	317	27.61	21424		40354	7623	7912
通州市档案馆(局)	Tongzhou Archive (Bureau)	195	6.3	1377		12279	3040	3626
海门市档案馆(局)	Haimen Archive (Bureau)	167	9.28	1945		19543	3084	2756
崇川区档案馆	Chongchuan Archive	23	1.13	131		1532	1200	4720
港闸区档案馆	Gangzha Archive	59	3.21	582	1418	308	3725	3500
开发区档案馆	Development Zone Archive	23	7.6	1577	308		861	925
二、专门档案馆	Specialized Archive							
城建档案馆	Urban Construction Archive	7	43.68	84318	93103			
三、部门档案馆	Deparment Archive							
农业科技档案馆	Agricultural S&T Archive	3	0.76	2536			80	92
房地产档案馆	Real Estate Archive	1	77.78				74839	89800
四、大型企业档案室	Large&Medium Enterprise Archive	25	139.26	22672	60369		4230	12031
五、中型企业档案室	Medium Enterprise Archive	6	13.65	2514	103024		1684	4516
六、机关事业单位档案室	Archive Room of Government Organizations And Institutions	109	590.29	114978			49191	52679

第十八篇 城市建设

Chapter 18

Urban Construction

18-1 市区城市设施水平(2014 年)

URBAN CIVIL FACILITIES(2014)

指标	Item	数值 Number	指标	Item	数值 Number
人口密度(人/平方公里)	Population Density of Urban Districts (person/km^2)	1536	污水处理率(%)	Sewage Disposal Rate (%)	92.8
人均日生活用水量(升)	Per Capita Daily Water Consumption (liter)	181.4	人均公园绿地面积(平方米)	Per Capita Public Green Area (m^2)	16.8
用水普及率(%)	Percentage of Population With Access to Tap Water (%)	100.0	建成区绿地率(%)	Rate of Green Area Developed (%)	39.6
燃气普及率(%)	Percentage of Population With Access to Gas (%)	100.0	建成区绿化覆盖率(%)	Coverage Rate of Green Area Developed (%)	42.6
人均城市道路面积(平方米)	Per Capita Urban Road Area (m^2)	29.2	生活垃圾无害化处理率(%)	Residential Garbage No-Harmful Disposal Rate (%)	100.0
建成区排水管道密度(公里/平方公里)	Density of Drainage Pipelines (km/km^2)	16.3	粪便无害化处理率(%)	Night Soil No-Harmful Disposal Rate (%)	100.0

18-2 市区城市建设用地(2014 年)

LAND USE OF URBAN CONSTRUCTION(2014)

单位:平方公里 (sq.km)

指标	Item	数值 Number	指标	Item	数值 Number
城市面积	Urban Area	1521	工业用地	Industrial Land	14.28
建成区面积	Developed Area	189.86	物流仓储用地	Logistics &Storage Land	3.72
城市建设用地	City Construction Land	222.00	交通设施用地	Communication Facilities Land	35.80
#居住用地	Residential Land	69.94	公共设施用地	Public Facilities Land	4.45
公共设施用地	Public Facilities Land	24.97	绿地与广场	Green Lands and Squares	10.62
商务服务业用地	Commercial and Service Land	58.22	征用土地面积	Area of Land of Requisition	6.30

18-3 市区城市园林绿化(2014 年)

URBAN PARKS, GARDENS & GREEN AREAS(2014)

指标	Item	数值 Number	指标	Item	数值 Number
绿化覆盖面积(公顷)	Green Coverage Area (hectare)	9213	公园绿地面积	Park Green Area	2592
#建成区	Developed Area	8085	公园个数(个)	Number of Parks	32
绿地面积(公顷)	Green Land Area(hectare)	8286	公园面积(公顷)	Park Space (hectare)	538
#建成区	Constructed Area	7513	人均公园绿地面积(平方米)	Per Capita Public Green Area (m^2)	16.8

18-4 市区城市市政工程(2014 年)
URBAN MUNICIPAL ENGINEERING(2014)

指 标	Item	数 值 Number	指 标	Item	数 值 Number
道路长度(公里)	Length of Road (km)	2557	排水管道长度(公里)	Length of Sewer Pipeline	3907
道路面积(万平方米)	Area of Road (10,000 m^2)	4523	#污水管道	Sewer Pipeline	1545
#人行道	Pavement	802	雨水管道	Rain Water Pipeline	2303
桥梁数(座)	Number of Bridges	1187	污水处理厂个数(个)	Sewage Disposal Plant	6
#立交桥	Overpass	34	污水日处理能力(万立方米/日)	Capability of Sewage Disposal Per Day (10,000 m^3/day)	52.7
道路照明灯盏数(盏)	Number of Street Lights	188343	污水年处理量(万立方米)	Annual Capability of Sewage Disposal(10,000 m^3/day)	18562

18-5 市区城市供水情况(2014 年)
URBAN WATER SUPPLY(2014)

指 标	Item	数 值 Number	指 标	Item	数 值 Number
综合生产能力(万立方米/日)	Comprehensive Generation Capacity (10,000 m^3/day)	168	居民家庭用水	Resident Household Water	9954
全年供水总量(万立方米)	Annual Water Supply Volume (10,000 m^3)	22686	其他用水	Others	969
全年售水量(万立方米)	Annual Water Sales (10,000 m^3)	18136	免费供水量	Free Water Supply	320
#生产运营用水	Production Running Water	6929	供水管道总长度(公里)	Total Length of Water Pipeline (km)	3086
公共服务用水	Public Service Water	284	人均日生活用水量(升)	Per Capita Daily Water Consumption (liter)	181.4

18-6 市区城市供气情况(2014年)

BASIC STATISTICS ON URBAN GAS SUPPLY(2014)

指　标	Item	数 值 Number	指　标	Item	数 值 Number
液化气	**Liquefied Gas**		**天然气**	**Natural Gas**	
储气能力(吨)	Capability of Gas Storage	2710	储气能力(万立方米)	Capability of Gas Storage (10,000 m³)	120
供气管道长度(公里)	Length of Gas Pipeline	5.0	供气管道长度(公里)	Length of Gas Pipeline(km)	2466
供气总量(吨)	Total Gas Supply	24869	供气总量(万立方米)	Total Gas Supply (10,000 m³)	20300
售气总量	Total Gas Sales	24869	售气总量(万立方米)	Total Gas Sales (10,000 m³)	19752
#家庭用量	Residential Use	19272	#家庭用量	Residential Use	4484
液化气汽车加气站(座)	Automobile Liquefied Gas Station	3	天然气汽车加气站(座)	Automobile Natural Gas Station	10

18-7 市区城市环境卫生情况(2014年)

URBAN ENVIRONMENT AND HYGIENIC CONDITIONS(2014)

指　标	Item	数 值 Number	指　标	Item	数 值 Number
道路清扫保洁面积(万平方米)	Sweeping Areas (10,000 sq.m)	3410	粪便清运量(万吨)	Night Soil Disposal Capacity (10,000 tons)	2.5
#机械化清扫	Mechanical Cleaning	2178	生活垃圾转运站(座)	Residential Garbage Transfer Station	17
生活垃圾无害化处理厂数(个)	Residential Garbage No-Harmful Disposal Plant	1	公厕数量(座)	Public Toilets	264
生活垃圾无害化处理能力(吨/日)	Residential Garbage No-Harmful Disposal Capability (ton/day)	500	#三类以上	above Three Level	264
生活垃圾无害化处理量(万吨)	Residential Garbage No-Harmful Disposal Capacity (10,000 tons)	53	环卫专用车辆(辆)	Environmental Sanitation Lorries	454

主要统计指标解释

年底自来水生产能力　指年底城建部门管理的自来水厂和自备水源的社会单位取水、净化、送水、出厂输水干管等环节的实际生产能力。

年底供水管理长度　指从送水泵到用户水表之间所有的管道的长度。

全年供水总量　指公用自来水厂和自备水源的社会单位全年的供水总量,包括有效供水量及损失水量。

生活用水量　指居民日常生活与公共福利设施的用水量。包括居民、饮食店、旅馆、医院、理发店、浴池、洗衣店、游泳池、商店、学校、机关、部队等单位的用水量。

城市人口用水普及率　指城市用水的非农业人口数(不包括临时人口和流动人口)与城市非农业人口总数之比。

计算公式:$用水普及率=\frac{城市用水的非农业人口数}{城市非农业人口数}\times100\%$

人工煤气生产能力　指城市煤气制气、净化、输送等环节的综合实际生产能力。

输气管道长度　指由压缩机、鼓风机、储气罐的出口到用户立管之间的全部管道长度。

全年供气总量　指全年售给各类用户的全部煤气量。包括工业用量、家庭用量和其他用量、

城市用气普及率　指使用煤气(包括人工煤气、液化石油气、天然气)的城市非农业人口数(不包括临时人口和流动人口)与城市非农业人口总数之比。

计算公式:$城市用气普及率=\frac{城市用气的非农业人口数}{城市非农业人口数}\times100\%$

年底实有铺装道路长度　指除土路外,路面经过铺装宽度在3.5米以上的道路,包括高级、次高等级路和普通道路。

城市桥梁　指城市范围内,修建在河道上的桥梁和道路与道路立交、道路跨越路的立交桥,以及人行天桥。包括永久性桥和半永久性桥,不包括临时性、铁路桥、涵洞。

城市下水道总长度　指所有排水总管、干管、支管及暗渠、检查井、连接井进出水口等长度之和。

城市污水日处理能力　指污水处理厂每昼夜处理污水量的设计能力。

年末实有公共汽(电)车　指年底可参加营运的全部车辆数,包括年底运营车辆和和库存查封未参加营运的车辆,不包括非营运车辆,如架线车、油罐车、工程车、货车及其他专用车辆和借入的客运车辆。

营运的线路长度　指设置的固定营运的线路长度,包括郊区营运线路长度。不包括临时行驶的线路长度。

城市园林绿地面积　指城市公共绿地、专用绿地、生产绿地、防护绿地、郊区风景名胜区的全部面积。

公共绿地　指供游览休息的各种公园、动物园、植物园、陵园以及花园、游园和供游览休息用的林荫绿地、广场绿地。不包括一般栽植的行道树及林荫道的面积。

废水排放总量　包括生产废水和生活污水。生产废水指企事业单位在生产、科研过程中向外排放的所有排放口的废水量总和。生活污水指城镇居民区和企、事业单位职工集中居住区的排放的污水量。

工业废水排放总量　指经过工业企业厂区所有排放口排到企业外部的工业废水量,包括外排的直接冷却水、超标排放的矿井地下水和与工业废水混排的厂区生活污水,不包括外排的间接冷却水(清污不分流的间接冷却水应计算在内)。

工业废水排放达标量　指全面达到国家、地方排放标准的外排工业废水量,包括经过处理后达标外排的和未经过处理达标外排的两部分工业废水。国家排放标准见国标(GB8978-88)。

工业废水处理量　指经过各种水处理装置净化处理后的外排工业废水量(包括虽经处理仍未达到国家或地方标准的外排工业废水量)。

废气排放总量　指燃料燃烧和生产工艺过程中排放的各种废气总量,以标准状态下每年万标立方米表示。

燃料燃烧过程废气排放量　指燃煤、燃油、燃气锅炉、烘干炉、锻造加热炉、退火炉和其他工业炉窑在燃烧过程(燃料和物料不混合的纯加热过程)中所排废气的总量。它可根据烟气计算公式或经验计算公式求得。

经过消烟除尘的燃料废气量　指燃料燃烧过程中排放的废气经过消烟除尘装置处理的量。

经过净化处理的生产工艺废气量 指生产工艺过程中排放的废气经过各种净化处理装置净化、处理的量。

工业粉尘排放量 指工业企业在生产工艺过程中排放的固体微粒总重量。如钢铁企业的耐火材料粉尘、焦化企业的筛焦系统粉尘、烧结机的粉尘、石灰窑的粉尘、建材企业的水泥粉尘等,不包括电厂排放大气的烟尘。

工业粉尘回收量 批经生产工艺废气净化处理装置处理回收的粉尘和尘泥量(包括干法和湿法)。不包括电厂的烟尘。通常情况下:工业粉尘产生量=工业粉尘排放量+工业粉尘回收量

工业固定废物产生量 指工业企业在生产过程中产生的固体状、半固体状和高浓度液体状废弃物的总量,包括冶炼为渣、粉煤灰、炉渣、煤矸石、化工废渣、尾矿、放射性废渣和其它废渣等;不包括矿山开采的剥离废石和掘进废石(煤矸石和呈酸性或碱性的废石除外)。酸性或碱性废石是指采掘的废石其流经水、雨淋水 PH 值小于 4 或 PH 值大于 10.5 者。

工业固体废物处理量 指以符合环境保护要求的方式将固体废物放置在不再回收的场所的固体废物量,如填埋、焚烧、经封场处理的专业贮存场(库)、深层罐注、回填矿井等(包括当年处置往年的堆存量)。

工业固体废物综合利用量 指已用作农业肥料、造田、生产建筑材料、筑路以及其他方式综合利用的固体废物量(包括当年利用往年的工业固体废物堆存量)。综合利用量由原产同体废物的单位统计。

“三废”综合利用产品产值 指工业企业回收利用“三废”作为主要原料生产的产品产值。按国发(1985)117 号文规定执行。

“三废”综合利用产品利润 指工业企业回收利用“三废”用为主要原料生产的产品自用或出售后所得的利润额。

第十九篇 19
城市交流 Chapter
Inter-City Exchanges

19-1 江苏省十三市主要指标(2014年)

指 标	Item	南京市 Nanjing	无锡市 Wuxi	徐州市 Xuzhou	常州市 Changzhou
年末户籍人口(万人)	Registered Population at Year-end(10,000 persons)	648.72	477.14	1023.52	368.64
年末常住人口(万人)	Permanent Resident Population at Year-end(10,000 persons)	821.61	650.01	862.83	469.64
#城镇人口	#Urban Population	664.85	484.06	513.04	322.64
从业人员(万人)	Employees (10,000 persons)	453.00	389.50	480.90	281.00
#第一产业	#Primary Industry	47.40	17.80	162.70	30.80
第二产业	Secondary Industry(10,000 persons)	149.90	220.50	150.70	145.80
第三产业	Tertiary Industry	255.70	151.20	167.50	104.40
#在岗职工人数(万人)	#Number of Employed Staff and Workers (10,000 persons)	175.52	114.40	99.88	69.69
行政区域土地面积(平方公里)	Administrative Region Land Area(Square km)	6587	4627	11765	4372
#建成区面积	#Construction Land Area	734	522	433	254
地区生产总值(亿元)	GDP (100 Million Yuan)	8820.75	8205.31	4963.91	4901.87
第一产业	Primary Industry	214.25	138.13	473.54	138.46
第二产业	Secondary Industry	3623.48	4095.89	2246.24	2408.11
#工业	#Industry	3119.12	3747.59	1883.70	2170.19
第三产业	Tertiary Industry	4983.02	3971.29	2244.13	2355.30
人均地区生产总值	PGDP	107545	126389	57655	104423
地区生产总值指数(上年=100)	GDP Index(preceding year=100)	110.1	108.2	110.5	110.1
第一产业	Primary Industry	103.5	103.2	103.7	103.3
第二产业	Secondary Industry	108.8	106.6	110.8	109.5
#工业	#Industry	109.3	106.5	109.2	109.8
第三产业	Tertiary Industry	111.5	110.3	111.3	111.5
人均地区生产总值指数(上年=100)	PGDP Index(preceding year=100)	109.7	107.9	110.1	110.0
固定资产投资(亿元)	Fixed Investments (100 Million Yuan)	5430.77	4610.77	3671.56	3310.05
#工业投资	#Industrial Investment	2151.97	1746.34	1976.93	1680.20
#服务业投资	#Investment In Services	3215.59	2874.42	1652.59	1621.52
#房地产开发投资	#Real Estate Development Investment	1125.49	1252.22	468.88	681.53
商品房销售面积(万平方米)	Sales Area of Commercial Residential Building (10,000 Square Meter)	1207.58	839.15	738.03	787.50
#住宅	#Residence	1124.73	738.48	650.39	674.66

LEADING INDICATORS OF THIRTEEN CITIES IN JIANGSU PROVINCE(YEAR 2014)

苏州市 Suzhou	南通市 Nantong	连云港市 Nantong	淮安市 Lianyungang	盐城市 Yancheng	扬州市 Yangzhou	镇江市 Zhenjiang	泰州市 Taizhou	宿迁市 Suqian
661.08	767.63	526.52	560.25	828.54	461.34	272.07	508.51	580.74
1060.40	729.80	445.17	485.21	722.28	447.79	317.14	463.86	484.32
784.17	446.27	254.33	273.95	422.82	274.05	211.31	279.01	260.27
693.40	462	251.10	281.90	445.50	265.60	192.70	285.00	279.20
24.50	101.7	79.40	80.20	126.00	50.70	23.60	69.20	104.80
419.80	216	80.90	87.60	151.40	118.30	90.00	119.30	97.00
249.10	144.3	90.80	114.10	168.10	96.60	79.10	96.50	77.40
307.21	157.88	41.33	64.02	75.79	89.42	45.75	101.27	46.60
8657	10549	7615	10030	16931	6591	3840	5787	8524
735	329	275	255	322	232	205	196	212
13760.89	5652.69	836.50	2455.39	3835.62	3697.91	3252.44	3370.89	1930.68
203.98	339.57	49.07	286.99	489.50	227.36	121.45	209.25	246.37
6892.98	2812.34	443.16	1085.96	1782.41	1885.75	1631.10	1697.45	933.24
6360.14	2290.68	365.88	903.34	1524.64	1634.48	1498.41	1462.03	780.91
6663.93	2500.78	344.27	1082.44	1563.71	1584.80	1499.89	1464.19	751.07
129926	77457	92697	50736	53115	82654	102652	72706	39963
108.3	110.5	110.2	110.9	110.9	111.0	110.9	110.8	110.8
103.3	103.5	103.6	103.6	103.5	103.8	103.4	103.3	103.5
106.2	110.3	111.7	111.2	111.8	111.0	110.8	110.5	112.6
106.2	111.1	112.6	112.3	112.5	111.5	111.1	110.9	113.7
111.1	111.9	110.3	112.5	112.1	112.1	111.6	112.3	111.0
108.0	110.5	109.6	110.3	110.8	110.8	110.6	110.6	110.2
6054.00	3896.39	1716.57	1795.73	2751.35	2416.66	2142.34	2197.34	1559.22
2250.34	2046.82	1040.24	1009.86	1663.23	1330.68	1148.70	1196.96	1023.12
3796.52	1839.66	662.89	753.20	1058.06	1070.83	991.02	983.39	526.98
1764.44	678.92	189.28	357.66	379.64	360.44	319.05	285.54	377.14
1599.16	919.17	337.64	614.53	624.52	635.07	520	440.21	584.12
1446.07	843.35	298.26	538.37	513.84	569.75	474	404.89	524.29

19-1 续表

	Item	南京市 Nanjing	无锡市 Wuxi	徐州市 Xuzhou	常州市 Changzhou
商品房待售面积(万平方米)	For-sale Area of Commercial Residential Building (10,000 Square Meter)	489.01	827.53	258.35	521.33
# 住宅	#Residence	324.44	476.71	219.62	250.37
一般公共预算收入	General public budget revenue	903.49	768.01	472.33	433.88
# 税收收入	#Tax Revenue	757.21	620.34	386.43	348.38
一般公共预算支出(亿元)	General public budget revenue expenditure(100 Million Yuan)	921.20	748.06	661.84	434.93
金融机构人民币存款余额(亿元)	RMB Balance of Financial Institutions(100 Million Yuan)	20161.86	11849.03	4286.46	6758.57
# 储蓄存款	#Saving Deposits	5055.77	4341.45	2377.44	2934.19
金融机构人民币贷款余额(亿元)	RMB Loan Balance of Financial Institutions(100 Million Yuan)	15628.53	8669.62	2724.79	4789.74
规模以上工业企业单位数(个)	Units of Industrial Enterprises above Designated Size (Individual)	2748	5163	2861	4350
规模以上工业总产值(当年价)(亿元)	Gross Output Value of Industrial Enterprises above Designated Size(Current Year's Prices)(100 Million Yuan)	13199.67	14425.66	11390.64	11037.46
# 轻工业	#Light Industry	2713.19	3625.16	3538.78	2442.16
规模以上工业主营业务收入(亿元)	Main Business Income of Industrial Enterprises above Designated Size(100 Million Yuan)	13003.84	14190.87	11311.94	11379.01
规模以上工业利润总额(亿元)	Total Profit of Industrial Enterprises above Designated Size(100 Million Yuan)	879.39	873.14	899.73	618.49
规模以上工业利税总额(亿元)	Total Profits and Taxes of Industrial Enterprises above Designated Size(100 Million Yuan)	1724.87	1263.99	1639.85	1006.41
规模以上工业综合能源消费量(万吨标煤)	Comprehensive Energy Consumption of Industrial Enterprises above Designated Size(10,000 Tonnes of Standard Coal Equivalent)	3624	2463	2408	1668
全年用电量(亿千瓦时)	Annual Electricity Consumption(100 Million Kilowatt-hour)	470.50	598.18	332.47	395.06
# 工业用电量	#Commercial Power Consumption	289.02	477.47	247.48	316.09
城乡居民生活用电	Domestic Consumption of Urban and Rural Residents	60.74	48.94	43.28	32.43
社会消费品零售总额(亿元)	Total Retail Sales of Consumer Goods(100 Million Yuan)	4167.19	2607.90	2099.20	1805.40
进出口总额(亿美元)	Total Export-import Volume(100 Million USD)	572.21	741.70	59.88	288.10
# 出口总额	#Total Export Volume	326.28	442.31	46.77	213.64
协议到账外资(亿美元)	Agreed Payable Foreign Capital(100 Million USD)	49.22	55.08	30.21	29.56
实际到帐外资(亿美元)	Collected Foreign Capital(100 Million USD)	32.91	29.04	16.58	24.09
全体居民人均可支配收入(元)	Per capita disposable income of all residents (Yuan)	37283	36468	18744	32662
城镇居民人均可支配收入(元)	urban residents' per capita disposable income(Yuan)	42568	41731	24080	39483
农村居民人均可支配收入(元)	Rural Per Capita Net Income(Yuan)	17661	22266	12811	20133

注:单位 GDP 能耗下降率为初步测算数

Note: Energy Consumption Per Unit GDP is Preliminary Accounting

CONTINUED

苏州市 Suzhou	南通市 Nantong	连云港市 Nantong	淮安市 Lianyungang	盐城市 Yancheng	扬州市 Yangzhou	镇江市 Zhenjiang	泰州市 Taizhou	宿迁市 Suqian
996.37	689.53	0.00	260.71	403.10	255.04	361	279.05	206.75
517.09	509.38	0.00	198.42	312.69	159.06	264	181.23	124.65
1443.82	550.00	261.77	308.51	418.02	295.19	277.76	277.95	210.10
1244.37	457.34	213.42	251.94	341.41	242.22	228.82	225.80	180.69
1304.83	649.58	375.95	431.65	603.21	367.73	311.85	371.21	345.59
21428.20	8339.54	1852.67	2005.72	3692.75	4269.75	3536.27	3955.84	1598.96
6753.44	4602.87	924.03	1044.52	2062.39	2117.09	1569.40	1984.80	813.20
17247.94	5130.38	1549.34	1617.55	2567.98	2732.42	2679.83	2751.51	1483.05
10432	5081	1649	2474	3002	2681	2938	2709	2517
30322.17	12499.70	4865.00	5643.77	7238.02	8840.99	8084.47	9456.36	3368.77
7831.81	3955.64	1437.97	2247.66	2428.65	2137.80	1417.96	2623.40	1700.87
30397.27	12351.36	4820.99	5618.24	7209.61	8640.76	7897.58	9355.94	3282.89
1460.13	937.85	372.29	304.64	509.32	606.82	516.58	713.87	333.59
2074.08	1477.71	612.09	547.59	900.30	1051.82	803.65	1220.77	481.36
5254	1502	772	828	970	936	1360	683	302
1268.12	333.23	157.51	151.53	278.55	204.36	209.41	232.30	146.38
1044.14	242.89	110.44	106.89	209.02	147.89	162.44	180.73	103.90
87.33	43.73	23.30	23.68	37.46	28.03	20.15	26.08	21.73
4095.09	2166.10	739.40	864.80	1312.70	1128.10	1003.80	903.60	564.80
3113.06	316.47	80.30	41.06	75.17	100.12	103.07	108.93	37.55
1811.78	224.80	43.55	31.61	43.94	76.82	66.02	61.78	29.40
85.79	50.99	15.15	21.02	12.78	19.86	23.82	24.79	13.91
81.20	23.05	9.54	11.99	10.47	13.88	12.95	9.39	6.65
39780	25340	17798	19110	20543	24157	28850	23833	15888
46677	33374	23595	25798	25854	30322	35752	31346	20396
23560.4	15821	11698	12010	14414	15284	17617	15076	11677

19-2 江苏省十三市市区主要指标(2014年)

	Item	南京市区 Nanjing	无锡市区 Wuxi	徐州市区 Xuzhou	常州市区 Changzhou
土地面积(平方公里)	Land area (km²)	6587.02	1643.88	3062.51	1861.95
年末户籍人口(万人)	Year-end household population (10,000 persons)	648.72	245.74	331.46	233.92
#女	Female	323.68	124.41	161.11	118.66
年末常住人口(万人)	Year-end permanent population (10,000 persons)	821.61	361.38	320.74	337.82
年末从业人员	Year-end employees	488.90	215.41	166.27	196.49
第一产业	Primary industry	27.80	3.77	33.79	12.59
第二产业	Secondary industry	176.30	116.67	51.54	103.50
第三产业	Tertiary industry	284.80	94.97	80.95	80.40
地区生产总值(亿元)	GDP (100 million yuan)	8820.75	4217.47	2792.94	3744.81
第一产业	Primary industry	214.25	42.06	91.60	64.10
第二产业	Secondary industry	3623.48	1932.20	1445.24	1872.89
第三产业	Tertiary industry	4983.02	2243.21	1256.10	1807.82
人均地区生产总值(元)	Per capita GDP (yuan)	107545	116861	87618	110923
地区生产总值指数(上年=100)	GDP indicator (last year=100)	110.1	108.5	110.0	110.0
规模以上工业企业单位数(个)	Above-designated industrial enterprises	2748	2809	804	3506
#大中型企业	Large and medium size enterprises	530	397	192	432
规模以上工业总产值(亿元)	Above-designated industrial output (100 million yuan)	13199.67	5984.13	5287.69	8484.43
#大中型企业	Large and medium size enterprises	9104.45	3941.63	3750.10	4887.58
主营业务收入	Main business revenue	13003.84	5924.59	5324.53	8795.21
利税总额	Total taxes and profits	1724.87	568.80	831.25	742.21
全年用电量(亿千瓦时)	Total power consumption of the year (100 million KWH)	470.50	272.02	197.92	280.49
#城乡居民生活用电	Household electricity consumption of urban and rural residents	60.74	28.11	19.60	24.45
固定资产投资(亿元)	Fixed-asset investment (100 million yuan)	5430.77	2986.09	1931.56	2603.06
房地产开发投资(亿元)	Real-estate development investment (100 million yuan)	1125.49	806.14	299.68	608.61

LEADING INDICATORS OF THIRTEEN CITIES IN JIANGSU PROVINCE(2014)

苏州市区 Suzhou	南通市区 Nantong	连云港市区 Lianyungang	淮安市区 Huaian	盐城市区 Yancheng	扬州市区 Yangzhou	镇江市区 Zhenjiang	泰州市区 Taizhou	宿迁市区 Suqian
4652.84	2140.29	3011.89	3202.59	2122.58	2305.68	1087.87	1567.13	2153.25
337.50	212.83	219.07	291.49	169.31	231.84	103.41	163.82	172.00
171.11	108.65	105.52	141.34	81.96	116.57	51.98	115.25	83.42
548.30	233.55	206.64	268.94	162.18	242.03	122.71	162.06	154.62
348.29	136.70	109.87	155.44	96.94	138.30	69.18	99.51	89.16
11.29	18.40	26.73	39.00	17.61	15.60	5.86	17.42	29.48
203.82	59.90	39.10	50.35	35.86	63.40	27.83	41.89	33.87
133.18	58.40	44.04	66.09	43.47	59.30	35.49	40.20	25.81
7086.92	2093.78	1072.34	1462.04	1095.68	2432.28	1440.38	1408.22	691.56
74.55	56.54	103.16	130.86	76.77	81.33	26.88	53.40	57.89
3560.26	1021.67	473.50	681.57	609.49	1251.27	732.79	772.53	345.38
3452.11	1015.57	495.68	649.61	409.42	1099.68	680.71	582.29	288.29
129426	89766	67673	54503	67641	100578	117544	86997	44991
108.4	110.2	109.9	110.7	111.1	111.5	110.9	110.9	111.1
4690	1580	752	1105	697	1484	1071	1062	621
965	185	83	116	138	411	138	110	81
11856.02	4204.21	2933.23	3386.17	2561.47	6154.36	3205.33	4254.93	1138.18
8488.63	2396.73	2131.10	1841.63	1737.82	4408.41	2137.04	2379.37	717.97
11821.76	4104.51	2935.06	3370.88	2538.13	5899.93	3128.80	4079.33	1097.63
869.41	449.31	400.85	357.20	401.91	705.37	347.40	514.85	177.64
545.46	136.86	95.45	93.37	47.19	112.53	104.49	78.44	71.02
46.14	16.26	12.55	13.51	9.20	17.22	8.52	9.71	7.00
3307.02	1589.61	1089.37	1058.30	857.51	1224.50	1281.37	1055.09	609.98
1027.36	445.70	128.05	224.65	195.72	247.60	167.50	158.21	163.23

19-2 续表

	Item	南京市区 Nanjing	无锡市区 Wuxi	徐州市区 Xuzhou	常州市区 Changzhou
商品房屋销售面积(万平方米)	Sales Area of Commercial Housing(10,000 m^2)	1207.58	586.01	369.42	648.83
#住宅	Housing	1124.73	517.94	304.20	555.01
社会消费品零售总额(亿元)	Gross retail sales of social consumer goods (100 million yuan)	4167.19	1500.41	1315.77	1348.58
进出口总值(亿美元)	Total import and export value (100 million USD)	572.64	463.20	36.95	262.77
#出口	Export	326.39	275.32	29.34	194.32
实际到账外资(亿美元)	Actual arrival foreign capital (100 million USD)	32.91	21.08	11.42	26.21
星级饭店数(个)	Star-rated hotels	102	31	79	39
一般公共预算收入(亿元)	General public budget revenue	903.49	472.90	241.06	353.14
#税收收入	Tax income	757.21	375.10	189.12	278.77
一般公共预算支出(亿元)	General public budget revenue expenditure(100 million yuan)	921.20	460.49	301.29	340.46
金融机构人民币存款余额(亿元)	RMB deposit balance of banking institutions (100 million yuan)	20161.86	7328.89	2845.60	5365.33
#居民储蓄存款	Residential savings	5055.77	2583.16	1297.02	2221.15
金融机构人民币贷款余额(亿元)	RMB loan balance of banking institutions (100 million yuan)	15628.53	5145.48	1796.50	3766.69
城镇居民人均可支配收入(元)	Per capita disposable income of urban residents (yuan)	42568	40335	27031	34906
城镇居民人均消费性支出(元)	Per capita consumptive expenditure of urban residents (yuan)	25855	25524	18203	21796
人均住房建筑面积(平方米)	Per capita housing area (m^2)	36.26	41.14	33.40	51.06
居民消费价格指数(上年=100)	Residential CPI (last year-100)	102.6	102.2	102.1	102.2
邮电业务收入(亿元)	Postal income (100 million yuan)	175.07	79.12	34.91	59.00
国际互联网用户(万户)	Internet subscribers (10,000 households)	325.48	159.50	55.61	122.84
高等学校在校学生数(万人)	College student enrollment (10,000)	80.53	10.04	13.72	12.54
专利申请受理量(件)	Patent application accepted	56108	34808	9399	34156
公共图书馆图书藏量(千册)	Books in public library (1000)	15672	2977	1700	2436
卫生机构床位数(万张)	Number of beds in health institutions (10,000)	4.37	2.25	2.62	1.83
执业(助理)医师(万人)	(assistant) medical practitioners (10,000)	2.16	0.97	0.87	0.85

CONTINUED

苏州市区 Suzhou	南通市区 Nantong	连云港市区 Lianyungang	淮安市区 Huaian	盐城市区 Yancheng	扬州市区 Yangzhou	镇江市区 Zhenjiang	泰州市区 Taizhou	宿迁市区 Suqian
829.33	583.88	191.01	387.52	271.47	355.79	247.96	245.99	176.43
754.28	538.42	170.03	357.13	220.40	310.41	229.73	230.96	158.30
2133.71	856.60	430.90	514.73	448.71	774.56	517.79	448.03	255.27
1597.17	175.54	72.48	29.02	36.73	77.90	63.95	48.98	17.52
941.57	127.33	37.03	21.21	16.20	60.25	34.62	30.60	10.79
47.16	11.08	7.77	8.83	3.58	12.58	5.75	5.59	3.50
72	36	44	23	15	42	11	14	15
763.62	242.62	153.86	204.39	139.59	203.94	146.97	141.88	88.00
660.62	200.71	120.82	164.14	112.60	166.18	117.13	113.30	77.71
693.37	260.88	205.93	260.38	166.90	233.33	158.56	174.96	132.29
12783.28	3831.16	1296.70	1242.57	1517.70	3071.67	1803.04	2010.46	782.57
3432.87	1718.21	560.13	611.27	555.70	1371.30	640.11	846.09	276.30
10532.51	2404.65	1125.06	1004.87	1097.90	2003.26	1240.10	1461.56	701.83
46643	29960	27057	26675	296167	28136	35315	31819	21248
29291	18352	17695	14623	17886	19870	22569	19683	13507
40.26	51.40	46.24	42.60	42.32	47.08	40.56	49.10	43.53
102.1	102.1	102.4	102.1	102.3	102.1	102.0	102.1	102.4
151.27	31.61	21.62	17.43	17.69	17.25	16.89	18.04	32.65
190.43	76.39	55.26	32.82	35.36	75.89	31.25	42.21	28.96
15.35	8.74	3.80	6.73	5.61	7.53	7.52	5.53	2.12
51393	14118	6079	7861	5029	13136	9686	11774	2413
3857	1838	1673	1890	1213	2254	1784	1322	615
2.97	1.51	1.00	1.48	0.99	1.29	0.84	0.90	0.64
1.27	0.71	0.50	0.68	0.41	0.58	0.39	0.41	0.26

19-3 江苏省各市辖区主要指标(2014 年)

指标名称	Item	土地面积(平方公里) Land Area(km²)	年末户籍人口(万人) Year-end Household Population (10,000)	从业人员(万人) Employers (10,000)		
					第一产业 Primary Industry	第二产业 Secondary Industry
南京市浦口区	Nanjing City Pukou District	910	62.66	41.19	2.12	18.20
南京市栖霞区	Nanjing City Xixia District	395	44.38	35.96	1.61	14.35
南京市雨花台区	Nanjing City Yuhuatai District	132	25.17	20.77	0.15	4.05
南京市江宁区	Nanjing City Jiangning District	1563	97.28	74.11	7.50	34.21
南京市六合区	Nanjing City Liuhe District	1471	90.25	48.91	6.48	23.70
南京市溧水区	Nanjing City Lishui District	1064	42.71	31.09	3.96	16.43
南京市高淳区	Nanjing City Gaochun District	790	43.83	31.25	5.73	15.93
无锡市锡山区	Wuxi City Xishan District	399	43.16	45.61	1.78	30.72
无锡市惠山区	Wuxi City Huishan District	325	44.89	45.69	1.48	29.43
无锡市滨湖区	Wuxi City Binhu District	628	47.07	34.90	0.48	15.41
徐州市贾汪区	Xuzhou City Jiawang District	620	51.76	24.11	7.09	9.63
徐州市铜山区	Xuzhou City Tongshan District	2004	131.56	65.63	25.86	19.48
常州市新北区	Changzhou City Xinbei District	453	48.63	40.57	2.39	22.70
常州市武进区	Changzhou City Wujin District	1246	104.00	95.86	9.90	59.87
苏州市吴中区	Suzhou City Wuzhong District	2231	62.45	74.70	5.32	43.88
苏州市相城区	Suzhou City Xiangcheng District	490	40.02	49.25	1.09	31.36
苏州市吴江区	Suzhou City Wujiang District	1237	81.44	86.56	3.88	54.58
南通市崇川区	Nantong City Chongchuan District	160	52.12	37.20	0.00	7.90
南通市港闸区	Nantong City Gangzha District	152	19.22	16.90	0.50	10.00
南通市通州区	Nantong City Tongzhou District	1562	126.66	70.20	17.30	33.80
连云港市连云区	Liangyungang City Lianyun District	797	13.33	7.83	0.39	2.18
连云港市赣榆区	Liangyungang City Ganyu District	1514	119.27	57.60	18.73	22.15
淮安市淮安区	Huaian City Huaian District	1452	120.06	56.83	19.21	17.68
淮安市淮阴区	Huaian City Huaiyin District	1307	93.15	45.67	15.30	14.25
盐城市盐都区	Yancheng City Yandu District	1050	71.50	39.93	9.41	14.70
扬州市邗江区	Yangzhou City Hanjiang District	553	58.27	37.70	1.30	16.20
扬州市江都区	Yangzhou City Jiangdu District	1330	106.90	61.60	12.10	27.60
镇江市丹徒区	Zhenjiang City Dantu District	617	29.11	19.70	3.94	8.41
泰州市海陵区	Taizhou City Hailin District	237	42.66	29.38	1.78	12.89
泰州市高港区	Taizhou City Gaogang District	287	26.23	15.53	2.98	6.83
泰州市姜堰区	Taizhou City Jiangyan District	928	79.44	44.84	11.76	17.14
宿迁市宿豫区	Suqian City Suyu District	1237	65.55	35.25	12.34	13.59

MAJOR INDICATORS OF MUNICIPAL DISTRICTS IN JIANGSU PROVINCE(2014)

第三产业 Tertiary Industry	地区生产总值(亿元) GDP (100 million yuan)					地区生产总值指数(上年=100) GDP Index (last year=100)	固定资产投资(亿元) Fixed Asset Investment (100 million yuan)	房地产开发投资(亿元) Real-estate Development Investment (100 million yuan)
		第一产业 Primary Industry	第二产业 Secondary Industry	#工业 Industry	第三产业 Tertiary Industry			
20.87	705.64	34.86	362.30	324.01	308.48	110.9	808.35	135.57
20.00	1165.77	7.81	792.59	745.96	365.37	110.4	460.17	140.04
16.57	468.73	1.06	137.80	110.36	329.87	110.4	237.11	101.58
32.40	1491.49	51.43	788.69	669.59	651.37	110.9	886.80	135.98
18.73	892.69	51.81	537.86	475.23	303.02	110.3	725.58	97.50
10.70	543.65	33.03	278.84	235.39	231.78	110.7	460.41	47.34
9.59	497.22	33.55	246.26	190.32	217.41	110.7	395.06	38.51
13.11	620.71	20.73	325.55	276.00	274.43	108.8	596.83	138.38
14.78	652.45	17.03	394.94	360.83	240.48	108.3	517.10	109.13
19.01	718.18	4.45	329.22	286.86	384.51	108.4	490.01	232.65
7.39	246.96	18.60	130.31	123.56	98.05	109.3	216.72	11.39
20.29	835.27	64.71	450.81	382.56	319.75	111.6	566.54	30.15
15.48	900.21	14.86	523.03	499.63	362.32	112.1	722.31	175.60
26.09	1905.33	49.04	1047.46	995.42	808.83	110.2	1003.14	191.96
25.50	915.18	20.56	459.56	419.56	435.06	108.3	499.21	137.71
16.80	578.26	10.65	289.65	229.22	277.96	108.7	445.32	169.74
28.10	1486.51	39.53	794.54	745.92	652.44	108.0	754.90	197.10
29.30	574.69	0.27	164.62	117.20	409.80	109.5	406.38	151.42
6.40	284.14	2.03	168.32	141.45	113.79	109.5	239.82	152.02
19.10	860.73	52.25	446.99	367.49	361.49	110.8	520.12	67.79
5.26	106.26	4.65	43.31	36.09	58.30	109.2	187.07	9.90
16.72	426.87	62.20	212.19	166.62	152.48	112.0	252.80	23.19
19.94	365.53	56.81	149.53	99.37	159.19	111.0	233.83	28.69
16.12	362.73	62.70	156.92	132.70	143.11	111.1	223.86	38.09
15.82	370.01	39.44	192.45	163.81	138.12	111.0	249.36	24.22
20.20	602.74	17.10	256.19	254.41	329.45	110.2	309.13	87.78
21.90	792.61	52.92	397.59	206.53	342.10	116.0	469.03	54.15
7.35	323.56	16.07	172.15	161.81	135.34	111.0	258.71	17.48
14.71	430.56	6.63	214.98	179.96	208.95	109.2	194.26	63.82
5.72	338.88	10.39	217.84	198.93	110.65	112.0	247.28	10.56
15.94	488.52	35.16	242.99	197.99	210.37	111.1	345.56	51.93
9.31	214.20	23.86	131.64	116.48	58.70	111.0	197.24	29.79

19-3 续表

指标名称	Item	一般公共预算收入 General public budget revenue	# 税收收入 Tax Income	一般公共预算支出 General public budget revenue expenditure	规模以上工业企业个数(个) Above-designated Industrial Enterprise	工业总产值(亿元) Total Industrial Output (100 million yuan)
南京市浦口区	Nanjing City Pukou District	83.09	69.46	73.56	354	1523.21
南京市栖霞区	Nanjing City Xixia District	77.20	71.64	43.38	234	3352.25
南京市雨花台区	Nanjing City Yuhuatai District	51.95	47.54	32.61	88	386.92
南京市江宁区	Nanjing City Jiangning District	166.82	152.79	124.95	677	2879.89
南京市六合区	Nanjing City Liuhe District	64.99	55.47	57.62	507	2622.58
南京市溧水区	Nanjing City Lishui District	41.07	33.96	41.53	460	900.91
南京市高淳区	Nanjing City Gaochun District	29.37	24.68	30.48	325	802.76
无锡市锡山区	Wuxi City Xishan District	60.55	50.52	55.71	663	1122.00
无锡市惠山区	Wuxi City Huishan District	70.76	56.62	64.42	864	1149.59
无锡市滨湖区	Wuxi City Binhu District	83.01	66.53	55.42	420	489.14
徐州市贾汪区	Xuzhou City Jiawang District	19.21	16.23	31.34	161	626.45
徐州市铜山区	Xuzhou City Tongshan District	68.32	57.34	94.59	433	2990.24
常州市新北区	Changzhou City Xinbei District	89.32	71.91	54.59	959	2276.32
常州市武进区	Changzhou City Wujin District	129.63	106.06	124.04	1911	4227.24
苏州市吴中区	Suzhou City Wuzhong District	110.90	101.59	82.55	905	1144.73
苏州市相城区	Suzhou City Xiangcheng District	65.82	58.09	50.66	730	1047.57
苏州市吴江区	Suzhou City Wujiang District	137.36	112.05	126.28	1537	3080.70
南通市崇川区	Nantong City Chongchuan District	68.68	58.00	33.79	100	381.73
南通市港闸区	Nantong City Gangzha District	36.45	29.09	20.54	245	440.19
南通市通州区	Nantong City Tongzhou District	68.40	56.89	82.75	764	1855.49
连云港市连云区	Liangyungang City Lianyun District	13.91	11.71	13.19	62	96.71
连云港市赣榆区	Liangyungang City Ganyu District	40.17	33.83	66.49	431	1290.83
淮安市淮安区	Huaian City Huaian District	32.43	26.70	57.25	336	621.12
淮安市淮阴区	Huaian City Huaiyin District	39.22	33.22	61.64	418	1090.78
盐城市盐都区	Yancheng City Yandu District	51.72	45.71	44.23	338	773.15
扬州市邗江区	Yangzhou City Hanjiang District	56.03	45.36	49.35	407	1265.99
扬州市江都区	Yangzhou City Jiangdu District	47.98	39.39	57.47	618	2281.79
镇江市丹徒区	Zhenjiang City Dantu District	24.95	22.22	25.14	364	1008.26
泰州市海陵区	Taizhou City Hailin District	36.05	31.62	23.28	238	1191.88
泰州市高港区	Taizhou City Gaogang District	28.68	23.58	24.65	204	1449.83
泰州市姜堰区	Taizhou City Jiangyan District	30.35	25.16	44.28	473	1131.30
宿迁市宿豫区	Suqian City Suyu District	20.82	18.33	33.49	252	415.62

CONTINUED

主营业务收入(亿元) Main Business Revenue (100 million yuan)	利润总额(亿元) Total Value of Interests and Taxes (100 million yuan)	利税总额(亿元) Total Value of Profits (100 million yuan)	社会消费品零售总额(亿元) Total Retail Sales of Social Consumer Goods (100 million yuan)	进出口总额(亿美元) Total Import and Export Volume (100 million USD)	出口总额(亿美元) Export Volume (100 million USD)	实际外商直接投资(亿美元) Actual Arrival of Foreign Direct Investment (100 million USD)	城镇居民人均可支配收入(元) Per-capita Disposable Income of Urban and Rural Residents (yuan)
1546.19	123.96	197.79	237.99	15.04	13.11	2.72	40289
3415.68	171.95	436.28	196.30	129.04	55.69	5.08	41179
411.27	12.53	24.89	297.00	31.34	21.89	1.65	41039
2450.15	292.74	432.50	379.58	115.32	66.34	7.18	41331
2584.21	57.24	164.53	309.29	19.65	9.94	3.85	39363
899.78	100.67	149.30	155.96	5.17	5.05	1.45	37659
819.11	59.38	95.01	154.79	5.18	4.60	1.21	38530
1131.74	56.98	87.19	135.87	46.22	35.63	3.30	
1104.56	76.50	111.68	147.78	27.11	22.46	3.03	
483.43	42.04	60.49	212.95	22.45	16.68	1.40	
611.45	34.89	65.93	56.40	1.82	1.31	0.41	23685
2950.43	277.80	437.38	190.26	8.62	7.38	2.20	27100
2281.39	106.39	181.97	232.52	107.39	75.75	8.00	41634
4441.74	215.14	354.42	450.30	100.03	70.01	8.19	41363
1131.55	57.93	88.60	313.01	115.55	71.21	5.00	48400
1038.87	48.04	71.45	180.79	43.21	29.86	1.84	42811
3065.24	106.51	164.62	392.50	233.36	144.88	9.70	46741
374.60	36.80	47.84	334.64	64.68	45.99	1.33	
428.01	35.73	50.16	111.91	29.48	23.43	0.47	
1822.02	126.10	213.54	279.88	33.19	29.38	3.31	34565
94.41	3.05	5.17	57.59	18.04	8.11	0.83	
1297.16	89.13	151.11	136.57	6.28	4.15	1.54	23004
613.47	21.78	48.13	136.38	2.91	2.78	1.11	22098
1085.61	77.64	107.48	94.47	4.82	3.24	1.51	24039
768.45	46.99	94.24	168.04	5.75	3.09	0.86	27788
1156.05	71.07	129.42	238.28	19.62	16.43	2.90	34376
2193.98	164.91	298.88	212.25	14.72	11.15	2.07	31035
993.71	73.81	117.60	55.54	5.73	4.96	1.70	34965
1155.44	61.08	139.39	199.61	14.87	11.79	0.54	32358
1403.39	122.91	195.80	40.35	10.31	3.02	1.84	31503
1050.23	78.44	123.94	137.63	10.69	9.06	1.50	31375
392.98	19.77	35.05	43.00	4.47	3.23	0.73	19946

19–4 江苏省各县(市)主要指标(2014 年)

指标名称	Item	年末户籍人口(万人) Year-end Household Population (10,000)	年末常住人口(万人) Year-end Permanent Population (10,000)	土地面积(平方公里) Area (km^2)	建成区面积(平方公里) Built Area (km^2)	从业人员(万人) Employers (10,000)
南京市	**Nanjing City**	**648.72**	**821.61**	**6587**	**734**	**453.0**
无锡市	**Wuxi City**	**477.14**	**650.01**	**4627**	**522**	**389.5**
江阴市	Jiangyin City	123.21	163.47	987	118	99.61
宜兴市	Yixing Cityh	108.19	125.16	1997	77	74.48
徐州市	**Xuzhou City**	**1023.52**	**862.83**	**11765**	**433**	**480.9**
丰县	Fen County	120.05	94.59	1450	28	56.31
沛县	Pei County	130.63	111.29	1806	36	66.55
睢宁县	Suining County	143.58	102.15	1769	33	59.93
新沂市	Xinyi City	111.89	90.74	1592	35	54.30
邳州市	Pizhou City	185.89	143.32	2085	45	77.54
常州市	**Changzhou City**	**368.64**	**469.64**	**4372**	**254**	**281.0**
溧阳市	Liyang City	79.39	76.02	1535	28	49.37
金坛市	Jintan City	55.34	55.80	976	22	35.13
苏州市	**Suzhou City**	**661.08**	**1060.40**	**8657**	**735**	**693.4**
常熟市	Changshu City	106.88	150.97	1276	98	105.10
张家港市	Zhangjiagang City	91.98	125.25	987	69	77.69
昆山市	Kunshan City	76.97	165.03	932	72	116.34
太仓市	Taicang City	47.74	70.85	810	49	45.98
南通市	**Nantong City**	**767.63**	**729.80**	**10549**	**329**	**462.0**
海安县	Haian County	94.26	86.62	1184	31	54.50
如东县	Rudong County	104.37	98.19	2791	25	62.30
启东市	Qidong City	112.32	95.60	1715	26	67.90
如皋市	Rugao City	143.69	125.61	1576	34	74.70
海门市	Haimen City	100.16	90.23	1144	25	65.90
连云港市	**Lianyungang City**	**526.52**	**445.17**	**7615**	**275**	**251.10**
东海县	Donghai County	121.95	95.87	2037	28	56.72
灌云县	Guanyun County	104.06	79.79	1538	28	47.98
灌南县	Guannan County	81.44	62.87	1028	26	36.53

MAJOR INDICATORS OF CITIES AND COUNTRIES IN JIANGSU PROVINCE(2014)

			地区生产总值（亿元）GDP (100 million yuan)				
第一产业 Primary Industry	第二产业 Secondary Industry	第三产业 Tertiary Industry		第一产业 Primary Industry	第二产业 Secondary Industry	# 工业 Industry	第三产业 Tertiary Industry
47.4	**149.9**	**255.7**	**8820.75**	**214.25**	**3623.48**	**3119.12**	**4983.02**
17.8	**220.5**	**151.2**	**8205.31**	**138.13**	**4095.89**	**3747.59**	**3971.29**
5.06	62.52	32.03	2753.95	46.14	1520.54	1453.57	1187.27
8.97	41.31	24.20	1233.89	49.93	643.15	547.32	540.81
162.7	**150.7**	**167.5**	**4963.91**	**473.54**	**2246.24**	**1883.70**	**2244.13**
27.68	15.50	13.13	341.63	62.97	153.97	114.69	124.69
25.01	23.66	17.88	564.96	80.46	260.78	210.11	223.72
18.15	22.68	19.10	419.97	70.98	182.44	140.45	166.55
24.96	14.92	14.42	473.54	57.35	200.05	170.05	216.14
33.12	22.40	22.02	684.48	95.81	294.59	243.15	294.08
30.8	**145.8**	**104.4**	**4901.87**	**138.46**	**2408.11**	**2170.19**	**2355.30**
11.35	25.81	12.21	716.29	43.92	375.11	329.63	297.26
6.86	16.48	11.79	471.48	30.43	243.03	202.60	198.02
24.5	**419.8**	**249.1**	**13760.89**	**203.98**	**6892.98**	**6360.14**	**6663.93**
4.13	65.51	35.46	2009.36	38.40	1061.55	1011.19	909.41
4.58	47.48	25.63	2180.25	28.64	1186.39	1131.02	965.22
1.83	75.67	38.84	3001.02	27.46	1687.10	1592.57	1286.46
2.68	27.32	15.98	1065.33	35.24	556.65	522.60	473.44
101.7	**216.0**	**144.3**	**5652.69**	**339.57**	**2812.34**	**2290.68**	**2500.78**
11.60	28.80	14.10	624.14	51.27	304.13	245.80	268.74
14.10	30.90	17.30	615.51	62.17	297.11	245.42	256.23
19.60	29.60	18.70	739.13	62.93	369.03	287.41	307.17
20.20	35.10	19.40	743.64	57.60	377.24	311.08	308.80
17.80	31.70	16.40	836.50	49.07	443.16	365.88	344.27
79.40	**80.90**	**90.80**	**1965.89**	**261.98**	**889.68**	**706.89**	**814.23**
18.81	17.86	20.05	359.32	56.95	163.13	140.75	139.24
18.65	12.95	16.38	274.98	55.12	125.50	94.52	94.36
21.6	40.7	15.7	610.13	71.98	371.42	310.33	166.73

19-4 续表 1

指标名称	Item	年末户籍人口(万人) Year-end Household Population (10,000)	年末常住人口(万人) Year-end Permanent Population (10,000)	土地面积(平方公里) Area (km²)	建成区面积(平方公里) Built Area (km²)	从业人员(万人) Employers (10,000)
淮安市	**Huaian City**	**560.25**	**485.21**	**10030**	**255**	**281.9**
涟水县	Lianshui County	113.70	84.53	1678	33	48.77
洪泽县	Hongze County	39.09	33.67	1273	18	20.17
盱眙县	Xuyi County	80.05	65.03	2497	33	38.30
金湖县	Jinhu County	35.92	33.04	1378	21	19.20
盐城市	**Yancheng City**	**828.54**	**722.28**	**16931**	**322**	**445.5**
响水县	Xiangshui County	62.48	50.25	1474	21	28.70
滨海县	Binghai County	121.48	94.28	1950	32	56.34
阜宁县	Funing County	112.09	83.88	1439	44	51.37
射阳县	Sheyang County	96.78	89.14	2606	24	56.95
建湖县	Jianhu County	80.13	73.70	1157	27	44.12
东台市	Dongtai City	113.73	98.66	3176	36	65.11
大丰市	Dafeng City	72.54	70.19	3008	28	45.97
扬州市	**Yangzhou City**	**461.34**	**447.79**	**6591**	**232**	**265.6**
宝应县	Baoying County	91.13	75.45	1462	32	41.90
仪征市	Yizheng City	56.56	56.40	902	39	39.50
高邮市	Gaoyou City	81.81	73.91	1922	26	45.90
镇江市	**Zhenjiang City**	**272.07**	**317.14**	**3840**	**205**	**192.7**
丹阳市	Danyang City	81.35	97.86	1047	33	63.01
扬中市	Yangzhong City	28.26	34.16	327	13	21.54
句容市	Jurong City	59.05	62.41	1378	25	38.97
泰州市	**Taizhou City**	**508.51**	**463.86**	**5787**	**196**	**285.0**
兴化市	Xinghua City	158.00	125.47	2395	38	77.12
靖江市	Jinjiang City	66.81	68.65	656	34	42.14
泰兴市	Taixing City	119.88	107.68	1170	25	66.23
宿迁市	**Suqian City**	**580.74**	**484.32**	**8524**	**212**	**279.2**
沭阳县	Shuyang County	193.57	155.20	2299	63	89.45
泗阳县	Siyang County	106.32	84.50	1378	36	48.71
泗洪县	Sihong County	92.43	90.00	2694	35	51.88

CONTINUED 1

第一产业 Primary Industry	第二产业 Secondary Industry	第三产业 Tertiary Industry	地区生产总值（亿元）GDP (100 million yuan)	第一产业 Primary Industry	第二产业 Secondary Industry	# 工业 Industry	第三产业 Tertiary Industry
80.2	**87.6**	**114.1**	**2455.39**	**286.99**	**1085.96**	**903.34**	**1082.44**
17.60	11.32	19.85	302.35	49.97	120.82	96.94	131.56
5.95	6.88	7.34	207.35	29.44	88.32	74.97	89.59
12.07	12.45	13.78	290.04	48.42	118.86	93.77	122.76
5.59	6.57	7.04	193.61	28.30	76.39	66.77	88.92
126.0	**151.4**	**168.1**	**3835.62**	**489.50**	**1782.41**	**1524.64**	**1563.71**
9.35	9.47	9.88	222.00	38.16	105.11	94.07	78.73
19.09	17.81	19.44	328.19	53.10	138.63	116.80	136.46
17.44	16.50	17.43	330.62	50.84	148.14	109.18	131.64
18.10	18.59	20.26	370.10	72.14	139.47	125.11	158.49
12.41	16.21	15.50	392.00	45.21	175.34	149.41	171.45
18.56	22.04	24.51	610.33	84.60	261.81	228.01	263.92
13.44	14.92	17.61	486.70	68.68	204.42	175.65	213.60
50.7	**118.3**	**96.6**	**3697.91**	**227.36**	**1885.75**	**1634.48**	**1584.80**
12.70	17.60	11.60	418.30	61.60	189.80	154.29	166.90
9.30	18.10	12.10	465.06	21.13	255.76	146.76	188.17
13.10	19.20	13.60	445.20	62.72	201.13	166.28	181.35
23.6	**90.0**	**79.1**	**3252.44**	**121.45**	**1631.10**	**1498.41**	**1499.89**
6.13	34.35	22.53	1008.96	47.22	518.58	497.75	443.16
1.41	11.94	8.19	445.35	10.86	237.90	228.89	196.59
10.17	15.91	12.89	440.96	37.26	215.42	195.43	188.28
69.2	**119.3**	**96.5**	**3370.89**	**209.25**	**1697.45**	**1462.03**	**1464.19**
24.23	29.87	23.02	624.83	89.08	264.28	228.22	271.47
8.11	21.04	12.99	666.19	19.84	349.18	314.50	297.17
19.44	26.50	20.29	675.84	46.93	348.68	303.84	280.23
104.8	**97.0**	**77.4**	**1930.68**	**246.37**	**933.24**	**780.91**	**751.07**
34.62	30.36	24.47	579.96	78.83	268.55	236.82	232.58
19.37	16.50	12.84	332.24	49.89	173.74	144.17	108.61
21.33	16.27	14.28	330.00	51.87	141.42	116.81	136.71

19–4 续表 2

指标名称	Item	人均地区生产总值(元) Per capita GDP (yuan)	农林牧渔业总产值(亿元) Total Output of Agriculture, Forestry, Husbandry and Fishery (100 million yuan)	工业总产值(亿元) Total Industrial Output (100 million yuan)	主营业务收入(亿元) Main Business Revenue (100 million yuan)	利税总额(亿元) Total Value of Interests and Taxes (100 million yuan)
南京市	**Nanjing City**	**107545**	**384.63**	**13199.67**	**13003.84**	**1724.87**
无锡市	**Wuxi City**	**126389**	**253.76**	**14425.66**	**14190.87**	**1263.99**
江阴市	Jiangyin City	168711	88.61	5657.14	5532.39	534.30
宜兴市	Yixing Cityh	98648	88.45	2784.39	2733.89	160.89
徐州市	**Xuzhou City**	**57655**	**893.65**	**11390.64**	**11311.94**	**1639.85**
丰　县	Fen County	36086	123.22	520.54	505.64	71.77
沛　县	Pei County	50772	150.19	1355.17	1305.33	163.63
睢宁县	Suining County	41087	134.26	782.69	773.19	121.14
新沂市	Xinyi City	52195	117.55	1394.28	1382.78	170.25
邳州市	Pizhou City	47761	187.36	2050.28	2020.47	281.81
常州市	**Changzhou City**	**104423**	**256.81**	**11037.46**	**11379.01**	**1006.41**
溧阳市	Liyang City	94224	81.67	1732.29	1738.41	166.57
金坛市	Jintan City	84495	62.16	820.74	845.39	97.35
苏州市	**Suzhou City**	**129926**	**392.49**	**30322.17**	**30397.27**	**2074.08**
常熟市	Changshu City	133150	72.28	3668.70	3642.64	247.11
张家港市	Zhangjiagang City	174148	56.18	4863.71	5044.54	240.29
昆山市	Kunshan City	182222	49.16	7852.39	7855.64	549.55
太仓市	Taicang City	150523	66.30	2081.35	2032.69	167.72
南通市	**Nantong City**	**77457**	**631.32**	**12499.70**	**12351.36**	**1477.71**
海安县	Haian County	72051	102.71	1789.96	1786.35	203.64
如东县	Rudong County	62631	126.86	1670.98	1662.68	214.35
启东市	Qidong City	77242	121.52	1508.48	1486.23	180.01
如皋市	Rugao City	59158	98.98	1589.78	1581.02	136.89
海门市	Haimen City	92697	86.38	1736.29	1730.57	293.51
连云港市	**Lianyungang City**	**44277**	**507.39**	**4865.00**	**4820.99**	**612.09**
东海县	Donghai County	37580	113.18	814.02	802.71	87.82
灌云县	Guanyun County	34532	109.09	538.88	510.20	51.91
灌南县	Guannan County	41364	83.69	578.87	573.03	71.51

CONTINUED 2

利润总额（亿元）Total Value of Profits (100 million yuan)	公路里程（公里）Highway Mileage (km)	公路客运量（万人）Highway Passenger Capacity (10,000 persons)	公路货运量（万吨）Highway Freight Volume (10,000 tons)	民用汽车拥有量（万辆）Civil Vehicles Possessed (10,000)	邮电业务总量（亿元）Post and Tele-communications Service (100 million yuan)	国际互联网用户（万户）Internet Subscribers (10,000 households)
879.39	**11309**	**10596**	**12143**	**172.20**	**237.94**	**226.98**
873.14	**7655**	**7222**	**12885**	**127.76**	**169.57**	**153.00**
356.16	2362	501	2871	31.86	28.38	54.58
105.46	2365	703	1640	20.31	17.67	36.94
899.73	**16428**	**15063**	**16967**	**75.60**	**100.72**	**107.65**
41.84	1847	573	1361	6.19	6.08	8.17
85.54	2290	984	1295	6.29	7.39	10.56
86.04	2462	1089	1603	6.93	7.67	10.19
90.88	2849	979	1646	5.88	7.67	10.62
170.94	3052	1063	2130	9.70	8.99	12.51
618.49	**8906**	**6769**	**10705**	**87.31**	**110.90**	**116.86**
95.46	2520	1181	1956	10.58	7.95	14.39
68.36	2073	836	1035	7.50	6.29	11.75
1460.13	**12665**	**39432**	**11855**	**240.79**	**337.66**	**295.70**
172.77	3093	4487	1363	31.34	31.32	47.17
131.34	1522	4112	2123	26.95	26.50	37.22
398.61	1796	4830	1481	36.95	47.33	61.07
112.70	1304	1975	1405	15.76	14.50	21.40
937.85	**18094**	**9998**	**11129**	**99.66**	**123.93**	**129.07**
131.75	2355	841	1830	9.51	7.51	23.61
131.70	2534	418	1121	10.66	7.72	20.95
107.85	3576	891	816	12.21	8.87	22.54
78.43	3219	441	1552	15.21	11.31	25.68
194.71	2488	705	640	11.79	9.19	21.73
372.29	**11914**	**5433**	**8406**	**36.87**	**63.41**	**68.18**
55.41	2966	581	1832	7.69	8.27	17.40
36.07	2592	513	887	5.22	5.10	10.43
38.69	1920	418	705	3.52	3.85	8.37

19-4 续表 3

指标名称	Item	人均地区生产总值(元) Per capita GDP (yuan)	农林牧渔业总产值(亿元) Total Output of Agriculture, Forestry, Husbandry and Fishery (100 million yuan)	工业总产值(亿元) Total Industrial Output (100 million yuan)	主营业务收入(亿元) Main Business Revenue (100 million yuan)	利税总额(亿元) Total Value of Interests and Taxes (100 million yuan)
淮安市	**Huaian City**	**50736**	**535.56**	**5643.77**	**5618.24**	**547.59**
涟水县	Lianshui County	35843	96.94	543.60	532.33	50.85
洪泽县	Hongze County	61812	59.96	550.97	543.25	58.83
盱眙县	Xuyi County	44714	90.42	751.59	761.73	53.64
金湖县	Jinhu County	58785	53.20	411.44	410.05	27.07
盐城市	**Yancheng City**	**53115**	**1035.82**	**7238.02**	**7209.61**	**900.30**
响水县	Xiangshui County	44170	71.20	583.35	599.98	93.77
滨海县	Binghai County	34806	99.95	561.64	563.23	59.31
阜宁县	Funing County	39411	103.27	536.15	523.83	46.80
射阳县	Sheyang County	41510	170.61	529.30	512.52	41.78
建湖县	Jianhu County	53178	86.79	790.02	743.33	94.94
东台市	Dongtai City	61868	189.68	948.78	987.51	92.89
大丰市	Dafeng City	69350	162.02	727.31	741.08	68.90
扬州市	**Yangzhou City**	**82654**	**431.98**	**8840.99**	**8640.76**	**1051.82**
宝应县	Baoying County	55525	115.39	886.33	823.55	73.78
仪征市	Yizheng City	82633	40.99	1396.11	1364.52	174.33
高邮市	Gaoyou City	60203	121.72	1020.37	995.47	109.57
镇江市	**Zhenjiang City**	**102652**	**214.02**	**8084.47**	**7897.58**	**803.65**
丹阳市	Danyang City	103187	77.76	2419.83	2381.81	200.08
扬中市	Yangzhong City	130467	21.69	1198.54	1157.91	132.91
句容市	Jurong City	70684	63.69	1260.78	1229.05	123.27
泰州市	**Taizhou City**	**72706**	**361.94**	**9456.36**	**9355.94**	**1220.77**
兴化市	Xinghua City	49803	155.84	1352.08	1327.20	141.78
靖江市	Jinjiang City	97063	35.00	1982.31	1902.10	257.22
泰兴市	Taixing City	62772	79.67	2054.46	2047.31	306.54
宿迁市	**Suqian City**	**39963**	**463.16**	**3368.77**	**3282.89**	**481.36**
沭阳县	Shuyang County	37525	152.27	1103.51	1084.36	153.98
泗阳县	Siyang County	39365	91.87	498.04	495.24	54.98
泗洪县	Sihong County	36484	111.72	629.04	605.65	94.76

CONTINUED 3

利润总额（亿元）Total Value of Profits (100 million yuan)	公路里程（公里）Highway Mileage (km)	公路客运量（万人）Highway Passenger Capacity (10,000 persons)	公路货运量（万吨）Highway Freight Volume (10,000 tons)	民用汽车拥有量（万辆）Civil Vehicles Possessed (10,000)	邮电业务总量（亿元）Post and Tele-communications Service (100 million yuan)	国际互联网用户（万户）Internet Subscribers (10,000 households)
304.64	**13071**	**8435**	**5572**	**34.72**	**73.95**	**58.57**
31.07	2535	0	0	5.16	4.18	6.26
39.97	1489	0	0	1.78	1.91	4.43
30.55	2699	0	0	3.25	3.32	6.06
18.70	1427	0	0	1.91	2.14	4.20
509.32	**19256**	**9440**	**5093**	**54.96**	**97.01**	**91.98**
67.91	1764	775	335	2.94	3.35	7.51
32.71	2156	364	701	5.85	5.70	10.68
25.10	1870	1091	166	4.71	5.43	11.11
20.92	2483	387	102	5.69	6.01	12.01
51.13	1767	895	271	3.73	5.57	11.45
52.02	3211	868	796	6.98	7.01	15.41
42.87	3088	974	404	6.66	6.47	14.80
606.82	**10525**	**4792**	**6504**	**48.82**	**84.42**	**82.80**
44.25	2263	697	554	4.67	6.92	13.43
106.37	1510	337	839	5.65	6.56	12.40
69.53	2535	718	796	5.40	7.75	13.85
516.58	**7263**	**4461**	**6905**	**38.49**	**64.39**	**61.98**
132.92	2165	950	1573	12.32	13.71	24.13
79.90	1008	449	420	4.57	5.11	8.23
65.07	2473	795	1037	3.21	6.91	11.25
713.87	**9457**	**8895**	**2487**	**47.03**	**76.61**	**75.29**
77.82	2716	2153	396	8.00	7.99	19.22
160.34	1323	1335	321	9.42	6.38	17.86
187.96	2109	1932	458	8.92	8.09	21.03
333.59	**10977**	**6734**	**3797**	**37.33**	**84.12**	**55.29**
104.89	3486	1958	1926	10.43	11.26	23.12
37.79	1735	1266	457	5.64	5.64	11.58
59.74	2436	2340	445	5.15	5.95	12.45

19-4 续表 4

指标名称	Item	全年用电量(亿千瓦时) Power Consumption of the Whole Year (100 million KWH)	# 工业用电 Industrial Power Consumption	固定资产投资(亿元) Fixed Asset Investment (100 million yuan)	房地产开发投资(亿元) Real-estate Development Investment (100 million yuan)	商品房屋销售建筑面积(万平方米) Sold Area of Commercial Housing (10,000 m²)
南京市	**Nanjing City**	**470.50**	**289.02**	**5430.77**	**1125.49**	**1207.58**
无锡市	**Wuxi City**	**598.18**	**477.47**	**4610.77**	**1252.22**	**839.15**
江阴市	Jiangyin City	237.87	212.09	1045.97	328.91	190.47
宜兴市	Yixing Cityh	88.28	69.51	602.15	134.43	86.02
徐州市	**Xuzhou City**	**332.47**	**247.48**	**3671.56**	**468.88**	**738.03**
丰　县	Fen County	18.04	10.80	180.14	27.68	47.77
沛　县	Pei County	31.93	23.94	409.06	17.31	46.11
睢宁县	Suining County	21.44	13.62	218.55	41.93	74.09
新沂市	Xinyi City	37.46	30.70	386.29	35.00	80.84
邳州市	Pizhou City	25.68	15.41	545.96	47.27	119.80
常州市	**Changzhou City**	**395.06**	**316.09**	**3310.05**	**681.53**	**787.50**
溧阳市	Liyang City	68.80	58.61	438.01	51.52	80.04
金坛市	Jintan City	45.77	38.56	268.99	21.39	58.63
苏州市	**Suzhou City**	**1268.12**	**1044.14**	**6054.00**	**1764.44**	**1599.16**
常熟市	Changshu City	155.20	130.63	631.82	147.81	144.36
张家港市	Zhangjiagang City	283.05	262.80	763.62	145.74	99.75
昆山市	Kunshan City	194.35	155.99	838.18	371.80	446.73
太仓市	Taicang City	90.05	77.08	513.36	71.74	78.99
南通市	**Nantong City**	**333.23**	**242.89**	**3896.39**	**678.92**	**919.17**
海安县	Haian County	43.01	33.96	448.95	52.48	63.11
如东县	Rudong County	41.94	31.39	427.93	31.47	29.10
启东市	Qidong City	26.87	17.35	483.41	47.03	87.84
如皋市	Rugao City	45.76	32.79	445.08	58.53	80.69
海门市	Haimen City	35.12	24.55	501.40	43.71	74.55
连云港市	**Lianyungang City**	**157.51**	**110.44**	**1716.57**	**189.28**	**337.64**
东海县	Donghai County	20.40	12.76	233.63	29.72	65.74
灌云县	Guanyun County	10.46	5.04	198.41	13.35	39.97
灌南县	Guannan County	31.20	26.04	195.17	18.15	40.92

CONTINUED 4

社会消费品零售总额(亿元) Total Retail Sales of Consumer Goods(100 Million Yuan)	进出口总值(亿美元) Total Export-import Volume (100 Million USD)	出口 Export	实际外商直接投资(亿美元) Collected Foreign Capital (100 Million USD)	一般公共预算收入(亿元) General public budget revenue (100 million yuan)	#税收收入 Tax Income	一般公共预算支出(亿元) General public budget revenue expenditure (100 million yuan)
4167.19	**572.21**	**326.28**	**32.91**	**903.49**	**757.21**	**921.20**
2607.90	**741.70**	**442.31**	**29.04**	**768.01**	**620.34**	**748.06**
643.07	223.04	130.23	8.55	200.66	164.88	187.28
464.42	55.46	36.76	1.53	94.45	80.36	100.29
2099.20	**59.88**	**46.77**	**16.58**	**472.33**	**386.43**	**661.84**
118.06	1.66	1.62	1.00	38.12	32.84	62.71
192.13	3.49	3.36	0.72	53.13	44.66	73.15
139.62	4.75	2.92	1.22	38.63	33.22	67.56
135.72	4.29	2.28	0.34	45.82	39.33	68.50
197.90	8.76	7.25	1.88	55.58	47.25	88.62
1805.40	**288.10**	**213.64**	**24.09**	**433.88**	**348.38**	**434.93**
259.22	10.08	7.32	4.00	50.62	43.11	57.01
197.61	15.25	12.20	1.00	30.12	26.50	37.46
4095.09	**3113.06**	**1811.78**	**81.20**	**1443.82**	**1244.37**	**1304.83**
618.67	201.80	125.53	10.52	147.40	122.90	138.02
458.32	328.26	148.10	6.72	162.66	133.67	152.78
650.09	847.91	535.77	12.84	263.66	236.19	222.98
239.04	137.91	60.80	3.96	106.47	90.97	97.68
2166.10	**316.47**	**224.80**	**23.05**	**550.00**	**457.34**	**649.58**
221.95	24.52	21.44	3.32	54.10	46.23	70.58
257.89	33.11	12.89	3.43	50.01	41.53	79.20
266.41	30.72	23.05	0.55	67.25	55.90	74.01
280.77	32.12	25.55	3.31	67.45	56.05	91.29
282.48	20.36	14.55	1.55	68.57	56.92	73.62
739.40	**80.30**	**43.55**	**9.54**	**261.77**	**213.42**	**375.95**
139.03	3.65	2.90	1.15	37.20	31.31	61.74
94.93	1.84	1.60	0.59	35.59	30.90	55.74
74.53	2.34	2.03	0.02	35.12	30.38	52.54

19-4 续表 5

指标名称	Item	全年用电量(亿千瓦时) Power Consumption of the Whole Year (100 million KWH)	# 工业用电 Industrial Power Consumption	固定资产投资(亿元) Fixed Asset Investment (100 million yuan)	房地产开发投资(亿元) Real-estate Development Investment (100 million yuan)	商品房屋销售建筑面积(万平方米) Sold Area of Commercial Housing (10,000 m²)
淮安市	**Huaian City**	**151.53**	**106.89**	**1795.73**	**357.66**	**614.53**
涟水县	Lianshui County	15.43	9.58	215.84	35.77	75.59
洪泽县	Hongze County	17.00	14.07	132.98	20.61	39.70
盱眙县	Xuyi County	15.29	9.43	260.08	57.83	76.75
金湖县	Jinhu County	10.44	7.31	128.53	18.80	34.97
盐城市	**Yancheng City**	**278.55**	**209.02**	**2751.35**	**379.64**	**624.52**
响水县	Xiangshui County	43.73	39.21	203.95	7.85	27.41
滨海县	Binghai County	25.19	18.14	265.45	16.00	49.22
阜宁县	Funing County	32.20	25.30	226.18	27.27	50.15
射阳县	Sheyang County	18.53	11.35	213.43	37.94	38.12
建湖县	Jianhu County	20.16	13.81	252.34	10.51	46.31
东台市	Dongtai City	38.82	29.92	409.82	48.02	74.62
大丰市	Dafeng City	52.74	44.62	322.67	36.33	67.22
扬州市	**Yangzhou City**	**204.36**	**147.89**	**2416.66**	**360.44**	**635.07**
宝应县	Baoying County	16.70	10.45	237.39	33.82	112.59
仪征市	Yizheng City	33.75	28.25	314.14	24.79	60.83
高邮市	Gaoyou City	29.86	22.56	280.20	54.23	105.86
镇江市	**Zhenjiang City**	**209.41**	**162.44**	**2142.34**	**319.05**	**520.15**
丹阳市	Danyang City	65.77	53.19	386.73	56.84	98.58
扬中市	Yangzhong City	16.45	12.06	216.09	15.11	23.89
句容市	Jurong City	22.69	15.36	258.16	79.60	149.73
泰州市	**Taizhou City**	**232.30**	**180.73**	**2197.34**	**285.54**	**440.21**
兴化市	Xinghua City	63.58	52.93	284.80	21.46	53.26
靖江市	Jinjiang City	36.01	26.48	405.76	53.65	48.20
泰兴市	Taixing City	54.26	44.47	454.53	55.07	94.84
宿迁市	**Suqian City**	**146.38**	**103.90**	**1559.22**	**377.14**	**584.12**
沭阳县	Shuyang County	39.67	27.86	383.91	82.01	110.17
泗阳县	Siyang County	20.11	12.63	283.44	56.50	93.62
泗洪县	Sihong County	15.58	7.95	281.89	75.40	203.90

CONTINUED 5

社会消费品零售总额(亿元) Total Retail Sales of Consumer Goods(100 Million Yuan)	进出口总值(亿美元) Total Export-import Volume (100 Million USD)		实际外商直接投资(亿美元) Collected Foreign Capital (100 Million USD)	一般公共预算收入(亿元) General public budget revenue (100 million yuan)		一般公共预算支出(亿元) General public budget revenue expenditure (100 million yuan)
		出口 Export			# 税收收入 Tax Income	
864.80	**41.06**	**31.61**	**11.99**	**308.51**	**251.94**	**431.65**
103.90	4.03	3.50	0.22	29.72	25.19	54.09
75.13	2.36	2.10	0.79	22.23	18.72	36.33
99.08	2.10	1.34	0.94	30.77	25.25	47.12
71.95	3.56	3.47	1.01	21.40	18.64	33.73
1312.70	**75.17**	**43.94**	**10.47**	**418.02**	**341.41**	**603.21**
53.60	4.09	3.36	0.75	27.82	22.85	43.67
88.99	4.63	3.22	0.86	33.45	27.32	58.07
104.45	2.17	1.85	0.76	33.57	27.92	56.46
135.28	3.13	1.58	0.60	17.50	12.48	45.07
139.09	3.99	3.76	0.90	44.76	36.77	65.88
203.37	6.61	6.24	0.96	61.31	51.95	84.26
139.21	13.82	7.75	2.06	60.02	49.52	82.90
1128.10	**100.12**	**76.82**	**13.88**	**295.19**	**242.22**	**367.73**
122.94	7.79	6.10	0.32	27.28	22.37	46.25
91.95	10.25	6.60	3.16	34.66	29.63	41.51
138.65	4.19	3.86	0.29	29.32	24.04	46.64
1003.80	**103.07**	**66.02**	**12.95**	**277.76**	**228.82**	**311.85**
255.71	27.73	22.41	3.48	64.16	54.81	74.93
114.22	5.60	4.48	1.16	30.72	26.23	34.71
116.07	5.79	4.52	2.57	35.91	30.65	43.65
903.60	**108.93**	**61.78**	**9.39**	**277.95**	**225.80**	**371.21**
139.97	5.83	5.25	1.16	36.95	30.61	73.56
144.85	27.35	12.71	0.26	54.04	44.42	61.49
170.75	26.75	13.25	2.38	45.08	37.47	61.20
564.80	**37.55**	**29.40**	**6.65**	**210.10**	**180.69**	**345.59**
145.53	9.21	8.02	1.47	64.04	53.85	100.49
80.00	6.96	6.88	0.96	30.05	25.35	54.84
84.00	3.85	3.70	0.73	28.01	23.79	57.97

19-4 续表 6

指标名称	Item	金融机构人民币存款余额(亿元) RMB Loan Balance of Financial Institutions(100 Million Yuan)	#居民储蓄存款 Residental Savings Deposit	金融机构人民币贷款余额(亿元) RMB Balance of Financial Institutions(100 Million Yuan)	公共图书馆图书藏量(千册) Books in public library (1000)	卫生机构床位数(张) Number of beds in health institutions (10,000)
南京市	**Nanjing City**	**20161.86**	**5055.77**	**15628.53**	**5188**	**43688**
无锡市	**Wuxi City**	**11849.03**	**4341.45**	**8669.62**	**4498**	**34998**
江阴市	Jiangyin City	2813.03	938.76	2198.16	996	7605
宜兴市	Yixing Cityh	1707.10	819.53	1325.98	524	4856
徐州市	**Xuzhou City**	**4286.46**	**2377.44**	**2724.79**	**3023**	**46213**
丰　县	Fen County	239.84	190.30	128.09	206	3969
沛　县	Pei County	336.53	252.34	157.33	320	4476
睢宁县	Suining County	282.79	214.29	169.40	411	3566
新沂市	Xinyi City	235.37	169.07	202.09	128	3117
邳州市	Pizhou City	346.34	254.42	271.39	438	4867
常州市	**Changzhou City**	**6758.57**	**2934.19**	**4789.74**	**3030**	**23634**
溧阳市	Liyang City	848.45	414.03	604.06	344	2879
金坛市	Jintan City	544.80	299.01	418.98	250	2444
苏州市	**Suzhou City**	**21428.20**	**6753.44**	**17247.94**	**15099**	**55218**
常熟市	Changshu City	2265.93	1021.99	1816.30	2356	7052
张家港市	Zhangjiagang City	2323.83	877.06	1787.62	1990	8588
昆山市	Kunshan City	2882.89	970.90	2043.47	2116	6300
太仓市	Taicang City	1172.26	450.61	1068.03	934	3577
南通市	**Nantong City**	**8339.54**	**4602.87**	**5130.38**	**4455**	**35136**
海安县	Haian County	975.91	565.35	682.49	429	4232
如东县	Rudong County	723.57	478.73	342.90	404	3286
启东市	Qidong City	944.22	637.96	550.04	417	3815
如皋市	Rugao City	849.56	576.27	519.70	855	5189
海门市	Haimen City	1015.12	626.34	630.58	511	3480
连云港市	**Lianyungang City**	**1852.67**	**924.03**	**1549.34**	**2485**	**18061**
东海县	Donghai County	242.53	162.74	181.51	984	2823
灌云县	Guanyun County	189.36	118.23	135.81	399	2439
灌南县	Guannan County	124.08	82.92	106.95	290	2770

CONTINUED 6

卫生技术人员（人） Health Technicians	城镇居民人均可支配收入（元） Per capita disposable income of urban residents (yuan)	城镇居民人均生活消费支出（元） Per capita consumptive expenditure of urban residents (yuan)	城镇居民人均住房建筑面积(平方米) Per capita housing area of urban and rural residents (m²)	农村居民人均可支配收入（元） Per capita disposable income of rural residents (yuan)	农村居民人均生活消费支出（元） Per capita consumptive expenditure of rural residents (yuan)	农村居民人均住房建筑面积(平方米) Per capita consumptive expenditure of rural residents (yuan)
62068	**42568**	**25855**	**36.3**	**17661**	**12818**	**55.4**
41563	**41731**	**27358**	**44.8**	**22266**	**15114**	**54.3**
8435	46880	24976	59.3	23965	15304	50.3
7226	39492	25035	46.5	20178	13792	61.4
47007	**24080**	**15005**	**40.5**	**12811**	**9011**	**49.7**
3883	19363	14573	42.1	11757	7641	46.9
4676	23078	14807	42.5	13249	8682	47.6
3356	19687	11315	46.6	11600	7293	51.4
4058	20984	14215	44.8	12140	7408	46.6
6271	24151	13726	61.8	12846	7990	63.7
28090	**39483**	**23590**	**43.7**	**20133**	**13529**	**59.7**
3812	35531	18900	38.3	18222	13701	47.2
2747	36902	19781	42.0	18733	11614	53.0
64281	**46677**	**28973**	**44.0**	**23560**	**15390**	**66.0**
8278	46571	27412	48.5	23767	17184	68.3
8441	46852	27760	56.7	23722	15430	69.3
10375	46920	28332	36.5	23921	15374	49.9
4143	46377	29250	58.2	23590	15838	77.8
39481	**33374**	**22035**	**46.3**	**15821**	**11051**	**58.6**
4153	31597	20125	49.3	15155	12447	54.6
3780	31557	18819	53.5	14494	10928	53.5
3721	31708	26249	41.1	16762	11931	59.6
5540	31026	19116	49.2	14210	10225	52.9
3800	34280	22830	43.0	17419	12081	60.0
21896	**23595**	**16016**	**45.3**	**11698**	**8282**	**47.9**
3201	23151	16504	44.9	12171	8370	48.6
2559	19486	12093	42.6	10864	7492	45.9
2723	20805	13569	49.0	10442	7288	50.6

19-4 续表 7

指标名称	Item	金融机构人民币存款余额(亿元) RMB Loan Balance of Financial Institutions(100 Million Yuan)	#居民储蓄存款 Residental Savings Deposit	金融机构人民币贷款余额(亿元) RMB Balance of Financial Institutions(100 Million Yuan)	公共图书馆图书藏量(千册) Books in public library (1000)	卫生机构床位数(张) Number of beds in health institutions (10,000)
淮安市	**Huaian City**	**2005.72**	**1044.52**	**1617.55**	**2368**	**24642**
涟水县	Lianshui County	238.69	138.76	164.07	580	3755
洪泽县	Hongze County	140.36	69.62	114.23	510	1503
盱眙县	Xuyi County	218.15	122.45	203.46	753	3106
金湖县	Jinhu County	165.96	102.42	130.92	273	1477
盐城市	**Yancheng City**	**3692.75**	**2062.39**	**2567.98**	**2831**	**35282**
响水县	Xiangshui County	115.37	67.32	103.47	73	2278
滨海县	Binghai County	207.93	131.76	156.74	206	4390
阜宁县	Funing County	283.95	193.77	198.17	272	3684
射阳县	Sheyang County	270.70	196.61	191.74	200	3252
建湖县	Jianhu County	306.53	217.38	235.52	238	3335
东台市	Dongtai City	553.89	425.48	301.01	263	5246
大丰市	Dafeng City	436.68	274.38	283.43	366	3216
扬州市	**Yangzhou City**	**4269.75**	**2117.09**	**2732.42**	**2937**	**19765**
宝应县	Baoying County	342.32	228.51	229.71	138	2203
仪征市	Yizheng City	461.08	248.13	257.85	338	2080
高邮市	Gaoyou City	394.68	269.15	241.60	207	2536
镇江市	**Zhenjiang City**	**3536.27**	**1569.40**	**2679.83**	**2829**	**14490**
丹阳市	Danyang City	872.00	453.55	791.74	565	3314
扬中市	Yangzhong City	441.25	238.25	332.59	306	970
句容市	Jurong City	419.98	237.50	315.41	174	1832
泰州市	**Taizhou City**	**3955.84**	**1984.80**	**2751.51**	**2439**	**20926**
兴化市	Xinghua City	514.93	374.06	352.54	239	4281
靖江市	Jinjiang City	785.81	381.47	549.05	493	3689
泰兴市	Taixing City	644.63	383.18	388.36	311	3964
宿迁市	**Suqian City**	**1598.96**	**813.20**	**1483.05**	**1132**	**20240**
沭阳县	Shuyang County	354.26	241.86	303.52	163	5608
泗阳县	Siyang County	228.50	146.71	240.19	262	4336
泗洪县	Sihong County	233.63	148.33	237.51	92	3904

CONTINUED 7

卫生技术人员（人）Health Technicians	城镇居民人均可支配收入（元）Per capita disposable income of urban residents (yuan)	城镇居民人均生活消费支出（元）Per capita consumptive expenditure of urban residents (yuan)	城镇居民人均住房建筑面积(平方米) Per capita housing area of urban and rural residents (m^2)	农村居民人均可支配收入（元）Per capita disposable income of rural residents (yuan)	农村居民人均生活消费支出（元）Per capita consumptive expenditure of rural residents (yuan)	农村居民人均住房建筑面积(平方米) Per capita consumptive expenditure of rural residents (yuan)
28976	**25798**	**14703**	**43.6**	**12010**	**7836**	**50.2**
4176	21389	13760	51.3	11206	6809	64.8
1702	25751	12250	37.5	13161	9199	46.0
3505	26041	13913	48.4	12175	6405	50.5
1713	26081	17137	41.4	13131	10892	59.7
36634	**25854**	**15372**	**42.7**	**14414**	**10782**	**48.0**
2561	21710	9924	32.5	11964	7922	43.1
4192	22432	13759	32.4	12524	9204	40.9
3087	21546	17578	33.8	12959	6672	42.6
3795	22440	19234	44.6	13848	6687	38.9
3364	25178	13801	41.8	14345	9111	40.7
4703	27800	15709	53.9	16565	10643	60.8
3529	26354	15331	40.0	16414	10988	55.8
23338	**30322**	**18417**	**42.1**	**15284**	**11266**	**53.7**
2668	22739	14026	37.3	14246	9923	47.8
2651	31123	18123	45.4	14860	13389	64.3
2968	26632	18024	38.5	14335	10898	42.4
18373	**35752**	**21310**	**44.2**	**17617**	**13081**	**55.8**
4371	35691	19498	48.8	18250	15352	59.9
1593	39237	20972	54.5	20078	13669	62.1
2349	34678	19980	42.0	15893	12241	46.9
22965	**31346**	**19517**	**48.0**	**15076**	**10849**	**62.0**
4330	28691	16571	38.0	14258	9594	45.0
4011	33864	23069	51.5	16570	13963	69.3
4611	31038	19644	52.6	15066	9681	73.7
23862	**20396**	**13463**	**46.5**	**11677**	**7702**	**49.8**
7116	20310	13691	46.1	11828	8187	49.2
4326	19909	13025	55.8	11690	8691	50.4
4708	19388	13202	43.2	11405	6362	42.8

中国统计出版社最新图书简目

（仅供参考，以实际出版为准）